Blackstone's Police Manua

General Police Duties

Blackstone's Police Manual

Volume 4

General Police Duties

2015

Glenn Hutton

BA, MPhil, FCIPD

Gavin McKinnon

LLB, LLM, MSt (Cantab), CMgr

and

Paul Connor

Cert Ed (FE), PG Cert Ed (ODE), LLB

Consultant Editor: Paul Connor

OXFORD
UNIVERSITY PRESS

OXFORD
UNIVERSITY PRESS

Great Clarendon Street, Oxford, OX2 6DP,
United Kingdom

Oxford University Press is a department of the University of Oxford.
It furthers the University's objective of excellence in research, scholarship,
and education by publishing worldwide. Oxford is a registered trade mark of
Oxford University Press in the UK and in certain other countries

© Oxford University Press 2014

The moral rights of the authors have been asserted

First Edition published in 1998
Seventeenth Edition published in 2014

Impression: 1

Published in the United States of America by Oxford University Press
198 Madison Avenue, New York, NY 10016, United States of America

British Library Cataloguing in Publication Data

Data available

ISBN 978–0–19–871901–4

Printed in Italy by
L.E.G.O. S.p.A.

Links to third party websites are provided by Oxford in good faith and
for information only. Oxford disclaims any responsibility for the materials
contained in any third party website referenced in this work.

Foreword for 2015 Blackstone's Police Manuals

The police service currently faces a series of challenges; from the changes that police forces must make to deliver savings and reduce crime to the increasing complexity of the threats to national security, public safety and public order. Underpinning the ability of officers to deal effectively with these challenges is the knowledge and understanding of relevant law and procedure and the ability to apply this on a daily basis. This understanding is the cornerstone in providing a professional policing service.

The College of Policing plays a vital role in the development of police officers and staff, helping them to obtain and retain the skills and knowledge they need to fight crime and protect the public. The College has a remit to develop, maintain and test standards to ensure suitability for promotion. Part of this responsibility requires the College to ensure a comprehensive and relevant syllabus is produced. As such, the College works alongside Oxford University Press to ensure these Manuals are an accurate and up-to-date source of information and that they reflect what is required by people working across policing.

The *Blackstone's Police Manuals 2015* are the definitive reference source and official study guide for the national legal examination which all candidates must successfully pass in order to be promoted to sergeant or inspector. Their content is derived from evidence gathered from operational sergeants and inspectors alongside input from the wider police service. Whilst they are primarily designed to support officers seeking to progress their careers in preparing for their promotion examinations, they also provide a reference point for officers and staff seeking to continue their professional development and maintain their knowledge as a professional in policing. If you are using these Manuals to prepare for your promotion examinations I would like to take this opportunity to wish you the very best of luck in your studies, and I hope these books will assist you in progressing your career within the police service.

Alex Marshall
Chief Executive Officer
of the College of Policing

Preface

The *Blackstone's Police Manuals* are the only official study guides for the Police Promotion Examinations—if the law is not in the Manuals, it will not be in the exams.

All the Manuals include explanatory keynotes and case law examples, providing clear and incisive analysis of important areas. As well as covering basic law and procedure they take full account of the PACE Codes of Practice and human rights implications. They can also be used as a training resource for police probationers, special constables and PCSOs, or as an invaluable reference tool for police staff of all ranks and positions.

By its very nature, policing covers a wide and widening range of activities. As society gets more complex and demanding, so too does the job of those who police it. Add to that the enormous political dimension, and it is no surprise that the legislative framework governing policing delivery has grown in depth and breadth. As a result, *General Police Duties* necessarily contains a wide range of powers, offences and considerations. Some parts of this Manual govern the practical application of the others in the series—an example is the Human Rights Act 1998 and the restrictions it places on the use of policing powers generally. Other areas involve the general powers of police constables and their CSO colleagues, the constitution of the police, the National Policing Plan, and the provisions governing misconduct and complaints. To that extent the areas of this Manual are absolutely fundamental to the effective delivery of policing across England and Wales.

The Manual also covers other areas of policing such as anti-social behaviour, harassment, public order and terrorism, weapons and knife crime, civil disputes, offences relating to land and premises, licensing, offences and powers relating to information, and diversity, discrimination and equality.

The 2015 edition has been edited and updated to incorporate all recent legislative changes and the revised PACE Codes of Practice. The legislation containing significant changes to the contents of the Manual includes the Policing and Crime Act 2009, the Crime and Courts Act 2013, the Marriage (Same Sex Couples) Act 2013, the Police and Fire Reform (Scotland) Act 2012, and the Criminal Procedure Rules 2013. The changes to the police disciplinary and misconduct Regulations in 2012 have also been included. This edition also includes a number of recent criminal cases decided by the appellate courts.

In addition to the very rapid and extensive changes in the law, these features mean that *General Police Duties* covers a lot of ground.

The aim of this Manual is to take this shifting and growing body of national and European law and analyse the essential elements in a practical and pragmatic context—without losing the specific meaning and applicability along the way. If we have achieved that, it is thanks to the contributions of the many police officers and staff, lawyers and practitioners who have helped in the development of this Manual, now in its fifteenth edition; if we haven't, it is not for the want of trying.

Oxford University Press are always happy to receive any useful written feedback from any reader on the content and style of the Manual, especially from those involved in or with the criminal justice system. Please email this address with any comments or queries: police.uk@oup.com.

The law is stated as at 1 June 2014.

Acknowledgements

Blackstone's Police Manuals have become firmly established as a 'household name' in the context of police law for which they are the leading text in England and Wales. Their growth and refinement year on year is a result, not simply of Parliament and the legislators, but also of the many and varied contributions of the Manuals' wide readership.

Thanks are due to all (except perhaps the legislators) and there is never space to mention everyone individually.

In particular, thanks to the staff of the Legal Services Department of the College of Policing (CoP) and Examinations and Assessment. The monthly Digest produced by the Legal Services Department is an invaluable reference and the informative syllabus review conducted by Examinations and Assessment has helped to shape the content and style of the Manual.

Thanks to George Cooper (Northamptonshire Police), Stuart K. Fairclough (Metropolitan Police), Paul Murphy (Greater Manchester Police) and Kevin Whitehouse (West Midlands Police).

Our thanks, as always, to all the staff involved in the production of the Manual in the Academic and Professional Law Department at Oxford University Press, especially Peter Daniell, Lucy Alexander, Emma Hawes, Pam Birkby and Lorna Richerby. Special thanks also to Sonal, Priya, Jayna, and Rosalie for their continued support and forbearance.

Glenn Hutton and Gavin McKinnon

Contents

PART III General Police Duties   **265**

Table of Cases

Table of Statutes

Table of Statutory Instruments

Table of Codes of Practice

Table of European Legislation

Table of Home Office Circulars

Table of International Treaties and Conventions

How to use this Manual

Volume numbers for the Manuals

The 2015 Blackstone's Police Manuals each have a volume number as follows:

Volume 1: *Crime*
Volume 2: *Evidence and Procedure*
Volume 3: *Road Policing*
Volume 4: *General Police Duties*

The first digit of each paragraph number in the text of the Manuals denotes the Manual number. For example, paragraph 2.3 is chapter 3 of the *Evidence and Procedure* Manual and 4.3 is chapter 3 of the *General Police Duties* Manual.

All index entries and references in the Tables of Legislation and the Table of Cases, etc. refer to paragraph numbers instead of page numbers, making information easier to find.

Material outside the scope of the police promotion examinations syllabus—blacklining

These Manuals contain some information which is outside the scope of the police promotion examinations. A full black line down the margin indicates that the text beside it is excluded from Inspectors' examinations.

PACE Code Chapters

The PACE Codes of Practice have been taken out of the appendices and are now incorporated within chapters in the main body of the *Blackstone's Police Manuals*. A thick grey line down the margin is used to denote text that is an extract of the PACE Code itself (i.e. the actual wording of the legislation) and does not form part of the general commentary of the chapter.

The PACE Codes of Practice form an important part of the police promotion examinations syllabus and are examinable for both Sergeants and Inspectors. They are not to be confused with 'blacklined' content that is excluded from the syllabus for Inspectors' examinations (see 'Material outside the scope of the police promotion examinations syllabus—blacklining').

Length of sentence for an offence

Where a length of sentence for an offence is stated in this Manual, please note that the number of months or years stated is the maximum number and will not be exceeded.

Any feedback regarding content or other editorial matters in the Manuals can be emailed to police.uk@oup.com.

Police Promotion Examinations Rules and Syllabus Information

The rules and syllabus for the police promotion examinations system are defined within the Rules & Syllabus document published by College of Policing Examinations and Assessment on behalf of the Police Promotions Examination Board (PPEB). The Rules & Syllabus document is published annually each September, and applies to all police promotion assessments scheduled for the calendar year following its publication. For example, the September 2014 Rules & Syllabus document would apply to all police promotion assessments held during 2015.

The document provides details of the law and procedure to be tested within the police promotion examinations, and also outlines the rules underpinning the police promotion examination system.

All candidates who are taking a police promotion examination are strongly encouraged to familiarise themselves with the Rules & Syllabus document during their preparation. The police promotion examination rules also apply to candidates who take the police promotion examination and then go on to apply for their force's work-based assessment promotion trials.

The document can be downloaded from the Recruitment, Assessment & Selection Section of the College of Policing website, which can be found at http://www.college.police.uk. Electronic versions are also supplied to all force police promotion examination contacts.

If you have any problems obtaining the Rules & Syllabus document from the above source, please email the police promotion examination Candidate Administration Team at:

osprecandidates@college.pnn.police.uk

Usually, no further updates to the Rules & Syllabus document will be issued during its year-long lifespan. However, in exceptional circumstances, the College of Policing (on behalf of the PPEB) reserves the right to issue an amended syllabus prior to the next scheduled annual publication date.

For example, a major change to a key area of legislation or procedure (e.g. the Codes of Practice) during the lifespan of the current Rules & Syllabus document would render a significant part of the current syllabus content obsolete. In such circumstances, it may be necessary for an update to the syllabus to be issued, which would provide guidance to candidates on any additional material which would be examinable within their police promotion examinations.

In such circumstances, an update to the Rules & Syllabus document would be made available through the College of Policing website, and would be distributed to all force police promotion examination contacts. The College of Policing will ensure that any syllabus update is distributed well in advance of the examination date, to ensure that candidates have sufficient time to familiarise themselves with any additional examinable material. Where possible, any additional study materials would be provided to candidates free of charge.

Please note that syllabus updates will only be made in *exceptional* circumstances, an update will not be made for every change to legislation included within the syllabus. For further guidance on this issue, candidates are advised to regularly check the College of Policing website, or consult their force police promotion examination contact, during their preparation period.

PART ONE

Police

4.1 The Policing Family

4.1.1 Introduction

How police officers are employed, promoted, remunerated, governed, and how the powers they hold are exercised (and by whom) is going through a period of major change. The Independent Review of Police Officer and Staff Remuneration and Conditions, led by Her Majesty's Chief Inspector of Constabulary Tom Winsor, has recommended far reaching changes which, if enacted, could bring about the biggest shift in the police workforce since the 1930s. A voluntary redundancy scheme for police officers came into effect in January 2013, and proposals to allow chief constables to make officers compulsorily redundant are under negotiation. New direct entry routes to the ranks of inspector, superintendent and chief constable have also been proposed, which cut across the legislation and practice requiring officers to work their way through the ranks from constable onwards. However, there remains much that is unique about the status of police officers, and their role is distinct from that of an employee in many regards.

4.1.2 Employment Status and Conditions of Police Officers

Police officers are not 'employees' for most purposes as they are not employed under contracts as such; they are public office holders (see *Fisher* v *Oldham Corporation* [1930] 2 KB 364; see also *Sheikh* v *Chief Constable of Greater Manchester Police* [1990] 1 QB 637). For this reason a significant number of the employment rights given to workers in other occupations do not apply to police officers. They cannot bring claims for wrongful dismissal because these are *contractual* claims. Similarly, they are prevented by statute from claiming unfair dismissal and some other protection that is given to ordinary employees by the Employment Rights Act 1996.

However, for some purposes (e.g. sex and race discrimination) chief officers are treated *as if they are employers* of their officers. This has caused some technical difficulties in practice and these categories have become blurred even further by recent events. So, for instance, some non-Home Office police officers *do have* a contract for service with their 'employer' (e.g. British Transport Police—see *Spence* v *British Railways Board* [2001] ICR 232).

Some of the Police Reform Act 2002 rules allow individuals who are employees in the strict sense to potentially be placed outside the full statutory protection for employees (by the Employment Rights Act 1996, s. 200) because they have the powers and privileges of constables. For some purposes, statutes refer to the European concept of 'workers' which, being a wider concept than 'employees', often *does* apply to the police. An example of this expression can be found in the Working Time Regulations 1998 (SI 1998/1833). These Regulations are a good example of an important area in which police officers are treated as though they were employees working under a contract of employment. One effect of this is that (for highly technical reasons) officers can rely on the annual leave year that is agreed from time to time by the force—something which has a knock-on effect on issues such as pension entitlements (see *Hyman* v *Chief Constable of South Wales Police* [2003] Po LR 166).

'Workers'—which include a number of healthcare and emergency personnel—are generally protected under the Public Interest Disclosure Act 1998 and this is a further area of recent importance to police officers (**see para. 4.1.19**).

The real practical importance of all this, however, lies in the fact that the police have had to be given their own statutory framework for dealing with complaints, conduct and efficiency—see **chapter 4.2**.

In April 1999 a number of very significant changes were made to the procedures governing the performance and conduct of, and complaints against, police officers. These changes have been further extended by amendments to the general employment laws and changes to the police conduct and complaints framework.

The Police Regulations 2003 (SI 2003/527) cover a number of areas that are central to the performance of police duties and good governance, as well as placing restrictions on the private lives of officers. The Police (Amendment No. 3) Regulations 2012 amend the 2003 Regulations which specifically restrict the business interests an officer and their relatives can have.

Voluntary Severance for Police Officers

The Police (Amendment No. 5) Regulations 2012 make an important change to the legal framework within which police officers are employed. They create a new Regulation 14A in the Police Regulations 2003 which allows the Secretary of State to create a voluntary early retirement scheme. This was a recommendation of the Winsor Review of Police Officers and Staff Remuneration and Conditions, and will allow officers to leave the service with a severance package—in effect a payment for cutting short their career.

More controversially, proposals to allow compulsory redundancy for police officers are currently under discussion at the Police Negotiating Board, and if agreed this will remove the current protections officers receive as office holders and make their jobs far more akin to that of an employee.

4.1.3   Part-time Appointments

Regulation 5 of the Police Regulations 2003 allows a chief constable, after consultation with local representatives of the staff associations, to appoint an officer to perform part-time service in any rank. Part-time officers may give notice in writing of their intention to be re-appointed as a full-time member and will be appointed within two months of the date on which the notice is received by the force, where there is a suitable vacancy, or when four months have elapsed since the day the notice was received, or from an earlier date if reasonably practicable. The Police (Amendment No. 4) Regulations 2012 extended these timescales in response to proposals contained in the Winsor Review.

4.1.4   Personal Records

The Police Regulations 2003 place a requirement on the chief constable to keep a personal record of each member of his/her force. Regulation 15(2) specifies that the record must contain:

- a personal description of the member;
- particulars of place and date of birth;
- particulars of marriage or civil partnership (if any) and children (if any);
- if applicable a record of service in any branch of the military or civil service;
- a record of service (if any) in any other police force and of transfers (if any) from one police force to another;
- a record of whether the officer passed or failed any qualifying examination at which he/she was a candidate;
- a record of service in the police force and the date on which the officer ceased to be a member of the police force with the reason thereof.

The record must also include particulars of all promotions, postings, removals, injuries received, periods of illness, commendations, rewards, sanctions other than cautions imposed under reg. 35 of the Police (Conduct) Regulations 2012.

4.1.5 Periods of Duty and Travelling Time

Regulation 22 of the Police Regulations 2003 allows the Home Secretary to determine the normal periods of duty of a member of a police force. It also gives the Home Secretary the authority to specify the periods allowed for refreshment, the variable shift arrangements which may be brought into operation by a force, the manner and timing of the publication of duty rosters and the matters to be contained therein.

The circumstances in which 'travelling time' may be treated as duty can also be determined by the Home Secretary under reg. 22. In this context 'travelling time' means time spent by members of a police force in travelling to and from their home where they are required to perform their normal daily period of duty in more than one tour of duty, between two tours, or where they are recalled to duty between two tours of duty, in consequence of their recall. The Home Secretary may confer on the chief officer discretion to fix a limit on the travelling time which is to be treated as duty and allow discretion to fix a limit on the amount of the expenses which may be reimbursed in respect of travelling time.

4.1.6 Overtime, Public Holidays and Rest Days

Regulation 25 of the Police Regulations 2003 permits the Home Secretary to determine the circumstances and manner in which a member of a police force shall be compensated in respect of overtime incurred when officers begin work earlier than their rostered time without 'due notice' and have completed their normal daily period of duty, or remain on duty after their tour of duty ends, or are recalled between two tours of duty. For the purposes of this regulation, 'due notice' means notice given at least eight hours before the revised starting time of the rostered tour of duty in question. 'Recall' does not include a warning to be in readiness for duty if required.

The Home Secretary can confer on the chief officer discretion to fix the day on which a period commences for the purposes of the determination, to fix the period within which time off in compensation for overtime is to be granted, and the discretion to allow time in addition to that specified in the determination to be taken into account in computing any period of overtime.

Likewise, reg. 26 allows the Home Secretary to determine the circumstances and manner in which a member of a police force shall be granted leave or otherwise compensated in respect of time spent on duty on days which a member of a police force has elected to treat as public holidays, or rostered rest days.

4.1.7 The Police Federation and Trade Union Membership

Part III of the Police Act 1996 makes provision for the establishment and maintenance of police representative institutions.

Section 59 provides for the continued existence of the Police Federation and specifies that it may represent a police officer in any proceedings brought under regulations made under s. 50(3) (e.g. efficiency and conduct; see chapters 4.2 and 4.3) or an appeal from such proceedings.

The Secretary of State may make Regulations in relation to matters concerning the Federation (s. 60(1)), e.g. the Police Federation Regulations 1969 (SI 1969/1787), as amended.

Provision is made under s. 61 for a Police Negotiating Board to represent the interests of persons and bodies who between them maintain the police forces in Great Britain in relation to:

- hours of duty
- leave
- pay and allowances
- pensions
- clothing, equipment and accoutrements.

Section 64 of the Police Act 1996 states:

(1) Subject to the following provisions of this section, a member of a police force shall not be a member of any trade union, or of any association having for its objects, or one of its objects, to control or influence the pay, pensions or conditions of service of any police force.

> **KEYNOTE**
>
> Where a person was a member of a trade union before becoming a member of a police service, he/she may, with the consent of the chief officer of police, continue to be a member of that union during the time of his/her service (s. 64(2)).

Section 64 also states:

(5) Nothing in this section applies to membership of the Police Federations, or of any body recognised by the Secretary of State for the purposes of this section as representing members of police forces who are not members of those Federations.

4.1.8 Special Constables

The terms under which special constables may be appointed and deployed are set out in the Special Constables Regulations 1965 (SI 1965/536). The Police Act 1996 covers how officers can be deployed, as well as allowing special constables to use their constabulary powers in forces throughout England and Wales. Amendments in 2006 brought special constables into line with regular officers, and allow greater flexibility in their deployment.

4.1.9 Extending the Policing Family

A feature of the Police Reform Act 2002 lies in what has been called the 'extended police family'. It has been recognised that police officers can spend too much time tied up with administrative or non-core tasks which, in turn, has led to the employment of civilian support staff in specific roles, for example as detention and escort officers, and giving them relevant powers to let them carry out their jobs. This allows police officers time to concentrate on the core policing tasks that require the full range of powers and training that police officers can offer, and provide the public with additional reassurance by having more officers visible and out working in the community.

Part 4 of the Police Reform Act 2002 introduced some novel developments in the law regulating policing powers by potentially extending some of those powers to a whole range of non-police individuals. These individuals will be designated in a particular role(s) or title(s) specifically used in the legislation. They will be given a number of different titles, including the titles specifically used in the legislation (such as Investigating

Officers and Detention Officers). The whole system works by allowing the relevant chief officer to confer certain powers on different groups of people by designating or accrediting them. The chief officer does not *have* to confer any powers on any such groups and he/she can decide to confer only a reduced number of powers or to place further limitations on those powers: the Act simply gives the chief officer the freedom and flexibility to do so.

4.1.10 Who Manages or Employs People with Police Powers?

When approaching these powers and their applicability to different individuals a good starting point is to consider who the relevant person's employer is. Some roles created under the Act (such as Police Community Support Officers) can only be carried out by police employees; if you do not work directly for the police, you cannot have these powers or perform these roles. In other roles (Detention Officers and Escort Officers), the person does not necessarily have to be employed by the police. If the person is not employed by the force, their employer must have a contract with the relevant Police and Crime Commissioner. These people will have their powers contained in a 'designation' from the relevant chief officer. Another group of people who can have powers conferred on them by a chief officer are not employees of either the police or a contractor. These people are 'accredited' with powers that can only come from their accreditation under a statutory Community Safety Accreditation Scheme. In order to perform *any* of the roles and exercise *any* of the powers under part 4 of the Act, an individual must be employed by somebody, because it is through the person's employer that the chief officer or the relevant constable can exercise a degree of control over those auxiliary staff who are not directly employed by the police. Therefore, if you are unemployed or self-employed, the legislation will not allow you to have these powers or to carry out any of the relevant functions.

4.1.11 The 'Chain of Control'

Another feature to note is that there is a sort of 'chain of control' linking the individual to a chief constable. The further along the chain people are, the less control a chief officer has over them—and therefore the fewer powers they can be given under the Act. In the case of staff directly employed by a particular police force, they will have a contract of employment with their own force as will any member of non-sworn civilian staff. Moving down the chain of control, you find individuals who are not police employees but are employed by an outside organisation which itself has a contract with the police. Examples would be security companies providing prisoner escort services. These employees can be given more limited powers and roles under the Act. Further still along the chain of control are people employed by entirely independent non-police organisations. These people could be working for any number of local businesses or organisations within a police area and the Act allows a chief officer to accredit their employees with limited policing powers.

4.1.12 Designated Police Employees

The first group of people who can be empowered under part 4 of the Police Reform Act 2002 are those employed by the police and under the direction and control of their chief officer. These police employees can be 'designated' under s. 38 by their chief officer as *one or more* of the following:

- Police Community Support Officers (PCSOs)
- Investigating Officers
- Detention Officers
- Escort Officers.

No one may be designated in these roles unless the chief officer is satisfied that they are a suitable person to carry out the designated functions, are capable of carrying out those functions effectively and have received adequate training. Adequate training is not defined but it would have to cover the exercise and performance of the relevant powers and duties to be conferred on the person (see s. 38(4)). Considerable weight was given to these safeguards—and the restrictions on any use of force (**see para. 4.1.18**)—during the passage of the Police Reform Bill through Parliament, and the provision of effective training was seen as an essential measure to the proper functioning of this new framework.

Because these designated staff are employees of the relevant force, the chief officer is responsible for dealing with reports of misconduct and complaints against them in the normal way. However, the Independent Police Complaints Commission (IPCC) also has jurisdiction over any such allegations or complaints.

4.1.13   Powers Conferred on Designated Police Employees

The specific powers that can be conferred by the chief officer on these designated employees depend on which designated role(s) they are given. The powers, which were extended by the Serious Organised Crime and Police Act 2005 and the Police and Justice Act 2006, are set out in sch. 4 to the Police Reform Act 2002. Schedule 4 is itself divided into further parts, 1–4, with each part containing a number of statutory powers. Helpfully the parts of sch. 4 correspond to the four roles set out in the list at **para. 4.1.12** so that the respective powers under parts 1–4 and the relative designated employee roles look like this:

Person	Powers
PCSO	Part 1
Investigating Officer	Part 2
Detention Officer	Part 3
Escort Officer	Part 4

The powers set out in sch. 4 are many and various but they do follow a degree of common sense when you consider the practical requirements of the roles they cover. For example, it makes sense for an Investigating Officer to be given investigative powers such as powers of entry, search and seizure, along with powers to arrest suspects during an interview where further offences are revealed. Similarly, Detention Officers need powers to fingerprint and search prisoners. People already employed by the police in certain roles can be designated under this part of the Act (e.g. scenes of crime officers can be given powers of entry and search).

The Police and Justice Act 2006, s. 7 allows for a standard set of Community Support Officer (CSO) powers and duties. The powers will be determined by an order from the Secretary of State. Section 38(5A) of the Police Reform Act 2002 adds a power for dealing with truants into the list of powers that may be conferred on persons designated as CSOs set out in sch. 4 to the Police Reform Act 2002. If designated with the power set out at para. 4C, CSOs now have the power that constables already have under s. 16 of the Crime and Disorder Act 1998 to deal with truants. This power would allow CSOs to remove from specified areas young people of school age that they believe are absent from school without lawful authority and to take them either to their school or to a place which has been specified by the local authority.

Also, s. 9 of the Police and Justice Act 2006 introduces sch. 5 which makes various amendments to provisions in the Police Reform Act 2002. Paragraph 2(3) inserts subs. (5B) into s. 38 of the 2002 Act so that when a chief constable first designates a person as a PCSO, he/she is required to ensure that the person has received adequate training in the exercise of the standard powers that are in force at that time. The effect of para. 3 of the schedule is to amend s. 42 of the 2002 Act so that CSOs, when exercising powers or duties, must produce on demand, evidence of their designation as a CSO and of any non-standard power which they exercise that has been conferred on them by their chief officer under s. 38.

Accordingly, CSOs will not have to carry with them details of all the standard powers which have been conferred upon them by an order under s. 38A. The requirement to produce evidence of a designation could be satisfied by production of the designation itself, but could also be satisfied by something less, such as some form of document or card.

The full list of powers is summarised in **appendix 4.2**.

4.1.14 Employees of Contracted-out Businesses

Moving further along the chain of control from a chief officer to the relevant employee you come across the next group of people who can be granted powers under sch. 4 to the Police Reform Act 2002. Although their employee status is the source of control over these employees' activities and performance, the first thing to note is that they are *not* employed by the police force. Where a police force has entered into a contract for the provision of services relating to the detention or escorting of people in custody, s. 39 allows the chief officer to designate employees *of the contractor* as either Detention Officers or Escort Officers or both. As such these people may be given some or all of the powers of those roles set out in parts 3 and 4 of sch. 4 to the Act (**see appendix 4.2**). These contracted-out personnel cannot be given the powers of PCSOs and Investigating Officers as they are not police employees—they are employees of the contractor.

Before designating anyone under this part of the Act, a chief officer must be satisfied that the person:

- is a suitable person to carry out the functions for which he/she is to be designated;
- is capable of effectively carrying out those functions; and
- has received adequate training in the carrying out of those functions and in the exercise of those powers and duties to be conferred on him/her (s. 39(4)).

As with the police employees given powers under parts 1–4 of sch. 4, a great deal of emphasis was placed on these safeguards in securing the passage of the Police Reform Bill through Parliament and, in particular, the provision of effective training was seen as essential for the proper functioning of the new measures. Further weight was given to the reassurances provided by the restrictions on the use of force (**see para. 4.1.18**).

If an employee stops being an employee of the contractor, or the contract between the employer and the police comes to an end, any designation ceases to have effect (s. 39(13)). Section 39 also allows for regulations to be made regarding the handling of complaints and misconduct issues arising out of the functions of designated employees.

4.1.15 Accredited Employees

Moving further still along the chain of control linking the force with the employee brings you to those people who are simply employed by local businesses and employers in the relevant police area. Those businesses do not have to have an existing contract with the force or the Police and Crime Commissioner and their employees only gain their accreditation from powers conferred under a Community Safety Accreditation Scheme (CSAS).

A CSAS is a scheme set up and maintained by a chief officer for the purposes of:

- contributing to community safety and security;
- combating crime and disorder, public nuisance and other forms of anti-social behaviour.

4.1.16 Community Safety Accreditation Schemes

Before establishing a CSAS, a chief officer must consult with the Police and Crime Commissioner maintaining that force and every local authority any part of whose area lies within his/her force (s. 40(4)). In the case of the Metropolitan Police the commissioner must consult the Deputy Mayor of London for Policing and Crime. Any CSAS must also appear in the policing plan of any force. A CSAS must contain provisions for making arrangements with local employers carrying on business (including those carrying out statutory functions) for the supervision of any of their employees who become accredited under the scheme (s. 40(8)). In addition, it is the duty of the chief officer to ensure that the employers of the persons on whom powers are conferred have established and maintain satisfactory arrangements for handling complaints relating to the carrying out of functions under the scheme (s. 40(9)). This is all the more important as the accredited employees will have no formal individual link with the force, either directly (as in the case of designated police employees under parts 1 to 4 of sch. 4) or indirectly (as with employees of contracted-out businesses whose employees are designated under parts 3 and 4 of the schedule).

Under a CSAS, s. 41 of the Police Reform Act 2002 allows a chief officer to accredit people with certain policing powers. These powers are set out in sch. 5 to the Act and in **appendix 4.2**.

Photographing of persons given fixed penalty notices—paragraph 9ZA

Under this paragraph an accredited employee will, within the relevant police area, have the power of a constable under s. 64A(1A) of the Police and Criminal Evidence Act 1984 (as to which **see** *Evidence and Procedure*, **para. 2.9.6**) to take a photograph, elsewhere than at a police station, of a person to whom the accredited person has given a penalty notice (or as the case may be a fixed penalty notice) in exercise of any power mentioned in para. 1(2).

OFFENCE: **Failing to Comply with Requirements—*Police Reform Act 2002, sch. 5, para. 2(2)***
- Triable summarily • Fine

The Police Reform Act 2002, sch. 5, para. 2 states:

(2) A person who fails to comply with a requirement under sub-paragraph (1) is guilty of an offence.

KEYNOTE

The reference to 'a requirement' under sub-para. (1) refers to the requirement for the person to give his/her name and address to the accredited employee.

In making the requirement it will be critical that the accredited person produces his/her authority and that, if relevant, he/she is in the correct uniform and wearing the proper badge etc.

4.1.17 General Considerations for Designated or Accredited Employees

Designated or accredited employees empowered under the Police Reform Act 2002 exercising any powers granted there under in relation to any person must produce their authority to that person if requested to do so (s. 42(1)). Their powers are only exercisable if the employee is wearing the relevant uniform as determined or approved by the chief officer and identified or described in the designation/accreditation (s. 42(2)). Any designation or accreditation will specify the extent, nature and duration of the powers conferred by it and also any uniform that the employee is required to wear. In the case of an accredited employee (i.e. acting under the authority of sch. 5 of the Act), he/she must also be wearing an appropriate badge as specified by the Secretary of State in the manner or place specified (s. 42(2)). Given the nature of some investigative functions carried out by Investigating Officers, a police officer of or above the rank of inspector may direct an Investigating Officer not to wear a uniform for the purposes of a particular operation (s. 42(2A)). If such a direction is given, s. 42(2) will not apply in relation to *that* Investigating Officer for the purposes of *that* operation. The officer giving this direction not to wear uniform must be from the same force as the chief officer who appointed the Investigating Officer under s. 38.

A chief officer of police may modify or withdraw an employee's designation or accreditation *at any time* simply by giving the employee notice (s. 42(3)). This power of revocation or amendment is absolute and there is no requirement for any misconduct or poor performance on the part of the employee. If a designation or accreditation is modified or withdrawn, the chief officer must send a copy of the notice to the relevant employer (see s. 42(5) and (6)). The Secretary of State can add to the relevant police powers that are extended to designated or accredited employees in a much simpler and quicker format in some circumstances and reference should be made to the most up-to-date version of the various schedules.

Any liability for civil wrongs (torts) arising out of conduct in the course of an employee's designation or accreditation will be apportioned jointly between the police force, the employer and the individual (see s. 42). This should make life interesting, particularly in the areas of remedies and the application of the Human Rights Act 1998.

4.1.18 Use of Force

There are two main sources of a designated employee's power to use reasonable force. The first source is the specific power granted under sch. 4 to the Police Reform Act 2002 as discussed at **para. 4.1.13**. The second source is to be found in s. 38(8) of the Act. This provides that if a designated employee has a power which, if exercised by a constable, would have a further power to use reasonable force then the designated employee will also have the same entitlement to use reasonable force. For instance, where a constable is exercising powers under the Police and Criminal Evidence Act 1984 where the consent of another person other than a police officer is not needed (e.g. most powers of arrest, search and seizure), s. 117 gives the officer a power to use reasonable force if necessary. If an Investigating Officer designated under part 2 of sch. 4 to the Police Reform Act 2002 uses a power to enter premises following an arrest (sch. 4, para. 18), he/she will be entitled to use reasonable force if necessary because a constable using the same power to enter and search would also have the power to use reasonable force. However, given the sensitivities around the use of force by the police and other agents of the State, there are further restrictions on the use of force by a designated employee. If, as in the above example, the designated employee uses force to enter premises, that power can *only* be used:

- in the company *and* under the supervision of a constable, or
- for the purpose of saving life or limb or preventing serious damage to property. (s. 38(9))

The accompanying constable in such circumstances can expect to be closely questioned over the extent and effectiveness of his/her 'supervision' in the event that the matter comes to trial or is investigated following a complaint, report or allegation of misconduct. It is unlikely that the requirements of s. 38(9) would be satisfied by a merely passive physical presence by a constable at a time when the power is exercised and the legislation envisages some form of active and effective supervision by the constable. Similarly, any designated employee using these powers will need to be able to show how the various criteria were met by the particular circumstances at the time.

The general rules and restrictions on the use of force will apply in these cases (**see para. 4.5.2.3**) and any use of force by a designated employee will come under close scrutiny— particularly where that person is a Detention Officer or Escort Officer employed by a contracted-out business under s. 39.

4.1.19 The Public Interest Disclosure Act 1998 and 'Whistle Blowing'

The Public Interest Disclosure Act 1998 was introduced to help create an atmosphere where workers both feel and *are* able to report certain cases of wrongdoing at work, primarily to their employers, but to outside bodies or individuals if appropriate. Often described as 'whistle blowing', the reporting of criminal, unlawful, dangerous or damaging practices and situations has been protected by the 1998 Act for most workers for several years—provided the Act's conditions are complied with. The framework that the legislation creates distinguishes between internal disclosures to the relevant employer and disclosures made to external bodies or individuals including the police—with the emphasis firmly on *internal* disclosure. It would clearly not be appropriate on all occasions when an employee believes something is amiss at work for that to be reported to an outside body, for instance by selling the story to the press or passing the information straight to an MP. The Act therefore differentiates between different types of situation which may need to be reported. These distinctions are less important where the employer *is* the police but it is still necessary to consider the relevant statutory procedure. Many employers have published detailed reporting procedures for making disclosure. In some areas of employment, the Secretary of State has made regulations prescribing those people and bodies to whom some disclosures can be made where appropriate. Examples are the IPCC, the Inland Revenue, the Charity Commissioners and the Health and Safety Executive (see the Public Interest Disclosure (Prescribed Persons) Order 1999 (SI 1999/1549)).

The Act works by inserting various provisions into the Employment Rights Act 1996. This has resulted in a fairly detailed piece of legislation and reference should be made to the full statutory text, along with any relevant regulations and guidance.

4.1.20 Protected Disclosures

Section 43B of the Employment Rights Act 1996 refers to 'protected disclosures'. These are generally disclosures made in accordance with the Act of information which, in the reasonable belief of the maker, tends to show *one or more* of the following:

- a criminal offence has been committed, is being committed or is likely to be committed;
- a person has failed, is failing or is likely to fail to comply with any legal obligation to which he/she is subject;
- a miscarriage of justice has occurred, is occurring or is likely to occur;
- the health or safety of any individual has been, is being or is likely to be endangered;
- the environment has been, is being or is likely to be damaged;
- information tending to show any matter falling within any one of the preceding paragraphs has been, is being or is likely to be deliberately concealed.

Clearly, although many of these things would be unusual in most employment contexts, the likelihood of some of the issues covered above arising is possibly greater in a policing or criminal justice environment than elsewhere.

It is immaterial that the relevant failure reported occurs or would occur outside the United Kingdom (Employment Rights Act 1996, s. 43B(2)). As discussed at **para. 4.1.19**, the disclosure should generally be made to the employer or other responsible or prescribed person. However, if:

- the employee reasonably believes that he/she will be subjected to a detriment by the employer if the disclosure is made, or
- there is no relevant or prescribed person and the employee reasonably believes that it is likely that evidence relating to the failure will be concealed or destroyed if a disclosure is made, or
- the employee has previously made a disclosure of substantially the same information to the employer or prescribed person

then he/she may make a protected disclosure to someone else. However, even if the above conditions are met, the employee must make any disclosure in good faith, must not be acting for personal gain and must reasonably believe that the information (and any allegation contained in it) is substantially true—and it must be reasonable in all the circumstances of the case for him/her to make the disclosure (see generally Employment Rights Act 1996, s. 43G). In determining whether it was reasonable to make the disclosure in all the circumstances here, regard will be had in particular to the identity of the person receiving it, the seriousness of the reported failure, any breach of confidentiality by the employee and the circumstances of any earlier disclosure.

If the relevant failure is of an exceptionally serious nature and the employee reasonably believes that the information (and any allegation contained in it) is substantially true, he/she may make a protected disclosure, in good faith and not for personal gain, to an external person provided it is reasonable in all the circumstances to do so (see Employment Rights Act 1996, s. 43H). Again, all the circumstances, and particularly the identity of the external party, will be relevant in determining whether it was reasonable to make the disclosure. It is important to note that, if the making of the disclosure would itself amount to an offence, the disclosure *will not* be protected. An example of where this might be the case is under the Regulation of Investigatory Powers Act 2000, s. 19—disclosing information as to the existence or non-existence of an interception warrant (**see para. 4.17.4**).

Initially the Public Interest Disclosure Act did not apply to the police, but under s. 43KA of the Employment Rights Act 1996, for the purposes of part IVA (Protected Disclosures), a police officer is to be treated as an employee.

As well as making the workplace safer and more open to scrutiny, the 1998 Act creates a number of key rights for individuals. For instance, it makes the dismissal of an employee automatically unfair if the reason (or principal reason if there is more than one) for the dismissal is that the employee made a protected disclosure (see Employment Rights Act 1996, s. 103A). While the Code of Conduct under the Police (Conduct) Regulations 2012 has always placed officers under a duty to report wrongdoing by fellow officers, there has not been any form of statutory protection for those who do so. In addition to being protected from dismissal, an employee also has the right under the Act not to be subjected to any other detriment by his/her employer (e.g. being disciplined, denied perks or promotion) on the grounds that he/she has made a protected disclosure (Employment Rights Act 1996, s. 47B). Employees can bring a complaint to the employment tribunal in respect of these matters and the usual statutory ceiling on the amount of the compensatory award that the tribunal can make is removed.

4.2 Complaints and Misconduct

4.2.1 Introduction

Police complaints and misconduct has always been a difficult and bureaucratically complex area of police law and procedure. The Taylor Review of police officer disciplinary arrangements was published in 2005 and recommended a new disciplinary procedure and a review of the unsatisfactory performance procedures for police officers.

One of the key points to emerge was the need to shift the emphasis and culture in police misconduct matters towards an environment focused on development and improvement as opposed to one focused on blame and punishment. In addition, the report stressed the importance of carrying out a full assessment of the alleged conduct at an early stage with a view to then implementing a proportionate and non-bureaucratic response.

Misconduct is defined as a breach of the Standards of Professional Behaviour (**see para. 4.2.2**); gross misconduct means a breach of the Standards of Professional Behaviour so serious that dismissal would be justified. Unsatisfactory performance or unsatisfactory attendance mean an inability or failure of a police officer to perform the duties of the role or rank he/she is currently undertaking to a satisfactory standard or level.

A series of Statutory Instruments provides the performance and misconduct framework:

- **The Police (Performance) Regulations 2012** set out the procedures for dealing with cases of unsatisfactory performance or attendance of police officers.
- **The Police (Conduct) Regulations 2012** set out the procedures for dealing with cases of misconduct or gross misconduct. The Conduct Regulations contain the 'Standards of Professional Behaviour' that police officers are expected to maintain.
- **The Police (Complaints and Misconduct) Regulations 2012** provide the link between the new misconduct procedures for police officers of all ranks and special constables, and the police complaints system that is governed by the provisions in sch. 3 to the Police Reform Act 2002.
- **The Police Appeals Tribunals Rules 2012** set out the procedures for an appeal to a police appeals tribunal and the grounds on which a police officer or special constable can appeal against a finding and/or a particular outcome from the Conduct and Performance Regulations.

The Home Office issued Home Office Circular 23/2012, *Changes to the police complaints system and procedures for dealing with police officer misconduct and unsatisfactory performance*, which came into effect on 16 November 2012.

The Police (Complaints and Conduct) Act 2013 has strengthened the role and powers of the Independent Police Complaints Commission (IPCC), particularly with regard to compelling officers to attend interviews, including those who have witnessed an event, not just officers whose conduct is under investigation.

4.2.2 The Standards of Professional Behaviour

The conduct procedures are supported by a code of ethics—the Standards of Professional Behaviour—which provide the yardstick by which the conduct of police officers is judged. They apply to police officers of all ranks, special constables, and to those subject to suspension. They are not intended to describe every situation but rather to set a framework which enables everybody to know what type of conduct by a police officer is acceptable and what is unacceptable. The standards are:

- **Honesty and Integrity**: Police officers are honest, act with integrity and do not compromise or abuse their position.
- **Authority, Respect and Courtesy**: Police officers act with self-control and tolerance, treating members of the public and colleagues with respect and courtesy. Police officers do not abuse their powers or authority and respect the rights of all individuals.
- **Equality and Diversity**: Police officers act with fairness and impartiality. They do not discriminate unlawfully or unfairly.
- **Use of Force**: Police officers only use force to the extent that it is necessary, proportionate and reasonable in all the circumstances.
- **Orders and Instructions**: Police officers only give and carry out lawful orders and instructions. Police officers abide by police regulations, force policies and lawful orders.
- **Duties and Responsibilities**: Police officers are diligent in the exercise of their duties and responsibilities.
- **Confidentiality**: Police officers treat information with respect and access or disclose it only in the proper course of police duties.
- **Fitness for Duty**: Police officers when on duty or presenting themselves for duty are fit to carry out their duties and responsibilities.
- **Discreditable Conduct**: Police officers behave in a manner which does not discredit the police service or undermine public confidence, whether on or off duty. Police officers report any action taken against them for a criminal offence, conditions imposed by a court or the receipt of any penalty notice.
- **Challenging and Reporting Improper Conduct**: Police officers report, challenge or take action against the conduct of colleagues which has fallen below the standards of professional behaviour.

4.2.3 The Role of the Police Friend

At all stages of the misconduct or performance proceedings (including any interview during an investigation into misconduct), police officers have the right to consult with and be accompanied by a police friend.

The police friend can be a police officer, a police staff member, or a person nominated by the police officer's staff association. A person asked to be a police friend is entitled to refuse, and cannot be appointed to act if he/she had any involvement in that particular case.

The police friend can:

- advise the police officer concerned throughout the proceedings under the Police (Conduct) Regulations 2012 or Police (Performance) Regulations 2012;
- unless the police officer concerned has the right to be legally represented and chooses to be so represented, represent the police officer concerned at the misconduct proceedings, performance proceedings, appeal meeting, a special case hearing or at a police appeals tribunal;
- make representations to the 'appropriate authority' concerning any aspect of the proceedings under the Conduct or Performance Regulations;
- accompany the police officer concerned to any interview, meeting or hearing which forms part of any proceedings under the Conduct or Performance Regulations.

The 'appropriate authority' under the Performance Regulations is the chief officer of police, who may delegate any of his/her functions to a police officer of at least the rank of chief inspector or a police staff member who is of at least a similar level of seniority to a chief inspector.

A police friend who has agreed to accompany a police officer is entitled to take a reasonable amount of duty time to fulfil those responsibilities and is considered to be on duty when attending interviews, meetings or hearings.

Subject to any timescales set out in the Conduct or Performance Regulations, at any stage of a case, up to and including a misconduct meeting or hearing or an unsatisfactory performance meeting, the police officer concerned or his/her police friend may submit that there are insufficient grounds upon which to base the case and/or that the correct procedures have not been followed, clearly setting out the reasons and submitting any supporting evidence. It will be for the person responsible for the relevant stage of the case to consider any such submission and determine how best to respond to it, bearing in mind the need to ensure fairness to the police officer concerned.

At a misconduct meeting, hearing or special case hearing under the Conduct Regulations or the Performance Regulations where the police friend attends, he/she may:

(a) put the police officer concerned's case;
(b) sum up that case;
(c) respond on the police officer concerned's behalf to any view expressed at the meeting;
(d) make representations concerning any aspect of the proceedings;
(e) confer with the police officer concerned;
(f) in a misconduct meeting or hearing, ask questions of any witness, subject to the discretion of the person(s) conducting that hearing.

A police officer is entitled to be legally represented at a misconduct hearing or special case hearing (in cases that fall to be dealt with under the Conduct Regulations) or a third stage performance meeting (for dealing with an issue of gross incompetence under the Performance Regulations). Where he/she decides to be so represented, the police friend can also attend and may consult with the police officer concerned, but will not carry out functions (a)–(d) and (f) described above.

Where a police officer is arrested or interviewed in connection with a criminal offence committed while off duty that has no connection with his/her role as a serving police officer, then the police friend has no right to attend the criminal interview.

4.2.4 Death or Serious Injury Matters

A death or serious injury (DSI) matter is defined in s. 12 (2A–D) of the Police Reform Act 2002. Where there is an investigation into a DSI case and there is no complaint or indication of any conduct matter, the investigation will focus on the circumstances of the incident. However, where during the course of the investigation into the DSI matter there is an indication that a person serving with the police may have committed a criminal offence or behaved in a manner that would justify the bringing of disciplinary proceedings, the DSI matter will be reclassified as a recordable conduct matter (or complaint if appropriate) and dealt with accordingly.

4.2.5 Misconduct Procedures

The procedures are intended to provide a fair, open and proportionate method of dealing with alleged misconduct and to encourage a culture of learning and development.

Where the conduct is linked to a complaint, recordable conduct matter or DSI matter the appropriate authority is required to follow the provisions in the Police Reform Act 2002, the accompanying Police (Complaints and Misconduct) Regulations 2012 and the IPCC statutory guidance which set out how complaints by members of the public are to be dealt with.

Probationer constables are not subject to the procedures for dealing with unsatisfactory performance, since there are separately established procedures for dealing with the performance of student police officers. However, they are subject to the misconduct procedures. The chief officer has discretion whether to use the misconduct procedures or the procedures set out at reg. 13 of the Police Regulations 2003 (Discharge of Probationer) as the most appropriate means of dealing with a misconduct matter. In exercising this discretion due regard should be had to whether the officer admits the conduct or not. Where the misconduct in question is not admitted then in most, if not all, cases the matter will fall to be determined under the misconduct procedures. If the reg. 13 procedure is used, the student police officer should be given a fair hearing (i.e. an opportunity to comment and present mitigation) under that procedure.

4.2.5.1 Suspension or Change of Duty

Suspension is not a formal misconduct outcome and does not suggest any prejudgement. The period of suspension should be as short as possible and any investigation into the conduct of a suspended police officer should be made a priority. The decision to suspend a police officer will only be taken where there is an allegation of misconduct/gross misconduct and:

- an effective investigation may be prejudiced unless the police officer is suspended; or
- the public interest, having regard to the nature of the allegation and any other relevant considerations, requires that the police officer should be suspended; and
- a temporary move to a new location or role has been considered but is not appropriate in the circumstances.

A temporary move to a new location or role must always be considered first as an alternative to suspension. While suspended, a police officer ceases to hold the office of constable and, in the case of a member of a police force, ceases to be a member of a police force, save for the purposes of the misconduct proceedings.

The police officer or his/her police friend may make representations against the initial decision to suspend (within seven working days beginning with the first working day after being suspended) and at any time during the course of the suspension if he/she believes the circumstances have changed and that the suspension is no longer appropriate.

The police officer should be told exactly why he/she is being suspended, or being moved to other duties and this should be confirmed in writing. If suspension is on public interest grounds, it should be clearly explained, so far as possible, what those grounds are. The use of suspension must be reviewed at least every four weeks, and sooner where facts have become known which suggest that suspension is no longer appropriate. In cases where the suspension has been reviewed and a decision has been made to continue that suspension, the police officer must be informed in writing of the reasons why. Suspension must be authorised by a senior officer although the decision can be communicated to the police officer by an appropriate manager.

In cases where the IPCC is supervising, managing or independently investigating a matter, the appropriate authority will consult with the IPCC before making a decision whether to suspend or not. It is the appropriate authority's decision whether to suspend a police officer or not. The appropriate authority must also consult the IPCC before making the decision to allow a police officer to resume his/her duties following suspension (unless the suspension ends because there will be no misconduct or special case proceedings or because these have concluded) in cases where the IPCC is supervising, managing or independently investigating a case involving that police officer.

The Standards of Professional Behaviour continue to apply to police officers who are suspended from duty. The appropriate authority can impose such conditions or restrictions on the police officer concerned as are reasonable in the circumstances, e.g. restricting access to police premises or police social functions.

4.2.5.2 Assessment of Misconduct

The initial assessment when an allegation of misconduct is made is conducted by the appropriate authority, and the purpose of the initial assessment is to:

- ensure a timely response to an allegation or an issue relating to conduct;
- identify the police officer subject to the allegation and to eliminate those not involved;
- ensure that the most appropriate procedures are used.

If it is not possible to make an immediate assessment, a process of fact finding should be conducted but only to the extent that it is necessary to determine which procedure should be used. It is perfectly acceptable to ask questions to seek to establish which police officers may have been involved in a particular incident and therefore to eliminate those police officers who are not involved.

Even if the person making the assessment has decided that the matter is not potentially one of misconduct he/she should consider whether there are any developmental or organisational issues which may need to be addressed by the individual (e.g. through management action) or the organisation.

Where an allegation is made which indicates that the conduct of a police officer did not meet the standards set out in the Standards of Professional Behaviour, the appropriate authority must decide whether, if proven or admitted, the allegation would amount to misconduct or gross misconduct. The assessment will also determine whether, if the matter was referred to misconduct proceedings, those proceedings would be likely to be a misconduct meeting (for cases of misconduct) or a misconduct hearing (for cases of gross misconduct or if the police officer concerned has a live final written warning at the time of the assessment and there is a further allegation of misconduct).

If new evidence emerges, a fresh assessment can be made. The matter may be moved up to a level of gross misconduct or down to a level of misconduct.

Unless there are good reasons to take no action, there are two ways by which line managers can deal with matters which have been assessed as potential misconduct: management action or a misconduct investigation. The purpose of management action is to deal with misconduct in a timely, proportionate and effective way that will: command the confidence of staff, police officers, the police service and the public; identify any underlying causes or welfare considerations; improve conduct; and prevent a similar situation arising in the future.

Where an appropriate manager decides at the severity assessment that management action is the most appropriate and proportionate way to deal with an issue of misconduct, there will be no requirement to conduct a formal investigation and therefore no requirement to give a written notice to the police officer concerned in accordance with the provisions in the Conduct Regulations. Where at a later stage, either following the investigation or on withdrawal of the case (under reg. 20 of the Conduct Regulations or reg. 7 of the Police (Complaints and Misconduct) Regulations 2012), an appropriate manager decides to take management action, written notice of this will be given to the police officer as soon as possible. Management action is not to be confused with management advice. Management advice is a disciplinary outcome that can only be imposed following a misconduct meeting or hearing.

Where it is felt that management action is not appropriate to deal with the alleged breach of the Standards of Professional Behaviour an investigation into the alleged misconduct may be necessary. Where, in cases of potential misconduct, management action is not considered appropriate, there will be an investigation under the Conduct Regulations and in cases where the allegation amounts to one of gross misconduct, the matter will always be investigated.

4.2.5.3 Written Notification to Officer

Written notification will be given to the police officer concerned by the investigator appointed to investigate the case, advising the officer that his/her conduct is under investigation—either under reg. 15 of the Conduct Regulations or under reg. 16 of the Complaint Regulations in the case of complaints subject to special requirements (during an investigation into a complaint if it appears to the person investigating that there is an indication that a person to whose conduct the investigation relates may have committed a criminal offence, or behaved in a manner which would justify the bringing of disciplinary proceedings, the person investigating must certify the investigation as one subject to special requirements (para. 19A of sch. 3 to the Police Reform Act 2002)).

The written notice will:

- inform the police officer that there is to be an investigation of his/her potential breach of the Standards of Professional Behaviour and inform the police officer of the name of the investigator who will investigate the matter;
- describe the conduct that is the subject of the investigation and how that conduct is alleged to have fallen below the Standards of Professional Behaviour;
- inform the police officer concerned of the appropriate authority's (or investigator's in a matter dealt with under the 2002 Act) assessment of whether the conduct alleged, if proved, would amount to misconduct or gross misconduct;
- inform the police officer of whether, if the case were to be referred to misconduct proceedings, those would be likely to be a misconduct meeting or misconduct hearing;
- inform the police officer that if the likely form of any misconduct proceedings changes, the police officer will be notified of this together with the reasons for that change;
- inform the police officer of his/her right to seek advice from his/her staff association or any other body, and whom the police officer may choose to act as his/her police friend;
- inform the police officer that if his/her case is referred to a misconduct hearing or special case hearing, he/she has the right to be legally represented by a relevant lawyer. If the police officer elects not to be so represented he/she may be represented by a police friend. The notice will also make clear that if he/she elects not to be legally represented he/she may be dismissed or receive any other disciplinary outcome without being so represented;
- inform the police officer that he/she may provide, within 10 working days of receipt of the notice (unless this period is extended by the investigator), a written or oral statement relating to any matter under investigation and he/she (or his/her police friend) may provide any relevant documents to the investigator within this time;
- inform the police officer that while he/she does not have to say anything, it may harm his/her case if he/she does not mention when interviewed or when providing any information within the relevant time limits something which he/she later relies on in any misconduct proceedings or special case hearing or at an appeal meeting or police appeals tribunal.

The written notification may be provided to a manager (including by email) to give to the police officer concerned or, where appropriate and with the agreement of the police friend, the notice may be given to the police friend to give to the police officer concerned. In both cases the notice must be given to the police officer in person. Alternatively, the notice can be posted by recorded delivery to his/her last known address. The responsibility for ensuring that the notice is served rests with the investigator (in cases dealt with under the 2002 Act) or the appropriate authority. In both cases it is the investigator who must cause the officer concerned to be given the written notice. Therefore while the appropriate authority may do it, the responsibility for ensuring that the notice is served rests with the investigator.

Where the IPCC is conducting an independent or managed investigation the responsibility for ensuring that the police officer is provided with the written notification (as soon as practicable) rests with the investigator appointed or designated to conduct that investigation.

4.2.5.4 Investigation

The purpose of an investigation is to:

- gather evidence to establish the facts and circumstances of the alleged misconduct;
- assist the appropriate authority to establish on the balance of probabilities, based on the evidence and taking into account all of the circumstances, whether there is a case to answer in respect of either misconduct or gross misconduct or that there is no case to answer;
- identify any learning opportunities for the individual or the organisation.

In cases which are not being managed or dealt with by the IPCC, the appropriate authority should ensure that a proportionate and balanced investigation is carried out as soon as possible after any alleged misconduct comes to the appropriate authority's attention and that the investigation is carried out as quickly as possible allowing for the complexity of the case. It is therefore crucial that any investigation is kept proportionate to ensure that an overly lengthy investigation does not lead to grounds for challenge. Where the investigation identifies that the issue is one of performance rather than misconduct, the police officer should be informed as soon as possible that the matter is now being treated as a performance issue.

The investigator is required to notify the police officer of the progress of the investigation at least every four weeks from the start of the investigation.

The investigator (under the Conduct Regulations or the 2002 Act) has a duty to consider the suggestions submitted to him/her. The investigator should consider and document reasons for following or not following any submissions made by the police officer or his/her police friend with a view to ensuring that the investigation is as fair as possible. The suggestions may involve a further suggested line of investigation or further examination of a particular witness. The purpose is to enable a fair and balanced investigation report to be prepared and, where appropriate, made available for consideration at a misconduct meeting/hearing and to negate the need (except where necessary) for witnesses to attend a meeting/hearing.

4.2.5.5 Interviews during Investigation

It will not always be necessary to conduct a formal interview with the police officer subject to the investigation. In some cases, particularly involving low level misconduct cases, it may be more appropriate, proportionate and timely to request a written account from the police officer. The police officer must attend the interview when required to do so and it may be a further misconduct matter to fail to attend.

If the police officer concerned or his/her police friend is not available at the date or time specified by the investigator, the police officer may propose an alternative time. Provided that the alternative time is reasonable and falls within a period of five working days beginning with the first working day after that proposed by the investigator the interview must be postponed to that time.

Where a police officer is on certificated sick leave, the investigator should seek to establish when the police officer will be fit for interview. It may be that the police officer is not fit for ordinary police duty but is perfectly capable of being interviewed. Alternatively the police officer concerned may be invited to provide a written response to the allegations within a specified period and may be sent the questions that the investigator wishes to be answered.

Where a police officer is alleged to have committed a criminal offence a normal criminal investigation will take place, with the police officer being cautioned in accordance with the PACE Code of Practice. Where the matter to be investigated involves both criminal and misconduct allegations, it should be made clear to the police officer concerned at the start of the interview whether he/she is being interviewed in respect of the criminal or misconduct allegations. This may be achieved by conducting two separate interviews, although this does not prevent the responses given in respect of the criminal interview being used in the misconduct investigation and therefore a separate misconduct interview may not be required.

Care should be taken when conducting a misconduct interview where the police officer is also the subject of a criminal investigation in respect of the same behaviour, as anything said by the police officer concerned in the misconduct interview when not under caution and used in the criminal investigation could be subject to an inadmissibility ruling by the court at any subsequent trial. At the beginning of a misconduct interview or when asking a police officer to provide a written response to an allegation, the police officer shall be reminded of the warning contained in reg. 15(1)(h) of the Conduct Regulations (or reg. 16(1)(h) of the Complaint Regulations for cases dealt with under the 2002 Act).

Prior to an interview with a police officer who is the subject of a misconduct investigation, the investigator must ensure that the police officer is provided with sufficient information and time to prepare for the interview. The information provided should always include full details of the allegations made against the police officer, including the relevant dates and places of the alleged misconduct if known. The investigator should consider whether there are good reasons for withholding certain evidence obtained prior to the interview and if there are no such reasons the police officer should normally be provided with all the relevant evidence obtained. The police officer will then have the opportunity to provide his/her version of the events together with any supporting evidence he/she may wish to provide. The police officer will be reminded that failure to provide any account or response to any questions at this stage of the investigation may lead to an adverse inference being drawn at a later stage.

Interviews do not have to be electronically recorded but if they are the person being interviewed shall be given a copy upon request. If the interview is not electronically recorded a written record or summary of the discussion must be given to the person being interviewed. The police officer concerned should be given the opportunity to check and sign that he/she agrees with the summary as an accurate record of what was said and should sign and return a copy to the investigator. Where a police officer refuses or fails to exercise his/her right to agree and sign a copy this will be noted by the investigator. The police officer may make a note of the changes he/she wants to make to the record and a copy of this will be given to the persons conducting the hearing/meeting along with the investigator's account of the record.

Other than for a joint criminal/misconduct investigation interview it will not be necessary for criminal-style witness statements to be taken. In misconduct investigations an agreed and signed written record of the information supplied will be sufficient.

4.2.5.6   Investigation Report and Supporting Documents

At the conclusion of the investigation the investigator must as soon as practicable submit his/her report of the investigation setting out an accurate summary of the evidence that has been gathered. It will also include a recommendation whether in the opinion of the investigator there is a case to answer in respect of misconduct or gross misconduct or whether there is no case to answer.

The appropriate authority shall make a decision based on the report and determine whether there is a case to answer in respect of misconduct or gross misconduct or that there is no case of misconduct to answer (reg. 19 of the Conduct Regulations). If it is decided that there is no case of misconduct to answer, management action may still be appropriate. In matters involving a complaint, where the complaint was subject to a local or supervised investigation under the 2002 Act, the decision of the appropriate authority may be subject to an appeal by the complainant to the IPCC. Similarly in cases where an investigation into a complaint, recordable conduct matter or DSI matter has been conducted under para. 18 (managed) or 19 (independent) of sch. 3 to the 2002 Act, the IPCC has the power to make recommendations and give directions as to whether there is a case to answer. If no further action is to be taken then it is good practice that the investigation report or part of the investigation report that is relevant to the police officer should be given, subject to the harm test, to the police officer on request.

4.2.5.7 Action Prior to Misconduct Meetings/Hearings

In cases where it is decided that there is a misconduct case to answer, the appropriate authority will need to determine whether the matter can be dealt with by means of immediate management action without the need to refer the case to a misconduct meeting. This will be particularly appropriate in cases where the police officer concerned has accepted that his/her conduct fell below the standards expected of a police officer and demonstrates a commitment to improve his/her conduct in the future and to learn from that particular case. In addition the appropriate authority will need to be satisfied that this is the case and that management action is an adequate and sufficient outcome having regard to all the circumstances of the case.

Where the appropriate authority consider that there is a case to answer in respect of misconduct and that management action would not be appropriate or sufficient (for example because the police officer has a live superintendent's warning issued under the previous procedures or the misconduct is serious enough to justify a written warning being given), a misconduct meeting/hearing should be arranged and the police officer shall, subject to the harm test, be given a copy of the investigation report (or the part of the report which is relevant to him/her), any other relevant documents gathered during the course of the investigation and a copy of his/her statement to the investigator.

In determining which documents are relevant, the test to be applied will be that under the Criminal Procedure and Investigations Act 1996, namely whether any document or other material undermines the case against the police officer concerned or would assist the police officer's case.

Where a determination has been made that the conduct amounts to gross misconduct, the case shall be referred to a misconduct hearing (or special case hearing if appropriate). The appropriate authority will also provide the police officer with a notice containing the matters discussed at reg. 21(1)(a) of the Conduct Regulations, including the particulars of the behaviour that is alleged to have fallen below the standards in the Standards of Professional Behaviour.

It is important to note that in cases where the misconduct to be considered was identified as a direct result of a complaint, any decision by the appropriate authority to hold or not to hold a particular misconduct proceeding may be subject to an appeal by the complainant. The appropriate authority, having made its decision on the outcome of the investigation into the complaint and whether there is a case to answer in respect of misconduct or gross misconduct, will notify the complainant of its determination and inform the complainant of his/her right of appeal. The police officer subject of the investigation into his/her conduct should be informed of the determination of the appropriate authority but also informed that the appropriate authority's decision could be subject to an appeal by the complainant to the IPCC. The appropriate authority should then wait until either a 28 plus 2 days period that the complainant may appeal in has elapsed or an appeal has been received and decided by the IPCC before serving the written notice described above (**see para. 4.2.5.3**) confirming how the proceedings are to be dealt with. There is no requirement to wait until the period the complainant has in which to appeal has elapsed in cases where the appropriate authority has determined that the case should be dealt with at a misconduct hearing or a special case hearing.

No final decision can be taken by the appropriate authority in the case of a recordable conduct matter where the IPCC is considering whether to recommend or direct that an appropriate authority take particular misconduct proceedings unless the appropriate authority intends to refer the matter to a misconduct hearing or special case hearing.

Within 14 working days (unless this period is extended by the person conducting the misconduct meeting/hearing for exceptional circumstances) beginning with the first working day after being supplied with the investigator's report and relevant documents and written notice, the police officer will be required to submit in writing:

- whether or not he/she accepts that the behaviour described in the particulars amounts to misconduct or gross misconduct as the case may be;
- where he/she accepts that his/her conduct amounts to misconduct or gross misconduct as the case may be, any written submission he/she wishes to make in mitigation;
- where he/she does not accept that his/her conduct amounts to misconduct or gross misconduct as the case may be, or he/she disputes part of the case, written notice of the particulars of the allegations he/she disputes and his/her account of the relevant events and any arguments on points of law he/she wishes the person conducting the meeting or hearing to consider.

The police officer concerned will also (within the same time limit) provide the appropriate authority and the person conducting the misconduct meeting or hearing with a copy of any document he/she intends to rely on at the misconduct proceedings. In addition, at a misconduct hearing the persons conducting that hearing have the right to have a relevant lawyer available to them for advice at the hearing.

The police officer shall be informed of the name of the persons holding the meeting/hearing together with the name of any person appointed to advise the persons conducting the meeting/hearing as soon as reasonably practicable after they have been appointed. The police officer may object to any person hearing or advising at a misconduct meeting or hearing within three working days starting with the first working day after he/she was notified of the person's name.

If the police officer concerned submits a compelling reason why such a person should not be involved in the meeting/hearing, a replacement should be found and the police officer will be notified of the name of the replacement and the police officer concerned will have the same right to object to that person. The police officer concerned may object to a person conducting a misconduct meeting or hearing or advising at such proceedings if, for example, the person has been involved in the case in a way that would make it difficult to make an objective and impartial assessment of the facts of the case.

4.2.5.8 Documents for the Meeting/Hearing

The person conducting the misconduct meeting/hearing shall be supplied with:

- a copy of the notice supplied to the police officer that sets out the fact that the case was to be referred to a misconduct meeting/hearing and details of the alleged misconduct etc.;
- a copy of the investigator's report or such parts of the report as relate to the police officer concerned, any other relevant documents gathered during the course of the investigation and a copy of any statement made by the officer;
- the notice provided by the police officer setting out whether or not the police officer accepts that his/her conduct amounts to misconduct or gross misconduct, any submission he/she wishes to make in mitigation where the conduct is accepted, and where he/she does not accept that the alleged conduct amounts to misconduct or gross

misconduct or he/she disputes part of the case, the allegations he/she disputes and his/her account of the relevant events; any arguments on points of law submitted by the police officer concerned as well as any documents he/she intends to rely on at the meeting/hearing, submitted under reg. 22 of the Conduct Regulations;

- where the police officer concerned does not accept that the alleged conduct amounts to misconduct or gross misconduct as the case may be or where he/she disputes any part of the case, any other documents that in the opinion of the appropriate authority should be considered at the meeting/hearing;
- any other documents that the persons conducting the meeting/hearing request that are relevant to the case.

4.2.5.9 Witnesses

Generally speaking, misconduct meetings and hearings will be conducted without witnesses. A witness will only be required to attend a misconduct meeting/hearing if the person conducting or chairing the meeting/hearing reasonably believes his/her attendance is necessary to resolve disputed issues in that case.

The appropriate authority and the officer concerned shall inform each other of any witnesses they wish to attend, including brief details of the evidence those persons can provide and their addresses. They should attempt to agree which witnesses are necessary to deal with the issues in dispute.

The appropriate authority shall supply the persons conducting the proceedings with a list of the witnesses agreed between the parties or, where there is no agreement, the lists provided by both the officer and the appropriate authority. The person conducting a misconduct meeting or the chair of a misconduct hearing will decide whether to allow such witnesses. The person conducting or chairing the misconduct proceedings may also decide that a witness other than one on such lists should be required to attend (if his/her attendance is considered necessary).

In special cases (fast track) no witnesses, other than the officer concerned, will provide evidence at the hearing.

4.2.6 Misconduct Proceedings

There are two types of misconduct proceedings:

- A **misconduct meeting** for cases where there is a case to answer in respect of misconduct and where the maximum outcome would be a final written warning.
- A **misconduct hearing** for cases where there is a case to answer in respect of gross misconduct or where the police officer has a live final written warning and there is a case to answer in respect of a further act of misconduct. The maximum outcome at this hearing would be dismissal from the police service without notice.

It is important that misconduct hearings are only used for those matters where the police officer has a live final written warning and has potentially committed a further act of misconduct that warrants misconduct proceedings or the misconduct alleged is so serious that it is genuinely considered that, if proven or admitted, dismissal from the police service would be justified.

4.2.6.1 Timing for Holding Meetings/Hearings

A misconduct meeting shall take place not later than 20 working days beginning with the first working day after the date on which the documents and material for the meeting have been supplied to the police officer under reg. 21 of the Conduct Regulations. Misconduct hearings shall take place not later than 30 working days beginning with the first working day after the date the documents for the hearing have been supplied to the police officer concerned. The time limit for holding a misconduct meeting or a misconduct hearing can be extended if in the interests of justice the person conducting or chairing the misconduct proceedings considers it appropriate to extend beyond that period.

In order to maintain confidence in the misconduct procedures it is important that the misconduct meetings/hearings are held as soon as practicable and extensions to the time-scales should be an exception rather than the rule.

4.2.6.2 Purpose of Misconduct Meeting/Hearing

The purpose of a formal misconduct meeting/hearing is to:

- give the police officer a fair opportunity to make his/her case having considered the investigation report, including supporting documents, and to put forward any factors the police officer wishes to be considered in mitigation (in addition to the submission which must be sent in advance to the person conducting or chairing the meeting/hearing for his/her consideration);
- decide if the conduct of the police officer fell below the standards set out in the Standards of Professional Behaviour based on the balance of probabilities and having regard to all of the evidence and circumstances;
- consider what the outcome should be if misconduct is proven or admitted. Consideration will be given to any live written warnings or final written warnings (and any previous disciplinary outcomes that have not expired) and any early admission of the conduct by the police officer.

4.2.6.3 Misconduct Meeting/Hearing—Non-senior Officers

A misconduct meeting for non-senior officers (police officers up to and including the rank of chief superintendent and all special constables) will be heard by a police officer (or other member of a police force) of at least one rank above the police officer concerned. However, in the case of a special constable, the member of the police force must be a sergeant or above or a senior human resources professional. Alternatively, a police staff member who, in the opinion of the appropriate authority, is a grade above that of the police officer concerned can be appointed, but not if the case substantially involves operational policing matters.

A misconduct hearing for non-senior officers will consist of a three person panel. The chair will be either a senior officer or a senior human resources professional. A senior human resources professional means a human resources professional who in the opinion of the appropriate authority has sufficient seniority, skills and experience to conduct the misconduct hearing.

4.2.6.4 Misconduct Hearings in Public

Where a misconduct hearing (not misconduct meetings) arises from a case where the IPCC has conducted an independent investigation (in accordance with para. 19 of sch. 3 to the 2002 Act) and the IPCC considers that because of its gravity or other exceptional circumstances it would be in the public interest to do so, the IPCC may, having consulted with the appropriate authority, the police officer concerned, the complainant and any witnesses, direct that the whole or part of the misconduct hearing will be held in public. The IPCC has published criteria for deciding when such cases will be held in public and a copy of this is available on the IPCC website at https://www.ipcc.gov.uk/sites/default/files/Documents/guidelines_reports/holding_hearings_in_public.pdf.

4.2.6.5 Joint Meetings/Hearings

Cases may arise where two or more police officers are to appear before a misconduct meeting or hearing in relation to apparent failures to meet the standards set out in the Standards of

Professional Behaviour stemming from the same incident. In such cases, each police officer may have played a different part and any alleged misconduct may be different for each police officer involved. It will normally be considered necessary to deal with all the matters together in order to disentangle the various strands of action, and therefore a single meeting/hearing will normally be appropriate.

A police officer may request a separate meeting/hearing if he/she can demonstrate that there would be a real risk of unfairness to that police officer if his/her case was dealt with in a joint meeting/hearing. It is for the person conducting the meeting or the chair of a misconduct hearing to decide if a separate meeting or hearing is appropriate.

4.2.6.6   Meeting/Hearing in Absence of Officer Concerned

It is in the interests of fairness to ensure that the misconduct meeting/hearing is held as soon as possible. Thus a meeting/hearing may take place if the police officer fails to attend. In cases where the police officer is absent (for example through illness or injury) a short delay may be reasonable to allow him/her to attend. If this is not possible or any delay is considered not appropriate in the circumstances the persons conducting the meeting/hearing may allow the police officer to participate by telephone or video link. In these circumstances a police friend will always be permitted to attend the meeting/hearing to represent the police officer in the normal way (and in the case of a misconduct hearing the police officer's legal representative where appointed).

If a police officer is detained in prison or other institution by order of a court, there is no requirement on the appropriate authority to have the officer concerned produced for the purposes of the misconduct meeting/hearing.

4.2.6.7   Conduct of Misconduct Meeting/Hearing

It will be for the persons conducting the meeting/hearing to determine the course of the meeting/hearing in accordance with the principles of natural justice and fairness. They will have read the investigator's report together with any account given by the police officer concerned during the investigation or when submitting his/her response under reg. 22 of the Conduct Regulations. They will also have had the opportunity to read any relevant documents attached to the investigator's report.

Any document or other material that was not submitted in advance of the meeting/hearing by the appropriate authority or the police officer concerned may still be considered at the meeting/hearing at the discretion of the persons conducting the meeting/hearing. Where any such document or other material is permitted to be considered, a short adjournment may be necessary to enable the appropriate authority or police officer concerned, as the case may be, to read or consider the document or other material and consider its implications.

Where there is evidence at the meeting or hearing that the police officer concerned, at any time after being given written notice under reg. 15 of the Conduct Regulations (or reg. 16 of the Complaint Regulations), failed to mention when interviewed or when making representations to the investigator or under reg. 22 of the Conduct Regulations, any fact relied on in his/her defence at the meeting/hearing, being a fact which in the circumstances existing at the time the police officer concerned could reasonably have been expected to mention when questioned or providing a written response, the persons conducting the meeting/hearing may draw such inferences from this failure as appear appropriate.

Where a witness does attend to give evidence, any questions to that witness should be made through the person conducting the meeting or in the case of a misconduct hearing the chair. This does not prevent the person conducting the meeting or the chair in a misconduct hearing allowing questions to be asked directly if he/she feels that is appropriate. It is for the persons conducting the meeting/hearing to control the proceedings and focus on the issues to ensure a fair meeting/hearing.

The persons conducting misconduct meetings/hearings will consider the facts of the case and will decide (on the balance of probabilities) whether the police officer's conduct amounted to misconduct, gross misconduct (in the case of a misconduct hearing) or neither. If the meeting decides that the police officer's conduct did not fall below the standards expected then as soon as reasonably practicable (and no later than five working days beginning with the first working day after the meeting or hearing) the police officer shall be informed and no entry will be made on his/her personal record.

4.2.6.8 Standard of Proof

In deciding matters of fact misconduct meetings/hearings must apply the standard of proof required in civil cases, that is, the balance of probabilities. Conduct will be proved on the balance of probabilities if the persons conducting the meeting/hearing are satisfied by the evidence that it is more likely than not that the conduct occurred.

4.2.6.9 Outcomes of Meetings/Hearings

If the persons conducting the misconduct meeting/hearing find that the police officer's conduct did fail to meet the Standards of Professional Behaviour, they will then determine the most appropriate outcome. In considering the question of outcome the persons conducting the meeting/hearing will need to take into account any previous written warnings (imposed under the Police (Conduct) Regulations 2012 but not superintendent's warnings issued under the previous procedures) that were live at the time of the initial assessment of the conduct in question, any aggravating or mitigating factors and have regard to the police officer's record of service, including any previous disciplinary outcomes that have not been expunged in accordance with reg. 15 of the Police Regulations 2003. The persons conducting the meeting/hearing may (only if deemed necessary and at their discretion) receive evidence from any witness whose evidence would in their opinion assist them in this regard.

The persons conducting the meeting/hearing are also entitled to take account of any early admission of the conduct on behalf of the police officer concerned and attach whatever weight to this he, she or they consider appropriate in the circumstances of the case.

In addition, the police officer concerned and his/her police friend (or where appropriate legal representative) will be given the opportunity to make representations on the question of the most appropriate outcome of the case. The appropriate authority also has the opportunity to make representations as to the most appropriate outcome.

4.2.6.10 Outcomes Available at Misconduct Meetings/Hearings

The meeting/hearing may record a finding that the conduct of the police officer concerned amounted to misconduct and take no further action or impose one of the following outcomes:

- **Management advice**—The police officer will be told the reason for the advice, that he/she has a right of appeal, and the name of the person to whom the appeal should be sent.
- **Written warning**—The police officer will be told the reason for the warning, that he/she has a right to appeal, and the name of the person to whom the appeal should be sent, and that the warning will be put on his/her personal file and remain live for 12 months from the date the warning is given. This means that any misconduct in the next 12 months is likely to lead to (at least) a final written warning.
- **Final written warning**—The police officer will be told the reason for the warning, that any future misconduct may result in dismissal, that he/she has a right to appeal and the

name of the person to whom the appeal should be sent, and that the final written warning will be put on his/her personal file and remain live for 18 months from the date the warning is given. This means that only in exceptional circumstances will further misconduct (that justifies more than management advice) not result in dismissal. (In exceptional circumstances only, the final written warning may be extended for a further 18 months on one occasion only.)

At a misconduct hearing, in addition to the three outcomes above, the persons conducting the hearing will also have available the outcomes of:

- **Dismissal with notice**—The notice period will be determined by the persons conducting the meeting subject to a minimum of 28 days.
- **Dismissal without notice**—Dismissal without notice will mean that the police officer is dismissed from the police service with immediate effect.

Where the persons conducting a misconduct hearing find that the police officer's conduct amounted to gross misconduct and decide that the police officer should be dismissed from the police service, that dismissal will be without notice. Where a police officer appears before a misconduct hearing for an alleged act of gross misconduct, and the persons conducting the hearing find that the conduct amounts to misconduct rather than gross misconduct, then (unless the police officer already has a live final written warning) the disciplinary outcomes available to the panel are those that are available at a misconduct meeting only.

4.2.6.11 Notification of the Outcome

In all cases the police officer will be informed in writing of the outcome of the misconduct meeting/hearing. This will be done as soon as practicable and in any case within five working days beginning with the first working day after the conclusion of the misconduct meeting/hearing. The notification in the case of a misconduct meeting will include notification to the police officer concerned of his/her right to appeal against the finding and/or outcome and the name of the person to whom any appeal should be sent. In the case of a police officer who has attended a misconduct hearing, the notification will include his/her right of appeal to a police appeals tribunal against any finding and/or outcome imposed. In cases involving a complainant, where the complaint was the subject of a local or supervised investigation the appropriate authority will be responsible for informing the complainant of the outcome. In cases managed or independently investigated by the IPCC, the IPCC will be responsible for informing the complainant of the outcome.

4.2.6.12 Expiry of Warnings

Notification of written warnings issued, including the date issued and expiry date, will be recorded on the police officer's personal record, along with a copy of the written notification of the outcome and a summary of the matter. Where a police officer has a live written warning and transfers from one force to another, the live warning will transfer with the police officer and will remain live until the expiry of the warning and should be referred to as part of any reference before the police officer transfers.

Where a police officer who has a live written warning or final written warning takes a career break in accordance with Police Regulations, any time on such a break will not count towards the 12 months (in the case of a written warning) or 18 months (in the case of a final written warning) or 36 months (in the case of an extended final written warning) that the warning is live.

4.2.6.13 Attendance of Complainant or Interested Person at Misconduct Proceedings

Where a misconduct meeting/hearing is being held as a direct result of a public complaint, the complainant or interested person will have the right to attend the meeting/hearing as an observer up until the point at which disciplinary action is considered (in addition to attending as a witness if required to do so). This right is subject to the right of the chair or person conducting the proceedings to exclude or impose conditions on the complainant's or interested party's attendance to facilitate the proper conduct of proceedings and to exclude him/her while evidence is being given, the disclosure of which to the complainant or interested party would be contrary to the harm test. He/she may be accompanied by one other person and, if he/she has a special need, one further person to accommodate that need (e.g. an interpreter, sign language expert etc.).

A complainant and any person accompanying the complainant will be permitted to remain in the meeting/hearing up to and including any finding by the persons conducting the meeting/hearing, after having given evidence (if appropriate). The complainant and any person accompanying the complainant will not be permitted to remain in the meeting/ hearing while character references or mitigation are being given or the decision of the panel as to the outcome is being given. However, the appropriate authority will have a duty to inform the complainant of the outcome of any misconduct meeting/hearing whether the complainant attends or not.

The persons conducting a misconduct meeting/hearing will have the discretion to allow a witness (who is not a complainant or interested person) who has attended and given evidence at the meeting/hearing to remain or to ask him/her to leave the proceedings after giving his/her evidence.

4.2.6.14 IPCC Direction and Attendance at Meetings/Hearings

Where the IPCC exercises its power (under para. 27 of sch. 3 to the 2002 Act) to direct an appropriate authority to hold a misconduct meeting/hearing, this will also include a direction as to whether the proceedings will be a misconduct meeting or hearing. In making such a direction the IPCC will have regard to the severity assessment that has been made in the case and been notified to the police officer concerned.

Where a misconduct meeting/hearing is to be held following:

- an investigation managed or independently investigated by the IPCC; or
- a local or supervised investigation where the IPCC has made a recommendation under para. 27(3) of sch. 3 to the Police Reform Act 2002 that misconduct proceedings should be taken and the recommendation has been accepted by the appropriate authority; or
- the IPCC has given a direction under para. 27(4) of that schedule that misconduct proceedings shall be taken,

the IPCC may attend the misconduct meeting/hearing to make representations. Such representations may be an explanation why the IPCC has directed particular misconduct proceedings to be brought or to comment on the investigation. Where the IPCC is to attend a misconduct hearing, it may instruct a relevant lawyer to represent it.

4.2.7 Right of Appeal

A police officer has a right of appeal against the finding and/or the outcome imposed at a misconduct meeting. The appeal is commenced by the police officer concerned giving written notice of appeal to the appropriate authority, clearly setting out the grounds for the appeal within seven working days beginning with the first working day after the receipt of the notification of the outcome of the misconduct meeting (unless this period is extended by the appropriate authority for exceptional circumstances). The police officer has the right to be accompanied by a police friend.

The police officer concerned may only appeal on the grounds that:

- the finding or disciplinary action imposed was unreasonable;
- there is evidence that could not reasonably have been considered at the misconduct meeting which could have materially affected the finding or decision on disciplinary action; or
- there was a serious breach of the procedures set out in the Regulations or other unfairness which could have materially affected the finding or decision on disciplinary action.

4.2.7.1 Appeal following Misconduct Meeting—Non-senior Officers

An appeal against the finding and/or the outcome of a misconduct meeting will be heard by a member of the police service of a higher rank or a police staff manager who is considered to be of a higher grade than the person who conducted the misconduct meeting. A police staff manager should not be appointed to conduct the appeal if the case substantially involves operational policing matters. A police officer or police staff member may be present to advise the person conducting the appeal on procedural matters. The person determining the appeal will be provided with the following documents:

- the notice of appeal from the police officer concerned setting out his/her grounds of appeal;
- the record of the original misconduct meeting;
- the documents that were given to the person who held the original misconduct meeting;
- any evidence that the police officer concerned wishes to submit in support of his/her appeal that was not considered at the misconduct meeting.

The person appointed to deal with the appeal must first decide whether the notice of appeal sets out arguable grounds of appeal. If he/she determines that there are no arguable grounds he/she shall dismiss the appeal and inform the police officer concerned accordingly setting out his/her reasons. Where the person appointed to hear the appeal determines that there are arguable grounds of appeal and the police officer concerned has requested to be present at the appeal meeting, the person appointed to conduct the proceedings will hold a meeting with the police officer concerned. Where the police officer fails to attend the meeting, the person conducting the appeal may proceed in the absence of the police officer concerned.

The person conducting the appeal may consider:

- whether the finding of the original misconduct meeting was unreasonable having regard to all the evidence considered or if the finding could now be in doubt due to evidence which has emerged since the meeting;
- any outcome imposed by the misconduct meeting which may be considered as too severe or too lenient having regard to all the circumstances of the case;
- whether the finding or outcome could be unsafe due to procedural unfairness and prejudice to the police officer (although the person conducting the appeal must also take into account whether the unfairness or prejudice could have materially influenced the outcome).

The person determining the appeal may confirm or reverse the decision appealed against. Where the person determining the appeal decides that the original disciplinary action imposed was too lenient he/she may increase the outcome up to a maximum of a final written warning. An appeal is not a repeat of the misconduct meeting. It is to examine a particular part of the misconduct case which is under question and which may affect the finding or the outcome.

The appeal will normally be heard within five working days beginning with the working day after the determination that the officer concerned has arguable grounds of appeal. The officer concerned can object to the person appointed to conduct the appeal in the same way as he/she could for the original misconduct meeting (**see para. 4.2.5.7**).

4.2.7.2 Appeal following Misconduct Hearing

Where a police officer has appeared before a misconduct hearing, any appeal against the finding or outcome is to the police appeals tribunal (**see paras 4.2.9 to 4.2.9.9**). The police officer should be informed that the police appeals tribunal can increase any outcome imposed as well as reduce or overturn the decision of the misconduct hearing or special case hearing.

Senior officers have the right to appeal against the finding and/or outcome of a misconduct meeting or hearing. The appeal in both cases will be made to the police appeals tribunal. The police officer should be informed that the police appeals tribunal can increase any outcome imposed as well as reduce or overturn the decision of the misconduct hearing or special case hearing.

4.2.8 Fast Track Cases ('Special Cases')

The operation of the fast track misconduct procedures, referred to as 'special cases', is set out in part 5 of the Conduct Regulations. The special case procedures can only be used if the appropriate authority certifies the case as a special case, having determined that the 'special conditions' are satisfied or if the IPCC has given a direction under para. 20H(7) of sch. 3 to the Police Reform Act 2002.

The 'special conditions' are that there is sufficient evidence, in the form of written statements or other documents, without the need for further evidence, whether written or oral, to establish on the balance of probabilities that the conduct of the police officer concerned constitutes gross misconduct, and it is in the public interest for the police officer concerned to cease to be a police officer without delay.

These procedures are therefore designed to deal with cases where the evidence is incontrovertible in the form of statements, documents or other material (e.g. CCTV, DNA) and is therefore sufficient without further evidence to prove gross misconduct and it is in the public interest, if the case is found or admitted, for the police officer to cease to be a member of the police service forthwith. Even where the criteria for special cases are met there may be circumstances where it would not be appropriate to certify the case as a special case, for instance, where to do so might prematurely alert others (police officers or non-police officers) who are, or may be, the subject of an investigation.

In the case of non-senior officers the case will be heard by the police officer's chief constable (assistant commissioner in the Metropolitan Police) or in cases where the chief constable is an interested party or is unavailable, another chief constable or an assistant commissioner. The police officer will have a right of appeal under reg. 56 of the Conduct Regulations to a police appeals tribunal against any finding of gross misconduct and the disciplinary action imposed.

Where a matter that meets the criteria for using the special case procedures has arisen from a complaint by a member of the public, the complainant or interested person will have the right to attend the special case hearing as an observer subject to any conditions imposed by the person conducting proceedings under reg. 52(3) of the Conduct Regulations. Where a complainant or interested person is to attend a special case hearing he/she will be entitled to be accompanied by one other person and if the complainant or interested person has a special need, by one further person to accommodate that need. A complainant or interested person and any person accompanying the complainant or interested person will be permitted to remain in the hearing up to and including any finding by the person (or persons in the case of a senior officer) conducting the hearing. The complainant or interested person and any person accompanying the complainant or interested person will not be permitted to remain in the hearing while character references or mitigation are being given or the decision of the person conducting the hearing (or persons in the case of a senior officer) as to the outcome is being given. However, the appropriate authority will have a duty (in cases investigated locally or supervised by the IPCC) to inform the complainant or interested person of the outcome of the hearing whether the complainant or interested person attends or not.

There will be no oral witness testimony at the special case hearing other than from the police officer concerned. There will be copies of the notice given to the police officer, the certificate certifying the case as a special case, the notice the police officer has supplied in response, including any documents he/she provides in support of his/her case, a copy of the investigator's report or such parts of that report as relate to the police officer concerned, statements made by the police officer during the investigation, and in a case where the police officer concerned denies the allegation against him/her, copies of all statements and documents that in the opinion of the appropriate authority should be considered at the meeting.

The hearing may proceed in the absence of the police officer concerned, but the persons conducting the hearing should ensure that the police officer concerned has been informed of his/her right to be legally represented at the hearing or to be represented by a police friend where the police officer chooses not to be legally represented.

4.2.8.1 Special Case Process

Where the appropriate authority determines that the special conditions are satisfied and unless it considers that the circumstances are such as to make it inappropriate to do so, it shall certify the case as a special case and refer it to a special case hearing. The decision as to whether a case is suitable for using the fast track procedure will be taken by the appropriate authority which must determine whether it believes the special conditions are satisfied having regard to the available evidence and any other relevant information.

If the appropriate authority decides that the special case procedures will not be used, it will refer the case back to the investigator if further investigation is required or to the appropriate authority to proceed under the standard procedures. If the appropriate authority decides that the special case procedures should be used, it will sign a 'Special Case Certificate' and will provide to the police officer concerned notice giving particulars of the conduct that is alleged to constitute gross misconduct and copies of:

- the Special Case Certificate;
- any statement the police officer may have made to the investigator during the course of the investigation;
- subject to the harm test:
    + the investigator's report (if any) or such parts of that report as relate to the police officer concerned, together with any documents attached to that report; and
    + any relevant statement or documents gathered during the course of the investigation.

The police officer concerned will also be told the date, time and place of the hearing and of his/her right to legal representation and to advice from a police friend. The date of the meeting will be not less than 10 working days and not more than 15 working days from the date the Special Case Certificate and other documents are provided to the police officer concerned.

Within seven working days of the first working day after the day on which the written notice and documents are supplied to the police officer concerned, the police officer shall provide a written notice to the appropriate authority of:

- whether or not he/she accepts that his/her conduct constituted gross misconduct;
- where he/she accepts that the conduct constituted gross misconduct, any submission he/she wishes to make in mitigation;
- where he/she does not accept that the conduct constituted gross misconduct;

+ the allegations he/she disputes and his/her version of the relevant events; and
+ any arguments on points of law he/she wishes to be considered by the person or persons conducting the hearing.

At the same time the police officer shall provide the person conducting or chairing the hearing with copies of any documents he/she intends to rely on at the hearing (in accordance with reg. 45).

4.2.8.2 Outcome of Special Case Hearing

Where the persons conducting the special case hearing find that the conduct of the police officer concerned constituted gross misconduct, then they shall impose disciplinary action, which may be dismissal without notice, a final written warning (unless a final written warning has been imposed on the police officer concerned within the previous 18 months), or an extension of a final written warning.

Where the police officer concerned has received a final written warning within the 18 months prior to the assessment of the conduct then, in exceptional circumstances only, the final written warning may be extended by a further 18 months. An extension of a final written warning can occur once.

Where the persons conducting the hearing determine that the conduct does not amount to gross misconduct, then he, she or they may dismiss the case. Alternatively, he, she or they may return the case to the appropriate authority to be dealt with at a misconduct meeting or hearing (where there is a live final written warning) under the standard procedures. This may be because the persons conducting the hearing consider that the conduct is misconduct rather than gross misconduct. There is power under reg. 42 for the appropriate authority to remit the case to be dealt with under the standard procedures at any time prior to the start of the special case hearing. This might be because it considers that a particular witness whose evidence is crucial to the case and is disputed must be called to give oral testimony.

Where the police officer admits the allegation or the persons conducting the hearing find it proved on the balance of probabilities, then the persons conducting the hearing:

- shall have regard to the record of police service of the police officer concerned as shown on his/her personal record;
- may consider such documentary evidence as would, in their opinion, assist him, her or them in determining the question; and
- shall give the police officer concerned, and his/her police friend or relevant lawyer, an opportunity to make oral or written representations.

The police officer concerned shall be informed of the finding and any disciplinary action imposed or a decision to dismiss the case or revert it back to be dealt with under the standard procedures as soon as practicable and in any event shall be provided with written notice of these matters and a summary of the reasons within five working days beginning with the first working day after the conclusion of the hearing.

4.2.9 Appeals to the Police Appeals Tribunal

The Police Appeals Tribunal Rules 2012 have introduced changes to the composition and operation of the Police Appeals Tribunal.

A police officer has a right of appeal to a police appeals tribunal against any disciplinary finding and/or disciplinary outcome imposed at a misconduct hearing or special case hearing held under the Conduct Regulations. Senior police officers, in addition, have the right to appeal to a police appeals tribunal against any disciplinary finding and/or outcome imposed at a misconduct meeting. A police officer may not appeal to a tribunal against a finding of misconduct or gross misconduct where that finding was made following acceptance by the officer that his/her conduct amounted to misconduct or gross misconduct (as the case may be). A police officer of a rank up to and including chief superintendent has a right of appeal to a police appeals tribunal against the finding and/or the following outcomes imposed following a third stage meeting under the Performance Regulations to dismiss or reduce in rank. In addition if the case has been dealt with at a stage three meeting, without having progressed through stages one and two, the police officer may appeal against redeployment to alternative duties, the issue of a final written improvement notice, or the issue of a written improvement notice.

4.2.9.1 Composition and Timing of Police Appeals Tribunals

Where the appeal is made by a police officer who is not a senior officer, the tribunal will consist of:

- a legally qualified chair drawn from a list maintained by the Home Office;
- a serving senior officer (ACPO rank); and
- a retired member of a police force who was a member of the Police Superintendents' Association of England and Wales or the Police Federation of England and Wales for Federated ranks.

A tribunal will take place as soon as reasonably practicable, no later than three months of the determination by a tribunal chair that a hearing should be held.

4.2.9.2 Grounds of Appeal

A police appeals tribunal is not a re-hearing of the original matter; rather its role is to consider an appeal based on specific grounds.

In the case of matters dealt with under the Police (Conduct) Regulations 2012 the grounds for appeal are:

- the finding or disciplinary action imposed was unreasonable; or
- there is evidence that could not reasonably have been considered at the misconduct meeting (in the case of senior police officers), the misconduct hearing or special case hearing (as the case may be); or
- there was a breach of the procedures set out in the Police (Conduct) Regulations 2012, the Police (Complaints and Misconduct) Regulations 2012, sch. 3 to the Police Reform Act 2002 or other unfairness which could have materially affected the finding or decision on disciplinary action.

In the case of matters dealt with under the Police (Performance) Regulations 2012 the grounds for appeal are:

- the finding of unsatisfactory performance or attendance or gross incompetence, or the outcome imposed, was unreasonable; or
- there is evidence that could not reasonably have been considered at the third stage meeting which could have materially affected the finding or decision on the outcome; or
- there was a breach of the procedures set out in the Police (Performance) Regulations 2012 or other unfairness which could have materially affected the finding or decision on the outcome; or
- where the police officer was required to attend a third stage meeting following a first and second stage meeting, the police officer concerned should not have been required to attend that meeting as his/her unsatisfactory performance or attendance was not similar to or connected with the unsatisfactory performance or attendance referred to in his/her final written improvement notice.

4.2.9.3 Notice of Appeal

Where a police officer wishes to appeal, he/she will need to give notice of his/her appeal in writing to the 'relevant local policing body'. The notice of appeal must be given within 10 working days, beginning with the first working day after the police officer is supplied with a written copy of the decision that he/she is appealing against. In cases where the police officer fails to submit his/her notice of appeal within the 10 working days period, he/she may, within a reasonable time after the end of that period, submit a notice of appeal which shall be accompanied by the reasons why it was not submitted within that period, and the reasons for the officer's view that it was served within a reasonable time after that period. The Tribunal Chair will then determine whether the appeal could have reasonably and practicably been submitted within the time limit.

4.2.9.4 Procedure on Notice of Appeal

As soon as reasonably practicable after receipt of a copy of the notice of appeal and in any case within 15 working days (beginning with the first working day following the day of such receipt) the Chief Constable shall provide to the relevant local policing body:

- a copy of the decision appealed against (namely the written judgment of the original panel/person);
- any documents that were available to the panel/person conducting the original hearing; and
- the transcript or part of the transcript of the proceedings at the original hearing requested by the appellant (a copy of the transcript (if applicable) shall also at the same time be sent to the appellant).

The appellant, within 20 working days beginning with the first working day following the day on which he/she is supplied with a copy of the transcript or, where no transcript is requested, within 35 working days (beginning with the first working day following the day on which the appellant gave notice of his/her appeal), shall provide to the relevant local policing body:

- a notice setting out the finding, disciplinary action or outcome appealed against and of his/her grounds for the appeal;
- any supporting documents;
- where the appellant is allowed to call witnesses (for appeals made only on the ground of there being evidence that could not reasonably have been considered at the original hearing and which could have materially affected the finding or outcome):
  + a list of any proposed witnesses; and
  + a witness statement from each of the proposed witness;
- if he/she consents to the appeal being determined without a hearing (that is, on the basis of the papers alone), notice in writing that he/she so consents.

In relation to the appellant, a 'proposed witness' is a person whom the appellant wishes to call to give evidence at the hearing, whose evidence was not and could not reasonably have been considered at the hearing and whose evidence could have materially affected the decision being appealed against.

4.2.9.5 Determination of an Appeal

Where the tribunal chair allows the appeal to go forward to a tribunal hearing the local policing body will be responsible for making the administrative arrangements prior to and at the tribunal and for ensuring that the members of the tribunal appointed to deal with the appeal are sent the papers together with a schedule of the documents that each of the members should have.

The tribunal chair who made the determination as to whether to allow the notice of appeal to proceed to a tribunal need not necessarily be the same tribunal chair who hears the subsequent appeal. However, the chair who makes the decision as to whether the appeal should be dealt with at a hearing or on the papers should be the chair appointed to hear the appeal itself.

Where an appeal has not been dismissed at the review stage, the tribunal chair shall determine whether the appeal should be dealt with at a hearing. It is expected that this decision will be made by the tribunal chair within 10 working days of receiving the papers. If the appellant has not consented to an appeal being dealt with on the papers then a hearing shall be held. If the appellant has consented, the tribunal chair may determine that the appeal shall be dealt with without a hearing. If the appeal is to be dealt with at a hearing, the chair shall give the appellant and the respondent his/her name and contact address.

4.2.9.6   Legal and Other Representation

The appellant can be represented at a hearing by a relevant lawyer or a police friend. Where the appellant is represented by a lawyer the appellant's police friend may also attend.

4.2.9.7   Procedure at Hearing

Where the case is to be heard at a tribunal hearing, the chair of the tribunal shall cause the appellant and the respondent to be given written notice of the time, date and place of the hearing, at least 20 working days or such shorter period as may with the agreement of both parties be determined, before the hearing begins.

The tribunal chair will determine in advance of the tribunal whether to allow any witness that the appellant or respondent proposes to call to give evidence at the tribunal. Witnesses will only be permitted where the ground for appeal is that there is evidence that could not reasonably have been considered at the original hearing which could have materially affected the finding or decision on outcome. No witnesses shall give evidence at the hearing unless the chair reasonably believes that it is necessary for the witness to do so. Any witness that does attend the tribunal may be subject to questioning and cross questioning. It is for the tribunal to decide on the admissibility of any evidence, or to determine whether or not any question should or should not be put to a witness. A verbatim record of the evidence given at the hearing shall be taken; and the relevant local policing body shall keep such record for a period of not less than two years from the date of the end of the hearing.

The tribunal has discretion to proceed with the hearing in the absence of either party, whether represented or not, if it appears to be just and proper to do so. Where it is decided to proceed in the absence of either party the tribunal should record its reasons for doing so. The tribunal may adjourn the appeal as necessary.

The hearing shall be held in private. The tribunal may allow a person to attend the hearing as an observer for the purposes of training. On the application of the appellant or the respondent or otherwise, the tribunal chair may require any observer to withdraw from all or any part of the hearing.

4.2.9.8   Attendance of Other Persons

Where the matter to be dealt with at the appeal is related directly to a complaint made against the appellant or a conduct matter involving an interested party, the chair of the tribunal shall cause the complainant or interested party to be given notice of the time, date and place of the tribunal. The complainant or interested party may attend the tribunal as an observer. The complainant or interested party may be accompanied by one other person and in addition, if the complainant or interested party has a special need, by one further person to accommodate that need. Where the complainant or interested party or any person accompanying him/her is to give evidence at the tribunal, then he/she or any person accompanying him/her may not attend the hearing before that evidence is given. Where the appeal is a 'specified appeal' then the tribunal chair shall cause the IPCC to be notified of the time, date and location of the tribunal. In such cases the IPCC may attend as an observer.

4.2.9.9 Determination and Outcome of Appeal

A tribunal, when determining any disciplinary or unsatisfactory performance outcome imposed, may impose any outcome that the original panel/person could have imposed. The tribunal has the power to increase as well as reduce the outcome imposed by the original panel/person. The decision of the tribunal will normally be made on the day of the tribunal hearing.

The tribunal chair shall, within three working days of the tribunal determining the appeal, give written notice to the appellant of the tribunal's decision.

A police officer ordered to be reinstated in his/her former force or rank will be deemed to have served in his/her force and/or rank continuously from the date of the original decision to the date of reinstatement. Reinstatement means that the officer is put back in the role that he/she would have been in if not dismissed or reduced in rank.

4.3 Unsatisfactory Performance and Attendance

4.3.1 Introduction

The formal procedures to deal with unsatisfactory performance and attendance are set out in the Police (Performance) Regulations 2012 and are referred to as 'UPPs'. The underlying principle of the procedures is to provide a fair, open and proportionate method of dealing with performance and attendance issues and to encourage a culture of learning and development for individuals and the organisation. It is envisaged that early intervention via management action should achieve the desired effect of improving and maintaining a police officer's performance or attendance to an acceptable level. There will, however, be cases where it will be appropriate for managers to take formal action under the procedures. The procedures in the Police (Performance) Regulations 2012 are largely the same whether applied to unsatisfactory performance or attendance (the differences that do exist are set out below). However, the issues that arise in attendance cases may be different from those in performance cases.

4.3.2 Applicability

The procedures apply to police officers up to and including the rank of chief superintendent, including special constables. However, given the nature of special constables as unpaid volunteers, cases where the procedures are initiated for special constables may be limited to those where the special constable either contests that his/her performance or attendance is unsatisfactory or agrees that it is unsatisfactory but expresses a desire to continue with his/her special constable duties. In other cases the special constable may choose to resign from his/her role as a special constable. In setting meeting dates and establishing panels, regard should be had to the nature of special constables as volunteers.

The procedures do not apply to student police officers during their probationary period. The procedures governing performance and attendance issues in respect of police students are determined locally by each force. These procedures are underpinned by reg. 13 of the Police Regulations 2003.

A police officer may seek legal advice at any time although legal representation is confined to third stage meetings where the procedure has been initiated at this stage. Police officers other than special constables can seek advice from their staff association and all police officers can be advised and represented by their police friend.

4.3.3 Ongoing Performance Assessment and Review

Every police officer should have some form of performance appraisal, or what is commonly referred to as a 'performance and development review' (PDR). The PDR should be the principal method by which the police officer's performance and attendance are monitored and assessed. The activities and behaviours expected of a police officer in order to achieve his/her objectives should be in accordance with the relevant national framework which will form the basis of the police officer's role profile.

4.3.4 Sources of Information

Unsatisfactory performance or attendance will often be identified by the immediate line manager of the police officer as part of his/her normal management responsibilities. Where the police officer currently works to a manager who has no line management responsibility for him/her, it is the responsibility of that manager to inform the police officer's line manager of any performance or attendance issues he/she has identified. It is also possible that line managers may be alerted to unsatisfactory performance or attendance on the part of one of their police officers as a result of information or complaint from a member of the public. Such cases must be dealt with in accordance with the established procedures for the handling of complaints.

It may be that the outcome of an investigation into a complaint alleging misconduct is that an issue of unsatisfactory performance or attendance has been identified. In such cases the outcome of the investigation may be that the appropriate authority will determine that there is no case to answer in respect of misconduct or gross misconduct but it may be appropriate to take action under the UPPs in order that the police officer may learn and improve.

UPPs are designed to deal with a pattern of unsatisfactory performance (except where there is a single incident of gross incompetence).

While the unsatisfactory performance and attendance procedures are internal management procedures, it may be necessary at times to inform public complainants of action taken with respect to the police officer to whom the complaint relates.

4.3.5 Management Action

There are some principles which should apply in management action:

- the line manager must discuss any shortcoming(s) or concern(s) with the individual at the earliest possible opportunity. It would be quite wrong for the line manager to accumulate a list of concerns about the performance or attendance of an individual and delay telling him/her about them until the occasion of the police officer's annual or mid-term PDR meetings;
- the reason for dissatisfaction must be made clear to the individual as soon as possible and there must be a factual basis for discussing the issues, i.e. the discussion must relate to specific incidents or omissions that have occurred;
- line managers should seek to establish whether there are any underlying reasons for the unsatisfactory performance or attendance;
- consideration should be given as to whether there is any health or welfare issue that is or may be affecting performance or attendance;
- in cases where the difficulty appears to stem from a personality clash with a colleague or line manager, or where for other reasons a change of duties might be appropriate, the police officer's line management may, in consultation with the appropriate human resources adviser, consider redeployment if this provides an opportunity for the police officer to improve his/her performance or attendance. Where a police officer is redeployed in this way, the police officer and his/her new line management should be informed of the reasons for the move and of the assessment of his/her performance or attendance in the previous role;
- the line manager must make it clear to the police officer that he/she is available to give further advice and guidance if needed;
- depending on the circumstances, it may be appropriate to indicate to the police officer that if there is no, or insufficient, improvement, then the matter will be dealt with under the UPPs;

- line managers are expected to gather relevant evidence and keep a contemporaneous note of interactions with the police officer;
- challenging unsatisfactory performance or attendance in an appropriate manner does not constitute bullying.

The principles outlined above cover the position when a line manager first becomes aware of some unsatisfactory aspect of the police officer's performance or attendance and is dealing with the issue as an integral part of normal line management responsibilities.

Management action taken as a result of identifying unsatisfactory performance or attendance should be put on record. In particular, the line manager should record the nature of the performance or attendance issue, the advice given, and steps taken to address the problems identified. Placing matters on record is important to ensure continuity in circumstances where one or more members of the management chain may move on to other duties or the police officer concerned moves to new duties.

Ideally, as a result of management action, performance or attendance will improve and continue to an acceptable level. Where there is insufficient or unsustained improvement, it will then be appropriate to use the UPPs. The period of time agreed or determined by the line manager for the police officer concerned to improve his/her performance or attendance prior to using the UPPs must be sufficient to provide a reasonable opportunity for the desired improvement or attendance to take place and must be time limited.

4.3.6 Performance Issues

Police officers should know what standard of performance is required of them and be given appropriate support to attain that standard and managers should let a police officer know when he/she is doing well or, if the circumstances arise, when there are the first signs that there is a need for improvement in his/her performance.

Unsatisfactory performance (or attendance) is defined in reg. 4 of the Police (Performance) Regulations 2012 as 'an inability or failure of a police officer to perform the duties of the role or rank he [or she] is currently undertaking to a satisfactory standard or level'.

There is no single formula for determining the point at which a concern about a police officer's performance should lead to formal procedures under the Police (Performance) Regulations being taken. Each case must be considered on its merits. However, the following points need to be emphasised:

- the intention of performance management, including formal action under the Police (Performance) Regulations, is to improve performance;
- occasional lapses below acceptable standards should be dealt with in the course of normal management activity and should not involve the application of the UPPs, which are designed to cover either repeated failures to meet such standards or more serious cases of unsatisfactory performance;
- managers should be able to demonstrate that they have considered whether management action is appropriate before using the UPPs.

4.3.7 Attendance Issues

It is envisaged that supportive action will in most cases achieve the desired effect of improving and maintaining a police officer's attendance to an acceptable level. There may however be cases where it will be appropriate for managers to take formal action under the Performance Regulations. Where the UPPs are used in relation to attendance matters, such matters will normally relate to periods of sickness absence such that the ability of the police officer to perform his/her duties is compromised. Other forms of absence not related to genuine sickness would normally be dealt with under the misconduct procedures, e.g. where a police officer's absence is unauthorised. Except where a police officer fails to co-operate, appropriate supportive action must be taken before formal action is taken under the Performance Regulations. A failure by a police officer to co-operate will not prevent formal action being taken or continued. If supportive action is taken, the police officer co-operates and the attendance improves and is maintained at a satisfactory level, there will be no need to take formal action under the Performance Regulations. Where police officers are injured or ill they should be treated fairly and compassionately. Managers should be able to demonstrate that they have acted reasonably in all actions taken at all stages of the attendance management process, including any action under the Police (Performance) Regulations. In cases where a decision is made at a third stage meeting to impose an out-come, including dismissal from the service, in most cases the police officer will have the right to appeal to a police appeals tribunal.

4.3.7.1 Monitoring Attendance

It is the responsibility of line managers, in conjunction with the force's human resources department if necessary, to monitor a police officer's attendance. A formal record of a police officer's period of illness will be kept in accordance with reg. 15 of the Police Regulations 2003. The force Occupational Health Service is an essential part of effective attendance management and should be involved as soon as any concerns about a police officer's attend-ance are identified. Where action is taken under the UPPs in respect of a police officer's attendance, the police officer may be referred to the Occupational Health Service for up-to-date information and advice at any stage within the procedure in accordance with force policy. This should enable the force to make an informed decision about a police officer's attendance. Where police officers do not attend appointments or otherwise fail to co-operate with the force's Occupational Health Service, an assessment will be made on the information available.

4.3.7.2 Action under the Police (Performance) Regulations 2012

Formal action under the Performance Regulations may be taken in cases of both unacceptable levels of persistent short-term absences and long-term absences due to sick-ness and/or injury. In deciding whether to take action under the procedures, managers must treat each case on its merits and consider all of the pertinent facts available to them, including:

- the nature of the illness, injury or condition;
- the likelihood of the illness, injury or condition (or some other related illness, injury or condition) recurring;
- the pattern and length of absence(s) and the period of good health between them;
- the need for the work to be done, i.e. what impact on the force's performance and work-load the absence is having;
- the extent to which a police officer has co-operated with supportive management action;
- whether the police officer was made aware, in the earlier supportive action, that unless an improvement was made, action under the Performance Regulations might be used;
- whether the selected medical practitioner (SMP) has been asked to consider the issue of permanent disablement and/or the police force is considering medical retirement;
- the impact of the Equality Act 2010 and the public sector equality duty (which came into effect on 6 April 2011).

4.3.8 The UPP Process—Improvement Notices

There are potentially three stages to the UPPs, each of which involves a different meeting composition and different possible outcomes. A line manager can ask a human resources professional or police officer (who should have experience of UPPs and be independent of the line management chain) to attend a UPP meeting to advise him/her on the proceedings at the first stage meeting. The second line manager may also have an adviser (as above) in respect of the second stage meeting. For stage three meetings, a human resources professional, police officer, counsel or solicitor may attend the meeting to advise the panel on the proceedings.

At the first and second stages, if it is found that the police officer's performance or attendance is unsatisfactory, an improvement notice will be issued. Improvement notices require a police officer to improve his/her performance or attendance and must state:

- in what respect the police officer's performance or attendance is considered unsatisfactory;
- the improvement in performance or attendance required to bring the police officer to an acceptable standard;
- a 'specified period' within which improvement is expected to be made; and
- the 'validity period' of the written improvement notice.

The 'specified period' of an improvement notice is a period specified by the manager conducting the meeting (having considered any representations made by or on behalf of the police officer) within which the police officer must improve his/her performance or attendance. It is expected that the specified period for improvement would not normally exceed three months. However, depending on the nature and circumstances of the matter, it may be appropriate to specify a longer or shorter period for improvement (but which should not exceed 12 months).

The 'validity period' of an improvement notice describes the period of 12 months from the date of the notice within which performance or attendance must be maintained (assuming improvement is made during the specified period). If the improvement is not maintained within this period the next stage of the procedures may be used. The period for improvement under an improvement notice and the validity period of an improvement notice do not include any time that the police officer is taking as a career break.

Improvement notices must be accompanied by the written record of the meeting and a notice informing the police officer of his/her right to appeal against the finding or terms of the improvement notice (or both of these). Following a second stage meeting, that documentation must also inform the police officer of his/her right to appeal against the decision to require him/her to attend the meeting. Any such appeal can only be made on the ground that the meeting did not concern unsatisfactory performance or attendance which was similar to or connected with that referred to in the written improvement notice.

An improvement notice would normally be followed by an action plan which should:

- identify any weaknesses which may be the cause of unsatisfactory performance or attendance;
- describe what steps the police officer must take to improve performance and/or attendance and what support is available from the organisation, e.g. training and support;
- specify a period within which actions identified should be followed up; and
- set a date for a staged review of the police officer's performance or attendance.

On the application of the police officer or otherwise (e.g. on the application of his/her line manager), the appropriate authority may extend the 'specified' period if it considers it appropriate to do so.

In setting an extension to the specified period, consideration should be given to any known periods of extended absence from the police officer's normal role, e.g. if the police officer is going to be on long periods of pre-planned holiday leave, study leave, or is due to undergo an operation. The extension should not lead to the improvement period exceeding 12 months unless the appropriate authority is satisfied that there are exceptional circumstances making this appropriate.

4.3.8.1 Initiation of Procedures at Stage Three

In very limited circumstances it is possible to commence the UPPs at the third stage. This is to allow for cases of a degree of severity such that initiation at this stage is the only appropriate option. In these cases only, the police officer is entitled to choose to be legally represented by counsel or a solicitor.

4.3.8.2 Multiple Instances of Unsatisfactory Performance

A police officer can move to a later stage of the UPPs only in relation to unsatisfactory performance or attendance that is similar to or connected with the unsatisfactory performance or attendance referred to in any previous written improvement notice. Where failings relate to different forms of unsatisfactory performance or attendance it will be necessary to commence the UPPs at the first stage (unless the failing constitutes gross incompetence). If more than one UPP is commenced, then, given that the procedures will relate to different failings and will have been identified at different times, the finding and outcome of each should be without prejudice to the others.

However, there may be circumstances where procedures have been initiated for a particular failing and an additional failing comes to light prior to the first stage meeting. In such circumstances it is possible to consolidate the two issues at the first stage meeting provided that there is sufficient time prior to the meeting to comply with the notification requirements explained in more detail below.

4.3.9 The First Stage

Where a line manager considers that a police officer's performance or attendance is unsatisfactory and decides that the UPPs are the most appropriate way of addressing the matter, he/she will notify the police officer in writing that he/she is required to attend a first stage meeting and include in that notification the following details:

- details of the procedures for determining the date and time of the meeting;
- a summary of the reasons why the line manager considers the police officer's performance or attendance unsatisfactory;
- the possible outcomes of a first stage, second stage and third stage meeting;
- that a human resources professional or a police officer (who should have experience of UPPs and be independent from the line management chain) may attend the meeting to advise the line manager on the proceedings;
- that if the police officer agrees, any other person specified in the notice may attend the meeting;
- that prior to the meeting the police officer must provide the line manager with any documentation he/she intends to rely on in the meeting; and
- the police officer's, rights, i.e. his/her right to seek advice from a representative of his/her staff association and to be accompanied and represented at the meeting by a police friend.

The notice shall be accompanied by copies of related documentation relied upon by the line manager in support of the view that the police officer's performance or attendance is unsatisfactory. In advance of the meeting, the police officer shall provide the line manager with any documents on which he/she intends to rely in support of his/her case. Any document or other material that was not submitted in advance of the meeting may be considered at the meeting at the discretion of the line manager. The purpose of allowing this discretion is to ensure fairness to all parties. However the presumption should be that such documents or material will not be permitted unless it can be shown that they were not previously available to be submitted in advance. Where such a document or other material is permitted to be considered, a short adjournment may be necessary to enable the line manager or the police officer, as the case may be, to read or consider the document or other material and consider its implications. The length of the adjournment will depend upon the case.

Wherever possible, the meeting date and time should be agreed between the line manager and the police officer. However, where agreement cannot be reached the line manager must specify a time and date. If the police officer or his/her police friend is not available at the date or time specified by the line manager, the police officer may propose an alternative time. Provided that the alternative time is reasonable and falls within a period of five working days beginning with the first working day after that specified by the line manager, the meeting must be postponed to that time. Once the date for the meeting is fixed, the line manager should send to the police officer a notice in writing of the date, time and place of the first stage meeting.

4.3.9.1 First Stage Meeting

At the first stage meeting the line manager will: explain to the police officer the reasons why the line manager considers that the performance or attendance of the police officer is unsatisfactory; provide the police officer with the opportunity to make representations in response; provide his/her police friend (if he/she has one) with an opportunity to make representations; and listen to what the police officer (and/or his/her police friend) has to say, ask questions and comment as appropriate.

Where the line manager finds that the performance or attendance of the police officer has been satisfactory during the period in question, he/she will inform the police officer that no further action will be taken. Where having considered any representations by either the police officer and/ or his/her police friend, the line manager finds that the performance or attendance of the police officer has been unsatisfactory he/she shall:

- inform the police officer in what respects his/her performance or attendance is considered unsatisfactory;
- inform him/her of the improvement that is required in his/her performance or attendance;
- inform the police officer that, if a sufficient improvement is not made within the period specified by the line manager, he/she may be required to attend a second stage meeting;
- inform the police officer that he/she will receive a written improvement notice;
- inform the police officer that if the sufficient improvement in his/her performance or attendance is not maintained during the validity period of such notice he/she may be required to attend a second stage meeting.

The specified period for improvement will not normally exceed three months.

4.3.9.2 Procedure following the First Stage Meeting

As soon as reasonably practicable, following the meeting, the line manager shall cause to be prepared a written record of the meeting and, where he/she found at the meeting that the performance or attendance of the police officer was unsatisfactory, a written improvement notice. The written record and any improvement notice shall be sent to the officer as soon as reasonably practicable after they have been prepared. The written record supplied to the police officer should comprise a summary of the proceedings at that meeting. Any improvement notice must be accompanied by a notice informing the police officer of his/her right to appeal and the name of the person to whom the appeal should be sent. The notice must also inform the police officer of his/her right to submit written comments on the written record of the meeting and of the procedure for doing so.

The police officer may submit written comments on the written record not later than the end of seven working days after the date that he/she received it (unless an extension has been granted by his/her line manager). However, if the police officer has exercised his/her right to appeal against the finding or outcome of the first stage meeting, the police officer may not submit comments on the written record. It is the responsibility of the line manager to ensure that the written record, written improvement notice and any written comments of the police officer regarding the written record are retained together and filed in accordance with force policies.

Normally it will be appropriate to agree an action plan setting out the actions which should assist the police officer to perform his/her duties to an acceptable standard. This may be agreed at the UPP meeting or at a later time specified by the line manager. It is expected that the police officer will co-operate with implementation of the action plan and take responsibility for his/her own development or improvement. Equally, the police officer's managers must ensure that any actions to support the police officer to improve are implemented.

4.3.9.3 Assessment of Performance or Attendance

It is expected that the police officer's performance or attendance will be actively monitored against the improvement notice and, where applicable, the action plan by the line manager throughout the specified period of the improvement notice. The line manager should discuss with the police officer any concerns that the line manager has during this period as regards his/her performance or attendance and offer advice and guidance where appropriate.

As soon as possible after the improvement notice period comes to an end, the line manager must formally assess the performance or attendance of the police officer during that period. If the line manager considers that the police officer's performance or attendance is satisfactory, the line manager should notify the police officer in writing of this. The notification should also inform the police officer that while the performance or attendance of the police officer is now satisfactory, the improvement notice is valid for a period of 12 months from the date printed on the notice so that it is possible for the second stage of the procedures to be initiated if the performance or attendance of the police officer falls below an acceptable level within the remaining period.

If the line manager considers that the police officer's performance or attendance is still unsatisfactory, the line manager should notify the police officer in writing of this. The line manager must also notify the police officer that he/she is required to attend a second stage meeting to consider these ongoing performance or attendance issues.

If the police officer has improved his/her performance or attendance to an acceptable standard within the specified improvement period, but then fails to maintain that standard within the 12 month validity period, it is open to the line manager to initiate stage two of the procedures. In such circumstances the line manager must notify the police officer in writing of his/her view that the police officer's performance or attendance is unsatisfactory as the police officer has failed to maintain the improvement and that as a consequence the police officer is required to attend a second stage meeting to discuss his/her failure to maintain a satisfactory standard of performance or attendance.

4.3.9.4 First Stage Appeals

A police officer has a right of appeal. However, any outcome of this first stage meeting will continue to apply up to the date that the appeal is determined. Therefore where the police officer contests the finding or outcome, he/she should continue to follow the terms of the improvement notice and any accompanying action plan pending the determination of the appeal. The notice of appeal must clearly set out the grounds and evidence for the appeal.

The grounds for appeal are:

- the finding of unsatisfactory performance or attendance is unreasonable;
- any of the terms of the improvement notice are unreasonable;
- there is evidence that could not reasonably have been considered at the first stage meeting which could have materially affected the finding of unsatisfactory performance or attendance or any of the terms of the written improvement notice;
- there was a breach of the procedures set out in the Police (Performance) Regulations or other unfairness which could have materially affected the finding of unsatisfactory performance or attendance or the terms of the improvement notice.

On the basis of the above grounds of appeal, the police officer may appeal against the finding of unsatisfactory performance or attendance or the terms of the written improvement notice, those being:

- the respect in which the police officer's performance or attendance is considered unsatisfactory;
- the improvement which is required of the police officer; and/or
- the length of the period specified for improvement by the line manager at the first stage meeting.

At the first stage appeal meeting the second line manager will provide the police officer with the opportunity to make representations and provide his/her police friend (if he/she has one) with an opportunity to make representations. Having considered any representations by either the police officer and/or his/her police friend, the second line manager may confirm or reverse the finding of unsatisfactory performance or attendance or endorse or vary the terms of the improvement notice appealed against.

The second line manager may deal with the police officer in any manner in which the line manager could have dealt with him/her at the first stage meeting. Where the second line manager has reversed the finding of unsatisfactory performance or attendance he/she must also revoke the written improvement notice.

Within three working days of the day following the conclusion of the appeal meeting, the police officer will be given written notice of the second line manager's decision. If the second line manager is in a position to send a written summary of the reasons for that decision, this may also accompany the written notice of the decision. Any decision made that changes the finding or outcome of the first stage meeting will take effect by way of substitution for the finding or terms appealed against and as from the date of the first stage meeting.

4.3.10 The Second Stage

Initiation of the second stage must be for matters similar to or connected with the unsatisfactory performance or attendance referred to in the improvement notice issued at the first stage. Where, at the end of the period specified in an improvement notice, the line manager finds that the police officer's performance or attendance has not improved to an acceptable standard during that period or that the police officer has not maintained an acceptable level of performance or attendance during the validity period of the notice, the second line manager will notify the police officer in writing that he/she is required to attend a second stage meeting. The notification will state:

- the details of the procedures for determining the date and time of the meeting;
- a summary of the reasons why the line manager considers the police officer's performance or attendance unsatisfactory;
- the possible outcomes of a second stage and third stage meeting;
- that the line manager may attend the meeting;
- that a human resources professional or a police officer (who should have experience of UPPs and be independent from the line management chain) may attend the meeting to advise the second line manager on the proceedings;
- that if the police officer agrees, any other person specified in the notice may attend the meeting;
- that prior to the meeting the police officer must provide the second line manager with any documentation he/she intends to rely on in the meeting; and
- the police officer's rights, i.e. his/her right to seek advice from a representative of his/her staff association (in the case of a member of the police force) and to be accompanied and represented at the meeting by a police friend.

The notice must also include copies of related documentation relied upon by the line manager in support of the view that the police officer's performance or attendance continues to be unsatisfactory.

In advance of the meeting, the police officer shall provide the second line manager with any documents on which he/she intends to rely on in support of his/her case. Any document or other material that was not submitted in advance of the meeting may be considered at the meeting at the discretion of the second line manager. The purpose of allowing this discretion is to ensure fairness to all parties. However, the presumption should be that such documents or other material will not be permitted unless it can be shown that they were not previously available to be submitted in advance.

The second line manager should explain that there is potentially a further stage to the procedures and that the maximum outcome of stage two is a final improvement notice. The second line manager will also explain that if the procedure is followed to the final stage, dismissal, a reduction in rank (in the case of a member of a police force and in performance cases only), redeployment to alternative duties or an extended improvement notice (in exceptional circumstances) are possible outcomes.

4.3.10.1 Second Stage Meeting

At the second stage meeting the second line manager will:

- explain to the police officer the reasons why he/she has been required to attend a second stage meeting;
- provide the police officer with the opportunity to make representations in response;
- provide the police officer's police friend (if he/she has one) with an opportunity to make representations;
- listen to what the police officer (and/or his/her police friend) has to say, ask questions and comment as appropriate.

The second line manager may adjourn the meeting at any time if he/she considers it is necessary or expedient to do so. Where, having considered any representations by either the police officer and/or his/her police friend, the second line manager finds that the performance or attendance of the police officer has been unsatisfactory (either during the period specified in the written improvement notice or during the validity period of the written improvement notice) he/she shall:

- inform the police officer in what respect(s) his/her performance or attendance is considered unsatisfactory;

- inform the police officer of the improvement that is required in his/her performance or attendance;
- inform the police officer that, if a sufficient improvement is not made within the period specified by the second line manager, he/she may be required to attend a third stage meeting.
- inform the police officer that he/she will receive a final written improvement notice; and
- inform the police officer that if the sufficient improvement in his/her performance or attendance is not maintained during the validity period of such notice, he/she may be required to attend a third stage meeting.

4.3.10.2 Procedure following the Second Stage Meeting

A written record of the meeting and any improvement notice shall be sent to the officer as soon as reasonably practicable after they have been prepared.

Any improvement notice must be accompanied by a notice informing the police officer of his/her right to appeal and the name of the person to whom the appeal should be sent. The notice must also inform the police officer of his/her right to submit written comments on the written record of the meeting and of the procedure for doing so.

The police officer may submit written comments on the written record not later than the end of seven working days after the date that he/she received it (unless an extension has been granted by the second line manager following an application by the police officer).

4.3.10.3 Second Stage Appeals

A police officer has a right of appeal against the finding and the terms of the improvement notice imposed at stage two of the UPPs and against the decision to require him/her to attend the meeting. However, any finding and outcome of this second stage meeting will continue to apply up to the date that the appeal is determined. Therefore where the police officer contests the finding or outcome, he/she should continue to follow the terms of the improvement notice and any accompanying action plan pending the determination of the appeal. Any appeal should be made in writing to the senior manager within seven working days following the day of the receipt of the improvement notice. The notice of appeal must clearly set out the grounds and evidence for the appeal. The grounds for appeal are as follows:

- the finding of unsatisfactory performance or attendance is unreasonable;
- any of the terms of the improvement notice are unreasonable;
- there is evidence that could not reasonably have been considered at the second stage meeting which could have materially affected the finding of unsatisfactory performance or attendance or any of the terms of the improvement notice;
- there was a breach of the procedures set out in the Police (Performance) Regulations or other unfairness which could have materially affected the finding of unsatisfactory performance or attendance or the terms of the written improvement notice;
- the police officer should not have been required to attend the second stage meeting as the meeting did not concern unsatisfactory performance or attendance which was similar to or connected with the unsatisfactory performance or attendance referred to in the written improvement notice that followed the first stage meeting.

On the basis of the above grounds of appeal, the police officer may appeal against the finding of unsatisfactory performance or attendance, the decision to require him/her to attend the second stage meeting or the terms of the written improvement notice, those being:

- the respect in which the police officer's performance or attendance is considered unsatisfactory;

- the improvement which is required of the police officer;
- the length of the period specified for improvement by the second line manager at the second stage meeting.

The police officer has the right to be accompanied and represented by a police friend at the second stage appeal meeting.

Once a date for the meeting is fixed, the senior manager should send to the police officer a notice in writing of the date, time and place of the second stage appeal meeting together with the information required to be provided under reg. 24 of the Performance Regulations.

At the second stage appeal meeting the senior manager will:

- provide the police officer with the opportunity to make representations;
- provide his/her police friend (if he/she has one) with an opportunity to make representations.

Having considered any representations by either the police officer and/or his/her police friend, the senior manager may:

- make a finding that the officer should not have been required to attend the second stage meeting, and reverse the finding made at that meeting;
- confirm or reverse the finding of unsatisfactory performance or attendance;
- endorse or vary the terms of the improvement notice.

Any decision made that changes the finding or outcome of the second stage meeting will take effect by way of substitution for the finding or terms appealed against and as from the date of the second stage meeting.

4.3.11   The Third Stage

With the exception of gross incompetence cases, initiation of the third stage must be for matters similar to or connected with the unsatisfactory performance or attendance referred to in the final written improvement notice.

Where, at the end of the period specified in the final written improvement notice, the line manager finds that the police officer's performance or attendance has not improved to an acceptable standard during that period or that the police officer has not maintained an acceptable level of performance or attendance during the validity period of the notice, the line manager must notify the police officer in writing that he/she is required to attend a third stage meeting to discuss these issues. As soon as reasonably practicable thereafter, the senior manager must give a notice to the officer informing him/her:

- that the meeting will be with a panel appointed by the appropriate authority;
- the procedures for determining the date and time of the meeting;
- a summary of the reasons why the police officer's performance or attendance is considered unsatisfactory;
- the possible outcomes of a third stage meeting;
- that a human resources professional or a police officer (who should have experience of UPPs and be independent from the line management chain) may attend to advise the panel on the proceedings;
- that counsel or a solicitor may attend the meeting to advise the panel on the proceedings and on any question of law that may arise at the meeting;
- where the police officer is a special constable, inform him/her that a member of the special constabulary will attend the meeting to advise the panel;
- that if the police officer agrees, any other person specified in the notice may attend, e.g. a person attending for development reasons; and

- the police officer's rights, i.e. his/her right to seek advice from a representative of his/her staff association (in the case of a member of the police force) and to be accompanied and represented at the meeting by a police friend.

The notice must also include copies of related documentation relied upon by the line manager in support of the view that the police officer's performance or attendance continues to be unsatisfactory. It is important to note that a third stage meeting may not take place unless the officer has been notified of his/her right to representation by a police friend. The notice does not at this stage need to give the names of the panel members as these may not be known at the time of issue. However, as soon as the panel has been appointed by the appropriate authority, the appropriate authority should notify the police officer of the members' names.

The purpose of the meeting is for the panel to hear the evidence of the unsatisfactory performance or attendance and to give the police officer the opportunity to put forward his/her views. It will also be an opportunity to hear of any factors that are continuing to affect the police officer's performance or attendance and what the police officer considers can be done to address them.

Where the police officer has reached stage three following stages one and two (i.e. not a gross incompetence meeting), the possible outcomes of this stage three meeting are as follows:

- redeployment;
- reduction in rank (in the case of a member of a police force and for performance cases only);
- dismissal (with a minimum of 28 days' notice); or
- extension of a final improvement notice (in exceptional circumstances).

Where the panel grants an extension to the final improvement notice, it will specify a new period within which improvement to performance or attendance must be made. The 12-month validity period of the extended final improvement notice will apply in full from the date of extension. The panel may also vary any of the terms in the notice.

4.3.11.1 Stage Three Gross Incompetence Meetings

There may be exceptional circumstances where the appropriate authority considers the performance (not attendance) of the police officer to be so unsatisfactory as to warrant the procedures being initiated at the third stage. This would be as a result of a single incident of 'gross incompetence'. It is not envisaged that an appropriate authority would initiate the procedures at the third stage in respect of a series of acts over a period of time. 'Gross incompetence' is defined in the Police (Performance) Regulations 2012 as '. . . a serious inability or serious failure of a police officer to perform the duties of the rank or role he is currently undertaking to a satisfactory standard or level, to the extent that dismissal would be justified, except that no account shall be taken of the attendance of a police officer when considering whether he has been grossly incompetent'.

Where the appropriate authority determines it is appropriate to initiate the procedures at this stage, then the police officer must be informed in writing that he/she is required to attend a third stage meeting to discuss his/her performance. Where the appropriate authority has informed the police officer that he/she is to attend a third stage only meeting, it must, as soon as reasonably practicable, send the police officer a notice in writing which will include the following details:

- that the meeting will be with a panel appointed by the appropriate authority;
- the procedure for determining the date and time of the meeting;
- a summary of the reasons why the police officer's performance is considered to constitute gross incompetence;

- the possible outcomes of a third stage only meeting;
- that a human resources professional and a police officer (who should have experience of UPPs and be independent from the line management chain) may attend to advise the panel on the proceedings;
- that counsel or a solicitor may attend the meeting to advise the panel on the proceedings and on any question of law that may arise at the meeting;
- where the police officer is a special constable, inform him/her that a member of the special constabulary will attend the meeting to advise the panel;
- if the police officer agrees, any other person specified in the notice may attend, e.g. a person attending for development reasons; and
- the police officer's rights, i.e. his/her right to seek advice from a representative of his/her staff association (in the case of a member of the police force) and to be accompanied at the meeting by a police friend.

The purpose of the meeting is for the panel to hear the evidence of the gross incompetence and to give the police officer and his/her representative the opportunity to make representations on the matter.

The appropriate authority will explain that the police officer is required to attend the third stage meeting and that the possible outcomes of the stage three meeting are:

- redeployment to alternative duties;
- the issue of a final written improvement notice;
- reduction in rank (with immediate effect);
- dismissal (with immediate effect); or
- the issue of a written improvement notice (if the panel considers that there has been unsatisfactory performance and not gross incompetence).

4.3.11.2 Panel Membership and Procedure

The panel will comprise a panel chair and two other members and be appointed by the appropriate authority of the force in which the police officer is a member. At least one of the three panel members must be a police officer and one should be a human resources professional. Membership will be as follows:

- First panel member (chair): Senior police officer or senior human resources professional.
- Second panel member: Police officer of at least the rank of superintendent or human resources professional who in the opinion of the appropriate authority is at least equivalent to that rank.
- Third panel member: Police officer of at least the rank of superintendent or police staff member who in the opinion of the appropriate authority is at least equivalent to that rank.

None of the panel members should be junior in rank to the police officer concerned. For the purposes of chairing a third stage meeting, the Police (Performance) Regulations 2012 define a 'senior human resources professional' as '...a human resources professional who, in the opinion of the appropriate authority, has sufficient seniority, skills and experience to be a panel chair'. The panel chair should be senior in rank (or, in the opinion of the appropriate authority, is senior in rank) to the police officer concerned.

The appropriate authority may appoint police officers or police staff managers from another police force to be members of a panel. No panel member should be an interested party, i.e. a person whose appointment could reasonably give rise to a concern as to whether he/she could act impartially under the procedures.

As soon as the appropriate authority has appointed a third stage panel, it should arrange for copies of all relevant documentation to be sent to those members. In particular, any document:

- that was available to the line manager in relation to any first stage meeting;
- that was available to the second line manager in relation to any second stage meeting;
- that was prepared or submitted in advance of the third stage meeting;
- that was prepared or submitted following those meetings, i.e. improvement notices, action plans and meeting notes;
- relating to any appeal.

As soon as the appropriate authority has appointed a third stage panel, it must send the police officer written confirmation of the names of panel members. The police officer has the right to object to any panel members appointed by the appropriate authority and any such objection must be made in writing to the appropriate authority no later than three working days after receipt of the notification of the names of the panel members. The police officer must include the ground of his/her objection to any panel member in that submission. The appropriate authority must inform the police officer in writing whether it upholds or rejects an objection to a panel member. If the appropriate authority upholds the objection, a new panel member will be appointed as a replacement. As soon as practicable after any such appointment, the police officer will be informed in writing of the name of the new panel member. The appropriate authority must ensure that the requirements for the composition of the panel are met. The police officer may object to the newly appointed panel member in the same way whereupon the appropriate authority must follow the same procedure again.

4.3.11.3 Special Constables and Third Stage Meetings

In cases where the police officer is a special constable, as indicated above (**see para. 4.3.11**), the force will appoint a member of the special constabulary to attend the meeting to advise the panel (this is for the purpose of fairness). The special constable advising the panel must have sufficient seniority and experience of the special constabulary to be able to advise the panel. The special constable advising the panel can be a police officer serving in a different force. The special constable adviser will not form part of the panel and will not have a role in determining whether or not the police officer's performance or attendance is unsatisfactory. In arranging a third stage meeting involving special constables, due consideration should be given to the fact that special constables are unpaid volunteers and may therefore have full-time employment or other personal commitments.

4.3.11.4 Third Stage Meeting Dates and Timeframes

Any third stage meeting should take place no later than 30 working days after the date that the notification has been sent to the police officer. Within that timeframe, wherever possible, the meeting date and time should be agreed between the panel chair and the police officer. However, where agreement cannot be reached the panel chair must specify a time and date. If the police officer or his/her police friend is not available at the date or time specified by the panel chair, the police officer may propose an alternative time. Provided that the alternative time is reasonable and falls within a period of five working days beginning with the first working day after that specified by the panel chair, the meeting must be postponed to that time. If the panel chair considers it to be in the interests of fairness to do so, he/she may extend the 30 working day period within which the meeting should take place and the reasons for any such extension must be notified in writing to both the appropriate authority and the police officer. As soon as a date for the meeting is fixed, the panel chair should send to the police officer a notice in writing of the date, time and place of the third stage meeting.

4.3.11.5 Procedure on Receipt of Notice of Third Stage Meeting

Within 14 working days of the date on which a notice has been sent to the police officer (unless this period is extended by the panel chair for exceptional circumstances), the police officer must provide to the appropriate authority:

- a written notice of whether or not he/she accepts that his/her performance or attendance has been unsatisfactory or that he/she has been grossly incompetent, as the case may be;
- where he/she accepts that his/her performance or attendance has been unsatisfactory or that he/she has been grossly incompetent, any written submission he/she wishes to make in mitigation.

Where the police officer does not accept that his/her performance or attendance has been unsatisfactory or that he/she has been grossly incompetent or where he/she disputes part of the matters referred to in the notice that he/she has received, he/she shall provide the appropriate authority with a written notice of:

- the matters he/she disputes and his/her account of the relevant events; and
- any arguments on points of law he/she wishes to be considered by the panel.

The police officer shall provide the appropriate authority and the panel with a copy of any document he/she intends to rely on at the third stage meeting.

Before the end of three working days following the officer's compliance the senior manager and the officer shall each supply a list of proposed witnesses or give notice that they do not have any witnesses. Where witnesses are proposed, this must be accompanied by brief details of their evidence and their address. The officer should try to agree a list of witnesses with the senior manager. Where agreement has not been reached, the officer shall send to the appropriate authority his/her list of witnesses. As soon as reasonably practicable after any list of witnesses has been agreed or, in the case where no agreement could be reached, supplied to the appropriate authority, the appropriate authority must send the lists to the panel chair together with, in the latter case, a list of its proposed witnesses. The panel chair will consider the list of proposed witnesses and will determine which, if any, witnesses should attend the third stage meeting.

The panel chair can determine that persons not named in the list should attend as witnesses. No witnesses will give evidence at a third stage meeting unless the panel chair reasonably believes that it is necessary in the interests of fairness for the witness to do so, in which case he/she will:

- in the case of a police officer, cause him/her to be ordered to attend the third stage meeting;
- in any other case, cause him/her to be given notice that his/her attendance at the third stage meeting is necessary.

Such notices will include the date, time and place of the meeting.

Where a witness attends to give evidence then any questions to that witness should be made through the panel chair. This would not prevent the panel chair allowing questions to be asked directly if he/she feels that this is appropriate.

The documents or other material to be relied upon at the meeting are required to be submitted in advance. Any document or other material that was not submitted in advance of the meeting may be considered at the meeting at the discretion of the panel chair. However, the presumption should be that such documents or other material will not be permitted unless it can be shown that they were not previously available to be submitted in advance or that they relate to mitigation following a finding of unsatisfactory performance or attendance that was contested by the police officer.

4.3.11.6 At the Third Stage Meeting

At the third stage meeting the panel chair will conduct the meeting and will explain to the police officer the reasons why he/she has been required to attend a third stage meeting and provide the police officer with the opportunity to make representations in response. Where the case is one of gross incompetence and the police officer has opted for legal representation, the chair will provide the police officer's legal representative with the opportunity to make representations (unless the police officer is entitled to be and has chosen to be legally represented, provide the police officer's police friend (if he/she has one) with an opportunity to make representations). The panel chair has a duty to listen to what the police officer and/or police friend has to say, and ask questions as appropriate.

Having considered any representations by either the police officer and/or his/her police friend or (where applicable) the police officer's legal representative, the panel will come to a finding as to whether or not the performance or attendance of the police officer has been unsatisfactory or whether or not his/her behaviour constitutes gross incompetence, as the case may be. If there is a difference of view between the three panel members, the finding or decision will be based on a simple majority vote, but it will not be indicated whether it was taken unanimously or by a majority.

The panel must prepare (or cause to be prepared) its decision in writing which shall also state the finding. Where the panel has found that the police officer's performance or attendance has been unsatisfactory or that he/she has been grossly incompetent, the decision must also state the panel's reasons and any outcome which it orders.

As soon as reasonably practicable after the conclusion of the meeting, the panel chair shall send a copy of the decision to the police officer and the line manager. However, the police officer must be given written notice of the finding of the panel within three working days of the conclusion of the meeting. Where the panel has made a finding of unsatisfactory performance or attendance or gross incompetence the copy of the decision sent to the police officer must also be accompanied by a notice informing him/her of the circumstances in which and the timeframe within which he/she may appeal to a police appeals tribunal. A verbatim record of the meeting should be taken. The police officer must, on request, be supplied with a copy of the record.

4.3.11.7 Postponement and Adjournment of a Third Stage Meeting

If the panel chair considers it necessary or expedient, he/she may direct that the third stage meeting should take place at a different time from that originally notified to the police officer. The panel chair's alternative time may fall after the period of 30 working days. In the event that the panel chair postpones a third stage meeting he/she should notify the following relevant parties in writing of his/her reasons and the revised time and place for the meeting:

- the police officer;
- other panel members; and
- the appropriate authority.

If the police officer informs the panel chair in advance that he/she is unable to attend the third stage meeting on grounds which the panel chair considers reasonable, the panel chair may allow the police officer to participate in the meeting by video link or other means. In cases where the police officer is absent (for example through illness or injury) a short delay may be reasonable to allow him/her to attend. If this is not possible or any delay is considered not appropriate in the circumstances then the persons conducting the meeting/hearing may allow the police officer to participate by telephone or video link. In these circumstances a police friend will always be permitted to attend the meeting/hearing to represent the police officer in the normal way (and, in the case of a gross incompetence meeting, the police officer's legal representative where appointed).

4.3.11.8 Assessment of Final and Extended Final Improvement Notices Issued at the Third Stage

Where the police officer has been issued with a final improvement notice or, in exceptional cases, the panel has extended a final improvement notice period, it is expected that the police officer's performance or attendance will be actively monitored by the line manager throughout the specified period of the final/extended final improvement notice. The line manager should discuss with the police officer any concerns that the line manager has during this period as regards his/her performance or attendance and offer advice and guidance where appropriate.

As soon as reasonably practicable after the specified period of the final/extended final improvement notice comes to an end, the panel will assess the performance or attendance of the police officer during that period. The panel chair must then inform the police officer in writing of the panel's conclusion following assessment, i.e. whether there has been sufficient improvement in his/her performance or attendance during the specified period. If the panel considers that there has been insufficient improvement the panel chair shall also notify the officer that he/she is required to attend another third stage meeting.

If, at the end of the validity period of the final/extended final improvement notice, the panel considers that sufficient improvement to the police officer's performance or attendance has not been made or maintained during this period, the panel chair will inform the police officer of the panel's assessment. Any such notification to the police officer must also include notification that he/she is required to attend a further third stage meeting. Where an officer is required to attend a further third stage meeting, the Regulations shall apply as if he/she were required to attend that meeting for the first time and following a second stage meeting.

As with the initiation of stages one and two for unsatisfactory performance or attendance, a further third stage meeting must relate to matters similar to or connected with the unsatisfactory performance or attendance or gross incompetence referred to in the final improvement notice extended or issued by the panel. The panel should (where possible) be composed of the same persons who conducted the previous third stage meeting. However, there may be cases where reconstitution of the panel is either inappropriate or not possible. In such circumstances the appropriate authority may substitute members as it sees fit subject to the requirements in **para. 4.3.11.2**. As soon as reasonably practicable after the appointment of any new panel members, the police officer should be notified in writing of the changes in panel membership. The police officer will have the opportunity to object to any new panel members.

A police officer may only be given an extension to a final improvement notice on one occasion. Therefore where the police officer is required to attend a reconvened third stage meeting and the panel finds that the police officer's performance or attendance continues to be unsatisfactory, the only outcomes available to the panel are redeployment, reduction in rank (only for a member of a police force and in performance cases) or dismissal (with notice).

In cases where a police officer was issued with an improvement notice (as opposed to a final improvement notice) for unsatisfactory performance at a gross incompetence third stage meeting, that written improvement notice will be equivalent to a written improvement notice issued at a first stage meeting. In that case the procedure for assessing the performance of the police officer will be the same as that following the first stage.

4.3.11.9 Third Stage Appeals

Following a third stage meeting, a police officer may be able to appeal to a police appeals tribunal. However, any finding and outcome of the third stage meeting will continue to apply up to the date that the appeal is determined.

4.3.12 Attendance at Each Stage of the Procedures and Ill-health

Attendance at any stage meeting is not subject to the same considerations as reporting for duty and the provisions of reg. 33 (sick leave) of the Police Regulations 2003 do not apply.

An illness or disability may render a police officer unfit for duty without affecting his/her ability to attend a meeting. However, if the police officer is incapacitated, the meeting may be deferred until he/she is sufficiently improved to attend. A meeting will not be deferred indefinitely because the police officer is unable to attend, although every effort should be made to make it possible for the police officer to attend if he/she wishes to be present. For example:

- the acute phase of a serious physical illness is usually fairly short-lived, and the meeting may be deferred until the police officer is well enough to attend;
- if the police officer suffers from a physical injury—a broken leg—for instance, it may be possible to hold the meeting at a location convenient to him/her.

Where such circumstances apply at a stage three meeting, the force may wish to consider the use of video, telephone or other conferencing technology. Where, despite such efforts having been made and/or the meeting having been deferred, the police officer either persists in failing to attend the meeting or maintains his/her inability to attend, the person conducting the meeting will need to decide whether to continue to defer the meeting or whether to proceed with it, if necessary in the absence of the police officer. The person conducting the meeting must judge the most appropriate course of action. Nothing in this paragraph should be taken to suggest that, where a police officer's medical condition is found to be such that he/she would normally be retired on medical grounds the UPPs should prevent or delay retirement.

4.3.13 The Use of Records under UPPs

Records of any part of the UPPs should not be taken into account after an improvement notice has ceased to be valid. Equally, where a police officer appeals and that appeal is successful, the record of that procedure should not be taken into consideration in any future proceedings or for any other purpose.

4.3.14 Misconduct, Performance and Attendance Issues for Seconded Officers

The procedures set out in the Police (Conduct) Regulations 2012 and Police (Performance) Regulations 2012 cannot be applied by the organisation to which the police officer is seconded under s. 97 of the Police Act 1996. However, the procedures set out in the Regulations can be applied by the parent force in respect of conduct, performance or attendance while on secondment. Those responsible for managing police officers on secondment are expected to manage any issue of unsatisfactory performance or attendance or minor misconduct in a proportionate, fair and timely manner without returning an officer to his/her parent force. Only if it is necessary to institute the formal procedures should an officer be returned to force, in accordance with the principles and procedures expressed below.

Where an officer is on secondment under the Police (Overseas Service) Act 1945, with the Police Ombudsman for Northern Ireland or with the Police Service of Northern Ireland, then he/she can be dealt with by the receiving organisation under its disciplinary arrangements. However, on return to his/her force, he/she can still be dealt with under the disciplinary arrangements in respect of the same matters.

It is important that police officers on secondment are clear about who has line management responsibility for them. The line managers for such police officers must ensure that the police officer continues to have a PDR and is made aware of these arrangements for dealing with issues of misconduct or unsatisfactory performance or attendance.

Where there is no or insufficient improvement in the performance or attendance of the police officer, the seconded police officer's line manager should prepare a written report which details the nature of the unsatisfactory performance or attendance together with the remedial and other measures taken, and send this report to the head of the organisation to which the police officer is seconded (or his/her nominated representative). The head of the organisation (or nominated representative), in conjunction with the appropriate authority for the police officer concerned, will decide whether it is appropriate that the police officer concerned should be returned to his/her parent force or whether the unsatisfactory performance or attendance can be addressed with the police officer remaining on secondment. Where a police officer who has been returned to his/her parent force under this procedure continues to demonstrate the same pattern of unsatisfactory performance or attendance, the details of the unsatisfactory performance or attendance while on secondment may be used to inform the decision whether it is appropriate to use the UPPs.

In alleged cases of misconduct by a secondee, the organisation to which the police officer has been seconded will need to make an initial assessment of the allegation of misconduct. If that assessment determines that the matter can be dealt with by management action, the seconded officer's manager is expected to deal with the matter in this way. As part of this decision making process, it may be necessary for the line manager to contact the appropriate authority for the seconded officer to assist in determining the nature of the conduct and whether it should be investigated. In this regard, the appropriate authority will need to consider its obligations under the Police Reform Act 2002 and any requirement to refer a matter to the IPCC.

However, where the line manager considers that an alleged breach of the Standards of Professional Behaviour is more serious and indicates that the police officer concerned may have committed a criminal offence, or behaved in a manner that would justify the bringing of disciplinary proceedings, the head of the organisation to which the police officer is seconded (or his/her nominated representative) will liaise with the appropriate authority from which the police officer concerned is seconded to assess whether the officer should be returned to the force while a preliminary assessment into the matter is conducted by the parent force. If, as a result of that preliminary assessment, the parent force considers it appropriate to issue a reg. 15 notice in relation to the matter, the officer must be returned to force.

Where it is determined by the appropriate authority for the seconded officer and the organisation to which he/she is seconded, that the conduct, if proved or admitted, would not justify the bringing of disciplinary proceedings, management action may still be taken where appropriate. At the conclusion of any disciplinary proceedings, where the police officer has been returned to the parent force, that force together with the organisation to which the police officer concerned was seconded will decide if it is appropriate for the police officer to be able to resume his/her secondment.

4.3.15 Vicarious Liability of Chief Officers

Section 88 of the Police Act 1996 originally provided that a chief officer will be vicariously liable for the 'torts' (civil wrongs) of his/her officers committed in the performance (or purported performance) of their duties. This meant that the chief officer was responsible for the payment of any damages arising out of a civil claim in respect of such a tort. The extent of this vicarious liability was wider than that imposed on employers generally (see comments of the Court of Appeal in *Weir* v *Chief Constable of Merseyside Police* [2003] EWCA Civ 111).

However, despite the fact that the vicarious liability of chief officers was broader than that of any ordinary employer, its limitation to strictly actionable civil wrongs was felt to have led to some inequities, denying remedies to individuals while failing to impose full accountability on the relevant chief officers. The Police Reform Act 2002 clarified the position and amends s. 88 to provide that chief officers will be liable for the 'unlawful conduct' (as opposed to purely civil wrongs) of their officers and employees when acting as such (s. 102).

4.3.16 Other Regulations

In addition to the specific provisions for conduct, complaints and efficiency, there are several other sources of regulation that govern the employment and deployment of police officers.

4.3.16.1 Restrictions on Private Lives

The Police Regulations 2003 (SI 2003/527) impose restrictions on the private lives of officers. Regulation 6 provides that the restrictions contained in sch. 1 shall apply to all members of a police force. It also provides that no restrictions other than those designed to secure the proper exercise of the functions of a constable shall be imposed by the chief officer of police on the private lives of members of a police force except such as may temporarily be necessary or such as may be approved by the Secretary of State after consultation with the Police Advisory Board for England and Wales.

Schedule 1

Schedule 1 provides that a member of a police force:

- shall at all times abstain from any activity which is likely to interfere with the impartial discharge of his/her duties or which is likely to give rise to the impression among members of the public that it may so interfere;
- shall in particular:
  + not take any active part in politics;
  + not belong to any organisation specified or described in a determination of the Secretary of State;

For this purpose the Secretary of State has determined that no member of a police force may be a member of the British National Party (BNP), Combat 18 or the National Front.

- shall not reside at premises which are not for the time being approved by the chief officer of police;
- shall not, without the previous consent of the chief officer of police, receive a lodger in a house or quarters with which he/she is provided, or sub-let any part of the house or quarters;
- shall not, unless he/she has previously given written notice to the chief officer of police, receive a lodger in a house in which he/she resides and in respect of which he/she receives an allowance under sch. 3, or sub-let any part of such a house;
- shall not wilfully refuse or neglect to discharge any lawful debt.

4.3.16.2 Business Interests

Some business interests preclude people from applying to be a police constable (reg. 7 of the Police Regulations 2003).

Regulation 8 provides that, if a member of a police force or a relative included in his/her family proposes to have, or has, a 'business interest', the member shall forthwith give written notice of that interest to the chief officer of police unless that business interest was disclosed at the time of the officer's appointment as a member of the force.

On receipt of such a notice, the chief officer shall determine whether or not the interest in question is compatible with the member concerned remaining a member of the force and shall notify the member in writing of his/her decision within 28 days.

If a business interest is felt to be incompatible, the chief officer may dispense with the member's services after giving him/her an opportunity to make representations. Regulation 7(2) provides that a member of a police force or relative has a business interest if:

- the member holds any office or employment for hire or gain or carries on any business;
- a shop is kept or a like business carried on by the member's spouse (not being separated) at any premises in the area of the police force in question or by any relative living with him/her at the premises where he/she resides; or
- the member, his/her spouse (not being separated) or any relative living with him/her has a pecuniary interest in any licence or permit granted in relation to liquor licensing, refreshment houses or betting and gaming or regulating places of entertainment in the area of the police force in question.

'Relative' includes a reference to a spouse, parent, son, daughter, brother or sister.

A police officer must notify his/her chief officer of any changes in a business interest.

4.3.17   Offences

The following criminal offences relate to the general abuse of public office and specific offences relating to police officers or impersonation of officers or officials.

4.3.17.1   Misconduct in a Public Office

OFFENCE: **Misconduct in a Public Office—*Common Law***
- Triable on indictment   • Imprisonment at large

It is a misdemeanour at common law for the holder of a public office to do anything that amounts to a malfeasance or a 'culpable' misfeasance (*R* v *Wyat* (1705) 1 Salk 380).

Where there is clear evidence of one or more statutory offences, they should usually form the basis of the case, with the 'public office' element being put forward as an aggravating factor for sentencing purposes. In *R* v *Rimmington, R* v *Goldstein* [2005] UKHL 63 at para. 30 the House of Lords confirmed this approach, saying:

...good practice and respect for the primacy of statute require that conduct falling within the terms of a specific statutory provision should be prosecuted under that provision unless there is good reason for doing otherwise.

The use of the common law offence should therefore be limited to the following situations:

- where there is no relevant statutory offence, but the behaviour or the circumstances are such that they should nevertheless be treated as criminal;
- where there is a statutory offence but it would be difficult or inappropriate to use it. This might arise because of evidential difficulties in proving the statutory offence in the particular circumstances;
- because the maximum sentence for the statutory offence would be entirely insufficient for the seriousness of the misconduct.

KEYNOTE

This offence has also been described as 'A man accepting an office of trust concerning the public is answerable criminally to the King for misbehaviour in his office…by whomsoever and in whatever way the officer is appointed' (*R* v *Bembridge* (1738) 3 Dougl 327).

Such offences can only be tried on indictment and the court has a power of sentence 'at large', that is, there is no limit on the sentence that can be passed. This ancient common law oddity is both a civil wrong (tort) giving rise to an action for damages in the county and High Court, and a criminal offence which is triable on indictment and punishable by an unlimited term of imprisonment.

Given the very wide scope of the 'offence' element, it can cover a multitude of transgressions by police officers, from mistreating prisoners to the improper use of criminal intelligence. The conduct can be separated into occasions of *mal*feasance and *mis*feasance. The first requires some degree of wrongful motive or intention on the part of the officer while the second is more likely to apply where there has been some form of wilful neglect of duty: both are notoriously difficult to prove.

The essence of both is generally an abuse of public power in bad faith (*Thomas* v *Secretary of State for the Home Office* [2000] Prison LR 188). There must at least be some real connection between the alleged misconduct and the public office—for instance where a man employed by a local council as a maintenance manager dishonestly caused his employees to carry out works on his girlfriend's premises (*R* v *Bowden* [1996] 1 WLR 98). Therefore, simply behaving badly while off duty would not of itself make a public office holder (such as a police officer) guilty of this offence (see *Elliott* v *Chief Constable of Wiltshire* (1996) *The Times*, 5 December—disclosure of previous convictions from PNC to a newspaper capable of amounting to misfeasance). It may, however, make the relevant *chief officer* vicariously liable under other heads of law if the off-duty officer was purporting to rely on his/her status as a constable (for a good example see *Weir* v *Chief Constable of Merseyside* [2003] EWCA Civ 111).

The key elements of the offence so far as it applies to public office holders (such as police officers) were set out by the Court of Appeal in *Attorney-General's Reference (No. 3 of 2003)* [2004] EWCA Crim 868). That case arose out of a death in police custody and the officers were charged with manslaughter by gross negligence, along with the alternative offence of misconduct in a public office. It was argued that misconduct in a public office is a 'conduct' crime, i.e. one where the acts (or omissions) themselves were the real consideration and not the consequences which those acts/omissions brought about (see *Crime*, chapter 1.2). Although reluctant to try to give an exhaustive definition of the offence, the Court of Appeal identified the elements of conduct and state of mind that must be proved in order to convict an officer of misfeasance, holding the main ingredients to be:

- Conduct (or omission) which involved the public office holder *acting as such*. In other words, this would need to arise from the actions (or omissions) of a police officer while acting in his/her capacity as a constable. A purely personal matter arising while the officer was off duty would not normally meet this first criterion.
- Evidence of wilful neglect and/or wilful misconduct. Simple inadvertence or accidental action/omission without more will not be enough.
- The degree of wilful neglect/misconduct must be such as to amount to an abuse of the public's trust in the office holder.
- Proof that the officer acted/omitted to act without any reasonable excuse or justification.

In the civil setting, even though there might be circumstances where officers could be criticised for failures, including incompetence, excess of zeal and even serious negligence, the absence of bad faith or deliberate misuse of power would generally mean that there is not enough to support an allegation of misfeasance (see *Ashley* v *Chief Constable of Sussex* [2005] EWHC 415 (QB)).

The ingredients of the civil wrong are fully set out in *Three Rivers District Council* v *Governor and Company of the Bank of England (No. 3)* [2003] 2 AC1. Their application, especially in the case of police officers, was discussed at length by the Court of Appeal in reviewing the relevant authorities in *Cornelius* v *London Borough of Hackney* [2002] EWCA Civ 1073. In *Three Rivers*, Lord Steyn confirmed that the civil and criminal wrongs bore some resemblance. Although many of the earlier cases involved an element of corruption, this is not a requirement for the offence (*R* v *Dytham* [1979] 2 QB 722). This offence might be committed where a police officer wilfully neglects to prevent a criminal assault (as in *Dytham*), or possibly where a supervisory officer fails to intervene in a situation where one of his/her officers is carrying out an unlawful act.

From the many authorities (especially the Court of Appeal in *Bowden*) it is arguable that this offence could be extended in appropriate circumstances to misconduct of non-sworn employees such as those designated (or perhaps even those accredited) under the Police Reform Act 2002 (as to which see chapter 4.4).

The Court of Appeal has held that, where the police wrote to the registered keepers of vehicles believed to have been stolen in another country, informing those keepers that they may not be the legal owners, the person who imported and sold the vehicles *might* be able to bring a claim for misfeasance—much would depend on the state of mind and intentions of the relevant individual in acting as they did—*R Cruickshank Ltd* v *Chief Constable of Kent* [2002] EWCA Civ 184.

4.3.17.2 Offences Relating to Impersonation

OFFENCE: **Impersonating a Police Officer—*Police Act 1996, s. 90(1)***
- Triable summarily • Six months' imprisonment

The Police Act 1996, s. 90 states:

(1) Any person who with intent to deceive impersonates a member of a police force or special constable, or makes any statement or does any act calculated falsely to suggest that he is such a member or constable, shall be guilty of an offence and liable ...

OFFENCE: **Wearing or Possessing Uniform—*Police Act 1996, s. 90(2) and (3)***
- Triable summarily • Fine *(No specific power of arrest)*

The Police Act 1996, s. 90 states:

(2) Any person who, not being a constable, wears any article of police uniform in circumstances where it gives him an appearance so nearly resembling that of a member of a police force as to be calculated to deceive shall be guilty of an offence ...

(3) Any person who, not being a member of a police force or special constable, has in his possession any article of police uniform shall, unless he proves that he obtained possession of that article lawfully and has possession of it for a lawful purpose, be guilty of an offence ...

KEYNOTE

'Article of police uniform' means:

- any article of uniform, or
- any distinctive badge or mark, or
- any document of identification

usually issued to members of police forces or special constables (s. 90(4)).

OFFENCE: **Impersonating Designated or Accredited Person—*Police Reform Act 2002, s. 46(3)***
- Triable summarily • Six months' imprisonment and/or a fine *(No specific power of arrest)*

The Police Reform Act 2002, s. 46 states:

(3) Any person who, with intent to deceive—
  (a) impersonates a designated person, an accredited person or an accredited inspector,
  (b) makes any statement or does any act calculated falsely to suggest that he is a designated person, that he is an accredited person or that he is an accredited inspector, or
  (c) makes any statement or does any act calculated falsely to suggest that he has powers as a designated or accredited person or as an accredited inspector that exceed the powers he actually has,
is guilty of an offence.

4.3.17.3 Causing Disaffection among the Police

OFFENCE: **Causing Disaffection—*Police Act 1996, s. 91(1)***
  • Triable either way • Two years' imprisonment on indictment • Six months'
  imprisonment and/or a fine summarily *(No specific power of arrest)*

The Police Act 1996, s. 91 states:

(1) Any person who causes, or attempts to cause, or does any act calculated to cause, disaffection amongst the members of any police force, or induces or attempts to induce, or does any act calculated to induce, any member of a police force to withhold his services, shall be guilty of an offence...

4.3.18 Health and Safety

Because police officers are not 'employees' in the conventional legal sense (they are holders of the office of constable), many of the statutory provisions regulating the workplace do not apply directly to them. The health and safety regime that was set up mainly by the Health and Safety at Work etc. Act 1974 applies principally to 'employees' and therefore did not cover police officers (though it clearly covers their non-sworn support colleagues who *are* employees). However, the Police (Health and Safety) Act 1997 made certain changes to the legislation by treating police officers for certain purposes relating to health and safety as if they were employees. Briefly, these areas include:

- the application of part 1 of the 1974 Act to the police;
- the right of police officers not to be subjected to a detriment in relation to health and safety issues (e.g. not to be punished for raising appropriate health and safety issues or undertaking duties as health and safety representatives—see s. 49A of the Employment Rights Act 1996);
- the right of police officers not to be unfairly dismissed in relation to health and safety issues—see s. 134A of the Employment Rights Act 1996.

Under the Health and Safety at Work etc. Act 1974, any prosecution of a chief officer of police for an offence under that Act will be brought against the office of chief constable rather than against the individual him/herself. This change to the law (brought in by the Serious Organised Crime and Police Act 2005) brings the position of a chief officer into line with that of police authorities and their liability for breaches of health and safety legislation in respect of police staff (who are their employees). However, a chief officer may also be prosecuted in a personal capacity if it can be shown that he/she personally consented to the commission of an offence or personally connived in its commission, or was personally negligent.

4.4 Human Rights

4.4.1 Introduction

The European Convention on Human Rights and the Human Rights Act 1998 have been included in this chapter in some detail because of the effect they have on the use of policing powers.

Procedural and constitutional issues affecting the Convention and the Act within the administration of justice system are largely dealt with in *Evidence and Procedure*. Other matters affecting substantive law and the particular effects of the Human Rights Act 1998 on existing legislation have been included throughout the relevant chapters of each Manual in this series.

4.4.2 Key Features of the Convention

The Convention sets out to protect most of what might be seen as the fundamental civil liberties within a democratic society. However, it is a very different concept from an Act of Parliament. There are several key features that need to be understood when considering the Convention and its effects. Those key features include:

- The balancing of competing rights and needs.
- Limitations and restrictions—the 'three tests'.
- The Convention as a 'living' instrument.
- The 'margin of appreciation'.
- Derogations and reservations.

Some of these features will now be considered in more detail.

4.4.2.1 Balancing Competing Rights and Needs

Some of the Convention's provisions are *absolute*, that is, they do not permit any infringement under any circumstances. An example would be the right to freedom from torture under Article 3. Other rights are often limited or restricted in some way, such as the right to liberty and security of person under Article 5. These rights have to be restricted if the 'democratic society' is going to work. If a person is lawfully arrested or detained, his/her right to liberty has been infringed, but the Convention takes account of such situations and imposes limitations on that right. Similarly, there will be times when the freedom of an individual conflicts with the general public interest—the right to freedom of assembly and freedom of association (protected under Article 11) and the need to maintain public order, for instance. A perfect example of the balancing act required in a policing context can be seen in the powers to seize and retain a motor vehicle that is being used in an anti-social manner. Here, the owner's rights to enjoy his/her personal possessions have to be balanced with the rights of the general population to enjoy their private and family lives, and the Police Reform Act 2002 created policing powers to deal with the situation where the two sets of rights collide— the real trick is exercising those powers lawfully, proportionately and sensibly. These categories of rights are generally referred to as 'qualified' rights and the areas of potential conflict they raise are of particular significance to the police and other law enforcement agencies.

In some cases, the rights of individuals may directly compete with one another. An example would be one person's right to freedom of expression (Article 10) and another person's freedom to respect for their private life (Article 8). What the Convention—and the European Court of Human Rights—sets out to do is to *balance* these rights against each other and against the needs of the democratic society within which they exist. For this reason many of the Convention's Articles include any relevant limitations or exceptions. Although each is different, a helpful practical approach when interpreting their extent is to apply the 'three tests'.

4.4.2.2 The Three Tests

Where the Convention gives individuals a particular right, any qualification or limitation on that right will be carefully defined and cautiously applied. Otherwise the effect of the Convention would be diluted by a series of 'get out' clauses or circumstances where the right could be easily overridden. This is particularly the case where the balancing of 'qualified' rights is concerned (**see para. 4.4.2.1**).

Very generally, any limitations on a Convention right must be:

- prescribed by, and in accordance with, the law
- intended to achieve a legitimate objective
- proportionate to the end that is to be achieved.

Each of these areas has a significant impact on the work of police officers and needs to be examined in turn.

Test one—prescribed by law

Any interference with a Convention right must first be traceable to a clear legal source (e.g. the Police and Criminal Evidence Act 1984). A person whose rights have allegedly been infringed is entitled to ask '*where did you get the power to act as you did?*' The public body concerned, whether it is a police service or a local authority or whatever, will have to point to a clear legal source and say '*that's where our authority to act in this way comes from*'. The source of this authority can be statutory or the common law; it can also be contractual (e.g. in matters relating to employment). This is one of the reasons why the need for police officers and anyone exercising policing powers to be able to identify the legal source of any power that they use has become even more important. If no such lawful authority can be identified, the consequent interference with a Convention right will be a violation of the Convention, *irrespective of any other justification*. Therefore if the relevant public authority (**see para. 4.4.3.5**) cannot point to a legal regulation that allows it to interfere with a Convention right, it will be in breach of its obligations (see e.g. the case involving the tapping of a senior police officer's telephone at work—*Halford* v *United Kingdom* (1997) 24 EHRR 523).

However, it is not enough that such a source of legal authority exists; it must also be readily accessible to the people of the relevant State (see *The Sunday Times* v *United Kingdom* (1979) 2 EHRR 245). This means that the law must be clearly and precisely defined and publicised so that people can make themselves aware of it and regulate their conduct accordingly. Acts of Parliament and statutory instruments would invariably meet this requirement. Our common law will probably meet this requirement in most cases (see the *Sunday Times* case) although it is arguable that there is so much lack of clarity in some areas that all aspects of this requirement are not met by our common law system.

Test two—legitimate objective

In addition to being authorised by a clear and accessible legal regulation, restrictions or limitations of qualified Convention rights must generally be directed at achieving a legitimate objective as set out under the Articles themselves. Such an objective might be the prevention of crime or the upholding of the rights of others. Given the broad nature of these objectives it should be relatively easy for a public authority, *when acting lawfully*, to meet this requirement.

Test three—proportionality and necessity

The test of proportionality asks *'were the measures you took necessary in a democratic society and in proportion to the ultimate objective?'* It is in this area that the 'balancing' of competing rights and needs takes place. It is also in this area that the use of police powers may be challenged most frequently. Any interference with a Convention right must be shown to have been relevant and proportional to the legitimate aim pursued (*Handyside* v *United Kingdom* (1979–80) 1 EHRR 737). A good example here would be police actions taken to prevent crime—forcibly entering and searching premises, for instance. Clearly, the prevention of crime would usually amount to a legitimate objective, but *the means employed by the officers would have to be in proportion to the crime that was to be prevented.*

If the manner and extent of an operation were shown to have infringed someone's Convention rights in a way that was out of all proportion to the legitimate aim being pursued, there would almost certainly have been a violation of those rights. As the authors of *Blackstone's Guide to the Human Rights Act 1998* put it: 'the State cannot use a sledgehammer to crack a nut'.

Although the decisions of public authorities, such as police services, have been open to the process of judicial review for some considerable time, the 'proportionality' test adopted by the European Court of Human Rights represents a much tighter constraint on the activities of public authorities than anything that has gone before. Generally under the judicial review procedure, the courts will not interfere with a decision of a public authority unless it can be shown to meet one of two criteria: unlawful or irrational (in short, 'wrong' or 'daft'). Under the *proportionality* test the Court in Strasbourg has taken a different approach and looks for a 'pressing social need' behind the actions complained of. If no such need can be found, the interference may be a violation of the Convention.

The overall practical result of the three tests means, in short, that the 'ways and means Act' has been repealed once and for all.

4.4.2.3 Discrimination

One final, generic test that will be applied to any limitation or restriction on Convention rights is whether the limitation or restriction is discriminatory, i.e. *'did the difference in treatment of the individuals affected have any objective and reasonable justification?'* (*Belgian Linguistic Case (No. 1)* (1967) 1 EHRR 241). Discrimination within the context of Convention rights is covered specifically by Article 14.

4.4.2.4 The Convention as a 'Living Instrument'

The Convention is different from the Acts of Parliament that appear elsewhere in this book. One difference is that the courts will interpret it in a 'purposive' way, i.e. in a way that gives effect to its central purposes, namely to protect the human rights of individuals and the ideals and values of a democratic society. Any such rights and ideals must not be theoretical, but practical and effective features of the lives of individuals within our democratic society. The Convention is also a 'living' instrument which must be interpreted in the light of present-day conditions (*Tyrer* v *United Kingdom* (1979–80) 2 EHRR 1). This means that its interpretation will develop alongside society without the need for older cases to be specifically overruled. If the acceptable standards within society become more tolerant (say, of consensual sexual activity or of behaviour in public), then the Convention should be interpreted and applied accordingly. Unlike our domestic common law where very old cases become well-established precedents, older case law relating to the Convention will not be followed slavishly by the courts and will therefore need to be considered carefully.

4.4.2.5 What are Derogations and Reservations?

Article 15 allows governments to 'derogate' from their obligations under the Convention *in time of war or other public emergency threatening the life of the nation.*

This provision allows governments to restrict the freedoms of individuals under such circumstances but *only to the extent that it is strictly necessary to do so.* Some of the individual rights protected by the Convention cannot be derogated from at all—these are Article 2, Article 3, Article 4(1) and Article 7.

The United Kingdom has attached a 'reservation' to its acceptance of one of the protocols to the Convention in relation to education (Protocol 1, Article 2). Article 2 says that no one shall be denied the right to education, and the reservation (which has also been registered by several other States) simply adds an amendment about compatibility with domestic provisions and unreasonable public expenditure.

4.4.3 The Human Rights Act 1998

The Human Rights Act 1998 came into force in October 2000. The 1998 Act effectively incorporates what are often called an individual's 'Convention rights' into our domestic law. These Convention rights are set out in the various Articles and Protocols of the Convention which appear in sch. 1 to the Act.

4.4.3.1 How Important is the Human Rights Act?

The 1998 Act is a very significant piece of legislation as not only does it give effect to the rights contained within the Convention, the Act also affects the way in which all other legislation will be interpreted and applied. Section 3 requires that, wherever possible, statutory provisions *and the common law* be read and given effect in a way that is compatible with Convention rights. This requirement, which also applies to new legislation, has an impact on all courts and tribunals in every jurisdiction, whether criminal or civil, where Convention rights are in issue.

A good example of this in action can be seen in a case involving the rights of a partner in a homosexual relationship to remain in their property when one partner died. Had the relationship been *heterosexual*, the survivor would have automatically become a statutory tenant entitled to remain in the home on the death of his partner. The House of Lords held that the relevant legislation should be read down and given effect in a way that was compatible with the Convention. The law as it stood discriminated against individuals on the basis of their sexuality (thereby breaching Article 14), within the context of their right to respect for their home as guaranteed by Article 8. As a result, the statute in question (the Rent Act 1977) was read and applied in a way that allowed the surviving partner to receive an assured tenancy and to remain in the property—(*Ghaidan* v *Godin-Mendoza* [2004] UKHL 30).

Although it creates avenues of redress against 'public authorities' (**see para. 4.4.3.5**), the Act does not create any new rights in private matters between individuals. The definition of 'public authorities' includes the courts (s. 6(3)) and therefore imposes an obligation for a court *in any matter*, criminal or civil, private or public, to give effect to the Act. This is why it is said that there will be occasions where the Act will be of 'indirect effect' as between individuals.

The 1998 Act still allows for occasions where an individual will need to petition the European Court of Human Rights in Strasbourg (see *Evidence and Procedure*, **chapter 2.1**).

4.4.3.2 Article 13—Real and Effective Remedy

It should be noted that Article 13—which requires States to ensure that individuals have a 'real and effective remedy' if their Convention rights are violated—has *not* been incorporated into the Human Rights Act 1998. It was the government's view that the introduction of the Act itself is enough to meet these requirements. Nevertheless, because Article 13 is very important in the case decisions of the European Court of Human Rights and s. 2 of the Act requires courts in England and Wales to have regard to those decisions made in Strasbourg, Article 13 will still have some significance in practice.

4.4.3.3 Breach of the Act—What Can You Do About It?

The Human Rights Act 1998, s. 6 states:

(1) It is unlawful for a public authority to act in a way that is incompatible with a Convention right.

KEYNOTE

The rights provided by the Convention are intended to be directly enforceable against 'public authorities'. Therefore, if it can be established that a person or organisation is a 'public authority' (as defined below), the Convention rights can be used directly against them in a number of ways. These ways include:

- Bringing proceedings against the public authority, e.g. for false imprisonment.
- Using the public authority's actions as a ground for judicial review.
- Using the public authority's actions as a defence to any action brought by it, e.g. someone charged with an offence of obstructing a police officer.

The first two ways of seeking a remedy are often referred to as using the Convention as a 'sword' while the last can be seen as making use of the Convention as a 'shield'. In using the Convention as a 'shield' in any legal proceedings, the person can do so *whenever the act complained of took place*. This will include citing acts by the public authority that have already taken place before the 1998 Act came into force. Where a person seeks to rely on their Convention rights as a 'sword', the restrictions and time limits under s. 7 will apply.

A good example of how the Convention can be used to launch a wide range of attacks on legislation and policing powers can be seen in *R (On the Application of Fuller and Secretary of State for the Home Department)* v *Chief Constable of Dorset Police* [2001] EWHC Admin 1057. There are many other examples throughout the text of the following chapters, particularly in the areas of public order, terrorism and anti-social behaviour.

In all cases where a person wishes to rely on the relevant Convention right in any proceedings (either as a sword or as a shield), he/she must meet the requirements of s. 7 (see para. 4.4.3.6).

If the person or organisation allegedly violating the individual's Convention rights cannot be shown to be a 'public authority', then there is no *direct* remedy against them (but, see para. 4.4.3.5). An 'act' will include a failure to act under certain circumstances (see para. 4.4.3.5).

4.4.3.4 Exceptions

Section 6 goes on to state:

(2) Subsection (1) does not apply to an act if—
   (a) as the result of one or more provisions of primary legislation, the authority could not have acted differently; or
   (b) in the case of one or more provisions of or made under, primary legislation which cannot be read or given effect in a way which is compatible with the Convention rights, the authority was acting so as to give effect to or enforce those provisions.

KEYNOTE

The 1998 Act is drafted in such a way as to preserve the concept of parliamentary sovereignty whereby Parliament's expressed intentions cannot be overruled. For this reason, s. 6(2) provides for circumstances where a public authority has acted in a way that is incompatible with a Convention right *but it only did so because it had no choice as a result of other legislation*. This means that if a public authority has a statutory duty to do

---

something and, in so doing, cannot avoid acting in a way that is incompatible with a Convention right, it does not commit a breach of s. 6(1) above. An example might be where there is a statutory requirement to pass on information, as under the Vehicle Excise and Registration Act 1994 and that requirement is enforced by the police or the DVLA. If an individual successfully claimed that such a requirement unnecessarily infringed his/her Convention right to privacy (Article 8), the actions of the police and the DVLA (as 'public authorities') may well be protected by s. 6(2). The proper remedy in such a case would be to seek a declaration from a higher court that the legislation concerned was in fact incompatible with the Convention (see *Evidence and Procedure,* chapter 2.1). This represents a key difference between the Human Rights Act 1998 and the legislation of the European Union. If there is a conflict between the domestic law of a Member State and the law of the European Union, the latter is able to override the domestic legislation even if it appears in a lawfully enacted Act of Parliament (see s. 2 of the European Communities Act 1972). In such circumstances, the courts in England and Wales are also under an obligation to disapply the inconsistent local legislation and give effect to European Union law (see e.g. *R* v *Secretary of State for Employment, ex parte Equal Opportunities Commission* [1995] 1 AC 1).

The effect of s. 6(2) only extends to *legislation*; it does not therefore appear to exempt the acts of people who are obeying, say, a court order such as a warrant. Moreover, the wording of s. 6(2)(a) suggests that it only applies where the legislation leaves the public authority no choice in the matter. Therefore this would not seem to apply to the exercise of *discretionary* powers such as powers of arrest, search and seizure. The bottom line is that an act or failure to act by a public authority will not be unlawful if:

- it is *not* incompatible with Convention rights;
- the authority could not have acted differently given the relevant primary legislation; or
- the authority acted so as to give effect to, or to enforce provisions made under, incompatible primary legislation.

4.4.3.5 Public Authorities

Section 6 goes on to state:

(3) In this section 'public authority' includes—
    (a) a court or tribunal, and
    (b) any person certain of whose functions are functions of a public nature, but does not include either House of Parliament or a person exercising functions in connection with proceedings in Parliament.
(4) …
(5) In relation to a particular act, a person is not a public authority by virtue only of subsection (3)(b) if the nature of the act is private.
(6) 'An act' includes a failure to act but does not include a failure to—
    (a) introduce in, or lay before Parliament a proposal for legislation; or
    (b) make any primary legislation or remedial order.

KEYNOTE

It can be seen from the text of s. 6(3) that there is no conclusive definition of what a public authority is; rather, there is a description of the functions that will make a person/organisation a 'public authority'. It can also be seen that there will be two groups of 'public authorities'—those who are named or who are concerned solely with discharging functions of a public nature ('pure' public authorities) and those who have *some* public functions ('quasi-public' authorities).

The first category (pure public authorities) would be:

- courts and tribunals
- police, fire and ambulance services
- local authorities and the Independent Police Complaints Commission.

These organisations, and the people working for them, have a duty to conform to the Convention rights of individuals when exercising *any and all* of their functions. Therefore a police service must act in conformity with the Convention in relation to its operational functions (preservation of law and order) and also in relation to its other functions (e.g. as an employee or contractor).

From the definition above it can be seen that not only are police *organisations* public authorities, but so are individual police officers—whether they are regular officers or special constables—and others who are employed by the police to exercise policing powers. As courts and tribunals are specified within s. 6(3), judges, magistrates and people chairing tribunals will be under a duty to ensure conformity with the Convention in deciding *any legal issue*—even if the hearing is one of private law between two individuals (e.g. a landlord and tenant dispute or a purely contractual matter).

It is difficult to identify accurately all the organisations that would fall into the second category. However, they might include a number of commercial or private organisations charged with some functions of a public nature, e.g.:

- rail operating companies
- security companies running prisons/prisoner escort services
- government contractors
- other bodies such as the BBC.

The important thing to establish with such groups is whether they were, at the material time, acting within the scope of their public functions or whether their actions were carried out purely within the ambit of their private functions. It would seem from the wording of s. 6(5) that quasi-public authorities will be accountable for acting in a way that is incompatible with the Convention *only while they are carrying out their public functions*. An example of this distinction might be a surgeon who both works for the NHS and has a private practice. While working for the NHS—an organisation having functions of a public nature—the surgeon's acts would probably be caught by s. 6(1). While acting in an entirely private capacity in his/her practice, the surgeon's acts would probably be excluded from the provisions of s. 6(1) by the wording of s. 6(5). This second category of organisations will be important to police services as the growth in public and private partnerships continues. In such cases the police service may be liable for acts committed by private partners in certain circumstances. This distinction will be particularly important where employees of private companies who have no other 'public' functions have been accredited under the Police Reform Act 2002.

4.4.3.6 Who Can Bring Proceedings?

The Human Rights Act 1998, s. 7 states:

(1) A person who claims that a public authority has acted (or proposes to act) in a way which is made unlawful by section 6(1) may—
  (a) bring proceedings against the authority under this Act in the appropriate court or tribunal, or
  (b) rely on the Convention right or rights concerned in any legal proceedings, but only if he is (or would be) a victim of the unlawful act.
(2) ...
(3) If the proceedings are brought on an application for judicial review, the applicant is to be taken to have a sufficient interest in relation to the unlawful act only if he is, or would be, a victim of that act.

KEYNOTE

Although the application of the 1998 Act is not restricted to natural persons and could include organisations, s. 7 limits the occasions where such 'people' can rely on Convention rights. To so rely on a Convention right, the person must be a 'victim'. The test to see if a person is a 'victim' for these purposes is taken directly from Article 34 of the Convention (which is not included in the Act) (s. 7(7)).

In order to qualify as a 'victim', a person must satisfy the same requirements as they would have to in order to bring a case before the Court in Strasbourg. These requirements are found in the case law from the European Court of Human Rights and principally mean that the person must show that he/she is:

- directly affected or
- at risk of being directly affected

by the act/omission complained of.

There is no need for the person to have actually *been* affected by the act/omission, as long as the person can show a real risk of him/her being directly affected by it in the future. An example can be seen in *Dudgeon* v *United Kingdom* (1983) 5 EHRR 573, where the petitioner was able to challenge the law proscribing consensual homosexual activity even though he had not been prosecuted under that legislation himself.

This limitation on 'victims' means that public interest groups will be excluded from bringing human rights actions directly, as will government organisations and local authorities.

The expression 'victim' is of particular relevance to people who are challenging the lawfulness of their arrest or detention under Article 5 (see para. 4.4.7).

There are significant restrictions on police officers relying on the Convention rights in the context of recruitment and disciplinary procedures. As the European Court of Justice regards police officers in Member States as being government servants, they cannot generally rely on their Convention rights against their employer (see *Pellegrin* v *France* (2001) 31 EHRR 26). Purely private matters such as police pensions disputes are, however, not precluded in this way and there are other examples of officers' Convention rights being taken into consideration by the courts (see para. 4.4.5).

The wording of s. 7(3) means that, if an application for judicial review is brought on human rights grounds, the applicant will have to meet the requirements of a 'victim' under s. 7 or he/she will not be allowed to bring the case *even though he/she might have sufficient legal standing under the rules governing judicial review generally*.

Time limits

Section 7 goes on to state:

(5) Proceedings under subsection (1)(a) must be brought before the end of—
    (a) the period of one year beginning with the date on which the act complained of took place; or
    (b) such longer period as the court or tribunal considers equitable having regard to all the circumstances,

but that is subject to any rule imposing a stricter time limit in relation to the procedure in question.

KEYNOTE

Any proceedings brought against a public authority under s. 7(1)(a) must be brought within one year from the date on which the act complained of took place (subject to the discretion of the relevant court/tribunal).

As the time for judicial review is three months, this stricter time limit will still apply in cases involving allegations of Convention rights infringement.

This time limit does not prevent people from raising the issue of Convention rights as a 'shield' in any other proceedings, neither does it affect the courts' general duty (under s. 3) to give effect to the Convention when interpreting and applying the law.

4.4.4   What are the 'Convention Rights'?

Having considered some of the key concepts and features of the Convention and the provisions of the Human Rights Act 1998, we can now examine some of the specific rights protected by them.

As Article 1 is simply a statement of the duty of governments signing up to the Convention to secure the relevant rights and freedoms to everyone within their jurisdiction, the starting point for the content of the Convention is Article 2.

4.4.5 Article 2—The Right to Life

Article 2 of the Convention states:

1. Everyone's right to life shall be protected by law. No one shall be deprived of his life intentionally save in the execution of a sentence of a court following his conviction of a crime for which this penalty is provided by law.
2. Deprivation of life shall not be regarded as inflicted in contravention of this Article when it results from the use of force which is no more than absolutely necessary:
   (a) in defence of any person from unlawful violence;
   (b) in order to effect a lawful arrest or to prevent the escape of a person lawfully detained;
   (c) in action lawfully taken for the purpose of quelling a riot or insurrection.

KEYNOTE

Article 2 provides what must be one of the most important and fundamental rights of individuals, namely, the right to life. There are two 'arms' to this Convention right, namely:

- a prohibition on the State from *taking* life, and
- a positive duty placed upon the State to *protect* life (see *X* v *United Kingdom* (1978) 14 DR 31).

The European Court of Human Rights said of Article 2 that it 'ranks as one of the most fundamental provisions in the Convention—indeed one which in peacetime admits of no derogation under Art. 15. Together with Art. 3 . . . it also enshrines one of the basic values of the democratic societies making up the Council of Europe . . . as such its provisions must be strictly construed' (*McCann* v *United Kingdom* (1996) 21 EHRR 97 at 160).

In a case concerning withholding medical treatment, the High Court considered the positive and negative duties under Article 2. The court held that the negative obligation was to refrain from taking a life intentionally. It held that this obligation was not breached by a decision made in the patient's best interests to withdraw life support facilities. The intentional deprivation of life had to involve a deliberate act as opposed to an omission. In relation to the positive obligation, the court held that this required the relevant public authority to take adequate and appropriate steps to safeguard life. Again, the taking of a responsible clinical decision to withhold treatment that was not in the patient's best interests met the State's positive obligation under Article 2 (*NHS Trust A* v *M* [2001] Fam 348). (In this judgment the court reaffirmed the pre-Convention decision (*Airedale NHS Trust* v *Bland* [1993] AC 789) to the same effect.)

Duties under Article 2 can arise in various practical policing situations such as deaths in police care and fatal shootings by officers. An example of where Article 2 was relied upon by police officers was *R (On the Application of A and B)* v *HM Coroner for Inner South District of Greater London* [2004] EWCA Civ 1439, where a coroner refused to allow officers involved in a fatal shooting of a suspect to give evidence anonymously at the inquest. The Divisional Court held that the risk of serious harm to the officers and their families was sufficient to engage Article 2 and the coroner ought to have protected the anonymity of the officers until the verdict or the occurrence of some other event requiring their identities to be disclosed in the interests of justice.

4.4.5.1 Taking Life

It can be seen from the wording of the first paragraph that Article 2 does not prohibit the taking of life by a lawful imposition of the death penalty.

It can be seen that the Article allows for a number of limited exceptions when the taking of life by the State may not be a violation of this Convention right. All of the situations covered by the exceptions are generally concerned with protecting life, preventing crime and preserving order. The exceptions include actions taken in defending another person (not property) from unlawful violence (**see *Crime*, chapter 1.4**) and effecting a lawful arrest (see para. 4.5.4). Therefore the Convention acknowledges that there will be occasions where the State is compelled to take the life of an individual, such as where a police officer has to use lethal force to protect the life of another.

However, while limited in themselves, these exceptions will also be subject to very restrictive interpretation by the courts. Given that Article 2 protects one of the most fundamental of all Convention rights, any claimed exceptions to the Article are extremely carefully examined by the courts.

When a life is taken under any of the three situations set out at para. 2(a)–(c) (**see para. 4.4.5**), the force used must be shown to have been *no more than absolutely necessary*—a more stringent test than the general test imposed in our domestic criminal law by s. 3 of the Criminal Law Act 1967 (as to which, **see *Crime*, chapter 1.4**). This very strict test was examined by the European Commission on Human Rights in a case where a young boy was killed by a baton round fired by a soldier during an outbreak of serious disorder (*Stewart* v *United Kingdom* (1985) 7 EHRR CD 453). There the Commission held that force will be absolutely necessary only if it is strictly proportionate to the legitimate purpose being pursued. In order to meet those criteria, regard must be had to:

- the nature of the aim being pursued,
- the inherent dangers to life and limb from the situation, and
- the degree of risk to life presented by the amount of force employed.

This test applies not only to cases where there has been an intentional taking of life, but also where there has been a permitted use of force that has led to the death of another. The test has been held to be a stricter one than even the general requirement of 'proportionality' that runs throughout the Convention (*McCann* v *United Kingdom* (1996) 21 EHRR 97).

This area is of critical importance to police officers in general, but to police supervisors and managers in particular. This is because not only are the courts concerned with any individual actions that directly lead to the death of another, but also because they will take into account 'other factors' surrounding and leading up to the incident that caused the loss of life.

Such other factors are likely to include:

- the planning and control of the operation,
- the training given to the officers concerned, and
- the briefing/instructions that they received.

Where the use of force by the police results in the deprivation of life, the training, briefing, deployment and overall competence of everyone involved in the relevant operation will potentially come under the scrutiny of the court. These considerations, which were made very clear by the European Court of Human Rights in the *McCann* case (a case involving the shooting of three terrorists by the SAS in Gibraltar in 1988), were applied by the Court to an incident when police officers shot and killed a gunman and his hostage (*Andronicou* v *Cyprus* (1998) 25 EHRR 491). In that case, the Court found that the police operation had been planned and managed in a way that was intended to minimise the risk to life, even though the officers ultimately made a mistake as to the extent of the gunman's weapons and ammunition when they took the decision to open fire. The Court found that the exceptional requirements of Article 2(2) had been made out and that there had been no violation of Article 2 by the police.

4.4.5.2 Protecting Life

A further area of importance for the police in Article 2 lies in the second arm—that of protecting the lives of others. This area was considered in the case of *Osman* v *United Kingdom* (2000) 29 EHRR 245. In this case a man had been killed by a person who had become fixated with the man's 15-year-old son. The dead man's relatives claimed that they had warned the police about the killer's fixation and tried to sue them for negligence in failing to protect

Mr Osman. Despite information being made available to the police the suspect's home had not been searched, nor had any special measures been put in place to protect the Osman family. The High Court dismissed the relatives' action on grounds of public policy and the relatives took their case to the European Court of Human Rights, claiming that the State had violated the second arm of Article 2 by failing to protect the life of Mr Osman. Although the Court held that there had been no such violation on the facts of the case, it went on to examine the positive obligation of the State under Article 2.

The positive obligation on the State to protect life is not an absolute one. In *Osman* the European Commission said that Article 2 must be interpreted as requiring preventive steps to be taken to protect life from '*known and avoidable dangers*' (emphasis added). The Commission went on to say that the extent of this obligation (which is clearly of the first importance to those tasked with investigating and preventing crime) will vary 'having regard to the source and degree of danger and the means available to combat it' (at 115). The European Court of Human Rights said in *Osman* (at 305) that it will be enough for an applicant to show that the authorities did not do all that could reasonably be expected of them to avoid a '*real and immediate risk to life*' (emphasis added) of which they have or ought to have knowledge. As such, whether a police officer or police force has failed in this positive obligation to protect life will only be answerable in the light of all the circumstances of a particular case. This requirement is therefore very similar to the test for negligence at civil law in England and Wales.

Under some circumstances, this requirement could make the police power to detain a person suffering from mental illness in a public place (**see para. 4.4.7.6**) a duty to do so.

4.4.6 Article 3—Torture

Article 3 of the Convention states:

No one shall be subjected to torture or to inhuman or degrading treatment or punishment.

> **KEYNOTE**
>
> Torture was made a specific criminal offence under s. 134 of the Criminal Justice Act 1988 (see *Crime*, chapter 1.10) but, whereas that offence has a statutory defence of 'lawful authority, justification or excuse', the prohibition contained in Article 3 is absolute. Irrespective of the prevailing circumstances, there can be no derogation from an individual's absolute right to freedom from torture, inhuman or degrading treatment or punishment.
>
> However, in a case where a French police officer kneed a prisoner, causing a ruptured testicle, the European Court of Human Rights accepted that general exceptions to criminal offences such as self-defence (see *Crime*, chapter 1.4) can apply (*RIVAS* v *France* [2004] Crim LR 305).
>
> The European Court of Human Rights has described Article 3 as enshrining one of the basic values of our democratic society and that, as such, its provisions must be strictly construed (see *McCann* v *United Kingdom* (1996) 21 EHRR 97 and Article 2 at **para. 4.4.5**).
>
> 'Degrading treatment' has been held to mean, in the interrogation of suspects, 'ill treatment designed to arouse in victims feelings of fear, anguish and inferiority, capable of humiliating and debasing them' (see *Ireland* v *United Kingdom* (1979–80) 2 EHRR 25).
>
> The behaviour envisaged by Article 3 therefore goes far beyond the traditional image of 'torture' and its three features can be identified as having the following broad characteristics:
>
> - Torture—deliberate treatment leading to serious or cruel suffering
> - Inhuman treatment—treatment resulting in intense suffering, both physical and mental
> - Degrading treatment—treatment giving rise to fear and anguish in the victim, causing feelings of inferiority and humiliation
>
> (see generally *Ireland* v *United Kingdom*).

It has been held by the European Commission of Human Rights that causing mental anguish without any physical assault could be a violation of Article 3 (see *Denmark* v *Greece* (1969) 12 YB Eur Conv HR special vol.).

As with the preceding Article, Article 3 has two 'arms' to it, namely, the duty of the State not to inflict torture etc. upon an individual and the correlative duty to prevent others from doing so.

It can be seen from the various categories of treatment above that Article 3 may be breached, not only by the deliberate application of pain and suffering to an individual, but also by a range of other behaviour. Oppressive interrogation techniques such as sleep deprivation, exposure to continuous loud noise and forcing suspects to adopt uncomfortable postures for prolonged lengths of time have been held to fall within the second and third categories of inhuman and degrading treatment (*Ireland* v *United Kingdom*). In each case, it must be shown that the prohibited behaviour went beyond the 'minimum level of severity'. In determining whether the behaviour did go beyond that level, and under which particular category that behaviour falls, the courts will take into account factors such as the age, sex, state of health and general life experience of the victim.

Where an individual was alleged to have been punched and kicked by police officers and pulled along by his hair, the Court found that there had been a violation of Article 3 in the form of inhuman and degrading treatment (*Ribitsch* v *Austria* (1996) 21 EHRR 573).

The government's positive duty to prevent individuals from suffering torture or inhuman and degrading treatment has been raised against proceedings to extradite a murder suspect to the United States where it was argued that he would face a long period awaiting the death penalty (*Soering* v *United Kingdom* (1989) 11 EHRR 439). It has also been used to prevent the deportation of a political activist to India where it was argued that he would be subjected to inhuman treatment by the authorities (*Chahal* v *United Kingdom* (1996) 23 EHRR 413). In each of these cases, the reasonable likelihood of ill-treatment at the hands of the State was held to be capable of giving rise to the positive obligation of the United Kingdom to prevent the extradition/deportation.

4.4.7 Article 5—The Right to Liberty and Security

Article 5 of the Convention states:

1. Everyone has the right to liberty and security of person. No one shall be deprived of his liberty save in the following cases and in accordance with a procedure prescribed by law:
   (a) the lawful detention of a person after conviction by a competent court;
   (b) the lawful arrest or detention of a person for non-compliance with the lawful order of a court or in order to secure the fulfilment of any obligation prescribed by law;
   (c) the lawful arrest or detention of a person effected for the purpose of bringing him before the competent legal authority on reasonable suspicion of having committed an offence or when it is reasonably considered necessary to prevent his committing an offence or fleeing after having done so;
   (d) the detention of a minor by lawful order for the purpose of educational supervision or his lawful detention for the purpose of bringing him before the competent legal authority;
   (e) the lawful detention of persons for the prevention of the spreading of infectious diseases, of persons of unsound mind, alcoholics or drug addicts or vagrants;
   (f) the lawful arrest or detention of a person to prevent his effecting an unauthorised entry into the country or of a person against whom action is being taken with a view to deportation or extradition.

KEYNOTE

This Article is of paramount importance to police officers.

The starting point is the general right to liberty and security of person. Although another fundamental right within a democratic society, this right to liberty is qualified under Article 5 and can be derogated from under Article 15 at certain times (**see para. 4.4.14**). However, a person can only be deprived of his/her general right to liberty under one of the conditions set out on the permitted grounds in Article 5(1)(a) to (f), and even then that deprivation must be carried out in accordance with *a procedure prescribed by law*. As noted at the beginning of this chapter, not only must the 'procedure' be set out in the domestic law of the country; it must also be recorded in such a way that people can appreciate the possible consequences of their actions and adapt their behaviour accordingly. If the legal authority used to deprive a person of his/her liberty is ambiguous or unclear, that may well provide grounds for challenge under Article 5.

Even if a lawful power is sufficiently clear and well established, the list of permitted grounds in Article 5(1)(a) to (f) will have to be construed narrowly by the courts (*Winterwerp* v *Netherlands* (1979–80) 2 EHRR 387).

That said, the House of Lords has ruled that, unlike part of Article 5(1)(c), 5(1)(f) does not require that detention has to be *necessary* in order to be justified. As a result, the temporary detention of asylum seekers pending their application to remain in the United Kingdom, is not of itself unlawful (*R (On the Application of Saadi)* v *Secretary of State for the Home Department* [2002] UKHL 41).

4.4.7.1 Permitted Grounds

Each of the situations envisaged in Article 5(1)(a) to (f) will now be examined. It should be noted at this point that Article 5 does not provide any *power* to arrest or detain; it simply sets out certain circumstances where the general right to liberty may be interfered with *by some existing lawful means*.

4.4.7.2 Lawful Detention after Conviction

This exception allows a person to be detained after their conviction by a 'competent court', i.e. a court having the jurisdiction to try that particular case. Article 6 provides a right to a fair trial. Those people who have been so convicted may be detained in accordance with the order of the court. Clearly, if the court does not have the power to pass the relevant order, the exception at Article 5(1)(a) will not apply and any detention will potentially amount to a violation of Article 5.

4.4.7.3 Lawful Arrest or Detention for Non-compliance

The exception under Article 5(1)(b) allows for the detention or arrest of a person who has failed to comply with the *lawful* order of a court. Failing to pay a fine or to observe the conditions of an injunction would be examples of such non-compliance. The exception also extends to the arrest or detention in order to secure the fulfilment of any obligation prescribed by law. Such an obligation might include an obligation to provide a roadside breath specimen or to surrender documents relating to a vehicle. Once again the circumstances of any arrest or detention will be examined by the courts who will need to consider whether the person was given a reasonable opportunity to comply with the order/obligation. The court will also need to consider whether the arrest or detention was a reasonable way to make sure that the order/obligation was met.

4.4.7.4 Lawful Arrest/Detention in Relation to an Offence

There are several aspects to the permitted grounds under Article 5(1)(c). The arrest/detention must first be lawful in itself. Any arrest/detention that is later shown to have been *unlawful* cannot be saved under any of the other headings. Even a lawful arrest/detention will only meet the requirements of Article 5(1)(c) if it can be shown to have been:

- effected for the purpose of bringing the person before the relevant 'competent legal authority' (i.e. a judge or magistrate) on reasonable suspicion that the person had committed an offence; or
- reasonably considered necessary to prevent the person committing an offence or from fleeing afterwards.

Where a person has been lawfully arrested for the purpose of bringing him/her before a competent legal authority, it is not necessary to show that he/she actually *was brought* before that authority (*Brogan v United Kingdom* (1989) 11 EHRR 117). It is the *purpose* of the arrest at the time that is relevant as opposed to its ultimate achievement. This accords with the provisions of s. 30(7) of the Police and Criminal Evidence Act 1984 which require an arrested person to be released if the grounds for detaining him/her cease to exist (**see para. 4.5.9**). Given the statutory status of a custody officer, he/she would probably not be a 'competent legal authority' for this purpose, which seems to be judicial in nature and requiring a degree of independence from the arresting authorities. However, it is hard to see how the expression 'competent legal authority' can be limited to judges and magistrates because Article 5(3) goes on to use a more restrictive expression (*judge or other officer authorised by law to exercise judicial power*) to define just such people (**see para. 4.4.7.8**). The lack of fit here between the wording and our own police and judicial roles is caused partly by the fact that those roles are different in nature from those in many other European Union countries.

'Reasonable suspicion' here will be assessed objectively and the court will look for 'the existence of facts or information which would satisfy an objective observer that the person may have committed the offence' (see *Fox v United Kingdom* (1991) 13 EHRR 157). Other tests applied to powers of arrest will need to be read in conjunction with this provision, as will powers to detain in connection with searches (as to which, **see para. 4.6.1**).

4.4.7.5 Lawful Detention of Minors

This ground refers solely to 'detention' rather than arrest, although Article 5 seems to use the two expressions interchangeably in places (e.g. Article 5(4) below) and there may be occasions where the two are difficult to distinguish anyway. As with Article 5(1)(c) (**see para. 4.4.7.4**), the initial detention must be lawful. A minor for these purposes is a person who has not attained the age of 18.

4.4.7.6 Lawful Detention of Others

Article 5(1)(e) also refers to 'detention' of certain people, in this case those who have various physical or mental ailments. It also extends to 'vagrants'. The reasoning behind Article 5(1)(e) is that the people described may need to be detained in their own interests. The permitted grounds set out here appear to allow the detention of people under the Mental Health Act 1983. Although there is a power under s. 34 of the Criminal Justice Act 1972 for a person to be taken after arrest to an approved alcohol treatment centre, it is unlikely that Article 5(1)(e) would apply as there is no further power to *detain* such a person once he/she arrives at the centre. In such cases, the permitted grounds under Article 5(1)(c) (**see para. 4.4.7.4**), would be more appropriate.

Whatever its extent, Article 5(1)(e) is likely to be very narrowly applied by the courts and the mere fact that an individual has, for example, an infectious disease, will not of itself justify his/her 'detention'.

4.4.7.7 Lawful Arrest/Detention for Deportation or Extradition

The House of Lords has ruled that, unlike part of Article 5(1)(c), 5(1)(f) does not require the detention to be *necessary* in order to be justified (*R (On the Application of Saadi) v Secretary of State for the Home Department* [2002] UKHL 41). In that case it was held that the temporary detention of asylum seekers pending their application to remain in the United Kingdom was not unlawful simply by reason of it not being strictly necessary.

4.4.7.8 Procedure

Article 5 goes on to state:

> 2. Everyone who is arrested shall be informed promptly, in a language which he understands, of the reasons for his arrest and of any charge against him.

3. Everyone arrested or detained in accordance with the provisions of paragraph 1(c) of this Article shall be brought promptly before a judge or other officer authorised by law to exercise judicial power and shall be entitled to trial within a reasonable time or to release pending trial. Release may be conditioned by guarantees to appear for trial.
4. Everyone who is deprived of his liberty by arrest or detention shall be entitled to take proceedings by which the lawfulness of his detention shall be decided speedily by a court and his release ordered if the detention is not lawful.
5. Everyone who has been the victim of arrest or detention in contravention of the provisions of this Article shall have an enforceable right to compensation.

KEYNOTE

The right to be informed of the reason for arrest is already enshrined in our domestic law under s. 28 of the Police and Criminal Evidence Act 1984 (**see para. 4.5.2.1**). The wording of Article 5(2) strengthens that requirement by specifying that the information must be given in a language that the person understands.

The reason for requiring this information to be given would appear to be to allow the arrested person to challenge the arrest and subsequent detention (*X* v *United Kingdom* (1982) 4 EHRR 188). The ability to challenge the lawfulness of that detention (and presumably, the arrest) is itself a Convention right under Article 5(4).

Article 5(3) clearly envisages the extension of bail where appropriate and for a discussion of this, together with the other implications of Article 5(3) and (4), see *Evidence and Procedure*, chapter 2.3.

Article 5(5) gives a person who is the 'victim' of an arrest or detention in contravention of the rest of the Article an enforceable right to compensation. This right applies not only to the people concerned in the arrest/detention itself, but is specifically extended to include the courts (see s. 9 of the Human Rights Act 1998).

Where a person was being extradited to Spain, the hearing was entitled to conclude that a delay of over five years between an individual's arrest and their extradition did not render the extradition unjust or oppressive (*Owalabi* v *Court Number Four at the High Court of Justice in Spain* [2005] EWHC 2849 (Admin)).

4.4.8 Article 6—The Right to a Fair Trial

Article 6 of the Convention states:

1. In the determination of his civil rights and obligations or of any criminal charge against him, everyone is entitled to a fair and public hearing within a reasonable time by an independent and impartial tribunal established by law. Judgment shall be pronounced publicly but the press and public may be excluded from all or part of the trial in the interest of morals, public order or national security in a democratic society, where the interests of juveniles or the protection of the private life of the parties so require, or to the extent strictly necessary in the opinion of the court in special circumstances where publicity would prejudice the interests of justice.
2. Everyone charged with a criminal offence shall be presumed innocent until proved guilty according to law.

KEYNOTE

The provisions of Article 6 affect both civil and criminal proceedings, although the Article goes on to provide specific safeguards in relation to criminal matters.

The key features of Article 6 are:

- a fair and public hearing
- held within a reasonable time
- by an independent and impartial legal tribunal.

Even a perception that the relevant court or tribunal is partial or biased can result in a breach of Article 6(1), reviving Lord Hewart's famous dictum that it is not enough that justice be done; it must manifestly be *seen* to be done.

Article 6 is restricted, however, to *procedural* issues and not to matters of fairness of the substantive law (see e.g. *R* v *G and R* [2002] EWCA Crim 1992).

Article 6 allows for the right to a public hearing to be restricted under certain circumstances, but requires any judgment to be publicly pronounced.

Article 6 has been interpreted as creating a requirement for 'equality of arms' in any civil or criminal proceedings (*Neumeister* v *Austria* (1968) 1 EHRR 91). Equality of arms requires that both parties be afforded the same opportunities to present their case and to cross-examine the other side. Additionally, both parties should be given the opportunity to be legally represented.

An example of where Article 6 has been used (unsuccessfully) as a 'shield' can be seen in the Scottish case of *Jardine* v *Crowe* 1999 JC 59. There the defendant refused to give details of the driver of his vehicle after a relevant offence when required to do so by the police under s. 172 of the Road Traffic Act 1988. He argued that the requirement infringed Article 6 on the grounds that it forced him to incriminate himself. This argument was disposed of in the English and Welsh courts in *DPP* v *Wilson* [2001] EWHC Admin 198.

4.4.9 Article 7—No Punishment without Crime

Article 7 of the Convention states:

1. No one shall be held guilty of any criminal offence on account of any act or omission which did not constitute a criminal offence under national or international law at the time when it was committed. Nor shall a heavier penalty be imposed than the one that was applicable at the time the criminal offence was committed.
2. This Article shall not prejudice the trial and punishment of any person for any act or omission which, at the time when it was committed, was criminal according to the general principles of law recognised by civilised nations.

KEYNOTE

The main purpose of Article 7 is to provide a safeguard against retrospective criminal legislation whereby a government passes laws that render previously lawful behaviour unlawful. It also prohibits the imposition of a heavier penalty for a crime than that which was available at the time the crime was committed. Both of these provisions are in accordance with the key principles underpinning the Convention, namely, that people should be able to look at the law and to adapt their behaviour in the full knowledge of what may happen to them if they break it.

In one case which illustrates the point, a defendant claimed that the change in the common law relating to marital rape (as to which, see *Crime*, para. **1.11.3**) violated Article 7 because he could not have foreseen that the law would be extended to protect wives. The European Court of Human Rights held that this did not amount to a violation of the Article (*SW* v *United Kingdom* [1996] 1 FLR 434).

Claims that football banning orders (see para. **4.12.3**) breached this Article have been unsuccessful (see *Gough* v *Chief Constable of Derbyshire Constabulary* [2002] EWCA Civ 351).

Article 7(2) is aimed at maintaining the rule *of* law rather than the rule *by* law. It provides for the situation where a person carries out activities that would be classified as 'crimes' according to the general principles of law among civilised nations but which were not necessarily criminal offences under the domestic law of that country (e.g. acts persecuting minority groups carried out with the acquiescence of the government). This very limited exception prevents States from legitimating what would otherwise be criminal acts by passing or repealing criminal laws.

4.4.10 Article 8—Right to Respect for Private and Family Life, Home and Correspondence

Article 8 of the Convention states:

1. Everyone has the right to respect for his private and family life, his home and his correspondence.

2. There shall be no interference by a public authority with the exercise of this right except such as is in accordance with the law and is necessary in a democratic society in the interests of national security, public safety or the economic well being of the country, for the prevention of disorder or crime, for the protection of health or morals, or for the protection of the rights and freedoms of others.

KEYNOTE

The provisions of Article 8 extend a right to respect for a person's:

- private life,
- family life,
- home, and
- correspondence.

The main aim of the Article is to protect these features of a person's life from the arbitrary interference by 'public authorities' (as to which, **see para. 4.4.3.5**) (*Kroon* v *Netherlands* (1995) 19 EHRR 263). However, the Convention does allow for individuals to raise issues of unjustified interference with their private lives and the courts have held that even celebrities have a basic right to privacy which will be protected by Article 8 (see *Campbell* v *Mirror Group Newspapers* [2004] UKHL 22); similar arguments (in a somewhat less genteel context) can be found in *Theakston* v *Mirror Group Newspapers* [2002] EWHC 137 (QB). A good practical example of how this Article can impact upon the actions of public authorities and decision-makers is *R (On the Application of Evans)* v *First Secretary of State* [2005] EWHC 149 (Admin). In that case a planning inspector refused an application to develop a gypsy caravan site in what was a green belt area. The appellant claimed that, as a 'gypsy', his special status and associated rights under Article 8 should have been preferred over any other considerations by the planning inspector and the Secretary of State on his appeal. The Divisional Court disagreed and held that, while the appellant's rights under Article 8 should be considered as part of the balancing process, gypsy status alone could not in effect be used to trump any other considerations in this way.

The State is under a duty not to interfere with these features of a person's life except in accordance with Article 8(2). Many police activities such as entry onto premises, surveillance and the seizure of property, touch upon the features covered by Article 8.

Article 8 was at the heart of the changes to the Sexual Offences Act 1956 as the European Court of Human Rights found that the law prohibiting consensual sexual acts between more than two men in private (s. 13) was an unjustifiable interference with Article 8 (see *ADT* v *United Kingdom* (2001) 31 EHRR 33).

Another reason why this Article is of importance to police services is that the State also has a positive obligation to prevent others from interfering with an individual's right to private life (see *Stjerna* v *Finland* (1994) 24 EHRR 194). How far the police would have to go in order to discharge this obligation is unclear, but Article 8 will be relevant in areas such as those set out in Part Two of this Manual (community safety), together with other areas such as civil disputes (as to which, **see chapter 4.14**).

It is here that the notion of balancing the rights and freedoms of individuals against each other and against those of the community at large can be seen most acutely. Article 8—and in particular the requirement for 'proportionality'—provides one of the main arguments that have been raised against the lawfulness of Anti-social Behaviour Orders (**see chapter 4.8**) and Sexual Offences Prevention Orders (**see** *Crime*, **chapter 1.12**).

A final reason that Article 8 is so important is that the Article appears to include the right to establish relationships with others, the right to privacy even within an office environment and the right to set up home, all of which have a significant impact on general supervisory and managerial functions. Failing to protect an individual from the unwanted advances of others, searching through an employee's office or directing an employee as to where he/she can and cannot live would all potentially fall within the remit of Article 8.

Article 8 also has implications for the law in relation to data protection and computer misuse (**see chapter 4.17**), and the lack of legal regulation governing the use of CCTV cameras has been raised with the European Commission (*R* v *Brentwood Borough Council, ex parte Peck* [1998] EMLR 697).

4.4.11   Article 10—Freedom of Expression

Article 10 of the Convention states:

1. Everyone has the right to freedom of expression. This right shall include freedom to hold opinions and to receive and impart information and ideas without interference by public authority and regardless of frontiers. This Article shall not prevent States from requiring the licensing of broadcasting, television or cinema enterprises.
2. The exercise of these freedoms, since it carries with it duties and responsibilities, may be subject to such formalities, conditions, restrictions or penalties as are prescribed by law and are necessary in a democratic society, in the interests of national security, territorial integrity or public safety, for the prevention of disorder or crime, for the protection of health or morals, for the protection of the reputation or rights of others, for preventing the disclosure of information received in confidence, or for maintaining the authority and impartiality of the judiciary.

KEYNOTE

Article 10 protects the freedom:

- of expression,
- to hold opinions, and
- to receive and impart information and ideas

in each case without interference by a public authority.

'Expression' here includes the creation of pictures and images (*Stevens* v *United Kingdom* (1986) 46 DR 245).

Although not providing a general 'right to freedom of information', Article 10 has been used in a number of different settings including the protection of artistic, political and economic expression. It has been used to protect journalists' sources (see *Goodwin* v *United Kingdom* (1996) 22 EHRR 123).

As the right to express freely has to be balanced against the rights of others and the needs of democratic society generally, this area of Convention rights has generated some considerable problems and is often intermingled with issues of freedom of thought, conscience and religion (under Article 9).

In a case where the defendant damaged the perimeter fence of a Trident defence base, the Divisional Court held that her acts could be characterised as an expression of her opinion under Article 10 but that the Convention required the expression of that opinion to be proportionate. There were other ways in which the defendant could have expressed her opinion without committing a crime and therefore her conviction for criminal damage was upheld (*Hutchinson* v *DPP* (2000) *The Independent*, 20 November).

Article 10(1) is drafted to allow for State licensing of broadcasts, television and cinema performances but, as you might expect, the courts will be unlikely to tolerate interference with the freedom of expression without compelling reasons. Once again, the courts will look for a 'pressing social need' and, indeed, one of the main cases setting out the requirement for proportionality (*Handyside* v *United Kingdom* (1979–80) 1 EHRR 737) involved an action under Article 10. A good example of how Article 10 can operate is the case in the Republic of Ireland where, although it was shown that injunctions used to prevent women from receiving information about abortion services were issued for a legitimate aim, the overall effect of such legal remedies was found to be disproportionate (*Open Door Counselling and Dublin Well Woman* v *Ireland* (1993) 15 EHRR 244).

Article 10(2) clearly allows for an individual's freedom of expression to be curtailed under a number of circumstances including the prevention of disorder or crime and the protection of morals. Balancing these competing needs is one area where the European Court of Human Rights has allowed a reasonable 'margin of appreciation'. Nevertheless, any restrictions on an individual's freedom of expression will be narrowly construed and closely scrutinised. It has been held that the exercise of the right to free speech could fall within the concept of harassment for the purposes of the Protection from Harassment Act 1997 where the ingredients for the offence were present (*Howlett* v *Harding* [2006] EWHC 41 (QB)).

The rights under this Article are subject to the restrictions allowed by Article 16 (political activities by aliens).

4.4.12 Article 11—Freedom of Assembly and Association

Article 11 of the Convention states:

1. Everyone has the right to freedom of peaceful assembly and to freedom of association with others, including the right to form and to join trade unions for the protection of his interests.
2. No restrictions shall be placed on the exercise of these rights other than such as are prescribed by law and are necessary in a democratic society in the interests of national security or public safety, for the prevention of disorder or crime, for the protection of health or morals or for the protection of the rights and freedoms of others. This Article shall not prevent the imposition of lawful restrictions on the exercise of these rights by members of the armed forces, of the police or of the administration of the State.

KEYNOTE

Article 11 is closely related to Article 10 and is often raised in conjunction with it, particularly in situations involving the arrest of demonstrators and protestors. In addition to refraining from interference with the individual's right to peaceful assembly, the State is also under a positive duty to prevent others from doing so. The assembly must, however, be *peaceful* and any intention to use violence or to cause disorder may take the individual's actions outside the protection of Article 11.

As with Article 10, there are allowances for reducing rights of assembly etc. under certain conditions including the prevention of disorder and crime and the interests of national security and public safety.

The right to freedom of association and to join trade unions means, among other things, that trade unions may be victims for the purposes of bringing an action under this Article. The State can impose 'lawful restrictions' on the exercise of these rights.

4.4.13 Article 14—Prohibition of Discrimination in Convention Rights

Article 14 of the Convention states:

The enjoyment of the rights and freedoms set forth in this Convention shall be secured without discrimination on any ground such as sex, race, colour, language, religion, political or other opinion, national or social origin, association with a national minority, property, birth or other status.

KEYNOTE

Article 14 simply provides a guarantee that access to the Convention's other provisions must be enjoyed equally by everyone under the jurisdiction of the particular State. The list set out in the Article is not exhaustive and other categories of people or grounds of discrimination may be added by the courts (and have been added by the European Court of Human Rights). A person claiming a breach of Article 14 must show that his/her own individual circumstances are similar to those of another person who has been treated differently in relation to the enjoyment of Convention rights.

Examples of Article 14 in practice can be found in a number of high-profile cases. One such case was the challenge to the prolonged detention without charge of suspects under s. 23 of the Anti-terrorism, Crime and Security Act 2001 (now repealed). Because the detention was only used against *foreign nationals* suspected of being international terrorists and not UK nationals, the practice was held by the House of Lords to discriminate on grounds of nationality—*A* v *Secretary of State for the Home Department* [2004] UKHL 56.

The open-ended wording of Article 14 means that a wide range of categories of people who can be grouped by reference to their status may be protected. That protection certainly extends to a person's sexuality, an area that has generally not been protected in our domestic law (see *Ghaidan* v *Godin-Mendoza* [2004] UKHL 30).

However, it does not make express provision for *indirect* discrimination (as to which, **see para. 4.18.3.8**) and the Divisional Court has expressed considerable doubt as to whether Article 14 provides protection

---

against indirect, as opposed to direct, discrimination (see *R (On the Application of Barber)* v *Secretary of State for Work and Pensions* [2002] EWHC 1915 (Admin)).

The rights under this Article are subject to the restrictions allowed by Article 16 (political activities by aliens).

4.4.14 Article 15—Derogation in Time of Emergency

Article 15 allows a State to derogate from some of its obligations under the Convention during times of war or other public emergency threatening the life of the nation. This is a very narrow restriction and even under those extreme circumstances the derogation may only be made to the extent that is strictly required by the exigencies of the situation.

The strict application of this requirement can be seen in the case involving detention of suspected international terrorists who were non-UK nationals. In that case the House of Lords held that the derogation made under the Anti-terrorism, Crime and Security Act 2001 went further than was strictly required by the exigencies of the situation and that, if the threat presented to national security by UK residents suspected of being terrorists could be addressed without infringing their Convention rights, then so could the threat posed by non-UK residents similarly suspected—*A* v *Secretary of State for the Home Department* [2004] UKHL 56.

The original derogation lodged by the United Kingdom at the time when the Act was passed permitted longer detention of terrorist suspects before charge. That derogation related to the ongoing unrest in Northern Ireland. With political developments in Northern Ireland, that derogation was removed but, since 11 September 2001, the United Kingdom lodged a further derogation under the Anti-terrorism, Crime and Security Act 2001 and the powers thereunder. Because those powers are potentially incompatible with parts of the Convention, Parliament passed the Human Rights (Amendment No. 2) Order 2001 (SI 2001/4032), giving effect to the derogation set out in part I of sch. 3 to the Human Rights Act 1998.

4.4.15 Protocol 1, Article 1—Protection of Property

The Convention itself has been extended by the addition of a number of Protocols, not all of which have been incorporated by the Human Rights Act 1998. Article 1 of the First Protocol sets out the right to peaceful enjoyment of one's possessions. This leaves room for the State to deprive a person of his/her possessions 'in the public interest' (e.g. by nationalisation of an industry) and courts are likely to allow a wide margin of appreciation in such cases. Broadly, to prove a violation of this part of Protocol 1, it must be shown that the State has:

- interfered with the applicant's peaceful enjoyment of possessions, or
- deprived him/her of those possessions, or
- subjected those possessions to some form of control.

Clear examples of where such State activity can be found is in the seizure of property by HM Revenue and Customs and the police. The term 'possessions' is likely to be interpreted very widely and, under European case law, has extended to land, contractual rights and intellectual property.

A different example of how this right might be used against a public authority can be seen in *AO* v *Italy* (2001) 29 EHRR CD 92. In that case the Italian police were held to have violated the applicant's right to peaceful enjoyment of his property when they continually failed to send any officers to his flat which he was trying to repossess from squatters. Although the action for repossession had been going on for over four years, this case illustrates one way in which private law matters can become issues of liability for public authorities such as police services.

Powers of Arrest (including Code G Codes of Practice) and Other Policing Powers

PACE Code of Practice for the Statutory Power of Arrest by Police Officers (Code G)

> A thick grey line down the margin denotes text that is an extract of the PACE Code itself (i.e. the actual wording of the legislation). This material is examinable for both Sergeants and Inspectors.

4.5.1 Introduction

This chapter scrutinises a number of key features that are relevant to powers of arrest and introduces certain shared points regarding arrest procedures before examining specific powers in detail (and consequently, Code G of the Codes of Practice). The chapter concludes with an examination of several eclectic policing powers and issues.

4.5.2 Powers of Arrest—Common Points

An arrest involves depriving a person of his/her liberty to go where he/she pleases (*Lewis* v *Chief Constable of South Wales Constabulary* [1991] 1 All ER 206). In a criminal context an arrest will usually be to answer an alleged charge, but occasionally an arrest may be preventive (such as where a person is arrested in connection with a breach of the peace), it may be to take samples or fingerprints, or it may be to return someone to prison or bring him/her before a court.

While the courts may issue warrants ordering the arrest of certain individuals on occasions, police officers are not under any general duty to arrest without warrant and should always consider the use of alternative methods of dealing with the incident or matter.

The source of a power of arrest may come from:

- the conditions at the time (e.g. allowing an arrest under s. 24 of the Police and Criminal Evidence Act 1984);
- the provisions of the particular Act (e.g. s. 7 of the Bail Act 1976, absconding from bail; **see *Evidence and Procedure*, para. 2.3.11**);
- the provisions of an order (e.g. a court order or warrant; **see *Evidence and Procedure*, para. 2.2.6**);
- common law (e.g. breach of the peace; **see para. 4.11.2**).

An arrest begins at the time when the arresting officer informs the person of it or when his/her words or actions suggest that the person is under arrest (*Murray* v *Ministry of Defence* [1988] 1 WLR 692).

It was held in *R v Fiak* [2005] EWCA Crim 2381 that an arrest had not been rendered unlawful by the police officer's failure to use the word 'arrest' until after a brief investigation into the defendant's story was completed.

Every arrest must be lawful, that is, the person carrying it out must be able to point to some legal authority which allows it; otherwise an arrest will be unlawful and actionable as an assault or a civil wrong (see *Spicer* v *Holt* [1977] AC 987). This position is reinforced by the Human Rights Act 1998, and the ability to challenge the lawfulness of detention and arrest is itself a Convention right under Article 5(4), while Article 5(5) gives a person who is the 'victim' of an arrest or detention in contravention of the rest of the Article an enforceable right to compensation.

Any unlawful arrest will also carry implications for the officers if they are assaulted during the course of making it, for their organisation, and for public confidence. Therefore an understanding of the legal powers and concepts underpinning arrests is critical to professional policing.

Where a power of arrest exists, any lawful arrest must be made for a proper purpose. In the past the courts have allowed the police a wide latitude in what amounts to a proper purpose, including bringing the person to a police station (*Holgate-Mohammed* v *Duke* [1984] AC 437), to obtain a confession even after a complainant has withdrawn his/her initial complaint (*Plange* v *Chief Constable of Humberside* (1992) *The Times*, 23 March), and arresting someone on a 'holding' offence (*R* v *Chalkley* [1998] QB 848). The courts have even accepted an arrest based on force policy (*Al Fayed* v *Commissioner of Police of the Metropolis* [2004] EWCA Civ 1579). However, all of these decisions will need to be reviewed in light of the changes to police powers of arrest under s. 24 of the Police and Criminal Evidence Act 1984.

The practice of arresting someone on a 'holding' offence was accepted by the Court of Appeal in *R* v *Chalkley* [1998] QB 848, *provided the arresting officers had reasonable grounds for suspecting that the person had actually committed that offence*. If that suspicion is present, then the fact that the officers making the arrest are doing so with the intention of investigating another, more serious offence does not render the arrest unlawful. If, however, there are no such grounds to suspect that the person had in fact committed the offence, or the officers know at the time of the arrest that there is no possibility of the person actually being charged with it, the arrest will be unlawful.

Section 30(7) of the Police and Criminal Evidence Act 1984 (in keeping with common law) requires that, if the grounds for detaining a person cease to exist before reaching a police station, the person must be released (**see para. 4.5.11**).

4.5.2.1 Information to be Given and Recorded on Arrest

Whether an arrest is made under the Police and Criminal Evidence Act 1984 or not, s. 28 makes clear provision for the information that *must* be given to a person on arrest. Section 28 states:

(1) Subject to subsection (5) below, where a person is arrested, otherwise than by being informed that he is under arrest, the arrest is not lawful unless the person arrested is informed that he is under arrest as soon as is practicable after his arrest.

(2) Where a person is arrested by a constable, subsection (1) above applies regardless of whether the fact of the arrest is obvious.

(3) Subject to subsection (5) below, no arrest is lawful unless the person arrested is informed of the ground for the arrest at the time of, or as soon as is practicable after, the arrest.

(4) Where a person is arrested by a constable, subsection (3) above applies regardless of whether the ground for the arrest is obvious.

(5) Nothing in this section is to be taken to require a person to be informed—
   (a) that he is under arrest; or
   (b) of the ground for the arrest,
   if it was not reasonably practicable for him to be so informed by reason of his having escaped from arrest before the information could be given.

KEYNOTE

The right to be informed of the reason for arrest is enshrined in our domestic law under s. 28 of the Police and Criminal Evidence Act 1984.

The formula used by courts in determining whether this has been properly carried out is taken from *Fox, Campbell and Hartley* v *United Kingdom* (1991) 13 EHRR 157, which stated:

Any person arrested must be told, in simple, non-technical language that he can understand, the essential legal and factual grounds for his arrest, so as to be able, if he sees fit, to apply to a court to challenge its lawfulness.

Therefore the key reason for requiring this information to be given is to allow the arrested person to challenge the arrest and subsequent detention (see also *X* v *United Kingdom* (1982) 4 EHRR 188).

Code C of the Police and Criminal Evidence Act 1984 also imposes requirements in this area.

The practical reality is that for certain types of offence (particularly those involving violence or disorder), it will be impractical to give each person arrested detailed particulars of the case against him/her. Whether or not the information actually given to a person on arrest was adequate for the purposes of the above legislation will have to be assessed objectively, *having regard to the information that was reasonably available to the arresting officer* (see *Taylor* v *Chief Constable of Thames Valley* [2004] EWCA Civ 858). It might suffice in some cases—such as the violent disorder in *Taylor*—for the police officer to tell the person he/she is being arrested on suspicion of taking part in violent disorder at a certain time and place.

Section 28 clearly makes provision for situations when the person cannot be told or would not be capable of understanding the information. However, as the failure to comply with s. 28 makes any arrest unlawful (see e.g. *Dawes* v *DPP* [1995] 1 Cr App R 65), it is perhaps better to 'err on the side of caution'.

In relation to the requirement at s. 28(2) and (3), particular care should be taken when giving a suspect details of exactly why he/she is being arrested. The Court of Appeal has held that it had been unfair—and unlawful—for an arresting officer to withhold facts which had led him to arrest the suspect on suspicion of having committed an offence (*Wilson* v *Chief Constable of Lancashire Constabulary* (2000) Po LR 367). In that case the court held that an arresting officer's minimum obligation was to give a suspect 'sufficient information as to the nature of an arrest to allow the suspect sufficient opportunity to respond'.

The reasons given for the arrest must be the *real* reasons in the officer's mind at the time (see *Christie* v *Leachinsky* [1947] AC 573) and he/she must clearly indicate to the person the fact that he/she is being arrested. This requirement might be met by using a colloquialism, provided that the person is familiar with it and understands its meaning (e.g. 'you're locked up' or 'you're nicked'; see *Christie* v *Leachinsky*). It does not matter that the words describe more than one offence (e.g. 'burglary' or 'fraud'), provided that they adequately describe the offence for which the person has been arrested (*Abbassy* v *Metropolitan Police Commissioner* [1990] 1 WLR 385).

4.5.2.2 Caution

The Police and Criminal Evidence Act 1984 Code of Practice, Code C, para. 10, requires that a person must be cautioned on arrest or further arrest (**see para. 4.5.5**).

There will be occasions where those involved with the custody and care of prisoners will overhear remarks by a defendant or will have comments made to them, which may be of relevance to the case in which the defendant is prosecuted. While such people may not be under a strict duty to administer the caution in the same way as police officers, the admissibility of the evidence will be tested against the general requirements of fairness and it might be appropriate to give a caution and/or to make a record of such comments as soon as possible (see *R* v *Ristic* [2004] EWCA Crim 2107—prison officer giving evidence of incriminating remarks overheard by a defendant).

Where police officers are themselves being interviewed or investigated, the caution used in such cases will follow the general criminal one from Code C, with the inclusion of an element relating to a failure to make a written statement.

4.5.2.3 Force

Section 117 of the Police and Criminal Evidence Act 1984 allows the use of reasonable force when making an arrest. Section 3 of the Criminal Law Act 1967 also allows the use of such force as is reasonably necessary in the arrest of people and the prevention of crime.

Whether any force used is 'reasonable' will be determined by the court in the light of all the circumstances, including the circumstances as the arresting officer believed them to be at the time. Such force may even be lethal to the defendant. Where serious harm is caused by an arrest, the courts will consider the time that was available to the officer to reflect on his/her actions and whether or not he/she believed that the danger presented to others by failing to arrest the person outweighed the harm caused to the person by the arrest (see *Attorney-General for Northern Ireland's Reference (No. 1 of 1975)* [1977] AC 105). This situation has been reinforced by the European Convention on Human Rights and the test for justifying the use of force has become more stringent (**see *Crime*, chapter 1.4**).

Use of excessive force, while amounting to possible misconduct and assault, does not render an otherwise lawful arrest unlawful (*Simpson* v *Chief Constable of South Yorkshire* (1991) 135 SJ 383).

4.5.3 | PACE Code of Practice for the Statutory Power of Arrest by Police Officers (Code G)

This Code applies to any arrest made by a police officer after midnight on 12 November 2012.

1 Introduction

1.1 This Code of Practice deals with statutory power of police to arrest a person who is involved, or suspected of being involved, in a criminal offence. The power of arrest must be used fairly, responsibly, with respect for people suspected of committing offences and without unlawful discrimination. The Equality Act 2010 makes it unlawful for police officers to discriminate against, harass or victimise any person on the grounds of the 'protected characteristics' of age, disability, gender reassignment, race, religion or belief, sex and sexual orientation, marriage and civil partnership, pregnancy and maternity when using their powers. When police forces are carrying out their functions they also have a duty to have regard to the need to eliminate unlawful discrimination, harassment and victimisation and to take steps to foster good relations.

1.2 The exercise of the power of arrest represents an obvious and significant interference with the Right to Liberty and Security under Article 5 of the European Convention on Human Rights set out in Part I of Schedule 1 to the Human Rights Act 1998.

1.3 The use of the power must be fully justified and officers exercising the power should consider if the necessary objectives can be met by other, less intrusive means. Absence of justification for exercising the powers of arrest may lead to challenges should the case proceed to court. It could also lead to civil claims against the police for unlawful arrest and false imprisonment. When the power of arrest is exercised it is essential that it is exercised in a non-discriminatory and proportionate manner which is compatible with the Right to Liberty under Article 5.

1.4 Section 24 of the Police and Criminal Evidence Act 1984 (as substituted by section 110 of the Serious Organised Crime and Police Act 2005) provides the statutory power for a constable to arrest without warrant for all offences. If the provisions of the Act and this Code are not observed, both the arrest and the conduct of any subsequent investigation may be open to question.

1.5 This code of practice must be readily available at all police stations for consultation by police officers and police staff, detained persons and members of the public.

4.5.3.1

4.5.3.1

KEYNOTE

Code G points out that juveniles should not be arrested at their place of education unless this is unavoidable. When a juvenile is arrested at their place of education, the principal or their nominee must be informed.

Section 24 of the Police and Criminal Evidence Act 1984 deals with a constable's power of arrest; s. 24A deals with the power of arrest by others and will be examined later in this chapter.

4.5.4

2 Elements of Arrest under section 24 PACE

2.1 A lawful arrest requires two elements:
A person's involvement or suspected involvement or attempted involvement in the commission of a criminal offence;
AND
Reasonable grounds for *believing* that the person's arrest is necessary.
- both elements must be satisfied, and
- it can never be necessary to arrest a person unless there are reasonable grounds to suspect them of committing an offence.

2.2 The arrested person must be informed that they have been arrested, even if this fact is obvious, and of the relevant circumstances of the arrest in relation to both the above elements. The custody officer must be informed of these matters on arrival at the police station. See Code C paragraph 3.4.

Involvement 'in the commission of an offence'

2.3 A constable may arrest without warrant in relation to any offence anyone:
- who is about to commit an offence or is in the act of committing an offence
- whom the officer has reasonable grounds for suspecting is about to commit an offence or to be committing an offence
- whom the officer has reasonable grounds to suspect of being guilty of an offence which he or she has reasonable grounds for suspecting has been committed
- anyone who is guilty of an offence which has been committed or anyone whom the officer has reasonable grounds for suspecting to be guilty of that offence.

2.3A There must be some reasonable, objective grounds for the suspicion, based on known facts and information which are relevant to the likelihood the offence has been committed and the person liable to arrest committed it.

4.5.4.1

KEYNOTE

For the purposes of this Code, 'offence' means any statutory or common law offence for which a person may be tried by a magistrates' court or the Crown Court and punished if convicted. Statutory offences include assault, rape, criminal damage, theft, robbery, burglary, fraud, possession of controlled drugs and offences under road traffic, liquor licensing, gambling and immigration legislation and local government by-laws. Common law offences include murder, manslaughter, kidnapping, false imprisonment, perverting the course of justice and escape from lawful custody.

This Code does not apply to powers of arrest conferred on constables under any arrest warrant, for example, a warrant issued under the Magistrates' Courts Act 1980, ss. 1 or 13, or the Bail Act 1976, s. 7(1), or to the powers of constables to arrest without warrant other than under s. 24 of PACE for an offence. These other powers to arrest without warrant do not depend on the arrested person committing any specific offence and include:

- PACE, s. 46A, arrest of person who fails to answer police bail to attend police station or is suspected of breaching any condition of that bail for the custody officer to decide whether they should be kept in police detention which applies whether or not the person commits an offence under s. 6 of the Bail Act 1976 (e.g. failing without reasonable cause to surrender to custody);

- Bail Act 1976, s. 7(3), arrest of person bailed to attend court who is suspected of breaching, or is believed likely to breach, any condition of bail to take them to court for bail to be re-considered;
- Children and Young Persons Act 1969, s. 32(1A) (absconding)—arrest to return the person to the place where they are required to reside;
- Immigration Act 1971, sch. 2, to arrest a person liable to examination to determine their right to remain in the United Kingdom;
- Mental Health Act 1983, s. 136, to remove person suffering from a mental disorder to place of safety for assessment;
- Prison Act 1952, s. 49, arrest to return person unlawfully at large to the prison etc. where they are liable to be detained;
- Road Traffic Act 1988, s. 6D, arrest of driver following the outcome of a preliminary roadside test requirement to enable the driver to be required to provide an evidential sample;
- Common law power to stop or prevent a breach of the peace—after arrest a person aged 18 or over may be brought before a justice of the peace court to show cause why they should not be bound over to keep the peace—not criminal proceedings.

4.5.4.2 Reasonable Grounds to Suspect

Central to the criteria set out in s. 24 is the concept of 'reasonable grounds for suspecting'. This expression has been developed by the courts over many years and, while the wording of s. 24 has yet to be developed by the courts, the interpretation of and approach to the pre-existing legislation are helpful in understanding the concepts involved.

Tests of 'reasonableness' impose an element of objectivity and the courts will consider whether, in the circumstances, a reasonable and sober person might have formed a similar view to that of the officer. Failing to follow up an obvious line of inquiry (e.g. as to the ownership of property found in the possession of the defendant) may well provide grounds for challenging the exercise of a power of arrest (see e.g. *Castorina* v *Chief Constable of Surrey* at **para. 4.5.4.3**).

4.5.4.3 The *Castorina* test

The key test for establishing the lawfulness of an arrest without warrant is set out by the Court of Appeal in *Castorina* v *Chief Constable of Surrey* (1996) 160 LG Rev 241.

The *Castorina* test effectively has three stages:

(1) Did the arresting officer suspect that the person who was arrested was guilty of the offence (or about to commit etc.)?
(2) If so, was there reasonable cause (i.e. reasonable grounds) for the arresting officer's suspicion?
(3) Was the arresting officer's exercise of his/her discretion reasonable in all the circumstances?

The first stage in the *Castorina* test is a subjective one in that it depends entirely on what was in the officer's mind at the time.

The test of 'reasonable suspicion' is lower than that of requiring an officer to provide *prima facie* evidence of guilt. It is (per Lord Devlin in *Hussein* v *Chong Fook Kam* [1970] AC 942): 'A state of conjecture or surmise where proof is lacking'. It is for the police to show on a balance of probabilities in relation to each arrested person that the arresting officer had reasonable grounds to suspect the commission of the offence(s) in question.

Another way of putting it is that a suspicion can be reasonable even if it is uncertain; this can provide reasonable grounds for a lawful arrest (see the Court of Appeal's decision in *Parker* v *Chief Constable of Hampshire Constabulary* [1999] All ER (D) 676).

Note that suspicion can take into account matters that could not be put in front of a court as 'evidence' at all (e.g. intelligence—see *Al Fayed* v *Commissioner of Police for the Metropolis* [2004] EWCA Civ 1579).

The second stage of the *Castorina* test is a purely objective one to be determined by the judge on facts found by the jury/court. This element means that it is not enough for the officer to claim reasonable suspicion in his/her own mind—a court will go on to look at whether there were reasonable grounds to suspect that an offence had been committed and that the person had committed it.

There is no need, however, for the officer to discount every possible defence or to seek complete proof of the relevant facts or circumstances before effecting an arrest (*Ward* v *Chief Constable of Avon and Somerset Constabulary* (1986) *The Times*, 26 June). However, the test that the courts will apply in assessing the lawfulness of an arrest where an offence is suspected is partly subjective. The arresting officer must have formed a genuine suspicion that the person being arrested was guilty of an offence, as well as having reasonable grounds for forming such a suspicion (*Jarrett* v *Chief Constable of the West Midlands Police* [2003] EWCA Civ 397).

It is not uncommon for police officers to be called to a situation where, while there might be only one or two people responsible for an offence, it is unclear which of a group of people is the culprit. The Court of Appeal has confirmed that where an offence has been committed and one of only a small number of people could have committed it, there is no reason why each member or all the group members cannot be arrested (*Cumming* v *Chief Constable of Northumbria Police* [2003] EWCA Civ 1844). In the absence of any information that could or should enable the police to reduce the number further, the fact that a person is in a small group, one of whom must have committed the offence, can amount to reasonable grounds for suspecting him/her.

What about the opposite case where only one person had the opportunity to commit the offence? Is 'opportunity' alone enough to justify reasonable grounds for suspicion? The view of Auld J in the *Al Fayed* case was that 'there is nothing in principle which prevents opportunity from amounting to reasonable grounds for suspicion. Indeed in some circumstances opportunity may be sufficient to found a conviction.'

However, merely being told to arrest someone by a more senior officer is not a reasonable ground for doing so (see *O'Hara* v *Chief Constable of the Royal Ulster Constabulary* [1997] AC 286).

Facts and information relevant to a person's suspected involvement in an offence should not be confined to those which tend to indicate the person has committed or attempted to commit the offence. Before making a decision to arrest, a constable should take account of any facts and information that are available, including claims of innocence made by the person, which might dispel the suspicion.

Particular examples of facts and information which might point to a person's innocence and may tend to dispel suspicion include those which relate to the statutory defence provided by the Criminal Law Act 1967, s. 3(1) which allows the use of reasonable force in the prevention of crime or making an arrest and the common law of self-defence. This may be relevant when a person appears, or claims, to have been acting reasonably in defence of themselves or others or to prevent their property or the property of others from being stolen, destroyed or damaged, particularly if the offence alleged is based on the use of unlawful force, e.g. a criminal assault.

When investigating allegations involving the use of force by school staff, the power given to all school staff under the Education and Inspections Act 2006, s. 93, to use reasonable force to prevent their pupils from committing any offence, injuring persons, damaging property or prejudicing the maintenance of good order and discipline may be similarly relevant. The Association of Chief Police Officers and the CPS have published joint guidance to help the public understand the meaning of reasonable force and what to expect from the police and CPS in cases which involve claims of self-defence. Separate advice for school staff on their powers to use reasonable force is available from the Department for Education.

Necessity criteria

2.4   The power of arrest is <u>only</u> exercisable if the constable has reasonable grounds for *believing* that it is necessary to arrest the person. The statutory criteria for what may constitute necessity are set out in paragraph 2.9 and it remains an operational decision at the discretion of the constable as to:
- which one or more of the necessity criteria (if any) applies to the individual; and
- if any of the criteria do apply, whether to arrest, grant street bail after arrest, report for summons or for charging by post, issue a fixed penalty notice or take any other action that is open to the officer.

2.5 In applying the criteria, the arresting officer has to be satisfied that at least one of the reasons supporting the need for arrest is satisfied.

2.6 Extending the power of arrest to all offences provides a constable with the ability to use that power to deal with any situation. However applying the necessity criteria requires the constable to examine and justify the reason or reasons why a person needs to be arrested or (as the case may be) further arrested, for an offence for the custody officer to decide whether to authorise their detention for that offence.

4.5.4.4 **KEYNOTE**

The officer must have reasonable grounds for *believing*—a higher test than mere suspicion—that the arrest is *necessary* for one of the statutory reasons.

For a constable to have reasonable grounds for believing it necessary to arrest, he/she is not required to be satisfied that there is no viable alternative to arrest. However, it does mean that in all cases, the officer should consider that arrest is the practical, sensible and proportionate option in all the circumstances at the time the decision is made. This applies equally to a person in police detention after being arrested for an offence who is suspected of involvement in a further offence and where the necessity to arrest them for that further offence is being considered.

2.7 The criteria in paragraph 2.9 below which are set out in section 24 of PACE as substituted by section 110 of the Serious Organised Crime and Police Act 2005 **are** exhaustive. However, the circumstances that may satisfy those criteria remain a matter for the operational discretion of individual officers. Some examples are given to illustrate what those circumstances may be and what officers might consider when deciding whether an arrest is necessary.

2.8 In considering the individual circumstances, the constable must take into account the situation of the victim, the nature of the offence, the circumstances of the suspect and the needs of the investigative process.

2.9 When it is practicable to tell a person why their arrest is necessary (as required by paragraphs 2.2 and 3.3), the constable should outline the facts, information and other circumstances which provide the grounds for believing that their arrest is necessary and which the officer considers satisfy one or more of the statutory criteria in sub-paragraphs (a) to (f) namely:

(a) to enable the name of the person in question to be ascertained (in the case where the constable does not know, and cannot readily ascertain, the person's name, or has reasonable grounds for doubting whether a name given by the person as his name is his real name):

An officer might decide that a person's name cannot be readily ascertained if they fail or refuse to give it when asked, particularly after being warned that failure or refusal is likely to make their arrest necessary. Grounds to doubt a name given may arise if the person appears reluctant or hesitant when asked to give their name or to verify the name they have given.

Where mobile fingerprinting is available and the suspect's name cannot be ascertained or is doubted, the officer should consider using the power under section 61(6A) of PACE (see Code D paragraph 4.3(e)) to take and check the fingerprints of a suspect as this may avoid the need to arrest solely to enable their name to be ascertained.

(b) correspondingly as regards the person's address:

An officer might decide that a person's address cannot be readily ascertained if they fail or refuse to give it when asked, particularly after being warned that such a failure or refusal is likely to make their arrest necessary. Grounds to doubt an address given may arise if the person appears reluctant or hesitant when asked to give their address or is unable to provide verifiable details of the locality they claim to live in.

When considering reporting to consider summons or charging by post as alternatives to arrest, an address would be satisfactory if the person will be at it for a sufficiently long period for it to be possible to serve them with the summons or requisition and charge; or, that some other person at that address specified by the person will accept service on their behalf. When considering issuing a penalty notice, the address should be one where the person will be in the event of enforcement action if the person does not pay the penalty or is convicted and fined after a court hearing.

(c) to prevent the person in question—

   (i) causing physical injury to himself or any other person;

   This might apply where the suspect has already used or threatened violence against others and it is thought likely that they may assault others if they are not arrested.

   (ii) suffering physical injury;

   This might apply where the suspect's behaviour and actions are believed likely to provoke, or have provoked, others to want to assault the suspect unless the suspect is arrested for their own protection.

   (iii) causing loss or damage to property;

   This might apply where the suspect is a known persistent offender with a history of serial offending against property (theft and criminal damage) and it is thought likely that they may continue offending if they are not arrested.

   (iv) committing an offence against public decency (only applies where members of the public going about their normal business cannot reasonably be expected to avoid the person in question);

   This might apply when an offence against public decency is being committed in a place to which the public have access and is likely to be repeated in that or some other public place at a time when the public are likely to encounter the suspect.

   (v) causing an unlawful obstruction of the highway;

   This might apply to any offence where its commission causes an unlawful obstruction which it is believed may continue or be repeated if the person is not arrested, particularly if the person has been warned that they are causing an obstruction.

(d) to protect a child or other vulnerable person from the person in question.

This might apply when the health (physical or mental) or welfare of a child or vulnerable person is likely to be harmed or is at risk of being harmed, if the person is not arrested in cases where it is not practicable and appropriate to make alternative arrangements to prevent the suspect from having any harmful or potentially harmful contact with the child or vulnerable person.

(e) to allow the prompt and effective investigation of the offence or of the conduct of the person in question.

This may arise when it is thought likely that unless the person is arrested and then either taken in custody to the police station or granted 'street bail' to attend the station later, further action considered necessary to properly investigate their involvement in the offence would be frustrated, unreasonably delayed or otherwise hindered and therefore be impracticable. Examples of such actions include:

   (i) interviewing the suspect on occasions when the person's voluntary attendance is not considered to be a practicable alternative to arrest, because for example:

     • it is thought unlikely that the person would attend the police station voluntarily to be interviewed.

     • it is necessary to interview the suspect about the outcome of other investigative action for which their arrest is necessary, see (ii) to (v) below.

     • arrest would enable the special warning to be given in accordance with Code C paragraphs 10.10 and 10.11 when the suspect is found:

       ~ in possession of incriminating objects, or at a place where such objects are found;

       ~ at or near the scene of the crime at or about the time it was committed.

     • the person has made false statements and/or presented false evidence;

- it is thought likely that the person:
  - ~ may steal or destroy evidence;
  - ~ may collude or make contact with, co-suspects or conspirators;
  - ~ may intimidate or threaten or make contact with, witnesses.

(ii) when considering arrest in connection with the investigation of an indictable offence, there is a need:
- to enter and search without a search warrant any premises occupied or controlled by the arrested person or where the person was when arrested or immediately before arrest;
- to prevent the arrested person from having contact with others;
- to detain the arrested person for more than 24 hours before charge.

(iii) when considering arrest in connection with any recordable offence and it is necessary to secure or preserve evidence of that offence by taking fingerprints, footwear impressions or samples from the suspect for evidential comparison or matching with other material relating to that offence, for example, from the crime scene.

(iv) when considering arrest in connection with any offence and it is necessary to search, examine or photograph the person to obtain evidence.

(v) when considering arrest in connection with an offence to which the statutory Class A drug testing requirements in Code C section 17 apply, to enable testing when it is thought that drug misuse might have caused or contributed to the offence.

(f) to prevent any prosecution for the offence from being hindered by the disappearance of the person in question.

This may arise when it is thought that:
- if the person is not arrested they are unlikely to attend court if they are prosecuted;
- the address given is not a satisfactory address for service of a summons or a written charge and requisition to appear at court because the person will not be at it for a sufficiently long period for the summons or charge and requisition to be served and no other person at that specified address will accept service on their behalf.

4.5.4.5

KEYNOTE

Arrested persons must be given sufficient information to enable them to understand they have been deprived of their liberty and the reason they have been arrested, as soon as practicable after the arrest, e.g. when persons are arrested on suspicion of committing an offence they must be informed of the nature of the suspected offence and when and where it was committed. Suspects must also be informed of the reason or reasons why arrest is considered necessary. Vague or technical language should be avoided. When explaining why one or more of the arrest criteria apply, it is not necessary to disclose any specific details that might undermine or otherwise adversely affect any investigative processes. An example might be the conduct of a formal interview when prior disclosure of such details might give the suspect an opportunity to fabricate an innocent explanation or to otherwise conceal lies from the interviewer.

4.5.4.6

Paragraph 2.9 (a), (b) and (c)

Although a warning is not expressly required, officers should, if practicable, consider whether to issue a warning which points out the person's offending behaviour, and explains why, if the person does not stop, the resulting consequences may make his/her arrest necessary. Such a warning might:

- if heeded, avoid the need to arrest, or
- if ignored, support the need to arrest and also help prove the mental element of certain offences, e.g. the person's intent or awareness, or help to rebut a defence that he/she was acting reasonably.

A person who is warned that he/she may be liable to arrest if his/her real name and address cannot be ascertained, should be given a reasonable opportunity to establish his/her real name and address before deciding that either or both are unknown and cannot be readily ascertained or that there are reasonable grounds to doubt that a name and address the person given is his/her real name and address. He/she should be told why his/her name is not known and cannot be readily ascertained and (as the case may be) of the grounds for doubting that a name and address he/she have given is his/her real name and address, including, for example, the reason why a particular document the person has produced to verify his/her real name and/or address is not sufficient.

4.5.4.7 Paragraph 2.9(e)

The meaning of 'prompt' should be considered on a case by case basis taking account of all the circumstances. It indicates that the progress of the investigation should not be delayed to the extent that it would adversely affect the effectiveness of the investigation. The arresting officer also has discretion to release the arrested person on 'street bail' as an alternative to taking the person directly to the station. Having determined that the necessity criteria have been met and having made the arrest, the officer can then consider the use of street bail on the basis of the effective and efficient progress of the investigation of the offence in question. It gives the officer discretion to compel the person to attend a police station at a date/time that best suits the overall needs of the particular investigation. Its use is not confined to dealing with child care issues or allowing officers to attend to more urgent operational duties, and granting street bail does not retrospectively negate the need to arrest.

4.5.4.8 Paragraph 2.9(e)(i)

An officer who believes that it is necessary to interview the person suspected of committing the offence must then consider whether his/her arrest is necessary in order to carry out the interview. The officer is not required to interrogate the suspect to determine whether he/she will attend a police station voluntarily to be interviewed but the officer must consider whether the suspect's voluntary attendance is a practicable alternative for carrying out the interview. If it is, then arrest would not be necessary. Conversely, an officer who considers this option but is not satisfied that it is a practicable alternative, may have reasonable grounds for deciding that the arrest is necessary at the outset 'on the street'. Without such considerations, the officer would not be able to establish that arrest was necessary in order to interview.

Circumstances which suggest that a person's arrest 'on the street' would not be necessary to interview him/her might be where the officer:

- is satisfied as to the person's identity and address and that he/she will attend the police station voluntarily to be interviewed, either immediately or by arrangement at a future date and time; and
- is not aware of any other circumstances which indicate that voluntary attendance would not be a practicable alternative. See paragraph 2.9(e)(i) to (v).

When making arrangements for the person's voluntary attendance, the officer should tell the person:

- that to properly investigate his/her suspected involvement in the offence he/she must be interviewed under caution at the police station, but in the circumstances his/her arrest for this purpose will not be necessary if he/she attends the police station voluntarily to be interviewed;
- that if he/she attends voluntarily, he/she will be entitled to free legal advice before, and to have a solicitor present at, the interview;
- that the date and time of the interview will take account of the person's circumstances and the needs of the investigation; and
- that if the person does not agree to attend voluntarily at a time which meets the needs of the investigation, or having so agreed, fails to attend, or having attended, fails to remain for the interview to be completed, his/her arrest will be necessary to enable him/her to be interviewed.

When the person attends the police station voluntarily for interview by arrangement (as above), his/her arrest on arrival at the station prior to interview would only be justified if:

- new information coming to light after the arrangements were made indicates that, from that time, voluntary attendance ceased to be a practicable alternative and the person's arrest became necessary; and
- it was not reasonably practicable for the person to be arrested before he/she attended the station.

If a person who attends the police station voluntarily to be interviewed decides to leave before the interview is complete, the police would at that point be entitled to consider whether the person's arrest was necessary to carry out the interview. The possibility that the person might decide to leave during the interview is therefore not a valid reason for arresting him/her before the interview has commenced. See Code C, paragraph 3.21.

4.5.4.9

Paragraph 2.9(e)(ii)

It should be remembered that certain powers available as the result of an arrest (e.g. entry and search of premises, detention without charge beyond 24 hours, holding a person incommunicado and delaying access to legal advice) only apply in respect of indictable offences and are subject to the specific requirements on authorisation as set out in PACE and the relevant Code of Practice.

4.5.4.10

Paragraph 2.9(e)(iii) and (iv)

The necessity criteria do not permit arrest solely to enable the routine taking, checking (speculative searching) and retention of fingerprints, samples, footwear impressions and photographs when there are no prior grounds to believe that checking and comparing the fingerprints etc. or taking a photograph would provide relevant evidence of the person's involvement in the offence concerned or would help to ascertain or verify his/her real identity.

The necessity criteria do not permit arrest for an offence solely because it happens to be one of the statutory drug testing 'trigger offences' (see Code C Note 17E) when there is no suspicion that Class A drug misuse might have caused or contributed to the offence (paragraph 2.9 (e)(v)).

4.5.5

3 Information to be given on Arrest

(a) Cautions—when a caution must be given (taken from Code C section 10)

3.1 Code C paragraphs 10.1 and 10.2 set out the requirement for a person whom there are grounds to suspect of an offence to be cautioned before being questioned or further questioned about an offence.

3.2 Not used.

3.3 A person who is arrested, or further arrested, must be informed at the time if practicable, or if not, as soon as it becomes practicable thereafter, that they are under arrest and the grounds and reasons for their arrest.

3.4 A person who is arrested, or further arrested, must also be cautioned unless:
   (a) it is impracticable to do so by reason of their condition or behaviour at the time;
   (b) they have already been cautioned immediately prior to arrest as in paragraph 3.1.

3.5 The caution, which must be given on arrest, should be in the following terms:
   'You do not have to say anything. But it may harm your defence if you do not mention when questioned something which you later rely on in Court. Anything you do say may be given in evidence.'
   Where the use of the Welsh Language is appropriate, a constable may provide the caution directly in Welsh in the following terms:
   'Does dim rhaid i chi ddweud dim byd. Ond gall niweidio eich amddiffyniad os na fyddwch chi'n sôn, wrth gael eich holi, am rywbeth y byddwch chi'n dibynnu arno nes ymlaen yn y Llys. Gall unrhyw beth yr ydych yn ei ddweud gael ei roi fel tystiolaeth.'

3.6 Minor deviations from the words of any caution given in accordance with this Code do not constitute a breach of this Code, provided the sense of the relevant caution is preserved.

3.7 Not used.

4.5.5.1

KEYNOTE

The Caution

Nothing in this Code requires a caution to be given or repeated when informing a person not under arrest he/she may be prosecuted for an offence. However, a court will not be able to draw any inferences under the Criminal Justice and Public Order Act 1994, s. 34, if the person was not cautioned.

If it appears a person does not understand the caution, the people giving it should explain it in their own words.

4 Records of Arrest

(a) General

4.1   The arresting officer is required to record in his pocket book or by other methods used for recording information:
   • the nature and circumstances of the offence leading to the arrest
   • the reason or reasons why arrest was necessary
   • the giving of the caution
   • anything said by the person at the time of arrest.

4.2   Such a record should be made at the time of the arrest unless impracticable to do. If not made at that time, the record should then be completed as soon as possible thereafter.

4.3   On arrival at the police station or after being first arrested at the police station, the arrested person must be brought before the custody officer as soon as practicable and a custody record must be opened in accordance with section 2 of Code C. The information given by the arresting officer on the circumstances and reason or reasons for arrest shall be recorded as part of the custody record. Alternatively, a copy of the record made by the officer in accordance with paragraph 4.1 above shall be attached as part of the custody record. See *paragraph 2.2* and *Code C paragraphs 3.4 and 10.3*.

4.4   The custody record will serve as a record of the arrest. Copies of the custody record will be provided in accordance with paragraphs 2.4 and 2.4A of Code C and access for inspection of the original record in accordance with paragraph 2.5 of Code C.

(b) Interviews and arrests

4.5   Records of interview, significant statements or silences will be treated in the same way as set out in sections 10 and 11 of Code C and in Codes E and F (audio and visual recording of interviews).

Arrest without Warrant—Arrest by Others

The Police and Criminal Evidence Act 1984 also makes provision for the so-called citizen's arrest powers. Far narrower than the police powers, these powers of arrest are set out in s. 24A, which states:

(1)   A person other than a constable may arrest without a warrant—
   (a) anyone who is in the act of committing an indictable offence;
   (b) anyone whom he has reasonable grounds for suspecting to be committing an indictable offence.
(2)   Where an indictable offence has been committed, a person other than a constable may arrest without a warrant—
   (a) anyone who is guilty of the offence;
   (b) anyone whom he has reasonable grounds for suspecting to be guilty of it.

KEYNOTE

Unlike the powers of arrest available to police officers (which apply to any and every offence), the citizen's power of arrest only applies where the relevant offence is *indictable*. This power is available to police staff and others in the wider policing family such as Police Community Support Officers.

Under s. 24A(3), an indictable offence must have been committed; it is not enough to suspect or even believe that such an offence has been committed, even if there are very good grounds for that suspicion or belief. This can cause difficulties for the person carrying out the arrest if the 'offender' is subsequently acquitted at court (see *R* v *Self* [1992] 1 WLR 657).

In addition to the criteria regarding the person's guilt/suspected guilt of an indictable offence (or his/her being about to commit one), there are two further elements to this power (see s. 24A(3)). These are:

- the person making the arrest must have *reasonable grounds for believing* that, for any of the reasons mentioned in s. 24A(4) (see below), it is necessary to arrest the person in question, and
- it appears to the person making the arrest that it is not reasonably practicable for a constable to make the arrest instead.

The specified reasons are to prevent the person in question:

- causing physical injury to him/herself or any other person;
- suffering physical injury;
- causing loss of or damage to property; or
- making off before a constable can assume responsibility for him/her.
  (s. 24A(4))

Racial and religious hatred offences provided by the Racial and Religious Hatred Act 2006 do not apply to this section (s. 24A(5)).

4.5.8 Arrest without Warrant—Other Powers of Arrest

Apart from the general power of arrest under s. 24 of the Police and Criminal Evidence Act 1984, several other powers of arrest exist.

4.5.8.1 Preserved Powers of Arrest

Section 26 of the Police and Criminal Evidence Act 1984 repealed all other powers of arrest without warrant which existed before the 1984 Act except those listed in sch. 2. This list has been further reduced by the provisions of the Serious Organised Crime and Police Act 2005.

The common law power of arrest for breach of the peace has been preserved by s. 26 of the 1984 Act (*DPP* v *Orum* [1989] 1 WLR 88).

4.5.8.2 Fingerprinting

The Police and Criminal Evidence Act 1984, s. 27 provides a power of arrest to take a person's fingerprints.

4.5.8.3 Failure to Answer Police Bail

Section 46A of the Police and Criminal Evidence Act 1984 provides a power of arrest when a person fails to answer police bail—this is discussed in detail in *Evidence and Procedure*, chapter 2.3.

4.5.8.4 Arrest to Take Samples

Section 63A of the Police and Criminal Evidence Act 1984 provides a power of arrest without warrant in respect of people:

- who have been charged with/reported for a recordable offence and who have not had a sample taken or the sample was unsuitable/insufficient for analysis;
- who have been convicted of a recordable offence and have not had a sample taken since conviction;
- who have been so convicted and have had a sample taken before or since conviction but the sample was unsuitable/insufficient for analysis.

This is simply a summary of s. 63A and reference should be made to the 1984 Act for the exact wording.

4.5.8.5 **Cross-border Arrest without Warrant**

The Criminal Justice and Public Order Act 1994 (ss. 136 to 140) makes provision for officers from one part of the United Kingdom to go into another part of the United Kingdom to arrest someone there in connection with an offence committed within their jurisdiction and gives them powers to search on arrest.

Under the 1994 Act an officer from a police service in England and Wales may arrest a person in Scotland where it appears to the officer that it would have been lawful for him/her to have exercised his/her powers had the suspected person been in England and Wales or where it would be impracticable to serve a summons for the same reasons which would justify an arrest in England and Wales.

A Scottish officer may arrest someone suspected of committing an offence in Scotland who is found in England, Wales or Northern Ireland if it would have been lawful to arrest that person had he/she been found in Scotland. In such a case the officer must take the person to a designated police station in Scotland or to the nearest designated police station in England or Wales (see s. 137(7)).

The 1994 Act sets out where a person arrested outside the relevant country should be taken on arrest (see s. 137(7)). The Act also provides wide powers of search in connection with arrests (see s. 139).

4.5.9 Arrest under Warrant

Arrest warrants may be issued by magistrates (generally under s. 1 of the Magistrates' Courts Act 1980 as amended) and the Crown Court (under the Senior Courts Act 1981, s. 80(2)) where the statute in question, together with the powers of the court allow. Warrants of arrest may also be issued to secure the attendance of witnesses (see s. 97 of the Magistrates' Courts Act 1980 and s. 4 of the Criminal Procedure (Attendance of Witnesses) Act 1965).

The police owe defendants a duty of care when drawing up and enforcing the contents of warrants. Therefore, where officers put the wrong date on an arrest warrant issued by a magistrates' court and, as a result, the defendant was not released by the Prison Service when he should have been, the police were liable in damages for the defendant's unlawful imprisonment (*Clarke* v *Chief Constable of Northamptonshire Police* (1999) *The Times*, 14 June). The creation of civilian enforcement officers (CEOs) and approved enforcement agencies (AEAs) has meant that there are a significant number of people who, though not employed by the police, are nevertheless empowered to execute arrest warrants in certain circumstances. Generally CEOs and AEAs will be able to execute warrants in connection with court matters such as failure to appear, breaching some bail conditions, or securing the attendance of the defendant at trial. CEOs and AEAs are also given further powers—including some powers to enter and search premises for the purposes of executing warrants—under the Domestic Violence, Crime and Victims Act 2004. The details of these specific provisions are beyond the scope of this Manual.

Warrants issued in relation to an offence may be backed for bail, in which case the person is then granted bail in accordance with the conditions on the warrant. If not backed for bail, the warrant will specify where the person is to be brought (i.e. before the next sitting of the court).

Warrants issued in England, Wales, Scotland or Northern Ireland may be executed by officers from the country where they are issued or in the country where the person is arrested (see s. 136 of the Criminal Justice and Public Order Act 1994).

Warrants from the Republic of Ireland (provided they are not issued for political offences) may be executed in England and Wales if so endorsed (s. 125 of the Magistrates' Courts Act 1980), as, indeed, may warrants issued in the Isle of Man or the Channel Islands if so endorsed (s. 13 of the Indictable Offences Act 1848).

Warrants issued in connection with 'an offence' do not need to be in the possession of the officer executing them at the time. The majority of warrants issued for the arrest of a person in England and Wales arise from matters such as failure to appear at court, breaching bail conditions or failing to pay fines. All of these were once a significant source of policing activity, but they are now enforceable by civilian enforcement officers and approved enforcement agencies.

The requirement under s. 28 of the Police and Criminal Evidence Act 1984 to tell a person why he/she is being arrested applies to arrests under warrant.

The long-awaited arrival of a European Arrest Warrant is covered by Council Framework Decision 2002/584. The detail of this new procedure is outside the scope of this Manual.

4.5.10 Voluntary Attendance at a Police Station

There are occasions where a person attends at a police station in a voluntary capacity. There are a variety of situations where this could arise, e.g. where the person is a suspect, by pre-arrangement with the officers in the case or where the person learns that the police want to speak to him/her. There will be those occasions where a person has elected to accompany a Police Community Support Officer to a police station rather than awaiting the arrival of a constable.

So far as the common law principles regarding arrest set out earlier are concerned, there is no distinction between a person being arrested at a police station after attending voluntarily, and a person arrested elsewhere, provided the arresting officers acted appropriately and reasonably (see *Al Fayed* v *Metropolitan Police Commissioner* [2004] EWCA Civ 1579).

However, there are certain statutory provisions with regard to the entitlements and treatment of people who are 'voluntary attendees' and these are set out below.

The Police and Criminal Evidence Act 1984, s. 29 states:

Where for the purpose of assisting with an investigation a person attends voluntarily at a police station or at any other place where a constable is present or accompanies a constable to a police station or any such other place without having been arrested—

(a) he shall be entitled to leave at will unless he is placed under arrest;

(b) he shall be informed at once that he is under arrest if a decision is taken by a constable to prevent him from leaving at will.

KEYNOTE

The person's attendance at a police station or other place must be for the purpose of 'assisting with an investigation', which would, on a strict interpretation, encompass witnesses and victims. The main principle behind s. 29 (and see also Code C, para. 3.2.1) is to avoid the situation where people find themselves at a police station (or any other place where there is a police officer present) and feel compelled to remain there but without the attendant procedural protection that follows a formal arrest. Section 29(b) is unusual in that it (along with s. 31 below) imposes an obligation on a police officer to make an arrest, an activity that is usually entirely within his/her discretion. The time when the need to arrest the person arises is when the officer takes the decision to prevent the person from leaving (e.g. the time when the officer decides him/herself)—it is not the time when the person is actually prevented from leaving or even when he/she is told of the decision.

If such a person is cautioned (under PACE Code C, para. 10), he/she must also be told that he/she is free to leave the police station. Although not in police detention (see s. 118), voluntary attendees should be given the opportunity to seek legal advice if they wish and should be given the appropriate notice (see Code C).

The Police and Criminal Evidence Act 1984, s. 31 states:

Where—

(a) a person—

   (i) has been arrested for an offence; and

   (ii) is at a police station in consequence of that arrest; and

(b) it appears to a constable that, if he were released from that arrest, he would be liable to arrest for some other offence, he shall be arrested for that other offence.

Like s. 29, this section also imposes an obligation to make an arrest under certain circumstances. In *R v Samuel* [1989] QB 615, the Court of Appeal said that the purpose of the s. 31 requirement was to prevent the release and immediate re-arrest of an offender—therefore, the court noted, s. 31 did not prevent any further arrest from being delayed until the release of the prisoner for the initial arrest was imminent. The Divisional Court has held that, where officers who had arrested a man for a breach of the peace failed to arrest him formally for the further offence of assault on the police, their omission did not impact on the magistrates' decision that there was a case to answer in respect of the assault charge (*Blench v DPP* [2004] EWHC 2717 (Admin)).

The power (though not, on the strict wording, the *obligation*) to arrest a person at a police station for a further offence under s. 31 is among those that can be conferred on an Investigating Officer designated under sch. 4 to the Police Reform Act 2002. Where this power is exercised by a designated Investigating Officer, the provisions of s. 36 of the Criminal Justice and Public Order Act 1994 (failing to account for objects etc.) will apply.

Where a person is re-arrested under this provision, the powers of search under s. 18 of the Police and Criminal Evidence Act 1984 apply (see para. 4.7.5.3).

4.5.11 After Arrest

The Police and Criminal Evidence Act 1984, s. 30 provides for the procedure to be adopted after a person has been arrested. Section 30 states:

(1) Subsection (1A) applies where a person is, at any place other than a police station—
  (a) arrested by a constable for an offence, or
  (b) taken into custody by a constable after being arrested for an offence by a person other than a constable.
(1A) The person must be taken by a constable to a police station as soon as practicable after the arrest.
(1B) Subsection (1A) has effect subject to section 30A (release on bail) and subsection (7) (release without bail).
(2) Subject to subsections (3) and (5) below, the police station to which an arrested person is taken under subsection (1A) above shall be a designated police station.
(3) A constable to whom this subsection applies may take an arrested person to any police station unless it appears to the constable that it may be necessary to keep the arrested person in police detention for more than six hours.
(4) Subsection (3) above applies—
  (a) to a constable who is working in a locality covered by a police station which is not a designated police station; and
  (b) to a constable belonging to a body of constables maintained by an authority other than a police authority.
(5) Any constable may take an arrested person to any police station if—
  (a) either of the following conditions is satisfied—
    (i) the constable has arrested him without the assistance of any other constable and no other constable is available to assist him;
    (ii) the constable has taken him into custody from a person other than a constable without the assistance of any other constable and no other constable is available to assist him; and
  (b) it appears to the constable that he will be unable to take the arrested person to a designated police station without the arrested person injuring himself, the constable or some other person.

(6)   If the first police station to which an arrested person is taken after his arrest is not a designated police station, he shall be taken to a designated police station not more than six hours after his arrival at the first police station unless he is released previously.

(7)   A person arrested by a constable at any place other than a police station must be released without bail if the condition in subsection (7A) is satisfied.

(7A)   The condition is that, at any time before the person arrested reaches a police station, a constable is satisfied that there are no grounds for keeping him under arrest or releasing him on bail under section 30A.

KEYNOTE

When arrested at a place other than a police station, the person must be taken to a designated police station unless the conditions under s. 30(5) and (6) apply.

Under s. 30(7) and (7A), the officer *must* de-arrest a person if he/she is satisfied, before reaching the police station, that there are no grounds for detaining that person. This may happen where the person has been arrested under one of the general arrest conditions and the particular condition has ceased to apply (e.g. the person gives a suitable name and address having originally failed to do so). An officer who releases a prisoner under s. 30(7) and (7A) must record the fact that he/she has done so and must make that record as soon as practicable after the release (s. 30(8) and (9)).

Section 30(10) allows the officer to delay taking the arrested person to a police station where his/her presence elsewhere is *necessary in order to carry out such investigations as it is reasonable to carry out immediately*. Where there is such a delay, the reasons for it must be recorded when the person first arrives at the police station (s. 30(11)).

Escort Officers designated under sch. 4 to the Police Reform Act 2002 may be authorised to take people who have been arrested by a constable in the relevant police area to a police station under the provisions of s. 30(1). The provisions for taking a prisoner to a non-designated police station (see s. 30(3) and 4(a)), and also the provisions allowing a delay in taking the prisoner to a police station (s. 30(10)) will also apply to any exercise of the powers by a designated Escort Officer (see the Police Reform Act 2002, sch. 4, part 4). Other exceptions in the application of s. 30(1) to terrorism and immigration are made by s. 30(12).

The delay permitted under s. 30(10) and (11) will only apply if the matter requires *immediate* investigation; if it can wait, the exception will not apply and the person must be taken straight to a police station (*R* v *Kerawalla* [1991] Crim LR 451).

Taking an arrested person to check out an alibi before going to a police station may be justified in some circumstances (see *Dallison* v *Caffery* [1965] 1 QB 348).

4.5.12   Other Policing Powers

Police officers are provided with many different powers to deal with a wide variety of situations. The majority of these powers are dealt with within the relevant chapters of these Manuals, but there are several powers that, whilst important, are either so isolated or so broad in their nature that they do not fit nicely into any particular category of police activity or offence. Some of those powers and features are dealt with in the following sections.

4.5.13   Acting Ranks

Many of the police powers considered in this—and subsequent—chapters are restricted to officers holding particular ranks. In particular, there are occasions when the Police and Criminal Evidence Act 1984 requires officers of certain ranks to perform roles. The 1984 Act recognises that there may be occasions when officers of the appropriate rank are not readily available and so in limited circumstances allows officers of a lower rank to perform their roles.

Section 107 of the Police and Criminal Evidence Act 1984 sets out occasions when an officer of a lower rank can perform the functions of that required by a higher rank.

Section 107 states:

(1) For the purpose of any provision of this Act or any other Act under which a power in respect of the investigation of offences or the treatment of persons in police custody is exercisable only by or with the authority of a police officer of at least the rank of superintendent, an officer of the rank of chief inspector shall be treated as holding the rank of superintendent if—

    (a) he has been authorised by an officer holding a rank above the rank of superintendent to exercise the power or, as the case may be, to give his authority for its exercise, or

    (b) he is acting during the absence of an officer holding the rank of superintendent who has authorised him, for the duration of that absence, to exercise the power or, as the case may be, to give his authority for its exercise.

(2) For the purpose of any provision of this Act or any other Act under which such a power is exercisable only by or with the authority of an officer of at least the rank of inspector, an officer of the rank of sergeant shall be treated as holding the rank of inspector if he has been authorised by an officer of at least the rank of superintendent to exercise the power or, as the case may be, to give his authority for its exercise.

The only mention of officers performing the higher rank of sergeant in the Police and Criminal Evidence Act 1984 is to be found in s. 36. Section 36 states:

(3) No officer may be appointed a custody officer unless he is of at least the rank of sergeant.

(4) An officer of any rank may perform the functions of a custody officer at a designated police station if a custody officer is not readily available to perform them.

However, in *Vince v Chief Constable of Dorset Police* [1993] 1 WLR 415, Steyn LJ (as he was then) made it clear that s. 36(4) should only be an exception:

> For my part I would start from the provisional premise that the legislature intended to introduce an effective system for the care and protection of detained suspects by custody officers. And on this basis section 36(4), which allows an independent officer of any rank to perform the function of a custody officer at a designated police station 'if a custody officer is not readily available to perform them', can be viewed as a concession to practicality in the light of the problems which will inevitably occur in a busy police station. In other words, there is much to be said for the view that it was not intended that chief constables would be entitled to arrange matters so that as a matter of routine officers below the rank of sergeant performed the functions of custody officers.

4.5.13.1 Temporary Promotion

Regulation 6 of the Police (Promotion) Regulations 1996 (SI 1996/1685) deals with temporary promotion. Regulation 6 states:

(1) A member of a police force who is required to perform the duties of a higher rank may, even if there is no vacancy for that rank, be promoted temporarily to it, but, in the case of promotion to the rank of sergeant or inspector only if he is qualified for the promotion under regulation 3.

(2) A member of a police force who is successful in the written paper under Part I of the qualifying assessment, and who has commenced the period of work-based assessment under Part IIB of the qualifying assessment, shall, at the commencement of the work-based assessment, be temporarily promoted to the rank of sergeant or inspector as the case may be.

4.5.14 Disorder Penalty Notices

The Criminal Justice and Police Act 2001 provides the police with powers for fast-track resolution of some lower-level criminal offences. This system relies on the issuing of penalty notices, though they are generally referred to as disorder penalty notices rather than fixed penalty notices. The powers in relation to some fixed penalty notices for low-level disorder are among those that can be given to Police Community Support Officers.

The offences which are subject to the fixed penalty scheme are set out in s. 1, along with the relevant penalties which are set out in the relevant statutory instrument issued under the 2001 Act. This has been amended several times since the initial Order was made in 2002 and the most up-to-date version should be consulted.

Part I Offences Attracting Penalty of £90 for People 16 and Over, or £40 for People under 16

Offence creating provision	Description of offence
Section 80 of the Explosives Act 1875	Throwing fireworks in a thoroughfare
Section 5(2) of the Criminal Law Act 1967	Wasting police time or giving false report
Section 91 of the Criminal Justice Act 1967	Disorderly behaviour while drunk in a public place
Section 1 of the Theft Act 1968	Theft
Section 1(1) of the Criminal Damage Act 1971	Destroying or damaging property
Section 5(2) of the Misuse of Drugs Act 1971 so far as relating to the following—Possession of cannabis etc.	Possession of a controlled drug
(a) cannabinol,	
(b) cannabinol derivatives (within the meaning of Part 4 of Schedule 2 to that Act),	
(c) cannabis or cannabis resin (within the meaning of that Act),	
(d) any stereoisomeric form of a substance specified in any of paragraphs (a) to (c),	
(e) any ester or ether of a substance specified in paragraph (a) or (b),	
(f) any salt of a substance specified in paragraphs (a) to (e),	
(g) any preparation or other product containing a substance or product specified in any of paragraphs (a) to (f), not being a preparation falling within paragraph 6 of Part 1 of Schedule 2 to that Act.	
Section 5 of the Public Order Act 1986	Behaviour likely to cause harassment, alarm or distress
Section 141 of the Licensing Act 2003	Sale of alcohol to a person who is drunk
Section 146(1) and (3) of the Licensing Act 2003	Sale of alcohol to children
Section 149(3) and (4) of the Licensing Act 2003	Purchase of alcohol on behalf of children
Section 151 of the Licensing Act 2003	Delivery of alcohol to children or allowing such delivery
Section 127(2) of the Communications Act 2003	Using a public electronic communications network in order to cause annoyance, inconvenience or needless anxiety
Section 11 of the Fireworks Act 2003	Contravention of a prohibition or failure to comply with a requirement imposed by or under fireworks regulations or making false statements
Section 49 of the Fire and Rescue Services Act 2004	Knowingly giving a false alarm to a person acting on behalf of a fire and rescue authority

Part II Offences Attracting Penalty of £60 for People 16 and Over, or £30 for People under 16

Offence creating provision	Description of offence
Section 12 of the Licensing Act 1872	Being drunk in a highway, other public place or licensed premises
Section 2(1) of the Parks Regulation (Amendment) Act 1926 so far as it creates an offence against the Parks Regulation Act 1872 relating to any of the following provisions of the Royal Parks and Other Open Spaces Regulations 1997:	Failing to comply with, or contravening those regulations by—

(a) Regulation 3(3)	Dropping or leaving litter or refuse except in a receptacle provided for the purpose
(b) Regulation 3(4)	Using a pedal cycle, a roller blade etc. except on a Park road or designated area
(c) Regulation 3(6)	Failing to remove immediately any faeces deposited by an animal of whom that person is in charge
Section 55 of the British Transport Commission Act 1949	Trespassing on a railway
Section 56 of the British Transport Commission Act 1949	Throwing stones etc. at trains or other things on railways
Section 87 of the Environmental Protection Act 1990	Depositing and leaving litter
Section 12 of the Criminal Justice and Police Act 2001	Consumption of alcohol in designated public place
Section 149(1) of the Licensing Act 2003	Purchase or attempt to purchase alcohol by children
Section 150 of the Licensing Act 2003	Consumption of alcohol by children or allowing such consumption

KEYNOTE

Section 3 sets out the form of the fixed penalty notice and the amounts permissible. The Secretary of State may add to this list by statutory instrument and may specify different amounts for people of different ages (s. 3(1A))—note the difference in the penalty payable by a person who is under 16 at the time of the offence.

There are restrictions on those occasions when theft and criminal damage can be dealt with by way of penalty notice (see *Crime*, chapters **1.14** and **1.16**, respectively).

The heading to s. 1 in the statute refers to 'on the spot' penalties. This is misleading as no payment will be required before 21 days (under s. 5).

Just as misleading is the description of the offence under s. 12 of the 2001 Act (described as 'consumption of alcohol in a public place'); this offence is wider than that (see chapter **4.16**).

The other offences listed above are set out in the relevant parts of this and other Manuals and are indicated in the respective Keynotes.

4.5.14.1 Form of Penalty Notice

The Criminal Justice and Police Act 2001, s. 3(3) states:

(3) A penalty notice must—
   (a) [revoked]
   (b) state the alleged offence;
   (c) give such particulars of the circumstances alleged to constitute the offence as are necessary to provide reasonable information about it;
   (d) specify the suspended enforcement period (as to which see section 5) and explain its effect;
   (e) state the amount of the penalty;
   (f) state the designated officer for a local justice area to whom, and the address at which, the penalty may be paid; and
   (g) inform the person to whom it is given of his right to ask to be tried for the alleged offence and explain how that right may be exercised.

4.5.14.2 Power to Issue Penalty Notices

The power to issue such notices in respect of the s. 1 offences is set out at s. 2. Basically, s. 2 allows a police officer in uniform (if away from a police station) or one that has been author-ised by his/her chief officer (if at a police station) to give a person aged 10 or over a penalty notice if he/she has reason to believe that the person has committed a s. 1 offence. A person given a penalty notice will have the option of requesting to be tried in the normal way or of paying the penalty within the suspended enforcement period. The right to request trial is intended as a safeguard of the defendant's right to a fair trial under Article 6 of the European Convention on Human Rights. If the person fails to pay within that period, a sum of one and a half times the amount of the penalty may be enforced against him/her as a fine. After the suspended enforcement period ends, proceedings may be brought against the person in the normal way for the relevant offence(s). Where a penalty notice is given to a person under the age of 16, the relevant chief officer of police must notify such parent or guardian as he/she thinks fit (see the Penalties for Disorderly Behaviour (Amendment of Minimum Age) Order 2004 (SI 2004/3166)). Any such notification must be in writing and must include a copy of the penalty notice and may be served by giving it to the parent or guardian personally or sending it to the parent or guardian at his/her usual or last-known address by first-class post before the end of the period of 28 days beginning with the date on which the penalty notice was given (see Article 3 of the 2004 Order).

If it transpires that a notification has been sent to a person who is not a parent or guardian of the person receiving the penalty notice (or that it would have been more appropriately sent to someone else), the chief officer can cancel the original notification and send out a fresh one (Article 4).

Where a parent or guardian of a young penalty recipient is notified in this way, then (unless the notification is cancelled) he/she is liable to pay the penalty under the original notice (Article 5). Full details surrounding the proposed operation of the whole scheme are available in the form of guidance from the Home Office under s. 6.

The power to issue penalty notices is among those that can be conferred on a designated person under sch. 4 to the Police Reform Act 2002.

4.5.15 Protection of People Suffering from Mental Disorders

The Mental Health Act 1983 provides for the care and treatment of people suffering from mental disorders and supplies powers for enforcing some of its provisions.

If those powers are executed in good faith, the 1983 Act also provides some protection against criminal and civil liability for the police officers and care workers who use them (see s. 139).

The 1983 Act is supported by a Code of Practice that sets out guidance for the police and other agencies when dealing with people suffering from mental disorders.

4.5.15.1 Mentally Disordered People Found in Public Places

Section 136 of the Mental Health Act 1983 creates a power for police officers to remove such a person under certain conditions.

Section 136 states:

(1) If a constable finds in a place to which the public have access a person who appears to him to be suffering from mental disorder and to be in immediate need of care or control, the constable may, if he thinks it necessary to do so in the interests of that person or for the protection of other persons, remove that person to a place of safety within the meaning of section 135 above.

(2) A person removed to a place of safety under this section may be detained there for a period not exceeding 72 hours for the purpose of enabling him to be examined by a registered medical practitioner and to be interviewed by an approved mental health professional and of making any necessary arrangements for his treatment or care.

(3) A constable, an approved mental health professional or a person authorised by either of them for the purposes of this subsection may, before the end of the period of 72 hours mentioned in subsection (2) above, take a person detained in a place of safety under that subsection to one or more other places of safety.

(4) A person taken to a place of safety under subsection (3) above may be detained there for a purpose mentioned in subsection (2) above for a period ending no later than at the end of the period of 72 hours mentioned in that subsection.

KEYNOTE

Given the number of people who are suffering from some form of mental disorder and who are receiving 'care in the community', this a significant power which is provided for the protection of the people themselves and of others.

The power places a lot of responsibility and latitude on the officer who must decide whether:

- the person is suffering from mental disorder (see below),
- the person is in immediate need of care or control, and
- it is necessary in the person's interest or for someone else's protection that he/she be removed to a place of safety,

before the power is applicable. This power appears to be consistent with Article 5 of the European Convention on Human Rights which sets out the limited circumstances where the detention or arrest of an individual will be permitted (see chapter 4.4).

The definition of 'mental disorder' under s. 1(2) is very wide and means:

- mental illness
- arrested or incomplete development of mind
- any other disorder or disability of mind.

Under s. 135(6), a 'place of safety' is:

- residential accommodation provided by social services
- a hospital
- a police station
- an independent hospital or care home for mentally disordered persons or
- any other suitable place where the occupier is willing to receive the patient temporarily.

Home Office Circular 07/2008 states that police stations should only be used as a place of safety in exceptional circumstances, e.g. where the person's behaviour would pose an unmanageably high risk to other patients, staff or users of a health care setting. Nor should police stations be assumed to be the automatic second choice if the first place of safety is not immediately available. Other options such as a residential care home or home of a friend/relative should also be considered. If a police station must be used, health and social care agencies should work with the police in supporting the care and welfare of the person while in police custody, and assist in arranging, where appropriate, the transfer of the person to a more suitable place of safety.

Section 136(3) and (4) are amendments made by the Mental Health Act 2007. These subsections enable a person detained at a place of safety to be transferred to another one, subject to an overall time limit for detention of 72 hours.

Anyone being taken to a place of safety or detained at such a place will be treated as being in legal custody (s. 137(1)). (This expression is only relevant in relation to escaping and assisting in an escape; it is very different from 'in police detention' used under s. 118 of the Police and Criminal Evidence Act 1984. A mentally disordered person removed from a public place is *not* in police detention even if taken to a police station.)

Note that this power is a power of removal from a public place; it is not a power of arrest nor does it provide a power to detain/further detain someone who is already in police detention.

It is an offence to assist someone removed under s. 136 to escape (see s. 128).

4.5.15.2 Warrant to Search for Patients

Where there is reasonable cause to suspect that a person believed to be suffering from a mental disorder has been, or is being ill-treated or neglected or is unable to care for himself/herself and is living alone, a warrant may be issued by a magistrate (s. 135).

The warrant allows a constable to enter any premises specified and to remove the person to a place of safety. In doing so, the officer must be accompanied by a social worker and a doctor (s. 135(4)).

A warrant may also be issued in respect of a patient ordered to be detained by a court.

4.5.15.3 Power to Retake Escaped Patients

Section 138 provides a power to retake people who have been in legal custody under the 1983 Act.

A person removed to a place of safety under s. 136 or a person removed under a warrant, who subsequently escapes while being taken to or detained in a place of safety, cannot generally be retaken after 72 hours have elapsed. That time period starts either when the person escapes or when his/her liability to be detained began, whichever expires first (s. 138(3)). This means that, if the person escapes *before* reaching the place of safety, the 72 hours begins then; if the person escapes *from* the place of safety, the 72 hours begins at the time he/she arrived there.

There is also a power for a court to issue a warrant for the arrest of a convicted mental patient who is unlawfully at large (Criminal Justice Act 1967, s. 72(3)).

4.5.15.4 Ambit of the Mental Health Act 1983

The ambit of the Mental Health Act 1983 was reviewed in *St George's Healthcare NHS Trust* v *S* [1998] 3 WLR 936, by the Court of Appeal. There it was held that:

- The 1983 Act should not be invoked to overrule the decision of a patient concerning medical treatment simply because that decision appears to be irrational.
- A person detained under the 1983 Act should not be forced to receive medical treatment which is not connected with his/her mental condition unless his/her capacity to give consent is seriously diminished.

4.5.15.5 The Mental Capacity Act 2005

The Mental Capacity Act 2005 provides a statutory framework to empower and protect vulnerable people who are not able to make their own decisions. It covers a wide range of situations in all areas of life and provides protection from legal liability for acts done in connection with care and treatment if done in a person's best interests and in keeping with the Act. Importantly, it can provide police officers with a power to act in a person's best interests, effectively as if they had the person's consent.

The Mental Capacity Act 2005, s. 5 states:

(1) If a person (D) does an act in connection with the care or treatment of another person (P), the act is one to which this section applies if—
  (a) before doing the act, D takes reasonable steps to establish whether P lacks capacity in relation to the matter in question, and
  (b) when doing the act, D reasonably believes—
    (i) that P lacks clarity in relation to the matter and
    (ii) that it will be in P's best interests for the act to be done.
(2) D does not incur any liability in relation to the act that he would not have incurred if P—
  (a) had had capacity to consent in relation to the matter, and
  (b) had consented to D's doing the act.
(3) ...
(4) ...

The Mental Capacity Act 2005, s. 6 states:

(1) If D does an act that is intended to restrain P, it is not an act to which section 5 applies unless two further conditions are satisfied.

(2) The first condition is that D reasonably believes that it is necessary to do the act in order to prevent harm to P.

(3) The second is that the act is a proportionate response to—

    (a) the likelihood of P's suffering harm, and

    (b) the seriousness of that harm.

(4) For the purposes of this section D restrains P if he—

    (a) uses, or threatens to use, force to secure the doing of an act which P resists, or

    (b) restricts P's liberty of movement, whether or not P resists.

(5) ...

(6) Section 5 does not authorise a person to do an act which conflicts with a decision made, within the scope of his authority and in accordance with this Part, by—

    (a) a donee of a lasting power of attorney granted by P, or

    (b) a deputy appointed for P by the court.

(7) But nothing in subsection (6) stops a person—

    (a) providing life-sustaining treatment, or

    (b) doing an act which he reasonably believes to be necessary to prevent a serious deterioration in P's condition, while a decision as respects any relevant issue is sought from the court.

KEYNOTE

This legislation provides a statutory footing for the actions of police officers when they are called to deal with an individual who lacks capacity. If no offence has been committed by the individual, the officer can act in that person's best interests in connection with care and treatment. Where the officer has used the capacity test (set out in s. 5), force can be used to move that person from one place to another. Simply put, the 'capacity test' is the question, 'Does this person have the capacity to make this decision at this time?' If the decision is that the person lacks capacity, the officer can act in the individual's best interests.

EXAMPLE

An officer on patrol finds an elderly man in the street. The man is extremely confused and is bleeding from a head injury. The elderly man refuses any assistance from the officer who is concerned for the man's welfare. The officer can consider the 'test of capacity' and if he/she decides that at that time the man lacks capacity, the officer can act in the man's best interests.

Section 6 defines restraint and before this is permitted it must be considered necessary and proportionate.

4.5.16 Road Checks

The power to stop vehicles generally is provided under s. 163 of the Road Traffic Act 1988 (officers exercising the power must be in uniform). Having caused a vehicle to stop, there are then certain other powers which may be employed by a police officer (or other authorised people).

Among those powers are the powers set out in the Police and Criminal Evidence Act 1984, s. 4 in relation to 'road checks'.

A road check is where the power under s. 163 of the Road Traffic Act 1988 is used in any locality in such a way as to stop all vehicles or vehicles selected by any criterion (s. 4(2) of the 1984 Act). That general power for uniformed officers to stop vehicles might be used in a particular geographical area to stop all vehicles on the road or all vehicles of a certain make, model or colour, or only those vehicles containing a certain number of adult occupants. In all these cases, there would be a 'road check' for the purposes of s. 4.

The power to carry out road checks following the appropriate authorisation under s. 4 of the Police and Criminal Evidence Act 1984 below is among those that can be conferred on a Police Community Support Officer designated under sch. 4 to the Police Reform Act 2002. In exercising this power, any such officer may also be given the power of a uniformed constable to stop vehicles (under s. 163 of the Road Traffic Act 1988).

The Police and Criminal Evidence Act 1984, s. 4 states:

(1) This section shall have effect in relation to the conduct of road checks by police officers for the purpose of ascertaining whether a vehicle is carrying—

    (a) a person who has committed an offence other than a road traffic offence or a vehicle excise offence;

    (b) a person who is a witness to such an offence;

    (c) a person intending to commit such an offence; or

    (d) a person who is unlawfully at large.

(2) ...

(3) Subject to subsection (5) below, there may only be such a road check if a police officer of the rank of superintendent or above authorises it in writing.

(4) An officer may only authorise a road check under subsection (3) above—

    (a) for the purpose specified in subsection (1)(a) above, if he has reasonable grounds—

        (i) for believing that the offence is an indictable offence; and

        (ii) for suspecting that the person is, or is about to be, in the locality in which vehicles would be stopped if the road check were authorised;

    (b) for the purpose specified in subsection (1)(b) above, if he has reasonable grounds for believing that the offence is an indictable offence;

    (c) for the purpose specified in subsection (1)(c) above, if he has reasonable grounds—

        (i) for believing that the offence would be an indictable offence; and

        (ii) for suspecting that the person is, or is about to be, in the locality in which vehicles would be stopped if the road check were authorised;

    (d) for the purpose specified in subsection (1)(d) above, if he has reasonable grounds for suspecting that the person is, or is about to be, in that locality.

KEYNOTE

Road checks may only be authorised for the purposes set out at s. 4(4) and for the duration set out at s. 4(11) (see para. 4.5.16.1). They must, subject to s. 4(5) (see para. 4.5.16.1), be authorised in writing by an officer of superintendent rank or above (s. 4(3)).

The locality in which vehicles are to be stopped must also be specified (s. 4(10)).

If it appears to an officer below the rank of superintendent that a road check is required as a matter of urgency for one of the purposes in s. 4(1), he/she may authorise such a road check (s. 4(5)). What amounts to 'urgency' is not defined, but it would appear to be a somewhat subjective requirement based on the apprehension of the officer concerned. Where such an urgent road check is authorised, the authorising officer must, *as soon as is practicable to do so*, make a written record of the time at which the authorisation is given and must cause an officer of superintendent rank or above to be informed of the authorisation (s. 4(6) and (7)). Where this occurs, the superintendent (or more senior officer) may authorise, *in writing*, that the road check continue (s. 4(8)). If the officer considers that the road check should not continue, he/she must make a written record that it took place as well as the purpose for which it took place (including the relevant 'indictable offence' (s. 4(9) and (14)).

Under s. 4(13), every written authorisation for a road check must include:

- the name of the authorising officer
- the purpose of the road check—including any relevant 'indictable offence'
- the locality in which vehicles are to be stopped
- the road check authorisation also requires the duration of the check to be recorded.

4.5.16.1 Duration of Road Check

The Police and Criminal Evidence Act 1984, s. 4 goes on to state:

(11) An officer giving an authorisation under this section, other than an authorisation under subsection (5) above—

    (a) shall specify a period, not exceeding seven days, during which the road check may continue; and

(b) may direct that the road check—

    (i) shall be continuous; or

    (ii) shall be conducted at specified times, during that period.

(12) If it appears to an officer of the rank of superintendent or above that a road check ought to continue beyond the period for which it has been authorised he may, from time to time, in writing specify a further period, not exceeding seven days, during which it may continue.

KEYNOTE

The road check may be extended—in writing—a number of times for further periods up to a total of seven days by a superintendent if it appears to him/her that it 'ought' to continue. There is no restriction of 'reasonableness' or requirement for the existence of particular grounds here and it seems that the judgement may be an entirely subjective one by the superintendent.

Where a vehicle is stopped during a road check, the person in charge of it is entitled to a written statement of the purpose of that road check if he/she applies for one no later than the end of the 12-month period from the day on which the vehicle was stopped (s. 4(15)).

4.5.17 The Aviation Security Act 1982

The Police and Justice Act 2006, s. 12 inserts s. 24B in part 3 of the Aviation Security Act 1982 (policing of aerodromes). This enables a police constable to stop and search, without warrant, any person, vehicle or aircraft in any area of an aerodrome (excluding a dwelling house), whether the aerodrome is designated or non-designated, for stolen or prohibited articles, where he/she has reasonable grounds to suspect that he/she will find such articles. Designation takes place under part 3 of the Aviation Security Act 1982. If applied to an aerodrome, it allows police constables' additional powers that are not available at non-designated aerodromes. The term 'aerodrome', as defined by s. 38(1) of the 1982 Act, is used rather than 'airport', as it has wider meaning and covers major airports as well as airfields used only by private flying clubs.

Section 24B(4) enables a constable to seize items discovered during a search which he/she reasonably suspects to be stolen or prohibited articles. Section 24B(5) defines a prohibited article as something made or adapted for use in the course of or in connection with criminal conduct, or an article intended for such use by the person having it with him/her or by some other person. 'Criminal conduct' under the 1982 Act is defined as conduct which constitutes an offence in the part of the United Kingdom in which the aerodrome is situated or conduct which would constitute an offence in that part of the United Kingdom if it occurred there.

Stop and Search

PACE Code of Practice for the Exercise by Police Officers of Statutory Powers of Stop and Search; Police Officers and Police Staff of Requirements to Record Public Encounters (Code A)

A thick grey line down the margin denotes text that is an extract of the PACE Code itself (i.e. the actual wording of the legislation). This material is examinable for both Sergeants and Inspectors.

4.6.1 Introduction

This chapter is, in essence, 'Code A of the Codes of Practice'. Code A deals with the exercise by police officers of statutory powers of stop and search and has been incorporated into this chapter with the addition of keynotes in appropriate places. This permits additional useful and explanatory detail to be presented to candidates that would not ordinarily be mentioned in any standard version of the code.

4.6.2 PACE Code of Practice for the Exercise by Police Officers of Statutory Powers of Stop and Search; Police Officers and Police Staff of Requirements to Record Public Encounters (Code A)

This code applies to any search by a police officer and the requirement to record public encounters taking place after midnight on 27 October 2013.

1.0 General

1.01 This code of practice must be readily available at all police stations for consultation by police officers, police staff, detained persons and members of the public.

1.02 The notes for guidance included are not provisions of this code, but are guidance to police officers and others about its application and interpretation. Provisions in the annexes to the code are provisions of this code.

1.03 This code governs the exercise by police officers of statutory powers to search a person or a vehicle without first making an arrest. The main stop and search powers to which this code applies are set out in Annex A, but that list should not be regarded as definitive. In addition, it covers requirements on police officers and police staff to record encounters not governed by statutory powers. This code does not apply to:

(a) the powers of stop and search under;

(i) Aviation Security Act 1982, section 27(2);

(ii) Police and Criminal Evidence Act 1984, section 6(1) (which relates specifically to powers of constables employed by statutory undertakers on the premises of the statutory undertakers).

(b) searches carried out for the purposes of examination under Schedule 7 to the Terrorism Act 2000 and to which the Code of Practice issued under paragraph 6 of Schedule 14 to the Terrorism Act 2000 applies.

(c) the powers to search persons and vehicles and to stop and search in specified locations to which the Code of Practice issued under section 47AB of the Terrorism Act 2000 applies.

4.6.3   1 Principles governing stop and search

1.1   Powers to stop and search must be used fairly, responsibly, with respect for people being searched and without unlawful discrimination. Under the Equality Act 2010, section 149, when police officers are carrying out their functions, they also have a duty to have due regard to the need to eliminate unlawful discrimination, harassment and victimisation, to advance equality of opportunity between people who share a relevant protected characteristic and people who do not share it, and to take steps to foster good relations between those persons.

1.2   The intrusion on the liberty of the person stopped or searched must be brief and detention for the purposes of a search must take place at or near the location of the stop.

1.3   If these fundamental principles are not observed the use of powers to stop and search may be drawn into question. Failure to use the powers in the proper manner reduces their effectiveness. Stop and search can play an important role in the detection and prevention of crime, and using the powers fairly makes them more effective.

1.4   The primary purpose of stop and search powers is to enable officers to allay or confirm suspicions about individuals without exercising their power of arrest. Officers may be required to justify the use or authorisation of such powers, in relation both to individual searches and the overall pattern of their activity in this regard, to their supervisory officers or in court. Any misuse of the powers is likely to be harmful to policing and lead to mistrust of the police. Officers must also be able to explain their actions to the member of the public searched. The misuse of these powers can lead to disciplinary action.

1.5   An officer must not search a person, even with his or her consent, where no power to search is applicable. Even where a person is prepared to submit to a search voluntarily, the person must not be searched unless the necessary legal power exists, and the search must be in accordance with the relevant power and the provisions of this Code. The only exception, where an officer does not require a specific power, applies to searches of persons entering sports grounds or other premises carried out with their consent given as a condition of entry.

4.6.4   2 Explanation of powers to stop and search

2.1   This code applies, subject to paragraph 1.03, to powers of stop and search as follows:

(a) powers which require reasonable grounds for suspicion, before they may be exercised; that articles unlawfully obtained or possessed are being carried;

(b) authorised under section 60 of the Criminal Justice and Public Order Act 1994, based upon a reasonable belief that incidents involving serious violence may take place or that people are carrying dangerous instruments or offensive weapons within any locality in the police area or that it is expedient to use the powers to find such instruments or weapons that have been used in incidents of serious violence, and

(c) Not used.

(d) powers to search a person who has not been arrested in the exercise of a power to search premises (see Code B paragraph 2.4); and

(e) the powers in Schedule 5 to the Terrorism Prevention and Investigation Measures (TPIM) Act 2011 to search an individual who has not been arrested, conferred by:

  (i) paragraph 6(2)(a) at the time of serving a TPIM notice;

  (ii) paragraph 8(2)(a) under a search warrant for compliance purposes; and

  (iii) paragraph 10 for public safety purposes.

See paragraph 2.18A.

4.6.4.1

KEYNOTE

This Code does not affect the ability of an officer to speak to or question a person in the ordinary course of the officer's duties without detaining the person or exercising any element of compulsion. It is not the purpose of the Code to prohibit such encounters between the police and the community with the cooperation of the person concerned and neither does it affect the principle that all citizens have a duty to help police officers to prevent crime and discover offenders. This is a civic rather than a legal duty; but when a police officer is trying to discover whether, or by whom, an offence has been committed he/she may question any person from whom useful information might be obtained, subject to the restrictions imposed by Code C. A person's unwillingness to reply does not alter this entitlement, but in the absence of a power to arrest, or to detain in order to search, the person is free to leave at will and cannot be compelled to remain with the officer.

The 'relevant protected characteristics' referred to in para. 1.1 include: age, disability, gender reassignment, pregnancy and maternity, race, religion/belief, sex and sexual orientation.

It is important to emphasise that Code A of the PACE Codes of Practice applies to *any* search by a police officer, i.e. the principles and processes created by Code A must be followed in *all* searches (there are exceptions for certain powers under the Aviation Security Act 1982 and those exercised by statutory undertakers).

Code A does not allow the routine searching of people with their consent and only permits very limited use of the power as a condition of entry (e.g. to a sports ground) (para. 1.5). This means the practice of conducting 'voluntary' searches in the street or other public places is not permitted.

There are many specific statutory authorities providing the police (and others) with powers to stop people and vehicles and search them (see Annex A of this Code at **appendix 4.1**). Perhaps the most important of these is the general power for police officers to stop and search people and vehicles under s. 1 of the Police and Criminal Evidence Act 1984 (PACE) referred to at para. 2.1(a).

A summary of s. 1 of the Police and Criminal Evidence Act 1984 is that it provides a constable with the power to stop, detain and search a person and/or a vehicle (or anything in or on a vehicle) for stolen articles, prohibited articles, bladed or sharply pointed articles and for fireworks. While such a summary is useful, a more detailed analysis of the power is required.

The Police and Criminal Evidence Act 1984, s. 1 states:

(1) A constable may exercise any power conferred by this section—

  (a) in any place to which at the time when he proposes to exercise the power the public or any section of the public has access, on payment or otherwise, as of right or by virtue of express or implied permission; or

  (b) in any other place to which people have ready access at the time when he proposes to exercise the power but which is not a dwelling.

(2) Subject to subsection (3) to (5) below, a constable—

  (a) may search—

    i) any person or vehicle;

    ii) anything which is in or on a vehicle, for stolen or prohibited articles or any article to which subsection (8A) below applies or any firework to which subsection (8B) below applies; and

  (b) may detain a person or vehicle for the purpose of such a search.

(3) This section does not give a constable power to search a person or vehicle or anything in or on a vehicle unless he has reasonable grounds for suspecting that he will find stolen or prohibited articles or any article to which subsection (8A) below applies or any firework to which subsection (8B) below applies.

(4) If a person is in a garden or yard occupied with and used for the purposes of a dwelling or on other land so occupied and used, a constable may not search him in the exercise of the power conferred by this section unless the constable has reasonable grounds for believing—

  (a) that he does not reside in the dwelling; and

  (b) that he is not in the place in question with the express or implied permission of a person who resides in the dwelling.

(5) If a vehicle is in a garden or yard occupied with and used for the purposes of a dwelling or on other land so occupied and used, a constable may not search the vehicle or anything in or on it in the exercise of the power conferred by this section unless he has reasonable grounds for believing—

(a) that the person in charge of the vehicle does not reside in the dwelling; and

(b) that the vehicle is not in the place in question with the express or implied permission of a person who resides in the dwelling.

(6) If in the course of such a search a constable discovers an article which he has reasonable grounds for suspecting to be stolen or a prohibited article or an article to which subsection (8A) below applies or a firework to which subsection (8B) below applies, he may seize it.

(7) An article is prohibited for the purposes of this Part of this Act if it is—

(a) an offensive weapon; or

(b) an article—

(i) made or adapted for use in the course of or in connection with an offence to which this sub-paragraph applies; or

(ii) intended by the person having it with him for such use by him or by some other person.

(8) The offences to which subsection (7)(b)(i) above applies are—

(a) burglary;

(b) theft;

(c) offences under section 12 of the Theft Act 1968 (taking motor vehicle or other conveyance without authority);

(d) fraud (contrary to section 1 of the Fraud Act 2006); and

(e) offences under section 1 of the Criminal Damage Act 1971 (destroying or damaging property).

(8A) This subsection applies to any article in relation to which a person has committed, or is committing or is going to commit an offence under section 139 of the Criminal Justice Act 1988.

(8B) This subsection applies to any firework which a person possesses in contravention of a prohibition imposed by fireworks regulations.

(8C) In this section—

(a) 'firework' shall be construed in accordance with the definition of 'fireworks' in section 1(1) of the Fireworks Act 2003; and

(b) 'fireworks regulations' has the same meaning as in that Act.

(9) In this Part of this Act 'offensive weapon' means any article—

(a) made or adapted for use for causing injury to persons; or

(b) intended by the person having it with him for such use by him or by some other person.

4.6.4.2 KEYNOTE

Search in a Garden, Yard or Land Connected to Dwelling

If the person to be searched is in a garden, yard or other land occupied with and used as part of a dwelling, the power to search *will not* apply unless the officer has 'reasonable grounds for *believing*' that the person does not live there and that he/she is not there with the permission (express or implied) of any person who does live there.

If the garden or yard is attached to a house that is not so 'occupied', the restriction at s. 1(4) would not appear to apply.

Similar restrictions are placed on the searching of vehicles found in such places by s. 1(5). For the meaning of 'in charge' of a vehicle, see *Road Policing*, chapter 3.1. For these purposes 'vehicle' includes vessels, aircraft and hovercraft (s. 2(10) of the 1984 Act).

4.6.4.3 KEYNOTE

Prohibited Articles

'Offensive weapon' is defined as any article made or adapted for use for causing injury to the person, or intended by the person having it with him for such use or by someone else. There are three categories of offensive weapons: those made for causing injury to the person; those adapted for such a purpose; and those not so made or adapted, but carried with the intention of causing injury to the person. A firearm, as defined by s. 57 of the Firearms Act 1968, would fall within the definition of offensive weapon if any of the criteria above apply.

The power under s. 1 of the Police and Criminal Evidence Act 1984 *does not* authorise an officer in plain clothes to stop a vehicle (s. 2(9)(b)). For the general power of police officers in uniform to stop vehicles, **see** *Road Policing*.

The power is restricted to those places set out in s. 1(1)(a) or (b) of the 1984 Act. This does not mean that the search itself must be carried out there; in fact Code A, paras 3.6 and 3.7 require certain searches to be carried out away from public view (**see para. 4.6.5**).

The power under s. 1 of PACE applies where the officer has 'reasonable grounds for suspecting' that he/she will find stolen or prohibited articles or articles falling under s. 139 of the Criminal Justice Act 1988 (bladed or sharply pointed articles; **see chapter 4.13**) or any firework to which s.1(8B) of the 1984 Act applies.

The existence of reasonable grounds for suspicion is at the heart of the power under s. 1 and for that reason, Code A devotes considerable attention to the concept.

Searches requiring reasonable grounds for suspicion

2.2 Reasonable grounds for suspicion depend on the circumstances in each case. There must be an objective basis for that suspicion based on facts, information, and/or intelligence which are relevant to the likelihood of finding an article of a certain kind. Reasonable suspicion can never be supported on the basis of personal factors. It must rely on intelligence or information about, or some specific behaviour by, the person concerned. For example, unless the police have a description of a suspect, a person's physical appearance (including any of the 'protected characteristics' set out in the Equality Act 2010 (see paragraph 1.1) or the fact that the person is known to have a previous conviction, cannot be used alone or in combination with each other, or in combination with any other factor, as the reason for searching that person. Reasonable suspicion cannot be based on generalisations or stereotypical images of certain groups or categories of people as more likely to be involved in criminal activity.

2.3 Reasonable suspicion may also exist without specific information or intelligence and on the basis of the behaviour of a person. For example, if an officer encounters someone on the street at night who is obviously trying to hide something, the officer may (depending on the other surrounding circumstances) base such suspicion on the fact that this kind of behaviour is often linked to stolen or prohibited articles being carried.

2.4 However, reasonable suspicion should normally be linked to accurate and current intelligence or information, such as information describing an article being carried, a suspected offender, or a person who has been seen carrying a type of article known to have been stolen recently from premises in the area. Searches based on accurate and current intelligence or information are more likely to be effective. Targeting searches in a particular area at specified crime problems increases their effectiveness and minimises inconvenience to law-abiding members of the public. It also helps in justifying the use of searches both to those who are searched and to the public. This does not however prevent stop and search powers being exercised in other locations where such powers may be exercised and reasonable suspicion exists.

2.5 Searches are more likely to be effective, legitimate, and secure public confidence when reasonable suspicion is based on a range of factors. The overall use of these powers is more likely to be effective when up-to-date and accurate intelligence or information is communicated to officers and they are well-informed about local crime patterns.

2.6 Where there is reliable information or intelligence that members of a group or gang habitually carry knives unlawfully or weapons or controlled drugs, and wear a distinctive item of clothing or other means of identification to indicate their membership of the group or gang, that distinctive item of clothing or other means of identification may provide reasonable grounds to stop and search a person.

2.7 A police officer may have reasonable grounds to suspect that a person is in innocent possession of a stolen or prohibited article or other item for which he or she is empowered to search. In that case the officer may stop and search the person even though there would be no power of arrest.

2.8 Not used.

2.9 An officer who has reasonable grounds for suspicion may detain the person concerned in order to carry out a search. Before carrying out a search the officer may ask questions about the person's behaviour or presence in circumstances which gave rise to the suspicion. As a result of questioning the detained person, the reasonable grounds for suspicion necessary to detain that person may be confirmed or, because of a satisfactory explanation, be eliminated. Questioning may also reveal reasonable grounds to suspect the possession of a different kind of unlawful article from that originally suspected. Reasonable grounds for suspicion however cannot be provided retrospectively by such questioning during a person's detention or by refusal to answer any questions put.

2.10 If, as a result of questioning before a search, or other circumstances which come to the attention of the officer, there cease to be reasonable grounds for suspecting that an article is being carried of a kind for which there is a power to stop and search, no search may take place. In the absence of any other lawful power to detain, the person is free to leave at will and must be so informed.

2.11 There is no power to stop or detain a person in order to find grounds for a search. Police officers have many encounters with members of the public which do not involve detaining people against their will. If reasonable grounds for suspicion emerge during such an encounter, the officer may search the person, even though no grounds existed when the encounter began. If an officer is detaining someone for the purpose of a search, he or she should inform the person as soon as detention begins.

4.6.4.4 KEYNOTE

Reasonable Grounds for Suspicion

In some circumstances preparatory questioning may be unnecessary, but in general a brief conversation or exchange will be desirable not only as a means of avoiding unsuccessful searches, but to explain the grounds for the stop/search, to gain cooperation and reduce any tension there might be surrounding the stop/search process.

Where a person is lawfully detained for the purpose of a search, but no search in the event takes place, the detention will not thereby have been rendered unlawful.

The issue of when an officer has reasonable grounds for suspicion has been developed by the courts for many years. This common law development is now supported by the inclusion of specific guidance on search powers that require reasonable grounds for suspicion (see Code A, paras 2.2 to 2.4).

Generally, the courts have held that 'suspicion' requires a lower degree of certainty than 'belief'. The distinction between the two expressions has been held to be a significant one, intended by Parliament (see *Baker* v *Oxford* [1980] RTR 315). In that particular case the court held that the statutory requirement for a reasonable *belief* imposed a greater degree of certainty on the officers concerned. Accordingly, police officers using powers that impose such an extra requirement must be prepared to justify their belief. Suspicion, on the other hand, has been described by Lord Devlin as 'a state of conjecture or surmise when proof is lacking' (*Shaaban bin Hussein* v *Chong Fook Kam* [1970] AC 942). That suspicion can be based on any evidence, even if the evidence itself would be inadmissible at trial (e.g. because it is hearsay). In fact Code A provides for occasions where a police officer has reasonable grounds to suspect that a person is in innocent possession of stolen or prohibited articles or other items which give rise to a power to search the person even though there would be no power of arrest, or no offence committed by that person. The Court of Appeal has reiterated the principle in *Hussein* in the context of an arrest of a person mistakenly thought to have been involved in an offence. The court went on to say that a state of mind of 'being suspicious but uncertain' would provide reasonable grounds to support an arrest where reasonable suspicion was required (*Parker* v *Chief Constable of Hampshire Constabulary* [1999] EWCA Civ 1685).

The courts have accepted that reasonable grounds for suspicion can arise from information given to the officer by a colleague, an informant or even anonymously (see *O'Hara* v *Chief Constable of the Royal Ulster Constabulary* [1997] AC 286).

The courts have held that it must be shown that any such grounds on which an officer acted would have been enough to give rise to that suspicion in a 'reasonable person' (*Nakkuda Ali* v *Jayaratne* [1951] AC 66).

However, the mere existence of such circumstances or evidence is not enough. The officer must actually have a 'reasonable suspicion' that the relevant articles will be found. If, in fact, the officer knows that there is little or no likelihood of finding the articles, the power could not be used (*R* v *Harrison* [1938] 3 All ER 134).

Paragraph 2.6 makes provision for the searching of members of gangs or groups who habitually carry knives unlawfully, weapons or drugs and wear a distinctive item of clothing or other means of identifying themselves with such a group, but only where there is reliable information or intelligence that members of the group or gang do so. Other means of identification might include jewellery, insignias, tattoos or other features which are known to identify members of the particular gang or group.

Searches authorised under section 60 of the Criminal Justice and Public Order Act 1994

2.12   Authority for a constable in uniform to stop and search under section 60 of the Criminal Justice and Public Order Act 1994 may be given if the authorising officer reasonably believes:

   (a) that incidents involving serious violence may take place in any locality in the officer's police area, and it is expedient to use these powers to prevent their occurrence;

   (b) that persons are carrying dangerous instruments or offensive weapons without good reason in any locality in the officer's police area; or

   (c) that an incident involving serious violence has taken place in the officer's police area, a dangerous instrument or offensive weapon used in the incident is being carried by a person in any locality in that police area, and it is expedient to use these powers to find that instrument or weapon.

2.13   An authorisation under section 60 may only be given by an officer of the rank of inspector or above and in writing, or orally if paragraph 2.12(c) applies and it is not practicable to give the authorisation in writing. The authorisation (whether written or oral) must specify the grounds on which it was given, the locality in which the powers may be exercised and the period of time for which they are in force. The period authorised shall be no longer than appears reasonably necessary to prevent, or seek to prevent incidents of serious violence, or to deal with the problem of carrying dangerous instruments or offensive weapons or to find a dangerous instrument or offensive weapon that has been used. It may not exceed 24 hours. An oral authorisation given where paragraph 2.12(c) applies must be recorded in writing as soon as practicable.

2.14   An inspector who gives an authorisation must, as soon as practicable, inform an officer of or above the rank of superintendent. This officer may direct that the authorisation shall be extended for a further 24 hours, if violence or the carrying of dangerous instruments or offensive weapons has occurred, or is suspected to have occurred, and the continued use of the powers is considered necessary to prevent or deal with further such activity or to find a dangerous instrument or offensive weapon that has been used. That direction must be given in writing unless it is not practicable to do so, in which case it must be recorded in writing as soon as practicable afterwards.

2.14A   The selection of persons and vehicles under s. 60 to be stopped and, if appropriate searched should reflect an objective assessment of the nature of the incident or weapon in question and the individuals and vehicles thought likely to be associated with that incident or those weapons. The powers must not be used to stop and search persons and vehicles for reasons unconnected with the purpose of the authorisation. When selecting persons and vehicles to be stopped in response to a specific threat or incident, officers must take care not to discriminate unlawfully against anyone on the grounds of any of the protected characteristics set out in the Equality Act 2010 (see paragraph 1.1).

2.14B   The driver of a vehicle which is stopped under section 60 and any person who is searched under section 60 are entitled to a written statement to that effect if they apply within twelve months from the day the vehicle was stopped or the person was searched. This statement is a record which states that the vehicle was stopped or (as the case may be) that the person was searched under s. 60 and it may form part of the search record or be supplied as a separate record.

4.6.4.5

KEYNOTE

Section 60 of the Criminal Justice and Public Order Act 1994

Section 60 of the 1994 Act states:

(1)   If a police officer of or above the rank of inspector reasonably believes—

    (a)   that incidents involving serious violence may take place in any locality in his police area, and that it is expedient to give an authorisation under this section to prevent their occurrence,

    (aa)   that—

        (i)   an incident involving serious violence has taken place in England and Wales in his police area;

        (ii)   a dangerous instrument or offensive weapon used in the incident is being carried in any locality in his police area by a person; and

        (iii)   it is expedient to give an authorisation under this section to find the instrument or weapon; or

    (b)   that persons are carrying dangerous instruments or offensive weapons in any locality in his police area without good reason, he may give an authorisation that the powers conferred by this section are to be exercisable at any place within that locality for a specified period not exceeding 24 hours.

(2)   (repealed)

(3)   ...

(3A)   ...

(4)   This section confers on any constable in uniform power—

    (a)   to stop any pedestrian and search him or anything carried by him for offensive weapons or dangerous instruments;

    (b)   to stop any vehicle and search the vehicle, its driver and any passenger for offensive weapons or dangerous instruments.

The powers under s. 60 are *separate from* and *additional to* the normal stop and search powers which require reasonable grounds to suspect an individual of carrying an offensive weapon (or other article). Their overall purpose is to prevent serious violence and the widespread carrying of weapons which might lead to persons being seriously injured by disarming potential offenders or finding weapons that have been used in circumstances where other powers would not be sufficient. They should not therefore be used to replace or circumvent the normal powers for dealing with routine crime problems. A particular example might be an authorisation to prevent serious violence or the carrying of offensive weapons at a sports event by rival team supporters when the expected general appearance and age range of those likely to be responsible, alone, would not be sufficiently distinctive to support reasonable suspicion (see para. 2.6).

4.6.4.6

KEYNOTE

Authorisation

Authorisations under s. 60 require a *reasonable belief* on the part of the authorising officer. This must have an objective basis, for example: intelligence or relevant information such as a history of antagonism and violence between particular groups; previous incidents of violence at, or connected with, particular events or locations; a significant increase in knife-point robberies in a limited area or reports that individuals are regularly carrying weapons in a particular locality.

It is for the authorising officer to determine the period of time during which the power may be exercised and in any event must not exceed 24 hours. The officer should set the minimum period he/she considers necessary to deal with the risk of violence, the carrying of knives or offensive weapons. A direction to extend the period authorised under the power may be given only once (by a superintendent for a further 24 hours). Thereafter further use of the powers requires a new authorisation.

It is for the authorising officer to determine the geographical area in which the use of the powers is to be authorised. In doing so the officer may wish to take into account factors such as the nature and venue of the anticipated incident or the incident which has taken place, the number of people who may be in the immediate area of that incident, their access to surrounding areas and the anticipated level of violence. The officer should not set a geographical area which is wider than he/she believes necessary for the purpose of preventing anticipated violence, the carrying of knives or offensive weapons or for finding a dangerous instrument or weapon that has been used. It is particularly important to ensure that constables exercising such powers are fully aware of where they may be used. If the area specified is smaller than the whole force area, the officer giving the authorisation should specify either the streets which form the boundary of the area or a divisional boundary within the force area. If the power is to be used in response to a threat or incident that straddles police force areas, an officer from each of the forces concerned will need to give an authorisation.

If it appears to an officer of or above the rank of superintendent that:

- having regard to offences that have been, or are reasonably suspected to have been, committed
- in connection with any activity falling within the authorisation, and
- it is expedient to do so

he/she may authorise the continuation of the authority to exercise the powers under s. 60(1) for a further period of 24 hours (s. 60(3) and Code A, para. 2.14).

This authorisation must be in writing, signed by the officer giving it, and must specify:

- the grounds on which it is given
- the locality in which it is to operate, and
- the period during which the powers are exercisable

and any direction for the authorisation to continue must also be given in writing at the time or reduced into writing as soon as it is practicable to do so (s. 60(9)).

4.6.4.7

KEYNOTE

Interpretation

'Serious violence' is not defined in the 1994 Act but, although violence could relate to property, the whole tenor of the section suggests that it is aimed at tackling violence against people. 'Dangerous instruments' are bladed or sharply pointed instruments, while offensive weapons have the same meaning as that under s. 1(9) of the Police and Criminal Evidence Act 1984. For the purposes of s. 60, 'carrying' will mean 'having in your possession' (s. 60(11A)), a much wider meaning than carrying usually conveys.

4.6.4.8

KEYNOTE

Powers, Offences and Entitlements

A significant difference between this power and the general powers of stop and search (which are not affected by the granting of this power (s. 60(12))), is that it does not require any grounds at all for the officer to suspect that the person/vehicle is carrying offensive weapons or dangerous instruments (s. 60(5)). However, para. 2.14A is clear in that it states that the stopping of people and/or vehicles should reflect the purpose of the authorisation. A further difference is that the power under s. 60 authorises *officers in uniform* to stop vehicles in order to search them and their occupants (but not in relation to the removal and seizure of face coverings; **see para. 2.15**).

The power allows the stopping and searching of pedestrians, vehicles (including caravans, aircraft, vessels and hovercraft) and passengers. If a dangerous instrument or anything reasonably suspected to be an 'offensive weapon' is found during the search, the officer may seize it (s. 60(6)).

Note the general requirements governing searches imposed by Code A apply to this power.

Failing to stop (or to stop a vehicle) when required to do so under this power is a summary offence punishable with one month's imprisonment and/or a fine (s. 60(8)(a)).

Powers to require removal of face coverings

2.15 Section 60AA of the Criminal Justice and Public Order Act 1994 also provides a power to demand the removal of disguises. The officer exercising the power must reasonably believe that someone is wearing an item wholly or mainly for the purpose of concealing identity. There is also a power to seize such items where the officer believes that a person intends to wear them for this purpose. There is no power to stop and search for disguises. An officer may seize any such item which is discovered when exercising a power of search for something else, or which is being carried, and which the officer reasonably believes is intended to be used for concealing anyone's identity. This power can only be used if an authorisation under section 60 or an authorisation under section 60AA is in force.

2.16 Authority for a constable in uniform to require the removal of disguises and to seize them under section 60AA may be given if the authorising officer reasonably believes that activities may take place in any locality in the officer's police area that are likely to involve the commission of offences and it is expedient to use these powers to prevent or control these activities.

2.17 An authorisation under section 60AA may only be given by an officer of the rank of inspector or above, in writing, specifying the grounds on which it was given, the locality in which the powers may be exercised and the period of time for which they are in force. The period authorised shall be no longer than appears reasonably necessary to prevent, or seek to prevent the commission of offences. It may not exceed 24 hours.

2.18 If an inspector gives an authorisation, he or she must, as soon as practicable, inform an officer of or above the rank of superintendent. This officer may direct that the authorisation shall be extended for a further 24 hours, if crimes have been committed, or is suspected to have been committed, and the continued use of the powers is considered necessary to prevent or deal with further such activity. This direction must also be given in writing at the time or as soon as practicable afterwards.

4.6.4.9 **KEYNOTE**

Section 60AA of the Criminal Justice and Public Order Act 1994

The Criminal Justice and Public Order Act 1994, s. 60AA states:

(1) Where—
    (a) an authorisation under section 60 is for the time being in force in relation to any locality for any period, or
    (b) an authorisation under subsection (3) that the powers conferred by subsection (2) shall be exercisable at any place in a locality is in force for any period,
    those powers shall be exercisable at any place in that locality at any time in that period.

(2) This subsection confers power on any constable in uniform—
    (a) to require any person to remove any item which the constable reasonably believes that person is wearing wholly or mainly for the purpose of concealing his identity;
    (b) to seize any item which the constable reasonably believes any person intends to wear wholly or mainly for that purpose.

(3) If a police officer of or above the rank of inspector reasonably believes—
    (a) that activities may take place in any locality in his police area that are likely (if they take place) to involve the commission of offences, and
    (b) that it is expedient, in order to prevent or control the activities, to give an authorization under this subsection,

he may give an authorisation that the powers conferred by this section shall be exercisable at any place within that locality for a specified period not exceeding twenty-four hours.

The purpose of the powers under s. 60AA is to prevent those involved in intimidatory or violent protests using face coverings to conceal identity.

These provisions are wider than those under s. 60 in that they are not restricted to anticipated outbreaks of serious violence. This is not simply a preventive power and can be used where the 'activities' are already under way.

4.6.4.10   **KEYNOTE**

Authorisation

The authorisation process closely follows that of an authorisation under s. 60 of the Act, i.e. the authorising officer reasonably believes that activities may take place in any locality in his/her police area that are likely (if they take place) to involve the commission of offences. This reasonable belief must have an objective basis, for example where the authorising officer is aware of previous incidents of crimes being committed while wearing face coverings to conceal identity. The requirements in relation to the further authority of a superintendent (or above) and the manner and form in which any authority is to be given are broadly similar to those set out in s. 60; the limitations and requirements as to the time and geographical extent of any authorisation are the same (see para. 4.6.4.9).

4.6.4.11   **KEYNOTE**

Interpretation

Any officer exercising these powers must reasonably *believe* (not merely 'suspect') that the person wearing the item is doing so *wholly or mainly for the purpose of concealing his/her identity*. Therefore if the person is a cyclist wearing a face mask to prevent the inhalation of traffic fumes, or a motorcyclist wearing a crash helmet, the fact that its *effect* is to conceal his/her identity will not be enough—concealing his/her identity has to be the purpose/main purpose of the wearer.

The expression 'item' is very wide and would clearly include balaclavas, scarves and crash helmets (if the officer believes that such items are being worn wholly or mainly to conceal identity). It is not specifically restricted to face coverings and extends to anything that could be worn wholly or mainly for the purpose of concealing identity (e.g. where offenders swap clothing after an offence). The purpose of the legislation is primarily to ensure that people are not allowed to commit offences anonymously in situations of public disorder.

4.6.4.12   **KEYNOTE**

Religious Sensitivities

Specific guidance in relation to religious sensitivities is provided by Code A. Many people customarily cover their heads or faces for religious reasons, e.g. Muslim women, Sikh men, Sikh or Hindu women or Rastafarian men or women. A police officer cannot order the removal of a head or face covering except where there is reason to believe that the item is being worn by the individual wholly or mainly for the purpose of disguising identity, not simply because it disguises identity. Where there may be religious sensitivities about ordering the removal of such an item, the officer should permit the item to be removed out of public view (perhaps in a police van or a police station if there is one nearby). Where practicable, the item should be removed in the presence of an officer of the same sex as the person and out of sight of anyone of the opposite sex.

4.6.4.13   **KEYNOTE**

Powers and Offences

Unlike s. 60, there is no specific power under this section to stop vehicles but, given that this is a power for police officers in uniform, the general power under s. 163 of the Road Traffic Act 1988 could be used.

There is no power to search for face coverings etc. under this power. The Divisional Court has held that the predecessor to this power (the old s. 60(4A)) neither involved nor required a 'search' and that therefore the provisions of s. 2 of the Police and Criminal Evidence Act 1984 did not apply (*DPP* v *Avery* [2001] EWHC Admin 748). The court went on to hold that, although the power amounted to a significant interference with a person's liberty, it was justified by the type of situation envisaged by the legislators whereby the police may need to call upon the law. Clearly if an item is found during a lawful search for other articles (say under s. 60(4)) which does not require any 'reasonable belief' by the officer, face coverings and masks could then be seized under subsection (b). The procedure to be followed in relation to the retention and disposal of items seized under s. 60 is set out in the Police (Retention and Disposal of Items Seized) Regulations 2002 (SI 2002/1372).

4.6.4.14

KEYNOTE

OFFENCE: **Failing to Comply with Requirement to Remove Items—*Criminal Justice and Public Order Act 1994, s. 60AA(7)***

- Triable summarily • One month's imprisonment and/or a fine

The Criminal Justice and Public Order Act 1994, s.60AA states:

(7) A person who fails to remove an item worn by him when required to do so by a constable in the exercise of his power under this section shall be liable.

The wording of this offence is absolute. There is no requirement that the person failed without reasonable excuse or without good reason etc.; simply that he/she failed to remove an item worn by him/her. However, it must be shown that:

- the requirement was made (and presumably understood)
- it was made by a police officer in uniform
- in the exercise of powers authorised under s. 60

in the reasonable belief that the person was wearing the item wholly or mainly for the purpose of concealing his/her identity.

Searches under Schedule 5 to the Terrorism Prevention and Investigation Measures Act 2011

2.18 A Paragraph 3 of Schedule 5 to the TPIM Act 2011 allows a constable to detain an individual to be searched under the following powers:

(i) paragraph 6(2)(a) when a TPIM notice is being, or has just been, served on the individual for the purpose of ascertaining whether there is anything on the individual that contravenes measures specified in the notice;

(ii) paragraph 8(2)(a) in accordance with a warrant to search the individual issued by a justice of the peace in England and Wales, a sheriff in Scotland or a lay magistrate in Northern Ireland who is satisfied that a search is necessary for the purpose of determining whether an individual in respect of whom a TPIM notice is in force is complying with measures specified in the notice (see *paragraph 2.20*); and

(iii) paragraph 10 to ascertain whether an individual in respect of whom a TPIM notice is in force is in possession of anything that could be used to threaten or harm any person.

See *paragraph 2.1(e)*.

2.19 The exercise of the powers mentioned in paragraph 2.18A does not require the constable to have reasonable grounds to suspect that the individual:

(a) has been, or is, contravening any of the measures specified in the TPIM notice; or

(b) has on them anything which:

- in the case of the power in sub-paragraph (i), contravenes measures specified in the TPIM notice;

- in the case of the power in sub-paragraph (ii) is not complying with measures specified in the TPIM notice; or
- in the case of the power in sub-paragraph (iii), could be used to threaten or harm any person.

2.20   A search of an individual on warrant under the power mentioned in paragraph 2.18A(ii) must carried out within 28 days of the issue of the warrant and:
- the individual may be searched on one occasion only within that period;
- the search must take place at a reasonable hour unless it appears that this would frustrate the purposes of the search.

2.21   *Not used.*

2.22   *Not used.*

2.23   *Not used.*

2.24   *Not used.*

2.24A   *Not used.*

2.25   *Not used.*

2.26   The powers under Schedule 5 only allow a constable to conduct a search of an individual only for specified purposes relating to a TPIM notice as set out above. However, anything found may be seized and retained if there are reasonable grounds for believing that it is or it contains evidence of any offence for use at a trial for that offence or to prevent it being concealed, lost, damaged, altered, or destroyed. However, this would not prevent a search being carried out under other search powers if, in the course of exercising these powers, the officer formed reasonable grounds for suspicion.

Powers to search in the exercise of a power to search premises

2.27   The following powers to search premises also authorise the search of a person, not under arrest, who is found on the premises during the course of the search:
    (a)   section 139B of the Criminal Justice Act 1988 under which a constable may enter school premises and search the premises and any person on those premises for any bladed or pointed article or offensive weapon;
    (b)   under a warrant issued under section 23(3) of the Misuse of Drugs Act 1971 to search premises for drugs or documents but only if the warrant specifically authorises the search of persons found on the premises; and
    (c)   under a search warrant or order issued under paragraph 1, 3 or 11 of Schedule 5 to the Terrorism Act 2000 to search premises and any person found there for material likely to be of substantial value to a terrorist investigation.

2.28   Before the power under section 139B of the Criminal Justice Act 1988 may be exercised, the constable must have reasonable grounds to suspect that an offence under section 139A or 139AA of the Criminal Justice Act 1988 (having a bladed or pointed article or offensive weapon on school premises) has been or is being committed. A warrant to search premises and persons found therein may be issued under section 23(3) of the Misuse of Drugs Act 1971 if there are reasonable grounds to suspect that controlled drugs or certain documents are in the possession of a person on the premises.

2.29   The powers in paragraph 2.27 do not require prior specific grounds to suspect that the person to be searched is in possession of an item for which there is an existing power to search. However, it is still necessary to ensure that the selection and treatment of those searched under these powers is based upon objective factors connected with the search of the premises, and not upon personal prejudice.

4.6.5 | 3 Conduct of searches

3.1 All stops and searches must be carried out with courtesy, consideration and respect for the person concerned. This has a significant impact on public confidence in the police. Every reasonable effort must be made to minimise the embarrassment that a person being searched may experience.

3.2 The cooperation of the person to be searched must be sought in every case, even if the person initially objects to the search. A forcible search may be made only if it has been established that the person is unwilling to co-operate or resists. Reasonable force may be used as a last resort if necessary to conduct a search or to detain a person or vehicle for the purposes of a search.

3.3 The length of time for which a person or vehicle may be detained must be reasonable and kept to a minimum. Where the exercise of the power requires reasonable suspicion, the thoroughness and extent of a search must depend on what is suspected of being carried, and by whom. If the suspicion relates to a particular article which is seen to be slipped into a person's pocket, then, in the absence of other grounds for suspicion or an opportunity for the article to be moved elsewhere, the search must be confined to that pocket. In the case of a small article which can readily be concealed, such as a drug, and which might be concealed anywhere on the person, a more extensive search may be necessary. In the case of searches mentioned in paragraph 2.1(b) and (d), which do not require reasonable grounds for suspicion, officers may make any reasonable search to look for items for which they are empowered to search.

3.4 The search must be carried out at or near the place where the person or vehicle was first detained.

3.5 There is no power to require a person to remove any clothing in public other than an outer coat, jacket or gloves except under section 60AA of the Criminal Justice and Public Order Act 1994 (which empowers a constable to require a person to remove any item worn to conceal identity). A search in public of a person's clothing which has not been removed must be restricted to superficial examination of outer garments. This does not, however, prevent an officer from placing his or her hand inside the pockets of the outer clothing, or feeling round the inside of collars, socks and shoes if this is reasonably necessary in the circumstances to look for the object of the search or to remove and examine any item reasonably suspected to be the object of the search. For the same reasons, subject to the restrictions on the removal of headgear, a person's hair may also be searched in public (see paragraphs 3.1 and 3.3).

3.6 Where on reasonable grounds it is considered necessary to conduct a more thorough search (e.g. by requiring a person to take off a T-shirt), this must be done out of public view, for example, in a police van unless paragraph 3.7 applies, or police station if there is one nearby. Any search involving the removal of more than an outer coat, jacket, gloves, headgear or footwear, or any other item concealing identity, may only be made by an officer of the same sex as the person searched and may not be made in the presence of anyone of the opposite sex unless the person being searched specifically requests it (see Annex F).

3.7 Searches involving exposure of intimate parts of the body must not be conducted as a routine extension of a less thorough search, simply because nothing is found in the course of the initial search. Searches involving exposure of intimate parts of the body may be carried out only at a nearby police station or other nearby location which is out of public view (but not a police vehicle). These searches must be conducted in accordance with paragraph 11 of Annex A to Code C except that an intimate search mentioned in paragraph 11(f) of Annex A to Code C may not be authorised or carried out under any stop and search powers. The other provisions of Code C do not apply to the conduct and recording of searches of persons detained at police stations in the exercise of stop and search powers.

KEYNOTE

A search of a person should be completed as soon as possible.

A person may be detained under a stop and search power at a place other than where the person was first detained, only if that place, be it a police station or elsewhere, is nearby. Such a place should be located within a reasonable travelling distance using whatever mode of travel (on foot or by car) is appropriate. This applies to all searches under stop and search powers, whether or not they involve the removal of clothing or exposure of intimate parts of the body (see paras 3.6 and 3.7) or take place in or out of public view. It means, for example, that a search under the stop and search power in s. 23 of the Misuse of Drugs Act 1971 which involves the compulsory removal of more than a person's outer coat, jacket or gloves cannot be carried out unless a place which is both nearby the place he/she was first detained and out of public view, is available. If a search involves exposure of intimate parts of the body and a police station is not nearby, particular care must be taken to ensure that the location is suitable in that it enables the search to be conducted in accordance with the requirements of para. 11 of Annex A to Code C.

A search in the street itself should be regarded as being in public for the purposes of paras 3.6 and 3.7, even though it may be empty at the time a search begins.

Although there is no power to require a person to do so, there is nothing to prevent an officer from asking a person *voluntarily to remove* more than an outer coat, jacket or gloves.

Steps to be taken prior to a search

3.8   Before any search of a detained person or attended vehicle takes place the officer must take reasonable steps, if not in uniform (see paragraph 3.9), to show their warrant card to the person to be searched or in charge of the vehicle to be searched and whether or not in uniform, to give that person the following information:

(a) that they are being detained for the purposes of a search;

(b) the officer's name (except in the case of enquiries linked to the investigation of terrorism, or otherwise where the officer reasonably believes that giving their name might put him or her in danger, in which case a warrant or other identification number shall be given) and the name of the police station to which the officer is attached;

(c) the legal search power which is being exercised; and

(d) a clear explanation of:

(i) the object of the search in terms of the articles or articles for which there is a power to search; and

(ii) in the case of

• the power under section 60 of the Criminal Justice and Public Order Act 1994 (see paragraph 2.1(b)), the nature of the power, the authorisation and the fact that it has been given;

• the powers under Schedule 5 to the Terrorism Prevention and Investigation Measures Act 2011 (see *paragraph 2.1(e)* and *2.18A*):

~ the fact that a TPIM notice is in force or, (in the case of paragraph 6(2) (a)) that a TPIM notice is being served;

~ the nature of the power being exercised.

For a search under paragraph 8 of Schedule 5, the warrant must be produced and the person be provided with a copy of it.

• all other powers requiring reasonable suspicion (see paragraph 2.1(a)), the grounds for that suspicion.

(e) that they are entitled to a copy of the record of the search if one is made (see section 4 below) if they ask within 3 months from the date of the search and:

>   (i) if they are not arrested and taken to a police station as a result of the search and it is practicable to make a record on the spot, that immediately after the search is completed they will be given, if they request, either:
>
> - a copy of the record, or
> - a receipt which explains how they can obtain a copy of the full record or access to an electronic copy of the record, or
>
>   (ii) if they are arrested and taken to a police station as a result of the search, that the record will be made at the station as part of their custody record and they will be given, if they request, a copy of their custody record which includes a record of the search as soon as practicable whilst they are at the station.

3.9   Stops and searches under the power mentioned in paragraph 2.1(b) may be undertaken only by a constable in uniform.

3.10   The person should also be given information about police powers to stop and search and the individual's rights in these circumstances.

3.11   If the person to be searched, or in charge of a vehicle to be searched, does not appear to understand what is being said, or there is any doubt about the person's ability to understand English, the officer must take reasonable steps to bring information regarding the person's rights and any relevant provisions of this Code to his or her attention. If the person is deaf or cannot understand English and is accompanied by someone, then the officer must try to establish whether that person can interpret or otherwise help the officer to give the required information.

4.6.5.2

KEYNOTE

This Code A requirement is mirrored by the specific requirements of s. 2 of the Police and Criminal Evidence Act 1984.

The Police and Criminal Evidence Act 1984, s. 2 states:

(1) A constable who detains a person or vehicle in the exercise—
 (a) of the power conferred by section 1 above; or
 (b) of any other power—
  (i) to search a person without first arresting him; or
  (ii) to search a vehicle without making an arrest,
need not conduct a search if it appears to him subsequently—
  (i) that no search is required; or
  (ii) that a search is impracticable.
(2) If a constable contemplates a search, other than a search of an unattended vehicle, in the exercise—
 (a) of the power conferred by section 1 above; or
 (b) of any other power, except the power conferred by section 6 below and the power conferred by section 27(2) of the Aviation Security Act 1982—
  (i) to search a person without first arresting him; or
  (ii) to search a vehicle without making an arrest,
it shall be his duty, subject to subsection (4) below, to take reasonable steps before he commences the search to bring to the attention of the appropriate person—
  (i) if the constable is not in uniform, documentary evidence that he is a constable; and
  (ii) whether he is in uniform or not, the matters specified in subsection (3) below; and the constable shall not commence the search until he has performed that duty.
(3) The matters referred to in subsection (2)(ii) above are—
 (a) the constable's name and the name of the police station to which he is attached;
 (b) the object of the proposed search;
 (c) the constable's grounds for proposing to make it; and
 (d) the effect of section 3(7) or (8) below, as may be appropriate.

Having stopped a person for the purposes of searching him/her, there is no requirement for the officer to conduct the search if it appears that to do so is not necessary or that it is impracticable.

The officer carrying out the search must take reasonable steps to bring the matters at s. 2(3)(a) to (d) to the person's attention before starting the search. This information must be given whether it is requested or not. Whether reasonable steps have been taken to communicate information will ultimately be a question of fact for the court to decide and what is 'reasonable' will vary with the particular circumstances of each search (e.g. what is reasonable outside a busy city centre nightclub may well be different from that which is required on a rural public footpath). The courts have taken a very firm position in interpreting and applying these requirements. For example, the requirements for officers to provide details of their names and police stations still apply even though that information is discernible from the officers' uniform; failure to provide the information in such circumstances will make any subsequent search unlawful and will mean that the person being searched may use reasonable force to resist it (*Osman* v *DPP* (1999) 163 JP 725). In a further case, the Divisional Court held that the officers conducting the stop and search had not informed the suspect of their intention to search him at an early enough stage before laying their hands on him. The suspect—who was standing with his hands in his pockets and who was suspected of drugs offences—had struggled with the officers when they took hold of him and had been arrested. The magistrates' court held that, where it was obvious that the people apprehending a suspect were police officers and where an officer was genuinely concerned for the safety of a fellow officer, it was not essential to comply with all the requirements of s. 2(3). However, the Divisional Court disagreed, quashing the conviction and holding that, where police officers contemplated a statutory search, they were required (by s. 2(2)) to comply with s. 2(3) before commencing the search—*Bonner* v *DPP* [2004] EWHC 2415 (Admin). The principle was restated in *R* v *Bristol* [2007] EWCA Crim 3214.

The 'effect of section 3(7) or (8)' referred to in s. 2(3)(d) means the person's entitlement to a copy of any search record made.

The 'appropriate person' is the person to be searched or the person in charge of the vehicle to be searched (s. 2(5)).

4.6.6 4 Recording requirements

(a) Searches which do not result in an arrest

4.1 When an officer carries out a search in the exercise of any power to which this Code applies, and the search does not result in the person searched or person in charge of the vehicle searched being arrested and taken to a police station, a record must be made of it, electronically or on paper, unless there are exceptional circumstances which make this wholly impracticable (e.g. in situations involving public disorder or where the recording officer's presence is urgently required elsewhere). If a record is to be made, the officer carrying out the search must make the record on the spot unless this is not practicable, in which case, the officer must make the record as soon as practicable after the search is completed.

4.2 If the record is made at the time, the person who has been searched or who is in charge of the vehicle that has been searched must be asked if they want a copy and if they do, they must be given immediately, either:
- a copy of the record, or
- a receipt which explains how they can obtain a copy of the full record or access to an electronic copy of the record.

4.2A An officer is not required to provide a copy of the full record or a receipt at the time if they are called to an incident of higher priority.

(b) Searches which result in an arrest

4.2B If a search in the exercise of any power to which this Code applies results in a person being arrested and taken to a police station, the officer carrying out the search is responsible for ensuring that a record of the search is made as a part of their custody record. The custody officer must then ensure that the person is asked if they want a copy of the record and if they do, that they are given a copy as soon as practicable.

4.6.6.1

(c) Record of search

4.3 The record of a search must always include the following information:

(a) A note of the self-defined ethnicity, and if different, the ethnicity as perceived by the officer making the search, of the person searched or of the person in charge of the vehicle (as the case may be);

(b) The date, time and place the person or vehicle was searched;

(c) The object of the search in terms of the article or articles for which there is a power to search;

(d) In the case of:

• the power under section 60 of the Criminal Justice and Public Order Act 1994 (see paragraph 2.1(b)), the nature of the power, the authorisation and the fact that it has been given;

• the powers under Schedule 5 to the Terrorism Prevention and Investigation Measures Act 2011 (see paragraphs 2.1(e) and 2.18A):

~ the fact that a TPIM notice is in force or, (in the case of paragraph 6(2)(a)), that a TPIM notice is being served;

~ the nature of the power, and

~ for a search under paragraph 8, the date the search warrant was issued, the fact that the warrant was produced and a copy of it provided and the warrant must also be endorsed by the constable executing it to state whether anything was found and whether anything was seized, and

• all other powers requiring reasonable suspicion (see paragraph 2.1A)), the grounds for that suspicion.

(e) subject to paragraph 3.8(b), the identity of the officer carrying out the search.

4.3A For the purposes of completing the search record, there is no requirement to record the name, address and date of birth of the person searched or the person in charge of a vehicle which is searched and the person is under no obligation to provide this information.

4.4 Nothing in paragraph 4.3 requires the names of police officers to be shown on the search record or any other record required to be made under this code in the case of enquiries linked to the investigation of terrorism or otherwise where an officer reasonably believes that recording names might endanger the officers. In such cases the record must show the officers' warrant or other identification number and duty station.

4.5 A record is required for each person and each vehicle searched. However, if a person is in a vehicle and both are searched, and the object and grounds of the search are the same, only one record need be completed. If more than one person in a vehicle is searched, separate records for each search of a person must be made. If only a vehicle is searched, the self-defined ethnic background of the person in charge of the vehicle must be recorded, unless the vehicle is unattended.

4.6 The record of the grounds for making a search must, briefly but informatively, explain the reason for suspecting the person concerned, by reference to the person's behaviour and/or other circumstances.

4.7 Where officers detain an individual with a view to performing a search, but the need to search is eliminated as a result of questioning the person detained, a search should not be carried out and a record is not required. [See paragraph 2.10]

4.8 After searching an unattended vehicle, or anything in or on it, an officer must leave a notice in it (or on it, if things on it have been searched without opening it) recording the fact that it has been searched.

4.9 The notice must include the name of the police station to which the officer concerned is attached and state where a copy of the record of the search may be obtained and how (if applicable) an electronic copy may be accessed and where any application for compensation should be directed.

4.10 The vehicle must if practicable be left secure.

4.10A Not used.

4.10B Not used.

4.6.6.2

KEYNOTE

Once again, Code A is mirrored by the requirements of s. 3 of the Police and Criminal Evidence Act 1984.

The Police and Criminal Evidence Act 1984, s. 3 states:

(6) The record of a search of a person or a vehicle—
  (a) shall state—
    (i) the object of the search;
    (ii) the grounds for making it;
    (iii) the date and time when it was made;
    (iv) the place where it was made;
    (v) except in the case of a search of an unattended vehicle, the ethnic origins of the person searched or the person in charge of the vehicle searched (as the case may be); and
  (b) shall identify the constable who carried out the search.
(6A) The requirement in subsection (6)(a)(v) above, for a record to state a person's ethnic origins is a requirement to state –
  (a) the ethnic origins of the person as described by the person, and
  (b) if different, the ethnic origins of the person as perceived by the constable.

Officers should record the self-defined ethnicity of every person stopped according to the categories used in the 2001 census question listed in Annex B. The person should be asked to select one of the five main categories representing broad ethnic groups and then a more specific cultural background from within this group. The ethnic classification should be coded for recording purposes using the coding system in Annex B. An additional 'Not stated' box is available but should not be offered to respondents explicitly. Officers should be aware and explain to members of the public, especially where concerns are raised, that this information is required to obtain a true picture of stop and search activity and to help improve ethnic monitoring, tackle discriminatory practice, and promote effective use of the powers. If the person gives what appears to the officer to be an 'incorrect' answer (e.g. a person who appears to be white states that he/she is black), the officer should record the response that has been given and then record his/her own perception of the ethnic background by using the PNC classification system. If the 'Not stated' category is used the reason for this must be recorded on the form.

It is important for monitoring purposes to specify if the authority for exercising a stop and search power was given under s. 60 of the Criminal Justice and Public Order Act 1994.

Where a person is lawfully detained for the purpose of a search, but no search in the event takes place, the detention will not thereby have been rendered unlawful.

The requirements of s. 3 will apply to the searches of vehicles, vessels, aircraft and hovercraft (s. 3(10)).

It has been held that a failure to make a record of a search does not thereby render the search unlawful (*Basher* v *DPP* [1993] COD 372). However, it is not only the lawfulness of a search that is of concern to police officers and the general principles set out in Code A should be borne in mind at all times.

Where a search record has been made, the person searched, the owner or the person who was in charge of any vehicle that was searched, will be entitled to a copy of the record if he/she requests one within three months.

In situations where it is not practicable to provide a written copy of the record or immediate access to an electronic copy of the record or a receipt of the search at the time (**see para. 4.2A**), the officer should consider providing the person with details of the station at which the person may attend for a record. A receipt may take the form of a simple business card which includes sufficient information to locate the record should the person ask for the copy, e.g. the date and place of the search, a reference number or the name of the officer who carried out the search (unless para. 4.4 applies).

Where a stop and search is conducted by more than one officer the identity of all the officers engaged in the search must be recorded on the record. Nothing prevents an officer who is present but not directly involved in searching from completing the record during the course of the encounter.

In the case of unattended vehicles, s. 2 of the Police and Criminal Evidence Act 1984 states:

(6) On completing a search of an unattended vehicle or anything in or on such a vehicle in the exercise of any such power as is mentioned in subsection (2) above a constable shall leave a notice—
  (a) stating that he has searched it;
  (b) giving the name of the police station to which he is attached;
  (c) stating that an application for compensation for any damage caused by the search may be made to that police station; and
  (d) stating the effect of section 3(8) below.
(7) The constable shall leave the notice inside the vehicle unless it is not reasonably practicable to do so without damaging the vehicle.

Recording of encounters not governed by Statutory Powers

4.11   Not used.
4.12   There is no national requirement for an officer who requests a person in a public place to account for themselves, i.e. their actions, behaviour, presence in an area or possession of anything, to make a record of the encounter or to give the person a receipt.
4.12A   Not used.
4.13   Not used.
4.14   Not used.
4.15   Not used.
4.16   Not used.
4.17   Not used.
4.18   Not used.
4.19   Not used.
4.20   Not used.

4.6.6.3   **KEYNOTE**

Where there are concerns which make it necessary to monitor any local disproportionality, forces have discretion to direct officers to record the self-defined ethnicity of persons they request to account for themselves in a public place or who they detain with a view to searching but do not search. Guidance should be provided locally and efforts made to minimise the bureaucracy involved. Records should be closely monitored and supervised in line with paras 5.1 to 5.4 and forces can suspend or reinstate recording of these encounters as appropriate.

A person who is asked to account for him/herself should, if he/she requests, be given information about how to report his/her dissatisfaction about how he/she has been treated.

5 Monitoring and supervising the use of stop and search powers

5.1 Supervising officers must monitor the use of stop and search powers and should consider in particular whether there is any evidence that they are being exercised on the basis of stereo-typed images or inappropriate generalisations. Supervising officers should satisfy themselves that the practice of officers under their supervision in stopping, searching and recording is fully in accordance with this Code. Supervisors must also examine whether the records reveal any trends or patterns which give cause for concern, and if so take appropriate action to address this.

5.2 Senior officers with area or force-wide responsibilities must also monitor the broader use of stop and search powers and, where necessary, take action at the relevant level.

5.3 Supervision and monitoring must be supported by the compilation of comprehensive statistical records of stops and searches at force, area and local level. Any apparently disproportionate use of the powers by particular officers or groups of officers or in relation to specific sections of the community should be identified and investigated.

5.4 In order to promote public confidence in the use of the powers, forces in consultation with police and crime commissioners must make arrangements for the records to be scrutinised by representatives of the community, and to explain the use of the powers at a local level.

KEYNOTE

Arrangements for public scrutiny of records should take account of the right to confidentiality of those stopped and searched. Anonymised forms and/or statistics generated from records should be the focus of the examinations by members of the public.

4.7 Entry, Search and Seizure

PACE Code of Practice for Searches of Premises by Police Officers and the Seizure of Property found by Police Officers on Persons or Premises (Code B)

A thick grey line down the margin denotes text that is an extract of the PACE Code itself (i.e. the actual wording of the legislation). This material is examinable for both Sergeants and Inspectors.

4.7.1 Introduction

The main police powers dealing with entry to premises, searching them and seizing evidence from them, are contained within the Police and Criminal Evidence Act 1984; Code B of the Codes of Practice provides detailed guidance in relation to these features.

Whilst PACE and Code B are predominant when considering entry with or without a warrant, there are many other statutes that allow such processes to take place. However, only one common law power of entry without warrant exists—to deal with a breach of the peace (see chapter 4.11). This power is preserved by s. 17(6) of the Police and Criminal Evidence Act 1984 and only applies where officers have a genuine and reasonable belief that a breach of the peace is happening or is about to happen in the immediate future (*McLeod* v *Commissioner of Police for the Metropolis* [1994] 4 All ER 553).

On a general point, it is worth remembering that where police officers enter premises *lawfully* (including where they are there by invitation), they are on the premises for *all lawful purposes* (see *Foster* v *Attard* [1986] Crim LR 627). This means that they can carry out any lawful functions while on the premises, even if that was not the original purpose for entry. For instance, if officers entered under a lawful power provided by the Misuse of Drugs Act 1971, they may carry out other lawful functions such as enforcing the provisions of the Gaming Act 1968. If officers are invited onto premises by someone entitled to do so, they are lawfully there unless and until that invitation is withdrawn. Once the invitation is withdrawn, the officers will become trespassers unless they have a power to be there, and the person may remove them by force (*Robson* v *Hallett* [1967] 2 QB 939). If that invitation is terminated, the person needs to communicate that clearly to the officer; it has been held that merely telling officers to 'fuck off' is not necessarily sufficient (*Snook* v *Mannion* [1982] RTR 321 (see *Road Policing*, chapter 3.5).

The above issues are of broad significance to police officers but the principal features of the Police and Criminal Evidence Act 1984 and Code B remain the most important for the purposes of operational policing and that is the central focus of this chapter.

4.7.2

PACE Code of Practice for Searches of Premises by Police Officers and the Seizure of Property found by Police Officers on Persons or Premises (Code B)

This Code applies to applications for warrants made after midnight 6 March 2011 and to searches and seizures taking place after midnight on 27 October 2013.

1 Introduction

1.1 This Code of Practice deals with police powers to:
- search premises
- seize and retain property found on premises and persons

1.1A These powers may be used to find:
- property and material relating to a crime
- wanted persons
- children who abscond from local authority accommodation where they have been remanded or committed by a court

1.2 A justice of the peace may issue a search warrant granting powers of entry, search and seizure, e.g. warrants to search for stolen property, drugs, firearms and evidence of serious offences. Police also have powers without a search warrant. The main ones provided by the Police and Criminal Evidence Act 1984 (PACE) include powers to search premises:
- to make an arrest
- after an arrest

1.3 The right to privacy and respect for personal property are key principles of the Human Rights Act 1998. Powers of entry, search and seizure should be fully and clearly justified before use because they may significantly interfere with the occupier's privacy. Officers should consider if the necessary objectives can be met by less intrusive means.

1.3A Powers to search and seize must be used fairly, responsibly, with respect for people who occupy premises being searched or are in charge of property being seized and without unlawful discrimination. Under the Equality Act 2010, section 149, when police officers are carrying out their functions, they also have a duty to have due regard to the need to eliminate unlawful discrimination, harassment and victimisation, to advance equality of opportunity between people who share a relevant protected characteristic and people who do not share it, and to take steps to foster good relations.

1.4 In all cases, police should therefore:
- exercise their powers courteously and with respect for persons and property
- only use reasonable force when this is considered necessary and proportionate to the circumstances.

1.5 If the provisions of PACE and this Code are not observed, evidence obtained from a search may be open to question.

KEYNOTE

In paragraph 1.3A, 'relevant protected characteristic' includes: age, disability, gender reassignment, pregnancy and maternity, race, religion/belief, sex and sexual orientation.

4.7.3

2 General

2.1 This Code must be readily available at all police stations for consultation by:
- police officers
- police staff
- detained persons
- members of the public

2.2 The *Notes for Guidance* (incorporated within Keynotes of this Manual) are not provisions of this Code.

2.3 This Code applies to searches of premises:

(a) by police for the purposes of an investigation into an alleged offence, with the occupier's consent, other than:

- routine scene of crime searches;
- calls to a fire or burglary made by or on behalf of an occupier or searches following the activation of fire or burglar alarms or discovery of insecure premises;
- searches when *paragraph 5.4* applies;
- bomb threat calls;

(b) under powers conferred on police officers by PACE, sections 17, 18 and 32;

(c) undertaken in pursuance of search warrants issued to and executed by constables in accordance with PACE, sections 15 and 16;

(d) subject to *paragraph 2.6*, under any other power given to police to enter premises with or without a search warrant for any purpose connected with the investigation into an alleged or suspected offence.

For the purposes of this Code, 'premises' as defined in PACE, section 23, includes any place, vehicle, vessel, aircraft, hovercraft, tent or movable structure and any offshore installation as defined in the Mineral Workings (Offshore Installations) Act 1971, section 1.

2.4 A person who has not been arrested but is searched during a search of premises should be searched in accordance with Code A.

2.5 This Code does not apply to the exercise of a statutory power to enter premises or to inspect goods, equipment or procedures if the exercise of that power is not dependent on the existence of grounds for suspecting that an offence may have been committed and the person exercising the power has no reasonable grounds for such suspicion.

2.6 This Code does not affect any directions or requirements of a search warrant, order or other power to search and seize lawfully exercised in England or Wales that any item or evidence seized under that warrant, order or power be handed over to a police force, court, tribunal, or other authority outside England or Wales. For example, warrants and orders issued in Scotland or Northern Ireland, and search warrants and powers provided for in sections 14 to 17 of the Crime (International Co-operation) Act 2003.

2.7 When this Code requires the prior authority or agreement of an officer of at least inspector or superintendent rank, that authority may be given by a sergeant or chief inspector authorised to perform the functions of the higher rank under PACE, section 107.

2.8 Written records required under this Code not made in the search record shall, unless otherwise specified, be made:

- in the recording officer's pocket book ('pocket book' includes any official report book issued to police officers) or
- on forms provided for the purpose.

2.9 Nothing in this Code requires the identity of officers, or anyone accompanying them during a search of premises, to be recorded or disclosed:

(a) in the case of enquiries linked to the investigation of terrorism; or

(b) if officers reasonably believe recording or disclosing their names might put them in danger.

In these cases officers should use warrant or other identification numbers and the name of their police station. Police staff should use any identification number provided to them by the police force.

2.10 The 'officer in charge of the search' means the officer assigned specific duties and responsibilities under this Code. Whenever there is a search of premises to which this Code applies one officer must act as the officer in charge of the search.

2.11 In this Code:

(a) 'designated person' means a person other than a police officer, designated under the Police Reform Act 2002, Part 4 who has specified powers and duties of police officers conferred or imposed on them;

(b) any reference to a police officer includes a designated person acting in the exercise or performance of the powers and duties conferred or imposed on them by their designation;

(c) a person authorised to accompany police officers or designated persons in the execution of a warrant has the same powers as a constable in the execution of the warrant and the search and seizure of anything related to the warrant. These powers must be exercised in the company and under the supervision of a police officer.

2.12 If a power conferred on a designated person:

(a) allows reasonable force to be used when exercised by a police officer, a designated person exercising that power has the same entitlement to use force;

(b) includes power to use force to enter any premises, that power is not exercisable by that designated person except:

(i) in the company and under the supervision of a police officer; or

(ii) for the purpose of:
- saving life or limb; or
- preventing serious damage to property.

2.13 Designated persons must have regard to any relevant provisions of the Codes of Practice.

4.7.3.1 **KEYNOTE**

Application for Warrant—s. 15 PACE

The Police and Criminal Evidence Act 1984, s. 15 states:

(1) This section and section 16 below have effect in relation to the issue to constables under any enactment, including an enactment contained in an Act passed after this Act, of warrants to enter and search premises; and an entry on or search of premises under a warrant is unlawful unless it complies with this section and section 16 below.

(2) Where a constable applies for any such warrant, it shall be his duty—

(a) to state—

(i) the ground on which he makes the application;

(ii) the enactment under which the warrant would be issued; and

(iii) if the application is for a warrant authorising entry and search on more than one occasion, the ground on which he applies for such a warrant, and whether he seeks a warrant authorising an unlimited number of entries, or (if not) the maximum number of entries desired;

(b) to specify the matters set out in subsection (2A) below; and

(c) to identify, so far as is practicable, the articles or persons to be sought.

(2A) The matters which must be specified pursuant to subsection (2)(b) above are—

(a) if the application relates to one or more sets of premises specified in the application each set of premises which it is desired to enter and search; and

(b) if the application relates to any premises occupied or controlled by a person specified in the application—

(i) as many sets of premises which it is desired to enter and search as it is reasonably practicable to specify;

(ii) the person who is in occupation or control of those premises and any others which it is desired to enter and search;

(iii) why it is necessary to search more premises than those specified under sub-paragraph (i); and

(iv) why it is not reasonably practicable to specify all the premises which it is desired to enter and search.

(3) An application for such a warrant shall be made ex parte and supported by information in writing.

(4) The constable shall answer on oath any question that the justice of the peace or judge hearing the application asks him.

(5) A warrant shall authorise an entry on one occasion only unless it specifies that it authorises multiple entries.

(5A) If it specifies that it authorises multiple entries, it must also specify whether the number of entries authorised is unlimited, or limited to a specified maximum.

(6) A warrant—

(a) shall specify—

(i) the name of the person who applies for it;

(ii) the date on which it is issued;

(iii) the enactment under which it is issued;

(iv) each set of premises to be searched, or (in the case of an all premises warrant) the person who is in occupation or control of premises to be searched, together with any premises under his occupation or control which can be specified and which are to be searched; and

(b) shall identify, so far as is practicable, the articles or persons to be sought.

(7) Two copies shall be made of a warrant (see section 8(1A)(a) above) which specifies only one set of premises and does not authorise multiple entries; and as many copies as are reasonably required may be made of any other kind of warrant.

(8) The copies shall be clearly certified as copies.

KEYNOTE

Execution of a Warrant—s. 16 PACE

The Police and Criminal Evidence Act 1984, s. 16 states:

(1) A warrant to enter and search premises may be executed by any constable.

(2) Such a warrant may authorise persons to accompany any constable who is executing it.

(2A) A person so authorised has the same powers as the constable whom he accompanies in respect of—

(a) the execution of the warrant, and

(b) the seizure of anything to which the warrant relates.

(2B) But he may exercise those powers only in the company, and under the supervision, of a constable.

(3) Entry and search under a warrant must be within three months from the date of its issue.

(3A) If the warrant is an all premises warrant, no premises which are not specified in it may be entered or searched unless a police officer of at least the rank of inspector has in writing authorised them to be entered.

(3B) No premises may be entered or searched for the second or any subsequent time under a warrant which authorises multiple entries unless a police officer of at least the rank of inspector has in writing authorised that entry to those premises.

(4) Entry and search under a warrant must be at a reasonable hour unless it appears to the constable executing it that the purpose of a search may be frustrated on an entry at a reasonable hour.

(5) Where the occupier of premises which are to be entered and searched is present at the time when a constable seeks to execute a warrant to enter and search them, the constable—

(a) shall identify himself to the occupier and, if not in uniform, shall produce to him documentary evidence that he is a constable;

(b) shall produce the warrant to him; and

(c) shall supply him with a copy of it.

(6) Where—

(a) the occupier of such premises is not present at the time when a constable seeks to execute such a warrant; but

(b) some other person who appears to the constable to be in charge of the premises is present, Subsection (5) above shall have effect as if any reference to the occupier were a reference to that other person.

(7) If there is no person present who appears to the constable to be in charge of the premises, he shall leave a copy of the warrant in a prominent place on the premises.

(8) A search under a warrant may only be a search to the extent required for the purpose for which the warrant was issued.

(9) A constable executing the warrant shall make an endorsement on it stating—

(a) whether the articles or persons sought were found; and

(b) whether any articles were seized, other than articles which were sought; and

unless the warrant is a warrant specifying one set of premises only, he shall do so separately in respect of each set of premises entered and searched, which he shall in each case state in the endorsement.

(10) A warrant shall be returned to the appropriate person mentioned in subsection (10A) below—

(a) when it has been executed; or

(b) in the case of a specific premises warrant which has not been executed, or an all premises warrant, or any warrant authorising multiple entries, upon the expiry of the period of three months referred to in subsection (3) above or sooner.

(10A) The appropriate person is—

(a) if the warrant was issued by a justice of the peace, the designated officer for the local justice area in which the justice was acting when he issued the warrant;

(b) if it was issued by a judge, the appropriate officer of the court from which he issued it.

(11) A warrant which is returned under subsection (10) above shall be retained for 12 months from its return—

(a) by the designated officer for the local justice area, if it was returned under paragraph (i) of that subsection; and

(b) by the appropriate officer, if it was returned under paragraph (ii).

(12) If during the period for which a warrant is to be retained the occupier of premises to which it relates asks to inspect it, he shall be allowed to do so.

KEYNOTE

General Points

If an application for a warrant is refused, no further application can be made unless it is supported by additional grounds.

'Premises' include any place, and in particular, (a) any vehicle, vessel, aircraft or hovercraft; (b) any offshore installation; (c) any renewable energy installation; (d) any tent or moveable structure (s. 23 of the 1984 Act).

The details of the extent of the proposed search should be made clear in the application and the officer swearing the warrant out must be prepared to answer *any* questions put to him/her on oath under s. 15(4). Many courts will go into background detail about the particular premises, or part of the premises, and who is likely to be present on the premises at the time the warrant is executed (e.g. children).

4.7.3.4

KEYNOTE

Examples

Sections 15 and 16 of the 1984 Act apply to all search warrants issued to and executed by constables under any enactment, e.g. search warrants issued by:

(a) a justice of the peace under:
- Theft Act 1968, s. 26—stolen property;
- Misuse of Drugs Act 1971, s. 23—controlled drugs;
- PACE, s. 8—evidence of an indictable offence;
- Terrorism Act 2000, sch. 5, para. 1;
- Terrorism Prevention and Investigation Measures Act 2011, sch. 5, para. 8(2)(b) search of premises for compliance purposes.

(b) a Circuit judge under:
- PACE, sch. 1;
- Terrorism Act 2000, sch. 5, para. 11.

Examples of the other powers in para. 2.3(d) include:

(a) Road Traffic Act 1988, s. 6E(1) giving police power to enter premises under s. 6E(1) to:
- require a person to provide a specimen of breath; or
- arrest a person following
  — a positive breath test;
  — failure to provide a specimen of breath;

(b) Transport and Works Act 1992, s. 30(4) giving police powers to enter premises mirroring the powers in (a) in relation to specified persons working on transport systems to which the Act applies;

(c) Criminal Justice Act 1988, s. 139B giving police power to enter and search school premises for offensive weapons, bladed or pointed articles;

(d) Terrorism Act 2000, sch. 5, paras 3 and 15 empowering a superintendent in urgent cases to give written authority for police to enter and search premises for the purposes of a terrorist investigation;

(e) Explosives Act 1875, s. 73(b) empowering a superintendent to give written authority for police to enter premises, examine and search them for explosives;

(f) search warrants and production orders or the equivalent issued in Scotland or Northern Ireland endorsed under the Summary Jurisdiction (Process) Act 1881 or the Petty Sessions (Ireland) Act 1851 respectively for execution in England and Wales.

The Criminal Justice Act 1988, s. 139B provides that a constable who has reasonable grounds for suspecting that an offence under the Criminal Justice Act 1988, s. 139A or 139AA has been or is being committed may enter school premises and search the premises and any persons on the premises for any bladed or pointed article or offensive weapon. Persons may be searched under a warrant issued under the Misuse of Drugs Act 1971, s. 23(3) to search premises for drugs or documents only if the warrant specifically authorises the search of persons on the premises. Powers to search premises under certain terrorism provisions also authorise the search of persons on the premises, for example, under paragraphs 1, 2, 11 and 15 of Schedule 5 to the Terrorism Act 2000 and section 52 of the Anti-terrorism, Crime and Security Act 2001.

The Immigration Act 1971, part III and sch. 2 gives immigration officers powers to enter and search premises, seize and retain property, with and without a search warrant. These are similar to the powers available to police under search warrants issued by a justice of the peace and without a warrant under ss. 17, 18, 19 and 32 of the 1984 Act except they only apply to specified offences under the Immigration Act 1971 and immigration control powers. For certain types of investigations and enquiries these powers avoid the need for the

Immigration Service to rely on police officers becoming directly involved. When exercising these powers, immigration officers are required by the Immigration and Asylum Act 1999, s. 145 to have regard to this Code's corresponding provisions. When immigration officers are dealing with persons or property at police stations, police officers should give appropriate assistance to help them discharge their specific duties and responsibilities.

The purpose of para. 2.9(b) of Code B is to protect those involved in serious organised crime investigations or arrests of particularly violent suspects when there is reliable information that those arrested or their associates may threaten or cause harm to the officers or anyone accompanying them during a search of premises. In cases of doubt, an officer of inspector rank or above should be consulted.

4.7.3.5 KEYNOTE

Officer in Charge of the Search

For the purposes of para. 2.10, the officer in charge of the search should normally be the most senior officer present. Some exceptions are:

(a) a supervising officer who attends or assists at the scene of a premises search may appoint an officer of lower rank as officer in charge of the search if that officer is:
- more conversant with the facts;
- a more appropriate officer to be in charge of the search;

(b) when all officers in a premises search are the same rank. The supervising officer if available must make sure one of them is appointed officer in charge of the search, otherwise the officers themselves must nominate one of their number as the officer in charge;

(c) a senior officer assisting in a specialist role. This officer need not be regarded as having a general supervisory role over the conduct of the search or be appointed or expected to act as the officer in charge of the search.

Except in (c), nothing in this keynote diminishes the role and responsibilities of a supervisory officer who is present at the search or knows of a search taking place.

An officer of the rank of inspector or above may direct a designated investigating officer not to wear a uniform for the purposes of a specific operation.

4.7.3.6 KEYNOTE

Exclusion of Evidence

If the provisions of these sections are not fully complied with, any entry and search made under a warrant will be unlawful. Although the officers executing the warrant may have some protection from personal liability where there has been a defect in the *procedure* by which the warrant was issued, failure to follow the requirements of ss. 15 and 16 may result in the exclusion of any evidence obtained under the warrant. Therefore, where officers failed to provide the occupier of the searched premises with a copy of the warrant (under s. 16(5)(c)), they were obliged to return the property seized during the search (*R* v *Chief Constable of Lancashire, ex parte Parker* [1993] QB 577).

If a warrant itself is invalid for some reason, any entry and subsequent seizure made under it are unlawful (*R* v *Central Criminal Court and British Railways Board, ex parte AJD Holdings Ltd* [1992] Crim LR 669). After a warrant has been executed, or if it has not been used within three months (or sooner) from its date of issue, it must be returned to the designated officer for the local justice area in which the justice of the peace issued the warrant, or where it was issued by a judge to the appropriate officer of the court from which it was issued (s. 16(10) and (10A)).

Very minor departures from the letter of the warrant, however, will not render any search unlawful (see *Attorney-General of Jamaica* v *Williams* [1998] AC 351).

KEYNOTE

Search Warrants for Indictable Offences—s. 8 PACE

The Police and Criminal Evidence Act 1984, s. 8 states:

(1) If on an application made by a constable a justice of the peace is satisfied that there are reasonable grounds for believing—
   (a) that an indictable offence has been committed; and
   (b) that there is material on premises mentioned in subsection (1A) below which is likely to be of substantial value (whether by itself or together with other material) to the investigation of the offence; and
   (c) that the material is likely to be relevant evidence; and
   (d) that it does not consist of or include items subject to legal privilege, excluded material or special procedure material; and
   (e) that any of the conditions specified in subsection (3) below applies in relation to each set of premises specified in the application

   he may issue a warrant authorising a constable to enter and search the premises.

(1A) The premises referred to in subsection (1)(b) above are—
   (a) one or more sets of premises specified in the application (in which case the application is for a 'specific premises warrant'); or
   (b) any premises occupied or controlled by a person specified in the application, including such sets of premises as are so specified (in which case the application is for an 'all premises warrant').

(1B) If the application is for an all premises warrant, the justice of the peace must also be satisfied—
   (a) that because of the particulars of the offence referred to in paragraph (a) of subsection (1) above, there are reasonable grounds for believing that it is necessary to search premises occupied or controlled by the person in question which are not specified in the application in order to find the material referred to in paragraph (b) of that subsection; and
   (b) that it is not reasonably practicable to specify in the application all the premises which he occupies or controls and which might need to be searched.

(1C) The warrant may authorise entry to and search of premises on more than one occasion if, on the application, the justice of the peace is satisfied that it is necessary to authorise multiple entries in order to achieve the purpose for which he issues the warrant.

(1D) If it authorises multiple entries, the number of entries authorised may be unlimited, or limited to a maximum.

(2) A constable may seize and retain anything for which a search has been authorised under subsection (1) above.

(3) The conditions mentioned in subsection (1)(e) above are—
   (a) that it is not practicable to communicate with any person entitled to grant entry to the premises;
   (b) that it is practicable to communicate with a person entitled to grant entry to the premises but it is not practicable to communicate with any person entitled to grant access to the evidence;
   (c) that entry to the premises will not be granted unless a warrant is produced;
   (d) that the purpose of a search may be frustrated or seriously prejudiced unless a constable arriving at the premises can secure immediate entry to them.

(4) In this Act 'relevant evidence', in relation to an offence, means anything that would be admissible in evidence at a trial for the offence.

(5) The power to issue a warrant conferred by this section is in addition to any such power otherwise conferred.

This section provides that a constable can apply for two different types of search warrant: a 'specific premises warrant' for the search of one set of premises; and an 'all premises warrant' when it is necessary to search all premises occupied or controlled by an individual, but where it is not reasonably practicable to specify all such premises at the time of applying for the warrant. The warrant allows access to all premises occupied or controlled by that person, both those which are specified on the application, and those which are not. Note that s. 8(1C) and (1D) provide that a warrant (either an 'all premises warrant' or a 'specific premises warrant') may authorise access on more than one occasion, and if multiple entries are authorised these may be unlimited or limited to a maximum.

The officer applying for a warrant under s. 8 must have reasonable grounds for believing that material which is *likely to be of substantial value to the investigation of the offence* is on the premises specified. Therefore, when executing such a warrant, the officer must be able to show that any material seized thereunder fell within that description (*R* v *Chief Constable of the Warwickshire Constabulary, ex parte Fitzpatrick* [1999] 1 WLR 564). Possession of a warrant under s. 8 does not authorise police officers to seize all material found on the relevant premises to be taken away and 'sifted' somewhere else (*R* v *Chesterfield Justices, ex parte Bramley* [2000] QB 576) (see s. 50 of the Criminal Justice and Police Act 2001 for the power to 'seize and sift'). This means that material which is solely of value for *intelligence* purposes may not be seized under a s. 8 warrant.

The power to apply for and execute a warrant under s. 8 and to carry out the actions under s. 8(2) are among those powers that can be conferred on a person designated as an Investigating Officer under sch. 4 to the Police Reform Act 2002.

The conditions set out under s. 8(1)(e) are part of the *application* process, not part of the general execution process (which is set out at s. 16 above). Therefore the officer swearing out a s. 8 warrant will have to satisfy the court that any of those conditions apply.

4.7.3.8 KEYNOTE

Legally Privileged Material

Material which falls within the definition in s. 10 of the 1984 Act is subject to legal privilege which means that it cannot be searched for or seized.

The Police and Criminal Evidence Act 1984, s. 10 states:

(1) Subject to subsection (2) below, in this Act 'items subject to legal privilege' means—
 (a) communications between a professional legal adviser and his client or any person representing his client made in connection with the giving of legal advice to the client;
 (b) communications between a professional legal adviser and his client or any person representing his client or between such an adviser or his client or any such representative and any other person made in connection with or in contemplation of legal proceedings and for the purposes of such proceedings; and
 (c) items enclosed with or referred to in such communications and made—
  (i) in connection with the giving of legal advice; or
  (ii) in connection with or in contemplation of legal proceedings and for the purposes of such proceedings,

when they are in the possession of a person who is entitled to possession of them.

Items held with the intention of furthering a criminal purpose are not subject to this privilege (s. 10(2)). When making an application for a warrant to search for and seize such material the procedure under sch. 1 should be used. Occasions where this will happen are very rare and would include instances where a solicitor's firm is the subject of a criminal investigation (see *R* v *Leeds Crown Court, ex parte Switalski* [1991] Crim LR 559). However, it may be possible during a search to ascertain which material is subject to legal privilege and which might be lawfully seized under the warrant being executed. Therefore, although a warrant cannot authorise a search for legally privileged material, the fact that such material is inadvertently seized in the course of a search authorised by a proper warrant does not render the search unlawful (*R* v *HM Customs & Excise, ex parte Popely* [2000] Crim LR 388).

4.7.3.9 KEYNOTE

Excluded Material

Access to 'excluded material' can generally only be gained by applying to a judge for a production order under the procedure set out in s. 9 of, and sch. 1 to, the 1984 Act and PACE Code B. That strict statutory procedure also applies to the application for and execution of warrants by Investigating Officers designated under sch. 4 to the Police Reform Act 2002.

The Police and Criminal Evidence Act 1984, s. 11 states:

(1) Subject to the following provisions of this section, in this Act 'excluded material' means—
 (a) personal records which a person has acquired or created in the course of any trade, business, profession or other occupation or for the purposes of any paid or unpaid office and which he holds in confidence;
 (b) human tissue or tissue fluid which has been taken for the purposes of diagnosis or medical treatment and which a person holds in confidence;
 (c) journalistic material which a person holds in confidence and which consists—
  (i) of documents; or
  (ii) of records other than documents.
(2) A person holds material other than journalistic material in confidence for the purposes of this section if he holds it subject—
 (a) to an express or implied undertaking to hold it in confidence; or

---

4.7.3.10

KEYNOTE

Special Procedure Material

Special procedure material can be gained by applying for a search warrant or a production order under sch. 1 to the 1984 Act.

The Police and Criminal Evidence Act 1984, s. 14 states:

(1) In this Act 'special procedure material' means—

(a) material to which subsection (2) below applies; and

(b) journalistic material, other than excluded material.

(2) Subject to the following provisions of this section, this subsection applies to material, other than items subject to legal privilege and excluded material, in the possession of a person who—

(a) acquired or created it in the course of any trade, business, profession or other occupation or for the purpose of any paid or unpaid office; and

(b) holds it subject—

(i) to an express or implied undertaking to hold it in confidence; or

(ii) to a restriction or obligation such as is mentioned in section 11(2)(b) above.

For items subject to 'legal privilege' and 'excluded material', see para. 4.7.3.8.

The person believed to be in possession of the material must have come by it under the circumstances set out at s. 14(2)(a) *and* must hold it under the undertakings or obligations set out at s. 14(2)(b).

4.7.4

3 Search warrants and production orders

(a) Before making an application

3.1 When information appears to justify an application, the officer must take reasonable steps to check the information is accurate, recent and not provided maliciously or irresponsibly. An application may not be made on the basis of information from an anonymous source if corroboration has not been sought.

3.2 The officer shall ascertain as specifically as possible the nature of the articles concerned and their location.

3.3 The officer shall make reasonable enquiries to:

(i) establish if:

- anything is known about the likely occupier of the premises and the nature of the premises themselves;

- the premises have been searched previously and how recently;

(ii) obtain any other relevant information.

3.4 An application:

    (a)   to a justice of the peace for a search warrant or to a Circuit judge for a search warrant or production order under PACE, Schedule 1 must be supported by a signed written authority from an officer of inspector rank or above:

Note: If the case is an urgent application to a justice of the peace and an inspector or above is not readily available, the next most senior officer on duty can give the written authority.

    (b)   to a circuit judge under the Terrorism Act 2000, Schedule 5 for

- a production order;
- search warrant; or
- an order requiring an explanation of material seized or produced under such a warrant or production order

        must be supported by a signed written authority from an officer of superintendent rank or above.

3.5   Except in a case of urgency, if there is reason to believe a search might have an adverse effect on relations between the police and the community, the officer in charge shall consult the local police/community liaison officer:

- before the search; or
- in urgent cases, as soon as practicable after the search.

(b) Making an application

3.6   A search warrant application must be supported in writing, specifying:

    (a)   the enactment under which the application is made;

    (b)

        (i)   whether the warrant is to authorise entry and search of:

- one set of premises; or
- if the application is under PACE section 8, or Schedule 1, paragraph 12, more than one set of specified premises or all premises occupied or controlled by a specified person; and

        (ii) the premises to be searched;

    (c)   the object of the search;

    (d)   the grounds for the application, including, when the purpose of the proposed search is to find evidence of an alleged offence, an indication of how the evidence relates to the investigation;

    (da) where the application is under PACE section 8, or Schedule 1, paragraph 12 for a single warrant to enter and search:

        (i)   more than one set of specified premises, the officer must specify each set of premises which it is desired to enter and search

        (ii) all premises occupied or controlled by a specified person, the officer must specify:

- as many sets of premises which it is desired to enter and search as it is reasonably practicable to specify;
- the person who is in occupation or control of those premises and any others which it is desired to search;
- why it is necessary to search more premises than those which can be specified;
- why it is not reasonably practicable to specify all the premises which it is desired to enter and search;

    (db) whether an application under PACE section 8 is for a warrant authorising entry and search on more than one occasion, and if so, the officer must state the grounds for this and whether the desired number of entries authorised is unlimited or a specified maximum;

    (e)   there are no reasonable grounds to believe the material to be sought, when making application to a:

        (i)   justice of the peace or a Circuit judge consists of or includes items subject to legal privilege;

        (ii) justice of the peace, consists of or includes excluded material or special procedure material;

Note: this does not affect the additional powers of seizure in the Criminal Justice and Police Act 2001, Part 2 covered in paragraph 7.7;

        (f) if applicable, a request for the warrant to authorise a person or persons to accompany the officer who executes the warrant.

3.7   A search warrant application under PACE, Schedule 1, paragraph 12(a), shall if appropriate indicate why it is believed service of notice of an application for a production order may seriously prejudice the investigation. Applications for search warrants under the Terrorism Act 2000, Schedule 5, paragraph 11 must indicate why a production order would not be appropriate.

3.8   If a search warrant application is refused, a further application may not be made for those premises unless supported by additional grounds.

4.7.4.1   KEYNOTE

The identity of an informant need not be disclosed when making an application, but the officer should be prepared to answer any questions the magistrate or judge may have about:

- the accuracy of previous information from that source
- any other related matters.

Under s. 16(2) of the 1984 Act, a search warrant may authorise persons other than police officers to accompany the constable who executes the warrant. This includes, for example, any suitably qualified or skilled person or an expert in a particular field whose presence is needed to help accurately identify the material sought or to advise where certain evidence is most likely to be found and how it should be dealt with. It does not give them any right to force entry, but it gives them the right to be on the premises during the search and to search for or seize property without the occupier's permission.

    The information supporting a search warrant application should be as specific as possible, particularly in relation to the articles or persons being sought and where in the premises it is suspected they may be found. The meaning of 'items subject to legal privilege', 'excluded material' and 'special procedure material' are defined by ss. 10, 11 and 14 of the 1984 Act respectively.

4.7.5   4 Entry without warrant—particular powers

(a) Making an arrest etc

4.1   The conditions under which an officer may enter and search premises without a warrant are set out in PACE, section 17. It should be noted that this section does not create or confer any powers of arrest.

4.7.5.1   KEYNOTE

Power of Entry—s.17 PACE

The Police and Criminal Evidence Act 1984, s. 17 states:

(1) Subject to the following provisions of this section, and without prejudice to any other enactment, a constable may enter and search any premises for the purpose—

  (a) of executing—

    (i) a warrant of arrest issued in connection with or arising out of criminal proceedings; or

    (ii) a warrant of commitment issued under section 76 of the Magistrates' Courts Act 1980;

  (b) of arresting a person for an indictable offence;

(c) of arresting a person for an offence under—

   (i) section 1 (prohibition of uniforms in connection with political objectives) of the Public Order Act 1936;

   (ii) any enactment contained in sections 6 to 8 or 10 of the Criminal Law Act 1977 (offences relating to entering and remaining on property);

   (iii) section 4 of the Public Order Act 1986 (fear or provocation of violence);

   (iiia) section 4 (driving etc when under influence of drink or drugs) or 163 (failure to stop when required to do so by constable in uniform) of the Road Traffic Act 1988;

   (iiib) section 27 of the Transport and Works Act 1992 (which relates to offences involving drink or drugs);

   (iv) section 76 of the Criminal Justice and Public Order Act 1994 (failure to comply with interim possession order);

   (v) any of sections 4, 5, 6(1) and (2), 7 and 8(1) and (2) of the Animal Welfare Act 2006 (offences relating to the prevention of harm to animals);

(ca) of arresting, in pursuance of section 32(1A) of the Children and Young Persons Act 1969, any child or young person who has been remanded or committed to local authority accommodation under section 23(1) of that Act;

(caa) of arresting a person for an offence to which section 61 of the Animal Health Act 1981 applies;

(cb) of recapturing any person who is, or is deemed for any purpose to be, unlawfully at large while liable to be detained—

   (i) in a prison, remand centre, young offender institution or secure training centre, or

   (ii) in pursuance of section 92 of the Powers of Criminal Courts (Sentencing) Act 2000 (dealing with children and young persons guilty of grave crimes), in any other place;

(d) of recapturing any person whatever who is unlawfully at large and whom he is pursuing; or

(e) of saving life or limb or preventing serious damage to property.

(2) Except for the purpose specified in paragraph (e) of subsection (1) above, the powers of entry and search conferred by this section—

   (a) are only exercisable if the constable has reasonable grounds for believing that the person whom he is seeking is on the premises; and

   (b) are limited, in relation to premises consisting of two or more separate dwellings, to powers to enter and search—

      (i) any parts of the premises which the occupiers of any dwelling comprised in the premises use in common with the occupiers of any other such dwelling; and

      (ii) any such dwelling in which the constable has reasonable grounds for believing that the person whom he is seeking may be.

(3) The powers of entry and search conferred by this section are only exercisable for the purposes specified in subsection (1)(c) (ii) or (iv) above by a constable in uniform.

(4) The power of search conferred by this section is only a power to search to the extent that is reasonably required for the purpose for which the power of entry is exercised.

(5) Subject to subsection (6) below, all the rules of common law under which a constable has power to enter premises without a warrant are hereby abolished.

(6) Nothing in subsection (5) above affects any power of entry to deal with or prevent a breach of the peace.

Force may be used in exercising the power of entry where it is necessary to do so. Generally, the officer should first attempt to communicate with the occupier of the premises, explaining by what authority and for what purpose entry is to be made, before making a forcible entry. Clearly though, there will be occasions where such communication is impossible, impracticable or even unnecessary; in those cases there is no need for the officer to enter into such an explanation (*O'Loughlin* v *Chief Constable of Essex* [1998] 1 WLR 374).

In a case where police had been called to an address by an abandoned 999 call, the officers had to move a man away from the front door in order to gain entry under s. 17. The Queen's Bench Divisional Court held that the officers had the power to use reasonable force in order to do so (*Smith (Peter John)* v *DPP* [2001] EWHC Admin 55). The source of the power to use force here is s. 117 of the Police and Criminal Evidence Act 1984.

'Unlawfully at large' does not have a particular statutory meaning and can apply to someone who is subject to an order under the Mental Health Act 1983 or someone who has escaped from custody. The pursuit of the person who is unlawfully at large must be 'fresh', that is, the power will only be available while the officer is actually 'pursuing' the person concerned (*D'Souza* v *DPP* [1992] 1 WLR 1073).

The power of a constable under s. 17(1)(d) to enter and search premises to recapture a person who is unlawfully at large and whom he/she is pursuing extends to entry to retake a mentally ill patient unlawfully at large provided that such a patient is liable to be retaken and returned to hospital and provided that the pursuit of such a person is almost contemporaneous with the entry to the premises, a term which is somewhat wider than 'hot pursuit'.

The officer must have reasonable grounds to *believe* that the person is on the premises in all cases except saving life and limb at s. 17(1)(e). This expression is narrower than 'reasonable cause to suspect' and you must be able to justify that belief before using this power (although see *Kynaston* v *DPP* (1988) 87 Cr App R 200, where the court accepted reasonable cause to *suspect*).

Note the requirement for an officer to be in uniform for the purposes of s. 17(1)(c)(ii) and (iv), and the restrictions on the power of search under s. 17(4) (i.e. that any such search is limited to the extent that is reasonably required for the purpose for which you entered the premises in the first place).

The power to enter and search any premises in the relevant police area for the purpose of saving life or limb or preventing serious damage to property above is among those that can be conferred on a designated person under sch. 4 to the Police Reform Act 2002.

(b) Search of premises where arrest takes place or the arrested person was immediately before arrest

4.2 When a person has been arrested for an indictable offence, a police officer has power under PACE, section 32 to search the premises where the person was arrested or where the person was immediately before being arrested.

4.7.5.2 **KEYNOTE**

Power to Search after Arrest—s. 32 PACE

The Police and Criminal Evidence Act 1984, s. 32 states:

(1) A constable may search an arrested person, in any case where the person to be searched has been arrested at a place other than a police station, if the constable has reasonable grounds for believing that the arrested person may present a danger to himself or others.

(2) Subject to subsections (3) to (5) below, a constable shall also have power in any such case—

    (a) to search the arrested person for anything—

        (i) which he might use to assist him to escape from lawful custody; or

        (ii) which might be evidence relating to an offence; and

    (b) if the offence for which he has been arrested is an indictable offence, to enter and search any premises in which he was when arrested or immediately before he was arrested for evidence relating to the offence.

(3) The power to search conferred by subsection (2) above is only a power to search to the extent that is reasonably required for the purpose of discovering any such thing or any such evidence.

(4) The powers conferred by this section to search a person are not to be construed as authorising a constable to require a person to remove any of his clothing in public other than an outer coat, jacket or gloves but they do authorise a search of a person's mouth.

(5) A constable may not search a person in the exercise of the power conferred by subsection (2)(a) above unless he has reasonable grounds for believing that the person to be searched may have concealed on him anything for which a search is permitted under that paragraph.

The power to search the arrested person under s. 32(1) is a general one relating to safety.

Section 32(2)(a) then goes on to provide a power to search the person in relation to anything that the arrested person might use to escape from lawful custody and anything that 'might be' evidence relating to *an offence*. There are restrictions placed on the extent and circumstances of the search (s. 32(3) and (4)) and the officer must have reasonable grounds to *believe* (as opposed to mere suspicion) that the person may have such things concealed on him/her (s. 32(5)). Nevertheless, this is still a very wide power. The House of Lords have confirmed that the police have a common law power to search for and seize property after a lawful arrest (*R* v *Governor of Pentonville Prison, ex parte Osman* [1990] 1 WLR 277). This decision was confirmed by the House of Lords in *R (On the Application of Rottman)* v *Commissioner of Police of the Metropolis* [2002] UKHL 20. In *Rottman* the House of Lords held that it was a well-established principle of the common law that an arresting officer had the power to search a room in which a person had been arrested (*per Ghani* v *Jones*

[1970] 1 QB 693). This extended power is not limited to purely 'domestic' offences, but also applies to cases involving extradition offences.

Section 32 also provides that a constable shall have the power in such a case to enter and search any premises in which the person was when arrested or immediately before being arrested for an indictable offence (s. 32(2)(b)). The search may be conducted for the purpose of finding evidence relating to the offence for which the person was arrested.

Section 32 also states:

(6) A constable may not search premises in the exercise of the power conferred by subsection (2)(b) above unless he has reasonable grounds for believing that there is evidence for which a search is permitted under that paragraph on the premises.

(7) In so far as the power of search conferred by subsection (2)(b) above relates to premises consisting of two or more separate dwellings, it is limited to a power to search—

(a) any dwelling in which the arrest took place or in which the person arrested was immediately before his arrest; and

(b) any parts of the premises which the occupier of any such dwelling uses in common with the occupiers of any other dwellings comprised in the premises.

(8) A constable searching a person in the exercise of the power conferred by subsection (1) above may seize and retain anything he finds, if he has reasonable grounds for believing that the person searched might use it to cause physical injury to himself or to any other person.

(9) A constable searching a person in the exercise of the power conferred by subsection (2)(a) above may seize and retain anything he finds, other than an item subject to legal privilege, if he has reasonable grounds for believing—

(a) that he might use it to assist him to escape from lawful custody; or

(b) that it is evidence of an offence or has been obtained in consequence of the commission of an offence.

(10) Nothing in this section shall be taken to affect the power conferred by section 43 of the Terrorism Act 2000.

Both 'reasonable grounds' and 'immediately' are questions of fact for a court to determine. It has been held that the power under s. 32(2)(b) is one for use at the time of arrest and should not be used to return to the relevant premises some time after the arrest in the way that s. 18 of the 1984 Act may be used (*R* v *Badham* [1987] Crim LR 202).

Officers exercising their power to enter and search under s. 32 must have a genuine belief (i.e. more than mere suspicion) that there is evidence on the premises; it is not a licence for a general fishing expedition (*R* v *Beckford* [1992] 94 Cr App R 43).

The Divisional Court has refused to allow s. 32 to be used in a situation where the arrested person had not been in the relevant premises (where he did not live) for a period of over two hours preceding his arrest and where there were no reasonable grounds for believing that he presented a danger to himself or others (*Hewitson* v *Chief Constable of Dorset Police* [2003] EWHC 3296 (QB)).

(c) Search of premises occupied or controlled by the arrested person

4.3 The specific powers to search premises which <u>are</u> occupied or controlled by a person arrested for an indictable offence are set out in PACE, section 18. They may not be exercised, except if section 18(5) applies, unless an officer of inspector rank or above has given written authority. That authority should only be given when the authorising officer is satisfied that the premises <u>are</u> occupied or controlled by the arrested person and that the necessary grounds exist. If possible the authorising officer should record the authority on the Notice of Powers and Rights and, subject to *paragraph 2.9*, sign the Notice. The record of the grounds for the search and the nature of the evidence sought as required by section 18(7) of the Act should be made in:

• the custody record if there is one, otherwise

• the officer's pocket book, or

• the search record.

KEYNOTE

Power to Search after Arrest for Indictable Offence—s.18 PACE

The Police and Criminal Evidence Act 1984, s. 18 states:

(1) Subject to the following provisions of this section, a constable may enter and search any premises occupied or controlled by a person who is under arrest for an indictable offence, if he has reasonable grounds for suspecting that there is on the premises evidence, other than items subject to legal privilege, that relates—

    (a) to that offence; or

    (b) to some other indictable offence which is connected with or similar to that offence.

(2) A constable may seize and retain anything for which he may search under subsection (1) above.

(3) The power to search conferred by subsection (1) above is only a power to search to the extent that is reasonably required for the purpose of discovering such evidence.

(4) Subject to subsection (5) below, the powers conferred by this section may not be exercised unless an officer of the rank of inspector or above has authorised them in writing.

(5) A constable may conduct a search under subsection (1)—

    (a) before the person is taken to a police station or released on bail under section 30A; and

    (b) without obtaining an authorisation under subsection (4), if the condition in subsection (5A) is satisfied.

(5A) The condition is that the presence of the person at a place (other than a police station) is necessary for the effective investigation of the offence.

(6) If a constable conducts a search by virtue of subsection (5) above, he shall inform an officer of the rank of inspector or above that he has made the search as soon as practicable after he has made it.

(7) An officer who—

    (a) authorises a search; or

    (b) is informed of a search under subsection (6) above, shall make a record in writing—

        (i) of the grounds for the search; and

        (ii) of the nature of the evidence that was sought.

(8) If the person who was in occupation or control of the premises at the time of the search is in police detention at the time the record is to be made, the officer shall make the record as part of his custody record.

The power under s. 18 only applies to premises which *are* occupied and controlled by a person under arrest for an indictable offence; reasonable *suspicion* that the person occupies or controls the premises *is not sufficient*.

The search is limited to evidence relating to the indictable offence for which the person has been arrested or another indictable offence which is similar or connected; it does not authorise a general search for anything that might be of use for other purposes (e.g. for intelligence reports). The extent of the search is limited by s. 18(3). If you are looking for a stolen fridge-freezer, you would not be empowered to search through drawers or small cupboards. You would be able to, however, if you were looking for packaging, receipts or other documents relating to the fridge-freezer.

That authority is for a search which is lawful *in all other respects*, that is, the other conditions imposed by s. 18 must be met. An inspector cannot make an otherwise unlawful entry and search lawful simply by authorising it (*Krohn* v *DPP* [1997] COD 345).

Where officers carry out a search under s. 18 they must, so far as is possible in the circumstances, explain to the occupier(s) the reason for it. If officers attempt to carry out an authorised search under s. 18 without attempting to explain to an occupier the reason, it may mean that the officers are not acting in the execution of their duty and their entry may be lawfully resisted (*Lineham* v *DPP* [2000] Crim LR 861).

The provision under s. 18(5) relates to cases where the presence of the person *is in fact necessary* for the effective investigation of the offence. This is a more stringent requirement than merely reasonable suspicion or grounds to believe on the part of the officer concerned. If such a search is made, the searching officer must inform an inspector (or above) as soon as practicable after the search.

If the person is in police detention after the arrest, the facts concerning the search must be recorded in the custody record. Where a person is re-arrested under s. 31 of the 1984 Act for an indictable offence, the powers to search under s. 18 begin again, that is, a new power to search is created in respect of each indictable offence.

4.7.6 | 5 Search with consent

5.1 Subject to *paragraph 5.4*, if it is proposed to search premises with the consent of a person entitled to grant entry the consent must, if practicable, be given in writing on the Notice of Powers and Rights before the search. The officer must make any necessary enquiries to be satisfied the person is in a position to give such consent.

5.2 Before seeking consent the officer in charge of the search shall state the purpose of the proposed search and its extent. This information must be as specific as possible, particularly regarding the articles or persons being sought and the parts of the premises to be searched. The person concerned must be clearly informed they are not obliged to consent, that any consent can be withdrawn at any time, including before the search starts or while it is underway and anything seized may be produced in evidence. If at the time the person is not suspected of an offence, the officer shall say this when stating the purpose of the search.

5.3 An officer cannot enter and search or continue to search premises under *paragraph 5.1* if consent is given under duress or withdrawn before the search is completed.

5.4 It is unnecessary to seek consent under *paragraphs 5.1* and *5.2* if this would cause disproportionate inconvenience to the person concerned.

4.7.6.1 | KEYNOTE

In a lodging house or similar accommodation, every reasonable effort should be made to obtain the consent of the tenant, lodger or occupier. A search should not be made solely on the basis of the landlord's consent.

If the intention is to search premises under the authority of a warrant or a power of entry and search without warrant, and the occupier of the premises cooperates in accordance with para. 6.4, there is no need to obtain written consent.

Paragraph 5.4 is intended to apply when it is reasonable to assume innocent occupiers would agree to, and expect, police to take the proposed action, e.g. if:

- a suspect has fled the scene of a crime or to evade arrest and it is necessary quickly to check surrounding gardens and readily accessible places to see if the suspect is hiding or;
- police have arrested someone in the night after a pursuit and it is necessary to make a brief check of gardens along the pursuit route to see if stolen or incriminating articles have been discarded.

4.7.7 | 6 Searching premises—general considerations

(a) Time of searches

6.1 Searches made under warrant must be made within three calendar months of the date of the warrant is issued or within the period specified in the enactment under which the warrant is issued if this is shorter.

6.2 Searches must be made at a reasonable hour unless this might frustrate the purpose of the search.

6.3 When the extent or complexity of a search mean it is likely to take a long time, the officer in charge of the search may consider using the seize and sift powers referred to in *section 7*.

6.3A A warrant under PACE, section 8 may authorise entry to and search of premises on more than one occasion if, on the application, the justice of the peace is satisfied that it is necessary to authorise multiple entries in order to achieve the purpose for which the warrant is issued. No premises may be entered or searched on any subsequent occasions without the prior written authority of an officer of the rank of inspector who is not involved in the investigation. All other warrants authorise entry on one occasion only.

6.3B Where a warrant under PACE section 8, or Schedule 1, paragraph 12 authorises entry to and search of all premises occupied or controlled by a specified person, no premises which are not specified in the warrant may be entered and searched without the prior written authority of an officer of the rank of inspector who is not involved in the investigation.

(b) Entry other than with consent

6.4 The officer in charge of the search shall first try to communicate with the occupier, or any other person entitled to grant access to the premises, explain the authority under which entry is sought and ask the occupier to allow entry, unless:

(i) the search premises are unoccupied;

(ii) the occupier and any other person entitled to grant access are absent;

(iii) there are reasonable grounds for believing that alerting the occupier or any other person entitled to grant access would frustrate the object of the search or endanger officers or other people.

6.5 Unless *sub-paragraph 6.4(iii)* applies, if the premises are occupied the officer, subject to *paragraph 2.9*, shall, before the search begins:

(i) identify him or herself, show their warrant card (if not in uniform) and state the purpose of, and grounds for, the search, and

(ii) identify and introduce any person accompanying the officer on the search (such persons should carry identification for production on request) and briefly describe that person's role in the process.

6.6 Reasonable and proportionate force may be used if necessary to enter premises if the officer in charge of the search is satisfied the premises are those specified in any warrant, or in exercise of the powers described in *paragraphs 4.1* to *4.3*, and if:

(i) the occupier or any other person entitled to grant access has refused entry;

(ii) it is impossible to communicate with the occupier or any other person entitled to grant access; or

(iii) any of the provisions of *paragraph 6.4* apply.

(c) Notice of Powers and Rights

6.7 If an officer conducts a search to which this Code applies the officer shall, unless it is impracticable to do so, provide the occupier with a copy of a Notice in a standard format:

(i) specifying if the search is made under warrant, with consent, or in the exercise of the powers described in *paragraphs 4.1* to *4.3*. Note: the notice format shall provide for authority or consent to be indicated, see *paragraphs 4.3* and *5.1*;

(ii) summarising the extent of the powers of search and seizure conferred by PACE and other relevant legislation as appropriate;

(iii) explaining the rights of the occupier, and the owner of the property seized;

(iv) explaining compensation may be payable in appropriate cases for damages caused entering and searching premises, and giving the address to send a compensation application, and

(v) stating this Code is available at any police station.

6.8 If the occupier is:

• present, copies of the Notice and warrant shall, if practicable, be given to them before the search begins, unless the officer in charge of the search reasonably believes this would frustrate the object of the search or endanger officers or other people

• not present, copies of the Notice and warrant shall be left in a prominent place on the premises or appropriate part of the premises and endorsed, subject to *paragraph 2.9* with the name of the officer in charge of the search, the date and time of the search

the warrant shall be endorsed to show this has been done.

(d) Conduct of searches

6.9 Premises may be searched only to the extent necessary to achieve the object of the search, having regard to the size and nature of whatever is sought.

6.9A A search may not continue under:
- a warrant's authority once all the things specified in that warrant have been found
- any other power once the object of that search has been achieved.

6.9B No search may continue once the officer in charge of the search is satisfied whatever is being sought is not on the premises. This does not prevent a further search of the same premises if additional grounds come to light supporting a further application for a search warrant or exercise or further exercise of another power. For example, when, as a result of new information, it is believed articles previously not found or additional articles are on the premises.

6.10 Searches must be conducted with due consideration for the property and privacy of the occupier and with no more disturbance than necessary. Reasonable force may be used only when necessary and proportionate because the cooperation of the occupier cannot be obtained or is insufficient for the purpose.

6.11 A friend, neighbour or other person must be allowed to witness the search if the occupier wishes unless the officer in charge of the search has reasonable grounds for believing the presence of the person asked for would seriously hinder the investigation or endanger officers or other people. A search need not be unreasonably delayed for this purpose. A record of the action taken should be made on the premises search record including the grounds for refusing the occupier's request.

6.12 A person is not required to be cautioned prior to being asked questions that are solely necessary for the purpose of furthering the proper and effective conduct of a search, see Code C, *paragraph 10.1(c)*. For example, questions to discover the occupier of specified premises, to find a key to open a locked drawer or cupboard or to otherwise seek cooperation during the search or to determine if a particular item is liable to be seized.

6.12A If questioning goes beyond what is necessary for the purpose of the exemption in Code C, the exchange is likely to constitute an interview as defined by Code C, *paragraph 11.1A* and would require the associated safeguards included in Code C, *section 10*.

(e) Leaving premises

6.13 If premises have been entered by force, before leaving the officer in charge of the search must make sure they are secure by:
- arranging for the occupier or their agent to be present
- any other appropriate means.

(f) Searches under PACE Schedule 1 or the Terrorism Act 2000, Schedule 5

6.14 An officer shall be appointed as the officer in charge of the search, see *paragraph 2.10*, in respect of any search made under a warrant issued under PACE Act 1984, Schedule 1 or the Terrorism Act 2000, Schedule 5. They are responsible for making sure the search is conducted with discretion and in a manner that causes the least possible disruption to any business or other activities carried out on the premises.

6.15 Once the officer in charge of the search is satisfied material may not be taken from the premises without their knowledge, they shall ask for the documents or other records concerned. The officer in charge of the search may also ask to see the index to files held on the premises, and the officers conducting the search may inspect any files which, according to the index, appear to contain the material sought. A more extensive search of the premises may be made only if:

- the person responsible for them refuses to:
  - produce the material sought, or
  - allow access to the index
- it appears the index is:
  - inaccurate, or
  - incomplete
  - for any other reason the officer in charge of the search has reasonable grounds for believing such a search is necessary in order to find the material sought.

4.7.7.1

KEYNOTE

Whether compensation is appropriate depends on the circumstances in each case. Compensation for damage caused when effecting entry is unlikely to be appropriate if the search was lawful, and the force used can be shown to be reasonable, proportionate and necessary to effect entry. If the wrong premises are searched by mistake everything possible should be done at the earliest opportunity to allay any sense of grievance and there should normally be a strong presumption in favour of paying compensation.

It is important that, when possible, all those involved in a search are fully briefed about any powers to be exercised and the extent and limits within which it should be conducted.

In all cases the number of officers and other persons involved in executing the warrant should be determined by what is reasonable and necessary according to the particular circumstances.

4.7.8

7 Seizure and retention of property

(a) Seizure

7.1 Subject to *paragraph 7.2*, an officer who is searching any person or premises under any statutory power or with the consent of the occupier may seize anything:
   (a) covered by a warrant
   (b) the officer has reasonable grounds for believing is evidence of an offence or has been obtained in consequence of the commission of an offence but only if seizure is necessary to prevent the items being concealed, lost, disposed of, altered, damaged, destroyed or tampered with
   (c) covered by the powers in the Criminal Justice and Police Act 2001, Part 2 allowing an officer to seize property from persons or premises and retain it for sifting or examination elsewhere.

7.2 No item may be seized which an officer has reasonable grounds for believing to be subject to legal privilege, as defined in PACE, section 10, other than under the Criminal Justice and Police Act 2001, Part 2.

7.3 Officers must be aware of the provisions in the Criminal Justice and Police Act 2001, section 59, allowing for applications to a judicial authority for the return of property seized and the subsequent duty to secure in section 60, see *paragraph 7.12(iii)*.

7.4 An officer may decide it is not appropriate to seize property because of an explanation from the person holding it but may nevertheless have reasonable grounds for believing it was obtained in consequence of an offence by some person. In these circumstances, the officer should identify the property to the holder, inform the holder of their suspicions and explain the holder may be liable to civil or criminal proceedings if they dispose of, alter or destroy the property.

7.5 An officer may arrange to photograph, image or copy, any document or other article they have the power to seize in accordance with *paragraph 7.1*. This is subject to specific restrictions on the examination, imaging or copying of certain property seized under the Criminal Justice and Police Act 2001, Part 2. An officer must have regard to their statutory obligation to retain an original document or other article only when a photograph or copy is not sufficient.

7.6 If an officer considers information stored in any electronic form and accessible from the premises could be used in evidence, they may require the information to be produced in a form:

- which can be taken away and in which it is visible and legible; or
- from which it can readily be produced in a visible and legible form.

4.7.8.1 **KEYNOTE**

General Powers of Seizure—s.19 PACE

The Police and Criminal Evidence Act 1984, s. 19 states:

(1) The powers conferred by subsections (2), (3) and (4) below are exercisable by a constable who is lawfully on any premises.

(2) The constable may seize anything which is on the premises if he has reasonable grounds for believing—
   (a) that it has been obtained in consequence of the commission of an offence; and
   (b) that it is necessary to seize it in order to prevent it being concealed, lost, damaged, altered or destroyed.

(3) The constable may seize anything which is on the premises if he has reasonable grounds for believing—
   (a) that it is evidence in relation to an offence which he is investigating or any other offence; and
   (b) that it is necessary to seize it in order to prevent the evidence being concealed, lost, altered or destroyed.

(4) The constable may require any information which is stored in any electronic form and is accessible from the premises to be produced in a form in which it can be taken away and in which it is visible and legible or from which it can readily be produced in a visible and legible form if he has reasonable grounds for believing—
   (a) that—
      (i) it is evidence in relation to an offence which he is investigating or any other offence; or
      (ii) it has been obtained in consequence of the commission of an offence; and
   (b) that it is necessary to do so in order to prevent it being concealed, lost, or destroyed.

(5) The powers conferred by this section are in addition to any power otherwise conferred.

(6) No power of seizure conferred on a constable under any enactment (including an enactment contained in an Act passed after this Act) is to be taken to authorise the seizure of an item which the constable exercising the power has reasonable grounds for believing to be subject to legal privilege.

For this power to apply, the officers concerned must be on the premises lawfully. If the officers are on the premises only with the consent of the occupier, they become trespassers once that consent has been withdrawn. Once the officers are told to leave, they are no longer 'lawfully' on the premises—even though they must be given a reasonable opportunity to leave—and cannot then seize any property that they may find. For this reason, it is far safer to exercise a power where one exists, albeit that the *cooperation* of the relevant person should be sought.

The power of seizure only applies where the officer has 'reasonable grounds for believing' that:

- the property has been obtained in consequence of the commission of an offence, or
- the property is *evidence* in relation to an offence, *and*

in each case, that its seizure is *necessary* to prevent the property being concealed, lost or destroyed.

Where the 'premises' searched is a vehicle (see s. 23), the vehicle can itself be seized (*Cowan* v *Commissioner of Police for the Metropolis* [2000] 1 WLR 254). In *Cowan* it was argued that the powers given by ss. 18 and 19 authorise the seizure of anything in or on the premises but not the *premises* themselves. The Court of Appeal disagreed, holding that the power to seize 'premises', where it was appropriate and practical to do so, was embodied in both ss. 18 and 19 and also at common law and the defendant's claim for damages following the seizure of his vehicle after his arrest for serious sexual offences was dismissed. Therefore, the powers of seizure conferred by ss. 18(2) and 19(3) of the Police and Criminal Evidence Act 1984 extend to the seizure of the whole premises when it is physically possible to seize and retain the premises in their totality and practical considerations make seizure desirable. The police may remove premises such as tents, vehicles or caravans to a police station for the purpose of preserving evidence. However, it does not extend to seizing things that are not on the premises, such as a car parked in a car park adjacent to the premises (*Wood* v *North Avon Magistrates' Court* [2009] EWHC 3614 (Admin)).

Unless the elements above are satisfied, the power under s. 19 will not apply. Therefore, the power does not authorise the seizure of property purely for intelligence purposes.

Section 19(5) expressly preserves any common law power of search and seizure; however, in *R (On the Application of Rottman)* v *Commissioner of Police for the Metropolis* [2002] UKHL 20, the House of Lords held that s. 19 was confined to 'domestic' offences (e.g. and did not extend to extradition offences). The same applies to powers under s. 18 of the Police and Criminal Evidence Act 1984.

If the warrant under which entry or seizure was made is invalid, the officers will not be on the premises lawfully.

The power of seizure under s. 19(1), along with the power to require information stored in any electronic form to be made accessible under s. 19(4), are among those that can be conferred on an Investigating Officer designated under sch. 4 to the Police Reform Act 2002. The safeguards provided by s. 19(6) in relation to privileged material also apply to the exercise of these powers by designated Investigating Officers.

4.7.8.2

KEYNOTE

Powers of Seizure and Information in Electronic Form

The Police and Criminal Evidence Act 1984, s. 20 states:

(1) Every power of seizure which is conferred by an enactment to which this section applies on a constable who has entered premises in the exercise of a power conferred by an enactment shall be construed as including a power to require any information stored in any electronic form and accessible from the premises to be produced in a form in which it can be taken away and in which it is visible and legible or from which it can readily be produced in a visible and legible form.

(2) This section applies—
  (a) to any enactment contained in an Act passed before this Act;
  (b) to sections 8 and 18 above;
  (c) to paragraph 13 of Schedule 1 to this Act; and
  (d) to any enactment contained in an Act passed after this Act.

This provision applies to:

• powers conferred under pre-PACE statutes;
• powers exercised under a s. 8 warrant (for 'indictable offences');
• powers exercised under s. 18 (following arrest for an indictable offence);
• powers under sch. 1 ('excluded' or 'special procedure material');
• powers exercised under s. 19 (officers lawfully on premises);
• powers of seizure exercised by Investigating Officers designated under sch. 4 to the Police Reform Act 2002.

4.7.8.3

KEYNOTE

Supply of Copies of Seized Material

Section 21 of the 1984 Act makes provision for the supplying of copies of records of seizure to certain people after property has been seized. If requested by the person who had custody or control of the seized property immediately before it was seized, the officer in charge of the investigation must allow that person access to it under police supervision. The officer must also make provisions to allow for the property be to photographed or copied by that person or to supply the person with photographs/copies of it within a reasonable time. Such a request need not be complied with if there are reasonable grounds to believe that to do so would prejudice any related investigation or criminal proceedings (s. 21(8)).

4.7.8.4

KEYNOTE

Retention of Seized Material

The provisions for accessing and copying of seized material as set out in ss. 21 and 22 of the Police and Criminal Evidence Act 1984 also apply to powers of seizure exercised by Investigating Officers designated under sch. 4 to the Police Reform Act 2002.

Section 22 of the 1984 Act makes provision for the retention of seized property. Section 22(1) provides that anything seized may be retained for as long as necessary in all the circumstances. However, s. 22(2) allows for property to be retained for use as evidence in a trial, forensic examination or further investigation *unless a photograph or copy would suffice*. Seized property may be retained in order to establish its lawful owner (s. 22(2)(b)). Once this power to retain property is exhausted, a person claiming it can rely on his/her right to possession at the time the property was seized as giving sufficient title to recover the property from the police. This situation was confirmed by the Court of Appeal in a case where the purchaser of a stolen car was allowed to rely upon his possession of the car at the time it was seized. As it could not be established that anyone else was entitled to the vehicle, the court allowed the claimant's action for return of the car to him (*Costello* v *Chief Constable of Derbyshire Constabulary* [2001] EWCA Civ 381). Clearly any claim based on previous possession where it would be unlawful for the police to return the property (e.g. a controlled drug) could not be enforced. Provisions amending this area of legislation are now contained in the Criminal Justice and Police Act 2001. There is no specific provision under s. 22 for the retention of property for purely intelligence purposes.

The importance of police officers being able to point clearly to the need for retaining property either in order to establish its owner or as a necessary part of the investigative or law enforcement process when relying on the above powers, was highlighted by the Court of Appeal in *Gough* v *Chief Constable of the West Midlands Police* [2004] EWCA Civ 206. In that case it was clear that neither of these purposes was being served and therefore the officers could not rely on the statutory power for retaining the property.

Property seized simply to prevent an arrested person from using it to escape or to cause injury, damage etc. cannot be retained for those purposes once the person has been released (s. 22(3)). This includes car keys belonging to someone who is released from police detention having been detained under the relevant drink driving legislation.

4.7.8.5

KEYNOTE

Prohibitions on Re-use of Information Seized

Information gained as a result of a lawful search may be passed on to other individuals and organisations for purposes of investigation and prosecution. It must not be used for private purposes (*Marcel* v *Commissioner of Police for the Metropolis* [1992] Ch 225; also **see chapter 4.1** for the requirements as to confidentiality in the Code of Conduct for police officers).

4.7.8.6

KEYNOTE

Disposal of Property in Police Possession

Any person claiming property seized by the police may apply to a magistrates' court under the Police (Property) Act 1897 for its possession and should, if appropriate, be advised of this procedure.

(b) Criminal Justice and Police Act 2001: Specific procedures for seize and sift powers

7.7 The Criminal Justice and Police Act 2001, Part 2 gives officers limited powers to seize property from premises or persons so they can sift or examine it elsewhere. Officers must be careful they only exercise these powers when it is essential and they do not remove any more material than necessary. The removal of large volumes of material, much of which may not ultimately be retainable, may have serious implications for the owners, particularly when they are involved in business or activities such as journalism or the provision of medical services. Officers must carefully consider if removing copies or images of relevant material or data would be a satisfactory alternative to removing originals. When originals are taken, officers must be prepared to facilitate the provision of copies or images for the owners when reasonably practicable.

7.8 Property seized under the Criminal Justice and Police Act 2001, sections 50 or 51 must be kept securely and separately from any material seized under other powers. An examination under section 53 to determine which elements may be retained must be carried out at the earliest practicable time, having due regard to the desirability of allowing the person from whom the property was seized, or a person with an interest in the property, an opportunity of being present or represented at the examination.

7.8A All reasonable steps should be taken to accommodate an interested person's request to be present, provided the request is reasonable and subject to the need to prevent harm to, interference with, or unreasonable delay to the investigatory process. If an examination proceeds in the absence of an interested person who asked to attend or their representative, the officer who exercised the relevant seizure power must give that person a written notice of why the examination was carried out in those circumstances. If it is necessary for security reasons or to maintain confidentiality officers may exclude interested persons from decryption or other processes which facilitate the examination but do not form part of it.

7.9 It is the responsibility of the officer in charge of the investigation to make sure property is returned in accordance with sections 53 to 55. Material which there is no power to retain must be:
- separated from the rest of the seized property
- returned as soon as reasonably practicable after examination of all the seized property.

7.9A Delay is only warranted if very clear and compelling reasons exist, e.g. the:
- unavailability of the person to whom the material is to be returned
- need to agree a convenient time to return a large volume of material.

7.9B Legally privileged, excluded or special procedure material which cannot be retained must be returned:
- as soon as reasonably practicable
- without waiting for the whole examination.

7.9C As set out in section 58, material must be returned to the person from whom it was seized, except when it is clear some other person has a better right to it.

7.10 When an officer involved in the investigation has reasonable grounds to believe a person with a relevant interest in property seized under section 50 or 51 intends to make an application under section 59 for the return of any legally privileged, special procedure or excluded material, the officer in charge of the investigation should be informed as soon as practicable and the material seized should be kept secure in accordance with section 61.

7.11 The officer in charge of the investigation is responsible for making sure property is properly secured. Securing involves making sure the property is not examined, copied, imaged or put to any other use except at the request, or with the consent, of the applicant or in accordance with the directions of the appropriate judicial authority. Any request, consent or directions must be recorded in writing and signed by both the initiator and the officer in charge of the investigation.

7.12 When an officer exercises a power of seizure conferred by sections 50 or 51 they shall provide the occupier of the premises or the person from whom the property is being seized with a written notice:
(i) specifying what has been seized under the powers conferred by that section;
(ii) specifying the grounds for those powers;
(iii) setting out the effect of sections 59 to 61 covering the grounds for a person with a relevant interest in seized property to apply to a judicial authority for its return and the duty of officers to secure property in certain circumstances when an application is made;
(iv) specifying the name and address of the person to whom:
- notice of an application to the appropriate judicial authority in respect of any of the seized property must be given;
- an application may be made to allow attendance at the initial examination of the property.

7.13　If the occupier is not present but there is someone in charge of the premises, the notice shall be given to them. If no suitable person is available, so the notice will easily be found it should either be:

- left in a prominent place on the premises
- attached to the exterior of the premises.

4.7.8.7　**KEYNOTE**

Seize and Sift Powers

These seize and sift powers only extend the scope of *some other existing power*. In other words, they do not provide free-standing powers to seize property—rather, they supplement other powers of search and seizure where the relevant conditions and circumstances apply. The full list of these powers is set out in sch. 1 to the Act and includes all the relevant powers under the Police and Criminal Evidence Act 1984, along with those under other key statutes such as the Firearms Act 1968 and the Misuse of Drugs Act 1971. If there is no existing power of seizure other than the Criminal Justice and Police Act 2001, then there is no power.

The Criminal Justice and Police Act 2001 powers allow officers to remove materials from the premises being searched where there are real practical difficulties in not doing so—e.g. because there will be insufficient time to examine all the material properly, where special equipment is needed to examine it or where the material is stored on a computer.

In summary, s. 50 of the Act provides the extended powers to seize material where it is not reasonably practicable to sort through it at the scene of the search. The factors that can be taken into account in considering whether or not it is reasonably practicable for something to be determined, or for relevant material to be separated from other materials, are set out in s. 50(3); these include the length of time and number of people that would be required to carry out the determination or separation on those premises within a reasonable period, whether that would involve damage to property, any apparatus or equipment that would be needed and (in the case of separation of materials) whether the separation would be likely to prejudice the use of some or all of the separated seizable property. Section 50 also allows for the seizure of material that is reasonably believed to be legally privileged where it is not reasonably practicable to separate it. In some cases, the power to 'seize' will be read as a power to take copies (see s. 63).

Section 51 provides for extended seizure of materials in the same vein as above but where the material is found on people who are being lawfully searched.

(i) Initial Examination

Where any property has been seized under ss. 50 or 51, the officer in possession of it is under a duty to make sure that a number of things are done (s. 53). These include ensuring that an initial examination of the property is carried out *as soon as reasonably practicable* after the seizure. In determining the earliest practicable time to carry out an initial examination of the seized property, due regard must be had to the desirability of allowing the person from whom it was seized (or a person with an interest in it) an opportunity of being present, or of being represented, at the examination (s. 53(4)). Officers should consider reaching agreement with owners and/or other interested parties on the procedures for examining a specific set of property, rather than awaiting the judicial authority's determination. Agreement can sometimes give a quicker and more satisfactory route for all concerned and minimise costs and legal complexities. What constitutes a relevant interest in specific material may depend on the nature of that material and the circumstances in which it is seized. Anyone with a reasonable claim to ownership of the material and anyone entrusted with its safe keeping by the owner should be considered.

The officer must also ensure that any such examination is confined to whatever is *necessary* for determining how much of the property:

- is property for which the person seizing it had power to search when making the seizure but is not property that has to be returned (by s. 54—see (ii) Protected Material);
- is property authorised to be retained (by s. 56—see (iii) Retention of Property); or
- is something which, in all the circumstances, it will not be reasonably practicable, following the examination, to separate from the property above (see generally s. 53(3)).

The officer must ensure that anything found not to fall within the categories above is separated from the rest of the seized property and *is returned as soon as reasonably practicable* after the examination of all the seized property. That officer is also under a duty to ensure that, until the initial examination of all the seized property has been completed and anything which does not fall within the categories above has been returned, the seized property is kept separate from anything seized under any other power. There are special provisions where the property is inextricably linked to relevant material (e.g. where the 'innocent' material is completely mixed up with or inseparable from the material that is properly the subject of the investigation). However, those provisions place very strict limits on what use can be made of this inextricably linked material (see s. 62).

(ii) Protected Material

If, at any time, after a seizure of anything has been made in exercise of *any statutory power of seizure*, it appears that the property is subject to legal privilege (or it has such an item comprised in it), s. 54 imposes a general duty on the officer in possession of the property to ensure that the item is returned as soon as reasonably practicable after the seizure. This general duty is subject to some exceptions (e.g. where in all the circumstances it is not reasonably practicable for that item to be separated from the rest of that property without prejudicing the use of the rest of that property—see s. 54(2)) but is otherwise very wide-ranging and absolutely clear. A similar duty is generally imposed in relation to property that appears to be excluded material or special procedure material (s. 55).

(iii) Retention of Property

The Act authorises the retention of certain seized property by the police. In order to be retained, the property must have been seized on any premises by a constable who was lawfully on the premises, by a person authorised under a relevant statute (see s. 56(5)) who was on the premises accompanied by a constable, or by a constable carrying out a lawful search of any person (s. 56). Generally property so seized will fall within these categories if there are reasonable grounds for believing:

- that it is property obtained in consequence of the commission of an offence; or
- that it is evidence in relation to any offence; *and* (in either case)
- that it is necessary for it to be retained in order to prevent its being concealed, lost, altered or destroyed

(for full details see s. 56(2) and (3)). Note, so far as s. 56(2) is concerned, property may be retained if it is necessary to prevent its being 'damaged', in addition to the other factors listed.

These are fairly wide provisions and, if the property fits the above description, it may be retained even if it was not being searched for. Section 57 goes on to make certain provisions for the retention of property under other statutes such as s. 5(4) of the Knives Act 1997, para. 7(2) of sch. 9 to the Data Protection Act 1998, and sch. 5 to the Human Tissue Act 2004.

(iv) Notice

Where a person exercises a power of seizure conferred by ss. 50 or 51, that person will be under a duty, on doing so, to give the occupier or person from whom property is seized a written notice (s. 52). That notice will specify:

- what has been seized and the grounds on which the powers have been exercised;
- the effect of the safeguards and rights to apply to a judicial authority for the return of the property (see (v) Return of Property Seized);
- the name and address of the person to whom notice of an application to a judge and an application to be allowed to attend the initial examination should be sent.

Where it appears to the officer exercising a power of seizure under s. 50 that the occupier of the premises is not present at the time of the exercise of the power, but there is some other person present who is in charge of the premises, the officer may give the notice to that other person (s. 52(2)). Where it appears that there is no one present on the premises to whom a notice can be given, the officer must, before leaving the premises, attach a notice in a prominent place to the premises (s. 53(3)).

(v) Return of Property Seized

There are specific obligations on the police to return property seized under these powers—particularly where the property includes legally privileged, excluded or special procedure material. The general rule is that any extraneous property initially seized under these provisions must be returned—usually—to the person from whom it was seized unless the investigating officer considers that someone else has a better claim to it (see ss. 53 to 58).

Any person with a relevant interest in the seized property may apply to the appropriate judicial authority, on one or more of the grounds in s. 59(3) for the return of the whole or a part of the seized property. Generally those grounds are that there was no power to make the seizure or that the seized property did not fall into one of the permitted categories (see s. 59). Where a person makes such an application, the police must secure the property in accordance with s. 61 (e.g. in a way that prevents investigators from looking at or copying it until the matter has been considered by a judge). There are other occasions where protected material is involved that will give rise to the duty to secure the property under s. 61 too. The mechanics of securing property vary according to the circumstances; 'bagging up', i.e. placing material in sealed bags or containers and strict subsequent control of access is the appropriate procedure in many cases. The 'judicial authority' (at least a Crown Court judge) will be able to make a number of wide-ranging orders in relation to the treatment of the seized property, including its return or examination by a third party. Failure to comply with any such order will amount to a contempt of court (s. 59(9)). Requirements to secure and return property apply equally to all copies, images or other material created because of seizure of the original property.

When material is seized under the powers of seizure conferred by the Police and Criminal Evidence Act 1984, the duty to retain it under the Code of Practice issued under the Criminal Procedure and Investigations Act 1996 is subject to the provisions on retention of seized material in s. 22 of the 1984 Act.

For further details on the extent and use of these powers, see Home Office Circular 19/2003.

(c) Retention

7.14 Subject to *paragraph 7.15*, anything seized in accordance with the above provisions may be retained only for as long as is necessary. It may be retained, among other purposes:
  (i) for use as evidence at a trial for an offence;
  (ii) to facilitate the use in any investigation or proceedings of anything to which it is inextricably linked;
  (iii) for forensic examination or other investigation in connection with an offence;
  (iv) in order to establish its lawful owner when there are reasonable grounds for believing it has been stolen or obtained by the commission of an offence.
7.15 Property shall not be retained under *paragraph 7.14(i), (ii)* or *(iii)* if a copy or image would be sufficient.

(d) Rights of owners etc

7.16 If property is retained, the person who had custody or control of it immediately before seizure must, on request, be provided with a list or description of the property within a reasonable time.
7.17 That person or their representative must be allowed supervised access to the property to examine it or have it photographed or copied, or must be provided with a photograph or copy, in either case within a reasonable time of any request and at their own expense, unless the officer in charge of an investigation has reasonable grounds for believing this would:
  (i) prejudice the investigation of any offence or criminal proceedings; or
  (ii) lead to the commission of an offence by providing access to unlawful material such as pornography.
A record of the grounds shall be made when access is denied.

KEYNOTE

Paragraph 7.14 (ii) applies if inextricably linked material is seized under the Criminal Justice and Police Act 2001, ss. 50 or 51. Inextricably linked material is material it is not reasonably practicable to separate from other linked material without prejudicing the use of that other material in any investigation or proceedings. For example, it may not be possible to separate items of data held on computer disk without damaging their evidential integrity. Inextricably linked material must not be examined, imaged, copied or used for any purpose other than for proving the source and/or integrity of the linked material.

4.7.9

8 Action after searches

8.1 If premises are searched in circumstances where this Code applies, unless the exceptions in *paragraph 2.3(a)* apply, on arrival at a police station the officer in charge of the search shall make or have made a record of the search, to include:

(i) the address of the searched premises;

(ii) the date, time and duration of the search;

(iii) the authority used for the search:
- if the search was made in exercise of a statutory power to search premises without warrant, the power which was used for the search:
- if the search was made under a warrant or with written consent;
  - a copy of the warrant and the written authority to apply for it, see paragraph 3.4; or
  - the written consent;

shall be appended to the record or the record shall show the location of the copy warrant or consent.

(iv) subject to paragraph 2.9, the names of:
- the officer(s) in charge of the search;
- all other officers and any authorised persons who conducted the search;

(v) the names of any people on the premises if they are known;

(vi) any grounds for refusing the occupier's request to have someone present during the search, see *paragraph 6.11*;

(vii) a list of any articles seized or the location of a list and, if not covered by a warrant, the grounds for their seizure;

(viii) whether force was used, and the reason;

(ix) details of any damage caused during the search, and the circumstances;

(x) if applicable, the reason it was not practicable:
  (a) to give the occupier a copy of the Notice of Powers and Rights, see *paragraph 6.7*;
  (b) before the search to give the occupier a copy of the Notice, see *paragraph 6.8*;

(xi) when the occupier was not present, the place where copies of the Notice of Powers and Rights and search warrant were left on the premises, see *paragraph 6.8*.

8.2 On each occasion when premises are searched under warrant, the warrant authorising the search on that occasion shall be endorsed to show:

(i) if any articles specified in the warrant were found and the address where found;

(ii) if any other articles were seized;

(iii) the date and time it was executed and if present, the name of the occupier or if the occupier is not present the name of the person in charge of the premises;

(iv) subject to paragraph 2.9, the names of the officers who executed it and any authorised persons who accompanied them;

(v) if a copy, together with a copy of the Notice of Powers and Rights was:
- handed to the occupier; or
- endorsed as required by paragraph 6.8; and left on the premises and where.

8.3 Any warrant shall be returned within three calendar months of its issue or sooner on completion of the search(es) authorised by that warrant, if it was issued by a:
- justice of the peace, to the designated officer for the local justice area in which the justice was acting when issuing the warrant; or
- judge, to the appropriate officer of the court concerned.

4.7.10

9 Search registers

9.1 A search register will be maintained at each sub-divisional or equivalent police station. All search records required under *paragraph 8.1* shall be made, copied, or referred to in the register.

4.7.10.1

KEYNOTE

Paragraph 9.1 also applies to search records made by immigration officers. In these cases, a search register must also be maintained at an immigration office.

4.7.11

10 Searches under Schedule 5 to the Terrorism Prevention and Investigation Measures Act 2011

10.1 This Code applies to the powers of constables under Schedule 5 to the Terrorism Prevention and Investigation Measures Act 2011 relating to TPIM notices to enter and search premises subject to the modifications in the following paragraphs.

10.2 In paragraph 2.3(d), the reference to the investigation into an alleged or suspected offence include the enforcement of terrorism prevention and investigation measures which may be imposed on an individual by a TPIM notice in accordance with the Terrorism Prevention and Investigation Measures Act 2011.

10.3 References to the purpose and object of the entry and search of premises, the nature of articles sought and what may be seized and retained include (as appropriate):

(a) in relation to the power to search *without a search warrant in paragraph 5* (for purposes of serving TPIM notice), finding the individual on whom the notice is to be served.

(b) in relation to the power to search *without a search warrant in paragraph 6* (at time of serving TPIM notice), ascertaining whether there is anything in the premises, that contravenes measures specified in the notice.

(c) in relation to the power to search *without a search warrant* under *paragraph 7* (suspected absconding), ascertaining whether a person has absconded or if there is anything on the premises which will assist in the pursuit or arrest of an individual in respect of whom a TPIM notice is in force who is reasonably suspected of having absconded.

(d) in relation to the power to search *under a search warrant* issued under *paragraph 8* (for compliance purposes), determining whether an individual in respect of whom a TPIM notice is in force is complying with measures specified in the notice.

KEYNOTE

Searches of individuals under sch. 5, paras 6(2)(a) (at time of serving TPIM notice) and 8(2)(a) (for compliance purposes) must be conducted and recorded in accordance with Code A. See Code A, para. 2.18A for details.

Community Safety

4.8 Harassment, Stalking, Hostility and Anti-social Behaviour

4.8.1 Introduction

There is a growing list of measures available to police officers, police staff and the wider police family to help them to tackle disorder, and protect quality of life within the community. The government introduced an Anti-Social Behaviour, Crime and Policing Bill to Parliament in December 2012 with the aim of overhauling the existing system of ASBOs and introducing further offences as well as greater victim and community involvement.

New offences relating to stalking came into force in November 2012, giving officers far greater powers to deal with this unpleasant behaviour, which up until now has mainly had to be addressed through the harassment legislation.

This chapter sets out the key areas of current legislation and common law that are available to address public and individual anxiety, threats to personal safety, and anti-social behaviour.

4.8.2 Offences Involving Racial and Religious Hatred

The Racial and Religious Hatred Act 2006 inserts part 3A into the Public Order Act 1986 created offences of stirring up hatred against persons on religious grounds. This section provides a summary of the offences introduced by the 1986 Act aimed at addressing incidents specifically motivated by racial hatred, and the new offences, created by the Racial and Religious Hatred Act 2006, motivated by religious hatred.

For the purposes of the offences contrary to ss. 18 to 23 of the 1986 Act, 'racial hatred' means hatred against a group of persons defined by reference to colour, race, nationality (including citizenship) or ethnic or national origins (s. 17).

For the purposes of offences contrary to ss. 29B to 29G of the 1986 Act, 'religious hatred' means hatred against a group of persons defined by reference to religious belief or lack of religious belief (s. 29A).

4.8.2.1 Use of Words, Behaviour or Display of Written Material

OFFENCE: **Use of Words or Behaviour or Display of Written Material—*Public Order Act 1986, s. 18***

> • Triable either way • Seven years' imprisonment and/or a fine on indictment • Six months' imprisonment and/or a fine summarily

The Public Order Act 1986, s. 18 states:

(1) A person who uses threatening, abusive or insulting words or behaviour, or displays any written material which is threatening, abusive or insulting, is guilty of an offence if—
   (a) he intends thereby to stir up racial hatred, or
   (b) having regard to all the circumstances racial hatred is likely to be stirred up thereby.
(2) An offence under this section may be committed in a public or a private place, except that no offence is committed where the words or behaviour are used, or the written material is displayed, by a person inside a dwelling and are not heard or seen except by other persons in that or another dwelling.

4.8.2.2 Defence

The Public Order Act 1986, s. 18 states:

> (4) In proceedings for an offence under this section it is a defence for the accused to prove that he was inside a dwelling and had no reason to believe that the words or behaviour used, or the written material displayed, would be heard or seen by a person outside that or any other dwelling.

4.8.2.3 Publishing or Distributing Written Material

OFFENCE: **Publishing or Distributing Written Material—*Public Order Act 1986, s. 19***
- Triable either way • Seven years' imprisonment and/or a fine on indictment
- Six months' imprisonment and/or a fine summarily

The Public Order Act 1986, s. 19 states:

> (1) A person who publishes or distributes written material which is threatening, abusive or insulting is guilty of an offence if—
>   (a) he intends thereby to stir up racial hatred, or
>   (b) having regard to all the circumstances racial hatred is likely to be stirred up thereby.
> (2) ...
> (3) References in this Part to the publication or distribution of written material are to its publication or distribution to the public or a section of the public.

4.8.2.4 Defence

The Public Order Act 1986, s. 19 states:

> (2) In proceedings for an offence under this section it is a defence for an accused who is not shown to have intended to stir up racial hatred to prove that he was not aware of the content of the material and did not suspect, and had no reason to suspect, that it was threatening, abusive or insulting.

4.8.2.5 Use of Words, Behaviour or Display of Written Material

OFFENCE: **Use of Words or Behaviour or Display of Written Material—*Public Order Act 1986, s. 29B***
- Triable either way • Not exceeding seven years' imprisonment and/or a fine on indictment • Not exceeding six months' imprisonment and/or a fine summarily

The Public Order Act 1986, s. 29B states:

(1) A person who uses threatening words or behaviour, or displays any written material which is threatening, is guilty of an offence if he intends thereby to stir up religious hatred or hatred on the grounds of sexual orientation.

(2) An offence under this section is committed in a public or private place, except that no offence is committed where the words or behaviour are used, or the written material is displayed, by a person inside a dwelling and are not heard or seen except by other persons in that or another dwelling.

KEYNOTE

This differs from the other sections under the 1986 Act which have no specific power of arrest since the provisions of the Serious Organised Crime and Police Act 2005 were introduced.

All of the new offences are similar to that under s. 18 in that they require the consent of the Attorney-General before proceedings can be taken (s. 29L), and the same defences apply to this particular section—no reason to believe the words or behaviour, etc., would be heard or seen outside the dwelling (s. 29B(4)), or where used solely for the purpose of being included in a programming service (s. 29B(5)).

Section 29J of the Act provides that the offences of stirring up religious hatred are not intended to limit or restrict discussion, criticism or expressions of antipathy, dislike, ridicule or insult or abuse of particular religions or belief systems or lack of religion or of the beliefs and practices of those who hold such beliefs or to apply to persons newly converted to a religious faith, evangelism or the seeking to convert people to a particular belief or to cease holding a belief.

4.8.2.6 Publishing or Distributing Material

OFFENCE: **Publishing or Distributing Written Material—*Public Order Act 1986, s. 29C***
  • Triable either way • Not exceeding seven years' imprisonment and/or a fine on indictment • Not exceeding six months' imprisonment and/or a fine summarily

The Public Order Act 1986, s. 29C states:

(1) A person who publishes or distributes written material which is threatening is guilty of an offence if he intends thereby to stir up religious hatred or hatred on the grounds of sexual orientation.

(2) References in this Part to the publication or distribution of written material are to its publication or distribution to the public or a section of the public.

4.8.3 Hatred on the Grounds of Sexual Orientation

Section 74 of and sch. 16 to the Criminal Justice and Immigration Act 2008 extends the offences of inciting hatred against people on religious grounds to cover hatred against people on grounds of sexual orientation, amending part 3A of the Public Order Act 1986 (hatred against persons on religious grounds) to create offences involving stirring up hatred on the grounds of sexual orientation.

Section 29AB of the 1986 Act defines 'hatred on the grounds of sexual orientation'. The definition covers hatred against a group of persons defined by reference to their sexual orientation, be they heterosexual, homosexual or bi-sexual. The amendments to ss. 29B to 29G of the 1986 Act extend the various religious hatred offences in those sections to cover hatred on the grounds of sexual orientation. These offences involve the use of words or behaviour or display of written material (s. 29B), publishing or distributing written material (s. 29C), the public performance of a play (s. 29D), distributing, showing or playing a recording (s. 29E), broadcasting or including a programme in a programme service (s. 29F), and possession of inflammatory material (s. 29G).

In relation to each extended offence the relevant act (namely, words, behaviour, written material or recordings or programme) must be threatening, and the offender must intend thereby to stir up hatred on the grounds of sexual orientation. In the case of the offence under s. 29B, there is a specific defence where the words or behaviour are used or displayed inside a private dwelling and the accused had no reason to believe that they can be heard or seen by a person outside that or any other private dwelling.

The offences differ from the offences of stirring up racial hatred in, part 3 of the 1986 Act, in two respects. First, the offences apply only to 'threatening' words or behaviour, rather than 'threatening, abusive or insulting' words or behaviour. Secondly, the offences apply only to words or behaviour if the accused 'intends' to stir up hatred on grounds of sexual orientation, rather than if hatred is either intentional or 'likely' to be stirred up.

4.8.4 Stalking and Harassment

The Protection from Harassment Act 1997 was introduced after a number of highly publicised cases of stalking. Although intended for such situations, the Act's extensive provisions have been applied—and interpreted—widely. In passing the legislation set out at **para. 4.8.5**, the government anticipated the number of prosecutions under the 1997 Act to be only several hundred; in fact, many thousands of prosecutions have been brought. However, stalking itself has not been a criminal offence.

The Protection of Freedoms Act 2012 dealt with this problem, and makes changes to the Protection from Harassment Act 1997 by creating specific offences of stalking. The new offences are stalking contrary to s. 2A of the 1997 Act which is a summary offence, and stalking involving fear of violence or serious alarm or distress, contrary to s. 4A of the 1997 Act, which is triable either way.

Under s. 2A(1), a person is guilty of an offence if:

- he/she pursues a course of conduct in breach of s. 1(1) of the 1997 Act (i.e. a course of conduct which amounts to harassment); and
- the course of conduct amounts to stalking.

For the purposes of s. 2A(1)(b) and s. 4A(1)(a), s. 2A(2) states that a course of conduct amounts to stalking of another person if:

- it amounts to harassment of that person (under s. 7(2) of the Protection from Harassment Act 1997, references to harassing a person include alarming the person or causing the person distress);
- the acts or omissions involved are ones associated with stalking; and
- the person whose course of conduct it is knows or ought to know that the course of conduct amounts to harassment of the other person.

Section 2A(3) lists examples of behaviours associated with stalking. The list is not exhaustive but gives an indication of the types of behaviour that may be displayed in a stalking offence. The listed behaviours are:

- following a person;
- contacting, or attempting to contact, a person by any means;
- publishing any statement or other material (i) relating or purporting to relate to a person, or (ii) purporting to originate from a person;
- monitoring the use by a person of the Internet, email or any other form of electronic communication;
- loitering in any place (whether public or private);
- interfering with any property in the possession of a person;
- watching or spying on a person.

The new s. 2A offence does not specify how to demonstrate a defence for stalking. This is because an offence of stalking can only be established where an offence of harassment has occurred.

The s. 2 offence does not have a defence for the charge of harassment. Therefore, both ss. 2 and 2A will have to rely on s. 1(3), which states that the prohibition on harassment does not apply to a course of conduct if the person who pursued it can demonstrate the matters set out in s. 1(3)(a) or (b) or (c). Section 1(3) of the 1997 Act provides that a course of conduct will not amount to harassment if the person who pursued it shows:

- that it was pursued for the purpose of preventing or detecting crime (this defence is most obviously available to the police, or other statutory investigating agencies);
- that it was pursued under any enactment or rule of law, or to comply with any condition or requirement imposed by any person under any enactment; or
- that in the particular circumstances the pursuit of the course of conduct was reasonable.

The changes to the 1997 Act include a new police power of entry in relation to the s. 2A stalking offence, which is contained in s. 2B. A constable can apply to a justice of the peace, who may issue a warrant authorising entry and search of premises providing there are reasonable grounds to believe the conditions in s. 2B are met. A constable may seize and retain anything for which a search was authorised, and may use reasonable force, if necessary, in the exercise of any power conferred by s. 2B.

Section 4A of the 1997 Act prohibits a course of conduct relating to the offence of stalking involving fear of violence or serious alarm or distress. The first arm of the offence prohibits a course of conduct that causes the victim to fear, on at least two occasions, that violence will be used against him/her (which is similar to the existing s. 4 offence). For the purposes of s. 4A(1)(b)(i) a person (A) ought to know that A's course of conduct will cause another (B) to fear that violence will be used against B on any occasion if a reasonable person in possession of the same information would think the course of conduct would cause B so to fear on that occasion. The second arm of the offence prohibits a course of conduct which causes 'serious alarm or distress' which has a 'substantial adverse effect on the day-to-day activities of the victim'. It is designed to recognise the serious impact that stalking may have on victims, even where an explicit fear of violence is not created by each incident of stalking behaviour.

The phrase 'substantial adverse effect on the usual day-to-day activities' is not defined in s. 4A, and thus its construction will be a matter for the courts via judicial interpretation. However, the Home Office considers that evidence of a substantial adverse effect caused by the stalker may include:

- victims changing their routes to work, work patterns, or employment;
- victims arranging for friends or family to pick up children from school (to avoid contact with the stalker);
- victims putting in place additional security measures in their home;
- victims moving home;
- physical or mental ill-health;
- victims' deterioration in performance at work due to stress;
- victims stopping or changing the way they socialise.

Although some victims try to continue their existing routines in defiance of a stalker, they may still be able to evidence substantial impact on their usual day-to-day activities, depending on the individual case.

For the purposes of s. 4A(1)(b)(ii), A ought to know that A's course of conduct will cause B serious alarm or distress which has a substantial adverse effect on B's usual day-to-day activities if a reasonable person in possession of the same information would think the course of conduct would cause B such alarm or distress.

Unlike the s. 2A offence above, there is a defence to the offence of stalking involving fear of violence or serious alarm or distress, as set out in s. 4A(4), where it can be shown that the course of conduct was:

- pursued for the purpose of preventing or detecting crime;
- pursued under any enactment or rule of law;
- reasonable for the protection of A or another or for the protection of A's or another's property.

4.8.4.1 Protection from Harassment Act Offences

OFFENCE: **Harassment—*Protection from Harassment Act 1997, ss. 1 and 2***
- Triable summarily • Six months' imprisonment and/or a fine

OFFENCE: **Racially or Religiously Aggravated Harassment—*Crime and Disorder Act 1998, s. 32(1)(a)***
- Triable either way • Two years' imprisonment and/or a fine on indictment
- Six months' imprisonment and/or a fine summarily

The Protection from Harassment Act 1997, ss. 1 and 2 state:

1.—(1) A person must not pursue a course of conduct—
    (a) which amounts to harassment of another, and
    (b) which he knows or ought to know amounts to harassment of the other.

(1A) A person must not pursue a course of conduct—
    (a) which involves harassment of two or more persons, and
    (b) which he knows or ought to know involves harassment of those persons, and
    (c) by which he intends to persuade any person (whether or not one of those mentioned above)—
        (i) not to do something that he is entitled or required to do, or
        (ii) to do something that he is not under any obligation to do.
    ...

2.—(1) A person who pursues a course of conduct in breach of section 1(1) or (1A) is guilty of an offence.

KEYNOTE

'Person' here does not include companies or corporate bodies and therefore they cannot apply for injunctions under this part of the legislation. However, their employees can do so if appropriate (*Daiichi UK Ltd v (1) Stop Huntingdon Cruelty, and (2) Animal Liberation Front* [2003] EWHC 2337 (QB)). For injunctions relating to companies see para. 4.8.4.9.

'Harassment' includes alarming the person or causing him/her distress (s. 7(2) of the 1997 Act). The inclusion of harm and distress is significant as it has been held that a person, in this case a police officer, can be alarmed for the safety of another (*Lodge v DPP* [1989] COD 179).

The s. 1(1A) offence was introduced by the Serious Organised Crime and Police Act 2005 specifically to protect employees working for certain companies from harassment by animal rights protestors. Because of the courts' strict interpretation of the elements of the s. 1 offence (as discussed above) it was unclear how far such employees could be protected by this provision when they had not previously been harassed *individually* even where fellow employees had been. Section 1(1A) makes it an offence for a person to pursue a course of conduct involving the harassment of two or more people on separate occasions which the defendant knows or ought to know involves harassment. The purpose of such harassment is to persuade *any person* (not necessarily one of the people being harassed) not to do something he/she is entitled to do—such as going to work—or to do something he/she is not under any obligation to do—such as releasing animals or passing on confidential information.

The sort of behaviour envisaged by the offence would be the making of threats and intimidation which forces an individual or individuals to stop doing lawful business with another company or with another person. The subsection is not intended to outlaw peaceful protesting or lobbying. For instance, a person simply distributing leaflets outside a shop would not commit this offence unless they threatened or intimidated the people to whom they were handing their leaflets and that person felt harassed, alarmed or distressed. There would also need to be at least two separate incidents amounting to 'a course of conduct'.

The meaning of 'course of conduct' provided in s. 7 of the Act was amended by the Serious Organised Crime and Police Act 2005 and states:

(3)   A 'course of conduct' must involve—

    (a) in the case of conduct in relation to a single person (see s. 1(1)), conduct on at least two occasions in relation to that person, or

    (b) in the case of conduct in relation to two or more persons (see s. 1(1A)), conduct on at least one occasion in relation to each of those persons.

(3A) A person's conduct on any occasion shall be taken, if aided, abetted, counselled or procured by another—

    (a) to be conduct on that occasion of the other (as well as conduct of the person whose conduct it is); and

    (b) to be conduct in relation to which the other's knowledge and purpose, and what he ought to have known, are the same as they were in relation to what was contemplated or reasonably foreseeable at the time of the aiding, abetting, counselling or procuring.

(4)   'Conduct' includes speech.

(5)   References to a person, in the context of the harassment of a person, are references to a person who is an individual.

KEYNOTE

As with the similarly worded offence under the Public Order Act 1986, it appears that doing something remotely which has the desired effect on the victim—such as deliberately making a dog bark at someone—could form part of a 'course of conduct' for the purposes of an offence under the 1997 Act (see *R (On the Application of Taffurelli)* v *DPP* [2004] EWHC 2791 (Admin)). However, simply *failing* to stop a dog barking is a different matter and one that the Divisional Court in *Taffurelli* did not resolve.

Home Office Circular 34/2005 provides guidance on the introduction of the changes to this section and s. 1(1A). Examples of 'course of conduct' provided in the Circular include:

Where an animal rights extremist sends a threatening letter on one occasion to an individual who works for a company and the same extremist sends a threatening email on another occasion to another individual who works for the same company, and his intention is to persuade the individuals that they should not work for that company because of the work that company does, or the contract that it has with other companies, he would commit an offence.

Where an animal rights extremist send a threatening letter on one occasion to an individual who works for company A and the same extremist sends a threatening email on another occasion to another individual who works for company B, and his intention is to persuade the individuals that they should not work for these companies because both companies supply company C, or he intends by his actions to persuade companies A and B not to supply company C, he would commit an offence. In both these examples, if the letters or emails were sent by separate extremists, yet it could be proved that they were acting together, they both would be guilty of an offence. Additionally, under the new s. 3A both an individual employee or a company can apply for an injunction (see para. 4.8.4.9).

Not all courses of conduct will satisfy the offence of harassment. *Lau* v *DPP* [2000] 1 FLR 799 involved a battery (slapping across the face) against the complainant on one occasion, followed sometime later by a threat being made to the complainant's boyfriend in her presence. The court held that the evidence of a 'course of conduct' by the defendant was insufficient to convict. It stated that regard should be had to the number of incidents and the relative times when they took place—the fewer the incidents and the further apart in time that they took place, the less likely it was that a court would find that harassment had taken place.

There are some incidents that do not amount to harassment. Where a defendant approached the victim to strike up conversations and had sent her a gift, this was insufficient to constitute harassment. However, such incidents could provide a background to later behaviour that included covertly filming the victim and rummaging through her rubbish (*King* v *DPP* [2001] ACD 7).

On occasions the courts have accepted that two instances of behaviour by the defendant several months apart will suffice. Where a defendant wrote two threatening letters to a member of the Benefits Agency staff, he was convicted of harassment even though there had been four and a half months' interval between the two letters (*Baron* v *CPS* (2000) 13 June, unreported). The opposite course of conduct was found to amount to harassment where a defendant made several calls to the victim's mobile phone in the space of five minutes. In this case several abusive and threatening messages were left on the victim's voicemail facility and later replayed one after the other (*Kelly* v *DPP* [2002] EWHC 1428 (Admin)). The court held that it was enough that the victim was alarmed or distressed by the course of conduct as a whole rather than by each act making up the course of conduct. This is a different requirement from the more serious offence under s. 4 where the victim must be caused to fear violence on at least two occasions. In relation to that more serious offence, a magistrates' court has been allowed to regard a defendant's conduct on the second occasion as almost retrospectively affecting previous conduct on the first occasion.

There is no specific requirement that the activity making up the course of conduct be of the same nature. Therefore two distinctly different types of behaviour by the defendant (e.g. making a telephone call on one occasion and damaging the victim's property on another) may suffice. In a case involving the racially or religiously aggravated offence, the aggravating element will need to be proved in relation to both instances of the defendant's conduct.

Some behaviour will be sufficiently disturbing or alarming for two instances alone to suffice (e.g. the making of overt threats). Other behaviour, however, may not be sufficient to establish 'harassment' after only two occasions (e.g. the sending of flowers and gifts) and may require more than the bare statutory minimum of two occasions.

Although it may be helpful in terms of proving the occurrence of two or more acts amounting to 'a course of conduct', the practice in some police areas of issuing warnings and maintaining a register of the same (particularly in relation to their own officers) is not a specific requirement of the Act and may raise some issues of procedural fairness.

A limited company cannot be the 'victim' of harassment, although an individual employee or a clearly defined group of individuals could be—*DPP* v *Dziurzynski* [2002] EWHC 1380 (Admin). However, in *Majrowski* v *Guy's and St Thomas's NHS Trust* [2005] EWCA Civ 251, the Appeal Court held that a company could be a 'person' capable of harassing 'another' within the meaning of the Act. This ruling could therefore have implications in relation to the self-employed, customers and suppliers of businesses and members of the public in general. Where it can be shown that the conduct was carried out in the course of employment the employer could be held to be vicariously liable for that conduct.

The definition of harassment in s. 7 of the Protection from Harassment Act 1997 is an inclusive but not exhaustive list. Although the words used in s. 7 are 'alarm *and* distress', the Divisional Court has held that they should be taken disjunctively and not conjunctively, that is, the court need only be satisfied that the behaviour involved one or the other; alarm *or* distress (*DPP* v *Ramsdale* [2001] EWHC Admin 106).

All in all, this has turned out to be a very prosecution-friendly piece of legislation extending to behaviour far beyond the stalking incidents which prompted its drafting.

The repeated commission of other offences (say, public order offences or offences against property) involving the same victim may also amount to harassment. In such cases the advice of the CPS should be sought as to which *charge(s) to prefer*.

In short, in order to prove the s. 1 offence you must show that:

- the defendant pursued a 'course of conduct',
- the course of conduct amounted to harassment as defined in s. 7(1), and
- the defendant knew, or ought to have known, that his/her conduct amounted to harassment.

To avoid the practical difficulties of proving the subjective *intention* of the defendant, the offence focuses on an objective test.

4.8.4.2 What a Reasonable Person Would Think Amounts to Harassment

In addition, s. 1 of the 1997 Act states:

   (2) For the purposes of this section, the person whose course of conduct is in question ought to know that it amounts to or involves harassment of another if a reasonable person in possession of the same information would think the course of conduct amounted to or involved harassment of the other.

4.8.4.3 Aiding and Abetting

As a result of incidents against the directors and staff of life science research companies, the Protection from Harassment Act 1997 was amended (see s. 44 of the Criminal Justice and Police Act 2001). Those changes mean that if someone aids, abets, counsels or procures another to commit an offence under the 1997 Act, the conduct of the 'primary' defendant will be taken to be the conduct of the aider, abettor, counsellor or procurer of the offence. This does not prevent the primary defendant's conduct from being relevant; what it does is to make the aider, abettor, etc. of the offence liable for the conduct which he/she has facilitated. The 2001 Act also makes provision for determining the knowledge and intention of aiders, abettors, etc. Although the Act refers to this area as 'collective harassment', it overlaps with the whole concept of incomplete offences (**see Crime, chapter 1.3**) and the advice of the CPS should be sought in formulating appropriate charges.

4.8.4.4 Defences

If the person concerned in the course of conduct can show that he/she did so:

- for the purpose of preventing or detecting crime, or
- under any enactment or rule of law to comply with a particular condition or requirement, or
- in circumstances whereby the course of conduct was reasonable

the offence under s. 1(1) and (1A) will not apply (s. 1(3)).

The burden of proving any of these features or circumstances lies with the defendant (on the balance of probabilities).

Examples might be police or DSS surveillance teams, or court officers serving summonses. (See also the defence under s. 12 at **para. 4.8.4.8.**)

Whether a course of conduct is 'reasonable' will be a question of fact for a court to decide in the light of all the circumstances. The wording of s. 1(2) suggests that such a test might be an *objective* one (i.e. as a reasonable bystander) and not one based upon the particular belief or perception of the defendant—otherwise the main effect of the 1997 Act would be considerably diluted.

4.8.4.5 Restraining Order and Injunctions

The courts have two significant sources of power available to them to deal with harassment under the 1997 Act. These are injunctions and restraining orders. Injunctions are issued in the ordinary way of any civil injunction and are governed by s. 3 (**see para. 4.8.4.9**), whereas restraining orders follow a *conviction* for an offence under ss. 2 or 4 of the Act and are governed by s. 5 (**see para. 4.8.4.11**).

4.8.4.6 Civil Claims for Harassment

Under s. 3(1) conduct or apprehended conduct falling within s. 1(1) and (1A) may be the subject of a civil claim by the victim/intended victim. This creates a 'statutory tort' of harassment in addition to the criminal offence.

4.8.4.7 Putting People in Fear of Violence

OFFENCE: **Putting People in Fear of Violence—*Protection from Harassment Act 1997, s. 4***
- Triable either way • Five years' imprisonment and/or a fine on indictment
- Six months' imprisonment and/or a fine summarily

OFFENCE: **Racially or Religiously Aggravated—*Crime and Disorder Act 1998, s. 32(1)(b)***
- Triable either way • Seven years' imprisonment and/or a fine on indictment
- Six months' imprisonment and/or a fine summarily

The Protection from Harassment Act 1997, s. 4 states:

(1) A person whose course of conduct causes another to fear, on at least two occasions, that violence will be used against him is guilty of an offence if he knows or ought to know that his course of conduct will cause the other so to fear on each of those occasions.

KEYNOTE

'Course of conduct' is discussed above.

The defendant's course of conduct must cause the victim to fear that violence *will* (rather than might) be used against him or her. This is quite a strict requirement and showing that the conduct caused the victim to be seriously frightened of what might happen in the future is not enough (*R v Henley* [2000] Crim LR 582).

You must show that the defendant knew, or ought to have known that their conduct would cause the other person to fear violence. This may be shown by any previous conversations or communications between the defendant and the victim, together with the victim's response to the defendant's earlier behaviour (e.g. running away, calling the police, etc.).

The fear of violence being used against the victim must be present on both occasions. If it is present on one occasion but not the other, the offence under s. 2 above may be appropriate. As with other parts of this legislation, this is not necessarily as straightforward as it may seem. What if the defendant's conduct on the first occasion (e.g. a threat to burn the victim's house down) did not cause the victim undue concern, but a second threat some time later to do the same thing *did* put the victim in fear of violence, partly because this was the second time the threat had been made? These were the circumstances in *R (On the Application of A) v DPP* [2004] EWHC 2454 (Admin), where the defendant argued that the victim had only been put in fear of violence by his threats to burn her house down on the second occasion and that therefore the offence had not been made out. The Divisional Court disagreed and held that the magistrates were entitled to find as a matter of fact that the two incidents had put the victim in fear of violence, notwithstanding her admission that, on the first occasion, she had not been too concerned.

> The course of conduct for the purpose of s. 4 has to cause a person to fear, on at least two occasions, that violence would be used against *him/her* rather than against a member of their family (*Mohammed Ali Caurti v DPP* [2001] EWHC Admin 867).
>
> Unlike some of the other racially or religiously aggravated offences, provisions are specifically made for alternative verdicts in relation to harassment (see s. 32(6) of the Crime and Disorder Act 1998). Where the racially or religiously aggravated form of the offence is charged, the aggravating element of the defendant's conduct must be shown in relation to both instances.
>
> As with the s. 2 offence, a single instance of behaviour may be enough to support a charge for another offence.
>
> Again, this offence is not one of *intent* but one which is subject to a test of reasonableness against the standard of an ordinary person in possession of the same information as the defendant.
>
> For the powers of a court to issue a restraining order or injunction in relation to this offence, see para. 4.8.4.9.

The Protection from Harassment Act 1997, s. 4 goes on to state:

> (2) For the purposes of this section, the person whose course of conduct is in question ought to know that it will cause another to fear that violence will be used against him on any occasion if a reasonable person in possession of the same information would think the course of conduct would cause the other so to fear on that occasion.

4.8.4.8   Defence

The Protection from Harassment Act 1997, s. 4 states:

> (3) It is a defence for a person charged with an offence under this section to show that—
>   (a) his course of conduct was pursued for the purpose of preventing or detecting crime,
>   (b) his course of conduct was pursued under any enactment or rule of law or to comply with any condition or requirement imposed by any person under any enactment, or
>   (c) the pursuit of his course of conduct was reasonable for the protection of himself or another or for the protection of his or another's property.

KEYNOTE

There is a slight difference in the wording of the defence when compared with that under s. 1(3) above. There, the defendant may show that his/her conduct was reasonable in the particular circumstances. In relation to the more serious offence under s. 4, the defendant must show that his/her conduct was reasonable *for the protection of him/herself, another person or his/her own/another's property.* These are the only grounds on which the defendant may argue reasonableness in answer to a charge under s. 4. He/she could not therefore argue, say, that the pursuit of the course of conduct was 'reasonable' in order to enforce a debt or to communicate with the victim.

In addition, s. 12 allows for the Secretary of State to certify that the conduct was carried out by a 'specified person' on a 'specified occasion' related to:

* national security,
* the economic well-being of the United Kingdom, or
* the prevention or detection of serious crime

on behalf of the Crown. If such a certification is made, the conduct of the specified person will not be an offence under the 1997 Act.

4.8.4.9   Injunctions

Under ss. 3 and 3A of the Protection from Harassment Act 1997, the High Court or a county court may issue an injunction in respect of civil proceedings brought in respect of an actual or apprehended breach of s. 1(1) and (1A). The effect of this is that a defendant may be made the subject of an injunction even though his/her behaviour has not amounted to an offence under the 1997 Act.

Section 3 also states:

(3) Where—
   (a) in such proceedings the High Court or a county court grants an injunction for the purpose of restraining the defendant from pursuing any conduct which amounts to harassment, and
   (b) the plaintiff considers that the defendant has done anything which he is prohibited from doing by the injunction,

the plaintiff may apply for the issue of a warrant for the arrest of the defendant.

The Serious Organised Crime and Police Act 2001 introduced a new s. 3A to the 1997 Act in relation to injunctions to protect persons from harassment within s. 1(1A) (**see para. 4.8.4.1**). The person who is the victim of the course of conduct, or any person at whom the persuasion is aimed, may apply for an injunction. Therefore, where people who work for a life science or fur company are being harassed in order to persuade them not to work for that company, or in order to persuade the company not to supply another company, either the employees themselves or the company in question could apply for an injunction.

Section 3A states:

(1) This section applies where there is an actual or apprehended breach of section 1(1A) by any person ('the relevant person').
(2) In such a case—
   (a) any person who is or may be a victim of the course of conduct in question, or
   (b) any person who is or may be a person falling within section 1(1A)(c),
   may apply to the High Court or the county court for an injunction restraining the relevant person from pursuing any conduct which amounts to harassment in relation to any person or persons mentioned or described in the injunction.
(3) Sections 3(3) to (9) apply in relation to an injunction granted under subsection (2) above as they apply in relation to an injunction granted as mentioned in section 3(3)(a).

KEYNOTE

Anyone arrested under a warrant issued under s. 3(3)(b) may be dealt with by the court at the time of his/her appearance. Alternatively, the court may adjourn the proceedings and release the defendant, dealing with him/her within 14 days of his/her arrest provided the defendant is given not less than two days' notice of the adjourned hearing (see the Rules of the Supreme Court (Amendment) 1998 (SI 1998/1898) and the County Court (Amendment) Rules 1998 (SI 1998/1899)).

In a case involving an injunction restraining the actions of an anti-vivisection group, the Divisional Court held that the 1997 Act was not a means of preventing individuals from exercising their right to protest over issues of public interest. Eady J said that such an extension of the law had clearly not been Parliament's intention and that the courts would resist any attempts to interpret the Act widely (*Huntingdon Life Sciences Ltd* v *Curtin* (1997) *The Times*, 11 December).

The application for an injunction is essentially a private matter being pursued by an individual. The point at which the matter becomes of concern to policing is where the injunction is breached without reasonable excuse. The civil standard of proof (balance of probabilities) will apply to injunction applications—*Hipgrave* v *Jones* [2004] EWHC 2901 (QB).

In harassment cases the High Court can grant an interlocutory injunction under s. 37(1) of the Senior Courts Act 1981. This injunction can restrain conduct which is not in itself tortious or unlawful but is reasonably necessary to protect the legitimate interests of others. This includes the power to impose an exclusion zone when granting a non-molestation injunction (*Burris* v *Azadani* [1995] 1 WLR 1372). However in *Hall* v *Save Newchurch Guinea Pigs (Campaign)* [2005] EWHC 372 (QB), the court held that a 200 km² exclusion zone was not reasonably necessary for the protection of the protected person's rights.

4.8.4.10 Breach of Injunctions

Of far greater significance is the offence created by s. 3(6) of the Protection from Harassment Act 1997 .

OFFENCE: **Breach of Injunction—*Protection from Harassment Act 1997, s. 3(6)***
   • Triable either way   • Five years' imprisonment and/or a fine on indictment
   • Six months' imprisonment and/or a fine summarily

The Protection from Harassment Act 1997, s. 3 goes on to state:

(6) Where—
   (a) the High Court or a county court grants an injunction for the purpose mentioned in subsection (3)(a), and
   (b) without reasonable excuse…
he is guilty of an offence.

KEYNOTE

Civil injunctions generally will only involve the police where a power of an arrest has been attached (e.g. under s. 3(3) above). In these cases the role of the police will be to bring the defendant before the court in order that he/she can explain his/her behaviour. There is therefore no investigative or prosecuting function on the part of the officers. Section 3(6), however, creates a specific offence of breaching the terms of an injunction.

If a defendant breaches an injunction and commits the offence under s. 3(6) above, he/she will be dealt with in the way of any other prisoner brought into police detention and will face a prison sentence of five years.

It is important to distinguish the offence under s. 3(6), breaching an injunction, from the provisions of s. 5 which deal with restraining orders.

4.8.4.11 Restraining Orders

The Protection from Harassment Act 1997, s. 5 states:

(2) The order may, for the purpose of protecting the victim or victims of the offence, or any other person mentioned in the order, from conduct which—
   (a) amounts to harassment, or
   (b) will cause a fear of violence,
prohibit the defendant from doing anything described in the order.

Sections 12 and 13 of the Domestic Violence, Crime and Victims Act 2004 amend s. 5 of the Protection from Harassment Act as amended in 2007, and insert s. 5A into the Act. This extends the powers of the courts in England and Wales to enable them to impose a restraining order, when sentencing for any offence, for the purpose of protecting a person from conduct which amounts to harassment or will cause a fear of violence by the defendant. The court will be able to make a restraining order on acquittal for any offence where it considers it necessary to protect a person from harassment. Section 12 also gives any person mentioned in the restraining order the right to make a representation if an application is made to vary or discharge the restraining order. Section 13 makes equivalent amendments in respect of Northern Ireland.

KEYNOTE

The Domestic Violence, Crime and Victims Act 2004 changes clearly amount to a considerable broadening of the scope of restraining orders.

Unlike the injunction under s. 3(3), restraining orders can be made in a criminal court.

The order may be made for the protection of the victim or anyone else mentioned and it may run for a specified period or until a further order. Any order must identify by name the parties it is intended to protect (*R v Mann* (2000) 97(14) LSG 41).

In a case arising out of protests against fur retailers, the Divisional Court held that restraining orders under the 1997 Act did not generally breach the right to freedom of speech and association as protected by Articles 10 and 11 of the European Convention on Human Rights (*Silverton v Gravett* (2001) LTL 31 October).

The prosecutor, the defendant or anyone else mentioned in the order may apply to the court that made it to have the order varied or discharged (s. 5(4)). The courts have the power to vary an order made for a specified period of time so as to extend the expiry date of the order (*DPP v Hall* [2005] EWHC 2612 (Admin)). In *R v Debnath* [2005] EWCA Crim 3472 an order prohibiting an offender from publishing information indefinitely was held to be lawful and not in breach of Article 10 (Freedom of Expression) of the European Convention on Human Rights.

Breach of a restraining order without reasonable excuse will amount to a significant criminal offence (**see para. 4.8.4.12**). A practical example of how restraining orders can operate can be seen in *R v Evans (Dorothy)* [2004] EWCA 3102. In that case the appellant had been convicted of harassing her neighbours and a restraining order under (s. 5(5)) had been made by the court. Among other things, the order prohibited the appellant from 'using abusive words or actions' towards her neighbours. Some time into the life of the order, the neighbour called a plumber out to their house and he parked his van in the street. It was alleged that the appellant then moved her own car—which was also parked in the street—into such a position that it effectively blocked the plumber's van. The appellant was convicted of the offence of breaching the order (**see para. 4.8.4.12**) and appealed, partly on the basis that her conduct could not properly be said to have amounted to 'abusive action'. The Court of Appeal held that such matters should be approached in the same way as specific legislation which outlaws abusive conduct, and that a jury was entitled to conclude that, as she had been motivated by spite, the appellant's actions could be 'abusive' for this purpose.

4.8.4.12 Breach of Restraining Order

OFFENCE: **Breach of Restraining Order—*Protection from Harassment Act 1997, s. 5(5)***
- Triable either way • Five years' imprisonment and/or a fine on indictment
- Six months' imprisonment and/or a fine summarily

The Protection from Harassment Act 1997, s. 5 states:

(5) If without reasonable excuse the defendant does anything which he is prohibited from doing by an order under this section, he is guilty of an offence.

KEYNOTE

The above offence is one of strict liability and therefore whether the defendant believed that the order was no longer in force is only relevant to the extent that he/she may have a reasonable excuse—*Barber* v *CPS* [2004] EWHC 2605 (Admin). The prosecution needs simply to prove the existence and terms of the order (which it can do by an admission from the defendant in interview) and the doing of anything prohibited by it. Once that is done the offence is complete.

For an example of the practical operation and interpretation of this offence **see para. 4.8.4.11**. In the case of *R v Evans (Dorothy)* [2004] EWCA Crim 3102, the Court of Appeal held that harassment takes many forms and therefore the courts need to be able to prohibit conduct in fairly wide terms (e.g. in the wording of the order). It is, however, unclear just how far the defendant's subjective understanding of the terms of the order will be relevant. If a defendant honestly believed that his/her conduct did not breach the terms of the order, this would certainly be relevant when considering whether or not he/she had a 'reasonable excuse'.

Substituting or failing to include a charge under ss. 2 or 4, removes the court's powers to make a restraining order which may be the main remedy sought by a victim. In any cases of doubt the guidance of the CPS should be sought.

4.8.5 Anti-social Behaviour

In the Crime and Disorder Act 1998 the government introduced the Anti-social Behaviour Order (ASBO). A significant feature of ASBOs lies in the fact that they are civil orders, made under the procedure set out in the Magistrates' Courts Act 1980. This point was confirmed by the Court of Appeal in a case where it was held that the purpose behind ASBOs was the protection of an identified section of the community, not 'crime and punishment' and that this purpose had to be borne in mind when determining the compatibility of ASBO proceedings with the Human Rights Act 1998 (*R (On the Application of M (a child))* v *Manchester Crown Court* [2001] EWCA Civ 281). In a case involving a sex offenders order (under earlier legislation) the Divisional Court reiterated that these proceedings are *civil* in nature for the purposes of Article 6 of the European Convention (see *B* v *Chief Constable of Avon & Somerset Constabulary* [2001] 1 WLR 340). Although applications for ASBOs are civil (not criminal) in nature, the House of Lords has held that although the standard of proof in civil proceedings (the balance of probabilities) should apply to applications for ASBOs, the criminal standard of proof (beyond reasonable doubt) should apply where allegations are made which, if proved, would have serious consequences for the defendant (*R (On the Application of McCann)* v *Manchester Crown Court* [2002] UKHL 39). It also means that the procedural requirements of Article 6(2) and (3) of the European Convention on Human Rights do not apply. While any proceedings have to be 'fair' in accordance with Article 6(1) and any restriction on the defendant's liberty in an order is an 'interference' with their private life (under Article 8), the whole point of such proceedings is to try to predict how far past behaviour gives reasonable cause to believe that an order is necessary under the circumstances to curb future misconduct (*Jones (Peter)* v *Greater Manchester Police Authority* [2001] EWHC Admin 189).

In *S* v *Poole Borough Council* [2002] EWHC 244 (Admin), a juvenile, who was the subject of an ASBO application, had already been convicted of several offences under the Education Act 1996. He objected to the same material being used from his criminal trial to support the application for an ASBO, arguing that the use of the ASBO had been intended as an alternative to criminal prosecution. Hearing the appeal by way of case stated, the Divisional Court held that it was 'perfectly proper' to use the same material in this way and that the ASBO is akin to an injunction.

One of the benefits of an ASBO lies in its potential effect as a deterrent to others. This benefit will only be realised if there is sufficient publicity given to the issuing of the order and the circumstances of it. The extent to which the police (and local authorities) can use such publicity and include a photograph of the person made the subject of an ASBO, was clarified by the Divisional Court in *R (On the Application of Stanley)* v *Metropolitan Police Commissioner, Brent London Borough and the Secretary of State for the Home Department* [2004] EWHC 2229 (Admin). In that case ASBOs had been made against a number of youths, all of whom had previous convictions. The local authority posted details of the proceedings on its website, there was extensive press coverage of the case, and the police approved publication of leaflets bearing photographs of the youths which were distributed in the area specified in the ASBOs. The youths challenged the decisions to publish their ASBOs in this way. The Divisional Court held that ASBOs required publicity in order to be effective as a civil remedy. If publicity intended to reassure members of the community, to inform, to assist in reinforcement and to deter others, was to be effective, it needed photographs, names and at least parts of addresses. The court found that people living in the community had been subjected to significant criminal behaviour for several years and, as the ASBOs had been obtained to bring that behaviour to an end, the material publicising it could say so. Although the court accepted that it was always necessary to consider the Human Rights Act 1998 issues in the area of post-ASBO publicity, it held that there was a need here for readers to know the identities of the people against whom the orders had been made—if only to avoid mis-identification—and even the 'colourful language' used in the publicity material might be necessary in order to attract the attention of readers. This decision does *not* mean that so-called 'name and shame' campaigns will be lawful—rather, it means that those behind the publicising of the ASBO (or part of it) must be able to show a link between the publicity and the practical effectiveness of the ASBO.

The government introduced an Anti-Social Behaviour, Crime and Policing Bill to Parliament in December 2012 in which it set out its desire to scrap ASBOs and replace them with Criminal Behaviour Orders, which would be issued by the courts after conviction and would ban individuals from certain activities or places and require them to address their behaviour.

4.8.5.1   The Anti-social Behaviour Order (ASBO)

The Crime and Disorder Act 1998, s. 1 states:

(1) An application for an order under this section may be made by a relevant authority if it appears to the authority that the following conditions are fulfilled with respect to any person aged 10 or over, namely—

    (a) that the person has acted, since the commencement date, in an anti-social manner, that is to say, in a manner that caused or was likely to cause harassment, alarm or distress to one or more persons not of the same household as himself; and

    (b) that such an order is necessary to protect relevant persons from further anti-social acts by him.

    ...

(1A) In this section and sections 1AA, 1B, 1C, 1CA, 1E, IF and 1K 'relevant authority' means—

    (a) the council for a local government area;

    (aa) in relation to England, a county council;

    (b) the chief officer of police of any police force maintained for a police area;

    (c) the chief constable of the British Transport Police Force;

    (ca) any non-profit registered provider of social housing which provides or manages any houses or hostel in a local government area;

    (d) any person registered under section 1 of the Housing Act 1996 (c 52) as a social landlord who provides or manages any houses or hostel in a local government area; or

    (e) a housing action trust established by order in pursuance of section 62 of the Housing Act 1988

(1B) In this section 'relevant persons' means—

    (a) in relation to a relevant authority falling within paragraph (a) of subsection (1A), persons within the local government area of that council;

    (aa) in relation to a relevant authority falling within paragraph (aa) of subsection (1A) persons within the county of the county council;

    (b) in relation to a relevant authority falling within paragraph (b) of that subsection, persons within the police area;

    (c) in relation to a relevant authority falling within paragraph (c) of that subsection—

      (i) persons who are within or likely to be within a place specified in section 31(1)(a) to (f) of the Railways and Transport Safety Act 2003 in a local government area; or

      (ii) persons who are within or likely to be within such a place;

    (d) in relation to a relevant authority falling within paragraph (ca), (d) or (e) of that subsection—

      (i) persons who are residing in or who are otherwise on or likely to be on premises provided or managed by that authority; or

      (ii) persons who are in the vicinity of or likely to be in the vicinity of such premises

(2) ...

(3) Such an application shall be made by complaint to a magistrates' court.

(4) If, on such an application, it is proved that the conditions mentioned in subsection (1) above are fulfilled, the magistrates' court may make an order under this section (an 'anti-social behaviour order') which prohibits the defendant from doing anything described in the order.

The Crime and Disorder Act 1998, s. 1A states:

(2) The Secretary of State may by order—

    (a) provide that a person or body of any other description specified in the order is, in such cases and circumstances as may be prescribed by the order, to be a relevant authority for the purposes of such of sections 1 above and 1B, 1CA, 1E and 1F below as are specified in the order; and

    (b) prescribe the description of persons who are to be 'relevant persons' in relation to that person or body.

KEYNOTE

Although ASBOs are prohibitory in their nature (in that they order people *not* to do certain things rather than to do certain things), the purpose of the prohibition is not to punish but to prevent anti-social behaviour and to protect members of the public from further instances of it. Therefore, there is nothing legally wrong with including a curfew provision in an ASBO if it is necessary for such protection (*Lonergan* v *Lewes Crown Court* [2005] EWHC 457 (Admin)).

In order to apply for an ASBO it must appear to the relevant authority that:

- a relevant person acted in a manner that caused, or was likely to cause harassment, alarm or distress to one or more people who are not of the same household as the relevant person, and
- that such an order is necessary to protect people from further anti-social acts by that person. The 'relevant authority' for the purposes of an ASBO is the local authority or the chief officer of police, any part of whose police area lies within the area of that local authority. However, the chief constable of the British Transport Police may also apply for an ASBO to protect people from anti-social behaviour within the force's jurisdiction and 'registered social landlords' (under s. 1 of the Housing Act 1996) may apply for orders in relation to such behaviour on or in the vicinity of premises owned by them. The Secretary of State may also add to this list of relevant authorities (see s. 1A).

However, the person against whom an application for an order is being considered has no legal right to be consulted (*Wareham* v *Purbeck District Council* [2005] EWHC 358 (Admin)).

A general requirement for local authorities and chief officers to consult before applying for an ASBO is imposed by s. 1E, meaning that, in practice, both of these sources of authority will have to work together in bringing any application for an ASBO. Applications by other relevant authorities must be made in consultation with the local chief officer and the local council in the area in which the person lives or appears to live. This imposition of multiple responsibility, which effectively enforces a collaborative approach between the police and local authorities, is another key feature of the 1998 Act (see also ss. 5 and 6, and **para. 4.1.4**).

Chief constables can delegate or devolve the functions set out in s. 1(1) and (2) of the Act to any officer(s) judged suitable by them—*R (On the Application of Chief Constable of West Midlands Police)* v *Birmingham Magistrates' Court* [2002] EWHC 1087 (Admin). Under s. 1F, inserted by the Serious Organised Crime and Police Act 2005, local authorities can make arrangements for the contracting out of their ASBO functions subject to the relevant order made by the Secretary of State.

The Drugs Act 2005 inserted ss. 1G and 1H into the 1998 Act and these relate to intervention orders. This type of order can be made alongside an ASBO when drug misuse has been a cause of the behaviour that led to the ASBO being made. An intervention order sets out the specified activities and attendance requirements of a defendant, and the duration of the order cannot exceed six months (s. 1G). The breach of an order is a summary offence (s. 1H).

For these purposes, the relevant local government areas are:

- in relation to England, a district or London borough, the City of London, the Isle of Wight and the Isles of Scilly;
- in relation to Wales, a county or county borough.

(s. 1(12))

In these circumstances it is the relevant authority who makes the application for an ASBO, thereby removing from the 'victim' of the conduct the burden of seeking a remedy him/herself (contrast this with the remedy using an injunction in cases of harassment; **see para. 4.8.4.9**).

The proviso at s. 1(1)(a)—which excludes people from the same household—shows that the ASBO is not intended as a remedy for domestic disputes (as to which, **see chapter 4.14**).

Chief constables can delegate or devolve the functions set out in s. 1(1) and (2) of the Act to any officer(s) judged suitable by them—*R (On the Application of Chief Constable of West Midlands Police)* v *Birmingham Magistrates' Court* [2002] EWHC 1087 (Admin).

An application may be made in respect of the behaviour of any person aged 10 or over.

Local councils and chief officers may now make applications to protect people in their respective areas whether or not the original anti-social behaviour occurred in that area or elsewhere.

Criminal courts can also make an ASBO in respect of a defendant where he/she has been convicted of an offence (s. 1C). The court can make such an order of its own volition, irrespective of whether any specific application has been made but it can only be made *in addition* to any sentence or conditional discharge (s. 1C(4)). This illustrates that the order is, as under the other methods of application, a preventive measure rather than a punishment. If the defendant is detained in legal custody (e.g. given a custodial sentence or remanded into police custody), the order may be suspended until he/she is released (see s. 1C(5)).

Criminal courts can also make an ASBO in respect of a defendant where he/she has been convicted of an offence (s. 1C). However, in *R (On the Application of Mills)* v *Birmingham Magistrates' Court* [2005] EWHC 2732 (Admin) it was held that cases of theft, including shoplifting, would not automatically fall within the criteria of s. 1. However, there may be circumstances where some thefts or acts of shoplifting could cause harassment, alarm or distress and so fall within this section.

The court may adjourn any proceedings in relation to an order under this section even after sentencing the offender (s. 1C(4A)). If the offender does not appear for any adjourned proceedings, the court may further adjourn the proceedings, or it may issue a warrant for his/her arrest but not unless it is satisfied that he/she has had adequate notice of the time and place of the adjourned proceedings (s. 1C(4B) and (4C)).

Under s. 1CA a relevant authority or the CPS can apply to vary or discharge an Anti-social Behaviour Order made on conviction. No s. 1C order will be discharged before two years have passed since the date of the order without the consent of the defendant and the DPP (s. 1CA(7)).

4.8.5.2 ASBOs and Youth Rehabilitation Orders in Court Proceedings

Section 1B of the Crime and Disorder Act 1998 allows relevant authorities to apply to a county court where they are, or have become, a party to the proceedings and similar conditions apply to such orders as those made by magistrates' courts.

Section 1(1) of the Criminal Justice and Immigration Act 2008 provides that where a person aged under 18 is convicted of an offence, the court by or before which the person is convicted may make a Youth Rehabilitation Order (YRO) which can impose on the person any one or more of a number of requirements.

The YRO (applicable only to offences committed on or after 30 November 2009) replaces 'community sentences' for under-18s. The Order has 18 potential requirements, each of which can operate as a stand-alone requirement or be combined with other requirements under the YRO. Examples of the type of requirements that may be made under a YRO include:

- Activity requirement
- Supervision requirement
- Attendance centre requirement
- Curfew requirement
- Drug treatment requirement
- Exclusion requirement
- Unpaid work requirement (16/17 year olds only).

A YRO will come into effect on the day on which it is made or at a later date specified by the court (Criminal Justice and Immigration Act 2008, sch. 1, para. 30).

4.8.5.3 Interim Orders

Either the magistrates' or the county court may make an interim ASBO under the provisions of s. 1D if it considers that it is just to do so. Courts have the power to grant an interim order in relation to an application for an order under s. 1 or 1B (**see para. 4.8.5.2**) or a request under s. 1C (**see para. 4.8.5.1**) pending a full hearing. Interim orders can be made in this way pending the determination of the main application and any such order must be for a fixed period; it can be varied, renewed or discharged and ceases to have effect once the main application has been determined (e.g. once a full ASBO has been made or the application refused (s. 1D(4)).

Section 1(5) states:

For the purpose of determining whether the condition mentioned in subsection (1)(a) above is fulfilled, the court shall disregard any act of the defendant which he shows was reasonable in the circumstances.

Section 1(6) states:

The prohibitions that may be imposed by an anti-social behaviour order are those necessary for the purpose of protecting persons (whether relevant persons or persons elsewhere in England and Wales) from further anti-social acts by the defendant.

KEYNOTE

This requirement clearly places the burden of showing the reasonableness of his/her behaviour on the defendant.

4.8.5.4 Power to Direct a Person to Leave a Place

The Serious Organised Crime and Police Act 2005, s. 112 states:

(1) A constable may direct a person to leave a place if he believes, on reasonable grounds, that the person is in the place at a time when he would be prohibited from entering it by virtue of—
   (a) an order to which subsection (2) applies, or
   (b) a condition to which subsection (3) applies.
(2) This subsection applies to an order which—
   (a) was made, by virtue of any enactment, following the person's conviction of an offence, and
   (b) prohibits the person from entering the place or from doing so during a period specified in the order.
(3) This subsection applies to a condition which—
   (a) was imposed, by virtue of any enactment, as a condition of the person's release from a prison in which he was serving a sentence of imprisonment following his conviction for an offence, and
   (b) prohibits the person from entering the place or from doing so during a period specified in the condition.
(4) A direction under this section may be given orally.

KEYNOTE

Prior to the introduction of this section the police could only ask an offender in breach of an exclusion order to leave the area and had no power of arrest if he/she refused. However, s. 112 provides the police with a new power to direct a person to leave an exclusion area if they reasonably believe that the person is prohibited from entering the area. In knowingly failing to obey that direction the person commits a new offence of contravening a direction to leave a place (see para. 4.8.5.5).

The power only applies to a breach of those exclusion orders imposed as part of an:

- exclusion order (s. 112(1))
- community sentence
- suspended sentence
- licence condition on release from custody (s. 112(3)).

Exclusion is imposed as part of a civil order, such as an Anti-social Behaviour Order or a restraining order, is not included.

Notification of a breach of an exclusion requirement may be made by a person who is aware the offender is in breach of his or her exclusion requirements or by electronic monitoring. Pilot schemes testing the use of satellite tracking technology are currently being conducted by three forces in England.

Home Office Circular 29/2005 explains the new power under this section.

4.8.5.5   Contravening a Direction to Leave a Place

OFFENCE: **Contravening a Direction to Leave a Place**—*Serious Organised Crime and Police Act 2005, s. 112(5)*
* • Triable summarily • 51 weeks' imprisonment or a fine

The Serious Organised Crime and Police Act 2005, s. 112 states:

> (5) Any person who knowingly contravenes a direction given to him under this section is guilty of an offence.

4.8.5.6   Duration of Anti-social Behaviour Order

An ASBO has a minimum period of two years' duration (s. 1(7)). Although an ASBO has to run for a minimum of two years, it does not follow that every prohibition within the order must endure for the life of the order. In many cases it is possible that a period of curfew could properly be set at less than the full life of the order or, in light of behavioural progress, an application to vary the curfew could be made under s. 1(8) of the 1998 Act (*Lonergan* v *Lewes Crown Court* [2005] EWHC 457 (Admin)).

Under s. 1(8) of the 1998 Act, either the applicant or the defendant may apply to have the order varied or discharged but, under s. 1(9), no ASBO shall be discharged before the end of two years except with the consent of both parties.

4.8.5.7   Breach of an Anti-social Behaviour Order

OFFENCE: **Breaching an Anti-social Behaviour Order**—*Crime and Disorder Act 1998, s. 1(10)*
* • Triable either way • Five years' imprisonment and/or a fine on indictment
* • Six months' imprisonment and/or a fine summarily

The Crime and Disorder Act 1998, s. 1 states:

> (10) If without reasonable excuse a person does anything which he is prohibited from doing by an anti-social behaviour order, he is guilty of an offence and liable—
> (a) on summary conviction, to imprisonment for a term not exceeding six months or to a fine not exceeding the statutory maximum, or to both; or
> (b) on conviction on indictment, to imprisonment for a term not exceeding five years or to a fine, or to both.

KEYNOTE

The above offence applies to all ASBOs, including interim orders and those made by the county court.

In proceedings for an offence under s. 1(10), a copy of the original ASBO, certified as such by the proper officer of the court which made it, is admissible as evidence of its having been made and of its contents to the same extent that oral evidence of those things is admissible in those proceedings (s. 1(10C)).

As the punishment provided by a conditional discharge (under the Powers of Criminal Courts (Sentencing) Act 2000) has the same general effect as an ASBO, a court cannot impose a conditional discharge on a defendant found guilty of committing an offence under s. 1(10) above (s. 1(11)).

Given the breadth of an ASBO, which may restrain a defendant from communicating with a particular person or from creating noise or nuisance, the behaviour required to commit this offence could be relatively minor. The advice of the CPS may need to be sought in cases involving what appear to be innocuous but technical breaches of such an order.

It appears from the wording of the 1998 Act that a person might have an ASBO made against him/her in his/her absence. Although a magistrates' court has the power to issue a summons and then a warrant (under the Magistrates' Courts Act 1980) in order to compel the person to come to court when an application for an ASBO is being heard, it does seem that the court can go on to make an ASBO *ex parte* (in the absence of the other party).

4.8.5.8   Appeal

The Crime and Disorder Act 1998, s. 4 states:

(1) An appeal shall lie to the Crown Court against the making by a magistrates' court of an anti-social behaviour order, an individual support order, an order under section 1D above, . . .

(2) On such an appeal the Crown Court—

(a) may make such orders as may be necessary to give effect to its determination of the appeal; and

(b) may also make such incidental or consequential orders as appear to it to be just.

KEYNOTE

The appeal process above applies to both full ASBOs and interim orders made by a magistrates' court; it does not apply to ASBOs made by the county court in civil proceedings under s. 1B.

There is no right of appeal open to the local authority or chief officer against a decision of a court not to make an order. That would not preclude the applicant from requiring the court to 'state a case' for consideration by the Divisional Court in appropriate circumstances.

4.8.5.9   People Acting in an Anti-social Manner

In addition to the ASBO system above, the police have other specific powers to deal with anti-social behaviour. If a constable in uniform has reason to believe that a person has been, or is, acting in an anti-social manner (within the meaning of s. 1 of the Crime and Disorder Act 1998—**see para. 4.8.4.1**), the constable may require the person to give their name and address (Police Reform Act 2002, s. 50). This power is among those that can be conferred on a Community Support Officer designated under sch. 4 to the Police Reform Act 2002 and a person accredited under sch. 5 to that Act.

Where motor vehicles are involved, there are further specific powers to stop the vehicle and to seize it.

Note that s. 91 of the Anti-social Behaviour Act 2003 allows a local authority to request a power of arrest to be attached to any provision of an injunction obtained under s. 222 of the Local Government Act 1972 where the injunction is to prohibit anti-social behaviour. The Police and Justice Act repealed s. 91 but the replacement provision still includes the power to attach a power of arrest. However, changes will be made as to the procedure following such an arrest.

OFFENCE: **Failing to Comply with Requirement to Give Name and Address—*Police Reform Act 2002, s. 50(2)***
• Triable summarily • Fine

The Police Reform Act 2002, s. 50 states:

(2) Any person who—

(a) fails to give his name and address when required to do so under subsection (1), or

(b) gives a false or inaccurate name or address in response to a requirement under that subsection, is guilty of an offence . . .

4.8.5.10 Closure Notices and Orders on Premises Associated with Persistent Disorder or Nuisance

Part 1A of the Anti-social Behaviour Act 2003, added by the Criminal Justice and Immigration Act 2008, makes provision for closure orders in respect of premises associated with persistent disorder or nuisance. The provisions are very similar to those in part 1 of the Act, which relate to closure orders in respect of premises where Class A drugs are used unlawfully.

Section 11A(1) sets out the test which must be satisfied before a police officer not below the rank of superintendent or a local authority can authorise the issue of a part 1A closure notice. The officer or authority must have reasonable grounds for believing that a person has engaged in anti-social behaviour on the premises in the preceding three months and that the premises are associated with significant and persistent disorder or persistent serious nuisance. Section 11A(2) requires that the authorising officer must be satisfied that the local authority has been consulted and that reasonable steps have been taken to identify those living on the premises or with an interest in them before the authorisation for the issue of the notice is given. The local authority must be satisfied that the chief officer of police for the area has been consulted and that reasonable steps have been taken to identify those living on the premises or with an interest in them before the authorisation for the issue of the notice is given. Authorisation for the issue of a closure notice can be given initially orally or in writing, but must be confirmed in writing as soon as practicable if not done so at the time.

A part 1A closure notice must give notice that an application will be made to court for a closure order and must include details of the time and place of the court hearing and a statement that access to the premises during the period of the notice is prohibited to anyone other than someone who is usually resident in, or is the owner of, the premises. It must explain the effects of the closure order, state that non-compliance with the notice amounts to an offence and also contain information about local providers of advice on legal and housing matters.

Once authorised, a constable or an employee of the local authority must serve the notice by fixing a copy of it to at least one prominent part of the premises in question, fixing it to each normal means of access and to any outbuildings. He/she must also give a copy to those people identified as living in or having an interest in the property, as well as to at least one person who appears to the server of the notice to have control of or responsibility for the premises. The notice must also be served on any person who occupies any other part of the building in which the premises are located if their access will be impeded should the part 1A closure order be made. Section 11A(9) allows the server of the notice to enter any premises for the purposes of fixing the closure notice to a prominent place, using reasonable force if necessary.

Once a part 1A closure notice has been issued, an application must be made to the magistrates' court for the making of a closure order, by either a constable or an employee of the local authority, depending on who issued the part 1A closure notice. The court must hear the application within 48 hours from the time the part 1A closure notice was fixed to a prominent place on the premises. The court must be satisfied that a person has engaged in anti-social behaviour on the premises (but not necessarily within the preceding three months), that the use of premises is associated with significant and persistent disorder or persistent serious nuisance, and that the making of the order is necessary to prevent future disorder or nuisance of that description. The court may adjourn the hearing for up to 14 days to allow the occupier or persons having control of or responsibility for, or an interest in, the premises to show why a part 1A closure order should not be made, for example because the problems have ceased or the occupiers have been evicted. A closure notice continues to have effect until the end of any such adjournment. A closure order may be made in relation to the whole or part of the premises affected by the notice.

When a closure order is made, a constable (or a person authorised by the chief officer of police in respect of orders applied for by a constable) or a person authorised by the local authority (in respect of orders applied for by that authority) may enter the premises and secure them against entry by any other person, using reasonable force if necessary. The same authorised persons may also enter the premises at any time to carry out essential maintenance or repairs.

The police or local authority may apply for an extension of up to three months for a part 1A closure order for which they originally applied. The closure order must not have effect for more than six months in total. Such an application must be authorised by a police officer not below the rank of superintendent or the local authority, who must:

- have reasonable grounds for believing that the extension of the order is necessary for the purpose of preventing the occurrence of significant and persistent disorder or persistent serious nuisance to the public; and
- be satisfied that the appropriate chief officer or local authority (whichever is not making the application) has been consulted about the intention to make the application.

Section 11D of the Anti-social Behaviour Act 2003 creates offences of remaining on or entering premises which are subject to a part 1A closure notice or order without reasonable excuse. It also creates an offence of obstructing a person who is serving a part 1A closure notice or securing closed premises against entry.

Appeals to the Crown Court against part 1A closure orders can be made under s. 11F by all interested parties, and against a refusal to make one by the police or local authority that made the application for the order.

4.8.6   Nuisance and the Environment

There are many forms of behaviour which, although not falling within some of the more 'serious' offences discussed elsewhere in this Manual, are nevertheless a source of annoyance or disquiet to the community. Some of these activities are usefully classified as 'nuisances', while others come under 'environmental' legislation. What follows is a brief summary of some of the main areas covered by both types of legislation.

4.8.6.1   Public Nuisance

Although many of the activities dealt with in this chapter are described as 'nuisances', there is a specific offence of creating or being responsible for a public nuisance, an offence that overlaps with some other aspects of criminal behaviour.

The common law concept of nuisance is separated into public and private nuisance. Private nuisance is dealt with under civil law as a *tort* ('wrong'). Public nuisance, however, can also be dealt with under criminal law.

A public nuisance is an unlawful act or an omission to discharge a duty which, in either case, obstructs or causes inconvenience or damage to the public in the exercise of their common rights (see *Attorney-General* v *PYA Quarries Ltd (No. 1)* [1957] 2 QB 169).

Although there is no 'magic number' of people who must suffer from the annoyance or obstruction in order for it to amount to a *public nuisance*, you must show that the act or omission affected the public in general as opposed to a small group of people (such as the employees of a firm). Therefore, in *R* v *Madden* [1975] 1 WLR 1379, where a person made a hoax bomb call to an organisation (**see paras 4.9.2 to 4.9.3**), it was held that such behaviour could in theory amount to a public nuisance, although in *Madden* it did not as the annoyance/obstruction was limited in its effect.

People who entered school premises for the purpose of glue sniffing were held to have committed a public nuisance by unduly interfering with the comfortable and convenient enjoyment of the land, even though the school was empty (*Sykes* v *Holmes* [1985] Crim LR 791). (For offences and powers in relation to educational premises specifically, **see chapter 4.15**.)

Given that the courts have unlimited sentencing power in relation to this offence, there may well be advantages in considering its application to cases where the only other offences disclosed would be summary offences. An example is the case of *R* v *Johnson* [1997] 1 WLR 367 where the defendant made several hundred obscene telephone calls to women across a county over a period of five years.

4.8.6.2 Offence of Public Nuisance

OFFENCE: **Public Nuisance—*Common Law***

- Triable either way   • Unlimited powers of sentence on indictment
- Statutory maxima apply summarily

It is an offence at common law for a person to cause a public nuisance.

KEYNOTE

As this offence is a common law 'misdemeanour', a court may pass sentence at its discretion on indictment, that is, its sentencing powers are unlimited.

Although the typical and obvious causes of public nuisance are now the subject of express statutory prohibition, the common law offence still exists and is not in breach of Article 7 (No Punishment without Crime) of the European Convention on Human Rights (*R* v *Rimmington; R* v *Goldstein* [2005] UKHL 63).

The behaviour of the defendant must interfere with the material rights enjoyed by a class of Her Majesty's subjects (*R* v *Johnson* [1997] 1 WLR 367).

It is not necessary to prove that every member within a class of people in the community has been affected by the defendant's behaviour; simply that a representative cross-section has been so affected (*Attorney-General* v *PYA Quarries Ltd (No. 2)* [1961] 2 QB 169). Such a cross-section might include members of a housing estate or users of a public transport facility such as a main-line railway station.

In Lord Denning's view (also in the *PYA* case), a nuisance would need to be 'so widespread in its range or so indiscriminate in its effect' that it would not be reasonable to expect one person to bring proceedings on his/her own to put a stop to it.

There is no need to show that the defendant intended his/her actions or omission to cause a public nuisance and it will be enough that he/she knew or ought to have known that the conduct would bring about a public nuisance (*R* v *Shorrock* [1994] QB 279).

A good practical example of how the law of public nuisance can be used in a policing context can be seen in *R* v *Harvey* [2003] EWCA Crim 112. In that case the defendant was convicted of causing a public nuisance after following different groups of children in his car, sounding the horn and smiling at them. Evidence was adduced to show that he presented a real threat to children with the possibility of his luring them into his car for unlawful purposes. Although the defendant was originally sentenced to life imprisonment, that was later reduced in the absence of features of sex or violence, to three years.

Other examples of criminal public nuisances have included:

- allowing a rave to take place in a field (*R* v *Shorrock* [1994] QB 279)
- making hundreds of nuisance telephone calls to at least 13 women (*R* v *Johnson* [1997] 1 WLR 367)
- contaminating 30 houses with dust and noise from a quarry (*Attorney-General* v *PYA Quarries Ltd (No. 2)* [1961] 2 QB 169)
- selling meat which was unfit for consumption (*R* v *Stephens* (1866) LR 1 QB 702).

In addition, s. 79 of the Environmental Protection Act 1990 sets out a list of 'statutory nuisances', any of which would potentially be capable of amounting to a criminal offence if it met the relevant conditions.

4.8.6.3 Defence

Statutory authorisation for a person's conduct (e.g. building a road or a railway), will be a defence provided the behaviour is specifically permitted by that statute (*Hammersmith and City Railway Co.* v *Brand and Louisa* (1869–70) LR 4 HL 171).

4.8.6.4 Enforcement

In addition to providing powers of arrest and sentencing for tackling public nuisance through the criminal process, there is always the preventive measure of a court injunction available. Historically, the Attorney-General has sought injunctions on behalf of the public at large. However, local authorities have the power to apply for a public nuisance injunction under the Local Government Act 1972 (see *Stoke-on-Trent City Council* v *B & Q (Retail) Ltd* [1984] AC 754) and there appears to be no reason why chief officers should not do the same.

4.8.6.5 Fireworks

The Fireworks Act 2003 regulates the sale and use of fireworks under certain circumstances and makes provision for further regulations by the Secretary of State. The principal regulations in this regard are the Fireworks Regulations 2004 (SI 2004/1836). The relevant aspects of this legislation affecting practical policing are summarised at **paras 4.8.6.6 to 4.8.6.10**.

4.8.6.6 Controls on Supplying Fireworks

Sections 2 and 3 of the Fireworks Act 2003 allow for regulations to ensure that there is no risk that the use of fireworks will lead to death, injury, or distress to people and animals or the destruction of, or damage to, property.

Generally 'fireworks' mean fireworks for the purposes of the British Standard Specification published on 30 November 1988 (BS 7114) or any British Standard Specification replacing it. The regulations go on to categorise specific types of firework according to the danger they present. These range from caps and party poppers to the elaborate pyrotechnic devices as used in public displays.

4.8.6.7 Possession of Fireworks

OFFENCE: **Possession of Fireworks—*Fireworks Regulations 2004, regs 4 and 5***
- Triable summarily • Six months' imprisonment and/or a fine

Regulations 4 and 5 state:

4.—(1) Subject to regulation 6 below, no person under the age of eighteen years shall possess an adult firework in a public place.

...

5. Subject to regulation 6 below, no person shall possess a category 4 firework.

4.8.6.8 Prohibition of Use of Certain Fireworks at Night

Regulation 7 states:

(1) Subject to paragraph (2) below, no person shall use an adult firework during night hours.

4.8.6.9 Other Fireworks Regulations

Sections 4 and 5 of the Act allow for regulations to prohibit the supply of fireworks in certain circumstances or the supply of certain types of firework (such as excessively loud fireworks which are defined and regulated by reg. 8 of the 2004 Regulations). In addition, reg. 9 imposes a general requirement for anyone supplying adult fireworks (or exposing them for supply) to be licensed. However, this requirement does *not* apply:

- on the first day of the Chinese New Year or on the day of Diwali and the three days immediately preceding it;
- during the period beginning on 15 October and ending on 10 November; or
- during the period beginning on 26 December and ending on 31 December.

These exemptions are designed to work in conjunction with 'permitted fireworks nights'.

'Supplying' includes selling, exchanging and giving fireworks (even as prizes) but does not include supplying otherwise than in the course of business (see s. 1(3)). People licensed by the local authority to supply adult fireworks have to comply with certain conditions. Where the supply or exposure for supply takes place on premises, the person must display in a prominent position a notice of the prescribed size stating that it is illegal to sell adult fireworks to anyone under the age of 18 and that it is illegal for anyone under the age of 18 to possess adult fireworks in a public place (reg. 10). There are also further requirements under reg. 10 for suppliers to provide full details as to their own suppliers and customers in cases of larger transactions of *any* fireworks (not just adult fireworks) and an absolute restriction on importing *any* fireworks unless certain information has been given to the Commissioners of Her Majesty's Revenue and Customs (see reg. 11).

The Act goes on to make provision for the regulation of public fireworks displays, the requirement of suppliers to attend training courses, the licensing of suppliers and the provision of information about fireworks generally.

4.8.6.10   Breach of Fireworks Regulations

OFFENCE: **Breach of Regulations—*Fireworks Act 2003, s. 11***
- Triable summarily • Six months' imprisonment and/or a fine

The Fireworks Act 2003, s. 11 states:

(1) Any person who contravenes a prohibition imposed by fireworks regulations is guilty of an offence.
(2) Any person who fails to comply with a requirement imposed by or under fireworks regulations to give or not to give information is guilty of an offence.
(3) Where a requirement to give information is imposed by or under fireworks regulations, a person is guilty of an offence if, in giving the information, he—
    (a) makes a statement which he knows is false in a material particular; or
    (b) recklessly makes a statement which is false in a material particular.

KEYNOTE

There is some overlap between regulations made under the Consumer Protection Act 1987 and this offence and both pieces of legislation should be checked.

In particular, the general defence of due diligence (under s. 39 of that Act) will apply to offences at s. 11(1) and (2) above.

The regulations are amended regularly and reference should be made to the latest version when considering the enforcement of their provisions. Many of the regulations are concerned with the way in which fireworks are advertised, displayed and sold.

In relation to the supply of, offer or agreement to supply fireworks to a child or young person, s. 11(8) creates a defence for the defendant to show that he/she had no reason to suspect that the person was under the relevant age.

The sections of the Consumer Protection Act 1987 allowing for enforcement measures such as test purchases and powers of search, generally apply to the above offences.

OFFENCE: **Throwing Fireworks into Highway or Street—*Explosives Act 1875, s. 80***
- Triable summarily • Fine

The Explosives Act 1875, s. 80 states:

If any person throw, cast, or fire any fireworks in or into any highway, street, thoroughfare, or public place, he shall be guilty of an offence and liable.

4.8.6.11 Noise

The creation of noise is another environmental issue that can severely affect quality of life in the community. As a result, there are several statutory provisions allowing the relevant agencies to address problems associated with noise and its sources.

Under the Anti-social Behaviour Act 2003 the chief executive of a relevant local authority can apply to a court for an order to close licensed premises in certain circumstances involving noise (**see chapter 4.15**).

In addition to the above legislation, the Noise Act 1996 provides powers to allow local authorities to tackle the problems of noise within their community. For instance, ss. 2 and 3 of the 1996 Act allow for the serving of warning notices in relation to 'excessive noise' emanating from one house which can be heard in another at night. Night is defined as being between 11 pm and 7 am (s. 2(6)). The Clean Neighbourhoods and Environment Act 2005 has extended s. 2 to include noise emitted from any premises in respect of which a premises licence (Licensing Act 2003—**see para. 4.16.4.1**), or a temporary event notice (Licensing Act 2003—**see para. 4.16.4.5**) has been issued, that can be heard in a dwelling (s. 2(2)(b) of the 1996 Act). The noise level must be measured using an 'approved device' (s. 6). Any warning must be served on the person who appears to be responsible for the noise or by leaving the warning notice at the 'offending premises' (s. 3(3)). (Note that, under the Environmental Protection Act 1990 there is no requirement for evidence of acoustic measurements and a court may convict on other evidence (e.g. evidence from an environmental enforcement officer of excessively loud music being played—*Lewisham Borough Council* v *Hall* [2002] EWHC 960 (Admin)).

OFFENCE: **Where Noise from Other Premises Exceeds Permitted Level after Service of Notice—*Noise Act 1996, s. 4A(1)***

  • Triable summarily • Fine

The Noise Act 1996, s. 4 states:

(1) If a warning notice has been served in respect of noise emitted from a dwelling, any person who is responsible for noise which—
   (a) is emitted from the dwelling in the period specified in the notice, and
   (b) exceeds the permitted level, as measured from within the complainant's dwelling, is guilty of an offence.
(2) It is a defence for a person charged with an offence under this section to show that there was a reasonable excuse for the act, default or sufferance in question.

OFFENCE: **Where Noise from a Dwelling Exceeds Permitted Level after Service of Notices—*Noise Act 1996, s. 4(1)***

  • Triable summarily • Fine

The Noise Act 1996, s. 4A states:

(1) If—
   (a) a warning notice has been served under section 3 in respect of noise emitted from premises,
   (b) noise is emitted from the premises in the period specified in the notice, and
   (c) the noise exceeds the permitted level, as measured from within the complainant's dwelling, the person responsible in relation to the offending premises at the time at which the noise referred to in paragraph (c) is emitted is guilty of an offence.

4.8.6.12 Litter

The law regulating the roles of local authorities in controlling litter can be found in the Litter Act 1983. The 1983 Act makes allowances for actions by 'litter authorities' (i.e. local councils, see s. 10) to discourage the dropping of litter and for the provision of litter bins.

Removing or interfering with local authority litter bins or litter notices is a summary offence under s. 5(9).

The remainder of the provisions regulating the dropping of litter are in the Environmental Protection Act 1990.

The law in this area has been extended recently by the Anti-social Behaviour Act 2003 and the Clean Neighbourhoods and Environment Act 2005. The Clean Neighbourhoods and Environment Act 2005 makes further provisions with regard to litter in public places and the use of fixed penalty notices to deal with litter offences. This has increased the powers of litter authorities and extended the powers of local authorities for dealing with unlawfully deposited waste.

OFFENCE: **Leaving Litter—*Environmental Protection Act 1990, s. 87(1)***
- Triable summarily • Fine

The Environmental Protection Act 1990, s. 87 states:

(1) A person is guilty of an offence if he throws down, drops or otherwise deposits any litter in any place to which this section applies and leaves it.

dogs if it involves one of the following matters: fouling of land by dogs and the removal of dog faeces; keeping dogs on leads; excluding dogs from land; restricting the number of dogs a person can take on to any land (s. 55(3)). The procedure to be followed is contained in the Dog Control Orders (Procedures) Regulations 2006 (SI 2006/798).

Section 59 of the 2005 Act allows authorised officers to issue a fixed penalty notice in respect of any offence under s. 55.

Similarly, s. 88 of the Environmental Protection Act 1990 makes provision for the issuing of fixed penalty notices in respect of the general litter offence above. Section 88 provides that, where a notice setting out the prescribed details is given to an offender, by an authorised officer of a litter authority, no proceedings can be instituted against that person for 14 days. Payment of the fixed penalty will prevent the person's prosecution for that offence. Where the offender pays by posting the required amount properly to the relevant address, payment will be regarded as having been made at the time of the expected *delivery* (not the time the letter is posted) in the normal course of post (s. 88(4)).

The power to issue fixed penalty notices in relation to the Clean Neighbourhoods and Environment Act 2005 and the Environmental Protection Act 1990 are among those that can be conferred on a Community Support Officer designated under sch. 4 to the Police Reform Act 2002 and a person accredited under sch. 5 to that Act, along with the relevant power to require the person to give their name and address.

The Clean Neighbourhoods and Environment Act 2005, clarifies that 'litter', for the purposes of part 4 of the Environmental Protection Act 1990, specifically includes cigarettes, cigars and like products and discarded chewing gum (including bubble gum).

Under s. 91 of the 1990 Act, a magistrates' court may act on a complaint of anyone who is aggrieved by the defacement by litter or refuse of any relevant road, highway or land occupied by relevant statutory undertakers or educational institutions. Before doing so, the court must notify the occupier of the complaint. The court may then issue a litter abatement order requiring the relevant person to remedy the situation and failure to comply with such an order is a summary offence under s. 91(9).

Section 99 and sch. 4 to the 1990 Act give local authorities powers to deal with problems involving the abandonment of shopping trolleys and luggage trolleys. Schedule 4 allows local authorities (after abiding by the procedure in s. 99) to seize, retain and ultimately dispose of such trolleys. The Clean Neighbourhoods and Environment Act 2005 has extended the powers of local authorities and they can now charge the person believed to be the owner of an abandoned shopping or luggage trolley for its removal, storage and disposal.

Section 87 also states:

> (4A) No offence is committed under subsection (1) above where the depositing of the litter is—
> (a) authorised by law; or
> (b) done by or with the consent of the owner, occupier or other person having control of the place where it is deposited.

4.8.6.13 Begging

Section 3 of the Vagrancy Act 1824 creates the ancient offence of begging or gathering alms in streets and public places. This summary offence is still relevant and the activities of so-called beggars have attracted increased interest over recent years. It has been held that the mischief to which the 1824 Act was directed was conduct that forces passers-by to deal with the defendant's activities (*Mathers* v *Penfold* [1915] 1 KB 514) and there is authority to suggest that a single act of approaching one person and asking for money is not, without more, enough to raise a *prima facie* case of begging (*R* v *Dalton* [1982] Crim LR 375). Where the person seeking money is doing something in exchange, such as singing as a busker, it has been held that this conduct does not amount to begging (see *Gray* v *Chief Constable of Greater Manchester Police* [1983] Crim LR 45).

There is a further summary offence of 'persistent' begging, and both offences (s. 3 and s. 4) are 'trigger offences' for the purposes of the Criminal Justice and Court Service Act 2000.

This has a number of consequences for those charged with such an offence. The principal consequence is that he/she will come within the provisions of s. 63B of the Police and Criminal Evidence Act 1984. This effectively allows (in certain circumstances) for a sample of urine or a non-intimate sample to be taken for the purpose of ascertaining the presence of any specified Class A drug in his/her body.

Offences Involving Communications

4.9.1 Introduction

As with many areas of criminal law and policing, the substantial terrorist threat in the past decade has made the offences set out below much more relevant to day-to-day policing. The making of direct threats to people's lives or their property is covered by a number of statutes. There are, however, specific offences which deal with the making of general threats and other communications which are intended to cause alarm or anxiety among people receiving them. The growth of social media has also brought challenges for police forces as complaints are frequently made about the use of platforms such as Facebook and Twitter to send malicious messages or make threats, such as in the case of *Chambers* v *DPP* [2012] EWHC 2157 (Admin) which examined a message interpreted as a bomb hoax at an airport.

4.9.2 Placing or Sending Material

OFFENCE: **Placing or Sending Substances—*Anti-terrorism, Crime and Security Act 2001, s. 114***
- Triable either way • Seven years' imprisonment on indictment
- Six months' imprisonment and/or a fine summarily

The Anti-terrorism, Crime and Security Act 2001, s. 114 states:

(1) A person is guilty of an offence if he—
  (a) places any substance or other thing in any place; or
  (b) sends any substance or other thing from one place to another (by post, rail or any other means whatever);
with the intention of inducing in a person anywhere in the world a belief that it is likely to be (or contain) a noxious substance or other noxious thing and thereby endanger human life or create a serious risk to human health.

OFFENCE: **Placing or Sending Articles—*Criminal Law Act 1977, s. 51(1)***
- Triable either way • Seven years' imprisonment on indictment
- Six months' imprisonment and/or a fine summarily

The Criminal Law Act 1977, s. 51 states:

(1) A person who—
  (a) places any article in any place whatever; or
  (b) dispatches any article by post, rail or any other means whatever of sending things from one place to another,
with the intention (in either case) of inducing in some other person a belief that it is likely to explode or ignite and thereby cause personal injury or damage to property is guilty of an offence.

In this subsection 'article' includes substance.

KEYNOTE

These definitions are very wide. The Criminal Law Act 1977 offence relates specifically to bomb threats while the 2001 offence (which is modelled on the earlier offence) is far broader and applies to creating a belief in someone anywhere in the world. For the purposes of the Anti-terrorism, Crime and Security Act 2001, 'substance' here includes any biological agent and any other natural or artificial substance (whatever its form, origin or method of production (s. 115(1)). The 'article' concerned in s. 51(1) can also be anything at all.

It is the inducing of a relevant belief in someone else that is the key element to the first offence, not any actual endangering of life or risk to human health. You do not have to show that the defendant had any particular person in mind in whom he/she intended to induce the belief in question (see the Anti-terrorism, Crime and Security Act 2001, s. 115(2) and the Criminal Law Act 1977, s. 51(3)).

The Home Office guidance to the Anti-terrorism, Crime and Security Act 2001 offence gives examples of acts which, though at one time would not have been seen as threatening, would now amount to an offence under this section—examples such as scattering white powder in a public place or spraying water droplets around in an underground train, in each case with the requisite intent.

4.9.3 Threats and Communication of False Information

OFFENCE: **Threats Involving Noxious Substances or Things—*Anti-terrorism, Crime and Security Act 2001, s. 114***
- Triable either way • Seven years' imprisonment on indictment
- Six months' imprisonment and/or a fine summarily

The Anti-terrorism, Crime and Security Act 2001, s. 114 states:

(2) A person is guilty of an offence if he communicates any information which he knows or believes to be false with the intention of inducing in a person anywhere in the world a belief that a noxious substance or other noxious thing is likely to be present (whether at the time the information is communicated or later) in any place and thereby endanger human life or create a serious risk to human health.

OFFENCE: **Communicating False Information—*Criminal Law Act 1977, s. 51(2)***
- Triable either way • Seven years' imprisonment on indictment
- Six months' imprisonment and/or a fine summarily

The Criminal Law Act 1977, s. 51 states:

(2) A person who communicates any information which he knows or believes to be false to another person with the intention of inducing in him or any other person a false belief that a bomb or other thing liable to explode or ignite is present in any place or location whatever is guilty of an offence.

KEYNOTE

The essence of these offences is the communication of information which the defendant knows or believes to be false. Again, the 1977 Act offence relates specifically to bomb hoaxes while the 2001 Act offence is far wider and applies to creating a belief in someone anywhere in the world. The meaning of 'substance' for the 2001 Act offence is the same as in the Keynote at **para. 4.9.2** and in neither case is there a need to show that the defendant had any particular person in mind. Under the Criminal Law Act 1977 it has been held that while the information communicated need not be specific, a message saying that there is a bomb somewhere has been held to be enough, even though no location was given (*R* v *Webb* (1995) 92(27) LSG 31).

The wording of the 1977 Act offence is in the *present* tense which suggests that a message threatening to place a bomb etc. sometime in the *future* would not suffice, while the 2001 Act specifically allows for such a situation.

The use of some form of code word is not a prerequisite of the offence but it does go towards proving the defendant's intention that the threat etc. be taken seriously; it may also be taken into account when passing sentence.

The 'communication' can be in any form (including, it would seem, on the Internet) and can be direct (e.g. to a railway station or department store where the bomb or device is alleged to be) or indirect (to a radio station switchboard).

There is no need for the person making the communication to have any particular person in mind at the time (s. 51(3)).

4.9.4   Misuse and Obstruction of Postal Services

OFFENCE: **Interfering with Mail—*Postal Services Act 2000, s. 84***
> • Triable summarily • Six months' imprisonment and/or a fine

The Postal Services Act 2000, s. 84 states:

> (1) A person commits an offence if, without reasonable excuse, he—
>   (a) intentionally delays or opens a postal packet in the course of its transmission by post, or
>   (b) intentionally opens a mail-bag
> (2) …
> (3) A person commits an offence if, intending to act to a person's detriment and without reasonable excuse, he opens a postal packet which he knows or reasonably suspects has been incorrectly delivered to him.

KEYNOTE

The Postal Services Act 2000 was introduced to make the extensive changes in the law that were required by the 'privatisation' of the Post Office and its functions.

The Act creates two offences in relation to interfering with the mail, along with a further offence of opening someone else's mail that has been incorrectly delivered.

The first general offence, under s. 84(1), applies to anyone. There is a second offence (under s. 83) which specifically applies to postal workers and which is triable either way, carrying a maximum of two years' imprisonment. Under the second, more specific, offence, you have to prove the same elements as the above offence but also need to show that the person was engaged in the business of a postal operator and that he/she was acting contrary to his/her duty.

To prove the above offence you must show that the defendant acted without any reasonable excuse and that he/she also acted intentionally. The offence does not apply where the actions were carried out under a lawful warrant or statutory provision (e.g. the Regulation of Investigatory Powers Act 2000). Similarly, any action carried out in accordance with the terms and conditions of postage will not attract criminal liability here. Delays (but not the opening of mail) caused by industrial action also fall outside this offence.

The offence under s. 84(3) looks simple enough, but requires proof of a number of elements. First, it must be shown that the defendant opened a postal packet (as opposed to delaying it under s. 84(1)). It must also be shown that he/she did so intending 'to act to another person's detriment'—this can be any other person's detriment, not simply the addressee, but it is nevertheless a key feature of the offence. It must also be shown that the defendant knew or reasonably suspected that the postal packet had been incorrectly delivered to him/her. This means that the packet must have been 'delivered'; it would be difficult to show that someone reasonably suspected a packet that is still in transit to have been 'incorrectly delivered' to him/her. As with the general offence under s. 84(1), any opening of postal packets that is done properly in pursuance of a warrant, statutory authority or under the conditions of postage will not be an offence under s. 84(3).

4.9.4.1   Sending Prohibited Article by Post

OFFENCE: **Sending Prohibited Article by Post—*Postal Services Act 2000, s. 85***
> • Triable either way • 12 months' imprisonment on indictment • Fine summarily

The Postal Services Act 2000, s. 85 states:

(1) A person commits an offence if he sends by post a postal packet which encloses any creature, article or thing of any kind which is likely to injure other postal packets in course of their transmission by post or any person engaged in the business of a postal operator.

(2) Subsection (1) does not apply to postal packets which enclose anything permitted (whether generally or specifically) by the postal operator concerned.

(3) A person commits an offence if he sends by post a postal packet which encloses—

    (a) any indecent or obscene print, painting, photograph, lithograph, engraving, cinematograph film or other record of a picture or pictures, book, card or written communication, or

    (b) any other indecent or obscene article (whether or not of a similar kind to those mentioned in paragraph (a)).

(4) A person commits an offence if he sends by post a postal packet which has on the packet, or on the cover of the packet, any words, marks or designs which are of an indecent or obscene character.

KEYNOTE

Section 85 creates a number of offences, all concerned with the sending of postal packets via the postal infrastructure. The first offence addresses the sending of things that are likely to harm either other postal packets or postal workers. Evidence that any article is in the course of transmission by post, or has been accepted by a postal operator for transmission by post, will be enough to prove that it is in fact a 'postal packet' (s. 109). This offence will not apply to the sending of things that are permitted by the relevant postal operator.

The other offences under s. 85 apply irrespective of whether the offending packets are permitted by the postal operator and include indecent or obscene contents or packaging.

Whether an article is obscene etc. is a question of fact for the court to determine in each case. That test will not look at the particular views or frailties of the recipient but will be an objective test based on a reasonable bystander (*Kosmos Publications Ltd* v *DPP* [1975] Crim LR 345).

4.9.4.2 Obstruction of Postal Service

OFFENCE: **Obstruction—*Postal Services Act 2000, s. 88***

        • Triable summarily • Fine

The Postal Services Act 2000, s. 88 states:

(1) A person commits an offence if, without reasonable excuse, he—

    (a) obstructs a person engaged in the business of a universal service provider in the execution of his duty in connection with the provision of a universal postal service, or

    (b) obstructs, while in any universal postal service post office or related premises, the course of business of a universal service provider.

(2) ...

(3) A person commits an offence if without reasonable excuse, he fails to leave a universal postal service post office or related premises when required to do so by a person who—

    (a) is engaged in the business of a universal service provider, and

    (b) reasonably suspects him of committing an offence under subsection (1).

(4) A person who commits an offence under subsection (3)—

    (a) ...

    (b) may be removed by any person engaged in the business of a universal service provider.

KEYNOTE

Section 88 creates two offences relating to obstruction. The first offence involves the general obstruction, without reasonable excuse, of someone engaged in the business of a 'universal service provider'. These providers are broadly organisations empowered under the 2000 Act to carry on many of the services that were formerly provided by the Post Office.

The second offence relates to conduct in a post office or related premises. Such conduct must be shown to have obstructed, without reasonable excuse, *the course of business* of a universal service provider. Therefore, it is not a member of staff who has to be obstructed here, but rather, the postal business itself.

Subsection (3) is of more immediate relevance to police officers. This offence is committed if a person fails without reasonable excuse to leave a post office or related premises when required to do so by someone engaged in the provider's business who reasonably suspects the other person of committing one of the obstruction offences under s. 88(1). Anyone failing to leave when properly required to do so under subs. (3) may be removed by the post office staff but also, subs. (5) provides that *'any constable shall on demand remove, or assist in removing, any such person'*. This places a clear duty on—as opposed to just granting a power to—individual police officers to help in removing offenders under these circumstances.

'Related premises' are any premises belonging to a universal postal service post office or used together with any such post office (s. 88(6)).

4.9.5 Malicious Communications

OFFENCE: **Malicious Communications—*Malicious Communications Act 1988, s. 1(1)***

  • Triable summarily • Six months' imprisonment and/or a fine

The Malicious Communications Act 1988, s. 1 states:

(1) Any person who sends to another person—
 (a) a letter, electronic communication or article of any description which conveys—
  (i) a message which is indecent or grossly offensive;
  (ii) a threat; or
  (iii) information which is false and known or believed to be false by the sender; or
 (b) any article or electronic communication which is, in whole or part, of an indecent or grossly offensive nature,

is guilty of an offence if his purpose, or one of his purposes, in sending it is that it should, so far as falling within paragraph (a) or (b) above, cause distress or anxiety to the recipient or to any other person to whom he intends that it or its contents or nature should be communicated.

KEYNOTE

The offence is not restricted to threatening or indecent communications and can include giving false information provided that *one* of the sender's purposes in so doing is to cause distress or anxiety. 'Purposes' is simply another way of saying 'intention'.

In addition to letters, the above offence also covers *any* article; it also covers electronic communications which include any oral or other communication by means of an electronic communications network. This will extend to communications in electronic form such as emails, text messages, pager messages etc. (see s. 1(2A)).

'Sending' will include transmitting.

The relevant distress or anxiety may be intended towards the recipient *or* any other person.

It is clear from s. 1(3) that the offence can be committed by using someone else to send, deliver or transmit a message. This would include occasions where a person falsely reports that someone has been a victim of a crime in order to cause anxiety or distress by the arrival of the police.

Section 1(1)(b) covers occasions where the article itself is indecent or grossly offensive (such as putting dog faeces through someone's letter box).

4.9.5.1 Defence Regarding Malicious Communications

Section 1 of the 1988 Act goes on to state:

(2) A person is not guilty of an offence by virtue of subsection (1)(a)(ii) above if he shows—
 (a) that the threat was used to reinforce a demand made by him on reasonable grounds; and
 (b) that he believed, and had reasonable grounds for believing, that the use of the threat was a proper means of reinforcing the demand.

KEYNOTE

The wording of the statutory defence has been changed (by the Criminal Justice and Police Act 2001) to make the relevant test objective. It will no longer be enough that the person claiming the defence under s. 1(2) believed that he/she had reasonable grounds; the defendant will have to show:

- that there were in fact reasonable grounds for making the demand;
- that he/she believed that the accompanying threat was a proper means of enforcing the demand; and
- that reasonable grounds existed for that belief.

Given the decisions of the courts in similarly worded defences under the Theft Act 1968 (e.g. blackmail; see *Crime*, chapter 1.14), it is unlikely that any demand could be reasonable where agreement to it would amount to a crime.

The defence is intended to cover financial institutions and other commercial concerns who often need to send forceful letters to customers. However, for the offence of unlawfully harassing debtors, see s. 40 of the Administration of Justice Act 1970.

4.9.6 Public Communications

OFFENCE: **Improper Use of Public Electronic Communications Network— *Communications Act 2003, s.127***

- Triable summarily • Six months' imprisonment and/or a fine

The Communications Act 2003, s. 127 states:

(1) A person is guilty of an offence if he—
    (a) sends by means of a public electronic communications network a message or other matter that is grossly offensive or of an indecent, obscene or menacing character; or
    (b) causes any such message or matter to be so sent.
(2) A person is guilty of an offence if, for the purpose of causing annoyance, inconvenience or needless anxiety to another, he—
    (a) sends by means of a public electronic communications network, a message that he knows to be false;
    (b) causes such a message to be sent; or
    (c) persistently makes use of a public electronic communications network.

KEYNOTE

These offences, like their predecessors, were designed to deal with 'nuisance' calls. They only apply to 'public' electronic communications networks. These are defined as an electronic communications network provided wholly or mainly for the purpose of making electronic communications services available to members of the public (s. 151) and would therefore not generally include internal calls in a workplace. The wording would apply to the sending of messages via the Internet (provided the system used comes within the definition under s. 151). They do, however, take in public social media systems such as Twitter, as the case of *Chambers v DPP* [2012] EWHC 2157 (Admin) has held. This involved a man posting a joke on his Twitter account about a bomb hoax at an airport. He was arrested and charged under s. 127.

There is no need to show a particular 'purpose' (intention) on the part of the defendant for the first offence under s. 127(1) and that offence is complete if the message is, as a matter of fact, grossly offensive, indecent, obscene or menacing. The offence also covers actions which cause others to send such a message. Unlike the offence under s. 51(2) of the Criminal Law Act 1977 (see para. 4.9.3), there is no need for any information passed to be 'false'. In determining whether a message is 'grossly offensive', it is the message and not the content that is the basic ingredient of the offence. What constitutes 'grossly offensive' has to be judged by considering the reaction of reasonable people and the standards of an open and just multiracial society (*DPP v Collins* [2005] EWHC 1308 (Admin)).

The second offence, under s. 127(2), requires that you show the defendant acted with the purpose of causing annoyance, inconvenience or needless anxiety. A person is to be treated as 'persistently misusing' a network or service in any case in which his/her misuse is repeated on a sufficient number of occasions for it to be clear that the misuse represents a pattern of behaviour or practice, or recklessness as to whether persons suffer annoyance, inconvenience or anxiety (s. 128(6)). In assessing these points it is immaterial that the misuse was in relation to a 'network' on some occasions and in relation to a communications 'service' on others, that different networks or services were involved on different occasions or that the people likely to suffer annoyance, inconvenience or anxiety were different on different occasions (s. 128(7)).

This second offence is a 'penalty offence' for the purposes of s. 1 of the Criminal Justice and Police Act 2001 (see para. 4.5.3).

Where a number of calls have been made to several different people within the community, the offence of public nuisance may also be considered.

4.9.6.1   False Alarms of Fire

OFFENCE: **Making False Alarm of Fire—*Fire and Rescue Services Act 2004, s. 49***
- Triable summarily
- Imprisonment for a term not exceeding 51 weeks and/or a fine (In relation to an offence committed before the commencement of s. 281(5) of the Criminal Justice Act 2003, the reference to 51 weeks is to be read as a reference to three months)

The Fire and Rescue Services Act 2004, s. 49 states:

(1) A person commits an offence if he knowingly gives or causes to be given a false alarm of fire to a person acting on behalf of a fire and rescue authority.

KEYNOTE

The offence requires proof that the defendant acted 'knowingly' (as opposed to e.g. mistakenly). The offence clearly applies where someone makes a malicious call to a fire and rescue authority. However, the wording 'causes to be given' potentially covers the making of a false report to a body other than a fire and rescue authority—e.g. the police—if the person knew that this would result in the police passing that call to the relevant fire and rescue authority.

This offence is a 'penalty offence' for the purposes of s. 1 of the Criminal Justice and Police Act 2001 (see para. 4.5.14).

4.10 Terrorism and Associated Offences

4.10.1 Introduction

The law on terrorism contained in this chapter relates to the Terrorism Act 2000, Terrorism Act 2006, Counter-Terrorism Act 2008 and the Terrorism Prevention and Investigation Measures Act 2011. Another piece of legislation dealing with terrorism is the Anti-terrorism, Crime and Security Act 2001. The 2001 Act, which is not the subject of this chapter, deals with offences designed to combat the potential use by terrorists of poisons and chemical, biological and nuclear weapons, as well as the forfeiture of assets and the disclosure of information by public bodies.

4.10.2 Terrorism Defined

Terrorism is defined in the Terrorism Act 2000, s. 1 as:

(1) ...the use or threat of action where—
  (a) the action falls within subsection (2),
  (b) the use or threat is designed to influence the government or an international governmental organisation, or to intimidate the public or a section of the public, and
  (c) the use or threat is made for the purpose of advancing a political, religious, ideological or racial cause.
(2) Action falls within this subsection if it—
  (a) involves serious violence against a person,
  (b) involves serious damage to property,
  (c) endangers a person's life, other than that of the person committing the action,
  (d) creates a serious risk to the health or safety of the public or a section of the public, or
  (e) is designed seriously to interfere with or seriously to disrupt an electronic system.
(3) The use or threat of action falling within subsection (2) which involves the use of firearms or explosives is terrorism whether or not subsection (1)(b) is satisfied.

KEYNOTE

This definition includes domestic terrorism, and is so broad that it should be considered when dealing with other, more familiar offences such as blackmail, contamination of goods and threats to kill.

The definition recognises that terrorist activity may be motivated by religious, racial or fundamental reasons rather than simply political ones. The purpose of advancing a 'racial' cause was inserted by s. 75 of the Counter-Terrorism Act 2008. Although a racial cause will in most cases be subsumed within a political or ideological cause, this amendment is designed to put the matter beyond doubt that such a cause is included. The definition also encompasses broad activities (including threats) which, though potentially devastating in their impact on society, may not be overtly violent. Examples of such activity might be interference with domestic water and power supplies or serious disruption of computer networks.

The provision at s. 1(3) means that, where the relevant criminal activity involves the use of firearms or explosives, there is no further need to show that the behaviour was designed to influence the government or to intimidate the public or a section of the public. An example of such activity might be the shooting of a senior military or political figure. A 'firearm' for this purpose includes air weapons (s. 121); it is not clear whether the definition includes imitation firearms.

The reference to 'action' here includes action outside the United Kingdom. Similarly, references to people, property, the public and governments apply to all those features whether in the United Kingdom or elsewhere (s. 1(4)).

4.10.2.1 Membership of a Proscribed Organisation

OFFENCE: **Membership of a Proscribed Organisation—*Terrorism Act 2000, s. 11***
- Triable either way • 10 years' imprisonment and/or a fine on indictment
- Six months' imprisonment and/or a fine summarily

The Terrorism Act 2000, s. 11 states:

(1) A person commits an offence if he belongs or professes to belong to a proscribed organisation.

(2) It is a defence for a person charged with an offence under subsection (1) to prove—

(a) that the organisation was not proscribed on the last (or only) occasion on which he became a member or began to profess to be a member, and

(b) that he has not taken part in the activities of the organisation at any time while it was proscribed.

KEYNOTE

Specific organisations are proscribed by the Secretary of State and include some of the most active and widely known terrorist groups across the world, including Al-Qa'ida (sch. 2 to the Act). What amounts to membership is likely to depend on the nature of an organisation, e.g. membership of a loose and unstructured organisation may not need any formal steps or express process by which a person becomes a member (*R* v *Ahmed* [2011] EWCA Crim 184).

The reverse burden of proof contained in s. 11(2) has been held as imposing an evidential, as opposed to a persuasive, burden of proof (*Attorney-General's Reference (No. 4 of 2002), Sheldrake* v *DPP* [2004] UKHL 43).

Other offences relating to proscribed organisations are provided by s. 12 and include: inviting support; arranging or managing (or assisting in doing so) a meeting of three or more people in public or private, to support, further the activities or be addressed by a person belonging to a proscribed organisation; or addressing a meeting to encourage support or further the activities of the organisation.

The Act also created a summary offence of wearing an item of clothing, or wearing, carrying or displaying an article in such a way or in such circumstances as to arouse reasonable suspicion that the defendant is a member or supporter of a proscribed organisation (s. 13).

4.10.3 Terrorism Act 2000: Financial Measures

The main financial measures under the Terrorism Act 2000 relate to terrorist fundraising, possession of property and funding arrangements, and include:

- *inviting* another to provide money or other property (s. 15(1));
- *providing* money or other property (s. 15(3));
- *receiving* money or other property (s. 15(2));
- *possessing* money or other property (s. 16(2));
- *arranging* for money or other property to be made available (s. 17);

in each case intending that, or having reasonable cause to suspect that, it may be used for the purposes of terrorism (ss. 15, 16(2) and 17);

- *using* money or other property for the purposes of terrorism (s. 16(1));
- *concealing, moving or transferring* any terrorist property (s. 18).

Each of these offences is punishable by a maximum of 14 years' imprisonment on indictment (s. 22).

4.10.4 Terrorism Act 2000: Duty of Disclosure and Tipping Off

The 2000 Act creates a number of offences in relation to the unlawful disclosure of information and provides where disclosure is permissible.

4.10.4.1 Disclosure of Information

OFFENCE: **Disclosure of Information—*Terrorism Act 2000, s. 19***
- Triable either way • Five years' imprisonment and/or a fine on indictment
- Six months' imprisonment and/or a fine summarily

The Terrorism Act 2000, s. 19 states:

(1) This section applies where a person—
    (a) believes or suspects that another person has committed an offence under any of sections 15 to 18, and
    (b) bases his belief or suspicion on information which comes to his attention—
        (i) in the course of a trade, profession or business, or
        (ii) in the course of his employment (whether or not in the course of a trade, profession or business).
(1A) But this section does not apply if the information came to the person in the course of a business in the regulated sector.
(2) The person commits an offence if he does not disclose to a constable as soon as is reasonably practicable—
    (a) his belief or suspicion, and
    (b) the information on which it is based.

KEYNOTE

In relation to s. 19(2), a constable includes an authorised member of staff of the National Crime Agency (s. 19(7B)).

This section requires banks and other businesses to report any suspicions they may have that someone is laundering terrorist money or committing any of the other terrorist property offences in ss. 15–18. Section 19(1)(b) ensures the offence is focused on suspicions which arise at work.

'Employment' means any employment (paid or unpaid) including work under a contract for services or as an office holder, work experience provided pursuant to a training course or programme or in the course of training for employment, and voluntary work (s. 22A).

It is a defence for a person to prove that he/she had a reasonable excuse for not making the disclosure (s. 19(3)), or that the matters specified were disclosed in accordance with an established procedure for the making of disclosures (s. 19(4)). Disclosure by a professional legal adviser is not required if the information was obtained in privileged circumstances (s. 19(5)).

Section 21A of the Act also provides for an offence of failure to disclose information in the 'regulated sector', i.e. accountancy firms, investment companies, etc., the definition of which is contained in sch. 3A to the Act.

4.10.4.2 Disclosure of Information: Permission

The Terrorism Act 2000, s. 20 states:

(1) A person may disclose to a constable—
    (a) a suspicion or belief that any money or other property is terrorist property or is derived from terrorist property;
    (b) any matter on which the suspicion or belief is based.
(2) A person may make a disclosure to a constable in the circumstances mentioned in section 19(1) and (2).
(3) Subsections (1) and (2) shall have effect notwithstanding any restriction on the disclosure of information imposed by statute or otherwise.
(4) Where—
    (a) a person is in employment, and

(b) his employer has established a procedure for the making of disclosures of the kinds mentioned in subsection (1) and section 19(2),

subsections (1) and (2) shall have effect in relation to that person as if any reference to disclosure to a constable included a reference to disclosure in accordance with the procedure.

KEYNOTE

Section 20 ensures that businesses can disclose information to the police without fear of breaching legal restrictions.

4.10.4.3 Information about Acts of Terrorism

OFFENCE: **Information about Acts of Terrorism—*Terrorism Act 2000, s. 38B***
- Triable either way • Five years' imprisonment and/or a fine on indictment
- Six months' imprisonment and/or a fine summarily

The Terrorism Act 2000, s. 38B states:

(1) This section applies where a person has information which he knows or believes might be of material assistance—
  (a) in preventing the commission by another person of an act of terrorism, or
  (b) in securing the apprehension, prosecution or conviction of another person, in the United Kingdom, for an offence involving the commission, preparation or instigation of an act of terrorism.
(2) The person commits an offence if he does not disclose the information as soon as reasonably practicable in accordance with subsection (3).
(3) Disclosure is in accordance with this subsection if it is made—
  (a) in England and Wales, to a constable . . .

KEYNOTE

This offence, unlike some of the Act's other provisions, relates to any person who has information that he/she knows or believes might help prevent an act of terrorism or help bring terrorists to justice.

A person resident in the United Kingdom could be charged with this offence notwithstanding that he/she was outside the country when he/she became aware of the information (s. 38B(6)).

It is a defence for a person charged to prove that he/she had a reasonable excuse for not making the disclosure (s. 38B(4)).

4.10.4.4 Disclosure of and Interference with Information Offences

OFFENCE: **Disclosure of Information etc.—*Terrorism Act 2000, s. 39***
- Triable either way • Five years' imprisonment and/or a fine on indictment
- Six months' imprisonment and/or a fine summarily

The Terrorism Act 2000, s, 39 states:

(1) Subsection (2) applies where a person knows or has reasonable cause to suspect that a constable is conducting or proposes to conduct a terrorist investigation.
(2) The person commits an offence if he—
  (a) discloses to another anything which is likely to prejudice the investigation, or
  (b) interferes with material which is likely to be relevant to the investigation.
(3) Subsection (4) applies where a person knows or has reasonable cause to suspect that a disclosure has been or will be made under any of sections 19 to 21B or 38B.
(4) The person commits an offence if he—
  (a) discloses to another anything which is likely to prejudice an investigation resulting from the disclosure under that section, or
  (b) interferes with material which is likely to be relevant to an investigation resulting from the disclosure under that section.

4.10.5 Terrorism Act 2000: Other Offences

The Terrorism Act 2000 also creates a number of other offences in relation to terrorism. In summary, the key offences are:

- *Directing* the activities of an organisation which is concerned in the commission of acts of terrorism (s. 56). This offence (which is often easier to prove than some of the better known offences) carries a maximum sentence of life imprisonment.
- *Providing or receiving instruction or training* in the making or use of firearms or explosives or radioactive material or weapons designed or adapted for the discharge of any radioactive material, or chemical, biological or nuclear weapons (s. 54).
- *Possessing articles* in circumstances which give rise to a reasonable suspicion that the possession is for a purpose connected with the commission, preparation or instigation of an act of terrorism (s. 57). It must be shown that the defendant(s) possessed extremist material for use in the future to incite the commission of terrorist acts (*R v Zafar* [2008] EWCA Crim 184). See also *R v G*; *R v J* [2009] UKHL 13.
- *Collecting or making a record* of information (including photographs and electronic records) of a kind likely to be useful to a person committing or preparing an act of terrorism, or possessing a document or record containing information of that kind (s. 58). The document, etc. concerned must be of a kind that is likely to provide practical assistance to a person, rather than simply encouraging the commission of terrorist acts (*R v K* [2008] EWCA Crim 185). See also *R v Muhammed* [2010] EWCA Crim 227. In *R v Brown* [2011] EWCA Crim 2751, it was held that s. 58 did not infringe the appellant's right to free speech under ECHR, Article 10, insofar as it penalised the collection and distribution of materials and advice (*The Anarchist Cookbook*) on bomb-making, poisoning and other such activities. This ruling also applies to s. 2 of the Terrorism Act 2006 (**see para. 4.10.6**).
- *Eliciting or attempting to elicit* information about a member of the armed forces or the intelligence services or a constable, which is likely to be useful to a person committing or preparing an act of terrorism, or publishing or communicating information of that kind (s. 58A—inserted by the Counter-Terrorism Act 2008).
- *Inciting* another person to commit an act of terrorism wholly or partly outside the United Kingdom (s. 59).

4.10.6 Terrorism Act 2006: Offences

For the purposes of the 2006 Act the offences are grouped into three specific areas; encouragement etc. of terrorism; preparation of terrorist acts and terrorist training; offences involving radioactive devices and materials and nuclear facilities and sites.

4.10.6.1 Encouragement etc. of Terrorism

The offences within this group are:

- publishes a statement to encourage the commission, preparation or instigation of acts of terrorism or Convention offences (s. 1(2));
- engages in the dissemination of terrorist publications (s. 2(1)).

For the purposes of both these sections it is necessary to prove that they glorify the act of terrorism and that members of the public could reasonably be expected to infer that what is being glorified is being glorified as conduct that should be emulated by them in existing circumstances. 'Glorification' includes any form of praise or celebration, and cognate expressions are to be construed accordingly (s. 20(2)). The 'Convention offences' mentioned in s. 1(2) are those offences listed in sch. 1 to the Act and include offences in relation to explosives, biological weapons, chemical weapons, nuclear weapons, hostage-taking, hijacking, terrorist funds, etc.

In relation to an offence under s. 2 of the Act it was held that videos uploaded onto the Internet of scenes showing attacks on soldiers of the Coalition forces in Iraq and Afghanistan by insurgents were depicting scenes of terrorism within the definition of s. 1 of the 2000 Act (*R* v *Gul* [2013] UKSC 64). Under this section, although the accused is free to argue that the prosecution constituted an unacceptable interference with the applicant's right to freedom of speech at common law, this defence is always a matter to be determined by the jury (see *R* v *Brown* [2011] EWCA Crim 2751 and *Faraz* v *R* [2012] EWCA Crim 2820).

Section 3(1) provides that the offences under ss. 1 and 2 can be committed by publishing a statement electronically, i.e. via the Internet. 'Statement' includes a communication of any description, including a communication without words consisting of sounds or images or both (s. 20(6)). Section 3(3) provides for a notice to be served by a constable on the person electronically publishing the statement declaring that it is, in the constable's opinion, unlawfully terrorism-related and requiring its removal or modification (s. 3(3)). The methods for giving such a notice are provided in s. 4 of the Act. The offences under ss. 1 and 2 are punishable on indictment by a term of imprisonment not exceeding seven years or a fine or both, and summarily by a term of imprisonment not exceeding six months or a fine or both.

4.10.6.2 Preparation of Terrorist Acts and Terrorist Training

The offences within this group are:

- preparation for terrorist acts (s. 5(1));
- providing instruction or training in any of the skills mentioned for the commission or preparation of acts of terrorism or Convention offences (s. 6(1));
- receiving instruction or training in any of the skills mentioned for the commission or preparation of acts of terrorism or Convention offences (s. 6(2));
- attendance at a place used for terrorist training s. 8(1)).

For an offence under s. 5(1) it is irrelevant whether the intention and preparations relate to one or more particular acts of terrorism, acts of terrorism of a particular description or acts of terrorism generally (s. 5(2) and see *R* v *Roddis* [2009] EWCA Crim 585 and *R* v *Khan* [2013] EWCA Crim 468). The punishment for an offence under this section is imprisonment for life.

In relation to the offences of providing or receiving instruction or training under s. 6, the skills mentioned include: the making, handling or use of a noxious substance, the use of any method or technique for doing anything capable of being done for the purposes of terrorism, and the design or adaptation for the purposes of terrorism of any method or technique for doing anything. In *R* v *Da Costa* [2009] EWCA Crim 482, it was held that the person delivering the training had to know that one or more of those receiving it intended to use it for a terrorist purpose. The punishment on indictment for an offence under s. 6(1) and (2) is a term of imprisonment not exceeding 10 years or a fine or both, or on summary conviction imprisonment for a term not exceeding six months or a fine, or both.

The offence under s. 8(1) may be committed either in the United Kingdom or elsewhere. It must be shown that the person either knew or believed that the instruction or training was wholly or partly for purposes connected with the commission or preparation of acts of terrorism, or that the person could not reasonably have failed to understand the purpose of such instruction or training (s. 8(2)). The punishment on indictment for an offence under this section is a term of imprisonment not exceeding 10 years or a fine or both, or on summary conviction imprisonment for a term not exceeding six months or a fine, or both.

4.10.6.3 Radioactive Devices and Materials and Nuclear Facilities and Sites

The offences within this group are:

- making and possession of devices or materials (s. 9(1));
- misuse of devices or material and misuse and damage of facilities (s. 10(1) and (2));
- terrorist threats relating to devices, materials or facilities (s. 11(1) and (2));
- trespassing etc. on nuclear sites (s. 12 which amends s. 128 of the Serious Organised Crime and Police Act 2005).

The offence under s. 9(1) is committed where a person intends using the device or material in the course of or in connection with the commission or preparation of an act of terrorism or for the purposes of terrorism, or making it available to be so used. The punishment for an offence under this section is imprisonment for life.

A person commits an offence under s. 10(1) if he/she uses a radioactive device or radioactive material in connection with an act of terrorism. For the offence under s. 10(2) the person must use or damage a nuclear facility in a manner which causes a release of radioactive material or creates or increases a risk that such material will be released. The punishment for both these offences is imprisonment for life.

In relation to s. 11(1), this offence deals with a demand for the supply of a radioactive device, radioactive material, a nuclear facility, or for access to such a facility, for him/herself or another, and supports such a demand with a threat that a reasonable person would assume that there is a real risk of the threat being carried out if the demand is not met. Section 11(2) deals with a threat to use radioactive material, a radioactive device, or use or damage a nuclear facility in a manner that releases radioactive material or creates or increases a risk of its release. The punishment for both these offences is imprisonment for life.

Where a person does anything outside the United Kingdom that would constitute an offence falling within ss. 1, 6 or 8 to 11 of the Act, he/she is deemed to be guilty of that offence. This includes conspiracy, incitement, attempt, aiding, abetting, counselling or procuring the commission of such offences. Proceedings for any such offence may be taken at any place in the United Kingdom irrespective of whether the person is a British citizen or, in the case of a company, a company incorporated in a part of the United Kingdom (s. 17). Proceedings for any of the offences may only be instituted in England and Wales with the consent of the DPP. However, where an offence has been committed outside the United Kingdom or for a purpose wholly or partly connected with the affairs of another country the DPP's consent may only be given with the permission of the Attorney-General (s. 19).

4.10.7 Terrorism Act 2000: Police Powers

The Terrorism Act 2000 provides the police with many wide-ranging powers which exist *in addition* to any more general powers that the police may have. They include powers of arrest, search of persons and vehicles, authorisations of stop and search in specified locations, and the power to set up cordons.

4.10.7.1 Arrest without Warrant

The Terrorism Act 2000, s. 41 states:

(1) A constable may arrest without a warrant a person whom he reasonably suspects to be a terrorist.

KEYNOTE

The definition of a terrorist is broadly a person who has committed one of the main terrorism offences under the Act (including ss. 11, 12, 15–18, 54 and 56–63), or is or has been concerned in the commission, preparation or instigation of acts of terrorism (s. 40).

A magistrate's warrant may be obtained authorising any constable to enter and search the specified premises for the purpose of arresting the person to whom s. 41 applies (s. 42).

4.10.7.2 Search of Persons

The Terrorism Act 2000, s. 43 states:

(1) A constable may stop and search a person whom he reasonably suspects to be a terrorist to discover whether he has in his possession anything which may constitute evidence that he is a terrorist.

(2) A constable may search a person arrested under section 41 to discover whether he has in his possession anything which may constitute evidence that he is a terrorist.

(3) ...

(4) A constable may seize and retain anything which he discovers in the course of a search of a person under subsection (1) or (2) and which he reasonably suspects may constitute evidence that the person is a terrorist.

(4A) Subsection (4B) applies if a constable, in exercising the power under subsection (1) to stop a person whom the constable reasonably suspects to be a terrorist, stops a vehicle (see section 116(2)).

KEYNOTE

Where a vehicle is stopped the constable may search the vehicle, and anything in or on it, to discover whether there is anything which may constitute evidence that the person concerned is a terrorist, and may seize and retain anything which the constable discovers in the course of such a search, and reasonably suspects may constitute evidence that the person is a terrorist (s. 43(4B)). Nothing in s. 43(4B) confers a power to search any person but the power to search in that subsection is in addition to the power in subsection (1) to search a person whom the constable reasonably suspects to be a terrorist (s. 43(4C)).

In relation to s. 43(4A), s. 116(2) provides that the power to stop a person includes the power to stop a vehicle (other than an aircraft which is airborne).

4.10.7.3 Search of Vehicles

The Terrorism Act 2000, s. 43A states:

(1) Subsection (2) applies if a constable reasonably suspects that a vehicle is being used for the purposes of terrorism.

(2) The constable may stop and search—

　(a) the vehicle;

　(b) the driver of the vehicle;

　(c) a passenger in the vehicle;

　(d) anything in or on the vehicle or carried by the driver or a passenger;

　to discover whether there is anything which may constitute evidence that the vehicle is being used for the purposes of terrorism.

4.10.7.4 Stop and Search in Specified Locations

The Terrorism Act 2000, s. 47A states:

(1) A senior police officer may give an authorisation under subsection (2) or (3) in relation to a specified area or place if the officer—
   (a) reasonably suspects that an act of terrorism will take place; and
   (b) reasonably considers that—
      (i) the authorisation is necessary to prevent such an act;
      (ii) the specified area or place is no greater than is necessary to prevent such an act; and
      (iii) the duration of the authorisation is no longer than is necessary to prevent such an act.
(2) An authorisation under this subsection authorises any constable in uniform to stop a vehicle in the specified area or place and to search—
   (a) the vehicle;
   (b) the driver of the vehicle;
   (c) a passenger in the vehicle;
   (d) anything in or on the vehicle or carried by the driver or a passenger.
(3) An authorisation under this subsection authorises any constable in uniform to stop a pedestrian in the specified area or place and to search—
   (a) the pedestrian;
   (b) anything carried by the pedestrian.

4.10.7.5 Designated Cordoned Areas

The Terrorism Act 2000, s. 33 states:

(1) An area is a cordoned area for the purposes of this Act if it is designated under this section.
(2) A designation may be made only if the person making it considers it expedient for the purposes of a terrorist investigation.
(3) If a designation is made orally, the person making it shall confirm it in writing as soon as is reasonably practicable.

4.10.7.6 Power to Designate

The Terrorism Act 2000, s. 34 states:

(1) Subject to subsections (1A), (1B) and (2), a designation under section 33 may only be made—
    (a) where the area is outside Northern Ireland and is wholly or partly within a police area, by an officer for the police area who is of at least the rank of superintendent, and
    (b) . . .

(1A) . . .

(1B) . . .

(1C) . . .

(2) A constable who is not of the rank required by subsection (1) may make a designation if he considers it necessary by reason of urgency.

(3) Where a constable makes a designation in reliance on subsection (2) he shall as soon as is reasonably practicable—
    (a) make a written record of the time at which the designation was made, and
    (b) ensure that a police officer of at least the rank of superintendent is informed.

(4) An officer who is informed of a designation in accordance with subsection (3)(b)—
    (a) shall confirm the designation or cancel it with effect from such time as he may direct, and
    (b) shall, if he cancels the designation, make a written record of the cancellation and the reason for it.

4.10.7.7 Cordons and Police Powers

The Terrorism Act 2000, s. 36 states:

(1) A constable in uniform may—
    (a) order a person in a cordoned area to leave it immediately,
    (b) order a person immediately to leave premises which are wholly or partly in or adjacent to a cordoned area,

(c) order the driver or person in charge of a vehicle in a cordoned area to move it from the area immediately,

(d) arrange for the removal of a vehicle from a cordoned area,

(e) arrange for the movement of a vehicle within a cordoned area,

(f) prohibit or restrict access to a cordoned area by pedestrians or vehicles.

KEYNOTE

The officer giving the order or making the arrangements and prohibitions set out here must be in uniform. Therefore detectives or other plain clothes officers involved in the terrorist investigation will not have these powers available to them.

The powers under s. 36 are among those that can be conferred on a Police Community Support Officer designated under sch. 4 to the Police Reform Act 2002.

Failing to comply with an order, prohibition or restriction under this section is a summary offence punishable by three months' imprisonment and/or a fine (s. 36(2) and (4)).

This wording will presumably cover refusal. There is a defence if the person can show that he/she had a reasonable excuse for the failure.

A superintendent or above may request passenger, service and crew information from an owner or agent of a ship or aircraft which is arriving, or expected to arrive, at any place in the United Kingdom or is leaving, or expected to leave, from any place in the United Kingdom (Immigration, Asylum and Nationality Act 2006, s. 32(2)). There is a similar power to request freight information from the owners or agents of a ship or aircraft, and in the case of a vehicle, the owner or hirer (s. 33(2) and (3)).

It is an offence if without reasonable excuse a person fails to comply with a requirement imposed under ss. 32(2) or 33(2). The request must be for a police purpose, i.e. the prevention, detection, investigation or prosecution of criminal offences; safeguarding national security; and such other purposes as may be specified (s. 33(5)).

4.10.8 Terrorism Prevention and Investigation Measures

Terrorism Prevention and Investigation Measures (TPIM), created by the Terrorism Prevention and Investigation Measures Act 2011, are a civil preventative measure intended to protect the public from the risk posed by suspected terrorists who can be neither prosecuted nor, in the case of foreign nationals, deported, by imposing restrictions intended to prevent or disrupt their engagement in terrorism-related activity.

The Secretary of State may impose requirements, restrictions and other provision which may be made in relation to an individual by serving a Terrorism Prevention and Investigation Measures notice on him/her if certain conditions are met (s. 2(1)).

The five conditions required to be met are provided by s. 3 of the Act which states:

(1) Condition A is that the Secretary of State reasonably believes that the individual is, or has been, involved in terrorism-related activity (the 'relevant activity').

(2) Condition B is that some or all of the relevant activity is new terrorism-related activity.

(3) Condition C is that the Secretary of State reasonably considers that it is necessary, for purposes connected with protecting members of the public from a risk of terrorism, for terrorism prevention and investigation measures to be imposed on the individual.

(4) Condition D is that the Secretary of State reasonably considers that it is necessary, for purposes connected with preventing or restricting the individual's involvement in terrorism-related activity, for the specified terrorism prevention and investigation measures to be imposed on the individual.

(5) Condition E is that—

(a) the court gives the Secretary of State permission under section 6, or

(b) the Secretary of State reasonably considers that the urgency of the case requires terrorism prevention and investigation measures to be imposed without obtaining such permission.

4.10.8.1 Contravening a Terrorism Prevention and Investigation Measure

OFFENCE: **Contravening a Terrorism Prevention and Investigation Measure—**
Terrorism Prevention and Investigation Measures Act 2011, s. 23

• Triable either way • Five years' imprisonment and/or a fine on indictment
• Six months' imprisonment and/or a fine summarily

The Terrorism Prevention and Investigation Measures Act 2011, s. 23 states:

(1) An individual is guilty of an offence if—
    (a) a TPIM notice is in force in relation to the individual, and
    (b) the individual contravenes, without reasonable excuse, any measure specified in the TPIM notice.

4.10.8.2 Terrorism Prevention and Investigation Measures: Police Powers

The Terrorism Prevention and Investigation Measures Act 2011, sch. 5 states:

1 This Schedule confers powers of entry, search, seizure and retention on constables in connection with the imposition of measures on individuals.
2 A power conferred on a constable by virtue of this Schedule—

(a) is additional to powers which the constable has at common law or by virtue of any other enactment, and

(b) is not to be taken as affecting those powers.

3 A constable may detain an individual for the purpose of carrying out a search of that individual under a power conferred by virtue of this Schedule.

4 A constable may use reasonable force, if necessary, for the purpose of exercising a power conferred on the constable by virtue of this Schedule.

KEYNOTE

The following is an extract of the PACE Code of Practice for the Exercise by: Police Officers of Statutory Powers of Stop and Search (Code A) (2013) in relation to sch. 5.

Searches under Schedule 5 to the Terrorism Prevention and Investigation Measures Act 2011

2.18 A Paragraph 3 of Schedule 5 to the TPIM Act 2011 allows a constable to detain an individual to be searched under the following powers:

(i) paragraph 6(2)(a) when a TPIM notice is being, or has just been, served on the individual for the purpose of ascertaining whether there is anything on the individual that contravenes measures specified in the notice;

(ii) paragraph 8(2)(a) in accordance with a warrant to search the individual issued by a justice of the peace in England and Wales, a sheriff in Scotland or a lay magistrate in Northern Ireland who is satisfied that a search is necessary for the purpose of determining whether an individual in respect of whom a TPIM notice is in force is complying with measures specified in the notice (see *paragraph 2.20*); and

(iii) paragraph 10 to ascertain whether an individual in respect of whom a TPIM notice is in force is in possession of anything that could be used to threaten or harm any person.

2.19 The exercise of the powers mentioned in paragraph 2.18A does not require the constable to have reasonable grounds to suspect that the individual:

(a) has been, or is, contravening any of the measures specified in the TPIM notice; or

(b) has on them anything which:

- in the case of the power in sub-paragraph (i), contravenes measures specified in the TPIM notice;
- in the case of the power in sub-paragraph (ii) is not complying with measures specified in the TPIM notice; or
- in the case of the power in sub-paragraph (iii), could be used to threaten or harm any person.

2.20 A search of an individual on warrant under the power mentioned in paragraph 2.18A(ii) must carried out within 28 days of the issue of the warrant and:

- the individual may be searched on one occasion only within that period;
- the search must take place at a reasonable hour unless it appears that this would frustrate the purposes of the search.

. . .

2.26 The powers under Schedule 5 only allow a constable to conduct a search of an individual only for specified purposes relating to a TPIM notice as set out above. However, anything found may be seized and retained if there are reasonable grounds for believing that it is or it contains evidence of any offence for use at a trial for that offence or to prevent it being concealed, lost, damaged, altered, or destroyed. However, this would not prevent a search being carried out under other search powers if, in the course of exercising these powers, the officer formed reasonable grounds for suspicion.

4.10.9 Offences Involving Explosive Substance

OFFENCE: **Causing Explosion Likely to Endanger Life or Property—*Explosive Substances Act 1883, s. 2***

- Triable on indictment • Life imprisonment

The Explosive Substances Act 1883, s. 2 states:

(1) A person who in the United Kingdom or (being a citizen of the United Kingdom and Colonies) in the Republic of Ireland unlawfully and maliciously causes by any explosive substance an explosion of a nature likely to endanger life or to cause serious injury to property shall, whether any injury to person or property has been actually caused or not, be guilty of an offence.

OFFENCE: **Attempting to Cause Explosion or Keeping Explosive with Intent—**
Explosive Substances Act 1883, s. 3

- Triable on indictment • Life imprisonment

The Explosive Substances Act 1883, s. 3 states:

(1) A person who in the United Kingdom or a dependency or (being a citizen of the United Kingdom and Colonies) elsewhere unlawfully and maliciously—
   (a) does any act with intent to cause, or conspires to cause, by an explosive substance an explosion of a nature likely to endanger life, or cause serious injury to property, whether in the United Kingdom or elsewhere, or
   (b) makes or has in his possession or under his control an explosive substance with intent by means thereof to endanger life, or cause serious injury to property, whether in the United Kingdom or elsewhere, or to enable any other person so to do
shall, whether any explosion does or does not take place, and whether any injury to person or property is actually caused or not, be guilty of an offence...

OFFENCE: **Making or Possessing Explosive under Suspicious Circumstances—**
Explosive Substances Act 1883, s. 4

- Triable on indictment • 14 years' imprisonment

The Explosive Substances Act 1883, s. 4 states:

(1) Any person who makes or knowingly has in his possession or under his control any explosive substance under such circumstances as to give rise to a reasonable suspicion that he is not making it or does not have it in his possession or under his control for a lawful object, shall, unless he can show that he made it or had it in his possession or under his control for a lawful object, be guilty of felony...

No proceedings for an offence under either of those sections may be instituted except by or with the consent of the DPP.

Further guidance on the implementation of this section can be found in Home Office Circular 34/2005.

4.10.11.2 Intimidation of Persons Connected with Animal Research Organisation

OFFENCE: **Intimidation of Persons Connected with Animal Research Organisation—*Serious Organised Crime and Police Act 2005, s. 146(1)***
- Triable either way • Five years' imprisonment and/or a fine on indictment
- 12 months' imprisonment and/or a fine summarily

The Serious Organised Crime and Police Act 2005, s. 146 states:

(1) A person (A) commits an offence if, with the intention of causing a second person (B) to abstain from doing something which B is entitled to do (or to do something which B is entitled to abstain from doing)—
   (a) A threatens B that A or somebody else will do a relevant act, and
   (b) A does so wholly or mainly because B is a person falling within subsection (2).

KEYNOTE

Subsection (2) is a lengthy and very comprehensive list. In summary, a person falls within this subsection if he/she is:

- an employee or officer of an animal research organisation;
- a student at an educational establishment that is an animal research organisation;
- a lessor or licensor of any premises occupied by an animal research organisation;
- a person with a financial interest in, or who provides financial assistance to, an animal research organisation;
- a customer or supplier of an animal research organisation. (s. 146(2)).

A person who is contemplating becoming someone within the categories covered by the third, fourth and fifth bullet points is covered, as is a person who is (or is contemplating becoming) a customer or supplier of such people/organisations.

Employees and employers of someone within these descriptions are covered, as are people with a financial interest in, or providing financial assistance to the above.

Subsection (2) also extends to spouses, civil partners, friends or relatives, or people known personally to someone within any of these descriptions.

As with the offence under s. 145, this section does not generally apply to any act done wholly or mainly in contemplation or furtherance of a trade dispute and no proceedings for an offence under either of those sections may be instituted except by or with the consent of the DPP.

Further guidance on the implementation of this section can be found in Home Office Circular 34/2005.

4.11 | Public Disorder

4.11.1 Introduction

Threats to public order or the 'normal state of society' can arise in many forms, from intimidating and anti-social behaviour to full-scale riots and acts of terrorism. The role of the police in maintaining the normal state of society is both extremely important but also increasingly challenging. It is one thing to provide police officers and auxiliary staff with statutory and common law powers to tackle disorder in all its many forms and, perhaps more importantly, to prevent anticipated disorder in advance; it is quite another to use those powers in a way that is sensitive to the competing needs and expectations of people and the communities in which they live. Although such powers help the police in their efforts to preserve a peaceful state of society, their use is frequently controversial and often confrontational. This area of constitutional law involves balancing the opposing rights of individuals with one another against the wider entitlements and requirements of society—a task that, in practical terms, can seem like trying to satisfy the insatiable.

4.11.2 Breach of the Peace

The lowest level of threat to public order is probably represented in the common law 'complaint' of a breach of the peace. Defined specifically in *R v Howell* [1982] QB 416, a breach of the peace generally occurs when an act is done, or threatened to be done:

- which harms a person or, in his/her presence, his/her property; or
- which is likely to cause such harm; or
- which puts someone in fear of such harm.

The common law provides a power of arrest and also the power to intervene and/or detain by force, in order to prevent any action likely to result in a breach of the peace in either public or private places.

Breach of the peace is dealt with by way of complaint and is not a criminal offence (*R v County of London Quarter Sessions Appeals Committee, ex parte Metropolitan Police Commissioner* [1948] 1 KB 670). Although not a criminal offence in domestic law, it may be treated as such for the purposes of the European Convention on Human Rights (*Steel v UK* (1999) 28 EHRR 603). In *Williamson v Chief Constable of West Midlands Police* [2003] EWCA Civ 337 the Court of Appeal held that a person arrested for a breach of the peace is not, strictly speaking, in police detention for the purposes of s. 118 of the Police and Criminal Evidence Act 1984 and the provisions in relation to bail do not apply. A person may be detained and placed before the next available court, or detained until there is no further likelihood of a reoccurrence of the breach of the peace. In *Williamson* it was considered good practice for people arrested and detained for breach of the peace to be treated in accordance with the provisions of PACE, and that they should also be cautioned.

4.11.2.1 Breach of the Peace on Private Premises

A breach of the peace may take place on private premises as well as in public places (*R v Chief Constable of Devon and Cornwall, ex parte Central Electricity Generating Board* [1982] QB 458). The police are entitled to enter premises to prevent a breach of the peace and to remain there in order to do so (*Thomas* v *Sawkins* [1935] 2 KB 249). This power has not been affected by the general powers of entry provided by the Police and Criminal Evidence Act 1984 (**see chapter 4.7** and s. 17(6) of the 1984 Act).

Where a breach of the peace takes place on private property, there is no requirement to show that the resulting disturbance affected members of the public outside that property—*McQuade* v *Chief Constable of Humberside Police* [2001] EWCA Civ 1330. The presence of a member (or members) of the public is, however, a highly relevant factor when dealing with a breach of the peace (see *McConnell* v *Chief Constable of Greater Manchester Police* [1990] 1 WLR 364).

4.11.2.2 Police Powers are Discretionary

Although the police have a general duty to preserve the Queen's peace, and enjoy common law powers to carry out that duty, they also have a wide discretion as to how they go about that function. The common law powers of the police allow them, where appropriate, to prevent people from travelling to certain locations (e.g. striking miners heading for a working coalfield where their presence would give reasonable grounds to apprehend a breach of the peace (*Moss* v *McLachlan* [1985] IRLR 76)). Such an 'anticipatory' power is, however, exceptional (*Foulkes* v *Chief Constable of Merseyside Police* [1998] 3 All ER 705) and requires a careful balancing of the individual rights of the people involved against the wider interests of public safety, the maintenance of public order and the prevention of crime. Such exceptional powers to impose anticipatory restrictions on the movement of individuals, falling short of arrest, only arise if there is an imminent threat to public order.

The policing practicalities involved in this careful balancing exercise were considered in *R (On the Application of Laporte)* v *Chief Constable of Gloucestershire* [2006] UKHL 55. That case produced a useful interpretation and examination of a number of operational policing powers. In *Laporte* a lawful assembly had been arranged under the provisions of ss. 12 and 14 of the Public Order Act 1986 in connection with protests against the war in Iraq. As the result of a stop and search order made under s. 60 of the Criminal Justice and Public Order Act 1994 (**see para. 4.6.4**) the police stopped a number of coaches en route to the lawful assembly at Fairford US Air Force base, and then escorted them back to London. Intelligence had been received that the passengers would cause disorder at the base. The House of Lords ruled that the police had acted unlawfully because a breach of the peace was not imminent when the coaches were stopped. This action interfered with the passengers' rights under Articles 10 and 11 of the European Convention on Human Rights (as to which, **see chapter 4.4**) and was disproportionate. In *Mengesha* v *Commissioner of Police of the Metropolis* [2013] EWHC 1695 (Admin) it was held to be unlawful for the police to require people to provide their personal details and submit to being filmed as the price of release from a containment, notwithstanding that a s. 60 authorisation was in force allowing the lawful search of those present.

4.11.2.3 Which Parties are Likely to Present Actual Threat?

When exercising discretionary powers to prevent disorder, police officers will be expected to focus their attention on those who are likely to present the actual threat of violence or disorder. This is the approach first taken by the Divisional Court in a case where people preaching on the steps of a church were warned by police that they were antagonising passers-by. Despite the warning, the preachers continued and, as there was an imminent likelihood of a recently gathered crowd attacking them, the preachers were arrested (*Redmond-Bate* v *DPP* [1999] Crim LR 998). The Divisional Court felt that the approach taken by the police was incompatible with Article 10 of the European Convention on Human Rights and that the officers' attention should have been directed at the crowd from whom the threat to the 'peace' was emanating. The individuals preaching were simply exercising their right to freedom of expression. It was the crowd who, in the court's view, ought to have received the warning and who should have been arrested in the event of their continuing to represent a threat to public order.

However, it will not always be practicable to separate those who are directly and individually presenting a threat to the peace and those who are part of a larger crowd. In *Austin v Commissioner of Police of the Metropolis* [2009] UKHL 5 it was held that in extreme and exceptional circumstances it would be lawful for the police to contain demonstrators and members of the public caught up in that demonstration, even though they themselves did not appear to be about to commit a breach of the peace. This would be the case where it was necessary to prevent an imminent breach of the peace by others, and no other means would achieve that. In *Austin v United Kingdom* (2012) 55 EHRR 14 the European Court of Human Rights decided, by a majority, that there had been no violation of Article 5 (right to liberty and security) of the European Convention on Human Rights. *Austin* [2009] was followed in *R (On the Application of Moos) v Commissioner of Police of the Metropolis* [2011] EWHC 957 (Admin) which related to a Climate Camp protest against the G20 Summit in London. The court reiterated that containment would only be lawful in very exceptional circumstances. It is only when the police reasonably believe that there is no other means whatsoever to prevent an imminent breach of the peace that they can as a matter of necessity curtail the lawful exercise of their rights of freedom of expression by third parties. The test of necessity is met only in truly extreme and exceptional circumstances. The action taken has to be both reasonably necessary and proportionate and taken in good faith. In *R (On the Application of McClure) v Commissioner of Police of the Metropolis* [2012] EWCA Civ 12, the Court of Appeal concluded that a decision to contain a substantial crowd of demonstrators whose behaviour, though at times unruly and somewhat violent, did not of itself justify containment. It was, however, justifiable on the ground that containment was the least drastic way of preventing what the police officer responsible for the decision reasonably apprehended would be imminent and serious breaches of the peace.

Where demonstrators were contained in a police pen, in a demonstration against Israel and its Head of State, it was held that the police may deploy reasonable force to prevent a breach of the peace that they reasonably apprehend as imminent (*Wright v Commissioner of Police for the Metropolis* [2013] EWHC 2739 (QB)).

Where officers were directed by senior officers to arrest persons for breach of the peace, it was held to be lawful where those senior officers had good reason to believe that had those persons been allowed to proceed to a nearby demonstration point there would have been a strong likelihood of a breach of the peace occurring (*R (On the Application of Hicks) v Commissioner of Police of the Metropolis* [2012] EWHC 1947 (Admin)).

Guidance on 'immediacy' in relation to conduct in a domestic setting is contained in *Wragg v DPP* [2005] EWHC 1389 (Admin). Police officers attending a domestic dispute found one of the parties, who had been in a heated argument with a relative also living in the house, to have consumed a large amount of alcohol. In relation to the immediacy or imminence test the police officers believed that a breach of the peace could take place in the house after they departed that night in so far as the other household member was at risk of immediate assault while the accused was still in drink. The arrest of the accused was held to be lawful. In *Demetriou v DPP* [2012] EWHC 2443 (Admin) it was also held that an arrest was lawful if a person willing to leave premises but who an officer believed would return to cause violence gave rise to a reasonable basis for fearing imminent violence.

4.11.2.4 Power of Arrest

A constable or any other person may arrest without warrant any person:

- who is committing a breach of the peace;
- whom he/she reasonably believes will commit a breach of the peace in the immediate future; or
- who has committed a breach of the peace, where it is reasonably believed that a recurrence of the breach of the peace is threatened.

This power of arrest may be exercised on private premises, even where there is no other member of the public present (*R v Howell* [1982] QB 416).

In *Bibby* v *Chief Constable of Essex Police* (2000) 164 JP 297, the Court of Appeal held that the power of arrest for breach of the peace was wholly exceptional and set out the conditions that must be met before this power should be used. These conditions are:

- there must be the clearest of circumstances and a real and present threat to the peace to justify the arrest
- the threat must be coming from the person who is ultimately arrested
- his/her conduct must be clearly interfering with the rights of another
- that conduct must be unreasonable.

Even if exercising the power under circumstances where a breach of the peace has not yet occurred, it is enough that a constable uses the wording 'I am arresting you for a breach of the peace' when arresting the person (*R* v *Howell* [1982] QB 416).

4.11.3 The Public Order Acts

Many of the most common offences regulating public disorder and threats to public order were formerly contained in the Public Order Act 1936. This left several key offences, such as riot and affray, to the common law. These provisions were felt to be inadequate and the Public Order Act 1986 was passed in an attempt to codify the law in this area.

4.11.4 Riot

OFFENCE: **Riot—*Public Order Act 1986, s. 1***
>   • Triable on indictment • 10 years' imprisonment and/or a fine

The Public Order Act 1986, s. 1 states:

(1) Where 12 or more persons who are present together use or threaten unlawful violence for a common purpose and the conduct of them (taken together) is such as would cause a person of reasonable firmness present at the scene to fear for his personal safety, each of the persons using unlawful violence for the common purpose is guilty of riot.
(2) It is immaterial whether or not the 12 or more use or threaten unlawful violence simultaneously.
(3) The common purpose may be inferred from conduct.
(4) No person of reasonable firmness need actually be, or be likely to be, present at the scene.
(5) Riot may be committed in private as well as in public places.

KEYNOTE

This offence requires the consent of the DPP before a prosecution can be brought. Although there may be occasions where 12 or more people behave in the way proscribed by s. 1, it is still very rare for a charge of riot to be brought.

It is not necessary that all 12 people concerned use or threaten unlawful violence at the same time. However, the courts have held that each defendant must be shown to have *used* unlawful violence and not merely threatened to do so (*R* v *Jefferson* [1994] 1 All ER 270). A defendant must be shown to have *intended* to use/threaten violence or to have *been aware* that his/her conduct may have been violent (s. 6(1)).

The offence may be committed in private as well as in a public place. There is no need to prove that a person of reasonable firmness was actually caused to fear for his/her safety, merely that such a person would be caused so to fear (although clearly one way to prove that element would be by the testimony of those witnessing the behaviour).

Although there must be a common purpose, this need not be part of a pre-determined plan, nor be unlawful in itself. A common purpose to get into a rock concert or even the January sales at a high street store could therefore be enough, provided all other elements are present.

4.11.4.1 Unlawful Violence

The Public Order Act 1986, s. 8 provides guidance on when conduct will amount to 'violence':

'violence' means any violent conduct, so that—

(a) except in the context of affray, it includes violent conduct towards property as well as violent conduct towards persons, and

(b) it is not restricted to conduct causing or intended to cause injury or damage but includes any other violent conduct (for example, throwing at or towards a person a missile of a kind capable of causing injury which does not hit or falls short).

KEYNOTE

It has been held that the use of the term 'unlawful' in the 1986 Act has been included to allow for the general defences—such as self-defence—to be applicable (see *R v Rothwell* [1993] Crim LR 626).

4.11.4.2 Drunkenness

The effect of drunkenness on criminal liability generally is discussed in *Crime*, **chapter 1.4**. However, Parliament has specifically catered for self-induced intoxication, not just for the offence of riot, but in relation to other offences under the 1986 Act, by s. 6 which states:

(5) For the purposes of this section a person whose awareness is impaired by intoxication shall be taken to be aware of that of which he would be aware if not intoxicated, unless he shows either that his intoxication was not self-induced or that it was caused solely by the taking or administration of a substance in the course of medical treatment.

(6) In subsection (5) 'intoxication' means any intoxication, whether caused by drink, drugs or other means, or by a combination of means.

4.11.5 Violent Disorder

OFFENCE: **Violent Disorder—*Public Order Act 1986, s. 2***

- Triable either way • Five years' imprisonment and/or a fine on indictment
- Six months' imprisonment and/or a fine summarily

The Public Order Act 1986, s. 2 states:

(1) Where 3 or more persons who are present together use or threaten unlawful violence and the conduct of them (taken together) is such as would cause a person of reasonable firmness present at the scene to fear for his personal safety, each of the persons using or threatening unlawful violence is guilty of violent disorder.

(2) It is immaterial whether or not the 3 or more use or threaten unlawful violence simultaneously.

(3) No person of reasonable firmness need actually be, or be likely to be, present at the scene.

(4) Violent disorder may be committed in private as well as in public places.

KEYNOTE

In order to convict a defendant of this offence, you must show that there were three or more people using or threatening unlawful violence. However, while three or more persons must have been present and used or threatened unlawful violence, it is not necessary that three or more persons should actually be charged or prosecuted with the offence. Further, where there are three defendants and two are acquitted of the charge, the remaining defendant can still be convicted of violent disorder (*R v Mahroof* (1989) 88 Cr App R 317) as long as *it can be proved that there were three or more people using or threatening violence* (perhaps from CCTV evidence of the incident). If it *cannot be proved* that there were three or more people using or threatening unlawful violence the court should acquit each defendant (*R v McGuigan* [1991] Crim LR 719).

In *R* v *NW* [2010] EWCA Crim 404, the circumstances of the case were that a person was violently resisting arrest by a police officer, during which time a crowd gathered and various members of the crowd used or threatened violence. The Court of Appeal held that for the purposes of this section it was not necessary for a person to act deliberately in combination with at least two other people present at the scene, but that it is sufficient that at least three people be present, each separately using or threatening unlawful violence. The court's view was that the phrase, 'where 3 or more persons who are present together use or threaten violence…' consists of ordinary words which must be given their ordinary meaning.

The requirements as to the hypothetical effects on an equally hypothetical person of reasonable firmness are the same as for the offence of riot. However, there is no requirement to prove a common purpose.

Again, a defendant must be shown to have *intended* to use/threaten violence or to have *been aware* that his/her conduct may have been violent (s. 6(2)) and the offence may be committed in private as well as in a public place. 'Violence' for these purposes can include violent conduct towards property (s. 8).

4.11.6   Affray

OFFENCE: **Affray—*Public Order Act 1986, s. 3***
- Triable either way   • Three years' imprisonment and/or a fine on indictment
- Six months' imprisonment and/or a fine summarily

The Public Order Act 1986, s. 3 states:

(1) A person is guilty of affray if he uses or threatens unlawful violence towards another and his conduct is such as would cause a person of reasonable firmness present at the scene to fear for his personal safety.
(2) Where 2 or more persons use or threaten the unlawful violence, it is the conduct of them taken together that must be considered for the purposes of subsection (1).
(3) For the purposes of this section a threat cannot be made by the use of words alone.
(4) No person of reasonable firmness need actually be, or be likely to be, present at the scene.
(5) Affray may be committed in private as well as in public places.

KEYNOTE

This offence can be committed by a single defendant although, if he/she acts with another, the conduct of them taken together will be the relevant factor in determining their criminal conduct (s. 3(2)).

The House of Lords has held that, in order to prove the offence of affray, the threat of unlawful violence has to be towards a person(s) present at the scene (*I* v *DPP* [2001] UKHL 10). Once this element has been proved, it will be necessary to prove the second element, namely, whether the defendant's conduct would have caused a hypothetical person present at the scene to fear for his/her personal safety (*R* v *Sanchez* (1996) 160 JP 321 and *R* v *Carey* [2006] EWCA Crim 17). However, where the likelihood of a hypothetical person of reasonable firmness being present was low this element of the offence was not satisfied. In *R (On the Application of Leeson)* v *DPP* [2010] EWHC 994 (Admin) a woman had issued a drunken threat to kill her long-term partner whilst holding a knife, in a bathroom, in an otherwise unoccupied house. In these circumstances the court held that there was no possibility of hypothetical bystanders fearing for their safety.

The threat cannot be made by words alone (s. 3(3)), therefore there must be some action by the defendant—even if that 'action' consists of utilising something else such as a dog to threaten the violence (*R* v *Dixon* [1993] Crim LR 579).

The effect of s. 3(4) is that it is not necessary to show that the defendant's behaviour either was or could have been seen by someone at the time. Contrast this with the lesser offence under s. 5 (see para. 4.11.9).

Although violence is 'not restricted to conduct causing or intended to cause injury or damage but includes any other violent conduct' (s. 8), the expression does not include conduct towards property as it does with the offences under ss. 1 and 2.

Once more, a defendant must be shown to have *intended* to use/threaten violence or to have *been aware* that his/her conduct may have been violent (s. 6(2)).

4.11.7 Fear or Provocation of Violence

> OFFENCE: **Fear or Provocation of Violence—*Public Order Act 1986, s. 4***
> - Triable summarily • Six months' imprisonment and/or a fine

> OFFENCE: **Racially or Religiously Aggravated—*Crime and Disorder Act 1998, s. 31(1)(a)***
> - Triable either way • Two years' imprisonment and/or a fine on indictment
> - Six months' imprisonment and/or a fine summarily

The Public Order Act 1986, s. 4 states:

(1) A person is guilty of an offence if he—
   (a) uses towards another person threatening, abusive or insulting words or behaviour, or
   (b) distributes or displays to another person any writing, sign or other visible representation which is threatening, abusive or insulting,

   with intent to cause that person to believe that immediate unlawful violence will be used against him or another by any person, or to provoke the immediate use of unlawful violence by that person or another, or whereby that person is likely to believe that such violence will be used or it is likely that such violence will be provoked.

(2) An offence under this section may be committed in a public or a private place, except that no offence is committed where the words or behaviour are used, or the writing, sign or other visible representation is distributed or displayed, by a person inside a dwelling and the other person is also inside that or another dwelling.

KEYNOTE

The phrase 'threatening, abusive or insulting' is not defined but it was interpreted by the courts under the Public Order Act 1936. Whether words or behaviour are threatening, abusive or insulting will be a question of fact for the magistrate(s) to decide in each case (see *Brutus* v *Cozens* [1973] AC 854).

It is not enough that conduct is 'offensive' but it has been held that masturbation towards a police officer in a public lavatory is capable of being insulting (*Parkin* v *Norman* [1983] QB 92).

'Immediate' unlawful violence does not have to be instantaneous but it must be shown that the defendant's conduct was likely to lead to more than some form of violence at some later date. Therefore publication and sale of material by the author Salman Rushdie, however insulting it may have been to some people, was not enough on its facts to support a charge against the publishers under s. 4 (*R* v *Horseferry Road Metropolitan Stipendiary Magistrate, ex parte Siadatan* [1991] 1 QB 260). 'Immediate' here requires some close proximity between the acts of the defendant and the apprehended violence, with no intervening occurrence.

To make out an offence under s. 4 the prosecution must prove that the accused intended the victim to fear immediate unlawful violence. This is not possible where it was the intention of the accused to take the victim by surprise so that he/she did not know he/she would be assaulted until the act had occurred. The court considered that the accused should have been charged with assault (*Hughes* v *DPP* [2012] EWHC 606 (Admin)).

There are a number of ways in which this offence can be committed (see below). In all of these, however, there must be the use of threatening/abusive/insulting words or behaviour (or distribution/display of writing, signs, etc.). This must be carried out with the requisite state of mind set out at s. 6(3) which states:

(3) A person is guilty of an offence under section 4 only if he intends his words or behaviour, or the writing, sign or other visible representation, to be threatening, abusive or insulting, or is aware that it may be threatening, abusive or insulting.

In addition, it must be shown that the person further *intended* to bring about the consequences set out below (at (a) and (b)) or that the consequences (at (c) and (d)) were likely.

The offence was broken down into four component parts in *Winn* v *DPP* (1992) 156 JP 881. For each of these parts it must be shown:

(a) that the defendant:
   - intended the person against whom the conduct was directed
   - to believe

- that immediate unlawful violence would be used
- either against him/her or against anyone else
- by the defendant or anyone else; *or*

(b) that he/she:
- intended to provoke the immediate use of unlawful violence
- by that person or anyone else; *or*

(c) that:
- the person against whom the words or behaviour (or distribution/display of writing etc.) were directed
- was likely to believe
- that immediate unlawful violence would be used; *or*

(d) that it was likely that immediate unlawful violence would be provoked.

In the case at (a) above, it does not have to be shown that the other person *actually believed* that immediate violence would be used; it has to be shown that the defendant *intended to cause* him/her to believe it (*Swanston* v *DPP* (1997) 161 JP 203).

The person in whom the defendant intends to create that belief must be the same person at whom the conduct is directed (*Loade* v *DPP* [1990] 1 QB 1052).

4.11.7.1 Definition of Dwelling

Under the Public Order Act 1986, s. 8, 'dwelling' is defined as:

...any structure or part of a structure occupied as a person's home or as other living accommodation (whether the occupation is separate or shared with others) but does not include any part not so occupied, and for this purpose 'structure' includes a tent, caravan, vehicle, vessel or other temporary or movable structure.

KEYNOTE

Given that the offence at s. 4 can be committed in private (under the restrictions in relation to dwellings by s. 4(2); see para. 4.11.7), it appears that the offence could be committed by a person sending out emails or other forms of communication from his/her house to other non-dwellings or from his/her place of work to people's houses.

Communal landings which form access routes to separate dwellings have been held not to constitute part of a dwelling even though they could only be entered by way of an entry phone system (*Rukwira* v *DPP* [1993] Crim LR 882). Similarly, in *Le Vine* v *DPP* [2010] EWHC 1128 (Admin) a laundry room, commonly used by tenants in sheltered housing, did not form part of a dwelling. Also a police cell has been held not to be living accommodation (*R* v *Francis* [2006] EWCA Crim 3323).

4.11.8 Intentional Harassment, Alarm or Distress

OFFENCE: **Intentionally Causing Harassment, Alarm or Distress—*Public Order Act 1986, s. 4A***
- Triable summarily • Six months' imprisonment and/or a fine

OFFENCE: **Racially or Religiously Aggravated—*Crime and Disorder Act 1998, s. 31(1)(b)***
- Triable either way • Two years' imprisonment and/or a fine on indictment
- Six months' imprisonment and/or a fine summarily

The Public Order Act 1986, s. 4A states:

(1) A person is guilty of an offence if, with intent to cause a person harassment, alarm or distress, he—
  (a) uses threatening or abusive ords or behaviour, or disorderly behaviour, or

(b) displays any writing, sign or other visible representation which is threatening, abusive or insulting,

thereby causing that or another person harassment, alarm or distress.

KEYNOTE

For the purpose of the racially or religiously aggravated form of causing fear or provocation of violence, any words used by the defendant have to be construed within the meaning that they are given in England and Wales. In construing those words, the courts should not have any regard to the *defendant's* own racial, national or ethnic origins—or presumably their religious beliefs or lack of such (*R* v *White (Anthony Delroy)* [2001] EWCA Crim 216).

In order to prove this offence you must show that the defendant *intended* to cause harassment, alarm or distress and, it seems, that by so doing, the defendant actually caused some harassment, alarm or distress. In *Steele* v *DPP* [2008] EWHC 438 (Admin) the defendant took a digital photograph of the complainant and posted it on the Internet with a speech bubble and text alleging the complainant had previous convictions for violence. It was several months later that the photograph was shown to the complainant by the police and the Divisional Court held that the time and the circumstances in which it had been brought fully to the attention of the complainant were immaterial.

Harassment, alarm or distress are not defined and it would appear that they are to be given their ordinary everyday meaning. A police officer can be caused such harassment, alarm or distress (*DPP* v *Orum* [1989] 1 WLR 88), and can also be the victim of the racially aggravated form of the offence (see *R* v *Jacobs* [2001] 2 Cr App R(S) 38), and he/she can feel that harassment, alarm or distress for someone else present (e.g. a child—see *Lodge* v *DPP* [1989] COD 179). Police officers are expected to display a degree of fortitude and, for an officer to be caused harassment, alarm or distress, the conduct complained of must go beyond that which he/she would regularly come across in the ordinary course of police duties.

Whether the use of a particular phrase, in the context and circumstances in which it was used, was intended to cause harassment, alarm or distress for the offences above is a question of fact for the relevant magistrate/ jury to decide (see *DPP* v *Weeks* (2000) *The Independent*, 17 July). Consequently, in that case where the defendant was alleged to have called the victim a 'black bastard' during a heated argument over a business transaction, the magistrates were still entitled to find him not guilty of the aggravated s. 4A offence if they were satisfied that the relevant intention was not present.

Posting a threatening, abusive or insulting letter through someone's letter box is not an offence under this section (*Chappell* v *DPP* (1989) 89 Cr App R 82). It may, however, amount to an offence under the Malicious Communications Act 1988 (**see para. 4.9.5**).

As with the offence under s. 4, an offence under s. 4A can be committed in a public or private place, but no offence is committed where the words or behaviour are used, etc. by a person inside a dwelling and the person who is harassed, alarmed or distressed is also inside that or another dwelling (s. 4A(2)). For the definition of a 'dwelling' **see para. 4.11.7.1**.

4.11.8.1 Defences

The Public Order Act 1986, s. 4A states:

(3) It is a defence for the accused to prove—
   (a) that he was inside a dwelling and had no reason to believe that the words or behaviour used, or the writing, sign or other visible representation displayed, would be heard or seen by a person outside that or any other dwelling, or
   (b) that his conduct was reasonable.

KEYNOTE

If is for the defendant to prove that one of the elements existed at the time of the offence. The standard of proof here will be that of the balance of probabilities, i.e. that it was more likely than not.

4.11.9 Harassment, Alarm or Distress

OFFENCE: **Harassment, Alarm or Distress—*Public Order Act 1986, s. 5***
  • Triable summarily • Fine

OFFENCE: **Racially or Religiously Aggravated—*Crime and Disorder Act 1998, s. 31(1)(c)***
  • Triable summarily • Fine

The Public Order Act 1986, s. 5 states:

(1) A person is guilty of an offence if he—
  (a) uses threatening or abusive words or behaviour, or disorderly behaviour, or
  (b) displays any writing, sign or other visible representation which is threatening or abusive,
  within the hearing or sight of a person likely to be caused harassment, alarm or distress thereby.

KEYNOTE

Note that the word 'insulting' in the original statutory text has been removed by the Crime and Courts Act 2013 (Commencement No. 6) Order 2013 (SI 2013/2981), thereby decriminalising the use of insulting words or behaviour within the hearing or sight of someone likely to be caused harassment, alarm or distress.

Unlike the other racially or religiously aggravated forms of public order offences, the offence under s. 5 remains triable summarily, even if aggravated by the conditions set out in s. 28 of the Crime and Disorder Act 1998 (s. 31(5)).

In a case where the defendant used the words 'You're fucking Islam' in an aggressive manner towards a Sikh police officer of Asian appearance, the Divisional Court held that the expression itself was almost undeniably abusive if not insulting (*R (On the Application of DPP)* v *Humphrey* [2005] EWHC 822 (Admin)). In *Kendall* v *DPP* [2008] EWHC 1848 (Admin), British National Party posters showing a photograph of three black men with the caption 'Illegal Immigrant Murder Scum' were found to be threatening, abusive and insulting and racially aggravated.

The racially or religiously aggravated circumstances set out at s. 28(1)(a) of the Crime and Disorder Act 1998 deal with situations where the defendant demonstrates racial or religious hostility at the time of (or immediately before or after) committing the offence, towards the *victim*. To clarify such situations in relation to the racially or religiously aggravated form of the above offence, s. 31(7) provides that the person 'likely to be caused harassment, alarm or distress' will be treated as the 'victim'. This appears to be a more useful provision than its counterpart in relation to the Criminal Damage Act 1971.

Note that 'disorderly' is not defined and ought to be given its ordinary everyday meaning. It need not be shown that the disorderly behaviour is itself threatening, abusive or insulting, nor that it brought about any feelings of apprehension in the person to whom it was directed (*Chambers and Edwards* v *DPP* [1995] Crim LR 896). The wording of s. 5 is not limited to rowdy behaviour and will extend to any behaviour that could be construed as threatening or abusive.

The discussion at **para. 4.11.8** in relation to intentional harassment, alarm or distress also applies to this offence, except here there needs to be a person within whose sight or hearing the conduct takes place. This requirement was confirmed in *Taylor* v *DPP* [2006] EWHC 1202 (Admin) where it was held that there must be at least evidence that there was someone who could see, or could hear, at the material time, what the individual was doing. However, there was no requirement for the prosecution to call evidence that that someone did actually hear the words spoken or see the behaviour. In *Harvey* v *DPP* [2011] EWHC 3992 (Admin), the defendant had used bad language when detained by the police (saying, e.g. 'I told you you wouldn't find fuck all') and although this might have been considered abusive or insulting, there was no evidence that anyone involved, or any bystanders, had suffered or were likely to have been caused any harassment, alarm or distress. All those involved would have heard such language on many occasions and in consequence the Appeal Court quashed the conviction. In *R (On the Application of Reda)* v *DPP* [2011] EWHC 1550 (Admin), where an accused was acquitted of a s. 5 offence but found guilty of assaulting a police officer, the High Court upheld the assault police conviction as the arrest for the s. 5 offence had been made in good faith, i.e. there were reasonable grounds to suspect that an offence had been committed.

Abdul v DPP [2011] EWHC 247 (Admin) related to a parade to celebrate soldiers returning from Afghanistan and Iraq and a group of protesters who carried placards, chanted slogans such as 'British soldiers burn in hell', and called the soldiers murderers, rapists and baby-killers. The defence contended that the prosecution under this section was disproportionate bearing in mind the right to freedom of expression. The court held that in striking the right balance when determining whether speech was threatening, abusive or insulting, the focus on minority rights was not to result in overlooking the rights of the majority. Where the line between legitimate freedom of expression and a threat to public order was crossed, freedom of speech would not be impaired by 'ruling out' threatening, abusive or insulting speech; the prosecution was a proportionate response.

This offence is a 'penalty offence' for the purposes of s. 1 of the Criminal Justice and Police Act 2001 (**see para. 4.5.14**).

As with the offence under s. 4, an offence under s. 5 can be committed in a public place or a private place, but no offence is committed where the words or behaviour are used, etc. by a person inside a dwelling and the other person is also inside that or another dwelling (s. 5(2)). For the definition of a 'dwelling' **see para. 4.11.7.1**.

4.11.9.1 State of Mind

The Public Order Act 1986, s. 6 states:

> (4) A person is guilty of an offence under section 5 only if he intends his words or behaviour, or the writing, sign or other visible representation, to be threatening or abusive, or is aware that it may be threatening or abusive or (as the case may be) he intends his behaviour to be or is aware that it may be disorderly.

4.11.9.2 Defences

The Public Order Act 1986, s. 5 states:

> (3) It is a defence for the accused to prove—
>   (a) that he had no reason to believe that there was any person within hearing or sight who was likely to be caused harassment, alarm or distress, or
>   (b) that he was inside a dwelling and had no reason to believe that the words or behaviour used, or the writing sign or other visible representation displayed, would be heard or seen by a person outside that or any other dwelling, or
>   (c) that his conduct was reasonable.

KEYNOTE

It is for the defendant to prove that one of the elements existed at the time of the offence. The standard of proof here will be that of the balance of probabilities, i.e. that it was more likely than not.

In deciding whether a defendant's conduct was reasonable under s. 5(3)(c) an objective test will be applied (*DPP* v *Clarke* (1992) 94 Cr App R 359).

The relationship between the Public Order Act 1986, s. 5(1), the ECHR, Article 10 and the supposed 'right' to go naked in public was considered in the 'naked rambler' case, *Gough* v *DPP* [2013] EWHC 3267 (Admin). It was held that the appellant foresaw the consequence of his voluntary decision to walk naked through a town centre and was at least aware that his behaviour may have been threatening, abusive, insulting or disorderly. Thus the intent required by the legislation was proved.

4.11.9.3 Police Direction to Prevent Harassment

In response to a number of campaigns against individuals believed to be involved in animal experiments, the Criminal Justice and Police Act 2001 gives the police specific powers to prevent the intimidation or harassment of people in their own or others' homes. Situations envisaged by the legislation typically arise where protestors gather outside a house where a particular individual is believed to be. Under such circumstances s. 42 provides the most senior ranking police officer at the scene with discretionary powers to give directions to people in the vicinity. The power arises where:

- the person is outside (or in the vicinity of) any premises that are used by any individual as his/her dwelling, and
- the constable believes, on reasonable grounds, that the person is there for the purpose of representing or persuading the resident (or anyone else)
- that he/she should not do something he/she is entitled or required to do or
- that he/she should do something that he/she is under no obligation to do, and
- the constable also believes, on reasonable grounds, that the person's presence amounts to, or is likely to result in, the harassment of the resident or is likely to cause alarm or distress to the resident.

Although the premises involved may be in use by any 'individual' (e.g. *not* a company) and the purpose may be to persuade that or any other 'individual', the officer must believe that the ultimate effect will be harassment, alarm or distress of the *resident*. The requirement for 'belief' by the police officer here is greater than mere concern or suspicion. The requirement for reasonable grounds means that their existence or otherwise will be judged objectively and not simply from the personal standpoint of the officer using the power. Nevertheless, the officer is given a great deal of individual discretion in using this power.

A direction given under s. 42 requires the person(s) to do all such things as the officer specifies as being *necessary* to prevent the harassment, alarm or distress of the resident, including:

- a requirement to leave the vicinity of the premises in question, and
- a requirement to leave that vicinity and not to return to it within such period as the constable may specify, not being longer than 3 months;

and (in either case) the requirement to leave the vicinity may be to do so immediately or after a specified period of time (s. 42(4)).

The direction may be given orally and, where appropriate, may be given to a group of people together (s. 42(3)). There is no requirement that the officer giving the direction be in uniform.

The power under s. 42 cannot be used to direct someone to refrain from conduct made lawful under s. 220 of the Trade Union and Labour Relations (Consolidation) Act 1992 (Peaceful picketing; **see chapter 4.14**).

For further offences and measures in relation to animal experiments **see para. 4.10.11**.

4.11.9.4   Contravening a s. 42 Direction

OFFENCE: **Knowingly Contravening a s. 42 Direction—*Criminal Justice and Police Act 2001, s. 42(7)***

> • Triable summarily • Three months' imprisonment and/or a fine

The Criminal Justice and Police Act 2001, s. 42 states:

> (7) Any person who knowingly fails to comply with a requirement in a direction given to him under this section (other than a requirement under subsection (4)(b)) shall be guilty of an offence.

KEYNOTE

The wording of this offence means that you will have to prove a number of key aspects. First, you will need to show that the person acted 'knowingly' in failing to comply with a requirement in a direction and secondly that it was 'given to them'. Generally the best proof of this will be to show that the person had received the direction (and the detail of its extent) personally and that he/she understood it. Therefore, although the section allows for directions to be given to groups, there may be practical benefits in giving personal directions where circumstances allow.

The reference to subs. (4)(b) means a requirement to leave that vicinity and not to return to it within such period as the constable may specify, not being for a period longer than three months.

Unlawfully Returning to Vicinity—*Criminal Justice and Police Act 2001, s. 42(7A)*

- Triable summarily • Imprisonment for a term not exceeding six months and/or a fine

The Criminal Justice and Police Act 2001, s. 42 states:

(7A) Any person to whom a constable has given a direction including a requirement under subsection (4)(b) commits an offence if he—
- (a) returns to the vicinity of the premises in question within the period specified in the direction beginning with the date on which the direction is given; and
- (b) does so for the purpose described in subsection (1)(b).

KEYNOTE

The offence is committed where a person who is subject to a direction to leave the vicinity, returns within a period of up to three months (the precise length of time will be specified by the police officer) for the 'purposes' described at s. 42A(1)(b) (**see para. 4.11.9.5**)—representing to or persuading a person not to do something he/she is entitled to do, or to do something he/she is not obliged to do.

4.11.9.5   Harassment etc. of Person in their Home

OFFENCE: **Harassment of a Person in their Home—*Criminal Justice and Police Act 2001, s. 42A***

- Triable summarily • Imprisonment for a term not exceeding six months and/or a fine

The Criminal Justice and Police Act 2001, s.42A states:

(1) A person commits an offence if—
- (a) that person is present outside or in the vicinity of any premises that are used by any individual ('the resident') as his dwelling;
- (b) that person is present there for the purpose (by his presence or otherwise) of representing to the resident or another individual (whether or not one who uses the premises as his dwelling), or of persuading the resident or such another individual—
  - (i) that he should not do something that he is entitled or required to do; or
  - (ii) that he should do something that he is not under any obligation to do;
- (c) that person—
  - (i) intends his presence to amount to the harassment of, or to cause alarm or distress to, the resident; or
  - (ii) knows or ought to know that his presence is likely to result in the harassment of, or to cause alarm or distress to, the resident; and
- (d) the presence of that person—
  - (i) amounts to the harassment of, or causes alarm or distress to, any person falling within subsection (2); or
  - (ii) is likely to result in the harassment of, or to cause alarm or distress to, any such person.
(2) A person falls within this subsection if he is—
- (a) the resident,
- (b) a person in the resident's dwelling, or
- (c) a person in another dwelling in the vicinity of the resident's dwelling.

KEYNOTE

This offence, has a number of elements, each of which must be proved if a successful prosecution is to be brought. The ingredients include:

- **Place**—the defendant must be shown to have been in the relevant place (outside or in the vicinity of a 'dwelling') which has the same meaning as in part 1 of the Public Order Act 1986.

- **Purpose**—the defendant's purpose in being there must be to represent to, or persuade the resident/another individual that he/she is should not do something he/she is entitled/required to do or that he/she should do something that he/she is not under any obligation to do.
- **Intention/knowledge**—you must prove that the defendant intended his/her presence to amount to harassment of, or to cause alarm or distress to, the resident or that he/she knew/ought to have known that his/her presence was likely to have that result.
- **Consequences**—you must show that the defendant's presence amounted to/was likely to result in the harassment of, or causing alarm or distress to, any resident, person in the resident's dwelling, or person in another dwelling in the vicinity of the resident's dwelling.

References in s. 42A(1)(c) and (d) to a person's presence are references either to his/her presence alone or together with that of any other people who are also present (s. 42A(3)).

For the purposes of this section a person ought to know that his/her presence is likely to result in the harassment of, or to cause alarm or distress to, a resident if a reasonable person in possession of the same information would think that it was likely to have that effect (s. 42A(4)).

'Dwelling' means any structure or part of a structure occupied as a person's home or as other living accommodation (whether the occupation is separate or shared with others) but does not include any part not so occupied (s. 42A(7)).

Further guidance on this section is provided by Home Office Circular 34/2005.

4.11.10   Causing Nuisance or Disturbance on NHS Premises

OFFENCE: **Causing a Nuisance or Disturbance on NHS Premises—*Criminal Justice and Immigration Act 2008, s. 119***
- Triable summarily

The Criminal Justice and Immigration Act 2008, s. 119 states:

(1) A person commits an offence if—
   (a) the person causes, without reasonable excuse and while on NHS premises, a nuisance or disturbance to an NHS staff member who is working there or otherwise there in connection with work,
   (b) the person refuses, without reasonable excuse, to leave the NHS premises when asked to do so by a constable or an NHS staff member, and
   (c) the person is not on the NHS premises for the purpose of obtaining medical advice, treatment or care for himself or herself.

KEYNOTE

A person ceases to be on NHS premises for the purpose of obtaining medical advice, treatment or care for him/herself once the person has received the advice, treatment or care. Also, a person is not on NHS premises for the purpose of obtaining medical advice, treatment or care for him/herself if the person has been refused the advice, treatment or care during the last eight hours (s. 119(3)).

If a constable reasonably suspects that a person is committing or has committed an offence under s. 119, the constable may remove the person from the NHS premises concerned (s. 120(1)).

If an authorised officer reasonably suspects that a person is committing or has committed an offence he/she may remove the person from the NHS premises concerned, or authorise an appropriate NHS staff member to do so (s. 120(2)).

Any person removing another person from NHS premises under this section may, if necessary, use reasonable force (s. 120(3)).

An authorised officer cannot remove the person or authorise another person to do so if it is reasonably believed he/she is in need of medical advice, etc. or that such removal would endanger his/her mental or physical health (s. 120(4)). An authorised officer is a duly authorised NHS staff member (s. 120(5)).

Note that at the time of writing ss. 119 and 120 are yet to be appointed in relation to Wales.

4.11.11 Public Processions and Assemblies

The law relating to public processions and assemblies is primarily provided by the Public Order Act 1986 and is discussed below.

4.11.11.1 Advance Notice of Public Processions

The Public Order Act 1986, s. 11 states:

(1) Written notice shall be given in accordance with this section of any proposal to hold a public procession intended—
   (a) to demonstrate support for or opposition to the views or actions of any person or body of persons,
   (b) to publicise a cause or campaign, or
   (c) to mark or commemorate an event,
   unless it is not reasonably practicable to give any advance notice of the procession.
(2) Subsection (1) does not apply where the procession is one commonly or customarily held in the police area (or areas) in which it is proposed to be held or is a funeral procession organised by a funeral director acting in the normal course of his business.
(3) The notice must specify the date when it is intended to hold the procession, the time when it is intended to start it, its proposed route, and the name and address of the person (or of one of the persons) proposing to organise it.
(4) Notice must be delivered to a police station—
   (a) in the police area in which it is proposed the procession will start, or
   (b) where it is proposed the procession will start in Scotland and cross into England, in the first police area in England on the proposed route.

KEYNOTE

In relation to s. 11(2) it was held that an organised cycle ride that started at the same time and place on the last Friday of every month, even though there was no fixed, settled or predetermined route, end-time or destination, was a commonly or customarily held procession *(R (On the Application of Kay)* v *Commissioner of Police of the Metropolis* [2008] UKHL 69).

If the notice is delivered not less than six clear days before the date when the procession is intended to be held, the notice may be delivered by post by the recorded delivery service (s. 11(5)). Otherwise, the notice must be delivered by hand not less than six clear days before the date when the procession is intended to be held or, if that is not reasonably practicable, as soon as delivery is reasonably practicable (s. 11(6)).

Where a public procession is held, each of the persons organising it is guilty of an offence if the requirements of this section as to notice have not been satisfied, or the date when it is held, the time when it starts, or its route, differs from the date, time or route specified in the notice (s. 11(7)).

It is a defence for the accused to prove that he/she did not know of, and neither suspected nor had reason to suspect, the failure to satisfy the requirements or (as the case may be) the difference of date, time or route (s. 11(8)). To the extent that an alleged offence turns on a difference of date, time or route, it is a defence for the accused to prove that the difference arose from circumstances beyond his/her control or from something done with the agreement of a police officer or by the officer's direction (s. 11(9)).

4.11.11.2 Imposing Conditions on Public Processions

The Public Order Act 1986, s. 12 states:

(1) If the senior police officer, having regard to the time or place at which and the circumstances in which any public procession is being held or is intended to be held and to its route or proposed route, reasonably believes that—
   (a) it may result in serious public disorder, serious damage to property or serious disruption to the life of the community, or
   (b) the purpose of the persons organising it is the intimidation of others with a view to compelling them not to do an act they have a right to do, or to do an act they have a right not to do,

he may give directions imposing on the persons organising or taking part in the procession such conditions as appear to him necessary to prevent such disorder, damage, disruption or intimidation, including conditions as to the route of the procession or prohibiting it from entering any public place specified in the directions.

KEYNOTE

This section may also apply to a commonly or customarily held procession as described in s. 11(2) (see para. **4.11.11.1**). It enables a senior police officer, who reasonably believes that a procession may result in serious disruption to the life of the community, to give such directions imposing conditions as to the route of the procession as appear to him necessary to prevent such disruption. This can be done days before the procession, or at the point of assembly or during the procession itself. The giving of directions is a preventive measure whenever given (*Powlesland* v *DPP* [2013] EWHC 3846 (Admin)).

In relation to a procession being held, or to a procession intended to be held in a case where persons are assembling with a view to taking part in it, the 'senior police officer' is the most senior in rank of the police officers present at the scene (s. 12(2)(a)). For any other intended procession it is the chief officer of police (s. 12(2)(b)), whose direction must be given in writing (s. 12(3)).

A person who organises a public procession and knowingly fails to comply with a condition imposed under this section is guilty of a summary offence, but it is a defence to prove that the failure arose from circumstances beyond his/her control (s. 12(4)).

A person who takes part in a public procession and knowingly fails to comply with a condition imposed under this section is guilty of a summary offence, but it is a defence to prove that the failure arose from circumstances beyond his/her control (s. 12(5)). Those participating in a public procession are entitled to leave it, but they are not entitled to move from the route of the procession while they remain as participants in it (*Jukes* v *DPP* [2013] EWHC 195 (Admin)).

A person who incites another to commit a summary offence under s. 12(5) is guilty of an offence (s. 12(6)).

4.11.11.3 Prohibiting Public Processions

The Public Order Act 1986, s. 13 states:

(1) If at any time the chief officer of police reasonably believes that, because of particular circumstances existing in any district or part of a district, the powers under section 12 will not be sufficient to prevent the holding of public processions in that district or part from resulting in serious public disorder, he shall apply to the council of the district for an order prohibiting for such period not exceeding 3 months as may be specified in the application the holding of all public processions (or of any class of public procession so specified) in the district or part concerned.

(2) On receiving such an application, a council may with the consent of the Secretary of State make an order either in the terms of the application or with such modifications as may be approved by the Secretary of State.

(3) Subsection (1) does not apply in the City of London or the metropolitan police district.

KEYNOTE

A person who organises a public procession the holding of which he/she knows is prohibited by virtue of an order under this section is guilty of a summary offence (s. 13(7)). A person who takes part in a public procession the holding of which he/she knows is prohibited by virtue of an order under this section is guilty of a summary offence (s. 13(8)), and a person who incites another to commit an offence under s. 13(8) is guilty of a summary offence (s. 13(9)).

4.11.11.4 Imposing Conditions on Public Assemblies

The Public Order Act 1986, s. 14 states:

(1) If the senior police officer, having regard to the time or place at which and the circumstances in which any public assembly is being held or is intended to be held, reasonably believes that—

(a) it may result in serious public disorder, serious damage to property or serious disruption to the life of the community, or

(b) the purpose of the persons organising it is the intimidation of others with a view to compelling them not to do an act they have a right to do, or to do an act they have a right not to do,

he may give directions imposing on the persons organising or taking part in the assembly such conditions as to the place at which the assembly may be (or continue to be) held, its maximum duration, or the maximum number of persons who may constitute it, as appear to him necessary to prevent such disorder, damage, disruption or intimidation.

(2) In subsection (1) 'the senior police officer' means—

(a) in relation to an assembly being held, the most senior in rank of the police officers present at the scene, and

(b) in relation to an assembly intended to be held, the chief officer of police.

(3) A direction given by a chief officer of police by virtue of subsection (2)(b) shall be given in writing.

KEYNOTE

A person who organises a public assembly and knowingly fails to comply with a condition imposed under this section is guilty of a summary offence, but it is a defence to prove that the failure arose from circumstances beyond his/her control (s. 14(4)). A person who takes part in a public assembly and knowingly fails to comply with a condition imposed under this section is guilty of a summary offence, but it is a defence to prove that the failure arose from circumstances beyond his/her control (s. 14(5)). A person who incites another to commit an offence under s. 14(5) is guilty of an summary offence (s. 14(6)).

The distinction between this section and s. 12 concerns the conditions that may be imposed under each section. In *DPP* v *Jones* [2002] EWHC 110 (Admin) demonstrators against the Huntingdon Life Sciences Centre were prosecuted for failing to comply with a condition set out in a police notice issued under s. 14. It was held that some of the conditions imposed were more properly concerned with a public procession and therefore were beyond the police powers under s. 14. The offending parts of the police notice were 'severed' leaving the enforceable parts intact. However it may be safer for the police to issue two separate notices, in appropriate circumstances, one relating to the conditions to be observed by participants in the 'procession' element of an operation and the other imposing conditions on the 'assembly' element.

Where a chief officer gives a direction he/she must identify what limb of s. 14(1) was being relied upon and in sufficient detail to enable demonstrators to understand why the decision was made and for a court to understand if a decision was reasonable or not (*R (On the Application of Brehony)* v *Chief Constable of Greater Manchester Police* [2005] EWHC 640 (Admin)).

A direction under this section was lawful where a senior police officer imposed a condition that a Climate Camp protest against the G20 Summit in London must stop. The demonstration had lasted the best part of 12 hours—quite long enough for the protestors to take advantage of their human rights under Article 10 (Freedom of Expression) and Article 11 (Freedom of Assembly and Association)—and those wishing to remain were intent on continuing to block the highway, the main thoroughfare into and out of the City. There was no justification to prolong the demonstration and its continuation would cause serious disturbances and disruption to traffic and pedestrians wishing to use the highway. The police had a duty to clear the highway that could not be done without removing the protestors by force if necessary (*R (On the Application of Moos)* v *Commissioner of Police of the Metropolis* [2011] EWHC 957 (Admin)).

4.11.11.5 Prohibiting Trespassory Assemblies

The provisions of s. 14 (**see para. 4.11.11.4**) apply to public assemblies. However, occasions have arisen where the assembly has been *trespassory*, that is, on land which is either private or where there is only a limited right of public access and the permission of the relevant landowner has not been granted. In such instances, s. 14A of the Public Order Act 1986 provides the police with certain powers.

The Public Order Act, s. 14A states:

(1) If at any time the chief officer of police reasonably believes that an assembly is intended to be held in any district at a place on land to which the public has no right of access or only a limited right of access and that the assembly—

    (a) is likely to be held without the permission of the occupier of the land or to conduct itself in such a way as to exceed the limits of any permission of his or the limits of the public's right of access, and

    (b) may result—

        (i) in serious disruption to the life of the community, or

        (ii) where the land, or a building or monument on it, is of historical, architectural, archaeological or scientific importance, in significant damage to the land, building or monument,

he may apply to the council of the district for an order prohibiting for a specified period the holding of all trespassory assemblies in the district or a part of it, as specified.

KEYNOTE

A classic example of a trespassory assembly might be found at sites such as Stonehenge.

On receiving an application from a chief officer the council may make an order either in the terms of the application, or with modifications, either of which must be approved by the Secretary of State (s. 14A(2)(a)), and the order must be in writing or reduced to writing as soon as practicable after being made (s. 14A(8)).

An order must not last for more than four days, nor must it apply to an area beyond a radius of five miles from a specified centre (s. 14A(6)).

An 'assembly' for the purpose of this section means 20 or more people, 'land' means land in the open air, and 'public' includes a section of the public (s. 14A(9)).

A person who organises an assembly the holding of which he/she knows is prohibited by an order under s. 14A is guilty of a summary offence (s. 14B(1)). A person who takes part in an assembly which he/she knows is prohibited by an order under s. 14A is guilty of a summary offence (s. 14B(2)), and a person who incites another to commit an offence under s. 14B(2) is guilty of a summary offence (s. 14B(3)). Even where an order has been made, there will be a need to show that the assembly was obstructive of the highway or at least that it exceeded the public's general right of access (*DPP* v *Jones* [1999] 2 AC 240).

4.11.11.6 Trespassory Assemblies Police Powers

The Public Order Act 1986, s. 14C states:

(1) If a constable in uniform reasonably believes that a person is on his way to an assembly within the area to which an order under section 14A applies which the constable reasonably believes is likely to be an assembly which is prohibited by that order, he may, subject to subsection (2) below—

    (a) stop that person, and

    (b) direct him not to proceed in the direction of the assembly.

(2) The power conferred by subsection (1) may only be exercised within the area to which the order applies.

(3) A person who fails to comply with a direction under subsection (1) which he knows has been given to him is guilty of an offence.

KEYNOTE

This power allows officers to stop people, though not, it would seem, vehicles (in which case the general power under s. 163 of the Road Traffic Act 1988 must be used).

4.11.11.7 Public Meetings

It is an offence to attempt to break up a public meeting.

OFFENCE: **Trying to Break up a Public Meeting—*Public Meeting Act 1908, s. 1***

> • Triable summarily • Six months' imprisonment and/or a fine *(No specific power of arrest)*

The Public Meeting Act 1908, s. 1 states:

> (1) Any person who at a lawful public meeting acts in a disorderly manner for the purpose of preventing the transaction of the business for which the meeting was called together shall be guilty of an offence and shall on summary conviction be liable to imprisonment for a term not exceeding six months or to a fine not exceeding £1,000 or to both...
>
> (2) Any person who incites others to commit an offence under this section shall be guilty of a like offence.

KEYNOTE

If a constable reasonably suspects any person of committing this offence, he/she may, *if requested by the person chairing the meeting*, require the offender to declare his/her name and address immediately. Failing to comply with such a request or giving false details is a summary offence (s. 1(3)).

'Public meeting' is not defined in the 1908 Act. There appears to be no requirement for the meeting to be lawfully assembled.

This offence does not apply to meetings held in relation to s. 97 of the Representation of the People Act 1983 (meetings concerned with public elections) (s. 1(4)). In the case of people acting or inciting others to act in a disorderly way at such meetings, there is a specific summary offence under s. 97(1) of the 1983 Act.

4.11.12 Dispersal of Groups

In addition to the organisation of public assemblies, processions and meetings, informal and *ad hoc* gatherings have implications for policing.

The Anti-social Behaviour Act 2003 provides further policing powers to deal with such occasions by allowing a senior police officer to authorise the use of powers of dispersal if the relevant conditions are met.

4.11.12.1 Authorisation of Powers

The Anti-social Behaviour Act 2003, s. 30 states:

> (1) This section applies where a relevant officer has reasonable grounds for believing—
>
> > (a) that any members of the public have been intimidated, harassed, alarmed or distressed as a result of the presence or behaviour of groups of two or more persons in public places in any locality in his police area (the 'relevant locality'), and
> >
> > (b) that anti-social behaviour is a significant and persistent problem in the relevant locality.
>
> (2) The relevant officer may give an authorisation that the powers conferred on a constable in uniform by subsections (3) to (6) are to be exercisable for a period specified in the authorisation which does not exceed 6 months.

KEYNOTE

'Relevant officer' means a police officer of or above the rank of superintendent (s. 36). This officer must be able to show that he/she had reasonable grounds for believing both conditions set out in s. 30(1)(a) and (b) were met. If they are met, the relevant officer can then authorise the use of the further powers set out in the paragraphs below.

The 'anti-social behaviour' referred to means behaviour by a person which causes (or is likely to cause) harassment, alarm or distress to one or more other people not of the same household as that person (s. 36).

The definition of public place is also contained in s. 36 and is fairly wide. It includes a highway and any place to which at the material time the public (or any section of it) has access, on payment or otherwise, as of right or by virtue of express or implied permission.

Any authorisation must be in writing, signed by the relevant officer giving it and must specify:

- the relevant locality;
- the grounds on which the authority is given;
- the period during which the relevant powers (conferred by s. 30(3) to (6)—see paras **4.11.12.2 and 4.11.12.3**) are exercisable (which is not to exceed six months).

(s. 31)

An authorisation may not be given without the consent of the local authority or each local authority whose area includes the whole or part of the relevant locality (s. 31(2)). In addition, the authorisation must be given publicity, either by publishing a notice in a newspaper circulating in the relevant locality or by posting an authorisation notice in some conspicuous place or places within the relevant locality (or both) (s. 31(3)). This publicity must be given *before* the specified date on which the powers of dispersal below (**see para. 4.11.12.2**) are to begin (s. 31(5)).

An authorisation can be withdrawn by the officer who made it or by another officer for that police area of the same or higher rank; however, the local authority must be consulted first.

In accordance with the CPS's Anti-Social Behaviour Guidance (May 2008), the validity of the authorisation must be proved at court, both as regards the reasons for making the authorisation and that proper publicity has been given (*Carter* v *CPS* [2009] EWHC 2197 (Admin)).

4.11.12.2   Powers of Dispersal

The Anti-social Behaviour Act 2003, s. 30 states:

(3) Subsection (4) applies if a constable in uniform has reasonable grounds for believing that the presence or behaviour of a group of two or more persons in any public place in the relevant locality has resulted, or is likely to result, in any members of the public being intimidated, harassed, alarmed or distressed.

(4) The constable may give one or more of the following directions, namely—

(a) a direction requiring the persons in the group to disperse (either immediately or by such time as he may specify and in such way as he may specify),

(b) a direction requiring any of those persons whose place of residence is not within the relevant locality to leave the relevant locality or any part of the relevant locality (either immediately or by such time as he may specify and in such way as he may specify), and

(c) a direction prohibiting any of those persons whose place of residence is not within the relevant locality from returning to the relevant locality or any part of the relevant locality for such period (not exceeding 24 hours) from the giving of the direction as he may specify;

but this subsection is subject to subsection (5).

KEYNOTE

Section 30(5) provides that a direction under s. 30(4) may not be given in respect of a group of persons who are engaged in lawful picketing (under s. 220 of the Trade Union and Labour Relations (Consolidation) Act 1992), or who are taking part in a lawfully notified and organised public procession (under s. 11(1) of the Public Order Act 1986).

The direction under s. 30(4) may be given orally, may be given to any person individually or to two or more people together, and may be withdrawn or varied *by the person who gave it* (s. 32(1)).

Note that any reference to the presence or behaviour of a group of people will include a reference to the presence or behaviour of *any one or more* of those people (s. 30(7)). Therefore it is not necessary to show that the presence or behaviour of all the people in a particular group meets each of the criteria above.

In *R (On the Application of Singh)* v *Chief Constable of West Midlands Police* [2006] EWCA Civ 1118 it was held that the use of dispersal orders, in respect of a group of protesters of two or more persons who were causing harassment, alarm and distress to members of the public, was lawful even though the authorisation order was already in force in respect of unrelated expected anti-social behaviour. In addition it was held that the use of the power did not override the applicants' fundamental human rights (European Convention on Human Rights, Articles 9 and 10—see para. 4.4.11), but was expressly subject to them.

Mere presence in a designated dispersal area, whilst capable of being the basis for the forming of a belief under s. 30(3), was not normally sufficient for giving a direction under s. 30(4). A reasonable belief under s. 30(4) depends on some behaviour by the group indicating that harassment, alarm or distress had resulted or would result (*Bucknell* v *DPP* [2006] EWHC 1888 (Admin)).

4.11.12.3   Power to Remove Under-16s

A further power, to remove people under 16 to their place of residence, is provided by the Act.

The Anti-social Behaviour Act 2003, s. 30 states:

(6) If, between the hours of 9pm and 6am, a constable in uniform finds a person in any public place in the relevant locality who he has reasonable grounds for believing—
   (a) is under the age of 16, and
   (b) is not under the effective control of a parent or a responsible person aged 18 or over,
   he may remove the person to the person's place of residence unless he has reasonable grounds for believing that the person would, if removed to that place, be likely to suffer significant harm.

KEYNOTE

This power, while appearing relatively straightforward, presents some practical difficulties. It presupposes a number of things, one of them being that the officer knows the person's place of residence. Additionally, in many cases, 'removing' teenagers to their home address will be far easier said than done. Careful reference will need to be made to the Code of Practice when exercising this power.

In *R (On the Application of W)* v *Metropolitan Police Commissioner* [2006] EWCA Civ 458 it was held that the word 'remove' in s. 30(6) naturally and compellingly means 'take away using reasonable force if necessary'. However, this is not an arbitrary power and, within a designated dispersal area, a constable must only use this power, (a) to protect children under 16 from the physical and social risks of anti-social behaviour by others, or (b) to prevent children from participating in anti-social behaviour themselves.

If this power is used, any local authority whose area includes the whole or part of the relevant locality must be notified of that fact (s. 32(4)).

4.11.12.4   Knowingly Contravening Direction

OFFENCE: **Knowingly Contravening Direction—*Anti-social Behaviour Act 2003*, s. 32**
   • Triable summarily • Three months' imprisonment and/or a fine

The Anti-social Behaviour Act 2003, s. 32 states:

(2) A person who knowingly contravenes a direction given to him under section 30(4) commits an offence...

KEYNOTE

You must show that the person contravened the direction(s) 'knowingly'. Therefore it is important to be able to prove that the direction was lawfully authorised, clearly given and that it was understood by the defendant.

In *Carter v CPS* [2009] EWHC 2197 (Admin) it was held that in order to prove that a police officer acted lawfully, the authorisation of the officer to give the direction under s. 30(4) must be properly proved, i.e. the reason for having the authorisation (s. 30(1)), its form (s. 31(1)), the consent of the local authority (s. 31(2)), and the extent to which it has been publicised (s. 31(3) to (5)).

4.11.12.5 Injunctions: Gang-related Violence

The Policing and Crime Act 2009 provides courts with the power to grant injunctions in relation to gang-related violence.

Section 34 of the 2009 Act states:

(1) A court may grant an injunction against a respondent aged 14 or over under this section if 2 conditions are met.
(2) The first condition is that the court is satisfied on the balance of probabilities that the respondent has engaged in, or has encouraged or assisted, gang-related violence.
(3) The second condition is that the court thinks it is necessary to grant the injunction for either or both of the following purposes—
  (a) to prevent the respondent from engaging in, or encouraging or assisting, gang-related violence;
  (b) to protect the respondent from gang-related violence.
(4) An injunction under this section may (for either or both of those purposes)—
  (a) prohibit the respondent from doing anything described in the injunction;
  (b) require the respondent to do anything described in the injunction.
(5) In this section "gang-related violence" means violence or a threat of violence which occurs in the course of, or is otherwise related to, the activities of a group that—
  (a) consists of at least 3 people,
  (b) uses a name, emblem or colour or has any other characteristic that enables its members to be identified by others as a group, and
  (c) is associated with a particular area.

KEYNOTE

These injunctions are a civil tool allowing the chief officer of police for a police area, the chief constable of the British Transport Police, or a local authority to apply to a county court (or the High Court) for an injunction against an individual who has been involved in gang-related violence (s. 37).

The aim of a gang injunction is to prevent a person from engaging in, encouraging or assisting gang-related violence and may also serve to protect that person from gang-related violence.

Courts (including youth courts) can place a range of prohibitions and requirements on the behaviour and activities of a person involved in gang-related violence. These conditions could include prohibiting someone from being in a particular place or requiring him/her to participate in rehabilitative activities (s. 35).

Section 36 provides that a court may attach a power of arrest in relation to (a) any prohibition in the injunction, or (b) any requirement in the injunction, other than one which has the effect of requiring the respondent to participate in particular activities (s. 36(6)). If the court attaches a power of arrest, it may specify that the power is to have effect for a shorter period than the prohibition or requirement to which it relates (s. 36(7)).

Where a power of arrest is attached to a provision of an injunction a constable may arrest without warrant a person whom the constable has reasonable cause to suspect to be in breach of the provision. The constable must inform the person who applied for the injunction of the arrest, and the person arrested must be brought before a relevant judge within the period of 24 hours beginning at the time of the arrest (s. 43).

In December 2011 the Home Office published 'Statutory Guidance: Injunctions to Prevent Gang-Related Violence' to help local partners apply for and manage gang injunctions effectively and appropriately.

4.12 Sporting Events

4.12.1 Introduction

In addition to the more general offences regulating public order, there are several offences and statutory measures which are specifically aimed at tackling disorder and anti-social behaviour at sporting events. The legislation in this area has developed piecemeal over a number of years and is sprinkled across a number of different Acts. However, one of the more important pieces of football legislation, the Football (Disorder) Act 2000 which amended the Football Spectators Act 1989, significantly altered the powers of courts and police in football-related matters.

4.12.2 Designated and Regulated Football Matches

Many of the offences and powers relating to football fixtures apply to 'designated' or 'regulated' football matches. These expressions have caused a number of practical anomalies and have been standardised by various statutory instruments. In summary, the expressions generally have the following meaning:

- An association football match (in the United Kingdom) as described below will be a regulated football match for the purposes of part II of the Football Spectators Act 1989. The description will cover association football matches in which one or both of the participating teams represents a club which is, for the time being, a member (whether a full or associate member) of the Football League, the Football Association Premier League, the Football Conference or the Welsh Premier League, the Scottish Premier League, or the Scottish Professional Football League, or represents a country or territory.
- An association football match (outside the United Kingdom) as described below will also be a regulated football match for the purposes of part II of the 1989 Act. The description will cover an association football match involving:
  + a national team appointed by the Football Association to represent England or the Football Association of Wales to represent Wales; or
  + a team playing in the Football Association Cup (other than in a preliminary or qualifying round); or
  + a team representing a club which is, at the time the match is played, a member (whether a full or associate member) of the Football League, the Football Association Premier League, the Football Conference or the Welsh Premier League, the Scottish Premier League, or the Scottish Professional Football League; or
  + any match involving a country or territory whose football association is for the time being a member of Fédération Internationale de Football Association (FIFA), where the match is part of a competition or tournament organised by or under the authority of FIFA or the Union des Associations Européennes de Football (UEFA), and where the competition or tournament is one in which the England or Wales national team is eligible to participate or has participated;
  + any match involving a club whose national football association is a member of FIFA, where the match is part of a competition or tournament organised by or under the authority of FIFA or UEFA, and where the competition or tournament is one in which a club from the Football League, the Football Association Premier League, the Football Conference or the League of Wales is eligible to participate or has participated; or

♦ any match involving a club whose home ground is outside England or Wales but they are playing within England or Wales.

4.12.2.1 The Football (Offences) Act 1991

OFFENCE: **Misbehaviour at Designated Football Match**—*Football (Offences) Act 1991, ss. 2, 3 and 4*
- Triable summarily • Fine

The Football (Offences) Act 1991, ss. 2,3 and 4 state:

2. It is an offence for a person at a designated football match to throw anything at or towards—
   (a) the playing area, or any area adjacent to the playing area to which spectators are not generally admitted, or
   (b) any area in which spectators or other persons are or may be present, without lawful authority or lawful excuse (which shall be for him to prove).
3. (1) It is an offence to engage or take part in chanting of an indecent or racialist nature at a designated football match.
   (2) For this purpose—
   (a) 'chanting' means the repeated uttering of any words or sounds (whether alone or in concert with one or more others); and
   (b) 'of a racialist' nature means consisting of or including matter which is threatening, abusive or insulting to a person by reason of his colour, race, nationality (including citizenship) or ethnic or national origins.
4. It is an offence for a person at a designated football match to go onto the playing area, or any area adjacent to the playing area to which spectators are not generally admitted, without lawful authority or lawful excuse (which shall be for him to prove).

KEYNOTE

Section 1(2) of the 1991 Act provides that references to things done at a 'designated football match' include anything done at the ground:

- within the period beginning two hours before the start of the match or (if earlier) two hours before the time at which it is advertised to start and ending one hour after the end of the match;
- where the match is advertised to start at a particular time on a particular day but does not take place, within the period beginning two hours before and ending one hour after the advertised starting time.

A 'designated' match for these purposes is the same as a 'regulated' match under the Football Spectators Act 1989 (see para. 4.12.2).

These offences can be separated into those affecting the playing area and adjacent parts of the ground (ss. 2 and 4) and the offence of indecent or 'racialist' chanting (s. 3).

In the case of the first offence (s. 2), throwing anything at or towards the playing area etc., there is a defence of having lawful authority or lawful excuse (which presumably would cover returning the ball to the field of play). Generally there seem to be few occasions on which a defendant would have lawful authority/reasonable excuse for the behaviour prohibited by s. 2.

Section 4 makes the same savings in relation to lawful authority/reasonable excuse and, in both cases, the burden of proof falls on the defendant. (The *standard* of proof will be that of the balance of probabilities.)

For the offence under s. 3, the defendant must be shown to have *repeated* the words or sounds before it can be classed as 'chanting'. The definition under subsection (2) was amended by the Football (Offences and Disorder) Act 1999 to cater for occasions where one person acting alone commits the offence.

'Indecent' is not defined and will be a question of fact for the court to decide in all the circumstances.

'Racialist' is a slightly outdated term. The wording of s. 3(2)(b) requires that the chanting *is* rather than might potentially be, threatening, abusive or insulting (compare with the wording under the other general public order offences above). Therefore, although there is no express requirement for a 'victim' of the offence under this section, the best way to prove that element of the offence would be to find someone who was so threatened, abused or insulted by the behaviour. For an example, shouting 'you're just a town full of Pakis' at supporters from Oldham fell squarely within the definition, see *DPP* v *Stoke on Trent Magistrates' Court* [2003] EWHC 1593 (Admin).

4.12.3 Banning Orders and Detention

The Football Spectators Act 1989 contains the powers to impose banning orders that exclude offenders from attendance at regulated football matches in England, Wales, Scotland and Northern Ireland and international football matches.

There are two ways in which a banning order can be made, first where a person is convicted of a relevant offence (s. 14A), and secondly, by way of complaint by the relevant chief officer, or the DPP (s. 14B(1)).

Convicted of Relevant Offences

The relevant offences are set out in sch. 1 to the 1989 Act and include offences relating to drunkenness, violence or threats of violence, or public order offences committed at or in connection with a football match or when travelling to or from a football match (whether or not the match was actually attended by the offender). In *R* v *Elliott* [2007] EWCA Crim 1002, banning orders were quashed where it was found that violence involving a group of men in a public house was unrelated to the match. See also *DPP* v *Beaumont* [2008] EWHC 523 (Admin). In making a banning order a court may take into account the potential deterrent effect of the order on persons other than the offender (*R (On the Application of White)* v *Blackfriars Crown Court* [2008] EWHC 510 (Admin) and *R* v *Curtis* [2010] EWCA Crim 123).

Rather than simply having the power to make such orders, courts are under a statutory duty to pass such orders if they are satisfied that there are reasonable grounds to believe that the orders would help prevent violence or disorder at or in connection with a 'regulated football match' (**see para. 4.12.2**). Violence here includes violence towards property, and disorder includes stirring up racial hatred (1989 Act, s. 14C). Where these criteria are established, there is no discretion not to make an order (*R* v *Allen* [2011] EWCA Crim 3076, and see also *R* v *Doyle* [2012] EWCA Crim 995).

The court may adjourn any proceedings in relation to an order even after sentencing the offender and may remand the offender (s. 14A(4A) and (4BA)). Where the offender is remanded on bail he/she may be required not to leave England and Wales before appearing before the court and to surrender his/her passport to a constable (s. 14A(4BB)).

If a magistrates' court fails to make a banning order, the prosecution have a right of appeal to the Crown Court, or to the Court of Appeal where the Crown Court failed to make an order (s. 14A(5A)). If the offender does not appear for any adjourned proceedings, the court may further adjourn the proceedings, or it may issue a warrant for his/her arrest but only after it is satisfied that he/she has had adequate notice of the time and place of the adjourned proceedings (s. 14A(4B) and (4C)).

A banning order may only be made in addition to a sentence imposed by the court but can be passed even if the originating offence is dealt with by way of a conditional or absolute discharge.

Complaint by Chief Officer or DPP

On such an application a magistrates' court can make an order if the person has at any time caused or contributed to any violence or disorder in the United Kingdom or elsewhere.

The court may impose conditions on banning orders and must require the surrender of the person's passport in connection with regulated football matches outside the United Kingdom (s. 14E(3)). Where proceedings are adjourned, as with the first way of obtaining a banning order, the offender may be remanded and, where bailed, be required to surrender his/her passport (s. 14B(5)). Again, where the magistrates have failed to make a banning order, the prosecution have a right of appeal to the Crown Court (s. 14D(1A)).

The effect of a banning order, unless a person is detained in legal custody, is that he/she must initially report to a specified police station in England, Wales, Scotland or Northern Ireland, within five days of the order being made (s. 14E(2)). He/she must also notify the enforcing authority of specified changes to his/her personal circumstances within seven days of the occurrence of any such changes (s. 14E(2B) and (2C)).

KEYNOTE

Banning orders made under s. 14A of the 1989 Act (on conviction of a relevant offence) in addition to an immediate sentence of imprisonment will have a minimum of six and a maximum of 10 years' duration (s. 14F(3)). Other banning orders made under s. 14A (i.e. where they do not accompany a sentence of immediate imprisonment) have a minimum of three and a maximum of five years' duration (s. 14F(4)). Banning orders made under s. 14B (on complaint by a chief officer of police) have a minimum of three and a maximum of five years' duration (s. 14F(5)). If a banning order has been in effect for at least two-thirds of its period, the person subject to it can apply to the court which passed the order for its termination. The National Crime Agency (NCA) has responsibility for monitoring the movement of football spectators and collating relevant intelligence. The Football Banning Orders Authority is the 'designated authority' for the purposes of the 1989 Act. Under the Football Disorder Act 2000, the NCA is empowered to disclose information for the purposes of the 1989 Act.

International banning orders do not contravene either the general European law on the free movement of people within the European Union, or the European Convention on Human Rights (*Gough* v *Chief Constable of Derbyshire* [2002] EWCA Civ 351).

In *Gough*, the Court of Appeal held that there was no absolute right to leave one's country. As banning orders were to be imposed only where there were strong grounds for concluding that the person had a propensity to take part in football hooliganism, the court held that it was appropriate that such people should be subject to a scheme that restricted their ability to indulge in that hooliganism. Like sexual offences prevention orders and anti-social behaviour orders, banning orders are not criminal charges, nor are the proceedings in applying for them 'criminal' proceedings (*Gough*). However, although the standard of proof is the civil standard in applying for banning orders, that standard is flexible and has to reflect the consequences that would follow if the case for a banning order were made out. In reality, this means that magistrates should apply a standard of proof which is hard to distinguish from the criminal one.

The Association of Chief Police Officers and the CPS have published a *Prosecution Policy for Football Related Offences* (August 2013). There will be a presumption of prosecution whenever there is sufficient evidence to bring offenders before a court on appropriate criminal charges and where a Football Banning Order is considered necessary. This publication can be found at http://www.cps.gov.uk/publications/prosecution/football_offences_policy.html.

4.12.3.1 Failing to Comply with Banning Order

OFFENCE: **Failing to Comply with Banning Order—*Football Spectators Act 1989,
s. 14J***

- Triable summarily • Six months' imprisonment and/or a fine

The Football Spectators Act 1989, s. 14J states:

(1) A person subject to a banning order who fails to comply with—
   (a) any requirement imposed by the order, or
   (b) any requirement imposed under section 19(2B) or (2C) below is guilty of an offence.

4.12.3.2 Power of Detention

The Football Spectators Act 1989, s. 21A states:

(1) This section and section 21B below apply during any control period in relation to a regulated football match outside the United Kingdom or an external tournament if a constable in uniform—

    (a) has reasonable grounds for suspecting that the condition in section 14B(2) above is met in the case of a person present before him, and

    (b) has reasonable grounds to believe that making a banning order in his case would help to prevent violence or disorder at or in connection with any regulated football matches.

(2) The constable may detain the person in his custody (whether there or elsewhere) until he has decided whether or not to issue a notice under section 21B below, and shall give the person his reasons for detaining him in writing.

This is without prejudice to any power of the constable apart from this section to arrest the person.

(3) A person may not be detained under subsection (2) above for more than four hours or, with the authority of an officer of at least the rank of inspector, six hours.

4.12.3.3 Service of Notice

The Football Spectators Act 1989, s. 21B states:

(1) A constable in uniform may exercise the power in subsection (2) below if authorised to do so by an officer of at least the rank of inspector.

(2) The constable may give the person a notice in writing requiring him—

(a) to appear before a magistrates' court at a time, or between the times, specified in the notice,

(b) not to leave England and Wales before that time (or the later of those times), and

(c) if the control period relates to a regulated football match outside the United Kingdom or to an external tournament which includes such matches, to surrender his passport to the constable and stating the grounds referred to in section 21A(1) above.

(3) The times for appearance before the magistrates' court must be within the period of 24 hours beginning with—

(a) the giving of the notice, or

(b) the person's detention under section 21A(2) above, whichever is the earlier.

KEYNOTE

The power above requires the police officer to be in uniform and the authority of an inspector or above. It applies during any control period in relation to a regulated football match outside England and Wales or an external tournament (as to which, see the Keynote at **para. 4.12.3.2**).

A constable may arrest a person to whom he/she is giving a notice if he/she has reasonable grounds to believe that it is *necessary* to do so in order to ensure that the person complies with the notice (s. 21B(5)).

For the purposes of s. 14B, the notice is to be treated as an application for a banning order made by complaint (s. 21B(4)).

As with the provision for detention under s. 21A, the powers conferred by s. 21B may be exercised only in relation to a person who is a British citizen (s. 21C(1)).

4.12.3.4 Failure to Comply with Notice under Section 21B

OFFENCE: **Failing to Comply with Notice—*Football Spectators Act 1989, s. 21C***
- Triable summarily • Six months' imprisonment and/or a fine

The Football Spectators Act 1989, s. 21C states:

(2) A person who fails to comply with a notice given to him under section 21B above is guilty of an offence...

KEYNOTE

The notice must have been lawfully given in order to attract liability for this offence. Where a person who has been given a notice appears before a magistrates' court as required by the notice (whether under arrest or not), the court may remand him/her and the court may require the person not to leave England and Wales as a condition of bail (s. 21C(3) and (4)). Also, if the control period relates to a regulated football match outside the United Kingdom or to an external tournament which includes such matches, the court can order the person to surrender his/her passport to a police constable, if he/she has not already done so.

4.12.4 The Sporting Events (Control of Alcohol etc.) Act 1985

OFFENCE: **Alcohol on Coaches and Trains—*Sporting Events (Control of Alcohol etc.) Act 1985, s. 1***
- Triable summarily • Three months' imprisonment and/or a fine (s. 1(3))
- Fine (s. 1(2) and (4))

The Sporting Events (Control of Alcohol etc.) Act 1985, s. 1 states:

(1) This section applies to a vehicle which—
  (a) is a public service vehicle or railway passenger vehicle, and
  (b) is being used for the principal purpose of carrying passengers for the whole or part of a journey to or from a designated sporting event.
(2) A person who knowingly causes or permits alcohol to be carried on a vehicle to which the section applies is guilty of an offence—
  (a) if the vehicle is a public service vehicle and he is the operator of the vehicle or the servant or agent of the operator, or
  (b) if the vehicle is a hired vehicle and he is the person to whom it is hired or the servant or agent of that person.
(3) A person who has alcohol in his possession while on a vehicle to which this section applies is guilty of an offence.
(4) A person who is drunk on a vehicle to which this section applies is guilty of an offence.

KEYNOTE

Section 1 creates a number of offences in relation to public service vehicles and trains being used principally (though not exclusively) to carry passengers for the whole or part of a journey, to or from a designated sporting event.

The offences can be committed by the vehicle operator/hirer or his/her servant or agent provided there is evidence of *knowingly* causing or permitting the carrying of alcohol.

The other offences are committed by people who have alcohol in their 'possession' and by people who are drunk on a relevant vehicle. Generally, any mature and competent witness may give evidence as to drunkenness.

Section 7(3) provides a power for a police officer to stop a public service vehicle in order to search it where he/she has reasonable grounds to suspect an offence under this section *is being or has been committed* in respect of that vehicle. It also provides a power to search a railway carriage (though not to stop the train) under the same circumstances. The power to search people in those vehicles comes from s. 7(2).

OFFENCE: **Alcohol on Other Vehicles—*Sporting Events (Control of Alcohol etc.) Act 1985, s. 1A***

  • Triable summarily • Three months' imprisonment and/or a fine (s. 1A(3))
  • Fine (s. 1A(2) and (4))

The Sporting Events (Control of Alcohol etc.) Act 1985, s. 1A states:

(1) This section applies to a motor vehicle which—
  (a) is not a public service vehicle but is adapted to carry more than 8 passengers, and
  (b) is being used for the principal purpose of carrying two or more passengers for the whole or part of a journey to or from a designated sporting event.
(2) A person who knowingly causes or permits alcohol to be carried on a motor vehicle to which this section applies is guilty of an offence—
  (a) if he is its driver, or
  (b) if he is not its driver but is its keeper, the servant or agent of its keeper, a person to whom it is made available (by hire, loan or otherwise) by its keeper or the keeper's servant or agent, or the servant or agent of a person to whom it is so made available.
(3) A person who has alcohol in his possession while on a motor vehicle to which this section applies is guilty of an offence.
(4) A person who is drunk on a motor vehicle to which this section applies is guilty of an offence.

KEYNOTE

This section creates similar offences to those set out under s. 1 but these relate to mechanically propelled vehicles that are intended or adapted for use on roads and that are adapted to carry more than eight passengers (not being PSVs).

For the purposes of the above offences, a vehicle's 'keeper' is the person having the duty to take out a vehicle excise licence for it (s. 1A(5)).

The power to stop and search vehicles and their occupants under s. 7(3) above also applies to an offence under this section.

4.12.4.1 Power to Prohibit Sale of Alcohol on Trains

The Licensing Act 2003, s. 157 states:

(1) A magistrates' court acting for a petty sessions area may make an order prohibiting the sale of alcohol, during such period as may be specified, on any railway vehicle—
  (a) at such station or stations as may be specified, being stations in that area, or
  (b) travelling between such stations as may be specified, at least one of which is in that area.

KEYNOTE

Unlike some other aspects relating to the control of pre- and post-match events, there is no specific restriction on the period over which such an order may be made. However, the court cannot make such an order unless it is satisfied that the order is *necessary* to prevent disorder (s. 157(3)).

A court may only make an order under this section on the application of a senior police officer (s. 157(2)). 'Senior police officer' means a police officer of, or above, the rank of inspector (s. 157(7)).

Where an order is made, the police officer who applied for the order (or, if the chief officer of police of the force in question has designated another senior police officer for the purpose, that other officer) must immediately serve a copy of the order on the train operator (or each train operator) affected by the order (s. 157(4)).

OFFENCE: **Contravening Prohibition Order for Sale of Alcohol on Trains—** *Licensing Act 2003, s. 157(5)*

  • Triable summarily • Three months' imprisonment and/or a fine not exceeding £20,000

The Licensing Act 2003, s. 157 states:

(5) A person commits an offence if he knowingly—
  (a) sells or attempts to sell alcohol in contravention of an order under this section, or
  (b) allows the sale of alcohol in contravention of such an order.

KEYNOTE

The defendant must be shown to have acted *knowingly*, and proof that the order was properly made and in force so far as that date and location were concerned will be critical.

4.12.4.2 Designated Sporting Event

For the purposes of the Sporting Events (Control of Alcohol etc.) Act 1985, a 'designated' sporting event means an event or proposed event which has been designated or is part of a class designated by order made by the Secretary of State. It also includes events designated under comparable Scottish legislation. Events which are to be held outside Great Britain can also be designated (s. 9).

4.12.4.3 Alcohol, Containers etc. at Sports Grounds

OFFENCE: **Alcohol at Sports Grounds—***Sporting Events (Control of Alcohol etc.) Act 1985, s. 2*

  • Triable summarily • Three months' imprisonment and /or a fine (s. 2(1)) • Fine (s. 2(2))

The Sporting Events (Control of Alcohol etc.) Act 1985, s. 2 states:

(1) A person who has alcohol or an article to which this section applies in his possession—
  (a) at any time during the period of a designated sporting event when he is in any area of a designated sports ground from which the event may be directly viewed, or
  (b) while entering or trying to enter a designated sports ground at any time during the period of a designated sporting event at that ground, is guilty of an offence.
(2) A person who is drunk in a designated sports ground at any time during the period of a designated sporting event at that ground or is drunk while entering or trying to enter such a ground at any time during the period of a designated sporting event at that ground is guilty of an offence.

KEYNOTE

The articles to which s. 2 applies are:

- articles capable of causing injury to a person struck by them, being
- bottles, cans or other portable containers (including ones that are crushed or broken), which
- are for holding any drink, and
- are of a kind which are normally discarded or returned to/left to be recovered by the supplier when empty

and include parts of those articles. Any such article that is for holding any medicinal product (within the meaning of the Medicines Act 1968) is excluded from this definition (s. 2(3)).

A constable may, at any time during the period of a designated sporting event at any designated sports ground, enter any part of the ground for the purpose of enforcing the provisions of this Act, and search a person he/she has reasonable grounds to suspect is committing or has committed an offence under this Act, and may arrest such a person (s. 7(1) and (2)).

Where a person is convicted of an offence under either s. 2(1) or s. 2(2) the court must consider imposing a banning order.

4.12.4.4 Fireworks, Flares and Similar Objects at Sports Grounds and Events

OFFENCE: **Having Fireworks, Flares etc.—*Sporting Events (Control of Alcohol etc.) Act 1985, s. 2A***

- • Triable summarily • Three months' imprisonment and/or a fine

The Sporting Events (Control of Alcohol etc.) Act 1985, s. 2A states:

(1) A person is guilty of an offence if he has an article or substance to which this section applies in his possession—
  (a) at any time during the period of a designated sporting event when he is in any area of a designated sports ground from which the event may be directly viewed, or
  (b) while entering or trying to enter a designated sports ground at any time during the period of a designated sporting event at the ground.
(2) ...
(3) This section applies to any article or substance whose main purpose is the emission of a flare for purposes of illuminating or signalling (as opposed to igniting or heating) or the emission of smoke or a visible gas; and in particular it applies to distress flares, fog signals, and pellets and capsules intended to be used as fumigators or for testing pipes, but not to matches, cigarette lighters or heaters.
(4) This section also applies to any article which is a firework.

KEYNOTE

There is a defence under s. 2A(2) for the person to prove that he/she had possession of the article or substance with lawful authority. 'Possession' is quite a broad concept going beyond 'carrying'.

As with the offence under s. 2 (**see para. 4.12.4.3**), the powers of entry, search and arrest under s. 7 also apply to this offence.

4.12.4.5 Designated Sports Ground

Under s. 9 of the 1985 Act, a 'designated sports ground' means:

> (2) ...any place—
> (a) used (wholly or partly) for sporting events where accommodation is provided for spectators, and
> (b) for the time being designated, or of a class designated, by order made by the Secretary of State, and an order under this subsection may include provision for determining for the purposes of this Act the outer limit of any designated sports ground.

The period of a 'designated sporting event' is also covered by s. 9:

> (4) The period of a designated sporting event is the period beginning two hours before the start of the event or (if earlier) two hours before the time at which it is advertised to start and ending one hour after the end of the event, but—
> (a) where an event advertised to start at a particular time on a particular day is postponed to a later day, the period includes the period in the day on which it is advertised to take place beginning two hours before and ending one hour after that time, and
> (b) where an event advertised to start at a particular time on a particular day does not take place, the period is the period referred to in paragraph (a) above.

KEYNOTE

The Sports Grounds and Sporting Events (Designation) Order 2005 (SI 2005/3204) provides for the classes of sporting events for the purposes of the 1985 Act. These differ slightly from those contained in the Football Spectators Act 1989 and include:

- Association football matches in which one or both of the participating teams represents a club which is for the time being a member (whether a full or associate member) of the Football League, the Football Association Premier League, the Football Conference National Division, the Scottish Professional Football League, or Welsh Premier League, or represents a country or territory.
- Association football matches in competition for the Football Association Cup (other than in a preliminary or qualifying round).
- Association football matches at a sports ground outside England and Wales in which one or both of the participating teams represents a club which is for the time being a member (whether a full or associate member) of the Football League, the Football Association Premier League, the Football Conference National Division, the Scottish Professional Football League, or Welsh Premier League, or represents the Football Association or the Football Association of Wales.

4.12.5 Ticket Touts

OFFENCE: **Ticket Touts—*Criminal Justice and Public Order Act 1994, s. 166***
- Triable summarily • Fine

The Criminal Justice and Public Order Act 1994, s. 166 states:

> (1) It is an offence for an unauthorised person to—
> (a) sell a ticket for a designated football match, or
> (b) otherwise to dispose of such a ticket to another person.
> (2) For this purpose—
> (a) a person is 'unauthorised' unless he is authorised in writing to sell or otherwise dispose of tickets for the match by the organisers of the match;
> (aa) a reference to selling a ticket includes a reference to—
> (i) offering to sell a ticket;
> (ii) exposing a ticket for sale;
> (iii) making a ticket available for sale by another;
> (iv) advertising that a ticket is available for purchase; and
> (v) giving a ticket to a person who pays or agrees to pay for some other goods or services or offering to do so;

(b) a 'ticket' means anything which purports to be a ticket; and

(c) a 'designated football match' means a football match of a description, or a particular football match, for the time being designated for the purposes of this section by order made by the Secretary of State.

KEYNOTE

Section 166A, is designed to ensure that the offence in s. 166 is compatible with European Directive 2000/31/EC. It ensures that the provisions in s. 166 do not apply to internet service providers based outside the UK, but makes it an offence for an internet service provider established in the UK to sell or otherwise dispose of tickets for designated football matches regardless of where the sale etc., takes place.

For the purposes of s. 166(2)(c) a 'designated football match' is currently described in the Ticket Touting (Designation of Football Matches) Order 2007 (SI 2007/790). Article 2 of the Order designates association football matches in England and Wales in which one or both participating teams represent a club which is a member of the Football League, Football Association Premier League, Football Conference or League of Wales, or represents a country or territory. Article 2(3) designates association football matches outside England and Wales involving a national team of England or Wales, or a team representing a club which is a member of the Football League, Football Association Premier League, Football Conference or League of Wales, or matches in competitions or tournaments organised by or under the authority of FIFA (Fédération Internationale de Football Association) or UEFA (Union des Associations Européennes de Football), in which any of such English or Welsh domestic or national teams is eligible to participate or has participated.

4.13 Weapons

4.13.1 Introduction

In considering the different offences and restrictions, it is important to look at the *particular weapons* covered by each piece of legislation, together with the *particular activity* that Parliament has sought to control.

Although it is convenient to refer to the *possession* of offensive weapons, that word has a wide meaning which goes beyond the expressions used in most offences involving the carrying of weapons.

When considering this area, it is important to remember that the carrying of weapons is a very different thing from the use of weapons. This is why simply picking up a handy object and hitting someone with it will not usually amount to an offence under the relevant legislation dealing with carrying of weapons.

It is also useful to bear in mind the differences between offensive weapons and *weapons of offence*. The latter are specifically concerned with the entry onto premises as a trespasser and are slightly wider in their definition than offensive weapons.

4.13.2 Having Offensive Weapon in Public Place

OFFENCE: **Having Offensive Weapon in Public Place—*Prevention of Crime Act 1953, s. 1(1)***
* Triable either way • Four years' imprisonment and/or a fine on indictment
* Six months' imprisonment and/or a fine summarily

The Prevention of Crime Act 1953, s. 1 states:

(1) Any person who without lawful authority or reasonable excuse, the proof whereof shall lie on him, has with him in any public place any offensive weapon shall be guilty of an offence.

Lawful Authority

'Lawful authority' means those occasions where people from time to time are required to carry weapons as a matter of duty, such as police officers or members of the armed forces (*Bryan* v *Mott* (1976) 62 Cr App R 71). Security guards carrying truncheons, even if required to do so by their contracts of employment, are not covered (*R* v *Spanner* [1973] Crim LR 704). If someone does not fall into this—very limited—group, he/she may still have a 'reasonable excuse' for having the weapon with him/her.

Reasonable Excuse

'Reasonable excuse' may arise from a number of circumstances. People having tools with them in the course of their trade (e.g. craft knives for fitting carpets or hammers for carpentry) may have a 'reasonable excuse' (see *Ohlson* v *Hylton* [1975] 1 WLR 724). If a person passing the scene of a recent disturbance sees a weapon lying on the ground and he/she picks it up and puts it in his/her car intending to take it to the nearest police station, those circumstances would amount to a reasonable excuse for having the weapon with him/her.

The issues arising out of reasonable excuses under this offence overlap greatly with those of 'good reason' under the Criminal Justice Act 1988 offence below (**see para. 4.13.3.1**) and the two should be read together to make any sense of the many decisions. This area of criminal legislation has provided some of the most extensive litigation in recent years, to the point that most arguments open to even the most creative defendants have been tried. Nevertheless, magistrates retain a wide degree of discretion in what they accept as a 'reasonable excuse' and the cases below do *not* mean that this discretion is fettered and that the courts must follow this reasoning in every case—*DPP* v *Patterson* [2004] EWHC 2744 (Admin) (magistrates' court finding that a defendant in possession of a butterfly knife in a shopping centre because 'he needed it for feeding and stabling horses' and had meant to deposit it in a safe place that day but had not had the chance to do so, had a 'reasonable excuse'). Against that background, however, the following situations have been considered and pronounced upon by the courts:

- Not being aware that you have an offensive weapon with you is *not* a reasonable excuse in itself (*R* v *Densu* [1998] 1 Cr App R 400).
- Neither is forgetting that you have a weapon with you (*R* v *Lorimer* [2003] EWCA Crim 721) generally, or forgetting that there is one in the car you are driving (*R* v *McCalla* (1988) 87 Cr App R 372).
- However, where a taxi driver was found with a piece of wood and a cosh in the back of his cab where they had been left by passengers earlier in the week, the Court of Appeal held that his forgetting to remove the weapons might have been accepted as a reasonable excuse and the question should have been left for the jury (*R* v *Glidewell* (1999) 163 JP 557).
- Under the Criminal Justice Act offence below (**see para. 4.13.3.1**), however, there can be circumstances where forgetfulness could be relevant to the defence of 'good reason' (e.g. where it results from illness or medication)—*Bayliss* v *DPP* [2003] EWHC 245 (Admin).

It is not reasonable to have a weapon with you as *a general precaution* in case you are attacked (*Evans* v *Hughes* [1972] 1 WLR 1452). It may be reasonable to have a weapon if you have good grounds to anticipate an unprovoked or unlawful attack (e.g. for a person guarding cash transits—see *Malnik* v *DPP* [1989] Crim LR 451). However, in *N* v *DPP* [2011] EWHC 1807 (Admin), the defence of reasonable excuse was not made out where a person picked up a metal bar for protection having been threatened five minutes earlier by a group of young men in a car who were found to have no weapons. Even if the defendant did believe that he was at risk of an imminent attack, his belief was not a reasonable one in the circumstances.

Having a weapon for some other reason may amount to a reasonable excuse and whether or not it does so is a matter of fact for the court/jury to decide (see e.g. *Houghton* v *Chief Constable of Greater Manchester Police* (1987) 84 Cr App R 319 where the defendant was in 'fancy dress' costume as a police officer and had a truncheon with him as part of the costume—held to amount to 'reasonable excuse').

The defendant's state of mind when deciding whether the defence of 'good reason' was made out, for example, whether they had an angry and/or intoxicated and/or traumatised state of mind, is a matter that should be left to a jury (*R* v *Clancy* [2012] EWCA Crim 8).

The burden of proving the reasonable excuse or lawful authority rests with the defendant, but only when the prosecution have established that the defendant had an offensive weapon with him/her at the time. That burden of proof will be judged against the balance of probabilities.

Has With Him

This expression shows that the offence is designed to prevent the carrying of weapons; it is not an offence of *intention* and the reported decisions of the courts have consistently reflected that fact. The reasonable excuse must relate to the *carrying* of the weapon or article and not the *intention* of the person carrying it (*R* v *Jura* [1954] 1 QB 503).

This is most apparent where an 'innocent' article is used offensively. In *Ohlson* v *Hylton* [1975] 1 WLR 724 the defendant had a bag of tools with him in the course of his trade. He produced a hammer from the bag and used it to hit someone. The court held that, as he had formed the intention to use the hammer *after* it came into his possession, the offence was not made out. Although the court accepted that there might be times where a later intention to use an innocent article offensively would amount to an offence under the 1953 Act, the main purpose of the law was to prevent people from arming themselves with weapons. Similar decisions have been reached in relation to picking up a discarded knife during a fight (*Bates* v *Bulman* [1979] 1 WLR 1190), brandishing a jack taken from a car (*R* v *Dayle* [1974] 1 WLR 181) and using a penknife—which the defendant happened to be carrying—to stab someone who attacked him (*R* v *Humphreys* [1977] Crim LR 225).

It is possible for more than one person to have the same weapon 'with them', provided you can show that they knew of its existence in the hands of another at the time (*R* v *Edmonds* [1963] 2 QB 142).

You must show that the defendant knew that he/she had *something* with him/her and that the 'something' was, in fact, an offensive weapon (*R* v *Cugullere* [1961] 1 WLR 858).

Public Place

The Prevention of Crime Act 1953, s. 1 states:

(4) In this section 'public place' includes any highway and any other premises or place to which at the material time the public have or are permitted to have access, whether on payment or otherwise.

KEYNOTE

What is a public place is a question of fact, but whether it is capable of being a public place is a question of law (*R* v *Hanrahan* [2004] EWCA Crim 2943).

Offensive Weapon

The Prevention of Crime Act 1953, s.1(4) also states:

'offensive weapon' means any article made or adapted for use for causing injury to the person, or intended by the person having it with him for such use by him or by some other person.

KEYNOTE

Offensive weapons fall into three categories for the purposes of this offence, namely, articles:

- made for causing injury (offensive weapons *per se*);
- adapted for causing injury; and
- intended by the person who has them, for causing injury.

Offensive weapons *per se* are those which have been manufactured for use for causing injury and include truncheons, PR-24 batons and bayonets. A swordstick has been held to be such a weapon (*R* v *Butler* [1988] Crim LR 695) as have flick-knives (*R* v *Simpson* [1983] 1 WLR 1494) and butterfly knives (*DPP* v *Hynde* [1998] 1 WLR 1222). In *Hynde* the court took notice of the fact that butterfly knives were outlawed under the Criminal Justice Act 1988 deciding that such knives were clearly 'made' for causing injury. A flick-knife that also operates as a lighter remains an offensive weapon *per se* despite its alternative function (*R* v *Vasili* [2011] EWCA Crim 615). In *R* v *R* [2007] EWCA Crim 3312, the Court of Appeal held that a pair of combat gloves containing powdered lead/sand in the knuckle area were designed or adapted as an offensive weapon.

Once it has been shown that the article in question was in fact an offensive weapon, there is no need for the prosecution to show any intention to use it for causing injury (*Davis* v *Alexander* (1970) 54 Cr App R 398).

Weapons *adapted* for causing injury can include virtually anything. Whether something has in fact been so adapted is a question of fact for the court/jury to decide in each case. Bottles or glasses which have been broken in order to create a jagged edge have been held to be 'adapted' (*R* v *Simpson* [1983] 1 WLR 1494), so, too, has a potato with razor blades protruding from it (*R* v *Williamson* (1978) 67 Cr App R 35). If the article itself has not been altered in any physical way (such as by putting ammonia in a 'Jif' lemon to squirt in people's eyes—*R* v *Formosa* [1991] 2 QB 1), it has not been adapted.

It is still unclear whether the adaptation has to be to cause injury to *another* person or whether its capacity for self-inflicted injury (as in a suicide attempt) is enough. It is submitted that, as it is the *adaptation* of the article which is relevant, and not the *intention* of the person carrying it, the ultimate 'victim' is irrelevant (see *Bryan* v *Mott* (1976) 62 Cr App R 71).

Weapons *intended* to be used for causing injury can also include virtually anything. Here the intention of the person carrying it *is relevant* and you must prove an intention to cause injury. An intention to cause shock can be enough to satisfy this condition (see the memorably named *R* v *Rapier* (1980) 70 Cr App R 17 and also *R* v *Ali* [2012] EWCA Crim 934) but simply using the article to scare potential attackers away will not (see the less menacingly named *R* v *Snooks* [1997] Crim LR 230). To an extent this overlaps with the issues of 'reasonable excuse' and 'has with him' discussed above. In *C* v *DPP* [2001] EWHC Admin 1093 the court held that it was necessary to examine how closely the adoption of the relevant object and the intention to use it occurred, along with the circumstances in which the offence took place.

4.13.2.1 Threatening with Offensive Weapon in Public

The Legal Aid, Sentencing and Punishment of Offenders Act 2012, s. 142 created a new offence under the Prevention of Crime Act 1953.

OFFENCE: **Threatening with Offensive Weapon in Public—*Prevention of Crime Act 1953, s. 1A***
- Triable either way • Four years' imprisonment and/or a fine on indictment
- Six months' imprisonment and/or a fine summarily

The Prevention of Crime Act 1953, s. 1A states:

(1) A person is guilty of an offence if that person—
   (a) has an offensive weapon with him or her in a public place,
   (b) unlawfully and intentionally threatens another person with the weapon, and
   (c) does so in such a way that there is an immediate risk of serious physical harm to that other person.

KEYNOTE

This section creates an offence relating to the aggravated use of an offensive weapon in a public place.

The offence is committed where a person (A) has an offensive weapon with him/her and intentionally uses the weapon to threaten another (B) creating an immediate risk of serious physical harm to B. A's use of the weapon must be unlawful, allowing A to raise relevant defences to the use such as self-defence, defence of others or property, and the prevention of crime. If raised, the burden of rebutting those defences will rest on the prosecution.

In this section 'physical harm' is serious if it amounts to grievous bodily harm for the purposes of the Offences against the Person Act 1861 (s. 1A(2)). 'Public place' and 'offensive weapon' have the same meaning as in s. 1 of the 1953 Act (s. 1A(3)).

4.13.3 Having Bladed or Pointed Article in Public Place

OFFENCE: **Having Bladed or Sharply Pointed Article in Public Place—*Criminal Justice Act 1988, s. 139(1)***
- Triable either way • Four years' imprisonment and/or a fine on indictment
- Six months' imprisonment and/or a fine summarily

The Criminal Justice Act 1988, s. 139 states:

(1) Subject to subsections (4) and (5) below, any person who has an article to which this section applies with him in a public place shall be guilty of an offence.

KEYNOTE

This offence applies to any sharply pointed article or article having a blade. Folding pocket knives are excluded unless the cutting edge of the blade exceeds three inches (7.62 cm). If the knife is a lock-knife, it will be covered by this offence irrespective of whether the blade is actually locked open at the time (*Harris* v *DPP* [1993] 1 WLR 82).

Whether an article falls within the parameters of s. 139 is a question of law for the judge/magistrate(s) to determine (*R* v *Deegan* [1998] 2 Cr App R 121—a case that concerned the carrying of a folding pocket-knife that *was* locked open). In *R* v *Davis* [1998] Crim LR 564 the Court of Appeal reiterated that the question of whether an article was 'bladed' or not was a matter of law for the judge to decide. In that case the defendant had been carrying a screwdriver which, the prosecution contended, was a 'bladed' article capable of causing injury. The court decided that the test to be applied in such cases was not whether the 'bladed' article was capable of causing injury, but whether it had a cutting edge. Deciding whether or not an article was caught by the provisions of s. 139 was not a matter of interpreting the ordinary English word 'blade', but required the straightforward construction of the statute. This decision does not mean that a screwdriver can *never* fall within the type of article outlawed under s. 139 and if the screwdriver is pointed or it has been sharpened, it may still be caught by the above offence. There is no requirement for the item to be sharp as long as it has a blade. In *Brooker* v *DPP* [2005] EWHC 1132 (Admin) a blunt butter knife was held to fall within s. 139.

The fact that an article prohibited under s. 139 is part of something that has other innocuous features (e.g. a utility tool or 'Swiss army knife'), does not save it from falling under this offence if the other ingredients are present (see *R* v *Giles* [2003] EWCA Crim 1287).

'Has with him' is discussed at **para. 4.13.2**. The need to prove that the defendant was aware that he/she had the weapon with him/her for this offence was re-affirmed by the Court of Appeal in *R* v *Daubney* (2000) 164 JP 519.

'Public place' is similar to that under the Prevention of Crime Act 1953. The front garden of a house has been held *not* to be a public place for the purposes of this offence even where that garden is very narrow and the defendant would be able to inflict injuries on passers by from within it (*R* v *Roberts* [2003] EWCA Crim 2753). It must also be determined whether public access was implied or tolerated (*Harriot* v *DPP* [2005] EWHC 965 (Admin)).

4.13.3.1 Defences

The defendant may show that he/she had 'good reason' or 'lawful authority' for having the article in a public place (s. 139(4) and (5)). Lawful authority is discussed at **para. 4.13.2**; good reason is similar to reasonable excuse, also discussed at **para. 4.13.2**. This approach was confirmed by the Court of Appeal in *R* v *Emmanuel* [1998] Crim LR 347 where it accepted that 'good reason' could include self-defence. Similarly, in *R* v *McAuley* [2010] EWCA Crim 2130 it was held that it could amount to a 'good reason' if the appellant was carrying the knife for his own protection and he could show on the balance of probabilities that he was in fear of an imminent attack. Again it will be for the defendant to prove this authority or reason on the balance of probabilities and, again, forgetting that you have the article with you is not a general defence (see *DPP* v *Gregson* (1993) 96 Cr App R 240 and *R (On the Application of Hilton)* v *Canterbury Crown Court* [2009] EWHC 2867 (Admin)). The Court of Appeal, in a case where self-defence was used as the 'good reason', held that it would normally be wise for this type of defence to be considered by a jury (*R* v *McAuley* [2009] EWCA Crim 2130).

Under s. 139 of the Criminal Justice Act 1988 there is a 'strong public interest' in bladed articles not being carried in public without good reason. The Divisional Court so held, finding that the requirement on the defendant to prove a good reason for having the relevant article (a lock-knife) is not an infringement of human rights legislation—*Lynch* v *DPP*

[2001] EWHC Admin 882. The Court of Appeal went on to consider the relevant issues here in *R v Matthews* [2003] EWCA Crim 813. There it was held that the plain and ordinary meaning of s. 139(4) and (5) was that these provisions imposed a persuasive burden on the defendant, not merely an evidential burden. As such, the defence made an inroad into Article 6(2) but, because the defendant is the only person who knows why he/she had a bladed article in a public place, there is an objective justification for this burden being imposed on a defendant. Such a measure was proportionate and struck a fair balance between the general interest of the community and the individual's rights.

The courts and commentators have had lots of debates about forgetfulness in this context and the relevance of 'forgetting' you have a knife or other article with you. The issues were summarised by the Court of Appeal in *R v Jolie* [2003] EWCA Crim 1543. While it is clear that forgetfulness alone cannot be a 'good reason', from a policing perspective the main thing is to gather any evidence that the defendant had the article with him/her in a public place and to record any explanation given. Whether the defendant had a 'good reason' (which might include forgetfulness combined with other circumstances) is then a matter for the court. In *R v Chahal* [2010] EWHC 439 (Admin), quashing a conviction under this section, the court held that relevant consideration should have been given where the defendant, who undertook casual work at a relative's factory, forgot about a knife he was carrying.

A defendant may also show that he/she had the article:

- for use at work, e.g. joiners, chefs, gardeners etc.;
- for religious reasons, e.g. members of the Sikh religion having a *kirpan*;
- as part of any national costume—such as someone in Highland Dress with a *skean dhu*.

In *Mohammed v Chief Constable of South Yorkshire* [2002] EWHC 406 (Admin) the court held that the defendant did not have possession of a meat cleaver for use at his place of work; he had it for the purpose of rendering it possible to use it at work. He had taken the cleaver on a Saturday night intending, he claimed, to have it sharpened the following Monday. It was considered that there was no reason for him not to have taken the cleaver on the Monday, taking it directly to be sharpened. His appeal was dismissed. The fact that the work for which a person needed a knife was casual work was not a relevant consideration (*Chalal v DPP* [2010] EWHC 439 (Admin)).

Strangely, whether or not an article is for the uses or reasons set out above appears to be a question of *fact* (see *R v Manning* [1998] Crim LR 198).

4.13.4 Having Article with Blade or Point (or Offensive Weapon) on School Premises

OFFENCE: **Having Bladed or Sharply Pointed Article on School Premises—*Criminal Justice Act 1988, s. 139A(1)***
- Triable either way • Four years' imprisonment and/or a fine on indictment
- Six months' imprisonment and/or a fine summarily

The Criminal Justice Act 1988, s. 139A states:

(1) Any person who has an article to which section 139 of this Act applies with him on school premises shall be guilty of an offence.

KEYNOTE

'School premises' means land used for the purposes of a school *excluding any land occupied solely as a dwelling by a person employed at the school*. This means that the provisions would not apply to someone found in the garden of a caretaker's house if that house was occupied solely as a dwelling by the school caretaker.

'School', under s. 4 of the Education Act 1996, means:

(1) ...an educational institution which is outside the further education sector and the higher education sector and is an institution for providing—
  (a) primary education;
  (b) secondary education, or
  (c) both primary and secondary education,
whether or not the institution also provides further education.

This offence applies to the same articles as those covered under s. 139(1), see para. 4.13.3.

OFFENCE: **Having Offensive Weapon on School Premises—***Criminal Justice Act 1988, s. 139A(2)*
  • Triable either way • Four years' imprisonment and/or a fine on indictment
  • Six months' imprisonment and/or a fine summarily

The Criminal Justice Act 1988, s. 139A states:

(2) Any person who has an offensive weapon within the meaning of section 1 of the Prevention of Crime Act 1953 with him on school premises shall be guilty of an offence.

KEYNOTE

For the purposes of this offence, 'offensive weapons' fall into the three categories discussed at para. 4.13.2.

4.13.4.1 Defences

The defences are the same as for s. 139(1) (**see para. 4.13.3.1**), although in relation to a s. 139A(1) offence, it is a defence for the person charged to prove that he/she had the article or weapon in question for educational purposes (see s. 139A(4)(b)).

4.13.4.2 Power of Entry

The Criminal Justice Act 1988, s. 139B states:

(1) A constable may enter school premises and search those premises and any person on those premises for—
  (a) any article to which section 139 of this Act applies, or
  (b) any offensive weapon within the meaning of section 1 of the Prevention of Crime Act 1953, if he has reasonable grounds for suspecting that an offence under section 139A of this Act is being, or has been, committed.
(2) If in the course of a search under this section a constable discovers an article or weapon which he has reasonable grounds for suspecting to be an article or weapon of a kind described in subsection (1) above, he may seize and retain it.
(3) The constable may use reasonable force, if necessary, in the exercise of the power of entry conferred by this section.

KEYNOTE

Note that the threshold for a constable to exercise his/her powers of entry and search is 'reasonable grounds for suspecting'.

4.13.4.3 Power of Members of Staff to Search Pupils for Prohibited Items

The Education Act 1996, s. 550ZA states:

(1) This section applies where a member of staff of a school in England—

(a) has reasonable grounds for suspecting that a pupil at the school may have a prohibited item with him or her or in his or her possessions; and

(b) falls within section 550ZB(1).

(2) The member of staff may search the pupil ('P') or P's possessions for that item.

(3) For the purposes of this section and section 550ZC each of the following is a 'prohibited item'—

(a) an article to which section 139 of the Criminal Justice Act 1988 applies (knives and blades etc);

(b) an offensive weapon, within the meaning of the Prevention of Crime Act 1953;

...

(5) In this section and section 550ZB—

'member of staff', in relation to a school, means—

(a) any teacher who works at the school; and

(b) any other person who, with the authority of the head teacher, has lawful control or charge of pupils for whom education is being provided at the school;

'possessions', in relation to P, includes any goods over which P has or appears to have control.

KEYNOTE

A person may carry out a search under s. 550ZA only if that person is the head teacher of the school, or has been authorised by the head teacher to carry out the search (s. 550ZB(1)). The search may be carried out only where the member of staff and the pupil are on the premises of the school, or they are elsewhere and the member of staff has lawful control or charge of the pupil (s. 550ZB(4)), and a person may use such force as is reasonable in the circumstances (s. 550ZB(5)).

The person carrying out a search may not require the pupil to remove any clothing other than outer clothing, must be of the same sex, and may carry out the search only in the presence of another member of staff who should be of the same sex if it is reasonably practicable (s. 550ZB(6)). The pupil's possessions may not be searched except in the presence of the pupil and another member of staff (s. 550ZB(7)).

The person carrying out a search may seize anything which that person has reasonable grounds for suspecting is a prohibited item, and any other thing which that person has reasonable grounds for suspecting is evidence in relation to an offence. Such force as is reasonable in the circumstances may be used for exercising this power (s. 550ZC(1) and (2)).

Note that the powers in relation to prohibited items only apply in England. In Wales the power of members of staff to search pupils is restricted to knives, blades, etc. and other offensive weapons (s. 550AA).

Where a person seizes an article to which s. 139 of the Criminal Justice Act 1988 applies (knives and blades etc.), an offensive weapon, or anything which that person has reasonable grounds for suspecting is evidence in relation to an offence, he/she must deliver it to a police constable as soon as reasonably practicable (s. 550ZC(8)).

The Further and Higher Education Act 1992 provides the power for members of staff of an institution within the further education sector in England to search students for prohibited items (s. 85AA). In Wales the 1992 Act restricts the power of members of staff in the further education sector to search students for knives, blades, etc. and offensive weapons (s. 85B). Members of staff at an attendance centre also have the power to search persons for knives, blades, etc. and offensive weapons (Violent Crime Reduction Act 2006, s. 47). In relation to all these powers a person who seizes anything as a result of the search must deliver it to a police constable as soon as reasonably practicable.

4.13.4.4 Threatening with Article with Blade or Point or Offensive Weapon in Public or on School Premises

The Legal Aid, Sentencing and Punishment of Offenders Act 2012, s. 142 created a new offence under the Criminal Justice Act 1988.

OFFENCE: **Threatening with Article with Blade or Point or Offensive Weapon—** *Criminal Justice Act 1988, s. 139AA*

- Triable either way • Four years' imprisonment and/or a fine on indictment
- Six months' imprisonment and/or a fine summarily

The Criminal Justice Act 1988, s. 139AA states:

(1) A person is guilty of an offence if that person—
  (a) has an article to which this section applies with him or her in a public place or on school premises,
  (b) unlawfully and intentionally threatens another person with the article, and
  (c) does so in such a way that there is an immediate risk of serious physical harm to that other person.

KEYNOTE

This new offence is similar to that created in s. 1A of the Prevention of Crime Act 1953 but extends the threats to those made on school premises and includes articles with a blade or point (both on school premises and in a public place).

'Public place' has the same meaning as in s. 139, 'school premises' has the same meaning as in s. 139A (s. 139AA(2) and (3)), and 'physical harm' is serious if it amounts to grievous bodily harm for the purposes of the Offences against the Person Act 1861 (s. 139AA(4)).

4.13.5 Trespassing with Weapon of Offence

There is another offence relating to weapons, namely that under the Criminal Law Act 1977, which is concerned with preventing people *trespassing* with weapons in much the same way as aggravated burglary.

OFFENCE: **Trespassing with Weapon of Offence—*Criminal Law Act 1977, s. 8(1)***
  • Triable summarily • Three months' imprisonment and/or a fine

The Criminal Law Act 1977, s. 8 states:

(1) A person who is on any premises as a trespasser, after having entered as such, is guilty of an offence if, without lawful authority or reasonable excuse, he has with him on the premises any weapon of offence.

KEYNOTE

The definition of 'weapon of offence' is the same as that for aggravated burglary, namely, any article made or adapted for use for causing injury to or incapacitating a person, or intended by the person having it with him/ her for that use (s. 8(2)).

This offence is restricted to a person who has entered the relevant premises as a trespasser. It does not therefore extend to a person who, having entered lawfully, then becomes a trespasser for whatever reason (e.g. because the occupier has told him/her to leave).

'Premises' for this purpose means:

• any building or
• any part of a building under separate occupation
• any land adjacent to and used/intended for use in connection with a building
• the site comprising any building(s) together with ancillary land
• any fixed structure
• any movable structure, vehicle or vessel designed or adapted for residential purposes. (s. 12 of the 1977 Act)

4.13.6 Manufacture and Sale of Weapons

In addition to the controls on the carrying of weapons, there are also restrictions on the sale, manufacture, hire and buying of some weapons. The legislation is aimed at restricting the supply of such weapons and their availability in England and Wales.

Some of the offences relate to *possession* for the purpose of sale, hire etc.; this is a much wider term than that used in the carrying offences ('has with him').

OFFENCE: **Manufacture, Sale or Hire of Weapons—*Restriction of Offensive Weapons Act 1959, s. 1(1)***

  • Triable summarily • Six months' imprisonment and/or a fine

The Restriction of Offensive Weapons Act 1959, s. 1 states:

(1) Any person who manufactures, sells or hires or offers for sale or hire or exposes or has in his possession for the purpose of sale or hire, or lends or gives to any other person—
   (a) any knife which has a blade which opens automatically by hand pressure applied to a button, spring or other device in or attached to the handle of the knife, sometimes known as a 'flick knife' or 'flick gun'; or
   (b) any knife which has a blade which is released from the handle or sheath thereof by the force of gravity or the application of centrifugal force and which, when released, is locked in place by means of a button, spring, lever, or other device, sometimes known as a 'gravity knife', shall be guilty of an offence.

OFFENCE: **Manufacture, Sale and Hire of Offensive Weapons—*Criminal Justice Act 1988, s. 141(1)***

  • Triable summarily • Six months' imprisonment and/or a fine

The Criminal Justice Act 1988, s. 141 states:

(1) Any person who manufactures, sells or hires or offers for sale or hire, exposes or has in his possession for the purpose of sale or hire, or lends or gives to any other person, a weapon to which this section applies shall be guilty of an offence...

KEYNOTE

The importation of the weapons described in these offences is also prohibited (under s. 141(2) and (4), respectively).

4.13.6.1 Weapons Covered by s. 141

The weapons to which the 1988 Act applies are set out in the schedule to the Criminal Justice Act 1988 (Offensive Weapons) Order 1988 (SI 1988/2019) (see ***Blackstone's Criminal Practice 2014*, para. B12.182**). The weapons listed include knuckledusters, swordsticks, some telescopic truncheons, butterfly knives, samurai swords and a whole range of martial arts weapons.

KEYNOTE

The courts take notice of the fact that a weapon has been outlawed under this legislation in deciding whether or not it is 'made' for causing injury under the Prevention of Crime Act 1953.

There are a number of defences provided that include Crown servants and visiting forces (s. 141(5) to (7)), transactions made by or to museums and galleries (s. 141(8) to (11)), theatrical performances/rehearsals, and the production of films or television programmes (s. 141(11A) and (11B)). For the purpose of these defences the onus is on the defendant to provide sufficient evidence and the contrary is not proved beyond reasonable doubt (s. 141(11C)).

4.13.7 Knives

Although some knives will fall into the categories of offence covered above, there are further restrictions which apply to knives specifically:

4.13.7.1 Sale of Knives etc. to Persons under 18

OFFENCE: **Selling Knives and Articles to under 18 s—*Criminal Justice Act 1988, s. 141A***

> • Triable summarily • Six months' imprisonment and/or a fine

The Criminal Justice Act 1988, s. 141A states:

(1) Any person who sells to a person under the age of eighteen years an article to which this section applies shall be guilty of an offence...

(2) Subject to subsection (3) below, this section applies to—

    (a) any knife, knife blade or razor blade,

    (b) any axe, and

    (c) any other article which has a blade or which is sharply pointed and which is made or adapted for use for causing injury to the person.

(3) This section does not apply to any article described in—

    (a) section 1 of the Restriction of Offensive Weapons Act 1959,

    (b) an order made under section 141(2) of this Act, or

    (c) an order made by the Secretary of State under this section.

KEYNOTE

This offence does not apply to folding pocket knives with a cutting edge not exceeding three inches (7.62cm), neither does it apply to certain types of razor blade in a cartridge where not more than 2mm of blade is exposed (Criminal Justice Act 1988 (Offensive Weapons) (Exemption) Order 1996 (SI 1996/3064)).

Similar to the absurdity of a butter knife falling within the definition of an offence under s. 139 of the 1998 Act, in *R (On the Application of the Royal Borough of Windsor and Maidenhead)* v *East Berkshire Justices* [2010] EWHC 3020 (Admin) it was held that a grapefruit knife is not just a gadget but a knife within the meaning of s. 141A(2)(a).

4.13.7.2 Defence

The Criminal Justice Act 1988, s. 141A states:

(4) It shall be a defence for a person charged with an offence under subsection (1) above to prove that he took all reasonable precautions and exercised all due diligence to avoid the commission of the offence.

4.13.7.3 Unlawful Marketing of Knives

OFFENCE: **Unlawful Marketing of Knives—*Knives Act 1997, s. 1***

> • Triable either way • Two years' imprisonment and/or a fine on indictment
> • Six months' imprisonment and/or a fine summarily

The Knives Act 1997, s. 1 states:

(1) A person is guilty of an offence if he markets a knife in a way which—

    (a) indicates, or suggests, that it is suitable for combat; or

    (b) is otherwise likely to stimulate or encourage violent behaviour involving the use of the knife as a weapon.

KEYNOTE

'Knife' for this purpose means any instrument which has a blade *or* which is sharply pointed (s. 10 of the 1997 Act).

Marketing will include selling, hiring, offering or exposing for sale or hire and possessing it for those purposes (s. 1(4)).

'Indicates or suggests' is a very loose concept requiring no *mens rea* on the part of the defendant (however, see defences at para. **4.13.7.4**).

'Suitable for combat' means suitable for use as a weapon for inflicting injury to anyone *or causing them to fear injury*, and 'violent behaviour' means an unlawful act inflicting injury *or causing a person to fear injury* (s. 10). The elements in italics (author's emphasis) show that the legislation is intended to address the fear of the use of knives as well as their actual use.

The suggestion that knives are suitable for combat may be express or it may be implied by the name given to a product (e.g. 'commando') or by the packaging or advertisement relating to it (s. 1(3)). Therefore such packaging or advertising material, together with any surrounding advertisements, can be produced in evidence.

4.13.7.4 Defences

The Knives Act 1997, ss. 3 and 4 state:

3.—(1) It is a defence for a person charged with an offence under section 1 to prove that—
    (a) the knife was marketed—
        (i) for use by the armed forces of any country;
        (ii) as an antique or curio; or
        (iii) as falling within such other category (if any) as may be prescribed;
    (b) it was reasonable for the knife to be marketed in that way; and
    (c) there were no reasonable grounds for suspecting that a person into whose possession the knife might come in consequence of the way in which it was marketed would use it for an unlawful purpose.

    ...

4.—(1) It is a defence for a person charged with an offence under section 1 to prove that he did not know or suspect, and had no reasonable grounds for suspecting, that the way in which the knife was marketed—
    (a) amounted to an indication or suggestion that the knife was suitable for combat; or
    (b) was likely to stimulate or encourage violent behaviour involving the use of the knife as a weapon...

KEYNOTE

The defences at s. 3 require the person to show that the knife was marketed/the material published:

- for one of the uses at s. 3(1)(a)(i) to (iii) and s. 3(2)(a)(i) to (iii) *and*
- that it was reasonable to market it in that way *and*
- that there were no reasonable grounds for suspecting that a person would use the knife for an unlawful purpose.

The defences at s. 4 require the person to show that he/she:

- did not know or suspect, or
- *have any reasonable grounds to suspect*
- that the marketing/the marketing material amounted to an indication or even a *suggestion* that the knife was suitable for combat *or*
- was likely to stimulate or encourage violent behaviour involving the use of the knife as a weapon.

There is also the general defence under s. 4(3) for the person to show that he/she took *all* reasonable precautions and exercised *all* due diligence to avoid committing the offence.

Section 5 allows a court to issue a warrant for the entry onto premises and for the search, seizure and removal of knives (or materials where an offence under s. 2 is involved). Any knives or publications which have been seized and removed by a constable under a warrant issued under this section may be retained until the conclusion of proceedings against the suspect (s. 5(4)).

4.13.7.5 Publications Relating to Knives

OFFENCE: **Publications Relating to Knives—*Knives Act 1997, s. 2(1)***
- Triable either way • Two years' imprisonment and/or a fine on indictment
- Six months' imprisonment and/or a fine summarily

The Knives Act 1997, s. 2 states:

(1) A person is guilty of an offence if he publishes any written, pictorial or other material in connection with the marketing of any knife and that material—
    (a) indicates, or suggests, that the knife is suitable for combat; or
    (b) is otherwise likely to stimulate or encourage violent behaviour involving the use of the knife as a weapon.

The Knives Act 1997, s. 3 states:

(2) It is a defence for a person charged with an offence under section 2 to prove that—
    (a) the material was published in connection with marketing a knife—
        (i) for use by the armed forces of any country;
        (ii) as an antique or curio; or
        (iii) as falling within such other category (if any) as may be prescribed;
    (b) it was reasonable for the knife to be marketed in that way; and
    (c) there were no reasonable grounds for suspecting that a person into whose possession the knife might come in consequence of the publishing of the material would use it for an unlawful purpose.

The Knives Act 1997, s. 4 states:

(2) It is a defence for a person charged with an offence under section 2 to prove that he did not know or suspect, and had no reasonable grounds for suspecting, that the material—
    (a) amounted to an indication or suggestion that the knife was suitable for combat; or
    (b) was likely to stimulate or encourage violent behaviour involving the use of the knife as a weapon.

KEYNOTE

This offence is aimed at the publishers of advertisements rather than those who are involved in the sale and marketing of knives. The defences are shown above.

A search warrant may be issued under s. 5 for relevant publications.

4.13.8 Crossbows

Even though they might fit into some of the other offences discussed above, crossbows are also subject to specific legislation.

The Crossbows Act 1987 provides three summary offences:

- Selling or letting on hire a crossbow or part of a crossbow to a person under the age of 18 (s. 1);
- A person under the age of eighteen buying or hiring a crossbow or a part of a crossbow (s. 2);
- A person under the age of eighteen having with him a crossbow capable of discharging a missile (s. 3).

KEYNOTE

The 1987 Act provides that where a constable has reasonable cause to suspect that a person is committing or has committed an offence under section 3, they may search that person or any vehicle for a crossbow or part of a crossbow (s. 4(1)) and detain them for the purpose of the search (s. 4(2)).

For the purpose of exercising their powers a constable may enter any land other than a dwelling (s. 4(4)).

PART THREE

General Police Duties

4.14 Civil Disputes

4.14.1 Introduction

This chapter deals with domestic violence and abuse, and trade disputes, areas that have been generally considered to be non-core police functions. However, it is now accepted that domestic violence and abuse requires the expertise and associated resources to deal with criminal acts involving the abuse by one partner against another in an intimate relationship such as marriage, civil partnership, cohabitation, dating or within the family.

4.14.2 Domestic Violence and Abuse

The shared ACPO, CPS and government definition of domestic violence as contained in Home Office Circular 003/2013 is:

Any incident or pattern of incidents of controlling, coercive or threatening behaviour, violence or abuse between those aged 16 or over who are or have been intimate partners or family members regardless of gender or sexuality. This can encompass, but is not limited to, the following types of abuse: psychological, physical, sexual, financial or emotional. Controlling behaviour is: a range of acts designed to make a person subordinate and/or dependent by isolating them from sources of support, exploiting their resources and capacities for personal gain, depriving them of the means needed for independence, resistance and escape and regulating their everyday behaviour.

Coercive behaviour is: an act or a pattern of acts of assault, threats, humiliation and intimidation or other abuse that is used to harm, punish, or frighten their victim.

KEYNOTE

This definition, which is not a legal definition, now includes coercive behaviour and lowers the age recognition for domestic abuse incidents to include those aged 16 and 17. It also includes so called 'honour' based violence, female genital mutilation and forced marriage, and is clear that victims are not confined to one gender or ethnic group.

ACPO Guidance on Investigating Domestic Abuse (2008) provides the police service with clear information about the policing of domestic abuse. It provides operational, tactical and strategic advice.

4.14.2.1 Domestic Violence Protection Notices and Orders

A Domestic Violence Protection Notice (DVPN) is the initial notice issued by the police to provide emergency protection to an individual believed to be the victim of domestic violence.

The power to issue a domestic violence protection notice is provided by s. 24 of the Crime and Security Act 2010, which states:

(1) A member of a police force not below the rank of superintendent ('the authorising officer') may issue a domestic violence protection notice ('a DVPN') under this section.
(2) A DVPN may be issued to a person ('P') aged 18 years or over if the authorising officer has reasonable grounds for believing that—
    (a) P has been violent towards, or has threatened violence towards, an associated person, and
    (b) the issue of the DVPN is necessary to protect that person from violence or a threat of violence by P.

(3) Before issuing a DVPN, the authorising officer must, in particular, consider—

    (a) the welfare of any person under the age of 18 whose interests the officer considers relevant to the issuing of the DVPN (whether or not that person is an associated person),

    (b) the opinion of the person for whose protection the DVPN would be issued as to the issuing of the DVPN,

    (c) any representations made by P as to the issuing of the DVPN, and

    (d) in the case of provision included by virtue of subsection (8), the opinion of any other associated person who lives in the premises to which the provision would relate.

(4) The authorising officer must take reasonable steps to discover the opinions mentioned in subsection (3).

(5) But the authorising officer may issue a DVPN in circumstances where the person for whose protection it is issued does not consent to the issuing of the DVPN.

KEYNOTE

The purpose of a DVPN is to secure the immediate protection of a victim of domestic violence (V) from future violence or a threat of violence from a suspected perpetrator (P). A DVPN prohibits P from molesting V and, where they cohabit, may require P to leave those premises.

Where a DVPN has been issued, a constable must apply to a magistrates' court for a Domestic Violence Protection Order (DVPO). The application must be heard by the magistrates' court not later than 48 hours after the DVPN was served (s. 27). The DVPO is an order lasting between 14 and 28 days, which prohibits P from molesting V and may also make provision about access to shared accommodation (s. 28).

A person who breaches a DVPN may be arrested without warrant (s. 25(1)(b)) and must be held in custody to appear before a magistrates' court within 24 hours when an application for a DVPO can be heard (s. 26).

The Home Office has published a Domestic Violence Chapter to add to the Guide on Firearms Licensing Law (July 2013) that is available on the gov.uk website. It outlines that general evidence of domestic violence and abuse will indicate that an individual should not be permitted to possess a firearm or shotgun, and all cases must be assessed by the police on their own merits. It also says that every incident of domestic violence should prompt a police review of whether a certificate holder should be allowed to hold a firearm without posing a danger to the public.

4.14.2.2 Domestic Violence Disclosure Scheme

The Domestic Violence Disclosure Scheme, also known as Clare's Law, gained momentum following the tragic case of Clare Wood, who was murdered by her former partner in 2009. Her partner had three previous convictions under the Protection from Harassment Act 1997.

The principal aim of the Scheme is to introduce recognised and consistent procedures for disclosing information which will enable a partner (A) of a previously violent individual (B) to make informed choices about whether and how A takes forward that relationship with B.

There are two distinct entry routes that may lead to a disclosure being made. The first entry route—'right to ask'—is modelled closely on the existing Child Sex Offender Disclosure Scheme, and is triggered when a person makes a *direct application* to the police for information about B. The second entry route—'right to know'—is triggered when the police receive *indirect* information or intelligence about the safety of A and where, after appropriate checks are made, the police judge that a disclosure should be made to safeguard A.

Every request made under the scheme is thoroughly checked by a panel made up of the police, probation services and other agencies such as social services who decide whether any disclosure is lawful, necessary and proportionate.

The Home Office has developed guidance, available on its website (www.homeoffice.gov.uk). This guidance was produced for the pilots of the scheme and may be further updated.

4.14.2.3 Court Orders

Any court having jurisdiction over family law matters can make an order under the Family Law Act 1996. This Act consolidated many aspects of the law regulating family proceedings. Part IV of the Act makes provisions relating to family homes and domestic violence.

4.14.2.4 Non-molestation Orders

Section 42 of the 1996 Act provides for 'non-molestation' orders. Section 42 states:

(1) In this Part a 'non-molestation order' means an order containing either or both of the following provisions—

    (a) provision prohibiting a person ('the respondent') from molesting another person who is associated with the respondent;

    (b) provision prohibiting the respondent from molesting a relevant child.

(2) The court may make a non-molestation order—

    (a) if an application for the order has been made (whether in other family proceedings or without any other family proceedings being instituted) by a person who is associated with the respondent; or

    (b) if in any family proceedings to which the respondent is a party the court considers that the order should be made for the benefit of any other party to the proceedings or any relevant child even though no such application has been made.

KEYNOTE

Non-molestation orders can be applied for even though no other proceedings have been begun and such orders do not relate just to spouses or former partners; they apply to anyone who is 'associated' with the respondent.

Under s. 62, a person is 'associated' with another person if:

(3) ...

    (a) they are or have been married to each other;

    (aa) they are or have been civil partners of each other;

    (b) they are cohabitants or former cohabitants;

    (c) they live or have lived in the same household, otherwise than merely by reason of one of them being the other's employee, tenant, lodger or boarder;

    (d) they are relatives;

    (e) they have agreed to marry one another (whether or not that agreement has been terminated);

    (ea) they have or have had an intimate personal relationship with each other which is or was of significant duration;

    (eza) they have entered a civil partnership agreement (as defined by section 73 of the Civil Partnership Act 2004) (whether or not that agreement has been terminated);

    (f) in relation to any child, they are both persons falling within subsection (4); or

    (g) they are parties to the same family proceedings (other than proceedings under this Part).

(4) A person falls within this subsection in relation to a child if—

    (a) he is a parent of the child; or

    (b) he has or has had parental responsibility for the child.

In deciding whether or not to make such an order, the court must consider all the circumstances, including the need to secure the health, safety and well-being of the applicant or any relevant child (s. 42(5)).

4.14.2.5 Breach of a Non-molestation Order

OFFENCE: **Breach of a Non-molestation Order—*Family Law Act 1996, s. 42A***

    • Triable either way • Five years' imprisonment and/or a fine on indictment

    • 12 months' imprisonment and/or a fine summarily

The Family Law Act 1996, s. 42A states:

(1) A person who without reasonable excuse does anything that he is prohibited from doing by a non-molestation order is guilty of an offence.

(2) In the case of a non-molestation order made by virtue of s. 45(1), a person can be guilty of an offence under this section only in respect of conduct engaged in at a time when he was aware of the existence of the order.

KEYNOTE

This section, introduced by the Domestic Violence, Crime and Victims Act 2004, made the breach of a non-molestation order a criminal offence. Note that there is a power of arrest for the breach of a non-molestation order under the provisions of s. 24(1) of the Police and Criminal Evidence Act 1984.

In relation to s. 42A(2), non-molestation orders made by virtue of s. 45(1) are *ex parte* orders where the respondent has not been present at the proceedings when the order was made.

The Domestic Violence, Crime and Victims Act 2004, s. 12, amended s. 5 of the Protection from Harassment Act 1997 in relation to restraining orders (**see para. 4.8.4.11**). These orders may be made on conviction for any offence, rather than only on conviction for offences under the 1997 Act. Consequently, these orders are available to be used in cases involving domestic violence.

4.14.3 Trade Disputes

Most of the conditions regulating trade disputes can be found in the Trade Union and Labour Relations (Consolidation) Act 1992.

The areas which have historically created the greatest need for police involvement arise from the differences between those who wish to exercise their right to strike and those who wish to continue to work.

4.14.3.1 Picketing

The Trade Union and Labour Relations (Consolidation) Act 1992, s. 220 states:

(1) It is lawful for a person in contemplation or furtherance of a trade dispute to attend—
   (a) at or near his own place of work, or
   (b) if he is an official of a trade union, at or near the place of work of a member of the union whom he is accompanying and whom he represents, for the purpose only of peacefully obtaining or communicating information, or peacefully persuading any person to work or abstain from working.
(2) If a person works or normally works—
   (a) otherwise than at any one place, or
   (b) at a place the location of which is such that attendance there for a purpose mentioned in subsection (1) is impracticable, his place of work for the purposes of that subsection shall be any premises of his employer from which he works or from which his work is administered.
(3) In the case of a worker not in employment where—
   (a) his last employment was terminated in connection with a trade dispute, or
   (b) the termination of his employment was one of the circumstances giving rise to a trade dispute, in relation to that dispute his former place of work shall be treated for the purposes of subsection (1) as being his place of work.
(4) A person who is an official of a trade union by virtue only of having been elected or appointed to be a representative of some of the members of the union shall be regarded for the purposes of subsection (1) as representing only those members; but otherwise an official of a union shall be regarded for those purposes as representing all its members.

KEYNOTE

Section 220 effectively restricts lawful picketing to 'primary' picketing outside the person's own place of work.

If there is a real danger of any offence (such as a public order offence), being committed, then pickets have no right to attend the place in question under s. 220 (*Piddington v Bates* [1961] 1 WLR 162).

The power for police officers to give directions to people in the vicinity of someone's dwelling (under s. 42 of the Criminal Justice and Police Act 2001) does not apply to any conduct made lawful by s. 220. Given the

---

restrictions on just what conduct s. 220 allows, there may be occasions where the Criminal Justice and Police Act power could be used in connection with a trade dispute.

Although s. 220 does not place any restriction on the numbers of pickets, if they gather in large enough numbers, there may be a presumption that the pickets intend to intimidate others (*Broome* v *DPP* [1974] AC 587).

Section 220 does not authorise pickets to enter onto private land (*British Airports Authority* v *Ashton* [1983] 1 WLR 1079).

A person's place of work does not include new premises of an employer who has moved since dismissing the people picketing (*News Group Newspapers Ltd* v *SOGAT'82 (No. 2)* [1987] ICR 181).

For the Code of Practice on Picketing, see the Code of Practice (Picketing) Order 1992 (SI 1992/476 made under s. 3 of the Employment Act 1980).

Note that the police powers to disperse groups under s. 30 of the Anti-social Behaviour Act 2003 do not apply to people picketing lawfully under the above provisions.

4.14.3.2 Meaning of 'Trade Dispute'

The Trade Union and Labour Relations (Consolidation) Act 1992, s. 244 states:

(1) In this Part a 'trade dispute' means a dispute between workers and their employer which relates wholly or mainly to one or more of the following—
  (a) terms and conditions of employment, or the physical conditions in which any workers are required to work;
  (b) engagement or non-engagement, or termination or suspension of employment or the duties of employment, of one or more workers;
  (c) allocation of work or the duties of employment between workers or groups of workers;
  (d) matters of discipline;
  (e) a worker's membership or non-membership of a trade union;
  (f) facilities for officials of trade unions; and
  (g) machinery for negotiation or consultation, and other procedures, relating to any of the above matters, including the recognition by employers or employers' associations of the right of a trade union to represent workers in such negotiation or consultation or in the carrying out of such procedures.

KEYNOTE

'Employment' includes any relationship whereby one person personally does work or performs services for another. 'Worker', in relation to a dispute with an employer, means a worker employed by that employer, or a person who has ceased to be so employed if his/her employment was terminated in connection with the dispute, or if the termination of his/her employment was one of the circumstances giving rise to the dispute (s. 244(5)).

4.14.3.3 Use of Violence or Intimidation

OFFENCE: **Intimidation or Annoyance by Violence or Otherwise—*Trade Union and Labour Relations (Consolidation) Act 1992, s. 241***
  • Triable summarily • Six months' imprisonment and/or a fine

The Trade Union and Labour Relations (Consolidation) Act 1992, s. 241 states:

(1) A person commits an offence who, with a view to compelling another person to abstain from doing or to do any act which that person has a legal right to do or abstain from doing, wrongfully and without legal authority—
  (a) uses violence to or intimidates that person or his spouse or civil partner or children, or injures his property,
  (b) persistently follows that person about from place to place,
  (c) hides any tools, clothes or other property owned or used by that person, or deprives him of or hinders him in the use thereof,

(d) watches or besets the house or other place where that person resides, works, carries on business or happens to be, or the approach to any such house or place, or

(e) follows that person with two or more other persons in a disorderly manner in or through any street or road.

KEYNOTE

'With a view to compelling' means with intent to compel. This is therefore an offence of 'specific intent'.

'Wrongfully' means a civil wrong.

Although the breach of a contract is generally not a criminal offence, this section imposes a duty on some contracted personnel not to breach their contract under certain conditions.

For this offence you would have to show that the person acted wilfully and maliciously; you would also have to show knowledge or reasonable cause to believe that the listed consequences would apply. This would clearly create practical difficulties and this offence is likely to be very rarely used.

4.15 Offences Relating to Land and Premises

4.15.1 Introduction

The law regulating the relationship between landlord and occupier falls largely within the province of 'civil' law. There are, however, a number of occasions and circumstances where the interests of landowners and occupiers conflict. Under some such circumstances the threat to public order, property or proprietary rights is considered to need the protection of the criminal law.

4.15.2 Criminal Trespass

The law of trespass, as with that of landlord and tenant, is generally dealt with as civil law and, contrary to the many notices that appear on premises, trespass is not usually a matter for a criminal prosecution.

Whether it be civil or criminal, trespass involves an interference with someone's occupation of land or premises. This chapter is concerned with the main aspects of such interference.

In the wake of several well-publicised encounters between police officers and groups of people who either had trespassed, or intended to trespass, on someone else's land, Parliament created a number of criminal offences (in the Criminal Justice and Public Order Act 1994). It also created specific police powers to deal with such occasions.

These powers have been extended to include trespassing in or on buildings as well as on land in the open air.

The types of trespass addressed by the 1994 Act can be categorised into four main groups:

- trespassing with the intention of disrupting or obstructing a lawful activity, or intimidating those engaged in it;
- two or more people trespassing with the purpose of residing on the land;
- 20 or more people attending a 'rave';
- residing in vehicles on land.

The offence of squatting in residential premises was created by s. 144 of the Legal Aid, Sentencing and Punishment of Offenders Act 2012.

4.15.3 Aggravated Trespass

OFFENCE: **Trespass Intending to Obstruct, Disrupt or Intimidate—*Criminal Justice and Public Order Act 1994, s. 68***

- Triable summarily • Three months' imprisonment and/or a fine

The Criminal Justice and Public Order Act 1994, s. 68 states:

(1) A person commits the offence of aggravated trespass if he trespasses on land and, in relation to any lawful activity which persons are engaging in or are about to engage in on that or adjoining land, does there anything which is intended by him to have the effect—

(a) of intimidating those persons or any of them so as to deter them or any of them from engaging in that activity,

(b) of obstructing that activity, or

(c) of disrupting that activity.

(2) Activity on any occasion on the part of a person or persons on land is 'lawful' for the purposes of this section if he or they may engage in the activity on the land on that occasion without committing an offence or trespassing on the land.

KEYNOTE

Examples of the sort of conduct envisaged would be environmental activists disrupting a building programme or disrupting the planting of genetically modified crops (see *DPP* v *Bayer* [2003] EWHC 2567 (Admin)).

It must be shown that the defendant intended to bring about the effects set out at s. 68(1)(a) to (c). There is no need to specify which of the intended activities (i.e. deterring, obstructing or disrupting) in any charge and use of all three expressions is not bad for duplicity (*Nelder* v *DPP* (1988) *The Times*, 11 June). However, proof is required of both the trespassing on land *and* of some overt act, other than the trespassing, which was intended to have the effects set out at s. 68(1)(a) to (c) (see *DPP* v *Barnard* [2000] Crim LR 371 and *Pepper-sharp* v *DPP* [2012] EWHC 474 (Admin)).

In *Bauer* v *DPP* [2013] EWHC 634 (Admin) it was held that a large group of protesters, known as 'UK Uncut', protesting against tax avoidance, who occupied Fortnum and Mason's store in London for a period of nearly two and a half hours were guilty of aggravated trespass by virtue of their presence which had the intention to intimidate staff and customers within the store. It was also held that if the facts showed that people were part of the group which had committed the aggravated trespass then they were as guilty as the rest as a joint principal.

Under s. 68(5) land does not include land forming part of a highway unless it is:

- a footpath, bridleway or byway open to all traffic or road used as a public path (as defined by s. 54 of the Wildlife and Countryside Act 1981) or
- a cycle track under the Highways Act 1980 or the Cycle Tracks Act 1984.

Section 68 originally included the phrase 'in the open air' but this was removed by the Anti-social Behaviour Act 2003. In *DPP* v *Chivers* [2010] EWHC 1814 (Admin) it was held that the purpose and effect of this amendment was quite plainly to negative the exclusion of buildings.

Lawful activity is defined at s. 68(2) and is a very wide concept. Arguments as to the lawfulness of activities such as protesting or canvassing support for a given cause are strengthened with the advent of the Human Rights Act 1998 (as to which, **see chapter 4.4**). This point has been determined in the context of anti-war protestors where it was argued that the war against Iraq was illegal and therefore the activities carried out by staff at airbases were also unlawful. The House of Lords determined that for the purposes of s. 68(2), an act of aggression against another State or a general crime against peace did not constitute an offence contrary to the law of England and Wales (*R* v *Jones* [2006] UKHL 16)—(see also *Ayliffe* v *DPP* [2005] EWHC 684 (Admin); *Nero* v *DPP* [2012] EWHC 1238 (Admin); *Richardson* v *Director of Public Prosecutions* [2014] UKSC 8).

4.15.3.1 Aggravated Trespass: Power to Remove Persons

The Criminal Justice and Public Order Act 1994, s. 69 states:

(1) If the senior police officer present at the scene reasonably believes—

(a) that a person is committing, has committed or intends to commit the offence of aggravated trespass on land; or

(b) that two or more persons are trespassing on land and are present there with the common purpose of intimidating persons so as to deter them from engaging in a lawful activity or of obstructing or disrupting a lawful activity,

he may direct that person or (as the case may be) those persons (or any of them) to leave the land.

(2) A direction under subsection (1) above, if not communicated to the persons referred to in subsection (1) by the police officer giving the direction, may be communicated to them by any constable at the scene.

4.15.3.2 Failure to Leave Land or Re-entry to Land when Directed to Leave

OFFENCE: **Failure to Leave or Re-entry when Directed to Leave—*Criminal Justice and Public Order Act 1994, s. 69(3)***
  • Triable summarily • Three months' imprisonment and/or a fine

The Criminal Justice and Public Order Act 1994, s. 69 states:

(3) If a person knowing that a direction under subsection (1) above has been given which applies to him—
  (a) fails to leave the land as soon as practicable, or
  (b) having left again enters the land as a trespasser within the period of three months beginning with the day on which the direction was given,
  he commits an offence...

4.15.4 Trespassing for Purpose of Residence: Power to Remove Trespassers on Land

The Criminal Justice and Public Order Act 1994, s. 61 states:

(1) If the senior police officer present at the scene reasonably believes that two or more persons are trespassing on land and are present there with the common purpose of residing there for any period, that reasonable steps have been taken by or on behalf of the occupier to ask them to leave and—
  (a) that any of those persons has caused damage to the land or to property on the land or used threatening, abusive or insulting words or behaviour towards the occupier, a member of his family or an employee or agent of his, or
  (b) that those persons have between them six or more vehicles on the land,
  he may direct those persons, or any of them, to leave the land and to remove any vehicles or other property they have with them on the land.

(2) Where the persons in question are reasonably believed by the senior police officer to be persons who were not originally trespassers but have become trespassers on the land, the officer must reasonably believe that the other conditions specified in subsection (1) are satisfied after those persons became trespassers before he can exercise the power conferred by that subsection.

(3) A direction under subsection (1) above, if not communicated to the persons referred to in subsection (1) by the police officer giving the direction, may be communicated to them by any constable at the scene.

KEYNOTE

The key features of this section can be broken down into two parts. First, the senior officer present at the scene must have a reasonable belief that:

- at least two people *are trespassing* on land *and*
- that they are there with the common purpose of residing there *and*
- that reasonable (though not *all* reasonable) steps have been taken by/on behalf of the occupier to ask them to leave.

If this is the case, the senior officer must also have a reasonable belief that:

- *any* of those people have caused damage to the land or to property on the land *or*
- *any* of those people have used threatening, abusive or insulting words or behaviour towards the occupier or a member of the occupier's family or staff or one of his/her agents *or*
- those people have between them six or more vehicles on the land.

If all the conditions under the first heading, together with any of the conditions under the second are met, the officer may direct the people to leave the land and to take their vehicles and other property with them.

Most of the terms used in this section are defined under s. 61(9). 'Land' does not include buildings other than agricultural buildings or scheduled monuments. It also has the same restrictions in relation to highways as those set out under s. 68 (see para. 4.15.3).

The damaging of property includes the deposit of any substance capable of polluting the land and property for the purposes of damage has the same meaning as under the Criminal Damage Act 1971.

'Vehicles' do not have to be in a fit state for use on a road and can include a chassis or body (with or without wheels) appearing to have formed part of a vehicle. They also include caravans (as defined under the Caravan Sites and Control of Development Act 1960).

A person may be regarded as having a purpose of residing on land even though he/she has a home elsewhere.

Where the land concerned is 'common land', any references to trespassing will be construed as acts that are an infringement of the rights of the occupier or 'commoners' rights'. Where the public has access to that common land, references to the occupier will include the local authority (s. 61(7)).

If the people concerned were not originally trespassers (e.g. because they were given limited permission to be there), the senior officer present must have a reasonable belief that the relevant conditions above came about after the people became trespassers.

Again, the direction to leave the land may be communicated to the relevant parties by any police officer at the scene and there is no requirement for either officer to be in uniform.

The Home Office provides guidance on the use of s. 61 and advises that the police must be able to demonstrate that all eviction and enforcement decisions are 'proportionate' in weighing individual harm against the wider public interest. The guidance further states that the use of this section is not prohibited by the equality legislation, providing that the police are able to show that they have properly considered the race and equalities implications of their policies and actions in relation to unauthorised encampments and unauthorised development by gypsies and Irish travellers, and can demonstrate that their policies and actions are proportionate bearing in mind all the circumstances of the case.

Failure to Leave or Re-entry to Land after Police Direction to Leave

OFFENCE: **Failure to Leave or Re-entry to Land—*Criminal Justice and Public Order Act 1994, s. 61(4)***
  - • Triable summarily • Three months' imprisonment and/or a fine

The Criminal Justice and Public Order Act 1994, s. 61 states:

(4) If a person knowing that a direction under subsection (1) above has been given which applies to him—
  (a) fails to leave the land as soon as reasonably practicable, or
  (b) having left again enters the land as a trespasser within the period of three months beginning with the day on which the direction was given,
  he commits an offence...

KEYNOTE

The requirements as to proof of knowledge here are the same as those under s. 69 (**see para. 4.15.3.2**). This offence is the same as that under s. 69 with the exception of the word *reasonably* before practicable. This suggests that the law provides more latitude to people directed to leave the land under s. 61 than under s. 69, a suggestion that is also borne out by the wording of the respective defences.

It is a defence for the accused to show that he/she was not trespassing on the land, or had a reasonable excuse for failing to leave the land as soon as reasonably practicable or for re-entering the land as a trespasser (s. 61(6)).

A police officer may seize and remove a vehicle where he/she reasonably suspects a person, to whom a s. 61 direction applies, to be the owner or in possession or control of that vehicle. This power also applies where a person entered the land as a trespasser with a vehicle within the period of three months beginning with the day when the direction was given (s. 62).

4.15.5 Trespassing for Purpose of Residence with Vehicle(s) when Alternative Site Available: Power to Remove Trespassers and Vehicles on Land

Section 62A of the Criminal Justice and Public Order Act 1994 creates a power for a senior police officer to direct people to leave land and remove any vehicle or other property with them on that land.

Section 62A states:

(1) If the senior police officer present at a scene reasonably believes that the conditions in subsection (2) are satisfied in relation to a person and land, he may direct the person—
  (a) to leave the land;
  (b) to remove any vehicle and other property he has with him on the land.
(2) The conditions are—
  (a) that the person and one or more others ('the trespassers') are trespassing on the land;
  (b) that the trespassers have between them at least one vehicle on the land;
  (c) that the trespassers are present on the land with the common purpose of residing there for any period;
  (d) if it appears to the officer that the person has one or more caravans in his possession or under his control on the land, that there is a suitable pitch on a relevant caravan site for that caravan or each of those caravans;
  (e) that the occupier of the land or a person acting on his behalf has asked the police to remove the trespassers from the land.

4.15.5.1 Failure to Leave Land on Police Direction after Occupier's Request

OFFENCE: **Failure to Comply with Direction under Section 62A—*Criminal Justice and Public Order Act 1994, s. 62B***

- Triable summarily • Three months' imprisonment and/or a fine

The Criminal Justice and Public Order Act 1994, s. 62B states:

(1) A person commits an offence if he knows that a direction under section 62A(1) has been given which applies to him and—
    (a) he fails to leave the relevant land as soon as reasonably practicable, or
    (b) he enters any land in the area of the relevant local authority as a trespasser before the end of the relevant period with the intention of residing there.

4.15.6 Power to Remove Persons Attending or Preparing for a Rave

The Criminal Justice and Public Order Act 1994, s. 63 states:

(2) If, as respects any land, a police officer of at least the rank of superintendent reasonably believes that—

(a) two or more persons are making preparations for the holding there of a gathering to which this section applies,

(b) ten or more persons are waiting for such a gathering to begin there, or

(c) ten or more persons are attending such a gathering which is in progress,

he may give a direction that those persons and any other persons who come to prepare or wait for or to attend the gathering are to leave the land and remove any vehicles or other property which they have with them on the land.

(3) A direction under subsection (2) above, if not communicated to the persons referred to in subsection (2) by the police officer giving the direction, may be communicated to them by any constable at the scene.

(4) Persons shall be treated as having had a direction under subsection (2) above communicated to them if reasonable steps have been taken to bring it to their attention.

(5) ...

KEYNOTE

Whereas the powers to direct people to leave land above can be exercised by the senior police officer present at the scene, the power under s. 63 is restricted to an officer of at least superintendent rank.

Again, the officer must have a reasonable belief that one of the circumstances set out in s. 63(2) applies in respect of any land in the open air. Those circumstances are that:

- at least two people are making preparations for the holding of a relevant gathering; *or*
- at least 10 people are waiting for such a gathering to begin or are attending such a gathering which is in progress.

Where this is the case, the officer may direct those people, together with any others who come to prepare, wait for or attend the gathering, to leave the land and to take their property with them.

Given the practical constraints on communicating with people at an open air 'rave', s. 63 makes provision for the communication of a direction to leave. If reasonable steps have been taken to bring the direction to the attention of the people concerned, s. 63(4) provides that the relevant person will be taken to have received it. Therefore a person cannot later argue that he/she had not been able to hear or understand the direction when it was given.

In common with the other sections above, the direction to leave the land may be communicated to the relevant people by any police officer at the scene and there is no requirement for the officer to be in uniform.

4.15.6.1 Type of Gathering

The elements of the type of gathering to which s. 63 applies are as follows:

(1) This section applies to a gathering on land in the open air of 20 or more persons (whether or not trespassers) at which amplified music is played during the night (with or without intermissions) and as such, by reason of its loudness and duration and the time at which it is played, is likely to cause serious distress to the inhabitants of the locality; and for this purpose—

    (a) such a gathering continues during intermissions in the music and, where the gathering extends over several days, throughout the period during which amplified music is played at night (with or without intermissions); and

    (b) 'music' includes sounds wholly or predominantly characterised by the emission of a succession of repetitive beats.

(1A) This section also applies to a gathering if—

    (a) it is a gathering on land of 20 or more persons who are trespassing on the land; and

    (b) it would be a gathering of a kind mentioned in subsection (1) above if it took place on land in the open air.

4.15.6.2 Failure to Leave Land or Re-entry to Land

OFFENCE: **Failure to Leave Land or Re-entry to Land**—*Criminal Justice and Public Order Act 1994, s. 63*

- Triable summarily • Three months' imprisonment and/or a fine

The Criminal Justice and Public Order Act 1994, s. 63 states:

(6) If a person knowing that a direction has been given which applies to him—
  (a) fails to leave the land as soon as reasonably practicable, or
  (b) having left again enters the land within the period of 7 days beginning with the day on which the direction was given,
  he commits an offence...
  ...
(7A) A person commits an offence if—
  (a) he knows that a direction under subsection (2) above has been given which applies to him, and
  (b) he makes preparations for or attends a gathering to which this section applies within the period of 24 hours starting when the direction was given.

KEYNOTE

In each of the above cases you will need to show that the defendant knew that the direction applied to him/her. For the practicalities of communicating any direction see the Keynote in **para. 4.15.7**.

The offence under s. 63(6) deals with failing to leave/returning to the *land*, while that under s. 63(7A) deals with preparing to attend or attending a *gathering*, in each case where a direction has been properly given.

It is a defence for the accused to show that he/she had a reasonable excuse for failing to leave the land as soon as reasonably practicable or, as the case may be, for again entering the land (s. 63(7)).

4.15.6.3 Police Powers

The Criminal Justice and Public Order Act 1994, s. 64 states:

(1) If a police officer of at least the rank of superintendent reasonably believes that circumstances exist in relation to any land which would justify the giving of a direction under section 63 in relation to a gathering to which that section applies he may authorise any constable to enter the land for any of the purposes specified in subsection (2) below.
(2) Those purposes are—
  (a) to ascertain whether such circumstances exist; and
  (b) to exercise any power conferred on a constable by section 63 or subsection (4) below.
(3) A constable who is so authorised to enter land for any purpose may enter the land without a warrant.
(4) If a direction has been given under section 63 and a constable reasonably suspects that any person to whom the direction applies has, without reasonable excuse—
  (a) failed to remove any vehicle or sound equipment on the land which appears to the constable to belong to him or to be in his possession or under his control; or
  (b) entered the land as a trespasser with a vehicle or sound equipment within the period of 7 days beginning with the day on which the direction was given,
  the constable may seize and remove that vehicle or sound equipment.

KEYNOTE

Section 64(4) does not authorise the seizure of any vehicle or sound equipment of an exempt person. An exempt person includes the occupier of the land, and family member, employee or agent and anyone whose home is situated on the land (s. 63(10)).

'Sound equipment' means equipment designed or adapted for amplifying music and any equipment suitable for use in connection with such equipment. 'Music' has the same meaning as in s. 63, and 'vehicle' has the same meaning as in s. 61 (s. 64(6)).

4.15.6.4 Powers to Stop People from Proceeding to 'Raves'

The Criminal Justice and Public Order Act 1994, s. 65 states:

(1) If a constable in uniform reasonably believes that a person is on his way to a gathering to which section 63 applies in relation to which a direction under section 63(2) is in force, he may, subject to subsections (2) and (3) below—
  (a) stop that person, and
  (b) direct him not to proceed in the direction of the gathering.
(2) The power conferred by subsection (1) above may only be exercised at a place within 5 miles of the boundary of the site of the gathering.
(3) No direction may be given under subsection (1) above to an exempt person.

KEYNOTE

A person who knowingly fails to comply with a direction given to him/her commits a summary offence, and a constable in uniform who reasonably suspects that a person is committing an offence under this section may arrest that person without a warrant (s. 65(4)).

People who are 'exempt' has the same meaning as in s. 63.

Unlike the other directions discussed above this one must be given by a police officer in uniform.

This power does not appear to authorise the stopping of vehicles, and the general power under the Road Traffic Act 1988 would need to be used.

4.15.7 Power of Local Authority to Direct Unauthorised Campers to Leave Land

The Criminal Justice and Public Order Act 1994, s. 77 states:

(1) If it appears to a local authority that persons are for the time being residing in a vehicle or vehicles within that authority's area—
  (a) on any land forming part of a highway;
  (b) on any other unoccupied land; or
  (c) on any occupied land without the consent of the occupier,
  the authority may give a direction that those persons and any others with them are to leave the land and remove the vehicle or vehicles and any other property they have with them on the land.

KEYNOTE

A person commits an offence if, knowing that a direction has been given which applies to him/her, he/she fails, as soon as practicable, to leave the land or remove from the land any vehicle or other property which is the subject of the direction, or having removed any such vehicle or property again enters the land with a vehicle within the period of three months beginning with the day on which the direction was given (s. 77(3)).

It is a defence for the accused to show that his/her failure to leave or to remove the vehicle or other property as soon as practicable or his/her re-entry with a vehicle was due to illness, mechanical breakdown or other immediate emergency (s. 77(5)).

A local authority may apply to a magistrates' court for a removal order where people continue to reside in their vehicles on land in contravention of a s. 77 notice (s. 78(1)). A person who wilfully obstructs any person in the exercise of any power conferred on him/her by an order under this section commits a summary offence (s. 78(4)).

4.15.8 Other Offences Involving Premises

There are several specific offences and provisions relating to various types of premises that impact on day-to-day policing.

4.15.8.1 Depriving Residential Occupier

OFFENCE: **Depriving Residential Occupier—*Protection from Eviction Act 1977, s. 1***
- Triable either way • Two years' imprisonment and/or a fine on indictment
- Six months' imprisonment and/or a fine summarily

The Protection from Eviction Act 1977, s. 1 states:

(2) If any person unlawfully deprives the residential occupier of any premises of his occupation of the premises or any part thereof, or attempts to do so, he shall be guilty of an offence unless he proves that he believed, and had reasonable cause to believe, that the residential occupier had ceased to reside in the premises.

(3) If any person with intent to cause the residential occupier of any premises—
   (a) to give up the occupation of the premises or any part thereof; or
   (b) to refrain from exercising any right or pursuing any remedy in respect of the premises or part thereof;

   does acts likely to interfere with the peace or comfort of the residential occupier or members of his household, or persistently withdraws or withholds services reasonably required for the occupation of the premises as a residence, he shall be guilty of an offence.

(3A) Subject to subsection (3B) below, the landlord of a residential occupier or an agent of the landlord shall be guilty of an offence if—
   (a) he does acts likely to interfere with the peace or comfort of the residential occupier or members of his household, or
   (b) he persistently withdraws or withholds services reasonably required for the occupation of the premises in question as a residence,

   and (in either case) he knows, or has reasonable cause to believe, that that conduct is likely to cause the residential occupier to give up the occupation of the whole or part of the premises or to refrain from exercising any right or pursuing any remedy in respect of the whole or part of the premises.

KEYNOTE

The first two offences can be committed by 'any person', whereas the offence under s. 1(3A) can only be committed by a landlord or his/her agent.

Where these offences are committed by a 'body corporate' (e.g. a company), then the company's officers may be guilty as well as the company itself (s. 1(6)).

Thankfully—from a police perspective—the Court of Appeal has refused to find that a duty of care is owed by the police to an assured tenant to prevent that tenant's eviction without the necessary court order in breach of the Protection from Eviction Act 1977 (*Cowan* v *Chief Constable of Avon & Somerset* [2002] HLR 44).

The actions envisaged by s. 1(2) are those which amount to an eviction for any length of time (*R* v *Yuthiwattana* (1985) 80 Cr App R 55), while anything less (e.g. changing the locks of an entrance door while the residential occupier is out) would amount to an offence under s. 1(3) (*Costelloe* v *Camden London Borough Council* [1986] Crim LR 249).

In addition to the defence provided by s. 1(2), there is a specific defence to an offence under s. 1(3A), namely where a person proves that he/she had reasonable grounds for doing the acts or withdrawing or withholding the services in question (s. 1(3B)).

A caravan may amount to 'premises' for these offences (*Norton* v *Knowles* [1969] 1 QB 572).

'Residential occupier', in relation to any premises, means a person occupying the premises as a residence, whether under a contract or by virtue of any enactment or rule of law giving him/her the right to remain in occupation or restricting the right of any other person to recover possession of the premises (s. 1(1)).

4.15.8.2 Using or Threatening Violence to Secure Entry

OFFENCE: **Using or Threatening Violence to Secure Entry to Premises—*Criminal Law Act 1977, s. 6(1)***
- Triable summarily • Six months' imprisonment and/or a fine

The Criminal Law Act 1977, s. 6 states:

(1) Subject to the following provisions of this section, any person who, without lawful authority, uses or threatens violence for the purpose of securing entry into any premises for himself or for any other person is guilty of an offence, provided that—
  (a) there is someone present on those premises at the time who is opposed to the entry which the violence is intended to secure; and
  (b) the person using or threatening the violence knows that that is the case.

KEYNOTE

This offence is not restricted to occasions involving 'residential occupiers'.

It is immaterial whether the violence used/threatened is against a person or property, or whether the purpose of the entry is to gain possession of the premises or any other purpose (s. 6(4)).

The fact that a person has any right or interest in premises will not constitute 'lawful authority' to use violence to secure entry into those premises (s. 6(2)).

4.15.8.3 Defence to Using or Threatening Violence to Secure Entry

The Criminal Law Act 1977, s. 6 states:

(1A) Subsection (1) above does not apply to a person who is a displaced residential occupier or a protected intending occupier of the premises in question or who is acting on behalf of such an occupier; and if the accused adduces sufficient evidence that he was, or was acting on behalf of, such an occupier he shall be presumed to be, or to be acting on behalf of, such an occupier unless the contrary is proved by the prosecution.

(2) Subject to subsection (1A) above, the fact that a person has any interest in or right to possession or occupation of any premises shall not for the purposes of subsection (1) above constitute lawful authority for the use or threat of violence by him or anyone else for the purpose of securing his entry into those premises.

A 'displaced residential occupier' is defined at s. 12, which states:

(3) Subject to subsection (4) below, any person who was occupying any premises as a residence immediately before being excluded from occupation by anyone who entered those premises, or any access to those premises, as a trespasser is a displaced residential occupier of the premises for the purposes of this Part of this Act so long as he continues to be excluded from occupation of the premises by the original trespasser or by any subsequent trespasser.

(4) A person who was himself occupying the premises in question as a trespasser immediately before being excluded from occupation shall not by virtue of subsection (3) above be a displaced residential occupier of the premises for the purposes of this Part of this Act.

KEYNOTE

The definition of a 'protected intending occupier' (s. 12A) must be one of the longest definitions in criminal law (if not criminal history) and takes up an entire page of the Act! The gist of it is that it will include someone with a freehold or leasehold interest in the premises which has at least two years left to run; where the person needs the premises for his/her own occupation as a residence; where he/she is excluded from those premises by a trespasser and where he/she has documentation to prove his/her right to occupy the premises. (For a full discussion, **see Blackstone's Criminal Practice 2014, para. B13.29**.)

A co-owner of a property who has been excluded from it by another co-owner may be guilty of an offence under this section if he/she uses force to enter it while the resident co-owner is inside, and he/she cannot then claim to be a 'protected intending occupier' within the meaning of s. 12A (*Wakolo* v *DPP* [2012] EWHC 611 (Admin)).

4.15.8.4 Failing to Leave Premises

OFFENCE: **Failing to Leave Premises—*Criminal Law Act 1977, s. 7***
  • Triable summarily • Six months' imprisonment and/or a fine

The Criminal Law Act 1977, s. 7 states:

(1) Subject to the following provisions of this section and to section 12A(9) below, any person who is on any premises as a trespasser after having entered as such is guilty of an offence if he fails to leave those premises on being required to do so by or on behalf of—
  (a) a displaced residential occupier of the premises; or
  (b) an individual who is a protected intending occupier of the premises.

KEYNOTE

Sections 7 and 12A of the 1977 Act provide defences in relation to s. 7(1). It is a defence for the accused to prove that he/she believed that the person requiring him/her to leave the premises was not a person as described in s. 7(1)(a) or (b), or that the premises were used mainly for non-residential purposes and he/she was not on any part of the premises used wholly or mainly for residential purposes (s. 7(2) and (3)).

Section 12A provides that it is a defence for the accused to prove that the person making the requirement for the accused to leave did not produce a written statement specifying his/her interest in the premises (s. 12A(2)(d) or (4)(d)), or a certificate or licence from a protected intending occupier in relation to his/her right to tenancy or occupancy of the premises (s. 12A(6)(d)).

4.15.8.5 Squatting in a Residential Building

OFFENCE: **Squatting in a Residential Building—*Legal Aid, Sentencing and Punishment of Offenders Act 2012, s. 144***

  • Six months' imprisonment and/or a fine summarily

The Legal Aid, Sentencing and Punishment of Offenders Act 2012, s. 144 states:

(1) A person commits an offence if—
  (a) the person is in a residential building as a trespasser having entered it as a trespasser,
  (b) the person knows or ought to know that he or she is a trespasser, and
  (c) the person is living in the building or intends to live there for any period.
(2) The offence is not committed by a person holding over after the end of a lease or licence (even if the person leaves and re-enters the building).

KEYNOTE

'Building' includes any structure or part of a structure (including a temporary or moveable structure), and a building is 'residential' if it is designed or adapted, before the time of entry, for use as a place to live (s. 144(3)).

For the purposes of this section the fact that a person derives title from a trespasser, or has the permission of a trespasser, does not prevent the person from being a trespasser (s. 144(4)).

Section 17 of the Police and Criminal Evidence Act 1984 gives uniformed police officers the power to enter and search premises for the purpose of arresting a person for the offence of squatting in a residential building.

4.15.8.6 Found on Enclosed Premises

It is a summary offence under s. 4 of the Vagrancy Act 1824 for any person to be found in or upon any dwelling house, warehouse, coach house, stable or outhouse or in any inclosed yard, garden or area for *any unlawful purpose*. The unlawful purpose must be to commit some specific criminal offence as opposed to simply trespassing and a purely immoral purpose, and without more will not suffice (*Hayes* v *Stevenson* (1860) 3 LT 296). Note that in *L* v *CPS* [2007] EWHC 1843 (Admin), hiding from the police is not regarded as an unlawful purpose.

Where the defendant is found on the relevant premises, he/she can be arrested elsewhere (*R* v *Lumsden* [1951] 2 KB 513). Where a defendant was found in the garden of a house peering through the window at a woman inside intending to frighten her, his conduct was held to amount to an 'unlawful purpose' (*Smith* v *Chief Superintendent of Woking Police Station* (1983) 76 Cr App R 234). Had there not been any intention to frighten, the 'unlawful' purpose would probably not have been made out.

An area may still be 'inclosed' even though there are spaces left in between buildings, arches etc. for access (*Goodhew* v *Morton* [1962] 1 WLR 210). Railway sidings have been held not to amount to 'inclosed' premises and the essential feature of yards and similar enclosed areas for the purposes of this offence would appear to be that they are small pieces of land ancillary to a building (see *Quatromini* v *Peck* [1972] 1 WLR 1318). However, a room within an office building has been held not to amount to an inclosed area for the purposes of this offence (*Talbot* v *Oxford City Justices* [2000] 1 WLR 1102). It appears from the findings of the Divisional Court in *Talbot* that the expression 'inclosed' relates only to yards, gardens and areas in the open air. If the defendant is found in a *building* then that building must be a 'dwelling house, warehouse, coach house, stable or outhouse' before the offence under s. 4 can be applied. In *Akhurst* v *DPP* [2009] EWHC 806 (Admin), it was held that an 'inclosed area' had to be interpreted in a restrictive manner that took into account the wording of s. 4. In this instance the campuses of a university could not amount to an 'inclosed area'.

There is no need to show that the person intended to carry out the relevant criminal offence at the time or at that particular place. If the person is found in a building and either intends to commit certain offences there or had that intention when entering, the relevant offences of burglary may well apply.

4.15.8.7 Housing and Accommodation

In some cases the policing problems presented within a particular area will arise directly or indirectly from the area's housing. Among the legislation available to the relevant agencies in this regard is the Housing Act 1996, which is itself reinforced by the Housing Act 2004, providing local authorities with a range of significant powers where use of premises or the state of the property itself presents a nuisance or hazard to the physical or mental health of others.

Injunctions

Under s. 153A of the 1996 Act, as amended by the Police and Justice Act 2006, a court may, on the application of a relevant landlord, grant an anti-social behaviour injunction if:

> (3) …the person against whom the injunction is sought is engaging, has engaged or threatens to engage in housing-related conduct capable of causing a nuisance or annoyance to:
>   (a) a person with a right (of whatever description) to reside in or occupy housing accommodation owned or managed by a relevant landlord,
>   (b) a person with a right (of whatever description) to reside in or occupy other housing accommodation in the neighbourhood of housing accommodation mentioned in paragraph (a),
>   (c) a person engaged in lawful activity in, or in the neighbourhood of, housing accommodation mentioned in paragraph (a), or
>   (d) a person employed (whether or not by a relevant landlord) in connection with the exercise of a relevant landlord's housing management functions.
>
> It is immaterial where conduct to which this section applies occurs, and an anti-social behaviour injunction prohibits the person from engaging in any such conduct as described above.

KEYNOTE

This section allows social landlords (which may include local authorities) to obtain injunctions against a wide range of persons, not just residents, in order to protect other residents, visitors and their own staff. It also applies to situations where the conduct in question is capable of causing nuisance or annoyance (even if a complaint has not been received), but which directly or indirectly affects the landlord's management of its housing stock.

Other injunctions are also available to social landlords. This includes where a person engages in conduct that consists of, or involves using, or threatening to use, housing accommodation for an unlawful purpose (s. 153B). Where the court considers that the conduct relates to the use or threatened use of violence, or that there is a significant risk of harm to a person mentioned in s. 153A(3)(a) to (d) (above), it may include a provision prohibiting the person from entering or being in any premises or area specified in the injunction, and may also attach a power of arrest.

4.15.8.8 Nuisance on Educational Premises

There has been increasing concern over recent years that schools and their premises are particularly vulnerable to crime and the fear of crime.

In relation to nuisances on educational premises, the Education Act 1996 applies to premises that provide primary or secondary education (or both) and which are maintained by a local education authority or are grant-maintained.

OFFENCE: **Causing or Permitting Nuisance—*Education Act 1996, s. 547(1)***
> • Triable summarily • Fine

The Education Act 1996, s. 547 states:

(1) Any person who without lawful authority is present on premises to which this section applies and causes or permits nuisance or disturbance to the annoyance of persons who lawfully use those premises (whether or not any such persons are present at the time) [shall be guilty of an offence].

KEYNOTE

This offence is designed to deal with many types of nuisance, from using school playing fields inappropriately to interrupting lessons and lectures.

To be guilty of the above offence the defendant must be on the relevant premises without lawful authority and have caused (been directly responsible for bringing about) or permitted a nuisance or disturbance.

This provision applies to playing fields and other premises for outdoor recreation of the relevant institution including playgrounds (s. 547(2)).

Police powers

The Education Act 1996, s. 547(3) states:

(3) If—
   (a) a police constable or
   (b) ..., a person whom the appropriate authority has authorised to exercise the power conferred by this subsection,
has reasonable cause to suspect that any person is committing or has committed an offence under this section, he may remove him from the premises in question.

KEYNOTE

The nuisance or disturbance may have finished by the time the police officer gets to the premises but the wording of the subsection allows for the removal of the offender provided there is reasonable cause to suspect that he/she committed the offence.

4.15.9 Trespass on Protected Sites

The Serious Organised Crime and Police Act 2005 provides that various public access rights, as provided by the Countryside and Rights of Way Act 2000 in England and Wales, are not exercisable in relation to land forming part of a protected site.

OFFENCE: **Trespassing on Protected Sites—*Serious Organised Crime and Police Act 2005, s. 128(1)***

> • Triable summarily • six months' imprisonment and/or a fine

The Serious Organised Crime and Police Act 2005, s. 128 states:

(1) A person commits an offence if he enters, or is on, any protected site in England and Wales . . . as a trespasser.

(1A) In this section 'protected site' means—

    (a) a nuclear site; or

    (b) a designated site.

KEYNOTE

A nuclear site means so much of any premises in respect of which a nuclear site licence (within the meaning of the Nuclear Installations Act 1965) is for the time being in force as lies within the outer perimeter of the protection provided for those premises (s. 128(1B)). Nuclear sites were included within this section as a result of the Terrorism Act 2006 provisions.

A 'designated' site means a site specified or described in an order made by the Secretary of State (s. 128(2)), and a schedule of these sites is contained in the Serious Organised Crime and Police Act 2005 (Designated Sites) Order 2005 (SI 2005/3447), which designates 13 sites of military significance, and the Serious Organised Crime and Police Act 2005 (Designated Sites under Section 128) Order 2007 (SI 2007/930 as amended by SI 2012/1769, SI 2012/2709 and SI 2013/1562), which designates 18 sites associated with the government, security services and the Royal family. Such a 'site' means the whole or part of any building or buildings, or any land, or both (s. 128(8)(a)).

It is a defence for a person charged with an offence under this section to prove that he/she did not know, and had no reasonable cause to suspect, that the site in relation to which the offence is alleged to have been committed was a protected site (s. 128(4)).

For the purposes of this section a person who is on any protected site as a trespasser does not cease to be a trespasser by virtue of being allowed time to leave the site (s. 128(7)).

4.16 Licensing and Offences Relating to Alcohol

4.16.1 Introduction

The sale, supply and consumption of alcohol, along with the proper control and management of relevant premises, is a significant part of everyday policing.

This chapter only provides a brief overview of these matters and concentrates on the specific offences and police powers contained within the relevant legislation.

4.16.2 Licensable Activities

The Licensing Act 2003, s. 1 states:

(1) For the purposes of this Act the following are licensable activities—
    (a) the sale by retail of alcohol,
    (b) the supply of alcohol by or on behalf of a club to, or to the order of, a member of the club,
    (c) the provision of regulated entertainment, and
    (d) the provision of late night refreshment.

> **KEYNOTE**
>
> A licensable activity may be carried on under a premises licence or in circumstances where the activity is a permitted temporary activity (s. 2(1)).
>
> There is a raft of exemptions to licensable activities which include aircraft, vessels, hovercraft, ports, railway vehicles, premises occupied by the armed forces and premises exempt for national security purposes (ss. 173–175).

4.16.3 Licensing Objectives

The purpose of the system of licensing for licensable activities it to promote four fundamental objectives—the licensing objectives (s. 4(2)). These objectives are:

(a) the prevention of crime and disorder;
(b) public safety;
(c) the prevention of public nuisance; and
(d) the protection of children from harm.

> **KEYNOTE**
>
> The aim of the licensing objectives is to ensure that carrying on licensable activities on or from premises is done in the public interest. The third objective, the prevention of public nuisance, will not extend to every activity where annoyance may be caused to other people but will cover behaviour which, when balanced against the public interest, is found to be unacceptable. The fourth objective is concerned with the harm to children beyond matters relating to physical safety.

4.16.4 The Licensing System

The 2003 Act sets out a single licensing system that governs all premises used for licensable activities. The system is administered by licensing authorities that include councils of a district, county or borough within England and Wales (s. 3(1)).

The key licensing authorisations that may be issued are:

- Premises Licence
- Personal Licence
- Club Premises Certificate
- Temporary Event Notice.

Carrying on a licensable activity other than in accordance with a premises licence, club premises certificate or temporary event notice is an offence (s. 136).

4.16.4.1 Premises Licence

A 'premises licence' means a licence in respect of any premises, which authorises them to be used for one or more licensable activities (s. 11).

The Licensing Act 2003, s. 16 provides that the following persons may apply for a premises licence:

(a) a person who carries on, or proposes to carry on, a business which involves the use of the premises for the licensable activities to which the application relates,

(b) a person who makes the application pursuant to—
   (i) any statutory function discharged by that person which relates to those licensable activities, or
   (ii) any function discharged by that person by virtue of Her Majesty's prerogative,

(c) a recognised club,

(d) a charity,

(e) the proprietor of an educational institution,

(f) a health service body,

(g) a person who is registered under Part 2 of the Care Standards Act 2000 in respect of an independent hospital, in Wales,

(ga) a person who is registered under Chapter 2 of Part 1 of the Health and Social Care Act 2008 in respect of the carrying on of a regulated activity (within the meaning of that Part) in an independent hospital in England,

(h) the chief officer of police of a police force in England and Wales,

(i) a person of such other description as may be prescribed.

KEYNOTE

In relation to s. 16(b)(ii), an example would be a body exercising functions by virtue of a royal charter.

An individual may not apply for a premises licence unless he/she is aged 18 or over (s. 16(2)).

Any application for a premises licence must be accompanied by an operating schedule. The operating schedule must set out various details relating to the operation of the premises when carrying on licensable activities. These details include the licensable activities to be carried out, the proposed hours of opening etc., the duration of the licence (if it is to have a fixed term), details about the individual (if any) who is to act as the designated premises supervisor, details of whether alcohol is to be supplied (if at all) for on-sales, off-sales or both, and a statement of how the applicant intends to promote the licensing objectives. For example, the arrangements to be put in place to prevent crime and disorder, such as door security (s. 17(4))).

The premises licence will name a designated premises supervisor who holds a valid personal licence. Every supply of alcohol under the licence must be made by a personal licence holder or a person authorised by such a holder (s. 19).

A constable or an authorised person may require production of a premises licence or a certified copy of it (s. 57(5)), and a person who fails, without reasonable excuse, to produce the licence, or certified copy, commits a summary offence (s. 57(7)).

4.16.4.2 Review of Premises Licence

A responsible authority or any other person may apply to the relevant licensing authority for a review of a premises licence (s. 51), for example, where it is considered a licensee is failing to take sufficient measures to prevent public nuisance. Similarly, the police may consider that the measures put in place to prevent crime and disorder are not being effective and need to be reviewed. The review may result in the licensing authority revoking the premises licence but the authority are under a duty to ensure that the requirements of Article 6 of the European Convention on Human Rights (right to a fair trial) are clearly engaged and rigorously tested (*R (On the Application of Harpers Leisure International Limited* v *Chief Constable of Surrey* [2009] EWHC 2160 (Admin)).

In addition to the above procedure, a chief officer of police may apply to the relevant licensing authority for a review of a premises licence where a senior police officer (of or above the rank of superintendent) has given a certificate that it is their opinion that the premises are associated with serious crime or serious disorder or both (s. 53A). On receipt of such an application, the relevant licensing authority must within 48 hours of the time of its receipt, consider under s. 53B whether it is appropriate to take interim steps pending the determination of a review of the premises licence, and within 28 days after the day of its receipt, review that licence in accordance with s. 53C and reach a determination on that review (s. 53A(2)(a) and (b)).

4.16.4.3 Personal Licences

The supply of alcohol is regulated generally by the granting of a personal licence to an individual. The Licensing Act 2003, s. 111 states:

(1) In this Act 'personal licence' means a licence which—
  (a) is granted by a licensing authority to an individual, and
  (b) authorises that individual to supply alcohol, or authorise the supply of alcohol, in accordance with a premises licence.
(2) In subsection (1)(b) the reference to an individual supplying alcohol is to him—
  (a) selling alcohol by retail, or
  (b) supplying alcohol by or on behalf of a club to, or to the order of, a member of the club.

> **KEYNOTE**
>
> The licensing of individuals is separate from the licensing of premises and enables personal licence holders to move from one set of premises to another.
>
> A mainstay of the personal licensing system is the ability to refuse to grant, or to suspend/revoke the licence as a result of the applicant's or licensee's previous character or other conduct.
>
> A personal licence, which is valid for 10 years, must be held by the designated premises supervisor and more than one individual at the licensed premises may hold a personal licence. It is not necessary for all staff to be licensed, but all supplies of alcohol under a premises licence must be made by or under the authority of a personal licence holder.
>
> A constable or an authorised person may require production of a personal licence (s. 135(2)), and a person who fails without reasonable excuse to produce the licence commits a summary offence (s. 135(4)).

4.16.4.4 Club Premises Certificate

A club premises certificate may be granted by a licensing authority certifying that the premises may be used by the club for one or more qualifying club activities specified in the certificate, and that the club is a qualifying club in relation to each of those activities (s. 60).

The general conditions that apply for a club to qualify as a qualifying club (s. 62):

• persons may not be admitted to membership, or be admitted, as candidates for membership, to any of the privileges of membership without an interval of at least two days between their nomination or application for membership and their admission;

- persons becoming members without prior nomination or application may not be admitted to the privileges of membership without an interval of at least two days between their becoming members and their admission;
- the club is established and conducted in good faith as a club;
- the club has at least 25 members;
- alcohol is not supplied, or intended to be supplied, to members on the premises otherwise than by or on behalf of the club.

KEYNOTE

Clubs falling within this category will include the Royal British Legion, Working Men's Clubs, cricket and rugby clubs, where activities are carried on from private premises and because alcohol and entertainment are provided otherwise than for profit. Generally, 'nightclubs' do not fall within this category.

Where a club holds a club premises certificate, a responsible authority or any other person may apply to the relevant licensing authority for a review of the certificate (s. 87(1)). However, the licensing authority may reject the review if it is not relevant to any of the licensing objectives or the application is considered frivolous, vexatious or repetitious (s. 87(4)). Where conditions are imposed following a review of a club premises certificate they must be proportionate in achieving the licensing objectives (see *R (On the Application of Merlot 73 Ltd)* v *City of Westminster Magistrates' Court* [2013] EWHC 3416 (Admin)).

A constable or authorised person may require production of a club premises certificate (s. 94(7)) and failure to produce a certificate without reasonable excuse is a summary offence (s. 94(9)).

A constable may enter and search the club premises where they have reasonable cause to believe that an offence under s. 4(3)(a), (b) or (c) of the Misuse of Drugs Act 1971 (supplying or offering to supply, or being concerned in supplying or making an offer to supply, a controlled drug), has been, is being, or is about to be committed there, or there is likely to be a breach of the peace there. The constable may use reasonable force if necessary (s. 97).

4.16.4.5 Temporary Event Notice

A Temporary Event Notice (TEN), issued by the licensing authority, is required where a person (the premises user) intends to carry out a licensable activity on unlicensed premises or wishes to operate outside the terms of their existing premises licence or club premises licence (s.100 of the 2003 Act).

A 'licensable activity' is the sale or supply of alcohol, regulated entertainment (e.g. music, singing or dancing), or provisions of late night refreshment (hot food or drink between the hours of 2300 and 0500). Such activities might include a publican engaged to run a temporary bar for a wedding at a venue not licensed for the sale of alcohol, or a person not being the holder of a personal licence who may wish to run a bar and provide a band at a party to celebrate a significant anniversary.

A personal licence holder is permitted fifty TENs per calendar year and an individual who is not the holder of a personal licence is permitted five TENs a year.

All premises are limited to twelve TENs in a calendar year. A TEN can last up to 168 hours but in total the twelve TENs cannot exceed 21 days in a calendar year.

A TEN can only be used when the number of persons at the event (including performers) does not exceed 499 persons at any one time.

KEYNOTE

Where the police consider the TEN would undermine the 'crime prevention objective' they must notify the premises user and licensing authority of their objection. The licensing authority may withdraw the TEN or it may be modified so that it no longer undermines the objective (s. 104).

At any reasonable time, a constable or an authorised person may enter premises to which a TEN relates to assess the likely effect of the notice on the promotion of the crime prevention objective (s. 108(1)). Obstructing a constable or authorised officer is an offence (s. 108(3)).

On the day of the event a copy of the TEN and any statement of conditions attached to the TEN following an objection, must be prominently displayed at the premises or be in possession of the premises user or their nominated representative. Failure to comply with these requirements is an offence (s. 109(4)) and failure to produce a TEN when required by a constable or authorised person is also an offence (s. 109(8)).

4.16.5   Police Powers

The Act creates a number of powers for police officers and other authorised persons to enter and inspect premises, to investigate licensable activities, to investigate offences, and to require the production of documents.

Power of entry to investigate licensable activities

Where a constable or an authorised person has reason to believe that any premises are being, or are about to be, used for a licensable activity, he may enter the premises with a view to seeing whether the activity is being, or is to be, carried on under and in accordance with an authorisation (s. 179(1)). An authorised person exercising the power must, if so requested, produce evidence of his authority to exercise the power (s. 179(2)).

A person exercising the power conferred by this section may, if necessary, use reasonable force (s. 179(3)), and a person commits an offence if he intentionally obstructs an authorised person exercising a power conferred by this section (s. 179(4)).

Right of entry to investigate offences

A constable may enter and search any premises in respect of which he has reason to believe that an offence under this Act has been, is being or is about to be committed (s. 180(1)), and may, if necessary, use reasonable force (s. 180(2)).

4.16.6   Regulated Entertainment

Licensing the provision of regulated entertainment is another key feature of the 2003 Act and detailed guidance on this provision is contained in sch. 1 to the Act.

Regulated entertainment covers entertainment, provided solely or partly for members of the public, or exclusively to club members and their guests, or for which a charge is made, which is provided for profit (which will include raising money for charities).

The forms of entertainment regulated by the Act include:

- plays, including both performance and rehearsal;
- films, or any exhibition of moving pictures;
- all indoor sporting events;
- outdoor boxing and wrestling matches;
- performance of live music and the playing of recorded music;
- performance of dance.

Schedule 1 provides a number of exemptions to regulated entertainment, for example, entertainment at a garden fete, Morris dancing (or dancing of a similar nature), and entertainment provided on vehicles in motion.

4.16.7 Offences

The main offences with which police officers will be involved are contained in the 2003 Act. These follow a fairly common-sense approach imposing requirements and obligations on those people who could have acted to prevent the relevant conduct or who could have made the relevant request, e.g. of a disorderly person to leave licensed premises.

4.16.7.1 Unauthorised Licensable Activities

OFFENCE: **Unauthorised Licensable Activities—*Licensing Act 2003, s. 136***
- Triable summarily • Six months' imprisonment and/or a fine up to £20,000

The Licensing Act 2003, s. 136 states:

(1) A person commits an offence if—
  (a) he carries on or attempts to carry on a licensable activity on or from any premises otherwise than under and in accordance with an authorisation, or
  (b) he knowingly allows a licensable activity to be so carried on.

KEYNOTE

This offence requires that the person carried on (or attempted to carry on) the licensable activity *either* in a manner not authorised by or in accordance with an appropriate authorisation, or *knowingly* allowing the activity to be carried on in that way. Therefore the element of knowledge on the part of the defendant is essential in any case where he/she is not directly involved.

If the relevant authorisation (e.g. a premises licence) has certain conditions attached and they are not adhered to, this offence would be committed.

'Authorisation' here means a premises licence, a club premises certificate or a temporary event notice in respect of which the relevant conditions have been met. While some offences apply only to 'relevant premises', the above is wider than that and applies to any premises.

Where the licensable activity in question is the provision of regulated entertainment, a person will generally not commit an offence under this section if his/her only involvement in the provision of the entertainment is that he/she played the music, performed the dance etc. (see s. 136(2)).

The statutory defence of due diligence applies to this offence.

4.16.7.2 Exposing Alcohol for Unauthorised Sale

OFFENCE: **Exposing Alcohol for Unauthorised Sale—*Licensing Act 2003, s. 137***
- Triable summarily • Six months' imprisonment and/or a fine up to £20,000

The Licensing Act 2003, s. 137 states:

(1) A person commits an offence if, on any premises, he exposes for sale by retail any alcohol in circumstances where the sale by retail of that alcohol on those premises would be an unauthorised licensable activity.
(2) For that purpose a licensable activity is unauthorised unless it is under and in accordance with an authorisation.

KEYNOTE

This offence concerns retail sales of alcohol on premises where to do so lawfully would ordinarily require some form of authorisation. There is no requirement for the person to have done so 'knowingly' or with any particular state of mind, neither is there a need for any *sale* actually to have taken place, and the exposing for sale under the relevant circumstances makes the offence complete.

While some offences apply only to 'relevant premises', the above is wider than that and applies to any premises.

There is a further summary offence (punishable by a fine) for a person to have in his/her possession or under his/her control alcohol which he/she intends to sell by retail or supply by or on behalf of a club to a member of the club in circumstances where that activity would be an unauthorised licensable activity (see s. 138). The statutory defence of 'due diligence' applies to both these offences.

The court by which a person is convicted of either of these offences may order the alcohol in question (and any container), to be forfeited and either destroyed or dealt with in such other manner as the court may order (s. 137(4)).

'Sale by retail' is specifically defined in s. 192. In essence it excludes wholesale transactions made with people (including personal licence holders) in the course of their trade and sales for consumption off the premises.

4.16.7.3 Defence of Due Diligence

The Licensing Act 2003 contains a specific defence of 'due diligence', and s. 139 states:

(1) In proceedings against a person for an offence to which subsection (2) applies, it is a defence that—
   (a) his act was due to a mistake, or to reliance on information given to him, or to an act or omission by another person, or to some other cause beyond his control, and
   (b) he took all reasonable precautions and exercised all due diligence to avoid committing the offence.

KEYNOTE

The offences to which this defence applies are:

- s. 136(1)(a) (carrying on unauthorised licensable activity);
- s. 137 (exposing alcohol for unauthorised sale); or
- s. 138 (keeping alcohol on premises for unauthorised sale).

The defence of due diligence has two limbs and both (a) and (b) must be shown for it to apply.

4.16.7.4 Allowing Disorderly Conduct on Licensed Premises

OFFENCE: **Allowing Disorderly Conduct on Licensed Premises etc.—*Licensing Act 2003, s. 140***
   - Triable summarily • Fine

The Licensing Act 2003, s. 140 states:

(1) A person to whom subsection (2) applies commits an offence if he knowingly allows disorderly conduct on relevant premises.
(2) This subsection applies—
   (a) to any person who works at the premises in a capacity, whether paid or unpaid, which authorises him to prevent the conduct,
   (b) in the case of licensed premises, to—
      (i) the holder of a premises licence in respect of the premises, and
      (ii) the designated premises supervisor (if any) under such a licence,
   (c) in the case of premises in respect of which a club premises certificate has effect, to any member or officer of the club which holds the certificate who at the time the conduct takes place is present on the premises in a capacity which enables him to prevent it, and
   (d) in the case of premises which may be used for a permitted temporary activity by virtue of Part 5, to the premises user in relation to the temporary event notice in question.

4.16.7.5 Sale of Alcohol to a Person who is Drunk

OFFENCE: **Sale of Alcohol to a Person who is Drunk—*Licensing Act 2003, s. 141***

- Triable summarily • Fine

The Licensing Act 2003, s. 141 states:

(1) A person to whom subsection (2) applies commits an offence if, on relevant premises, he knowingly—
    (a) sells or attempts to sell alcohol to a person who is drunk, or
    (b) allows alcohol to be sold to such a person.
(2) This subsection applies—
    (a) to any person who works at the premises in a capacity, whether paid or unpaid, which gives him authority to sell the alcohol concerned,
    (b) in the case of licensed premises, to—
        (i) the holder of a premises licence in respect of the premises, and
        (ii) the designated premises supervisor (if any) under such a licence,
    (c) in the case of premises in respect of which a club premises certificate has effect, to any member or officer of the club which holds the certificate who at the time the sale (or attempted sale) takes place is present on the premises in a capacity which enables him to prevent it, and
    (d) in the case of premises which may be used for a permitted temporary activity by virtue of Part 5, to the premises user in relation to the temporary event notice in question.

4.16.7.6 Obtaining Alcohol for a Person who is Drunk

OFFENCE: **Obtaining Alcohol for a Person who is Drunk—*Licensing Act 2003, s. 142***

- Triable summarily • Fine

The Licensing Act 2003, s. 142 states:

(1) A person commits an offence if, on relevant premises, he knowingly obtains or attempts to obtain alcohol for consumption on those premises by a person who is drunk.

KEYNOTE

'Relevant premises' means licensed premises, premises in respect of which there is in force a club premises certificate, and premises which may be used for a permitted temporary activity by virtue of part 5 (s. 159).

The requirement to show that the defendant acted *knowingly* is critical to prove this offence.

The intended consumption must be on the premises where the alcohol is obtained/attempted to be obtained.

4.16.7.7   Failure to Leave Licensed Premises

OFFENCE: **Failure to Leave Licensed Premises etc.—*Licensing Act 2003, s. 143***
> • Triable summarily • Fine

The Licensing Act 2003, s. 143 states:

(1) A person who is drunk *or* disorderly commits an offence if, without reasonable excuse—
  (a) he fails to leave relevant premises when requested to do so by a constable or by a person to whom subsection (2) applies, or
  (b) he enters or attempts to enter relevant premises after a constable or a person to whom subsection (2) applies has requested him not to enter.
(2) This subsection applies—
  (a) to any person who works at the premises in a capacity, whether paid or unpaid, which gives him authority to sell the alcohol concerned,
  (b) in the case of licensed premises, to—
    (i) the holder of a premises licence in respect of the premises, and
    (ii) the designated premises supervisor (if any) under such a licence,
  (c) in the case of premises in respect of which a club premises certificate has effect, to any member or officer of the club which holds the certificate who is present on the premises in a capacity which enables him to make such a request, and
  (d) in the case of premises which may be used for a permitted temporary activity by virtue of Part 5, to the premises user in relation to the temporary event notice in question.

KEYNOTE

The above offence requires that the person concerned is shown to be *either* drunk *or* disorderly (contrast the offence under the Criminal Justice Act 1967, see para. 4.16.7.8).

The absence of a reasonable excuse is an important ingredient in this offence, and it should be shown that the request to leave/not to enter was both heard and understood by the defendant.

On being requested to do so by a person to whom s. 143(2) applies, a constable must:

- help to expel from relevant premises a person who is drunk or disorderly;
- help to prevent such a person from entering relevant premises.

s. 143(4)

If requested to do so by one of the above people, a police officer is under a duty (rather than simply having a power) to help them expel anyone who is drunk or disorderly. The wording of the section means that police officers are also under a similar duty to help to prevent such a person from entering relevant premises.

In assisting the removal of an individual a police officer is entitled to use force (*Semple v Luton & South Bedfordshire Magistrates' Court* [2009] EWHC 3241 (Admin)).

'Relevant premises' means licensed premises, premises in respect of which there is in force a club premises certificate, and premises which may be used for a permitted temporary activity by virtue of part 5 (s. 159).

4.16.7.8 Drunk and Disorderly

OFFENCE: **Drunk and Disorderly—*Criminal Justice Act 1967, s. 91(1)***

- Triable summarily • Fine

The Criminal Justice Act 1967, s. 91 states:

(1) Any person who in any public place is guilty, while drunk, of disorderly behaviour shall be liable...

KEYNOTE

In *Carroll* v *DPP* [2009] EWHC 554 (Admin) the court stated that drunk and disorderly was one of the most basic of offences and that it required proof of three elements: the accused was drunk; he/she was in a public place; and he/she was guilty of disorderly behaviour.

The drunkenness must be as a result of excessive consumption of alcohol; if the person's state is caused by some other intoxicant (e.g. glue solvents), the offence is not made out (*Neale* v *R.M.I.E. (a minor)* (1985) 80 Cr App R 20). The same ruling applies to a person 'found drunk' in a public place (*Lanham* v *Rickwood* (1984) 148 JP 737).

'Drunkenness' here means where the defendant has taken intoxicating liquor (alcohol) to an extent that affects his/her steady self-control (per Goff LJ in *Neale*).

Where there are *several* causes of a person's incapacitated state, one of which is alcohol, a court can find that the person was in fact 'drunk', even though some additional intoxicant had an exacerbating effect on his/her loss of 'steady self-control'.

In *McMillan* v *CPS* [2008] EWHC 1457 (Admin), it was held that where a police officer took hold of a drunken person by the arm to steady her for her own safety it was not an arrest. The circumstances entailed the officer leading the drunken person from a private garden to a public place. It was then legitimate for the officer to arrest for this offence where the accused displayed disorderly behaviour. However, this offence is not committed where a person did not commit any disorderly act until after the arrest (*H* v *DPP* [2005] EWHC 2459 (Admin)).

This offence is a 'penalty offence' for the purposes of s. 1 of the Criminal Justice and Police Act 2001. Note that a penalty notice for s. 91(1) cannot be given to a person aged under 18, and a constable giving a notice to a person other than at a police station does not need to be in uniform (Legal Aid, Sentencing and Punishment of Offenders Act 2012 (Consequential Amendments) Regulations 2013 (SI 2013/903)).

Where a person is arrested for committing this offence, under the powers contained within s. 24 of the Police and Criminal Evidence Act 1984, a constable may take him/her to an approved treatment centre for alcoholism (a 'detoxification' centre) and he/she will be treated as being in lawful custody for the purposes of that journey (see s. 34(1) of the Criminal Justice Act 1972).

The conduct of passengers who are drunk on an aircraft has a potential impact on the safety of the aircraft and the people therein, therefore they can be dealt with under s. 61 of the Civil Aviation Act 1982 and the relevant regulations made thereunder (see e.g. *R* v *Tagg* [2001] EWCA Crim 1230 and Air Navigation Order 2009 (SI 2009/3015, part 19) made under Civil Aviation Act 1982 and the Airports Act 1986).

4.16.7.9 Found Drunk

OFFENCE: **Being Found Drunk—*Licensing Act 1872, s. 12***

- Triable summarily • Fine

The Licensing Act 1872, s. 12 states:

Every person found drunk in any highway or other public place, whether a building or not, or on any licensed premises, shall be liable ...

Every person who is drunk while in charge on any highway or other public place of any carriage, horse, cattle, or steam engine, or who is drunk when in possession of any loaded firearms, shall be liable to a penalty not exceeding level 1 on the standard scale or in the discretion of the court to imprisonment for any term not exceeding one month.

4.16.7.10 Being Drunk While in Charge of Child

OFFENCE: **Being Drunk While in Charge of Child—*Licensing Act 1902, s. 2***
* One month's imprisonment and/or a fine summarily

The Licensing Act 1902, s. 2 states:

(1) If any person is found drunk in any highway or other public place, whether a building or not, or on any licensed premises, while having the charge of a child apparently under the age of seven years, he may be apprehended...

(2) If the child appears to the court to be under the age of seven, the child shall, for the purposes of this section, be deemed to be under that age unless the contrary is proved.

4.16.8 Children

The Licensing Act 2003 makes provision for offences and breaches of the regulatory framework with the protection of children as one of its primary objectives. The Act left in place the offence of giving alcohol to a child under five years old (s. 5 of the Children and Young Persons Act 1933), except on a doctor's order, or in cases of sickness, apprehended sickness or other urgent cause.

4.16.8.1 Unaccompanied Children Prohibited from Certain Premises

OFFENCE: **Unaccompanied Children Prohibited from Certain Premises—*Licensing Act 2003, s. 145***
* Triable summarily * Fine

The Licensing Act 2003, s. 145 states:

(1) A person to whom subsection (3) applies commits an offence if—
    (a) knowing that relevant premises are within subsection (4), he allows an unaccompanied child to be on the premises at a time when they are open for the purposes of being used for the supply of alcohol for consumption there, or

(b) he allows an unaccompanied child to be on relevant premises at a time between the hours of midnight and 5 a.m. when the premises are open for the purposes of being used for the supply of alcohol for consumption there.

(2) ...

(3) This subsection applies—

    (a) to any person who works at the premises in a capacity, whether paid or unpaid, which authorises him to request the unaccompanied child to leave the premises,

    (b) in the case of licensed premises, to—

      (i) the holder of a premises licence in respect of the premises, and

      (ii) the designated premises supervisor (if any) under such a licence,

    (c) in the case of premises in respect of which a club premises certificate has effect, to any member or officer of the club which holds the certificate who is present on the premises in a capacity which enables him to make such a request, and

    (d) in the case of premises which may be used for a permitted temporary activity by virtue of Part 5, to the premises user in relation to the temporary event notice in question.

KEYNOTE

The two limbs to this offence are either:

- that the child is unaccompanied on the premises at a time when they are open for the purposes of supplying alcohol for consumption on those premises, and the defendant knows that the premises fall within s. 145(4); or
- that the child is unaccompanied on the premises at a time between midnight and 5 am when the premises are being so used.

The people to whom this offence applies are those identified within other offences under the Act and cover the roles that would allow the person to take the appropriate action in preventing the presence of children in the way prohibited.

'Child' means an individual aged under 16 (s. 145(2)(a)).

A child is unaccompanied if he/she is not in the company of an individual aged 18 or over (s. 145(2)(b)). Relevant premises are within s. 145(4) if:

- they are exclusively or primarily used for the supply of alcohol for consumption on the premises; or
- they are open for the purposes of being used for the supply of alcohol for consumption on the premises by virtue of part 5 (permitted temporary activities) and, at the time the temporary event notice in question has effect, they are exclusively or primarily used for such supplies (s. 145(4)).

'Supply of alcohol' means the sale by retail of alcohol, or the supply of alcohol by or on behalf of a club to, or to the order of, a member of the club (s. 145(10)).

No offence is committed if the unaccompanied child is on the premises solely for the purpose of passing to or from some other place to or from which there is no other convenient means of access or egress (s. 145(5)).

As with some other offences, there are specific defences where the person is charged as a result of his/her own conduct and where the conduct is that of someone else.

4.16.8.2 Defence

Where a person is charged with an offence under this section by *reason of his own conduct*, it is a defence that:

- he believed that the unaccompanied child was aged 16 or over or that an individual accompanying him was aged 18 or over, *and*
- either:
  - he had taken all reasonable steps to establish the individual's age, or
  - nobody could reasonably have suspected from the individual's appearance that he was aged under 16 or, as the case may be, under 18.

Where a person is charged with an offence under this section *by reason of the act or default of some other person*, it is a defence that the person charged exercised all due diligence to avoid committing it (s. 145(6) and (8)).

A person will have taken all reasonable steps to establish an individual's age if:

- he/she asked the individual for evidence of his/her age, and
- the evidence would have convinced a reasonable person.

(s. 145(7))

4.16.8.3 Sale of Alcohol to Children

> OFFENCE: **Sale of Alcohol to Children—*Licensing Act 2003, s. 146***
> - Triable summarily - Fine

The Licensing Act 2003, s. 146 states:

(1) A person commits an offence if he sells alcohol to an individual aged under 18.
(2) A club commits an offence if alcohol is supplied by it or on its behalf—
　　(a) to, or to the order of, a member of the club who is aged under 18, or
　　(b) to the order of a member of the club, to an individual who is aged under 18.
(3) A person commits an offence if he supplies alcohol on behalf of a club—
　　(a) to, or to the order of, a member of the club who is aged under 18, or
　　(b) to the order of a member of the club, to an individual who is aged under 18.

KEYNOTE

The main offence under subs. (1) is straightforward and covers any type of 'selling' of alcohol to people under 18 *anywhere* (not just on licensed premises).

As with some other offences there are specific defences where the person is charged as a result of his/her own conduct or where the conduct is that of someone else.

4.16.8.4 Defence

Where a person is charged with an offence under this section *by reason of his own conduct*, it is a defence that:

- he believed that the individual was aged 18 or over, and
- either:
  - ◆ he had taken all reasonable steps to establish the individual's age, or
  - ◆ nobody could reasonably have suspected from the individual's appearance that he was aged under 18.

Where a person is charged with an offence under this section *by reason of the act or default of some other person*, it is a defence that the person charged exercised all due diligence to avoid committing it (s. 146(4) and (6)).

A person will have taken all reasonable steps to establish an individual's age if:

- he/she asked the individual for evidence of his/her age, and
- the evidence would have convinced a reasonable person.

(s. 146(5))

4.16.8.5 Allowing the Sale of Alcohol to Children

> OFFENCE: **Allowing the Sale of Alcohol to Children—*Licensing Act 2003, s. 147***
> - Triable summarily - Fine

The Licensing Act 2003, s. 147 states:

(1) A person to whom subsection (2) applies commits an offence if he knowingly allows the sale of alcohol on relevant premises to an individual aged under 18.

(2) This subsection applies to a person who works at the premises in a capacity, whether paid or unpaid, which authorises him to prevent the sale.

(3) A person to whom subsection (4) applies commits an offence if he knowingly allows alcohol to be supplied on relevant premises by or on behalf of a club—

(a) to or to the order of a member of the club who is aged under 18, or

(b) to the order of a member of the club, to an individual who is aged under 18.

KEYNOTE

The offences above require proof that the person *knowingly* allowed the sale (or, in the case of s. 147(3), the supply) to a person under 18. Unlike the offence under s. 146 (Sale of Alcohol to Children), the offence at s. 147 relates to 'relevant premises'. These are licensed premises, premises in respect of which there is in force a club premises certificate, and premises which may be used for a permitted temporary activity by virtue of part 5 (s. 159).

So far as the second offence relating to clubs (under s. 147(3)) is concerned, s. 147(4) to which it refers applies to:

- a person who works on the premises in a capacity, whether paid or unpaid, which authorises him/her to prevent the supply, and
- any member or officer of the club who at the time of the supply is present on the relevant premises in a capacity which enables him/her to prevent it.

Every local weights and measures authority in England and Wales has a statutory duty to enforce within its area the above provisions so far as they apply to sales of alcohol made on or from premises to which the public have access, and a weights and measures inspector may make (or authorise any person to make on his/her behalf) test purchases of goods for the purpose of determining whether those provisions are being complied with (s. 154).

4.16.8.6 Persistently Selling Alcohol to Children

OFFENCE: **Persistently Selling Alcohol to Children—*Licensing Act 2003, s. 147A***
- Triable summarily • Fine

The Licensing Act 2003, s. 147A states:

(1) A person is guilty of an offence if—

(a) on 2 or more different occasions within a period of 3 consecutive months alcohol is unlawfully sold on the same premises to an individual aged under 18;

(b) at the time of each sale the premises were either licensed premises or premises authorised to be used for a permitted temporary activity by virtue of Part 5; and

(c) that person was a responsible person in relation to the premises at each such time.

(2) For the purposes of this section alcohol sold to an individual aged under 18 is unlawfully sold to him if—

(a) the person making the sale believed the individual to be aged under 18; or

(b) that person did not have reasonable grounds for believing the individual to be aged 18 or over.

(3) For the purposes of subsection (2) a person has reasonable grounds for believing an individual to be aged 18 or over only if—

(a) he asked the individual for evidence of his age and that individual produced evidence that would have convinced a reasonable person; or

(b) nobody could reasonably have suspected from the individual's appearance that he was aged under 18.

4.16.8.7 Sale of Liqueur Confectionery to Children

OFFENCE: **Sale of Liqueur Confectionery to Children under 16—*Licensing Act 2003, s. 148***

- Triable summarily • Fine

The Licensing Act 2003, s. 148 states:

(1) A person commits an offence if he—
   (a) sells liqueur confectionery to an individual aged under 16, or
   (b) supplies such confectionery, on behalf of a club—
      (i) to or to the order of a member of the club who is aged under 16, or
      (ii) to the order of a member of the club, to an individual who is aged under 16.

4.16.8.8 Defence

Where a person is charged with an offence under this section *by reason of his own conduct*, it is a defence that:

- he believed that the individual was aged 16 or over, and
- either:
  - he had taken all reasonable steps to establish the individual's age, or
  - nobody could reasonably have suspected from the individual's appearance that he was aged under 16.

Where a person is charged with an offence under this section *by reason of the act or default of some other person*, it is a defence that the person charged exercised all due diligence to avoid committing it (s. 148(3) and (5)).

Again, a person will have taken all reasonable steps to establish an individual's age if:

- he/she asked the individual for evidence of his/her age, and
- the evidence would have convinced a reasonable person (s. 148(4)).

4.16.8.9 Purchase of Alcohol by or on behalf of Children

OFFENCE: **Purchase of Alcohol by or on behalf of Children—*Licensing Act 2003, s. 149***

> - Triable summarily • Fine

The Licensing Act 2003, s. 149 states:

(1) An individual aged under 18 commits an offence if—
  (a) he buys or attempts to buy alcohol, or
  (b) where he is a member of a club—
    (i) alcohol is supplied to him or to his order by or on behalf of the club, as a result of some act or default of his, or
    (ii) he attempts to have alcohol supplied to him or to his order by or on behalf of the club.
(2) …
(3) A person commits an offence if—
  (a) he buys or attempts to buy alcohol on behalf of an individual aged under 18, or
  (b) where he is a member of a club, on behalf of an individual aged under 18 he—
    (i) makes arrangements whereby alcohol is supplied to him or to his order by or on behalf of the club, or
    (ii) attempts to make such arrangements.
(4) A person ('the relevant person') commits an offence if—
  (a) he buys or attempts to buy alcohol for consumption on relevant premises by an individual aged under 18, or
  (b) where he is a member of a club—
    (i) by some act or default of his, alcohol is supplied to him, or to his order, by or on behalf of the club for consumption on relevant premises by an individual aged under 18, or
    (ii) he attempts to have alcohol so supplied for such consumption.

KEYNOTE

This wide offence covers all forms of under-18-year-olds buying (or trying to buy) alcohol or someone else doing it for them.

Section 149(1) does not apply where the individual buys or attempts to buy the alcohol at the request of a constable, or a weights and measures inspector who is acting in the course of his/her duty (s. 149(2)).

The offence at s. 149(4) does not apply where:

- the relevant person is aged 18 or over,
- the individual is aged 16 or 17,
- the alcohol is beer, wine or cider,
- its purchase or supply is for consumption at a table meal on relevant premises, and
- the individual is accompanied at the meal by an individual aged 18 or over. (s. 149(5))

'Table meal' here means a meal eaten by a person seated at a table (or at a counter or other structure which serves the purpose of a table) and is not used for the service of refreshments for consumption by people who are not seated at such a table or structure (s. 159).

Where a person is charged with an offence under s. 149(3) or (4) it is a defence that he/she had no reason to suspect that the individual was aged under 18 (s. 149(6)).

4.16.8.10 Consumption of Alcohol by Children

OFFENCE: **Consumption of Alcohol by Children—*Licensing Act 2003, s. 150***
  • Triable summarily • Fine

The Licensing Act 2003, s. 150 states:

(1) An individual aged under 18 commits an offence if he knowingly consumes alcohol on relevant premises.

(2) A person to whom subsection (3) applies commits an offence if he knowingly allows the consumption of alcohol on relevant premises by an individual aged under 18.

(3) This subsection applies—
 (a) to a person who works at the premises in a capacity, whether paid or unpaid, which authorises him to prevent the consumption, and
 (b) where the alcohol was supplied by a club to or to the order of a member of the club, to any member or officer of the club who is present at the premises at the time of the consumption in a capacity which enables him to prevent it.

KEYNOTE

These offences address the consumption of alcohol by under-18-year-olds on relevant premises.

'Relevant premises' are generally licensed premises, in respect of which there is in force a club premises certificate, and premises which may be used for a permitted temporary activity by virtue of part 5 (s. 159).
 Subsections (1) and (2) do not apply where:

- the individual is aged 16 or 17;
- the alcohol is beer, wine or cider;
- its consumption is at a table meal on relevant premises; and
- the individual is accompanied at the meal by an individual aged 18 or over.

(s. 150(4))

4.16.8.11 Delivering Alcohol to Children

OFFENCE: **Delivering Alcohol to Children—*Licensing Act 2003, s. 151***
  • Triable summarily • Fine

The Licensing Act 2003, s. 151 states:

(1) A person who works on relevant premises in any capacity, whether paid or unpaid, commits an offence if he knowingly delivers to an individual aged under 18—
 (a) alcohol sold on the premises, or
 (b) alcohol supplied on the premises by or on behalf of a club to or to the order of a member of the club.

(2) A person to whom subsection (3) applies commits an offence if he knowingly allows anybody else to deliver to an individual aged under 18 alcohol sold on relevant premises.

(3) This subsection applies to a person who works on the premises in a capacity, whether paid or unpaid, which authorises him to prevent the delivery of the alcohol.

(4) A person to whom subsection (5) applies commits an offence if he knowingly allows anybody else to deliver to an individual aged under 18 alcohol supplied on relevant premises by or on behalf of a club to or to the order of a member of the club.

(5) This subsection applies—
 (a) to a person who works on the premises in a capacity, whether paid or unpaid, which authorises him to prevent the supply, and
 (b) to any member or officer of the club who at the time of the supply in question is present on the premises in a capacity which enables him to prevent the supply.

4.16.8.12 Sending a Child to Obtain Alcohol

The Licensing Act 2003, s. 152 states:

OFFENCE: **Sending a Child to Obtain Alcohol—*Licensing Act 2003, s. 152***

- Triable summarily • Fine

(1) A person commits an offence if he knowingly sends an individual aged under 18 to obtain—
   (a) alcohol sold or to be sold on relevant premises for consumption off the premises, or
   (b) alcohol supplied or to be supplied by or on behalf of a club to or to the order of a member of the club for such consumption.

4.16.8.13 Prohibition of Unsupervised Sales by Children

OFFENCE: **Prohibition of Unsupervised Sales by Children—*Licensing Act 2003, s. 153***

- Triable summarily • Fine

The Licensing Act 2003, s. 153 states:

(1) A responsible person commits an offence if on any relevant premises he knowingly allows an individual aged under 18 to make on the premises—
   (a) any sale of alcohol, or
   (b) any supply of alcohol by or on behalf of a club to or to the order of a member of the club,
   unless the sale or supply has been specifically approved by that or another responsible person.

- in relation to licensed premises:
  - the holder of a premises licence in respect of the premises,
  - the designated premises supervisor (if any) under such a licence, or
  - any individual aged 18 or over who is authorised for the purposes of this section by such a holder or supervisor,
- in relation to premises in respect of which there is in force *a* club premises certificate, any member or officer of the club present on the premises in a capacity which enables him/her to prevent the supply in question, and
- in relation to premises which may be used for a permitted temporary activity by virtue of part 5:
  - the premises user, or
  - any individual aged 18 or over who is authorised for the purposes of this section by the premises user.

(s. 153(4))

'Relevant premises' are generally the same premises as those set out under the various descriptions of 'responsible person' above (see s. 159).

The offence is not committed where:

- the alcohol is sold or supplied for consumption with a table meal,
- it is sold or supplied in premises which are being used for the service of table meals (or in a part of any premises which is being so used), *and*
- the premises are (or the part is) not used for the sale or supply of alcohol otherwise than to persons having table meals there and for consumption by such persons as an ancillary to their meal.

(s. 153(2))

4.16.8.14 Persistently Possessing Alcohol in a Public Place

OFFENCE: **Persistently Possessing Alcohol in a Public Place—*Policing and Crime Act 2009, s. 30***

- Triable summarily • Fine

The Policing and Crime Act 2009, s. 30 states:

(1) A person under the age of 18 is guilty of an offence if, without reasonable excuse, the person is in possession of alcohol in any relevant place on 3 or more occasions within a period of 12 consecutive months.

(2) 'Relevant place', in relation to a person, means—
  (a) any public place, other than excluded premises, or
  (b) any place, other than a public place, to which the person has unlawfully gained access.
  . . .

(4) For the purposes of subsection (2) a place is a public place if at the material time the public or any section of the public has access to it, on payment or otherwise, as of right or by virtue of express or implied permission.

KEYNOTE

A person under 18 commits this offence if he/she is in possession of alcohol in a public place on three or more occasions within a 12 month period.

In relation to s. 30 (2)(a), 'excluded premises' means premises with a premises licence or permitted temporary activity used for the supply of alcohol, and premises with a club premises certificate used for the supply of alcohol to members or guests.

The original Home Office guidance set out the steps to be taken to deter young people from drinking and possessing alcohol in public places, including engagement with their parents or guardians. It was intended that this offence be used in conjunction with s. 1 of the Confiscation of Alcohol (Young Persons) Act 1997 (see para. 4.16.8.15), to enable a constable to confiscate alcohol from those under 18 years of age, and to ensure that the young person was required to give his/her name and address to the constable.

4.16.8.15   Confiscation of Alcohol when Person under 18 may be involved

The Confiscation of Alcohol (Young Persons) Act 1997, s. 1 states:

(1)   Where a constable reasonably suspects that a person in a relevant place is in possession of alcohol, and that either—

     (a) he is under the age of 18; or

     (b) he intends that any of the alcohol should be consumed by a person under the age of 18 in that or any other relevant place; or

     (c) a person under the age of 18 who is, or has recently been, with him has recently consumed alcohol in that or any other relevant place, the constable may require him to surrender anything in his possession which is, or which the constable reasonably believes to be, alcohol or a container for such alcohol.

(1AA) A constable who imposes a requirement on a person under subsection (1) shall also require the person to state the person's name and address.

(1AB) A constable who imposes a requirement on a person under subsection (1) may, if the constable reasonably suspects that the person is under the age of 16, remove the person to the person's place of residence or a place of safety.

KEYNOTE

This is a discretionary power for police officers to exercise as they deem fit.

It is unusual that the wording of the section says 'either', then goes on to give *three* instances where the power will be available. However, if one of the instances at s. 1(1)(a) to (c) applies, the police officer may require the person concerned to surrender anything that is, or that the officer reasonably *believes* (a narrower expression than 'suspects') to be, alcohol or a container for such alcohol.

Subsection (1AA) states the constable *shall* require the person to state his/her name and address, whereas the previous subsection (now omitted) stated that a constable *may* require the person to give his/her name and address. Subsection (1AB) was part of a government initiative intended to prevent low-level crime and disorder. Although a 'place of safety' is not defined, this may be a relative or friend, or where necessary, a police station or social services accommodation.

The wording of this section is similar to that relating to powers to confiscate items in a designated public place (see para. 4.16.10). There is no requirement for the officer to be in uniform.

Under s. 1(2), the officer may dispose of *anything* surrendered to him/her in answer to the making of such a requirement. This wide discretionary power is not limited to alcohol and the officer could dispose of any other drink surrendered under this section (see HC Official Report SC C, 12 February 1997).

4.16.8.16   Failure to Surrender Items believed to be Alcohol

OFFENCE: **Failing to Surrender Alcohol—*Confiscation of Alcohol (Young Persons) Act 1997, s 1(3)***

     • Triable summarily • Fine

The Confiscation of Alcohol (Young Persons) Act 1997, s. 1 states:

(3) A person who fails without reasonable excuse to comply with a requirement imposed on him under subsection (1)or (1AA) commits an offence.

KEYNOTE

Where a constable imposes a requirement on a person under s. 1(1) or 1(1AA) (see para. 4.16.8.15), he/she must inform that person of his/her suspicion and that to fail without reasonable excuse to comply with such a requirement is an offence (s. 1(4)).

Under s. 1(6), a 'relevant place' is:

• any public place, other than licensed premises; or

• any place, other than a public place, to which that person has unlawfully gained access;

---

and for this purpose a place is a public place if, at the material time, the public or any section of the public has access to it—on payment or otherwise—as of right or by virtue of express or implied permission. Therefore the power may be exercised in any public place (as defined above) not being 'licensed premises'. It may also be exercised in any other place that is not a public place to which the person has gained access unlawfully. This second expression suggests that the person must, as a matter of fact, have gained access to the place unlawfully—as opposed to the officer simply 'suspecting' or 'believing' that to be the case. It also suggests that, if the person was originally in the place lawfully but was later asked to leave, the power would not apply as the person's access would not have been 'unlawfully gained'. The section does not provide the police officer with a power of entry or a power to search.

The 1997 Act provides a useful power which might be considered in relation to events such as parties and 'raves'.

4.16.8.17 Closure Notices for Persistently Selling Alcohol to Children

Section 169A of the Licensing Act 2003, provides that a senior police officer (of the rank of superintendent or higher), or an inspector of weights and measures, may give a closure notice where there is evidence that a person has committed the offence of persistently selling alcohol to children at the premises in question (**see para. 4.16.8.6**), and he/she considers that the evidence is such that there would be a realistic prospect of conviction if the offender was prosecuted for it. A closure notice can only be given within three months of the last offence (s. 169A(9)).

A closure notice will propose a prohibition on sales of alcohol at the premises in question for at least 48 hours but not more than 336 hours (s. 169A(4)), and will offer the opportunity to discharge all criminal liability in respect of the alleged offence by the acceptance of the prohibition proposed in the notice (s. 169A(2)). The premises licence holder will have fourteen days to decide whether or not to accept the proposed prohibition or to elect to be tried for the offence (s. 169A(4)). Where the licence holder decides to accept the prohibition, it must take effect not less than fourteen days after the date on which the notice was served at a time specified in the closure notice (s. 169A(5)).

A closure notice may be served on the premises to which it applies only by being handed by a constable or trading standards officer to a person on the premises who appears to the constable or trading standards officer to have control of or responsibility for the premises (s. 169A(7)). The closure notice can only be served at a time when licensable activities are being carried on at the premises.

4.16.9 Alcohol Consumption in Designated Public Places

The Criminal Justice and Police Act 2001 introduced a statutory framework to regulate the drinking of alcohol in certain public places and to reinforce existing licensing laws.

Home Office Circular 13/2007, *The Local Authorities (Alcohol Consumption in Designated Public Places) Regulations 2007*, provides guidance on the use of Designated Public Places Orders issued by local authorities.

4.16.9.1 Designated Public Places: Local Authority Order

The Criminal Justice and Police Act 2001, s. 13 states:

(1) A place is, subject to section 14, a designated public place if it is —
  (a) a public place in the area of a local authority; and
  (b) identified in an order made by that authority under subsection (2).
(2) A local authority may for the purposes of subsection (1) by order identify any public place in their area if they are satisfied that —

(a) nuisance or annoyance to members of the public or a section of the public; or

(b) disorder; has been associated with the consumption of alcohol in that place.

(3) The power conferred by subsection (2) includes power —

(a) to identify a place either specifically or by description;

(b) to revoke or amend orders previously made.

KEYNOTE

The expression 'has been associated' is a fairly loose one that does not appear to impose a particularly heavy burden on the local authority, which will clearly rely on evidence from the police in establishing whether such a situation exists.

Premises in respect of which a premises licence, club premises licence, or temporary event notice is in force cannot be designated public places for the purposes of this section. However, this only applies when alcohol is actually being sold or supplied in accordance with the licence or notice and for another 30 minutes thereafter (s. 14).

'Public place' means any place to which the public (or a section of the public) has access, on payment or otherwise, as of right or by virtue of any express or implied permission (s. 16(1)).

4.16.9.2   Police Powers

The Criminal Justice and Police Act 2001, s. 12 states:

(1) Subsection (2) applies if a constable reasonably believes that a person is, or has been, consuming in a designated public place or intends to consume in such a place.

(2) The constable may require the person concerned —

(a) not to consume in that place anything which is, or which the constable reasonably believes to be, alcohol;

(b) to surrender anything in his possession which is, or which the constable reasonably believes to be, alcohol or a container for alcohol.

(3) A constable may dispose of anything surrendered to him under subsection (2) in such manner as he considers appropriate.

KEYNOTE

A constable who imposes a requirement on a person under s. 12(2) must inform the person concerned that failing without reasonable excuse to comply with the requirement is an offence (s. 12(5)). There is no requirement for the constable imposing a requirement to be in uniform. The offence is a 'penalty offence' for the purposes of s. 1 of the 2001 Act.

4.16.9.3   Directions to Individuals who Represent a Risk of Disorder

The Violent Crime Reduction Act 2006 provides the police with a power to issue a direction to an individual to leave a locality to minimise the risk of alcohol-related crime or disorder arising and/or taking place. Section 27 of the Act states:

(1) If the test in subsection (2) is satisfied in the case of an individual aged 10 or over who is in a public place, a constable in uniform may give a direction to that individual—

(a) requiring him to leave the locality of that place; and

(b) prohibiting the individual from returning to that locality for such period (not exceeding 48 hours) from the giving of the direction as the constable may specify.

(2) That test is—

(a) that the presence of the individual in that locality is likely, in all the circumstances, to cause or to contribute to the occurrence of alcohol-related crime or disorder in that locality, or to cause or to contribute to a repetition or continuance there of such crime or disorder; and

(b) that the giving of a direction under this section to that individual is necessary for the purpose of removing or reducing the likelihood of there being such crime or disorder in that locality during the period for which the direction has effect or of there being a repetition or continuance in that locality during that period of such crime or disorder.

(3) A direction under this section—

    (a) must be given in writing;

    (b) may require the individual to whom it is given to leave the locality in question either imme-diately or by such time as the constable giving the direction may specify;

    (c) must clearly identify the locality to which it relates;

    (d) must specify the period for which the individual is prohibited from returning to that locality;

    (e) may impose requirements as to the manner in which that individual leaves the locality, in-cluding his route; and

    (f) may be withdrawn or varied (but not extended so as to apply for a period of more than 48 hours) by a constable.

KEYNOTE

A constable may not give a direction that prevents a person from having access to a place where he/she, resides or works, is attending education or training, receiving medical treatment, is under an obligation imposed under any enactment, or by the order of a court or tribunal (s. 27(4)).

A constable who gives a direction under this section may, if the constable reasonably suspects that the individual to whom it is given is aged under 16, remove the person to a place where the person resides or a place of safety (s. 27(4A).

The constable giving a direction must record the terms of the direction and locality to which it relates, the name of the person to whom it is given, the time it is given, and the specified period (s. 27(5)).

A person who fails to comply with a direction under this section is guilty of a summary offence (s. 27(6)).

4.16.9.4   Late Night Levy

Section 125 of the Police Reform and Social Responsibility Act 2011 introduced provisions for a Late Night Levy on licensed premises. The levy may be applied by a licensing authority in its area if it considers it desirable to raise revenue in relation to the costs of policing and other arrangements for the reduction or prevention of crime and disorder, in connection with the supply of alcohol between midnight and 6 am.

The period can be for any length of time within these parameters but must be the same every day. The levy is payable by the holders of premises licences or club premises certifi-cates which authorise the supply of alcohol during those hours.

The licensing authority is expected to consider the need for a levy with the chief officer of police and police and crime commissioner.

4.16.9.5   Drinking Banning Orders

The Violent Crime Reduction Act 2006 s. 1 provides for a civil order, a drinking banning order, which is designed to protect persons and their property from criminal or disorderly conduct by an individual while he/she is under the influence of alcohol.

Persons aged 16 or over who are responsible for alcohol-related disorder may be excluded from licensed premises in a defined geographic area for a given length of time under a drinking banning order. Other relevant prohibitions may also be included in the order. Such orders must be for not less than two months and not more than two years in duration.

OFFENCE: **Breach of a Drinking Banning Order—*Violent Crime Reduction Act 2006, s. 11(1)***

    • Triable summarily • Fine

The Violent Crime Reduction Act 2006, s. 11(1) states:

If the subject of a drinking banning order or of an interim order does, without reasonable excuse, anything that he is prohibited from doing by the order, he is guilty of an offence.

4.16.9.6 Early Morning Alcohol Restriction Orders

The Licensing Act 2003, ss. 172A–172E, gives licensing authorities the powers they need to effectively manage and police the night-time economy and take action against those premises that are causing problems.

These orders can be applied to areas between midnight and 6 am, where the licensing authority considers that restricting the late night supply of alcohol is appropriate to promote the licensing objectives.

The Licensing Act 2003 (Early Morning Alcohol Restriction Orders) Regulations 2012 (SI 2012/2551) prescribe the requirements in relation to the process for making an early morning alcohol restriction order and the kinds of premises that will be exempt from the orders.

4.16.10 Closure Orders for Licensed Premises

Further powers are provided by the Licensing Act 2003 to tackle disorder and disturbances connected with both licensed and unlicensed premises. These powers are relatively straightforward, and provide for the two distinct types of closure order outlined below.

4.16.10.1 Orders to Close Premises in Area Experiencing Disorder

The Licensing Act 2003, s.160 states:

(1) Where there is or is expected to be disorder in any local justice area, a magistrates' court acting in the area may make an order requiring all premises—
    (a) which are situated at or near the place of the disorder or expected disorder, and
    (b) in respect of which a premises licence or a temporary event notice has effect, to be closed for a period, not exceeding 24 hours, specified in the order.
(2) A magistrates' court may make an order under this section only on the application of a police officer who is of the rank of superintendent or above.
(3) A magistrates' court may not make such an order unless it is satisfied that it is necessary to prevent disorder.

OFFENCE: **Contravening Closure Order—*Licensing Act 2003, s. 160***

• Triable summarily • Fine

The Licensing Act 2003, s. 160 states:

(4) Where an order is made under this section, a person to whom subsection (5) applies commits an offence if he knowingly keeps any premises to which the order relates open, or allows any such premises to be kept open, during the period of the order.

(5) This subsection applies—

(a) to any manager of the premises,

(b) in the case of licensed premises, to—

(i) the holder of a premises licence in respect of the premises, and

(ii) the designated premises supervisor (if any) under such a licence, and

(c) in the case of premises in respect of which a temporary event notice has effect, to the premises user in relation to that notice.

KEYNOTE

Proof that the person acted *knowingly* is an essential element of this offence. Proof that the order was properly made and in force so far as that date and location were concerned will also be an essential part of any prosecution.

4.16.10.2   Closure Orders for Identified Premises

The Licensing Act 2003, s. 161 states:

(1) A senior police officer may make a closure order in relation to any relevant premises if he reasonably believes that—

(a) there is, or is likely imminently to be, disorder on, or in the vicinity of and related to, the premises and their closure is necessary in the interests of public safety, or

(b) a public nuisance is being caused by noise coming from the premises and the closure of the premises is necessary to prevent that nuisance.

KEYNOTE

A 'senior police officer' for this purpose is a police officer of, or above, the rank of inspector (s. 161(8)). In deciding whether to make a closure order, the police officer must have regard to the conduct of certain defined individuals at the premises. The purpose of this provision is to allow discretion in cases where, for example, it is clear that those managing the premises are treating the disorder or disturbance with sufficient gravity and are taking steps to reduce it or bring it under control (s. 161(3)).

This power can be used where disorder is happening or is likely *imminent* to be so. This differs from the power under s. 160 where the disorder is happening or *expected* to happen. The disorder must be on the premises or in the vicinity *and* related to them, and their closure is *necessary* in the interests of public safety. Also an order under this section can be made where a public nuisance is being caused by noise from the premises and their closure is necessary to prevent it.

The order requires the relevant premises be closed for a period not exceeding 24 hours (s. 161(2)). 'Relevant premises' means premises in respect of which a premises licence or a temporary event notice has effect (s. 161(8)).

The order comes into force at the time *any* constable gives notice of it to an appropriate person who is connected with any of the activities to which the disorder or nuisance relates (s. 161(5)). 'Appropriate person' includes any person who holds a premises licence in respect of the premises, any designated premises supervisor under such a licence, and a manager of the premises (s. 171(5)).

A closure order must specify the premises to which it relates, the period for which the premises are to be closed, the grounds on which it is made; and state the effects of the court and extension procedures under ss. 162–168 (s. 161(4)).

The senior police officer who made the order, or another designated senior police officer *must* cancel a closure order and any extension of it if he/she no longer reasonably believes that closure is necessary for the purposes under s. 161(1)(a) or (b) (see s. 163(2)).

A constable may use such force as may be necessary for the purposes of closing premises in compliance with a closure order (s. 169).

4.16.10.3 Extension of Closure Order

The Licensing Act 2003, s. 162 states:

(1) Where, before the end of the period for which relevant premises are to be closed under a closure order or any extension of it (the 'closure period'), the responsible senior police officer reasonably believes that—
   (a) a relevant magistrates' court will not have determined whether to exercise its powers under section 165(2) in respect of the closure order, and any extension of it, by the end of the closure period, and
   (b) the conditions for an extension are satisfied, he may extend the closure period for a further period not exceeding 24 hours beginning with the end of the previous closure period.

KEYNOTE

The conditions referred to in s. 162(1)(b) are:

- in the case of an order made under s. 161(1)(a), closure is necessary in the interests of public safety because of disorder or likely disorder on, or in the vicinity of and related to, the premises;
- in the case of an order made under s. 161(1)(b), closure is necessary to ensure that no public nuisance is, or is likely to be, caused by noise coming from the premises.

An extension in relation to any relevant premises comes into force when *any* constable gives notice of it to an appropriate person connected with any of the activities to which the disorder or nuisance relates or is expected to relate, but the extension does not come into force *unless the notice is given before the end of the previous closure period* (see s. 162(3) and (4)).

4.16.10.4 Application to Magistrates' Court by Police

The Licensing Act 2003, s. 164 states:

(1) The responsible senior police officer must, as soon as reasonably practicable after a closure order comes into force in respect of any relevant premises, apply to a relevant magistrates' court for it to consider the order and any extension of it.
(2) Where an application is made under this section in respect of licensed premises, the responsible senior officer must also notify the relevant licensing authority—
   (a) that a closure order has come into force,
   (b) of the contents of the order and of any extension of it, and
   (c) of the application under subsection (1).

KEYNOTE

As soon as reasonably practicable after receiving an application, the magistrates' court must hold a hearing to consider whether it is appropriate to exercise any of its relevant powers in relation to the closure order (or any extension), and decide whether to exercise them (s. 165(1)). Generally, the court has powers to revoke the order, to add conditions or exceptions to it, or to leave the order in place until it has carried out a review of the order under s. 167. Any person aggrieved by a decision of a magistrates' court under s. 165 may appeal to the Crown Court against the decision (s. 166).

The Act makes extensive provisions for the review of closure orders and poses a number of obligations on the courts and the licensing authorities in this regard. In particular, the authority must reach a determination on the review no later than 28 days after receiving notification of a closure order from the court (s. 167).

4.16.10.5 Contravening Closure Order

OFFENCE: **Contravening Closure Order—*Licensing Act 2003, s. 161 and s. 165***
- Triable summarily • s. 161(6) offence—fine • s. 165(7) offence—three months' imprisonment and/or a fine

The Licensing Act 2003, s. 161 states:

(6) A person commits an offence if, without reasonable excuse, he permits relevant premises to be open in contravention of a closure order or any extension of it.

The Licensing Act 2003, s. 165 states:

(7) A person commits an offence if, without reasonable excuse, he permits relevant premises to be open in contravention of a magistrates' court order.

KEYNOTE

There is no requirement for the defendant to have acted *knowingly* here, only that he/she acted without reasonable excuse in permitting the premises to be open. Proof that the order was properly made (either by the police or the court), and in force so far as that date and location were concerned, will be critical.

Clearly there are practical reasons why certain people will need to be allowed to come and go from the premises. The legislation takes account of this and specifies when premises will be regarded as being open. Basically, relevant premises are 'open' if someone other than a person who works at, manages, holds a licence for or usually lives at the premises enters the premises and buys or is otherwise supplied with food, drink or anything usually sold on the premises, or while on the premises, the premises are used for the provision of regulated entertainment (s. 171(2)).

4.16.10.6 Closure Notices for Unlicensed Premises

The Criminal Justice and Police Act 2001, s. 19 states:

(1) Where a constable is satisfied that any premises are being, or within the last 24 hours have been, used for the unauthorised sale of alcohol for consumption on, or in the vicinity of, the premises, he may serve under subsection (3) a notice in respect of the premises.

(2) Where a local authority is satisfied that any premises in the area of the authority are being, or within the last 24 hours have been, used for the unauthorised sale of alcohol for consumption on, or in the vicinity of, the premises, the authority may serve under subsection (3) a notice in respect of the premises.

(3) A notice under subsection (1) or (2) ('a closure notice') shall be served by the constable or local authority concerned on a person having control of, or responsibility for, the activities carried on at the premises.

(4) A closure notice shall also be served by the constable or local authority concerned on any person occupying another part of any building or other structure of which the premises form part if the constable or (as the case may be) the local authority concerned reasonably believes, at the time of serving notice under subsection (3), that the person's access to the other part of the building or other structure would be impeded if an order under section 21 providing for the closure of the premises were made.

(5) A closure notice may also be served by a constable or the local authority concerned on—
   (a) any other person having control of, or responsibility for, the activities carried on at the premises;
   (b) any person who has an interest in the premises.

KEYNOTE

The power provided by this section is available to any police officer irrespective of rank.

The closure notice must specify the alleged use of the premises, the grounds on which it has been issued, the steps that are required to be taken to ensure that the alleged use of the premises ceases or does not recur, and state the effects of s. 20 (s. 19(6)).

Where a closure notice has been served under s. 19(3), a constable or the local authority concerned may make a complaint to a justice of the peace for a closure order (s. 20(1)). The complaint must be made not less than seven days, and not more than six months, after the service of the closure notice (s. 20(2)). However, a complaint cannot be made under this subsection if the constable or the local authority is satisfied that the use of the premises for the unauthorised sale of alcohol for consumption on, or in the vicinity of, the premises has ceased, and there is no reasonable likelihood that the premises will be so used in the future (s. 20(3)).

Where a closure order is made by the court a constable or authorised person may enter the premises, if necessary using reasonable force, at any reasonable time to do anything necessary to secure compliance with the order (s. 25(1)). The constable or authorised person must produce identification if so required by the owner, occupier or person in charge of the premises (s. 25(2)). Intentionally obstructing a constable or authorised person is a summary offence (s. 25(3)). Permitting premises to be open in contravention of the order is an offence (s. 25(4), as is failing to comply with a closure order generally (s. 25(5)).

4.16.11   Keeping of Smuggled Goods

OFFENCE: **Keeping of Smuggled Goods—*Licensing Act 2003, s. 144***

> • Triable summarily • Fine

The Licensing Act 2003, s. 144 states:

(1) A person to whom subsection (2) applies commits an offence if he knowingly keeps or allows to be kept, on any relevant premises, any goods which have been imported without payment of duty or which have otherwise been unlawfully imported.

(2) This subsection applies—

  (a) to any person who works at the premises in a capacity, whether paid or unpaid, which gives him authority to prevent the keeping of the goods on the premises,

  (b) in the case of licensed premises, to—

   (i) the holder of a premises licence in respect of the premises, and

   (ii) the designated premises supervisor (if any) under such a licence,

  (c) in the case of premises in respect of which a club premises certificate has effect, to any member or officer of the club which holds the certificate who is present on the premises at any time when the goods are kept on the premises in a capacity which enables him to prevent them being so kept, and

  (d) in the case of premises which may be used for a permitted temporary activity by virtue of Part 5, to the premises user in relation to the temporary event notice in question.

KEYNOTE

This offence was primarily created in an attempt to control the influx of tobacco and alcohol products on which the relevant duty had not been paid, but it is far wider than that.

The requirement that the defendant acted *knowingly* is an essential element of this offence.

The court by which a person is convicted of this offence may order the goods in question (and any container for them) to be forfeited and either destroyed or dealt with in such other manner as the court may order (s. 144(4)).

4.17 Offences and Powers Relating to Information

4.17.1 Introduction

This chapter examines the provisions of the Freedom of Information Act 2000, Computer Misuse Act 1990, Data Protection Act 1998 and the Regulation of Investigatory Powers Act 2000.

4.17.1.1 Access to Information Held by Public Authorities

The Freedom of Information Act 2000, s. 1 provides for the general right of access to information held by public authorities, and states:

> (1) Any person making a request for information to a public authority is entitled—
>   (a) to be informed in writing by the public authority whether it holds information of the description specified in the request, and
>   (b) if that is the case, to have that information communicated to him.

KEYNOTE

Public authorities for the purposes of this section include the police, the CPS and government departments, along with national health service bodies, schools and colleges (s. 3 and sch. 1). These public authorities are required to adopt and maintain a publication scheme and to publish information in accordance with it that sets out their specific plans for making certain types of information available (s. 19).

Requests for information must be in writing, state the name of the applicant and an address for correspondence, and describe the information requested (s. 8(1)). A request is to be treated as made in writing where the text of the request is transmitted by electronic means, is received in legible form, and is capable of being used for subsequent reference (s.8(2)). A fee may be charged for complying with the request (s. 9). Generally, a public authority must comply with a request for information promptly and in any event not later than the twentieth working day following the date of receipt (s. 10).

A number of exemptions and qualifications are imposed by the Act on the general 'right to know' and these usually arise due to the nature or the quantity of the material sought or the excessive costs involved in providing the information.

The Act creates the role of Information Commissioner (s. 18), and places a duty on the Commissioner to promote good practice by public authorities and promote the observance of the requirements of the Act and the codes of practice (s. 47).

The Freedom of Information Code of Practice, issued on 17 July 2013 under s. 45 of the Act, sets out the practices which public authorities should follow when dealing with requests for information under the Act and is available at http://www.justice.gov.uk/information-access-rights/foi-guidance-for-practitioners/code-of-practice.

4.17.1.2 Duty to Share Information

Under the provisions of the Criminal Justice Act 2003, a number of public agencies have a duty to share information in relation to violent or dangerous offenders.

This duty arises under the Multi-Agency Public Protection Arrangements (MAPPAs), the primary obligations of which are imposed on 'responsible authorities'. These authorities are the chief officer of police, the local probation board and the Home Secretary (see s. 325(1)).

The primary duty is for the responsible authority to establish arrangements, in co-operation with other listed bodies, for the purpose of assessing and managing risks posed by those convicted of certain violent or sexual offences. Those other listed bodies include youth offending teams, local education and housing authorities, NHS authorities and some registered social landlords.

MAPPAs involve the sharing of information about offenders across agencies, though due regard needs to be given to other legislative requirements such as the Data Protection Act 1998. Statutory guidance is issued by the Secretary of State under s. 325(8) of the 2003 Act: MAPPA Guidance Version 4 2012 available on the Ministry of Justice website (http://www.justice.gov.uk).

4.17.2 Offences under the Computer Misuse Act 1990

The Computer Misuse Act 1990 was enacted to address the growth in the use of computers and the inadequacy of the existing legislation in dealing with offences involving computers, such as 'hacking'.

The Police and Justice Act 2006 amended the 1990 Act to ensure the United Kingdom's compliance with the European Union Framework Decision on Attacks Against Information Systems. This compliance requires that penalties relating to 'hacking' into computer systems, unauthorised access to computer material, and the intentional serious hindering of a computer system, reflect the seriousness of the criminal activities that can be involved in committing these offences.

4.17.2.1 Unauthorised Access to Computer Materials

OFFENCE: **Unauthorised Access to Computer Material ('Hacking')—*Computer Misuse Act 1990, s. 1***
- Triable either way • Two years' imprisonment and/or a fine on indictment
- Six months' imprisonment and/or a fine summarily

The Computer Misuse Act 1990, s. 1 states:

(1) A person is guilty of an offence if—
- (a) he causes a computer to perform any function with intent to secure access to any program or data held in any computer, or to enable any such access to be secured;
- (b) the access he intends to secure, or to enable to be secured, is unauthorised; and
- (c) he knows at the time when he causes the computer to perform the function that that is the case.
(2) The intent a person has to have to commit an offence under this section need not be directed at—
- (a) any particular program or data;
- (b) a program or data of any particular kind; or
- (c) a program or data held in any particular computer.

KEYNOTE

This offence involves 'causing a computer to perform any function', which means more than simply looking at material on a screen or having any physical contact with computer hardware. In the latter case an offence of criminal damage may be appropriate. Any attempt to log on would involve getting the computer to perform a function (even if the function is to deny you access!). 'Computer' is not defined and therefore must be given its ordinary meaning. Given the multiple functions of many electronic devices such as mobile phones, this could arguably bring them within the ambit of the Act.

Any access must be 'unauthorised'. If the defendant is authorised to *access* a computer, albeit for restricted purposes, then it was originally held that he/she did not commit this offence if he/she then *used* any information for some other unauthorised purpose (e.g. police officers using data from the Police National Computer

(PNC) for private gain (*DPP* v *Bignell* [1998] 1 Cr App R 1)). However, this case was overruled by the House of Lords where an employee of American Express accessed accounts that fell outside her normal scope of work and passed on the information to credit card forgers. Their Lordships held that, although she was authorised to access certain data generally, she was not authorised to access the specific data involved—*R* v *Bow Street Metropolitan Stipendiary Magistrate, ex parte Government of the USA* [2000] 2 AC 216. This case still illustrates that the purpose of the Act is to address unauthorised access as opposed to unauthorised use of data and behaviour such as looking over a computer operator's shoulder to read what is on the screen would not be covered.

In order to prove the offence under s. 1 you must show that the defendant intended to secure access to the program or data. This is therefore an offence of 'specific intent' and lesser forms of *mens rea* such as recklessness will not do.

You must also show that the defendant knew the access was unauthorised.

The Privacy and Electronic Communications (EC Directive) Regulations 2003 (SI 2003/2426) regulate the use of cookies and Internet tracking devices, along with the use of unsolicited email and text messages. Guidance in their extent and practical effect is prepared by the Office of the Information Commissioner.

The powers of entry, search and seizure under the Police and Criminal Evidence Act 1984 apply to this offence.

4.17.2.2 Definition of Terms

The 1990 Act defines a number of its terms at s. 17 which states:

(2) A person secures access to any program or data held in a computer if by causing a computer to perform any function he—
  (a) alters or erases the program or data;
  (b) copies or moves it to any storage medium other than that in which it is held or to a different location in the storage medium in which it is held;
  (c) uses it; or
  (d) has it output from the computer in which it is held (whether by having it displayed or in any other manner);
and references to access to a program or data (and to an intent to secure such access or to enable such access to be secured) shall be read accordingly.

(3) For the purposes of subsection (2)(c) above a person uses a program if the function he causes the computer to perform—
  (a) causes the program to be executed; or
  (b) is itself a function of the program.

(4) For the purposes of subsection (2)(d) above—
  (a) a program is output if the instructions of which it consists are output; and
  (b) the form in which any such instructions or any other data is output (and in particular whether or not it represents a form in which, in the case of instructions, they are capable of being executed or, in the case of data, it is capable of being processed by a computer) is immaterial.

(5) Access of any kind by any person to any program or data held in a computer is unauthorised if—
  (a) he is not himself entitled to control access of the kind in question to the program or data; and
  (b) he does not have consent to access by him of the kind in question to the program or data from any person who is so entitled,
but this subsection is subject to section 10.

(6) References to any program or data held in a computer include references to any program or data held in any removable storage medium which is for the time being in the computer; and a computer is to be regarded as containing any program or data held in any such medium.
  ...

(8) An act done in relation to a computer is unauthorised if the person doing the act (or causing it to be done)—
  (a) is not himself a person who has responsibility for the computer and is entitled to determine whether the act may be done; and
  (b) does not have consent to the act from any such person.
In this subsection 'act' includes a series of acts.

4.17.2.3   Unauthorised Access to Computers with Intent

OFFENCE: **Unauthorised Access with Intent to Commit Further Offences—** *Computer Misuse Act 1990, s. 2*
- Triable either way • Five years' imprisonment and/or a fine on indictment
- Six months' imprisonment and/or a fine summarily

The Computer Misuse Act 1990, s. 2 states:

(1) A person is guilty of an offence under this section if he commits an offence under section 1 above ('the unauthorised access offence') with intent—
   (a) to commit an offence to which this section applies; or
   (b) to facilitate the commission of such an offence (whether by himself or by any other person); and the offence he intends to commit or facilitate is referred to below in this section as the further offence.
(2) This section applies to offences—
   (a) for which the sentence is fixed by law; or
   (b) for which a person of twenty-one years of age or over (not previously convicted) may be sentenced to imprisonment for a term of five years (or, in England and Wales, might be so sentenced but for the restrictions imposed by section 33 of the Magistrates' Courts Act 1980).
(3) It is immaterial for the purposes of this section whether the further offence is to be committed on the same occasion as the unauthorised access offence or on any future occasion.
(4) A person may be guilty of an offence under this section even though the facts are such that the commission of the further offence is impossible.

4.17.2.4   Unauthorised Acts with Intent to Impair Operation of Computer, etc.

OFFENCE: **Unauthorised Acts with Intent to Impair, or with Recklessness as to Impairing, Operation of Computer, etc.—***Computer Misuse Act 1990, s. 3*
- Triable either way • 10 years' imprisonment and/or a fine on indictment
- 12 months' imprisonment and/or a fine summarily

The Computer Misuse Act 1990, s. 3 states:

(1) A person is guilty of an offence if—
    (a) he does any unauthorised act in relation to a computer;
    (b) at the time when he does the act he knows that it is unauthorised; and
    (c) either subsection (2) or subsection (3) below applies.
(2) This subsection applies if the person intends by doing the act—
    (a) to impair the operation of any computer;
    (b) to prevent or hinder access to any program or data held in any computer; or
    (c) to impair the operation of any such program or the reliability of any such data.
(3) This subsection applies if the person is reckless as to whether the act will do any of the things mentioned in paragraphs (a) to (c) of subsection (2) above.

KEYNOTE

This section is designed to ensure that adequate provision is made to criminalise all forms of denial of service attacks in which the attacker denies the victim(s) access to a particular resource, typically by preventing legitimate users of a service accessing that service. An example of this is where a former employee, acting on a grudge, impaired the operation of a company's computer by using a program to generate and send 5 million emails to the company (*DPP* v *Lennon* [2006] EWHC 1201 (Admin)).

The seriousness of this offence is displayed in the fact that the sentencing for s. 3 is 10 years' imprisonment on indictment.

The intention referred to in s. 3(2), or the recklessness referred to in s. 3(3), need not relate to any particular computer, any particular program or data, or a program or data of any particular kind (s. 3(4)). An 'unauthorised act' can include a series of acts, and a reference to impairing, preventing or hindering something includes a reference to doing so temporarily (s. 3(5)).

The 'serious hindering' provided by this section is intended to cover programs that generate denial of service attacks, or malicious code such as viruses.

Causing a computer to record that information came from one source when it in fact came from another clearly affects the reliability of that information for the purposes of s. 3(2)(c) (*Zezev* v *USA*; *Yarimaka* v *Governor of HM Prison Brixton* [2002] EWHC 589 (Admin)).

4.17.2.5   Making, Supplying or Obtaining Articles for Use in Offences under sections 1 or 3

OFFENCE: **Making, Supplying or Obtaining Articles for Use in Offences under sections 1 or 3—*Computer Misuse Act 1990, s. 3A***
- Triable either way   • Two years' imprisonment and/or a fine on indictment
- 12 months' imprisonment and/or a fine summarily

The Computer Misuse Act 1990, s. 3A states:

(1) A person is guilty of an offence if he makes, adapts, supplies or offers to supply any article intending it to be used to commit, or to assist in the commission of, an offence under section 1 or 3.
(2) A person is guilty of an offence if he supplies or offers to supply any article believing that it is likely to be used to commit, or to assist in the commission of, an offence under section 1 or 3.
(3) A person is guilty of an offence if he obtains any article with a view to its being supplied for use to commit, or to assist in the commission of, an offence under section 1 or 3.
(4) In this section 'article' includes any program or data held in electronic form.

KEYNOTE

This section creates three offences designed to combat the growing market in electronic tools, such as 'hacker tools' which can be used for hacking into computer systems, and the increase in the use of such tools in connection with organised crime. These offences comply with Article 6(1)(a) of the 2001 Council of Europe

---

Cybercrime Convention requiring the criminalisation of the distribution or making available of a device, program or computer password or similar data by which a computer system is capable of being accessed with the intention to commit an offence.

4.17.3 The Data Protection Act 1998

The Data Protection Act 1998 brought UK law into line with the European Union Data Protection Directive 95/46/EC that requires Member States to protect people's fundamental rights and freedoms and in particular their right to privacy with respect to the processing of personal data.

The 1998 Act is intended to strike a balance between the rights of individuals to privacy and the ability of organisations to use data for the purposes of their business. It introduced basic rules of registration for users of data and rights of access to that data for the individuals to which it related.

Data protection law applies whenever a data controller processes personal data. A data controller is the person who determines the purposes for which, and the manner in which, any personal data is, or is likely to be, processed (s. 1(1)). A typical example of a data controller is an employer. The data controller must register with the Information Commissioner who has overall responsibility to ensure that personal data is protected in observance with the Act.

The Information Commissioner provides guidance and information, resolves complaints, and prosecutes those who commit offences under the Act. The DPP may also prosecute offences or give consent to such prosecutions.

4.17.3.1 Personal Data

The Data Protection Act 1998, s. 1 states:

(1) In this Act, unless the context otherwise requires— 'data' means information which—
  (a) is being processed by means of equipment operating automatically in response to instructions given for that purpose,
  (b) is recorded with the intention that it should be processed by means of such equipment,
  (c) is recorded as part of a relevant filing system or with the intention that it should form part of a relevant filing system, or
  (d) does not fall within paragraph (a), (b) or (c) but forms part of an accessible record as defined by section 68, or
  (e) is recorded information held by a public authority and does not fall within any of paragraphs (a) to (d).

The 1998 Act seeks to protect 'personal data', that is,

data which relate to a living individual who can be identified, (a) from those data, or (b) from those data and other information which is in the possession of, or is likely to come into the possession of, the data controller, and includes any expression of opinion about the individual and any indication of the intentions of the data controller or any other person in respect of the individual (s. 1(1)).

KEYNOTE

In *Johnson v Medical Defence Union Ltd (No. 2)* [2007] EWCA Civ 262 it was held that the compilation of information from various manual and electronic files in a computer-related document is not necessarily the creation of data capable of being processed under s. 1(1).

The individual must be capable of being identified from the data that the data controller has or is likely to get. This does not mean that the person's name and/or address must be known. If it is possible to distinguish the individual from other people (e.g. by email addresses which contain the person's name or from CCTV film of that person) then it may be that the above test is satisfied.

Data controllers must give data subjects the right of access to their personal data. An individual may request access to all personal data of which he/she is the subject and which is being processed by the data controller. There are exemptions from these access rules in certain limited circumstances.

'Personal data' means data which relates to a living individual who can be identified from those data, or from those data and other information which are in the possession of, or are likely to come into the possession of, the data controller. It includes any expression of opinion about the individual and any indication of the intentions of the data controller or any other person in respect of the individual.

The definition of personal data would apply to data held on police computers about suspected and convicted offenders and may well apply to other similar paper records. Personal data held on the PNC clearly falls within this category (see *R* v *Rees* [2000] LTL 20 October).

4.17.3.2 Sensitive Personal Data

The 1998 Act makes special provision in relation to 'sensitive personal data' which it defines (at s. 2) as:

personal data consisting of information as to—
(a) the racial or ethnic origin of the data subject,
(b) his political opinions,
(c) his religious beliefs or other beliefs of a similar nature,
(d) whether he is a member of a trade union (within the meaning of the Trade Union and Labour Relations (Consolidation) Act 1992),
(e) his physical or mental health or condition,
(f) his sexual life,
(g) the commission or alleged commission by him of any offence, or
(h) any proceedings for any offence committed or alleged to have been committed by him, the disposal of such proceedings or the sentence of any court in such proceedings.

KEYNOTE

Data controllers are not permitted to process sensitive data about an individual unless: the processing is in connection with current or prospective legal proceedings or consultations; or is in the substantial public interest; or the explicit, informed and freely given consent of the individual has been obtained. This consent of the individual must be in writing, he/she must be informed of what information is to be processed, and no detriment must be suffered by an individual refusing to give consent.

4.17.3.3 Data Protection Principles

A crucial element in the 1998 Act is the data protection principles set out at sch. 1. As well as introducing the principles, s. 4(4) makes it clear that it is the duty of the relevant 'data controller' to comply with those principles wherever they apply. Part I of sch. 1 sets out the principles as being:

1. Personal data shall be processed fairly and lawfully and, in particular, shall not be processed unless—
   (a) at least one of the conditions in Schedule 2 is met, and
   (b) in the case of sensitive personal data, at least one of the conditions in Schedule 3 is also met.
2. Personal data shall be obtained only for one or more specified and lawful purposes, and shall not be further processed in any manner incompatible with that purpose or those purposes.
3. Personal data shall be adequate, relevant and not excessive in relation to the purpose or purposes for which they are processed.
4. Personal data shall be accurate and, where necessary, kept up to date.
5. Personal data processed for any purpose or purposes shall not be kept for longer than is necessary for that purpose or those purposes.
6. Personal data shall be processed in accordance with the rights of data subjects under this Act.
7. Appropriate technical and organisational measures shall be taken against unauthorised or unlawful processing of personal data and against accidental loss or destruction of, or damage to, personal data.

8. Personal data shall not be transferred to a country or territory outside the European Economic Area unless that country or territory ensures an adequate level of protection for the rights and freedoms of data subjects in relation to the processing of personal data.

KEYNOTE

Under the first data protection principle, a data controller must justify its processing of personal data under one of the following conditions:

- the data subject has given his/her consent to the processing;
- the processing is necessary for the performance of a contract or the entering into of a contract to which the data subject is a party;
- the processing is necessary for compliance with any legal obligation to which the data controller is subject;
- the processing is necessary in order to protect the vital interests of the data subject;
- the processing is necessary for the administration of justice; or
- the processing is necessary for the purposes of legitimate interests pursued by the data controller provided such processing does not harm the rights and freedoms or legitimate interests of data subjects.

The 1998 Act creates certain offences from the first data protection principle. Section 55 of the Act provides that a person must not knowingly or recklessly, without the consent of the data controller, obtain or disclose data or the information contained in personal data, or procure its disclosure to another person (s. 55(1)). However, this subsection does not apply where the obtaining, disclosing or procuring was necessary for the purpose of preventing or detecting crime (s. 55(2)(a)). In *R (On the Application of Catt)* v *ACPO* [2013] EWCA Civ 192, it was held that the personal information relating to the appellant held on the National Domestic Extremism Database was in breach of Article 8 of the European Convention on Human Rights (Right to respect for privacy and family life). For many years the appellant had been an ardent and frequent protestor against what he saw as a variety of forms of injustice. The appellant's entry on the database arose from his attendance at protests where he associated with those who have a propensity to violence and crime. However, he personally had never been the specific target of any observations and it was not suggested that he indulged in criminal activity or actively encouraged those that do.

Other exemptions from subs. (1) are contained within s. 55.

4.17.4 The Regulation of Investigatory Powers Act 2000

The Regulation of Investigatory Powers Act 2000, or 'RIPA' as it is commonly known, is the law governing the use of covert techniques by public authorities. It requires that when the police or other law enforcement bodies (e.g. the Serious Fraud Office or the National Crime Agency (NCA)), the security and intelligence services (MI5, MI6 and GCHQ), as well as a large number of other public bodies, including local government, need to use covert techniques to obtain private information about someone, they do it in a way that is necessary, proportionate, and compatible with human rights. Surveillance measures necessarily involve some interference with private life, but have the legitimate aim of protecting national security and economic well-being (*Kennedy* v *United Kingdom* (2011) 52 EHRR 4).

Part II of the 2000 Act and associated Codes of Practice apply to actions such as:

- intercepting communications, such as the content of telephone calls, emails or letters;
- acquiring communications data: the 'who, when and where' of communications, such as telephone billing or subscriber details;
- conducting covert surveillance, either in private premises or vehicles (intrusive surveillance) or in public places (directed surveillance);
- the use of covert human intelligence sources, such as informants or undercover officers;
- access to electronic data protected by encryption or passwords.

In a policing context, any breach of the Act's provisions, or the provisions contained in the Codes of Practice, issued by the Secretary of State under s. 71, can have three main consequences:

- any evidence obtained may be excluded by a court or tribunal as being unfair;
- proceedings may be taken under the relevant police conduct regulations; or
- a person may make a claim before the Investigatory Powers Tribunal.

4.17.4.1 Surveillance and Covert Human Intelligence Sources

The Regulation of Investigatory Powers Act 2000, s. 26 provides:

(1) This Part applies to the following conduct—
    (a) directed surveillance;
    (b) intrusive surveillance; and
    (c) the conduct and use of covert human intelligence sources.

KEYNOTE

Although only the third of these expressly uses the word 'covert' for the nature of the activity, it is relevant to *all three* of these areas. Part II is concerned with *covert* activity and so, as a general rule, if it is not covert, it is not covered.

Some law enforcement activities fall outside the scope of the Act—an example is 'property interference' which is a very intrusive form of intelligence gathering such as attaching listening devices within people's homes. This type of activity is covered by part III of the Police Act 1997 and is beyond the scope of this Manual.

4.17.4.2 Covert Human Intelligence Sources (CHIS): Definition

The following is an extract from the Covert Human Intelligence Sources Code of Practice, Chapter 2, which states:

Definition of a covert human intelligence source (CHIS)
  2.1 Under the 2000 Act, a person is a CHIS if:
    (a) he establishes or maintains a personal or other relationship with a person for the covert purpose of facilitating the doing of anything falling within paragraph b) or c);
    (b) he covertly uses such a relationship to obtain information or to provide access to any information to another person; or
    (c) he covertly discloses information obtained by the use of such a relationship or as a consequence of the existence of such a relationship.
    See section 26(8) of the 2000 Act.
  2.2 A relationship is established or maintained for a covert purpose if and only if it is conducted in a manner that is calculated to ensure that one of the parties to the relationship is unaware of the purpose.
    See section 26(9)(b) of the 2000 Act for full definition.
  2.3 A relationship is used covertly, and information obtained is disclosed covertly, if and only if the relationship is used or the information is disclosed in a manner that is calculated to ensure that one of the parties to the relationship is unaware of the use or disclosure in question.
    See section 26(9)(c) of the 2000 Act for full definition.

KEYNOTE

A purpose is 'covert' here only if the relationship (and the subsequent disclosure of information) is conducted in a manner that is calculated to ensure that one of the parties is unaware of that purpose. Therefore the definition would not usually apply to members of the public generally supplying information to the police. Similarly, people who have come across information in the ordinary course of their jobs who suspect criminal activity (such as bank staff, local authority employees, etc.) do not have a covert relationship with the police simply by passing on information.

Great care will be needed, however, if the person supplying the information is asked by the police to do something further in order to develop or enhance it. Any form of direction or tasking by the police in this way could make the person a CHIS and thereby attract all the statutory provisions and safeguards.

Practically, there are two broad areas to be considered when considering covert human intelligence sources: the 'use' of a CHIS and 'conduct' as a CHIS. Both areas are strictly controlled by the legislation and require the relevant authorisation if they are to be lawful. The 'use' of a CHIS involves any action on behalf of a public authority to induce, ask or assist a person to engage in the conduct of a CHIS, or to obtain information by means of the conduct of a CHIS (s. 26(7)(b)). The conduct of a CHIS is any conduct of a CHIS which falls within para. 2.1 above, that is, steps taken by the CHIS on behalf, or at the request, of a public authority (s. 26(7)(a)). Most CHIS authorisations will be for both use and conduct as public authorities usually task the CHIS to under-take covert action, and because the CHIS will be expected to take action in relation to the public authority, such as responding to particular tasking.

Generally, covertly recording conversations and other personal information about a particular person will amount to some form of 'surveillance' (and therefore will be governed by the strict rules regulating such op-erations). However, such use of a CHIS will not amount to 'surveillance' (s. 48(3)).

Note that, apart from the many other considerations of using a CHIS, the police owe a duty to take reason-able care to avoid unnecessary disclosure to the general public of information which a CHIS has provided (*Swinney* v *Chief Constable of Northumbria (No. 2)* (1999) 11 Admin LR 811).

4.17.4.3   CHIS: General Rules on Authorisations

In relation to the authorisation of a CHIS by the police the Regulation of Investigatory Powers Act 2000, s. 29 states:

(1) Subject to the following provisions of this Part, the persons designated for the purposes of this section shall each have power to grant authorisations for the conduct or the use of a covert human intelligence source.

(2) A person shall not grant an authorisation for the conduct or the use of a covert human intelli-gence source unless he believes—

(a) that the authorisation is necessary on grounds falling within subsection (3);

(b) that the authorised conduct or use is proportionate to what is sought to be achieved by that conduct or use; and

(c) that arrangements exist for the source's case that satisfy—

(i) the requirements of subsection (4A), in the case of a source of a relevant collaborative unit;

. . .

(iii) the requirements of subsection (5), in the case of any other source;

and that satisfy such other requirements as may be imposed by order made by the Secretary of State.

(3) An authorisation is necessary on grounds falling within this subsection if it is necessary—

(a) in the interests of national security;

(b) for the purpose of preventing or detecting crime or of preventing disorder;

(c) in the interests of the economic well-being of the United Kingdom;

(d) in the interests of public safety;

(e) for the purpose of protecting public health;

(f) for the purpose of assessing or collecting any tax, duty, levy or other imposition, contribu-tion or charge payable to a government department; or

(g) for any purpose (not falling within paragraphs (a) to (f)) which is specified for the purposes of this subsection by an order made by the Secretary of State.

KEYNOTE

Note that in relation to s. 29(3)(b), preventing and detecting crime is defined in s. 81(5) and goes beyond the prosecution of offenders and includes actions taken to avert, end or disrupt the commission of criminal offences.

The following extract from the Covert Human Intelligence Sources Code of Practice, Chapter 3, explains the terms 'necessary' and 'proportionate' contained within s. 29(2):

Necessity and Proportionality

3.2 The 2000 Act stipulates that the authorising officer must believe that an authorisation for the use or conduct of a CHIS is necessary in the circumstances of the particular case for one or more of the statutory grounds listed in section 29(3) of the 2000 Act.

3.3 If the use or conduct of the CHIS is deemed necessary, on one of more of the statutory grounds, the person granting the authorisation must also believe that it is proportionate to what is sought to be achieved by carrying it out. This involves balancing the seriousness of the intrusion into the private or family life of the subject of the operation (or any other person who may be affected) against the need for the activity in investigative and operational terms.

3.4 The authorisation will not be proportionate if it is excessive in the overall circumstances of the case. Each action authorised should bring an expected benefit to the investigation or operation and should not be disproportionate or arbitrary. The fact that a suspected offence may be serious will not alone render the use or conduct of a CHIS proportionate. Similarly, an offence may be so minor that any deployment of a CHIS would be disproportionate. No activity should be considered proportionate if the information, which is sought, could reasonably be obtained by other less intrusive means.

3.5 The following elements of proportionality should therefore be considered:

- balancing the size and scope of the proposed activity against the gravity and extent of the perceived crime or offence;
- explaining how and why the methods to be adopted will cause the least possible intrusion on the subject and others;
- considering whether the activity is an appropriate use of the legislation and a reasonable way, having considered all reasonable alternatives, of obtaining the necessary result;
- evidencing, as far as reasonably practicable, what other methods had been considered and why they were not implemented.

Authorising officers are also required to take into account collateral intrusion, namely, the risk of interference with the private and family life of persons who are not the intended subjects of the CHIS activity. They will also need to be aware of any particular sensitivities in the local community. Consideration should also be given to any adverse impact on community confidence or safety that may result from the use or conduct of a CHIS or use of information obtained from that CHIS.

4.17.4.4   CHIS: Authorisation Procedures

The regulatory framework sets out specific conditions in relation to the deployment of different types of CHIS, from undercover operatives who change their entire identity to infiltrate criminal organisations, to 'decoys' that have no direct communication with suspects.

The following extract from the Covert Human Intelligence Sources Code of Practice, Chapter 5, outlines authorisation procedures for the use or conduct of a CHIS:

Authorisation Procedures

5.4 Responsibility for authorising the use or conduct of a CHIS rests with the authorising officer and all authorisations require the personal authority of the authorising officer. The Regulation of Investigatory Powers (Directed Surveillance and Covert Human Intelligence Sources) Order 2010 designates the authorising officer for each different public authority and the officers entitled to act only in urgent cases. In certain circumstances the Secretary of State will be the authorising officer (see section 30(2) of the 2000 Act).

5.5 The authorising officer must give authorisations in writing, except in urgent cases, where they may be given orally. In such cases, a statement that the authorising officer has expressly authorised the action should be recorded in writing by the applicant (or the person with whom the authorising officer spoke) as a priority. This statement need not contain the full detail of the application, which should however subsequently be recorded in writing when reasonably practicable (generally the next working day).

5.6 Other officers entitled to act in urgent cases may only give authorisation in writing...

5.7 A case is not normally to be regarded as urgent unless the time that would elapse before the authorising officer was available to grant the authorisation would, in the judgment of the person giving the authorisation, be likely to endanger life or jeopardise the operation or investigation for which the authorisation was being given. An authorisation is not to be regarded as urgent where the need for an authorisation has been neglected or the urgency is of the applicant's or authorising officer's own making.

KEYNOTE

Authorising officers should, where possible, be independent of the investigation. However, it is recognised that this is not always possible, especially in the cases of small organisations, or where it is necessary to act urgently or for security reasons.

The Regulation of Investigatory Powers (Directed Surveillance and Covert Human Intelligence Sources) Order 2010 (SI 210/521, as amended by SI 2013/2788) prescribes the ranks of those within the police service and the NCA who can authorize a CHIS. The relevant rank of an authorising officer for a CHIS is an assistant chief constable/commander or in urgent cases a superintendent. For the NCA it is a deputy director or in urgent cases a grade 2 senior manager. Such authorisations cease to have effect after 12 months, or in urgent cases will, unless renewed, cease to have effect after 72 hours, beginning with the time when the authorisation was granted. Authorisations may also be made on an application made by a member of another police force where such police forces are party to a collaborative agreement that provides for them (s. 33(3ZA)–(3ZC)).

Long term authorisations (those exceeding 12 months) can only be given by a Chief Constable/Commissioner, or in the case of the NCA, the Deputy Director General. These authorisations are also subject to approval by an independent Surveillance Commissioner.

Special safeguards apply in relation to juveniles and vulnerable individuals. Juveniles are those under 18 years of age. On no occasion should the use or conduct of a CHIS under 16 years of age be authorised to give information against his parents or any person who has parental responsibility for him. In other cases, authorisations should not be granted unless the special provisions contained within the Regulation of Investigatory Powers (Juveniles) Order 2000 (SI 2000/2793) are satisfied. A vulnerable individual is a person who is or may be in need of community care services by reason of mental or other disability, age or illness and who is or may be unable to take care of him/herself, or unable to protect him/herself against significant harm or exploitation.

The authorisation levels for juveniles and vulnerable individuals are assistant chief constable/commander where they are to be used as sources, or chief constable/commissioner when knowledge of confidential information is likely to be acquired. For the NCA authorisation levels are deputy director in both instances. In relation to juveniles the duration of such authorisations is one month.

Regular reviews of authorisations are required to assess whether it remains necessary and proportionate to use a CHIS and whether the authorisation remains justified. An authorisation must be cancelled if the use or conduct of the CHIS no longer satisfies the criteria for authorisation.

The Regulation of Investigatory Powers (Covert Human Intelligence Sources: Matters Subject to Legal Privilege) Order 2010 (SI 2010/521, as amended by SI 2013/2788) deals with cases where through the use or conduct of a CHIS it is likely that knowledge of legally privileged material or other confidential information will be acquired. In such cases the deployment of the CHIS is subject to an enhanced regime of prior approval. Confidential information consists of matters subject to legal privilege, confidential personal information, confidential constituent information or confidential journalistic material.

The Code of Practice sets out clear guidelines for the management of a CHIS (Chapter 6), i.e. the control and monitoring of CHIS activities, the keeping of records (Chapter 7), and the handling, storage and destruction of materials (Chapter 8).

4.17.4.5 Covert Surveillance

The Covert Surveillance and Property Interference Code of Practice, Chapter 1 provides:

The surveillance activity to which this code applies

1.8 Part II of the 2000 Act provides for the authorisation of covert surveillance by public authorities where that surveillance is likely to result in the obtaining of private information about a person.

1.9 Surveillance, for the purpose of the 2000 Act, includes monitoring, observing or listening to persons, their movements, conversations or other activities and communications. It may be conducted with or without the assistance of a surveillance device and includes the recording of any information obtained.
(See section 48(2) of the 2000 Act)

1.10 Surveillance is covert if, and only if, it is carried out in a manner calculated to ensure that any persons who are subject to the surveillance are unaware that it is or may be taking place.
(As defined in section 26(9)(a) of the 2000 Act)

1.11 Specifically, covert surveillance may be authorised under the 2000 Act if it is either intrusive or directed:

- Intrusive surveillance is covert surveillance that is carried out in relation to anything taking place on residential premises or in any private vehicle (and that involves the presence of an individual on the premises or in the vehicle or is carried out by a means of a surveillance device);
- Directed surveillance is covert surveillance that is not intrusive but is carried out in relation to a specific investigation or operation in such a manner as is likely to result in the obtaining of private information about any person (other than by way of an immediate response to events or circumstances such that it is not reasonably practicable to seek authorisation under the 2000 Act).

KEYNOTE

Some surveillance activity does not constitute intrusive or directed surveillance for the purposes of part II of the 2000 Act and includes:

- covert surveillance by way of an immediate response to events, e.g. where police officers conceal themselves to observe suspicious persons that they come across in the course of a routine patrol;
- covert surveillance as part of general observation activities, e.g. where plain clothes police officers are on patrol to monitor a high street crime hot-spot or prevent and detect shoplifting;
- covert surveillance not relating to specified grounds, e.g. where a specific investigation or operation does not relate to the grounds specified at s. 28(3) of the 2000 Act;
- overt use of CCTV and ANPR systems, e.g. members of the public will be aware that such systems are in use, and their operation is covered by the Data Protection Act 1998 and the CCTV Code of Practice 2008, and the overt use of ANPR systems to monitor traffic flows or detect motoring offences does not require an authorisation under the 2000 Act;
- certain other specific situations, e.g. the use of a recording device by a CHIS in respect of whom an appropriate use or conduct authorisation has been granted permitting him to record any information obtained in his presence (s. 48(3));
- the recording, whether overt or covert, of an interview with a member of the public where it is made clear that the interview is entirely voluntary and that the interviewer is a member of a public authority.

4.17.4.6 Directed Surveillance

Chapter 2 of the Covert Surveillance and Property Interference Code of Practice provides further guidance on what is directed surveillance and states:

Directed surveillance

2.2 Surveillance is directed surveillance if the following are all true:

- it is covert, but not intrusive surveillance;
- it is conducted for the purposes of a specific investigation or operation;

- it is likely to result in the obtaining of *private information* about a person (whether or not one specifically identified for the purposes of the investigation or operation);
- it is conducted otherwise than by way of an immediate response to events or circumstances the nature of which is such that it would not be reasonably practicable for an authorisation under Part II of the 2000 Act to be sought.

2.3 Thus, the planned covert surveillance of a specific person, where not intrusive, would constitute directed surveillance if such surveillance is likely to result in the obtaining of *private information* about that, or any other person.

KEYNOTE

Private information includes any information relating to a person's private or family life (s. 26(10)). It should be taken generally to include any aspect of a person's private or personal relationship with others, including family. Family should be treated as extending beyond the formal relationships created by marriage or civil partnership and may include professional or business relationships.

Private information may include personal data, such as names, telephone numbers and address details. Where such information is acquired by means of covert surveillance of a person having a reasonable expectation of privacy, a directed surveillance authorisation is appropriate. The fact that a directed surveillance authorisation is available does not mean it is required. There may be other lawful means of obtaining personal data that do not involve directed surveillance.

While a person may have a reduced expectation of privacy when in a public place, covert surveillance of that person's activities in public may still result in the obtaining of private information. This is likely to be the case where that person has a reasonable expectation of privacy even though acting in public and where a record is being made by a public authority of that person's activities for future consideration or analysis. Note also that a person in police custody will have certain expectations of privacy.

As with a CHIS, an authorisation for directed surveillance should not be granted unless it is believed to be proportionate to what is sought to be achieved and necessary on the specified grounds (see para. 4.17.4.3 in relation to 'necessary' and 'proportionate'). The specified grounds, contained in s. 28(3), are:

- in the interests of national security;
- for the purpose of preventing or detecting crime or of preventing disorder;
- in the interests of the economic well-being of the United Kingdom;
- in the interests of public safety;
- for the purpose of protecting public health;
- for the purpose of assessing or collecting any tax, duty, levy or other imposition, contribution or charge payable to a government department; or
- for any purpose (not falling within paragraphs (a) to (f)) which is specified for the purposes of this subsection by an order made by the Secretary of State.

The Regulation of Investigatory Powers (Directed Surveillance and Covert Human Intelligence Sources) Order 2003 (SI 2003/3171), as amended, sets out the relevant roles and ranks for those who can authorise directed surveillance. In the case of the police the relevant rank will generally be at superintendent level and above, and the authorisation must be in writing except in urgent cases where oral authorisation may be given (s. 43(1)(a)). A written authorisation ceases to have effect after three months beginning on the day it was granted, and if given orally will only last 72 hours unless renewed (s. 43(3)). Where it is not reasonably practicable to have the application considered by a superintendent or above, having regard to the urgency of the case, then an inspector may give the relevant authorisation which will only last 72 hours unless renewed by a superintendent. For the NCA the authorising officer is a Senior Manager (Grade 2) and for urgent cases a Principal Officer (Grade 3).

Authorisations may also be made on an application made by a member of another police force where such police forces are party to a collaborative agreement that provides for them (s. 33(3ZA)–(3ZC)).

As with a CHIS the codes of practice provide additional procedural safeguards regarding where the material sought by the surveillance is subject to legal privilege, is confidential personal information or some journalistic material. It is of interest to note that the House of Lords has held that the 2000 Act permits covert surveillance of communications between lawyers and their clients even though these may be subject to legal professional privilege *(Re McE (Northern Ireland)* [2009] UKHL 15).

4.17.4.7   Intrusive Surveillance

The Covert Surveillance and Property Interference Code of Practice, Chapter 2, provides further guidance on what is intrusive surveillance and states:

Intrusive Surveillance

2.11   Intrusive surveillance is covert surveillance that is carried out in relation to anything taking place on residential premises or in any private vehicle, and that involves the presence of an individual on the premises or in the vehicle or is carried out by a means of a surveillance device.

2.12   The definition of surveillance as intrusive relates to the location of the surveillance, and not any other consideration of the nature of the information that is expected to be obtained. In addition, surveillance under the ambit of the 2010 Order is to be treated as intrusive surveillance. Accordingly, it is not necessary to consider whether or not intrusive surveillance is likely to result in the obtaining of private information.

KEYNOTE

'Residential premises' are considered to be so much of any premises as is for the time being occupied or used by any person, however temporarily, for residential purposes or otherwise as living accommodation. This specifically includes hotel or prison accommodation that is so occupied or used (s. 48)(1)). However, common areas (such as hotel dining areas) to which a person has access in connection with their use or occupation of accommodation are specifically excluded (s. 48(7)). The Act further states that the concept of premises should be taken to include any place whatsoever, including any vehicle or movable structure, whether or not occupied as land (s. 48(8)).

A 'private vehicle' is defined as any vehicle, including vessels, aircraft or hovercraft, which is used primarily for the private purposes of the person who owns it or a person otherwise having the right to use it. This would include, for example, a company car, owned by a leasing company and used for business and pleasure by the employee of a company (see s. 48(1) and (7)).

In *R* v *Plunkett* [2013] EWCA Crim 261, in admitting evidence of statements and admissions by the accused in a police van which were covertly recorded, it was held that a police van is not a private vehicle for the purposes of s. 26(3) and that the authorisation given by a superintendent under s. 28 for directed surveillance was appropriate. Interestingly, evidence arising from the use of a bug in police transport, which was obtained in circumstances that meant there was a technical breach of the RIPA authority, was held admissible in that the officers had not acted in bad faith knowing they were exceeding their authority (*Khan* v *R* [2013] EWCA Crim 2230).

Surveillance is not intrusive if it is carried out by means only of a surveillance device designed or adapted principally for the purpose of providing information about the location of a vehicle (s. 25(4)(a)).

The elements of intrusive surveillance require the presence of people or devices on residential premises or in any private vehicle. However, if the surveillance is carried out by means of a surveillance device in relation to anything taking place on the premises or private vehicle, but is carried out without that device being present on the premises or in the vehicle, it is not intrusive unless the device is such that it consistently provides information of the same quality and detail as might be expected to be obtained from a device actually present on the premises or in the vehicle (s. 25(5)).

The Regulation of Investigatory Powers (Extension of Authorisation Provisions: Legal Consultations) Order 2010 (SI 2010/461) provides that directed surveillance carried out in relation to anything taking place on any premises specified in the Order that are being used for the purpose of legal consultations shall be treated as 'intrusive surveillance'. The 'any premises' includes prisons, police stations, high security psychiatric hospitals, the place of business of any professional legal adviser; and any place used for the sittings and business of any court, tribunal, inquest or inquiry.

Authorisations for intrusive surveillance will generally be granted by Chief Constables/Commissioners and the Director General of the NCA (s. 32), or in some cases designated deputies. As with the other authorisations under the Act the authorising officer shall not grant an authorisation for the carrying out of intrusive surveillance unless he/she believes that the authorisation is necessary on the specified grounds and that the author-

---

ised surveillance is proportionate to what is sought to be achieved by carrying it out (s. 32(2)). The specified grounds, contained in s. 32(3) are:

- in the interests of national security;
- for the purpose of preventing or detecting serious crime;
- in the interests of the economic well-being of the United Kingdom.

In relation to 'national security' a senior authorising officer or designated deputy of a law enforcement agency shall not issue an authorisation for intrusive surveillance where the investigation or operation is within the responsibilities of one of the intelligence services and properly falls to be authorised by warrant issued by the Secretary of State. 'Serious crime' is defined in ss. 81(2) and (3) as crime that comprises an offence for which a person who has attained the age of 21 and has no previous convictions could reasonably be expected to be sentenced to imprisonment for a term of three years or more, or which involves the use of violence, results in substantial financial gain or is conduct by a large number of persons in pursuit of a common purpose.

Except in urgent cases, authorisation granted for intrusive surveillance will not take effect until a Surveillance Commissioner has approved it and written notice of the Commissioner's decision has been given to the person who granted the authorisation. This means that the approval will not take effect until the notice has been received in the office of the person who granted the authorisation within the relevant force or organisation (s. 35(3)(a)). When the authorisation is urgent it will take effect from the time it is granted provided notice is given to the Surveillance Commissioner (s. 35(3)(b)).

A written authorisation will cease to have effect (unless renewed) at the end of a period of three months. Oral authorisations given in urgent cases will cease to have effect (unless renewed) at the end of the period of 72 hours beginning with the time when they took effect.

Authorisations may also be made on an application made by a member of another police force where such police forces are part to a collaborative agreement that provides for them (s. 33(3ZA)–(3ZC)).

4.17.4.8 Interception of Communications

The interception and monitoring of some communications have become important tools for the police and other investigatory bodies, particularly in proving a defendant's involvement in some of the incomplete offences covered by this chapter. Also of increasing importance is the interception of communications for intelligence-gathering purposes, particularly when monitoring terrorism and organised crime.

The 2000 Act creates two interception offences: one concerned with the interception of communications transmitted by either public postal or public communication systems; and the other concerned with the interception of communications transmitted by private telecommunication systems.

4.17.4.9 Unlawful Interception of Public Communications

OFFENCE: **Unlawful Interception of Public Communications—*Regulation of Investigatory Powers Act 2000, s. 1(1)***
- Triable either way • Two years' imprisonment and/or a fine on indictment
- Fine summarily

The Regulation of Investigatory Powers Act 2000, s. 1 states:

(1) It shall be an offence for a person intentionally and without lawful authority to intercept, at any place in the United Kingdom, any communication in the course of its transmission by means of—
   (a) a public postal service; or
   (b) a public telecommunication system.

4.17.4.10 Unlawful Interception of Private Communications

OFFENCE: **Unlawful Interception of Private Communications—*Regulation of Investigatory Powers Act 2000, s. 1(2)***

- Triable either way • Two years' imprisonment and/or a fine on indictment
- Fine summarily

The Regulation of Investigatory Powers Act 2000, s. 1 states:

(2) It shall be an offence for a person—
  (a) intentionally and without lawful authority, and
  (b) otherwise than in circumstances in which his conduct is excluded by subsection (6) from criminal liability under this subsection,
  to intercept, at any place in the United Kingdom, any communication in the course of its transmission by means of a private telecommunication system.

4.17.4.11 What Amounts to Interception?

The Regulation of Investigatory Powers Act 2000, s. 2 states:

(2) For the purposes of this Act, but subject to the following provisions of this section, a person intercepts a communication in the course of its transmission by means of a telecommunication system if, and only if, he—

 (a) so modifies or interferes with the system, or its operation,

 (b) so monitors transmissions made by means of the system, or

 (c) so monitors transmissions made by wireless telegraphy to or from apparatus comprised in the system,

as to make some or all of the contents of the communication available, while being transmitted, to a person other than the sender or intended recipient of the communication.

KEYNOTE

A communication is 'being transmitted' for the purposes of this offence when it is stored on the system for the intended recipient to collect or access (s. 2(7)). This means that email messages awaiting collection/access by the intended recipient are still 'being transmitted', as are unreceived or uncollected pager messages. This also includes a situation where a voicemail message has been saved by the recipient on the voicemail facility of a public telecommunications system (*R* v *Edmondson* [2013] EWCA Crim 1026).

The expression 'in the course of its transmission' is critical in applying the extent of the definition of interception. In a case where a listening device installed by the police in the defendant's car had recorded the defendant speaking on his mobile phone, the Court of Appeal held that this did not amount to an 'interception', and mere eavesdropping on a conversation between one person at one end of a mobile telephone or two people face-to-face could not constitute communication in the course of transmission (*R* v *Allsopp* [2005] EWCA Crim 703; see also *R* v *E (Admissibility: Covert Listening Device)* [2004] EWCA Crim 1243).

There is no equivalent definition for the interception of postal communications and this will presumably be a question of fact to be addressed on the merits of each case.

Having set out what the offence covers, the Act goes on to specify particular activities that will *not* be caught by this section. These include:

* the interception of any communication broadcast for general reception—this covers broadcasts such as television and radio; it does not extend to pagers and mobile phone communications and these *are* covered by the Act;
* the interception of certain types of 'traffic data'—this means certain types of information that are needed to deliver or route the communication.

4.17.4.12 Lawful Authority

The Regulation of Investigatory Powers Act 2000, s. 1 states:

(5) Conduct has lawful authority for the purposes of this section if, and only if—

 (a) it is authorised by or under section 3 or 4;

 (b) it takes place in accordance with a warrant under section 5 ('an interception warrant'); or

 (c) it is in exercise, in relation to any stored communication, of any statutory power that is exercised (apart from this section) for the purpose of obtaining information or of taking possession of any document or other property;

and conduct (whether or not prohibited by this section) which has lawful authority for the purposes of this section by virtue of paragraph (a) or (b) shall also be taken to be lawful for all other purposes.

The conduct authorised by the warrant must be proportionate to what is sought to be achieved by it (s. 5(2)(b)).

Conduct Authorised under section 3 or 4

Section 3 of the 2000 Act authorises certain *types of interception* without the need for a warrant. In general, it covers interception where:

- both the sender and intended recipient have consented to it;
- either the sender or intended recipient has consented and surveillance by means of that interception has been authorised under part II (as to which, **see para. 4.17.4.15**)—this might cover the situation where the police are monitoring threatening telephone calls made to a victim or calls made in connection with black-mail demands;
- the interception is by/on behalf of the provider of the postal or telecommunication service for purposes connected with it (examples of this conduct would include postal workers who need to open mail in order to return it to the sender);
- the person is authorised under s. 48 of the Wireless Telegraphy Act 2006 (as to which, **see para. 4.17.4.17**).

Section 4 of the 2000 Act sets out occasions where *other authorities* might permit the interception of certain communications without the need for a warrant such as communications to or from prisons and high security psychiatric hospitals. Section 4 also makes provision for interception of communications involving people who are (or are believed to be) outside the United Kingdom.

Interception Warrants

The issuing, exercising and oversight of interception warrants are subject to extensive statutory procedures (ss. 5–11). They are issued by the Secretary of State where he/she *believes* that the warrant is *necessary* on grounds falling within s. 5(3) and proportionate to what is sought to be achieved by the conduct authorised by the warrant.

Section 5(3) states that the warrant is *necessary* on grounds falling within this subsection if it is necessary: in the interests of national security; for the purpose of preventing or detecting serious crime (including the provisions of any international mutual assistance agreement); or for the purpose of safeguarding the economic well-being of the United Kingdom (s. 7). 'Serious crime' means an offence(s) for which a person who has attained the age of 21 and has no previous convictions could reasonably be expected to be sentenced to imprisonment for a term of three years or more, or that the conduct involves the use of violence, results in substantial financial gain, or is conduct by a large number of persons in pursuit of a common purpose (s. 81(3)).

The actions taken under an interception warrant are probably the most important means of making an interception lawful.

Stored Communication

This relates to occasions where the person is exercising a statutory power, other than s. 1 of the 2000 Act, for the purpose of obtaining information or taking possession of any document or other property *in relation to any stored communication*. The example given by the Home Office of such a situation is where police officers have recovered a pager from a person in custody and they apply to a circuit judge for an order under sch. 1 to the Police and Criminal Evidence Act 1984 to access its messages.

4.17.4.13   **Unauthorised Disclosures**

OFFENCE: **Unauthorised Disclosures—*Regulation of Investigatory Powers Act 2000, s. 19***
- Triable either way • Five years' imprisonment and/or a fine on indictment
- Six months' imprisonment and/or a fine summarily

The Regulation of Investigatory Powers Act 2000, s. 19 states:

(1) Where an interception warrant has been issued or renewed, it shall be the duty of every person falling within subsection (2) to keep secret all the matters mentioned in subsection (3).

(2) The persons falling within this subsection are—

(a) the persons specified in section 6(2);

(b) every person holding office under the Crown;

[...]

(e) every person employed by or for the purposes of a police force;

(f) persons providing postal services or employed for the purposes of any business of providing such a service;

(g) persons providing public telecommunications services or employed for the purposes of any business of providing such a service;

(h) persons having control of the whole or any part of a telecommunication system located wholly or partly in the United Kingdom.

(3) Those matters are—

(a) the existence and contents of the warrant and of any section 8(4) certificate in relation to the warrant;

(b) the details of the issue of the warrant and of any renewal or modification of the warrant or of any such certificate;

(c) the existence and contents of any requirement to provide assistance with giving effect to the warrant;

(d) the steps taken in pursuance of the warrant or of any such requirement; and

(e) everything in the intercepted material, together with any related communications data.

(4) A person who makes a disclosure to another of anything that he is required to keep secret under this section shall be guilty of an offence...

KEYNOTE

This offence imposes a very clear duty on the people set out in s. 19(2) and makes no specific requirement as to state of mind.

It is clearly intended to apply to police officers and others involved in an investigation, and it also extends to support staff.

Section 19(5) provides a defence for a person charged with this offence to show that he/she could not reasonably have been expected, after first becoming aware of the matter disclosed, to take steps to prevent the disclosure. Further defences exist for some communications with professional legal advisers (s. 19(6) and (7)), and other proper communications with the Interception of Communications Commissioner (s. 19(9)).

4.17.4.14   Communications Data

The Regulation of Investigatory Powers Act 2000 provides the legislative framework to cover the requisition, provision and handling of communications data. It explains the duties and responsibilities placed upon each party involved in these processes and creates a system of safeguards, reflecting the requirements of Article 8 of the European Convention on Human Rights (Right to Respect for Private and Family Life, Home and Correspondence).

4.17.4.15   Lawful Acquisition and Disclosure of Communications Data

The Regulation of Investigatory Powers Act 2000, s. 21 states:

(1) This Chapter applies to—

(a) any conduct in relation to a postal service or telecommunication system for obtaining communications data, other than conduct consisting in the interception of communications in the course of their transmission by means of such a service or system; and

(b) the disclosure to any person of communications data.

(2) Conduct to which this Chapter applies shall be lawful for all purposes if—

(a) it is conduct in which any person is authorised or required to engage by an authorisation or notice granted or given under this Chapter; and

(b) the conduct is in accordance with, or in pursuance of, the authorisation or requirement.

4.17.4.16 Obtaining and Disclosing Communications Data

The Regulation of Investigatory Powers Act 2000, s. 22 states:

(1) This section applies where a person designated for the purposes of this Chapter believes that it is necessary on grounds falling within subsection (2) to obtain any communications data.

(2) It is necessary on grounds falling within this subsection to obtain communications data if it is necessary—

    (a) in the interests of national security;

    (b) for the purpose of preventing or detecting crime or of preventing disorder;

    (c) in the interests of the economic well-being of the United Kingdom;

    (d) in the interests of public safety;

    (e) for the purpose of protecting public health;

    (f) for the purpose of assessing or collecting any tax, duty, levy or other imposition, contribution or charge payable to a government department;

    (g) for the purpose, in an emergency, of preventing death or injury or any damage to a person's physical or mental health, or of mitigating any injury or damage to a person's physical or mental health; or

    (h) for any purpose (not falling within paragraphs (a) to (g)) which is specified for the purposes of this subsection by an order made by the Secretary of State.

(3) Subject to subsection (5), the designated person may grant an authorisation for persons holding offices, ranks or positions with the same relevant public authority as the designated person to engage in any conduct to which this Chapter applies.

The 'designated person' who can authorise communications data to be obtained is the person holding a specified rank or office in one of the relevant public authorities. Those public authorities here include police forces, the National Crime Agency, HM Revenue and Customs and any other public authority specified by the Secretary of State in appropriate regulations. A person who is a designated person by reference to an office, rank or position with one police force is permitted to grant an authorisation for persons holding offices, ranks or positions with another police force where the forces are parties to a police force collaboration agreement which provides for them (s. 22(3A)–(3D)).

The above is merely a summary of the key aspects of the legislation relating to communications data. To find the full extent of the powers and duties under the 2000 Act, the statutory text should be used along with the relevant Codes of Practice in force at the time.

4.17.4.17 Wireless Telegraphy

The unauthorised interception of radio communications is a summary offence under s. 48 of the Wireless Telegraphy Act 2006, and a similar offence under the previous legislation was used where defendants had deliberately tuned in to police radio messages (*DPP* v *Waite* [1997] Crim LR 123).

The Regulation of Investigatory Powers Act 2000 greatly restricts the ability of a designated person to authorise interception of wireless telegraphy, but this type of interception is outside the scope of this Manual.

4.18 Equality

4.18.1 Introduction

The Equality Act 2010 has two main purposes—to harmonise discrimination law, and to strengthen the law to support progress on equality. It provides a framework of protection against direct and indirect discrimination, harassment and victimisation in services and public functions; premises; work; education; associations; and transport.

This chapter briefly sets out the key features of the 2010 Act. This is a specialised area of the law with equality continuing to be an important and sensitive issue for the police service.

4.18.2 Protected Characteristics

The words 'on the grounds of race, sex, sexual orientation, religion or belief, age' used in the previous anti-discrimination legislation have been replaced by the term 'protected characteristics'.

The protected characteristics covered by the Act are:

- Age
- Disability
- Gender reassignment
- Marriage and civil partnerships
- Race
- Religion or belief
- Sex
- Sexual Orientation

> **KEYNOTE**
>
> Although Pregnancy and Maternity are also protected characteristics they are dealt with separately in the Act (see para. 4.18.3.6).

4.18.2.1 Age

The Equality Act 2010, s. 5 states:

(1) In relation to the protected characteristic of age—
   (a) a reference to a person who has a particular protected characteristic is a reference to a person of a particular age group;
   (b) a reference to persons who share a protected characteristic is a reference to persons of the same age group.
(2) A reference to an age group is a reference to a group of persons defined by reference to age, whether by reference to a particular age or to a range of ages.

4.18.2.2 Disability

The Equality Act 2010, s. 6 states:

(1) A person (P) has a disability if—
   (a) P has a physical or mental impairment, and
   (b) the impairment has a substantial and long-term adverse effect on P's ability to carry out normal day-to-day activities.
(2) A reference to a disabled person is a reference to a person who has a disability.
(3) In relation to the protected characteristic of disability—
   (a) a reference to a person who has a particular protected characteristic is a reference to a person who has a particular disability;
   (b) a reference to persons who share a protected characteristic is a reference to persons who have the same disability.

4.18.2.3 Gender Reassignment

The Equality Act 2010, s. 7 states:

(1) A person has the protected characteristic of gender reassignment if the person is proposing to undergo, is undergoing or has undergone a process (or part of a process) for the purpose of re-assigning the person's sex by changing physiological or other attributes of sex.

(2) A reference to a transsexual person is a reference to a person who has the protected characteristic of gender reassignment.

(3) In relation to the protected characteristic of gender reassignment—

    (a) a reference to a person who has a particular protected characteristic is a reference to a transsexual person;

    (b) a reference to persons who share a protected characteristic is a reference to transsexual persons.

KEYNOTE

Gender reassignment for the purposes of the Act means where a person has proposed, started or completed a process to change his/her sex.

A woman making the transition to being a man and a man making the transition to being a woman both share the characteristic of gender reassignment, as does a person who has only just started out on the process of changing his/her sex and a person who has completed the process.

The established legal principle in law is that gender is set at birth—if you are born male you remain male and vice versa (see *Corbett* v *Corbett* [1970] 2 WLR 1306). However, in *A* v *Chief Constable of West Yorkshire and the Secretary of State for Work and Pensions* [2004] UKHL 21 it was held that it was no longer possible in the context of employment to regard a transsexual as being his/her birth gender. But public interest considerations in relation to the police service may determine that a gender reassigned applicant is not offered employment.

4.18.2.4 Marriage and Civil Partnerships

The Equality Act 2010, s. 8 states:

(1) A person has the protected characteristic of marriage and civil partnership if the person is married or is a civil partner.

(2) In relation to the protected characteristic of marriage and civil partnership—

    (a) a reference to a person who has a particular protected characteristic is a reference to a person who is married or is a civil partner;

    (b) a reference to persons who share a protected characteristic is a reference to persons who are married or are civil partners.

KEYNOTE

People who are not married or civil partners do not have this characteristic. A married man and a woman in a civil partnership both share the protected characteristic of marriage and civil partnership.

The Marriage (Same Sex Couples) Act 2013 has extended marriage to same sex couples which means that marriage has the same effect in law in relation to such a couple as it does in relation to an opposite sex couple (s. 11(1)). Section 11(2) ensures that the law of England and Wales, including all existing and new England and Wales legislation, will be interpreted in this way. The Act also enables civil partners who had their partnership formed in England and Wales to have their partnership converted into a marriage (s. 9(1)).

4.18.2.5 Race

The Equality Act 2010, s. 9 states:

(1) Race includes—

    (a) colour;

    (b) nationality;

    (c) ethnic or national origins.

(2) In relation to the protected characteristic of race—

    (a) a reference to a person who has a particular protected characteristic is a reference to a person of a particular racial group;

    (b) a reference to persons who share a protected characteristic is a reference to persons of the same racial group.

(3) A racial group is a group of persons defined by reference to race; and a reference to a person's racial group is a reference to a racial group into which the person falls.

(4) The fact that a racial group comprises two or more distinct racial groups does not prevent it from constituting a particular racial group.

KEYNOTE

People who have or share characteristics of colour, nationality or ethnic or national origins can be described as belonging to a particular racial group. A racial group can be made up of two or more different racial groups.

'Nationality' has been held to include citizenship acquired by birth, and in *Souster* v *BBC Scotland* [2001] IRLR 150, it was held that an English applicant can be discriminated against by a Scottish employer.

'Ethnic group' may include any group with a shared culture or history (*Mandla* v *Dowell Lee* [1983] 2 AC 548). Sikhs (*Mandla* v *Dowell Lee* [1983] 2 AC 548), Jews (*Seide* v *Gillette Industries Ltd* [1980] IRLR 427), Romany Gypsies (*Commission for Racial Equality* v *Dutton* [1989] QB 783), and Irish Travellers (*O'Leary* v *Allied Domecq Inns Ltd* (CL 950275 July 2000, Central London County Court), have all been held to be ethnic groups, but Scots, Welsh and English are however not an ethnic group (*Dawkins* v *Department of the Environment* [1993] IRLR 284).

'National origins' may overlap with nationality but the two concepts can be distinguished since 'nationality' is concerned with membership of a particular nation, and 'national origins' describes a persons connection by birth with a nation (see *Ealing LBC* v *Race Relations Board* [1972] AC 342).

'Racial group' includes a group of people who have or share a colour, ethnic, or national origin or nationality.

A Minister of the Crown may amend the Act so as to add 'caste' to the current definition of 'race' (s. 9(5)). The term 'caste' denotes a hereditary, endogamous (marrying within the group) community associated with a traditional occupation and ranked accordingly on a perceived scale of ritual purity, e.g. the four classes (varnas) of Hindu tradition (the Brahmin, Kshatriya, Vaishya and Shudra communities).

4.18.2.6 Religion or Belief

The Equality Act 2010, s. 10 states:

(1) Religion means any religion and a reference to religion includes a reference to a lack of religion.

(2) Belief means any religious or philosophical belief and a reference to belief includes a reference to a lack of belief.

(3) In relation to the protected characteristic of religion or belief—
   (a) a reference to a person who has a particular protected characteristic is a reference to a person of a particular religion or belief;
   (b) a reference to persons who share a protected characteristic is a reference to persons who are of the same religion or belief.

KEYNOTE

The section provides a broad definition in line with the freedom of thought, conscience and religion guaranteed by Article 9 of the European Convention on Human Rights. The main limitation is that the religion must have a clear structure and belief system. Denominations or sects within a religion can be considered to be a religion or belief, such as Protestants and Catholics within Christianity.

In *Eweida* v *United Kingdom* (2013) 57 EHRR 8 it was held that prohibiting a woman from visibly wearing a cross at work amounted to an interference with her right to manifest her Christian religion and this was in breach of the positive obligation under Article 9 of the European Convention on Human Rights (Right to freedom of thought, conscience and religion). However, in three other applications in the same case, which related to practising Christians, there was held to be no breach of either Article 9 or Article 14 (The rights and freedoms set forth in the Convention shall be secured without discrimination on any ground such as religion). These applications included: a nurse wearing a cross where the discrimination was based on health and safety rather than religious grounds; a registrar of births, deaths and marriages who believed that same-sex civil partnerships are contrary to God's law and refused to carry out civil partnerships; a Relate counsellor who refused to work with couples on same-sex sexual practices.

In response to the ruling in *Eweida*, the Equality and Human Rights Commission has issued fresh guidance for employers on how to handle religious beliefs at work. Details of the guidance can be found at http://www.equalityhumanrights.com.

Religious belief can vary from individual to individual within the same. Some Jews believe men should wear the Kippah (skull cap) at all times; and some Muslims believe women should cover their entire body and face with the Jilbab and Burqa (*R (On the Application of Begum)* v *Governors of Denbigh High School* [2006] UKHL 15). In *Power v Greater Manchester Police Authority* [2011] Eq LR 16 where a person was dismissed on grounds of his beliefs, it was not the belief itself but the expression of those beliefs which was in part the cause of his dismissal.

The criteria for determining what is a 'philosophical belief' are that it must be genuinely held; be a belief and not an opinion or viewpoint based on the present state of information available; be a belief as to a weighty and substantial aspect of human life and behaviour; attain a certain level of cogency, seriousness, cohesion and importance; and be worthy of respect in a democratic society, compatible with human dignity and not conflict with the fundamental rights of others. For example, a belief in 'climate change' affecting how a person lived his/her life is protected by the Act (*Grainger plc* v *Nicholson* [2010] 2 All ER 253).

4.18.2.7 Sex

The Equality Act 2010, s. 11 states:

In relation to the protected characteristic of sex—
(a) a reference to a person who has a particular protected characteristic is a reference to a man or to a woman;
(b) a reference to persons who share a protected characteristic is a reference to persons of the same sex.

KEYNOTE

This is a new provision which explains that references in the Act to people having the protected characteristic of sex are to mean being a man or a woman, and that men share this characteristic with other men, and women with other women.

The Act contains provisions (ss. 66 to 70) designed to achieve equality between men and women in pay and other terms of employment where the work of an employee and his/her comparator—a person of the opposite sex—is equal. It does so by providing for a sex equality clause to be read into the employee's contract of employment. This is designed to ensure parity of terms between the employee and his/her comparator.

For work to be equal, a claimant must establish that he/she is doing like work, work rated as equivalent or work of equal value to a comparator's work (s. 65). For example, in *Blackburn* v *West Midlands Police* [2008] EWCA Civ 1208 it was held that where police officers needed to work hours compatible with their child care responsibilities they were not entitled to special payments received by officers working 24/7 shift patterns.

4.18.2.8 Sexual Orientation

The Equality Act 2010, s. 12 states:

(1) Sexual orientation means a person's sexual orientation towards—
   (a) persons of the same sex,
   (b) persons of the opposite sex, or
   (c) persons of either sex.
(2) In relation to the protected characteristic of sexual orientation—
   (a) a reference to a person who has a particular protected characteristic is a reference to a person who is of a particular sexual orientation;
   (b) a reference to persons who share a protected characteristic is a reference to persons who are of the same sexual orientation.

4.18.3 Discrimination

The Equality Act 2010 provides for the following seven different types of discrimination which are discussed within this section:

- **Direct discrimination**: discrimination because of a protected characteristic.
- **Associative discrimination**: direct discrimination against someone because he/she is associated with another person with a protected characteristic.
- **Indirect discrimination**: a rule or policy that applies to everyone but disadvantages a person with a protected characteristic.
- **Harassment**: behaviour deemed offensive by the recipient.
- **Harassment by a third party**: harassment of staff or customers by people they do not directly employ.
- **Victimisation**: discrimination against someone because he/she made or supported a complaint under Equality Act legislation.
- **Discrimination by perception**: direct discrimination against someone because others think he/she has a protected characteristic.

4.18.3.1 Direct Discrimination

The Equality Act 2010, s. 13 states:

(1) A person (A) discriminates against another (B) if, because of a protected characteristic, A treats B less favourably than A treats or would treat others.

(2) If the protected characteristic is age, A does not discriminate against B if A can show A's treatment of B to be a proportionate means of achieving a legitimate aim.

(3) If the protected characteristic is disability, and B is not a disabled person, A does not discriminate against B only because A treats or would treat disabled persons more favourably than A treats B.

(4) If the protected characteristic is marriage and civil partnership, this section applies to a contravention of Part 5 (work) only if the treatment is because it is B who is married or a civil partner.

(5) If the protected characteristic is race, less favourable treatment includes segregating B from others.

(6) If the protected characteristic is sex—
  (a) less favourable treatment of a woman includes less favourable treatment of her because she is breast-feeding;
  (b) in a case where B is a man, no account is to be taken of special treatment afforded to a woman in connection with pregnancy or childbirth.

4.18.3.2 Combined Discrimination: Dual Characteristics

The Equality Act 2010, s. 14 states:

(1) A person (A) discriminates against another (B) if, because of a combination of two relevant protected characteristics, A treats B less favourably than A treats or would treat a person who does not share either of those characteristics.

4.18.3.3 Discrimination Arising from Disability

The Equality Act 2010, s. 15 states:

> (1) A person (A) discriminates against a disabled person (B) if—
>   (a) A treats B unfavourably because of something arising in consequence of B's disability, and
>   (b) A cannot show that the treatment is a proportionate means of achieving a legitimate aim.
> (2) Subsection (1) does not apply if A shows that A did not know, and could not reasonably have been expected to know, that B had the disability.

KEYNOTE

This section provides that it is discrimination to treat a disabled person unfavourably not because of the person's disability itself but because of something arising from, or in consequence of, that disability, such as the need to take a period of disability-related absence. It is, however, possible to justify such treatment if it can be shown to be a proportionate means of achieving a legitimate aim. For this type of discrimination to occur, the employer or other person must know, or reasonably be expected to know, that the disabled person has a disability.

This section is a new provision. In the judgment of *Lewisham London Borough Council* v *Malcolm* [2008] UKHL 43, it was held that the previous legislative provisions no longer provided the degree of protection from disability-related discrimination that is intended for disabled people. This section is aimed at re-establishing an appropriate balance between enabling a disabled person to make out a case of experiencing a detriment which arises because of his/her disability, and providing an opportunity for an employer or other person to defend the treatment.

4.18.3.4 Adjustments for Disabled Persons

The duty to make reasonable adjustments is a key element of a range of measures intended to eliminate barriers to access and participation for disabled people.

The Equality Act 2010, s. 20 states:

> (1) Where this Act imposes a duty to make reasonable adjustments on a person, this section, sections 21 and 22 and the applicable Schedule apply; and for those purposes, a person on whom the duty is imposed is referred to as A.
> (2) The duty comprises the following three requirements.
> (3) The first requirement is a requirement, where a provision, criterion or practice of A's puts a disabled person at a substantial disadvantage in relation to a relevant matter in comparison with persons who are not disabled, to take such steps as it is reasonable to have to take to avoid the disadvantage.
> (4) The second requirement is a requirement, where a physical feature puts a disabled person at a substantial disadvantage in relation to a relevant matter in comparison with persons who are not disabled, to take such steps as it is reasonable to have to take to avoid the disadvantage.
> (5) The third requirement is a requirement, where a disabled person would, but for the provision of an auxiliary aid, be put at a substantial disadvantage in relation to a relevant matter in comparison with persons who are not disabled, to take such steps as it is reasonable to have to take to provide the auxiliary aid.

KEYNOTE

This section defines what is meant by the duty to make reasonable adjustments for the purposes of the Act. The duty comprises three requirements which apply where a disabled person is placed at a substantial disadvantage in comparison with non-disabled people.

The first requirement covers changing the way things are done (such as changing a practice), the second covers making changes to the built environment (such as providing access to a building), and the third covers providing auxiliary aids and services (such as providing special computer software or providing a different service).

It sets out that under the second requirement, taking steps to avoid the disadvantage will include removing, altering or providing a reasonable means of avoiding the physical feature, where it would be reasonable to do so (s. 209). Where the first or third requirements involve the way in which information is provided, a reasonable step includes providing that information in an accessible format (s. 20(6)). It also makes clear that, except where the Act states otherwise, it would never be reasonable for a person bound by the duty to pass on the costs of complying with it to an individual disabled person (s. 20(7)).

The section contains only one threshold for the reasonable adjustment duty, that of 'substantial disadvantage'. Section 212(1) defines 'substantial' as more than minor or trivial.

Section 21 provides that a failure to comply with any one of the reasonable adjustment requirements amounts to discrimination against a disabled person to whom the duty is owed. It also provides that, apart from under this Act, no other action can be taken for failure to comply with the duty. The test of reasonableness is an objective one (*Collins* v *Royal National Theatre Board Ltd* [2004] IRLR 395), and will always depend on the particular circumstances in an individual case (*Archibald* v *Fife County Council* [2004] IRLR 651).

Although accepting the difficult role the police are often called upon to play, in *ZH* v *Commissioner of Police for the Metropolis* [2012] EWHC 604 (QB) it was held that the police dealing with a person who was severely autistic had a duty to make reasonable adjustments in dealing with that person irrespective of the fact that they acted in a well-intentioned but misguided manner.

In *Chief Constable of South Yorkshire* v *Jelic* [2010] IRLR 744 it was determined that the force had not acted 'reasonably' when it failed to allow an officer suffering from chronic anxiety syndrome to swap jobs with another officer. Also, in *Hinsley* v *Chief Constable of West Mercia Constabulary* [2010] UKEAT 0200 10 0911, it was decided that there was a breach of duty to make reasonable adjustments where there was a failure to reinstate a probationary police officer who had resigned whilst depressed. However, where an officer was perceived to have a dangerous mental condition the adjustments made to ensure he did not present a danger to colleagues or to the public were considered reasonable (*Aitken* v *Commissioner of Police of the Metropolis* [2011] EWCA Civ 582). In *Cordell* v *Foreign and Commonwealth Office* [2012] ICR 280 a tribunal dismissed claims of direct discrimination and discrimination by way of failure to make reasonable adjustments where the costs of providing an English-speaking lip-speaker support for a deaf employee were about £230,000 a year.

It was held that police officers lawfully searching the home of a man whom they knew to be profoundly deaf did not have any effect on the ability of the man and the officers to communicate with each other effectively without a British Sign Language interpreter being present. Officers who had had previous dealings with the man were satisfied on the basis of these dealings that they could achieve a basic level of communication with him without the benefit of an interpreter (*Finnegan* v *Chief Constable of Northumbria* [2013] EWCA Civ 1191).

4.18.3.5   Gender Reassignment Discrimination: Cases of Absence from Work

The Equality Act 2010, s. 16 states:

(1) This section has effect for the purposes of the application of Part 5 (work) to the protected characteristic of gender reassignment.
(2) A person (A) discriminates against a transsexual person (B) if, in relation to an absence of B's that is because of gender reassignment, A treats B less favourably than A would treat B if—
  (a) B's absence was because of sickness or injury, or
  (b) B's absence was for some other reason and it is not reasonable for B to be treated less favourably.
(3) A person's absence is because of gender reassignment if it is because the person is proposing to undergo, is undergoing or has undergone the process (or part of the process) mentioned in section 7(1).

KEYNOTE

This section is designed to replicate the effect of a similar provision in the previous legislation.

A person's absence is 'because of gender reassignment' if it is because the person is proposing to undergo, is undergoing, or has undergone gender reassignment. For example, where a female to male transsexual person takes time off work to receive hormone treatment as part of his gender reassignment his employer cannot discriminate against him because of his absence from work for this purpose.

4.18.3.6 Pregnancy and Maternity Discrimination: non-work cases

The Equality Act 2010, s. 17 states:

(1) This section has effect for the purposes of the application to the protected characteristic of pregnancy and maternity of—
    (a) Part 3 (services and public functions);
    (b) Part 4 (premises);
    (c) Part 6 (education);
    (d) Part 7 (associations).
(2) A person (A) discriminates against a woman if A treats her unfavourably because of a pregnancy of hers.
(3) A person (A) discriminates against a woman if, in the period of 26 weeks beginning with the day on which she gives birth, A treats her unfavourably because she has given birth.
(4) The reference in subsection (3) to treating a woman unfavourably because she has given birth includes, in particular, a reference to treating her unfavourably because she is breast-feeding.
(5) For the purposes of this section, the day on which a woman gives birth is the day on which—
    (a) she gives birth to a living child, or
    (b) she gives birth to a dead child (more than 24 weeks of the pregnancy having passed).

KEYNOTE

Note that pregnancy and maternity are 'protected characteristics' even though they are not grouped with the other protected characteristics in the Act.

Pregnancy and maternity discrimination is excluded from the definition of direct sex discrimination (s. 17(6)) and is dealt with under this separate provision and s. 18 (work situations, **see para. 4.18.3.7**).

4.18.3.7 Pregnancy and Maternity Discrimination: work cases

The Equality Act 2010, s. 18 states:

(1) This section has effect for the purposes of the application of Part 5 (work) to the protected characteristic of pregnancy and maternity.
(2) A person (A) discriminates against a woman if, in the protected period in relation to a pregnancy of hers, A treats her unfavourably—
    (a) because of the pregnancy, or
    (b) because of illness suffered by her as a result of it.
(3) A person (A) discriminates against a woman if A treats her unfavourably because she is on compulsory maternity leave.
(4) A person (A) discriminates against a woman if A treats her unfavourably because she is exercising or seeking to exercise, or has exercised or sought to exercise, the right to ordinary or additional maternity leave.

KEYNOTE

In relation to s. 18(2), if the treatment of a woman is in implementation of a decision taken in the protected period, the treatment is to be regarded as occurring in that period (even if the implementation is not until after the end of that period (s. 18(5)).

The duration of the protected period depends on the statutory maternity leave entitlements as set out in the Employment Rights Act 1996 which defines the right to compulsory, ordinary and additional maternity leave. The protected period starts when a woman becomes pregnant and ends either:

- if she has the right to ordinary and additional maternity leave, at the end of the additional maternity leave period or (if earlier) when she returns to work after the pregnancy; or
- if she does not have that right, at the end of the period of two weeks beginning with the end of the pregnancy.

As with s. 17 of the 2010 Act, sex discrimination does not apply to treatment of a woman in so far as it is in the protected period, or it is for a reason mentioned in s. 18(3) or (4).

Unfavourable treatment suffered because of an association with a pregnant woman or because of being perceived to be pregnant are not covered by this section, though such treatment might constitute direct discrimination under s. 13.

In *Maksymiuk* v *Bar Roma Partnership* [2012] Eq LR 917 an employee who was the only one of a number of bar staff who was selected for dismissal by reason of purported redundancy only a matter of days after she had announced that she was pregnant, had her claim of discrimination on the ground of pregnancy or sickness related to pregnancy dismissed.

4.18.3.8 Indirect Discrimination

The Equality Act 2010, s. 19 states:

(1) A person (A) discriminates against another (B) if A applies to B a provision, criterion or practice which is discriminatory in relation to a relevant protected characteristic of B's.

(2) For the purposes of subsection (1), a provision, criterion or practice is discriminatory in relation to a relevant protected characteristic of B's if—

(a) A applies, or would apply, it to persons with whom B does not share the characteristic,

(b) it puts, or would put, persons with whom B shares the characteristic at a particular disadvantage when compared with persons with whom B does not share it,

(c) it puts, or would put, B at that disadvantage, and

(d) A cannot show it to be a proportionate means of achieving a legitimate aim.

KEYNOTE

Apart from pregnancy and maternity, indirect discrimination applies to all the protected characteristics.

Indirect discrimination occurs when a policy which applies in the same way for everybody has an effect which particularly disadvantages people with a protected characteristic. Where a particular group is disadvantaged in this way, a person in that group is indirectly discriminated against if he/she is put at that disadvantage, unless the person applying the policy can justify it.

When a policy would put a person at a disadvantage if it were applied, e.g. where a person is deterred from applying for a job or taking up an offer of service because a policy which would be applied would result in his/her disadvantage, this may also be indirect discrimination. Examples of indirect discrimination have included: requiring all employees to work within 'normal office hours' (*Bhudi* v *IMI Refiners* [1994] IRLR 204); requiring all workers to have short hair thereby making it difficult for some groups such as Sikhs to comply (*Mandla* v *Dowell Lee* [1983] 2 AC 548); where 100 per cent of males could comply with a policy relating to rostering of duties, but only 95.2 per cent of women were able to do so, the policy discriminated indirectly against females (*London Underground Ltd* v *Edwards (No. 2)* [1998] IRLR 364).

4.18.3.9 Harassment

The Equality Act 2010, s. 26 states:

(1) A person (A) harasses another (B) if—

(a) A engages in unwanted conduct related to a relevant protected characteristic, and

(b) the conduct has the purpose or effect of—

(i) violating B's dignity, or

(ii) creating an intimidating, hostile, degrading, humiliating or offensive environment for B.

(2) A also harasses B if—

(a) A engages in unwanted conduct of a sexual nature, and

(b) the conduct has the purpose or effect referred to in subsection (1)(b).

(3) A also harasses B if—

(a) A or another person engages in unwanted conduct of a sexual nature or that is related to gender reassignment or sex,

(b) the conduct has the purpose or effect referred to in subsection (1)(b), and

(c) because of B's rejection of or submission to the conduct, A treats B less favourably than A would treat B if B had not rejected or submitted to the conduct.

4.18.3.10 Employees and Applicants: Harassment

The Equality Act 2010, s. 40 states:

(1) An employer (A) must not, in relation to employment by A, harass a person (B)—
    (a) who is an employee of A's;
    (b) who has applied to A for employment.

(2) The circumstances in which A is to be treated as harassing B under subsection (1) include those where—
    (a) a third party harasses B in the course of B's employment, and
    (b) A failed to take such steps as would have been reasonably practicable to prevent the third party from doing so.

(3) Subsection (2) does not apply unless A knows that B has been harassed in the course of B's employment on at least two other occasions by a third party; and it does not matter whether the third party is the same or a different person on each occasion.

(4) A third party is a person other than—
    (a) A, or
    (b) an employee of A's.

4.18.3.11 Victimisation

The Equality Act 2010, s. 27 states:

(1) A person (A) victimises another person (B) if A subjects B to a detriment because—

(a) B does a protected act, or

(b) A believes that B has done, or may do, a protected act.

(2) Each of the following is a protected act—

(a) bringing proceedings under this Act;

(b) giving evidence or information in connection with proceedings under this Act;

(c) doing any other thing for the purposes of or in connection with this Act;

(d) making an allegation (whether or not express) that A or another person has contravened this Act.

(3) Giving false evidence or information, or making a false allegation, is not a protected act if the evidence or information is given, or the allegation is made, in bad faith.

KEYNOTE

The section replaces similar provisions in previous legislation, though under the Act victimisation is technically no longer treated as a form of discrimination, so there is no longer a need to compare treatment of an alleged victim with that of a person who has not made or supported a complaint under the Act.

Victimisation takes place where one person treats another badly because he/she in good faith has done a 'protected act', e.g. taken or supported any action taken for the purpose of the Act, including in relation to any alleged breach of its provisions. It also provides that victimisation takes place where one person treats another badly because he/she is suspected of having done this or of intending to do this. The test to be applied in assessing whether or not victimisation has taken place is, 'was the real reason for the victim's treatment the fact that they had carried out a protected act' (*Chief Constable of West Yorkshire Police* v *Khan* [2001] UKHL 48). In *Bayode* v *Chief Constable of Derbyshire* [2008] UKEAT 0499 07 2205 it was held that a police constable, who was black African and Nigerian by national origin, had not been victimised where his colleagues recorded any problems they encountered with him in their PNBs for fear of a race discrimination claim at some future date.

Only an individual can bring a claim for victimisation, and a person is not protected from victimisation where he/she maliciously makes or supports an untrue complaint.

4.18.4 Police Officers

The 2010 Act also prohibits discrimination, victimisation, and harassment in other non-employment work relationships and this specifically includes police officers.

The Equality Act 2010, s. 42 states:

(1) For the purposes of this Part, holding the office of constable is to be treated as employment—

(a) by the chief officer, in respect of any act done by the chief officer in relation to a constable or appointment to the office of constable;

(b) by the responsible authority, in respect of any act done by the authority in relation to a constable or appointment to the office of constable.

KEYNOTE

This section provides that police constables (and police cadets—s. 42(2)) are treated as employees. The relevant employer is either the chief officer (or, in Scotland, the chief constable) or the responsible authority (s. 43), depending on who commits the act in question. For example, if a chief officer refused to allocate protective equipment to female constables he/she would be treated as the employer in a direct discrimination claim.

Constables serving with the Civil Nuclear Constabulary are treated as employees of the Civil Nuclear Constabulary. A constable seconded to the National Crime Agency (NCA) is treated as employed by the NCA.

4.18.5 Employees and Applicants

The Equality Act 2010, s. 39 makes it unlawful for an employer to discriminate against or victimise employees and people seeking work. It applies where the employer is making arrangements to fill a job, and in respect of anything done in the course of a person's employment.

KEYNOTE

Section 39 replaces similar provisions in previous legislation, and examples of direct discrimination in relation to work have included: rescinding an officer's posting on the grounds of force policy that spouses should not work in the same Division because neither officer would be compellable as a witness against the other (*Graham* v *Chief Constable of Bedfordshire Constabulary* [2002] IRLR 239); treating a police officer of one racial group, who was under investigation for disciplinary matters, differently from another officer under such investigation belonging to a different racial group (*Virdi* v *Commissioner of Police for the Metropolis* (2000) LTL 5 February); acceding to a request by a customer not to be served by someone of a particular colour (*Eldridge & Barbican Car Hire Ltd* v *Zhang* (2001) LTL 10 May).

There are a number of exceptions and defences to the provisions of the Act but two of the more relevant defences in relation to discrimination or victimisation in employment are 'genuine occupational requirement' and 'positive action'.

The principle behind 'genuine occupational requirement' is that, in certain jobs and roles, there may well be a legitimate reason that an employee is of a particular sex or belongs to a particular racial group (sch. 1, part 1, para. 1(1)(a)). In reality there are far more potential exceptions to discrimination on the grounds of sex and sexual orientation than for reasons of the other protected characteristics.

'Positive action' refers to measures to alleviate disadvantage experienced by people who share a protected characteristic, reduce their under-representation in relation to particular activities, and meet their particular needs (s. 158). It allows for measures to be targeted to particular groups, including training to enable them to gain employment, but any such measures must be a proportionate way of achieving the relevant aim.

An employer may also take a protected characteristic into consideration when deciding whom to recruit or promote, where people having the protected characteristic are at a disadvantage or are under-represented (s. 159). This can be done only where the candidates are as qualified as each other. The aim is to help employers achieve a more diverse workforce by giving them the option, when faced with candidates of equal merit, to choose a candidate from an under-represented group.

4.18.6 Liability for Discrimination in Employment

The Equality Act 2010, s. 109 states:

(1) Anything done by a person (A) in the course of A's employment must be treated as also done by the employer.

(2) ...

(3) It does not matter whether that thing is done with the employer's or principal's knowledge or approval.

KEYNOTE

This section makes employers and principals liable for acts of discrimination, harassment and victimisation carried out by their employees in the course of employment. It does not matter whether or not the employer or principal knows about or approves of those acts. For example, where police officers engage in inappropriate sexual behaviour towards a colleague at a work-related function, the chief officer may be liable for the acts of his/her officers at that function (*Chief Constable of Lincolnshire* v *Stubbs* [1999] IRLR 81).

Employers who can show that they took all reasonable steps to prevent their employees from acting unlawfully will not be held liable (s. 109(4)).

An employee is also personally liable for unlawful acts committed in the course of employment where, because of s. 109, the employer is also liable (s. 110).

4.18.7 Public Sector Equality Duty

The Act imposes a duty, known as the public sector equality duty, on public bodies, which includes a local policing body or police authority.

The Equality Act 2010, s. 149 states:

(1) A public authority must, in the exercise of its functions, have due regard to the need to—

    (a) eliminate discrimination, harassment, victimisation and any other conduct that is prohibited by or under this Act;

    (b) advance equality of opportunity between persons who share a relevant protected characteristic and persons who do not share it;

    (c) foster good relations between persons who share a relevant protected characteristic and persons who do not share it.

KEYNOTE

In relation to s.149(1)(b) and (c), these matters apply to all the protected characteristics except marriage and civil partnership.

An example of this duty could be where a local policing body reviews its recruitment procedures to ensure they do not unintentionally deter applicants from ethnic minorities with the aim of eliminating unlawful discrimination.

The Equality Act 2010 (Specific Duties) Regulations 2011 (SI 2011/2260) impose duties on public authorities listed in the Schedules to the Regulations. The purpose of the duties is to ensure better performance by the public authorities concerned of their duty to have due regard to the matters set out in s. 149(1).

Guidance in relation to the Public Sector Equality Duty is available on the Home Office website (https://www.gov.uk/equality-act-2010-guidance).

Appendix 4.1

PACE Code of Practice for the Exercise by Police Officers of Statutory Powers of Stop and Search; Police Officers and Police Staff of Requirements to Record Public Encounters (Code A), Annexes A–C

ANNEX A —SUMMARY OF MAIN STOP AND SEARCH POWERS

THIS TABLE RELATES TO STOP AND SEARCH POWERS ONLY. INDIVIDUAL STATUTES BELOW MAY CONTAIN OTHER POLICE POWERS OF ENTRY, SEARCH AND SEIZURE

Power	Object of Search	Extent of Search	Where Exercisable
Unlawful articles general			
1. Public Stores Act 1875, s. 6	HM Stores stolen or unlawfully obtained	Persons, vehicles and vessels	Anywhere where the constabulary powers are exercisable
2. Firearms Act 1968, s. 47	Firearms	Persons and vehicles	A public place, or anywhere in the case of reasonable suspicion of offences of carrying firearms with criminal intent or trespassing with firearms
3. Misuse of Drugs Act 1971, s. 23	Controlled drugs	Persons and vehicles	Anywhere
4. Customs and Excise Management Act 1979, s. 163	Goods: (a) on which duty has not been paid; (b) being unlawfully removed, imported or exported; (c) otherwise liable to forfeiture to HM Customs and Excise	Vehicles and vessels only	Anywhere
5. Aviation Security Act 1982, s. 27(1)	Stolen or unlawfully obtained goods	Airport employees and vehicles carrying airport employees or aircraft or any vehicle in a cargo area whether or not carrying an employee	Any designated airport

Power	Object of Search	Extent of Search	Where Exercisable
6. Police and Criminal Evidence Act 1984, s. 1	Stolen goods; articles for use in certain Theft Act offences; offensive weapons, including bladed or sharply-pointed articles (except folding pocket knives with a bladed cutting edge not exceeding 3 inches); prohibited possession of a category 4 (display grade) firework, any person under 18 in possession of an adult firework in a public place.	Persons and vehicles	Where there is public access
	Criminal damage: articles made, adapted or intended for use in destroying or damaging property	Persons and vehicles	Where there is public access
7. Sporting events (Control of Alcohol etc.) Act 1985, s. 7	Intoxicating liquor	Persons, coaches and trains	Designated sports grounds or coaches and trains travelling to or from a designated sporting event
8. Crossbows Act 1987, s. 4	Crossbows or parts of crossbows (except crossbows with a draw weight of less than 1.4 kilograms)	Persons and vehicles	Anywhere except dwellings
9. Criminal Justice Act 1988 s. 139B	Offensive weapons, bladed or sharply pointed article	Persons	School premises

Evidence of game and wildlife offences

Power	Object of Search	Extent of Search	Where Exercisable
10. Poaching Prevention Act 1862, s. 2	Game or poaching equipment	Persons and vehicles	A public place
11. Deer Act 1991, s. 12	Evidence of offences under the Act	Persons and vehicles	Anywhere except dwellings
12. Conservation of Seals Act 1970, s. 4	Seals or hunting equipment	Vehicles only	Anywhere
13. Protection of Badgers Act 1992, s. 11	Evidence of offences under the Act	Persons and vehicles	Anywhere
14. Wildlife and Countryside Act 1981, s. 19	Evidence of wildlife offences	Persons and vehicles	Anywhere except dwellings

Other

Power	Object of Search	Extent of Search	Where Exercisable
15. Paragraphs 6 & 8 of Schedule 5 to the Terrorism Prevention and Investigation Measures Act 2011	Anything that contravenes measures specified in a TPIM notice.	Persons in respect of whom a TPIM notice is being served or is in force	Anywhere

Power	Object of Search	Extent of Search	Where Exercisable
16. Paragraph 10 of Schedule 5 to the Terrorism Prevention and Investigation Measures Act 2011.	Anything that could be used to threaten or harm any person.	Persons in respect of whom a TPIM notice is in force.	Anywhere
17. *Not used*			
18. Paragraphs 7 and 8 of Schedule 7 to the Terrorism Act 2000	Anything relevant to determining if a person being examined falls within section 40(1)(b)	Persons, vehicles, vessels etc. *(Note: These searches are subject to the Code of Practice issued under paragraph 6 of Schedule 14 to the Terrorism Act 2000)*	*Ports and airports*
19. Section 60 Criminal Justice and Public Order Act 1994	Offensive weapons or dangerous instruments to prevent incidents of serious violence or to deal with the carrying of such items or find such items which have been used in incidents of serious violence	Persons and vehicles	Anywhere within a locality authorised under subsection (1)

ANNEX B —SELF-DEFINED ETHNIC CLASSIFICATION CATEGORIES

White	**W**
A. White—British	W1
B. White—Irish	W2
C. Any other White background	W9
Mixed	**M**
D. White and Black Caribbean	M1
E. White and Black African	M2
F. White and Asian	M3
G. Any other Mixed Background	M9
Asian/Asian—British	**A**
H. Asian—Indian	A1
I. Asian—Pakistani	A2
J. Asian—Bangladeshi	A3
K. Any other Asian background	A9
Black/Black—British	**B**
L. Black—Caribbean	B1
M. Black African	B2
N. Any other Black background	B9
Other	**O**
O. Chinese	O1
P. Any other	O9
Not Stated	NS

ANNEX C —SUMMARY OF POWERS OF COMMUNITY SUPPORT OFFICERS TO SEARCH AND SEIZE

The following is a summary of the search and seizure powers that may be exercised by a community support officer (CSO) who has been designated with the relevant powers in accordance with Part 4 of the Police Reform Act 2002.

When exercising any of these powers, a CSO must have regard to any relevant provisions of this Code, including section 3 governing the conduct of searches and the steps to be taken prior to a search.

1. Not used

2. Powers to search requiring the consent of the person and seizure

A CSO may detain a person using reasonable force where necessary as set out in Part 1 of Schedule 4 to the Police Reform Act 2002. If the person has been lawfully detained, the CSO may search the person provided that person gives consent to such a search in relation to the following:

Designation	Power conferred	Object of Search	Extent of Search	Where Exercisable
Police Reform Act 2002, Schedule 4, paragraph 7A	(a) Criminal Justice and Police Act 2001, s. 12(2)	(a) Alcohol or a container for alcohol	(a) Persons	(a) Designated public place
	(b) Confiscation of Alcohol (Young Persons) Act 1997, s. 1	(b) Alcohol	(b) Persons under 18 years old	(b) Public place
	(c) Children and Young Persons Act 1933, s. 7(3)	(c) Tobacco or cigarette papers	(c) Persons under 16 years old found smoking	(c) Public place

3. Powers to search not requiring the consent of the person and seizure

A CSO may detain a person using reasonable force where necessary as set out in Part 1 of Schedule 4 to the Police Reform Act 2002. If the person has been lawfully detained, the CSO may search the person without the need for that person's consent in relation to the following:

Designation	Power conferred	Object of Search	Extent of Search	Where Exercisable
Police Reform Act 2002, Schedule 4, paragraph 2A	Police and Criminal Evidence Act 1984, s. 32	(a) Objects that might be used to cause physical injury to the person or the CSO	Persons made subject to a requirement to wait	Any place where the requirement to wait has been made
		(b) Items that might be used to assist escape		

4. Powers to seize without consent

This power applies when drugs are found in the course of any search mentioned above.

Designation	Power conferred	Object of Search	Where Exercisable
Police Reform Act 2002, Schedule 4, paragraph 7B	Police Reform Act 2002, Schedule 4, paragraph 7B	Controlled drugs in a person's possession	Any place where the person is in possession of the drug

Appendix 4.2

Powers of Police Community Support Officers

Police Community Support Officers

Part 1 of Schedule 4 to the Police Reform Act 2002—Police Community Support Officers

Each of the following paragraphs will only apply if the designation specifically applies it to the Police Community Support Officer (PCSO) concerned.

Power to issue fixed penalty notices—paragraph 1

(1) Where a designation applies this paragraph to any person, that person shall have the powers specified in sub-paragraph (2) in relation to any individual who he has reason to believe has committed a relevant fixed penalty offence at a place within the relevant police area.

(2) Those powers are the following powers so far as exercisable in respect of a relevant fixed penalty offence—

    (a) the powers of a constable in uniform and of an authorised constable to give a penalty notice under Chapter 1 of Part 1 of the Criminal Justice and Police Act 2001 (fixed penalty notices in respect of offences of disorder);

    (aa) the power of a constable to give a penalty notice under section 444A of the Education Act 1996 (penalty notice in respect of failure to secure regular attendance at school of registered pupil);

    (ab) the power of a constable to give a penalty notice under s. 105 of the Education and Inspections Act 2006 (penalty notice in respect of presence of excluded pupil in public place);

    (b) the power of a constable in uniform to give a person a fixed penalty notice under section 54 of the Road Traffic Offenders Act 1988 (fixed penalty notices) in respect of an offence under section 72 of the Highway Act 1835 (riding on a footway) committed by cycling;

    (c) ...

    (ca) the power of an authorised officer of a local authority to give a notice under section 43(1) of the Anti-social Behaviour Act 2003 (penalty notices in respect of graffiti or fly-posting); and

    (d) the power of an authorised officer of a litter authority to give a notice under section 88 of the Environmental Protection Act 1990 (fixed penalty notices in respect of litter); and

    (e) the power of an authorised officer of a primary or secondary authority, within the meaning of section 59 of the Clean Neighbourhoods and Environment Act 2005, to give a notice under that section (fixed penalty notices in respect of offences under dog control orders).

(2A) The reference to the powers mentioned in sub-paragraph (2)(a) does not include those powers so far as they relate to an offence under the provisions in the following list—
section 1 of the Theft Act 1968, section 87 of the Environmental Protection Act 1990.

(3) In this paragraph 'relevant fixed penalty offence', in relation to a designated person, means an offence which—

    (a) is an offence by reference to which a notice may be given to a person in exercise of any of the powers mentioned in sub-paragraph (2)(a) to (e); and

    (b) is specified or described in that person's designation as an offence he has been designated to enforce under this paragraph.

(4) In its application to an offence which is an offence by reference to which a notice may be given to a person in exercise of the power mentioned in sub-paragraph (2)(aa), sub-paragraph (1) shall

have effect as if for the words from 'who he has reason to believe' to the end there were substituted 'in the relevant police area who he has reason to believe has committed a relevant fixed penalty offence'.

Power to require name and address—paragraph 1A

(1) This paragraph applies if a designation applies it to any person.

(2) Such a designation may specify that, in relation to that person, the application of sub-paragraph (3) is confined to one or more only (and not to all) relevant offences or relevant licensing offences, being in each case specified in the designation.

(3) Subject to sub-paragraph (4), where that person has reason to believe that another person has committed a relevant offence in the relevant police area, or a relevant licensing offence (whether or not in the relevant police area), he may require that other person to give him his name and address.

(4) In its application to an offence which is an offence by reference to which a notice may be given to a person in exercise of the power mentioned in sub-paragraph (2)(aa) or (ab), sub-paragraph (1) shall have effect as if for the words from 'who he has reason to believe' to the end there were substituted 'in the relevant police area who he has reason to believe has committed a relevant fixed penalty offence'.

(5) A person who fails to comply with a requirement under sub-paragraph (3) is guilty of an offence and shall be liable, on summary conviction, to a fine not exceeding level 3 on the standard scale.

(6) In its application to an offence which is an offence by reference to which a notice may be given to a person in exercise of the power mentioned in paragraph 1(2)(aa), sub-paragraph (3) of this paragraph shall have effect as if for the words 'has committed a relevant offence in the relevant police area' there were substituted 'in the relevant police area has committed a relevant offence'.

(7) In this paragraph, 'relevant offence', 'relevant licensing offence' and 'relevant byelaw' have the meaning given in paragraph 2 (reading accordingly the references to 'this paragraph' in paragraph 2(6)).

Power to detain—paragraph 2

(1) This paragraph applies if a designation applies it to any person.

(2) A designation may not apply this paragraph to any person unless a designation also applies paragraph 1A to him.

(3) Where, in a case in which a requirement under paragraph 1A(3) has been imposed on another person—
   (a) that other person fails to comply with the requirement, or
   (b) the person who imposed the requirement has reasonable grounds for suspecting that the other person has given him a name or address that is false or inaccurate,
   the person who imposed the requirement may require the other person to wait with him, for a period not exceeding thirty minutes, for the arrival of a constable.
   This sub-paragraph does not apply if the requirement was imposed in connection with a relevant licensing offence mentioned in paragraph (a), (c) or (f) of sub-paragraph (6A) believed to have been committed on licensed premises (within the meaning of the Licensing Act 2003).

(3A) Where—
   (a) a designation applies this paragraph to any person ('the CSO'); and
   (b) by virtue of a designation applying paragraph 1A to the CSO, the CSO has the power to impose a requirement under sub-paragraph (3) of that paragraph in relation to an offence under a relevant byelaw,
   the CSO shall also have any power a constable has under the relevant byelaw to remove a person from a place.

(3B) Where a person to whom this paragraph applies ('the CSO') has reason to believe that another person is committing an offence under section 3 or 4 of the Vagrancy Act 1824, and requires him to stop doing whatever gives rise to that belief, the CSO may, if the other person fails to stop as required, require him to wait with the CSO, for a period not exceeding thirty minutes, for the arrival of a constable.

(4) A person who has been required under sub-paragraph (3) or (3B) to wait with a person to whom this paragraph is applied may, if requested to do so, elect that (instead of waiting) he

will accompany the person imposing the requirement to a police station in the relevant police area.

(4A) If a person has imposed a requirement under sub-paragraph (3) or (3B) on another person ('P'), and P does not make an election under sub-paragraph (4), the person imposing the requirement shall, if a constable arrives within the thirty-minute period, be under a duty to remain with the constable and P until he has transferred control of P to the constable.

(4B) If, following an election under sub-paragraph (4), the person imposing the requirement under sub-paragraph (3) or (3B) ('the CSO') takes the person upon whom it is imposed ('P') to a police station, the CSO—

    (a)   shall be under a duty to remain at the police station until he has transferred control of P to the custody officer there;

    (b)   until he has so transferred control of P, shall be treated for all purposes as having P in his lawful custody; and

    (c)   for so long as he is at the police station, or in its immediate vicinity, in compliance with, or having complied with, his duty under paragraph (a), shall be under a duty to prevent P's escape and to assist in keeping P under control.

(5) A person who—

    (a)   ...

    (b)   makes off while subject to a requirement under sub-paragraph (3) or (3B), or

    (c)   makes off while accompanying a person to a police station in accordance with an election under sub-paragraph (4),

is guilty of an offence and shall be liable, on summary conviction, to a fine not exceeding level 3 on the standard scale.

(6) In this paragraph 'relevant offence', in relation to a person to whom this paragraph applies, means any offence which is—

    (a)   a relevant fixed penalty offence for the purposes of the application of paragraph 1 to that person; or

    (aa) an offence under section 32(2) of the Anti-social Behaviour Act 2003; or

    (ab) an offence committed in a specified park which by virtue of section 2 of the Parks Regulation (Amendment) Act 1926 is an offence against the Parks Regulation Act 1872; or

    (ac) an offence under section 3 or 4 of the Vagrancy Act 1824; or

    (ad) an offence under a relevant byelaw; or

    (b)   an offence the commission of which appears to that person to have caused—

        (i) injury, alarm or distress to any other person; or

        (ii) the loss of, or any damage to, any other person's property;

but a designation applying this paragraph to any person may provide that an offence is not to be treated as a relevant offence by virtue of paragraph (b) unless it satisfies such other conditions as may be specified in the designation.

(6A) In this paragraph 'relevant licensing offence' means an offence under any of the following provisions of the Licensing Act 2003—

    (a)   section 141 (otherwise than by virtue of subsection (2)(c) or (3) of that section);

    (b)   section 142;

    (c)   section 146(1);

    (d)   section 149(1)(a), (3)(a) or (4)(a);

    (e)   section 150(1);

    (f)   section 150(2) (otherwise than by virtue of subsection (3)(b) of that section);

    (g)   section 152(1) (excluding paragraph (b)).

(6B) In this paragraph 'relevant byelaw' means a byelaw included in a list of byelaws which—

    (a)   have been made by a relevant body with authority to make byelaws for any place within the relevant police area; and

    (b)   the chief officer of the police force for the relevant police area and the relevant body have agreed to include in the list.

(6C) The list must be published by the chief officer in such a way as to bring it to the attention of members of the public in localities where the byelaws in the list apply.

(6D) A list of byelaws mentioned in sub-paragraph (6B) may be amended from time to time by agreement between the chief officer and the relevant body in question, by adding byelaws to it or removing byelaws from it, and the amended list shall also be published by the chief officer as mentioned in sub-paragraph (6C).

(6E) A relevant body for the purposes of sub-paragraph (6B) is—
- (a) in England, a county council, a district council, a London borough council or a parish council; or in Wales, a county council, a county borough council or a community council;
- (b) the Greater London Authority;
- (c) Transport for London;
- (d) a metropolitan county passenger transport authority established under section 28 of the Local Government Act 1985;
- (e) any body specified in an order made by the Secretary of State.

(6F) An order under sub-paragraph (6E)(e) may provide, in relation to any body specified in the order, that the agreement mentioned in sub-paragraph (6B)(b) and (6D) is to be made between the chief officer and the Secretary of State (rather than between the chief officer and the relevant body).

(7) ...

(8) The application of any provision of this paragraph by paragraph 3(2), 3A(2), 7A(8) or 7C(2) has no effect unless a designation has applied this paragraph to the CSO in question.

Powers to search individuals and to seize and retain items—paragraph 2A

(1) Where a designation applies this paragraph to any person, that person shall (subject to sub-paragraph (3)) have the powers mentioned in sub-paragraph (2) in relation to a person upon whom he has imposed a requirement to wait under paragraph 2(3) or (3B) (whether or not that person makes an election under paragraph 2(4)).

(2) Those powers are the same powers as a constable has under section 32 of the 1984 Act in relation to a person arrested at a place other than a police station—
- (a) to search the arrested person if the constable has reasonable grounds for believing that the arrested person may present a danger to himself or others; and to seize and retain anything he finds on exercising that power, if the constable has reasonable grounds for believing that the person being searched might use it to cause physical injury to himself or to any other person;
- (b) to search the arrested person for anything which he might use to assist him to escape from lawful custody; and to seize and retain anything he finds on exercising that power (other than an item subject to legal privilege) if the constable has reasonable grounds for believing that the person being searched might use it to assist him to escape from lawful custody.

(3) If in exercise of the power conferred by sub-paragraph (1) the person to whom this paragraph applies seizes and retains anything by virtue of sub-paragraph (2), he must—
- (a) tell the person from whom it was seized where inquiries about its recovery may be made; and
- (b) comply with a constable's instructions about what to do with it.

Power to require name and address of person acting in an anti-social manner—paragraph 3

(1) Where a designation applies this paragraph to any person, that person shall, in the relevant police area, have the powers of a constable in uniform under section 50 to require a person whom he has reason to believe to have been acting, or to be acting, in an anti-social manner (within the meaning of section 1 of the Crime and Disorder Act 1998 (anti-social behaviour orders)) to give his name and address.

(2) Sub-paragraphs (3) to (5) of paragraph 2 apply in the case of a requirement imposed by virtue of sub-paragraph (1) as they apply in the case of a requirement under paragraph 1A(3).

Power to require name and address: road traffic offences—paragraph 3A

(1) Where a designation applies this paragraph to any person, that person shall, in the relevant police area, have the powers of a constable—
- (a) under subsection (1) of section 165 of the Road Traffic Act 1988 to require a person mentioned in paragraph (c) of that subsection who he has reasonable cause to believe has committed, in the relevant police area, an offence under subsection (1) or (2) of section 35 of that Act (including that section as extended by paragraphs 11B(4) and 12(2) of this Schedule) to give his name and address; and
- (b) under section 169 of that Act to require a person committing an offence under section 37 of that Act (including that section as extended by paragraphs 11B(4) and 12(2) of this Schedule) to give his name and address.

(2) Sub-paragraphs (3) to (5) of paragraph 2 apply in the case of a requirement imposed by virtue of sub-paragraph (1) as they apply in the case of a requirement under paragraph 1A(3).

(3) The reference in section 169 of the Road Traffic Act 1988 to section 37 of that Act is to be taken to include a reference to that section as extended by paragraphs 11B(4) and 12(2) of this Schedule.

Power to use reasonable force to detain person—paragraphs 4, 4ZA and 4ZB

(1) Sub-paragraph (3) applies where a designation—
   (a) applies this paragraph to a person to whom any or all of paragraphs 1 to 3 are also applied; and
   (b) sets out matters in respect of which that person has the power conferred by this paragraph.

(2) The matters that may be set out in a designation as matters in respect of which a person has the power conferred by this paragraph shall be confined to—
   (a) offences that are relevant penalty notice offences for the purposes of the application of paragraph 1 to the designated person;
   (b) offences that are relevant offences or relevant licensing offences for the purposes of the application of paragraph 1A or 2 to the designated person; and
   (c) behaviour that constitutes acting in an anti-social manner (within the meaning of section 1 of the Crime and Disorder Act 1998 (anti-social behaviour orders)).

(3) In any case in which a person to whom this paragraph applies has imposed a requirement on any other person under paragraph 1A(3) or 3(1) in respect of anything appearing to him to be a matter set out in the designation, he may use reasonable force to prevent that other person from making off and to keep him under control while he is either—
   (a) subject to a requirement imposed in that case by the designated person under sub-paragraph (3) of paragraph 2; or
   (b) accompanying the designated person to a police station in accordance with an election made in that case under sub-paragraph (4) of that paragraph.

Where a designation applies this paragraph to any person, that person may, if he has imposed a requirement on any person to wait with him under paragraph 2(3B) or by virtue of paragraph 7A(8) or 7C(2)(a), use reasonable force to prevent that other person from making off and to keep him under control while he is either—
   (a) subject to that requirement; or
   (b) accompanying the designated person to a police station in accordance with an election made under paragraph 2(4).

Where a designation applies this paragraph to any person, that person, if he is complying with any duty under sub-paragraph (4A) or (4B) of paragraph 2, may use reasonable force to prevent P (as identified in those sub-paragraphs) from making off (or escaping) and to keep him under control.

Power to disperse groups and remove young persons to their place of residence—paragraphs 4A and 4B

Where a designation applies this paragraph to any person, that person shall, within the relevant police area, have the powers which, by virtue of an authorisation under section 30 of the Anti-social Behaviour Act 2003, are conferred on a constable in uniform by section 30(3) to (6) of that Act (power to disperse groups and remove persons under 16 to their place of residence).

(1) Where a designation applies this paragraph to any person, that person shall, within the relevant police area, have the power of a constable under section 15(3) of the Crime and Disorder Act 1998 (power to remove child to their place of residence).

(2) Section 15(1) of that Act shall have effect in relation to the exercise of that power by that person as if the reference to a constable in that section were a reference to that person.

(3) Where that person exercises that power, the duty in section 15(2) of that Act (duty to inform local authority of contravention of curfew notice) is to apply to him as it applies to a constable.

Power to remove truants [and excluded pupils] to designated premises etc—paragraph 4C

Where a designation applies this paragraph to any person, that person shall—
   (a) as respects any area falling within the relevant police area and specified in a direction under section 16(2) of the Crime and Disorder Act 1998, but
   (b) only during the period specified in the direction,

have the powers conferred on a constable by *section 16(3) of that Act (power to remove truant found in specified area to designated premises or to the school from which truant is absent)* [section 16(3) or (3ZA) of that Act (power to remove truant or excluded pupil found in specified area to designated premises or, in case of truant, to the school from which he is absent)].

NB Paragraph 4C has been amended but the amendments are only in force for England, not Wales (so far). The text which applies to Wales is italicised; that which applies only to England is in square brackets.

Powers relating to alcohol consumption in designated public places—paragraph 5

Where a designation applies this paragraph to any person, that person shall, within the relevant police area, have the powers of a constable under section 12 of the Criminal Justice and Police Act 2001 (alcohol consumption in public places)—
   (a) to impose a requirement under subsection (2) of that section; and
   (b) to dispose under subsection (3) of that section of anything surrendered to him;
and that section shall have effect in relation to the exercise of those powers by that person as if the references to a constable in subsections (1) and (5) were references to that person.

Power to serve closure notice for licensed premises persistently selling to children—paragraph 5A

Where a designation applies this paragraph to any person, that person shall have—
   (a) within the relevant police area, and
   (b) if it appears to him as mentioned in subsection (7) of section 169A of the Licensing Act 2003 (closure notices served on licensed premises persistently serving children),
the capacity of a constable under that subsection to be the person by whose delivery of a closure notice that notice is served.

Power to confiscate alcohol—paragraph 6

Where a designation applies this paragraph to any person, that person shall, within the relevant police area, have the powers of a constable under section 1 of the Confiscation of Alcohol (Young Persons) Act 1997 (confiscation of intoxicating liquor)—
   (a) to impose a requirement under subsection (1) of that section; and
   (b) to dispose under subsection (2) of that section of anything surrendered to him;
and that section shall have effect in relation to the exercise of those powers by that person as if the references to a constable in subsections (1) and (4) (but not the reference in subsection (5) (arrest)) were references to that person.

Confiscation of tobacco etc—paragraph 7

Where a designation applies this paragraph to any person, that person shall, within the relevant police area, have—
   (a) the power to seize anything that a constable in uniform has a duty to seize under subsection (3) of section 7 of the Children and Young Persons Act 1933 (seizure of tobacco etc from young persons); and
   (b) the power to dispose of anything that a constable may dispose of under that subsection;
and the power to dispose of anything shall be a power to dispose of it in such manner as the police authority may direct.

Search and seizure powers: alcohol and tobacco—paragraph 7A

(1) Where a designation applies this paragraph to any person ('the CSO'), the CSO shall have the powers set out below.
(2) Where—
   (a) in exercise of the powers referred to in paragraph 5 or 6 the CSO has imposed, under section 12(2) of the Criminal Justice and Police Act 2001 or under section 1 of the Confiscation of Alcohol (Young Persons) Act 1997, a requirement on a person to surrender alcohol or a container for alcohol;
   (b) that person fails to comply with that requirement; and

    (c) the CSO reasonably believes that the person has alcohol or a container for alcohol in his possession,

the CSO may search him for it.

(3) Where—
- (a) in exercise of the powers referred to in paragraph 7 the CSO has sought to seize something which by virtue of that paragraph he has a power to seize;
- (b) the person from whom he sought to seize it fails to surrender it; and
- (c) the CSO reasonably believes that the person has it in his possession,

the CSO may search him for it.

(4) The power to search conferred by sub-paragraph (2) or (3)—
- (a) is to do so only to the extent that is reasonably required for the purpose of discovering whatever the CSO is searching for; and
- (b) does not authorise the CSO to require a person to remove any of his clothing in public other than an outer coat, jacket or gloves.

(5) A person who without reasonable excuse fails to consent to being searched is guilty of an offence and shall be liable, on summary conviction, to a fine not exceeding level 3 on the standard scale.

(6) A CSO who proposes to exercise the power to search a person under sub-paragraph (2) or (3) must inform him that failing without reasonable excuse to consent to being searched is an offence.

(7) If the person in question fails to consent to being searched, the CSO may require him to give the CSO his name and address.

(8) Sub-paragraph (3) of paragraph 2 applies in the case of a requirement imposed by virtue of sub-paragraph (7) as it applies in the case of a requirement under paragraph 1A(3); and sub-paragraphs (4) to (5) of paragraph 2 also apply accordingly.

(9) If on searching the person the CSO discovers what he is searching for, he may seize it and dispose of it.

Powers to seize and detain: controlled drugs—paragraphs 7B and 7C

(1) Where a designation applies this paragraph to any person ('the CSO'), the CSO shall, within the relevant police area, have the powers set out in sub-paragraphs (2) and (3).

(2) If the CSO—
- (a) finds a controlled drug in a person's possession (whether or not the CSO finds it in the course of searching the person by virtue of any paragraph of this Part of this Schedule being applied to the CSO by a designation); and
- (b) reasonably believes that it is unlawful for the person to be in possession of it,

the CSO may seize it and retain it.

(3) If the CSO—
- (a) finds a controlled drug in a person's possession (as mentioned in sub-paragraph (2)); or
- (b) reasonably believes that a person is in possession of a controlled drug,

and reasonably believes that it is unlawful for the person to be in possession of it, the CSO may require him to give the CSO his name and address.

(4) If in exercise of the power conferred by sub-paragraph (2) the CSO seizes and retains a controlled drug, he must—
- (a) if the person from whom it was seized maintains that he was lawfully in possession of it, tell the person where inquiries about its recovery may be made; and
- (b) comply with a constable's instructions about what to do with it.

(5) A person who fails to comply with a requirement under sub-paragraph (3) is guilty of an offence and shall be liable, on summary conviction, to a fine not exceeding level 3 on the standard scale.

(6) In this paragraph, 'controlled drug' has the same meaning as in the Misuse of Drugs Act 1971.

(1) Sub-paragraph (2) applies where a designation applies this paragraph to any person ('the CSO').

(2) If the CSO imposes a requirement on a person under paragraph 7B(3)—
- (a) sub-paragraph (3) of paragraph 2 applies in the case of such a requirement as it applies in the case of a requirement under paragraph 1A(3); and
- (b) sub-paragraphs (4) to (5) of paragraph 2 also apply accordingly.

Park trading offences—paragraph 7D

(1) This paragraph applies if—
    (a) a designation applies it to any person ('the CSO'), and
    (b) the CSO has under paragraph 2(3) required another person ('P') to wait with him for the arrival of a constable.

(2) If the CSO reasonably suspects that P has committed a park trading offence, the CSO may take possession of anything of a non-perishable nature which—
    (a) P has in his possession or under his control, and
    (b) the CSO reasonably believes to have been used in the commission of the offence.

(3) The CSO may retain possession of the thing in question for a period not exceeding 30 minutes unless P makes an election under paragraph 2(4), in which case the CSO may retain possession of the thing in question until he is able to transfer control of it to a constable.

(4) In this paragraph 'park trading offence' means an offence committed in a specified park which is a park trading offence for the purposes of the Royal Parks (Trading) Act 2000.

Power of entry to save life or limb or prevent serious damage to property—paragraph 8

Where a designation applies this paragraph to any person, that person shall have the powers of a constable under section 17 of the 1984 Act to enter and search any premises in the relevant police area for the purpose of saving life or limb or preventing serious damage to property.

Power of entry to investigate licensing offences—paragraph 8A

(1) Where a designation applies this paragraph to any person, that person shall have the powers of a constable under section 180 of the Licensing Act 2003 to enter and search premises other than clubs in the relevant police area, but only in respect of a relevant licensing offence (as defined for the purposes of paragraph 2).

(2) Except as mentioned in sub-paragraph (3), a person to whom this paragraph applies shall not, in exercise of the power conferred by sub-paragraph (1), enter any premises except in the company, and under the supervision, of a constable.

(3) The prohibition in sub-paragraph (2) does not apply in relation to premises in respect of which the person to whom this paragraph applies reasonably believes that a premises licence under Part 3 of the Licensing Act 2003 authorises the sale of alcohol for consumption off the premises.

Power to seize vehicles used to cause alarm—paragraph 9

(1) Where a designation applies this paragraph to any person—
    (a) that person shall, within the relevant police area, have all the powers of a constable in uniform under section 59 of this Act which are set out in subsection (3) of that section; and
    (b) references in that section to a constable, in relation to the exercise of any of those powers by that person, are references to that person.

(2) A person to whom this paragraph applies shall not enter any premises in exercise of the power conferred by section 59(3)(c) except in the company, and under the supervision, of a constable.

Powers to deal with abandoned vehicles—paragraph 10

Where a designation applies this paragraph to any person, that person shall have any such powers in the relevant police area as are conferred on persons designated under that section by regulations under section 99 of the Road Traffic Regulation Act 1984 (c 27) (removal of abandoned vehicles).

Power to stop vehicle for testing—paragraph 11

Where a designation applies this paragraph to any person, that person shall, within the relevant police area, have the power of a constable in uniform to stop a vehicle under subsection (3) of section 67 of the Road Traffic Act 1988 for the purposes of a test under subsection (1) of that section.

Power to stop cycles—paragraph 11A

(1) Subject to sub-paragraph (2), where a designation applies this paragraph to any person, that person shall, within the relevant police area, have the power of a constable in uniform under section 163(2) of the Road Traffic Act 1988 to stop a cycle.

(2) The power mentioned in sub-paragraph (1) may only be exercised by that person in relation to a person who he has reason to believe has committed an offence under section 72 of the Highway Act 1835 (riding on a footway) by cycling.

Power to control traffic for purposes other than escorting a load of exceptional dimensions—paragraph 11B

(1) Where a designation applies this paragraph to any person, that person shall have, in the relevant police area—
   (a) the power of a constable engaged in the regulation of traffic in a road to direct a person driving or propelling a vehicle to stop the vehicle or to make it proceed in, or keep to, a particular line of traffic;
   (b) the power of a constable in uniform engaged in the regulation of vehicular traffic in a road to direct a person on foot to stop proceeding along or across the carriageway.
(2) The purposes for which those powers may be exercised do not include the purpose mentioned in paragraph 12(1).
(3) Where a designation applies this paragraph to any person, that person shall also have, in the relevant police area, the power of a constable, for the purposes of a traffic survey, to direct a person driving or propelling a vehicle to stop the vehicle, to make it proceed in, or keep to, a particular line of traffic, or to proceed to a particular point on or near the road.
(4) Sections 35 and 37 of the Road Traffic Act 1988 (offences of failing to comply with directions of constable engaged in regulation of traffic in a road) shall have effect in relation to the exercise of the powers mentioned in sub-paragraphs (1) and (3), for the purposes for which they may be exercised and by a person whose designation applies this paragraph to him, as if the references to a constable were references to him.
(5) A designation may not apply this paragraph to any person unless a designation also applies paragraph 3A to him.

Power to control traffic for purposes of escorting a load of exceptional dimensions—paragraph 12

(1) Where a designation applies this paragraph to any person, that person shall have, for the purpose of escorting a vehicle or trailer carrying a load of exceptional dimensions either to or from the relevant police area, the power of a constable engaged in the regulation of traffic in a road—
   (a) to direct a vehicle to stop;
   (b) to make a vehicle proceed in, or keep to, a particular line of traffic; and
   (c) to direct pedestrians to stop.
(2) Sections 35 and 37 of the Road Traffic Act 1988 (offences of failing to comply with directions of constable engaged in regulation of traffic in a road) shall have effect in relation to the exercise of those powers for the purpose mentioned in sub-paragraph (1) by a person whose designation applies this paragraph to him as if the references to a constable engaged in regulation of traffic in a road were references to that person.
(3) The powers conferred by virtue of this paragraph may be exercised in any police area in England and Wales.
(4) In this paragraph 'vehicle or trailer carrying a load of exceptional dimensions' means a vehicle or trailer the use of which is authorised by an order made by the Secretary of State under section 44(1)(d) of the Road Traffic Act 1988.

Power to carry out road checks—paragraph 13

Where a designation applies this paragraph to any person, that person shall have the following powers in the relevant police area—
   (a) the power to carry out any road check the carrying out of which by a police officer is authorised under section 4 of the 1984 Act (road checks); and
   (b) for the purpose of exercising that power, the power conferred by section 163 of the Road Traffic Act 1988 (power of police to stop vehicles) on a constable in uniform to stop a vehicle.

Power to place traffic signs—paragraph 13A

(1) Where a designation applies this paragraph to any person, that person shall have, in the relevant police area, the powers of a constable under section 67 of the Road Traffic Regulation Act 1984 to place and maintain traffic signs.

(2) Section 36 of the Road Traffic Act 1988 (drivers to comply with traffic directions) shall apply to signs placed in the exercise of the powers conferred by virtue of sub-paragraph (1).

Cordoned areas—paragraph 14

Where a designation applies this paragraph to any person, that person shall, in relation to any cordoned area in the relevant police area, have all the powers of a constable in uniform under section 36 of the Terrorism Act 2000 (enforcement of cordoned area) to give orders, make arrangements or impose prohibitions or restrictions.

Power to stop and search in authorised areas—paragraph 15

(1) Where a designation applies this paragraph to any person—
    (a) that person shall, in any authorised area within the relevant police area, have all the powers of a constable in uniform by virtue of section 44(1)(a) and (d) and (2)(b) and 45(2) of the Terrorism Act 2000 (powers of stop and search)—
        (i) to stop and search vehicles;
        (ii) to search anything in or on a vehicle or anything carried by the driver of a vehicle or any passenger in a vehicle;
        (iii) to search anything carried by a pedestrian; and
        (iv) to seize and retain any article discovered in the course of a search carried out by him or by a constable by virtue of any provision of section 44(1) or (2) of that Act;
    and
    (b) the references to a constable in subsections (1) and (4) of section 45 of that Act (which relate to the exercise of those powers) shall have effect in relation to the exercise of any of those powers by that person as references to that person.
(2) A person shall not exercise any power of stop, search or seizure by virtue of this paragraph except in the company, and under the supervision, of a constable.

Photographing of persons arrested, detained or given fixed penalty notices—paragraph 15ZA

Where a designation applies this paragraph to any person, that person shall, within the relevant police area, have the power of a constable under section 64A(1A) of the 1984 Act (photographing of suspects etc) to take a photograph of a person elsewhere than at a police station.

Investigating Officers

Part 2 of schedule 4 to the police reform act 2002—investigating officers

Each of the following paragraphs will only apply if the designation specifically applies it to the Investigating Officer concerned.

Search warrants—paragraph 16

Where a designation applies this paragraph to any person—
    (a) he may apply as if he were a constable for a warrant under section 8 of the 1984 Act (warrants for entry and search) in respect of any premises whether in the relevant police area or not;
    (b) the persons to whom a warrant to enter and search any such premises may be issued under that section shall include that person;
    (c) that person shall have the power of a constable under section 8(2) of that Act in any premises in the relevant police area to seize and retain things for which a search has been authorised under subsection (1) of that section;
    (d) section 15 of that Act (safeguards) shall have effect in relation to the issue of such a warrant to that person as it has effect in relation to the issue of a warrant under section 8 of that Act to a constable;
    (e) section 16 of that Act (execution of warrants) shall have effect in relation to any warrant to enter and search premises that is issued (whether to that person or to any other person), but in respect of premises in the relevant police area only, as if references in that section to a constable included references to that person;

(f) section 19(6) of that Act (protection for legally privileged material from seizure) shall have effect in relation to the seizure of anything by that person by virtue of sub-paragraph (c) as it has effect in relation to the seizure of anything by a constable;

(g) section 20 of that Act (extension of powers of seizure to computerised information) shall have effect in relation the power of seizure conferred on that person by virtue of sub-paragraph (c) as it applies in relation to the power of seizure conferred on a constable by section 8(2) of that Act;

(h) section 21(1) and (2) of that Act (provision of record of seizure) shall have effect in relation to the seizure of anything by that person in exercise of the power conferred on him by virtue of sub-paragraph (c) as if the references to a constable and to an officer included references to that person; and

(i) sections 21(3) to (8) and 22 of that Act (access, copying and retention) shall have effect in relation to anything seized by that person in exercise of that power, or taken away by him following the imposition of a requirement by virtue of sub-paragraph (g)—

   (i) as they have effect in relation to anything seized in exercise of the power conferred on a constable by section 8(2) of that Act or taken away by a constable following the imposition of a requirement by virtue of section 20 of that Act; and

   (ii) as if the references to a constable in subsections (3),(4) and (5) of section 21 included references to a person to whom this paragraph applies.

Warrants for Stolen Goods—paragraph 16A

Where a designation applies this paragraph to any person—

(a) the persons to whom a warrant may be addressed under section 26 of the Theft Act 1968 (search for stolen goods) shall, in relation to persons or premises in the relevant police area, include that person; and

(b) in relation to such a warrant addressed to him, that person shall have the powers under subsection (3) of that section.

Misuse of Drugs Act 1971—paragraph 16B

Where a designation applies this paragraph to any person, subsection (3), and (to the extent that it applies subsection (3)) subsection (3A), of section 23 of the Misuse of Drugs Act 1971 (powers to search and obtain evidence) shall have effect as if, in relation to premises in the relevant police area, the reference to a constable included a reference to that person.

Access to excluded and special procedure material—paragraph 17

Where a designation applies this paragraph to any person—

(a) he shall have the powers of a constable under section 9(1) of the 1984 Act (special provisions for access) to obtain access, in accordance with Schedule 1 to that Act and the following provisions of this paragraph, to excluded material and special procedure material;

(b) that Schedule shall have effect for the purpose of conferring those powers on that person as if—

   (i) the references in paragraphs 1, 4, 5, 12 and 13 of that Schedule to a constable were references to that person; and

   (ii) the references in paragraphs 12 and 14 of that Schedule to premises were references to premises in the relevant police area (in the case of a specific premises warrant) or any premises, whether in the relevant police area or not (in the case of an all premises warrant);

(bb) section 15 of that Act (safeguards) shall have effect in relation to the issue of any warrant under paragraph 12 of that Schedule to that person as it has effect in relation to the issue of a warrant under that paragraph to a constable;

(bc) section 16 of that Act (execution of warrants) shall have effect in relation to any warrant to enter and search premises that is issued under paragraph 12 of that Schedule (whether to that person or to any other person), but in respect of premises in the relevant police area only, as if references in that section to a constable included references to that person;

(c) section 19(6) of that Act (protection for legally privileged material from seizure) shall have effect in relation to the seizure of anything by that person in exercise of the power conferred on him by paragraph 13 of Schedule 1 to that Act as it has effect in relation to the seizure of anything under that paragraph by a constable;

(d) section 20 of that Act (extension of powers of seizure to computerised information) shall have effect in relation the power of seizure conferred on that person by paragraph 13 of Schedule 1 to that Act as it applies in relation to the power of seizure conferred on a constable by that paragraph;

(e) section 21(1) and (2) of that Act (provision of record of seizure) shall have effect in relation to the seizure of anything by that person in exercise of the power conferred on him by paragraph 13 of Schedule 1 to that Act as if the references to a constable and to an officer included references to that person; and

(f) sections 21(3) to (8) and 22 of that Act (access, copying and retention) shall have effect in relation to anything seized by that person in exercise of that power or taken away by him following the imposition of a requirement by virtue of sub-paragraph (d), and to anything produced to him under paragraph 4(a) of Schedule 1 to that Act—

    (i) as they have effect in relation to anything seized in exercise of the power conferred on a constable by paragraph 13 of that Schedule or taken away by a constable following the imposition of a requirement by virtue of section 20 of that Act or, as the case may be, to anything produced to a constable under paragraph 4(a) of that Schedule; and

    (ii) as if the references to a constable in subsections (3),(4) and (5) of section 21 included references to a person to whom this paragraph applies.

Entry and search after arrest—paragraph 18

Where a designation applies this paragraph to any person—

(a) he shall have the powers of a constable under section 18 of the 1984 Act (entry and search after arrest) to enter and search any premises in the relevant police area and to seize and retain anything for which he may search under that section;

(b) subsections (5) and (6) of that section (power to carry out search before arrested person taken to police station and duty to inform senior officer) shall have effect in relation to any exercise by that person of those powers as if the references in those subsections to a constable were references to that person;

(c) section 19(6) of that Act (protection for legally privileged material from seizure) shall have effect in relation to the seizure of anything by that person by virtue of sub-paragraph (a) as it has effect in relation to the seizure of anything by a constable;

(d) section 20 of that Act (extension of powers of seizure to computerised information) shall have effect in relation the power of seizure conferred on that person by virtue of sub-paragraph (a) as it applies in relation to the power of seizure conferred on a constable by section 18(2) of that Act;

(e) section 21(1) and (2) of that Act (provision of record of seizure) shall have effect in relation to the seizure of anything by that person in exercise of the power conferred on him by virtue of sub-paragraph (a) as if the references to a constable and to an officer included references to that person; and

(f) sections 21(3) to (8) and 22 of that Act (access, copying and retention) shall have effect in relation to anything seized by that person in exercise of that power or taken away by him following the imposition of a requirement by virtue of sub-paragraph (d)—

    (i) as they have effect in relation to anything seized in exercise of the power conferred on a constable by section 18(2) of that Act or taken away by a constable following the imposition of a requirement by virtue of section 20 of that Act; and

    (ii) as if the references to a constable in subsections (3),(4) and (5) of section 21 included references to a person to whom this paragraph applies.

General power of seizure—paragraph 19

Where a designation applies this paragraph to any person—

(a) he shall, when lawfully on any premises in the relevant police area, have the same powers as a constable under section 19 of the 1984 Act (general powers of seizure) to seize things;

(b) he shall also have the powers of a constable to impose a requirement by virtue of subsection (4) of that section in relation to information accessible from such premises;

(c) subsection (6) of that section (protection for legally privileged material from seizure) shall have effect in relation to the seizure of anything by that person by virtue of sub-paragraph (a) as it has effect in relation to the seizure of anything by a constable;

(d) section 21(1) and (2) of that Act (provision of record of seizure) shall have effect in relation to the seizure of anything by that person in exercise of the power conferred on him by virtue of sub-paragraph (a) as if the references to a constable and to an officer included references to that person; and

(e) sections 21(3) to (8) and 22 of that Act (access, copying and retention) shall have effect in relation to anything seized by that person in exercise of that power or taken away by him following the imposition of a requirement by virtue of sub-paragraph (b)—

    (i) as they have effect in relation to anything seized in exercise of the power conferred on a constable by section 19(2) or (3) of that Act or taken away by a constable following the imposition of a requirement by virtue of section 19(4) of that Act; and

    (ii) as if the references to a constable in subsections (3),(4) and (5) of section 21 included references to a person to whom this paragraph applies.

Access and copying in the case of things seized by constables—paragraph 20

Where a designation applies this paragraph to any person, section 21 of the 1984 Act (access and copying) shall have effect in relation to anything seized in the relevant police area by a constable or by a person authorised to accompany him under section 16(2) of that Act as if the references to a constable in subsections (3),(4) and (5) of section 21 (supervision of access and photographing of seized items) included references to a person to whom this paragraph applies.

Arrest at a police station for another offence—paragraph 21

(1) Where a designation applies this paragraph to any person, he shall have the power to make an arrest at any police station in the relevant police area in any case where an arrest—

    (a) is required to be made under section 31 of the 1984 Act (arrest for a further offence of a person already at a police station); or

    (b) would be so required if the reference in that section to a constable included a reference to a person to whom this paragraph applies.

(2) Section 36 of the Criminal Justice and Public Order Act 1994 (consequences of failure by arrested person to account for objects etc) shall apply (without prejudice to the effect of any designation applying paragraph 23) in the case of a person arrested in exercise of the power exercisable by virtue of this paragraph as it applies in the case of a person arrested by a constable.

Power to transfer persons into custody of investigating officers—paragraph 22

(1) Where a designation applies this paragraph to any person, the custody officer for a designated police station in the relevant police area may transfer or permit the transfer to him of a person in police detention for an offence which is being investigated by the person to whom this paragraph applies.

(2) A person into whose custody another person is transferred under sub-paragraph (1)—

    (a) shall be treated for all purposes as having that person in his lawful custody;

    (b) shall be under a duty to keep that person under control and to prevent his escape; and

    (c) shall be entitled to use reasonable force to keep that person in his custody and under his control.

(3) Where a person is transferred into the custody of a person to whom this paragraph applies, in accordance with sub-paragraph (1), subsections (2) and (3) of section 39 of the 1984 Act shall have effect as if—

    (a) references to the transfer of a person in police detention into the custody of a police officer investigating an offence for which that person is in police detention were references to that person's transfer into the custody of the person to whom this paragraph applies; and

    (b) references to the officer to whom the transfer is made and to the officer investigating the offence were references to the person to whom this paragraph applies.

Powers in respect of detained persons—paragraph 22A

Where a designation applies this paragraph to any person, he shall be under a duty, when in the course of his employment he is present at a police station—

    (a) to assist any officer or other designated person to keep any person detained at the police station under control; and

    (b) to prevent the escape of any such person,

and for those purposes shall be entitled to use reasonable force.

Power to require arrested person to account for certain matters—paragraph 23

Where a designation applies this paragraph to any person—

    (a) he shall have the powers of a constable under sections 36(1)(c) and 37(1)(c) of the Criminal Justice and Public Order Act 1994 to request a person who—

        (i) has been arrested by a constable, or by any person to whom paragraph 21 applies, and

        (ii) is detained at any place in the relevant police area,

    to account for the presence of an object, substance or mark or for the presence of the arrested person at a particular place; and

    (b) the references to a constable in sections 36(1)(b) and (c) and (4) and 37(1)(b) and (c) and (3) of that Act shall have effect accordingly as including references to the person to whom this paragraph is applied.

Extended powers of seizure—paragraph 24

Where a designation applies this paragraph to any person—

    (a) the powers of a constable under Part 2 of the Criminal Justice and Police Act 2001 (c 16) (extension of powers of seizure) that are exercisable in the case of a constable by reference to a power of a constable that is conferred on that person by virtue of the provisions of this Part of this Schedule shall be exercisable by that person by reference to that power to the same extent as in the case of a constable but in relation only to premises in the relevant police area and things found on any such premises; and

    (b) section 56 of that Act (retention of property seized by a constable) shall have effect as if the property referred to in subsection (1) of that section included property seized by that person at any time when he was lawfully on any premises in the relevant police area.

Persons accompanying investigating officers—paragraph 24A

(1) This paragraph applies where a person ('an authorised person') is authorised by virtue of section 16(2) of the 1984 Act to accompany an investigating officer designated for the purposes of paragraph 16 (or 17) in the execution of a warrant.

(2) The reference in paragraph 16(h) (or 17(e)) to the seizure of anything by a designated person in exercise of a particular power includes a reference to the seizure of anything by the authorised person in exercise of that power by virtue of section 16(2A) of the 1984 Act.

(3) In relation to any such seizure, paragraph 16(h) (or 17(e)) is to be read as if it provided for the references to a constable and to an officer in section 21(1) and (2) of the 1984 Act to include references to the authorised person.

(4) The reference in paragraph 16(i) (or 17(f)) to anything seized by a designated person in exercise of a particular power includes a reference to anything seized by the authorised person in exercise of that power by virtue of section 16(2A) of the 1984 Act.

(5) In relation to anything so seized, paragraph 16(i)(ii) (or 17(f)(ii)) is to be read as if it provided for—

    (a) the references to the supervision of a constable in subsections (3) and (4) of section 21 of the 1984 Act to include references to the supervision of a person designated for the purposes of paragraph 16 (or paragraph 17), and

    (b) the reference to a constable in subsection (5) of that section to include a reference to such a person or an authorised person accompanying him.

(6) Where an authorised person accompanies an investigating officer who is also designated for the purposes of paragraph 24, the references in sub-paragraphs (a) and (b) of that paragraph to the designated person include references to the authorised person.

Accredited Employees

Schedule 5 to the Police Reform Act 2002—accredited employees

Each of the following paragraphs will only apply if the designation specifically applies it to the employee accredited under an authorised Community Safety Accreditation Scheme, established and maintained under s. 40.

Power to issue fixed penalty notices—paragraph 1

The powers below may be conferred on an Accredited Employee in relation to any individual who the employee has reason to believe has committed a relevant fixed penalty offence at a place within the relevant police area. Those powers are:

(a) the power of a constable in uniform to give a person a fixed penalty notice under s. 54 of the Road Traffic Offenders Act 1988 (fixed penalty notices—see **Road Policing, para. 3.11.4.1**) in respect of an offence under s. 72 of the Highway Act 1835 (riding on a footway) committed by cycling;

(aa) the powers of a constable in uniform to give a penalty notice under chapter 1 of part 1 of the Criminal Justice and Police Act 2001 (fixed penalty notices in respect of offences of disorder) except in respect of an offence under s. 12 of the Licensing Act 1872 or s. 91 of the Criminal Justice Act 1967 or notices under s. 1 of the Theft Act 1968, s. 1(1) of the Criminal Damage Act 1971 or s. 87 of the Environmental Protection Act 1990;

(ab) the power of a constable to give a penalty notice under s. 444A of the Education Act 1996 (penalty notice in respect of failure to secure regular attendance at school of registered pupil);

(ac) the power of a constable to give a penalty notice under s. 105 of the Education and Inspections Act 2006 (penalty notice in respect of presence of excluded pupil in public place);

(b) the power of an authorised officer of a local authority to give a notice under s. 4 of the Dogs (Fouling of Land) Act 1996 (fixed penalty notices in respect of dog fouling—**see chapter 4.8**);

(c) the power of an authorised officer of a litter authority to give a notice under s. 88 of the Environmental Protection Act 1990 (fixed penalty notices in respect of litter—**see chapter 4.8**);

(ca) the power of an authorised officer of a local authority to give a notice under s. 43(1) of the Anti-social Behaviour Act 2003 (penalty notice in respect of graffiti or fly-posting—**see Crime, para. 1.16.7**);

(d) the power of an authorised officer of a primary or secondary authority, within the meaning of section 59 of the Clean Neighbourhoods and Environment Act 2005, to give a notice under that section (fixed penalty notices in respect of offences under dog control orders).

'Relevant fixed penalty offence' = an offence which—

- is an offence by reference to which a notice may be given to a person in exercise of any of the powers mentioned in (a) to (d) above; and
- is specified or described in the Accredited Employee's accreditation as an offence he/she has been accredited to enforce (para. 1(3)).

The Secretary of State may extend the above powers under para. 1(2)(A) beyond simply issuing fixed penalty notices (see sch. 4, para. 15A).

Power to require giving of name and address—paragraph 2

Under this paragraph, where an Accredited Employee has reason to believe that another person has committed a relevant offence in the relevant police area, he/she may require that other person to give his/her name and address. 'Relevant offence' = any offence which is—

- a relevant fixed penalty offence for the purposes of the application of paragraph 1 above; or
- an offence under s. 3 or 4 of the Vagrancy Act 1824; or
- an offence the commission of which appears to the Accredited Employee to have caused—
  (i) injury, alarm or distress to any other person; or
  (ii) the loss of, or any damage to, any other person's property (para. 2(3)).

Note that an accreditation applying this paragraph to an Accredited Employee may provide that an offence is not to be treated as a 'relevant offence' unless some other specified conditions are satisfied.

Power to require name and address of person acting in an anti-social manner—paragraph 3

Under this paragraph an Accredited Employee will, in the relevant police area, have the powers of a constable in uniform under s. 50 to require a person whom he/she has reason to believe to have been acting, or to be acting, in an anti-social manner (within the meaning of s. 1 of the Crime and Disorder Act 1998—Anti-social Behaviour Orders—**see chapter 4.8**) to give his/her name *and* address (para. 3(1)).

Power to require name and address: road traffic offences—paragraph 3A

Under this paragraph an Accredited Employee will, in the relevant police area, have the following powers of a constable under the Road Traffic Act 1988 to require the person to give their name and address:

(a) under s. 165(1)—a person whom he/she has reasonable cause to believe has committed an offence under s. 35(1) or (2) of that Act (failing to comply with directions) in the relevant police areas and

(b) under s. 169—a person committing an offence under s. 37 of that Act (pedestrian failing to comply with directions).

Powers relating to alcohol consumption in designated public places—paragraph 4

Under this paragraph an Accredited Employee will have the powers of a constable under s. 12 of the Criminal Justice and Police Act 2001 (alcohol consumption in public places—**see para. 4.16.9.2**) in the relevant police area—

(a) to impose a requirement under subsection (2) of that section; and

(b) to dispose under subsection (3) of that section of anything surrendered to him/her;

and that section will have effect in relation to the exercise of those powers by that Accredited Employee as if the references to a constable in subsections (1) and (5) were references to the Accredited Employee.

Power to confiscate alcohol—paragraph 5

Under this paragraph an Accredited Employee will have the powers of a constable under s. 1 of the Confiscation of Alcohol (Young Persons) Act 1997 (confiscation of alcohol—**see chapter 4.16**) in the relevant police area—

(a) to impose a requirement under subsection (1) of that section; and

(b) to dispose under subsection (2) of that section of anything surrendered to him/her;

and that section shall have effect in relation to the exercise of those powers by that Accredited Employee as if the references to a constable in subsections (1) and (4) (but not the reference in subsection (5) (power of arrest)) were references to the Accredited Employee.

Power to confiscate tobacco—paragraph 6

Under this paragraph an Accredited Employee will have within the relevant police area—

(a) the power to seize anything that a constable in uniform has a duty to seize under subsection (3) of s. 7 of the Children and Young Persons Act 1933 (seizure of tobacco etc. from young persons); and

(b) the power to dispose of anything that a constable may dispose of under that subsection;

and the power to dispose of anything shall be a power to dispose of it in such manner as the Accredited Employee's employer may direct.

Powers to deal with abandoned vehicles—paragraph 7

Under this paragraph an Accredited Employee will have all such powers in the relevant police area as are conferred on people accredited under that section by regulations under s. 99 of the Road Traffic Regulation Act 1984 (removal of abandoned vehicles).

Power to stop vehicle for testing—paragraph 8

Under this paragraph an Accredited Employee will have the power of a constable in uniform to stop a vehicle under s. 67(3) the Road Traffic Act 1988 (see *Road Policing*) within the relevant police area for the purposes of a test under s. 67(1) of that section.

Power to stop cycles—paragraph 8A

Under this paragraph an Accredited Employee will, within the relevant police area, have the power of a constable in uniform under s. 163(2) of the Road Traffic Act 1988 to stop a cycle, in relation to a person whom he has reason to believe has committed an offence under s. 72 of the Highway Act 1835 (riding on a footway) by cycling.

Power to control traffic (purposes *other than* escorting load of exceptional dimensions)— paragraph 8B

Under this paragraph an Accredited Employee will, in the relevant police area, have the power of a constable engaged in the regulation of traffic in a road:

(a) to direct a person driving or propelling a vehicle to stop the vehicle, or

(b) to make it proceed in, or keep to, a particular line of traffic

and the power of a constable in uniform engaged in the regulation of vehicular traffic to direct a person on foot to stop proceeding along or across the carriageway.

Paragraph 8B(2) prevents these powers from being for the purposes of escorting loads of exceptional dimensions (as to which see para. 9).

Where their designation authorises it, an Accredited Employee under this paragraph will, in the relevant police area, have the powers of a constable for the purposes of a traffic survey to direct a person driving or propelling a vehicle to stop the vehicle, to make it proceed in, or keep to, a particular line of traffic or to proceed to a particular point on or near a road (para. 8B(3)).

Sections 35 and 37 of the Road Traffic Act 1988 (offences of failing to comply with direction) will apply to a direction lawfully given by an appropriately Accredited Employee (para. 8B(4)).

This paragraph can only be applied to an Accredited Employee where their accreditation contains the powers in para. 3A (power to require name and address for road traffic offences) (para. 8B(5)).

Power to control traffic for purposes of escorting a load of exceptional dimensions— paragraph 9

Under this paragraph an Accredited Employee will have, for the purpose of escorting a vehicle or trailer carrying a load of exceptional dimensions either to or from the relevant police area, the power of a constable engaged in the regulation of traffic in a road—

(a) to direct a vehicle to stop;

(b) to make a vehicle proceed in, or keep to, a particular line of traffic; and

(c) to direct pedestrians to stop (para. 9(1)).

Sections 35 and 37 of the Road Traffic Act 1988 (offences of failing to comply with directions of constable engaged in regulation of traffic in a road) will have effect in relation to the exercise of those powers by an Accredited Employee as if the references to a constable engaged in regulation of traffic in a road were references to that Accredited Employee (para. 9(2)) and will have effect in any police area in England and Wales (para. 9(3)).

'Vehicle or trailer carrying a load of exceptional dimensions' = a vehicle or trailer the use of which is authorised by an order made by the Secretary of State under s. 44(1)(d) of the Road Traffic Act 1988 (para. 9(4)).

Index